The Rāmāyaṇa of Vālmīki

The Rāmāyaṇa of Vālmīki

An Epic of Ancient India

Introduction, Annotation and Translation by
Sheldon I. Pollock

Edited by
Robert P. Goldman

Volume III: Araṇyakāṇḍa

MOTILAL BANARSIDASS PUBLISHERS
PRIVATE LIMITED • DELHI

First Indian Edition : Delhi, 2007

(Vol. III) ISBN : 81-208-3164-0
(Set) ISBN: 81-208-3089-x

MOTILAL BANARSIDASS
41 U.A. Bungalow Road, Jawahar Nagar, Delhi 110 007
8 Mahalaxmi Chamber, Warden Road, Mumbai 400 026
203 Royapettah High Road, Mylapore, Chennai 600 004
236, 9th Main III Block, Jayanagar, Bangalore 560 011
Sanas Plaza, 1302 Baji Rao Road, Pune 411 002
8 Camac Street, Kolkata 700 017
Ashok Rajpath, Patna 800 004
Chowk, Varanasi 221 001

Frontispiece: Rāma, Sītā, and Lakṣmaṇa dwelling on Mount Citrakūṭa. From the "Jagat Singh Rāmāyaṇa," 17th c. British Library Add. 15296. By permission of the British Library.

PRINTED IN INDIA

BY JAINENDRA PRAKASH JAIN AT SHRI JAINENDRA PRESS,
A-45 NARAINA, PHASE-I, NEW DELHI 110 028
AND PUBLISHED BY NARENDRA PRAKASH JAIN FOR
MOTILAL BANARSIDASS PUBLISHERS PRIVATE LIMITED,
BUNGALOW ROAD, DELHI 110 007

For My Beloved Daughters
Mica and Nira

pāpam ācaratāṃ ghoraṃ lokasyāpriyam icchatām
aham āsādito rājā prāṇān hantuṃ niśācara

I come as king, nightstalker, to end the life of evildoers
and all who wish the world ill.
—*Rām* 3.28.10

Contents

List of Abbreviations ix

Preface xv

Guide to Sanskrit Pronunciation xvii

PART I. INTRODUCTION

1. The Problem of the *Araṇyakāṇḍa* 3
2. Summary of the *Araṇyakāṇḍa* 7
3. The *Rāmāyaṇa*: Myth and Romance? 10
4. The Divine King of the *Rāmāyaṇa* 15
5. Rāma's Madness 55
6. *Rākṣasas* and Others 68

PART II. ARAṆYAKĀṆḌA 85

PART III. NOTES 245

Glossary of Important Sanskrit Words, Proper Nouns, and Epithets 359

Emendations and Corrections of the Critical Edition 363

Bibliography of Works Consulted 365

Index 379

List of Abbreviations

Manuscripts, Commentaries, and Editions Used in Volume III, Following the Conventions Established in the Critical Edition of the Araṇyakāṇḍa (see pp. ix–xi)

I. MANUSCRIPTS

Northern Manuscripts (N) forming the Northern Recension (NR) (14 MSS, including 5 Devanāgarī)

NW Northwestern Manuscripts
- i. Ś Śāradā
  - Ś1 undated

NE Northeastern Manuscripts
- i. Ñ Nepālī
  - Ñ1 A.D. 1020
  - Ñ2 A.D. 1675
- ii. V Maithilī
  - V1 undated
  - V2 1675
- iii. B Bengālī
  - B1 undated
  - B2 undated
  - B3 A.D. 1833
  - B4 undated

D Devanāgarī manuscripts allied with N
- D1 A.D. 1773 NW
- D2 A.D. 1659 NW
- D3 A.D. 1731 NW
- D5 undated NE
- D7 A.D. 1829 NE

Southern Manuscripts (S) forming the Southern Recension (SR) (15 MSS, including 6 Devanāgarī)
- i. T Telegu
  - T1 undated
  - T2 undated
  - T3 undated
- ii. G Grantha
  - G1 A.D. 1818
  - G2 undated
  - G3 undated
- iii. M Malayālam
  - M1 A.D. 1690
  - M2 A.D. 1823
  - M3 undated
- iv. D Devanāgarī manuscripts allied with S
  - Dg1 the version of Govindarāja A.D. 1774
  - Dt1 the version of Tilaka undated
  - Dm1 the version of Maheśvaratīrtha A.D. 1698
  - D4 A.D. 1766
  - D6 A.D. 1795
  - D8 undated

II. COMMENTARIES

(Note: Spelling follows the conventions established by the critical edition, see vol. 7, pp. 655–56.)

Cg the commentary called *Bhūṣaṇa* (the name of the commentary on the *Araṇyakāṇḍa* is the *Ratnamekhalā*) of Govindarāja
Ck the commentary called the *Amṛtakataka* of Kataka Mādhav Yogīndra
Cm the commentary called *Tattvadīpikā* of Maheśvaratīrtha
Cnā the commentary of Sarvajña Nārāyaṇa (as cited by Lokanātha Cakravartī)
Cr the commentary called *Śiromaṇi* of Bansidhara Śivasahāya*
Crā the commentary of Rāmānuja*
Cs the commentary of Satyatīrtha
Ct the commentary called Tilaka of Nāgeśa Bhaṭṭa, composed in the name of Rāmavarmā
Ctr the commentary called *Dharmākūtam* of Tryambakarāya Makhi(Yajvan)
Ctś the commentary called Taniślokī of Ātreya Ahobala
Cv the commentary called *Vivekatilaka* of Varadarāja Uḍāli (Uḍāri)

* The critical edition uses Cr for the commentary of Rāmānuja, and gives no abbreviation for that of Bansidhara Śivasahāya.

III. EDITIONS

GPP Gujarati Printing Press (also called the vulgate). *Rāmāyan of Vālmīki*. 7 volumes. Bombay: Gujarati Printing Press, 1914–1920. With three commentaries called Tilaka, Shiromani, and Bhooshana. Edited by Shastri Shrinivasa Katti Mudholkar.
VSP Veṅkateśvara Steam Press. *Śrīmadvālmīkirāmāyaṇa*. 3 volumes. Bombay: Lakṣmīveṅkateśvara Mudraṇālaya, 1935. Edited by Gaṅgāviṣṇu Śrīkṛṣṇadāsa.

Journals

ABORI *Annals of the Bhandarkar Oriental Research Institute*
ALB *Adyar Library Bulletin*
Annales *Annales: économies, sociétés, civilisations*
BSOAS *Bulletin of the School of Oriental and African Studies*
HR *History of Religions*
JA *Journal asiatique*
JAOS *Journal of the American Oriental Society*
JAS *Journal of Asian Studies*

JBBRAS	*Journal of the Bombay Branch of the Royal Asiatic Society*
JIP	*Journal of Indian Philosophy*
JOIB	*Journal of the Oriental Institute, Baroda*
KZ	*Kuhns Zeitschrift*
PMLA	*Publications of the Modern Language Association of America*
WZKSA	*Wiener Zeitschrift für die Kunde Südasiens*
WZKSOA	*Wiener Zeitschrift für die Kunde Süd-und Ostasiens*
ZDMG	*Zeitschrift der deutschen morgenländischen Gesellschaft*

Other Important Abbreviations

App.	Appendices to the critical edition of the *Rāmāyaṇa*
crit. app.	critical apparatus
crit. ed.	critical edition
PW	Petersburg Wörterbuch: Böhtlingk, Otto and Rudolph Roth. *Sanskrit-Wörterbuch*. St. Petersburg: Kaiserliche Akademie der Wissenschaften, 1855–1875. Reprint in seven volumes, Osnabrück/Wiesbaden, 1966.
pw	Petersburg Wörterbuch (abridged): Böhtlingk, Otto. *Sanskrit-Wörterbuch im kürzerer Fassung*. St. Petersburg: Kaiserliche Akademie de Wissenschaften, 1879–1889. Reprint in three volumes, Graz, 1959.
v.l.	varia lectio (a variant reading)

Sanskrit Texts Cited

AhirbuS	*Ahirbudhnyasaṃhitā*
AmaK	*Amarakoṣa*
ĀpaŚS	*Āpastambaśrautasūtra*
ArthŚā	*Arthaśāstra*
Āru	*Āruṇikopaniṣad*
ĀśvaGS	*Āśvalāyanagṛhyasūtra*
ĀśvaŚS	*Āśvalāyanaśrautasūtra*
AtriSm	*Atrismṛti*
AV	*Atharvavedasaṃhitā*
Bālrā	*Bālarāmāyaṇa*
BaudhDS	*Baudhāyanadharmasūtra*
BhagGī	*Bhagavadgītā*
BhāgP	*Bhāgavatapurāṇa*
BhāGS	*Bhāradvājagṛhyasūtra*
BrahmP	*Brahmapurāṇa*
BṛĀraU	*Bṛhadāraṇyakopaniṣad*
BṛDharmaP	*Bṛhaddharmapurāṇa*
BṛSaṃ	*Bṛhatsaṃhitā*

BuddhaC	*Buddhacarita*
ChāndoU	*Chāndogyopaniṣad*
DaśKuC	*Daśakumāracarita*
DevīBhāP	*Devībhāgavatapurāṇa*
Dhvanyā	*Dhvanyāloka*
DūtVā	*Dūtavākya*
GautDS	*Gautamapraṇītadharmasūtra*
HariVaṃ	*Harivaṃśa*
KālikāP	*Kālikāpurāṇa*
KāmSū	*Kāmasūtra*
KāśiVṛ	*Kāśikāvṛtti*
KāṭhU	*Kāṭhakopaniṣad*
KātyŚS	*Kātyāyanaśrautasūtra*
Kirātā	*Kirātārjunīya*
KumāSaṃ	*Kumārasaṃbhava*
KūrmaP	*Kūrmapurāṇa*
LaṅkāSū	*Saddharmalaṅkāvatārasūtra*
LiṅgaP	*Liṅgapurāṇa*
MahāBh	*Vyākaraṇamahābhāṣya*
MahāN	*Mahānāṭaka*
MaiS	*Maitrāyanīsaṃhitā*
MaiU	*Maitrāyaṇyupaniṣad*
MālaMā	*Mālatīmādhava*
ManuSm	*Manusmṛti*
MatsyaP	*Matsyapurāṇa*
MBh	*Mahābhārata*
Meghdū	*Meghadūta*
Mitā	*Mitākṣarā*
Mṛcch	*Mṛcchakaṭika*
MudrāRā	*Mudrārākṣasa*
MūlaMākā	*Mūlamādhyamikakārikā*
NalaCarNā	*Nalacaritranāṭaka*
NaraP	*Narasiṃhapurāṇa*
NāraSm	*Nāradasmṛti*
NāṭyaŚā	*Nāṭyaśāstra*
NītiSā	*Nītisāra*
Pā	*Pāṇini's Aṣṭādhyāyī*
PadmaP	*Padmapurāṇa*
PañcBr	*Pañcaviṃśabrāhmaṇa* = *Tāṇḍyamahābrāhmaṇa*
ParaS	*Paramāsaṃhitā*
PrasaRā	*Prasannarāghava*

RaghuVa	*Raghuvaṃśa*
RahaTrSā	*Rahasyatrayasāra*
Rām	*Rāmāyaṇa*
RāmāCam	*Rāmāyaṇacampū*
RāmS	*Rāmāyaṇasaṃgraharaghuvīrastava*
RāmU	*Rāmopākhyāna*
RasGañ	*Rasagaṅgādhara*
RatiRaha	*Ratirahasya*
ṚV	*Ṛgvedasaṃhitā*
ṢaḍviBr	*Ṣaḍviṃśabrāhmaṇa*
SāhiDa	*Sāhityadarpaṇa*
Śāk	*Abhijñānaśākuntala*
ŚāstDī	*Śāstradīpikā*
ŚatBr	*Śatapathabrāhmaṇa*
SkandP	*Skandapurāṇa*
SubhāRaBh	*Subhāṣitaratnabhāṇḍāgāra*
SūktiRa	*Sūktiratnahāra*
SuśruS	*Suśrutasaṃhitā*
TaiBr	*Taittirīyabrāhmaṇa*
TaiS	*Taittirīyasaṃhitā*
TaiU	*Taittirīyopaniṣad*
TāṇMaBr	*Tāṇḍyamahābrāhmaṇa* = *Pañcaviṃśabrāhmaṇa*
UnmaRā	*Unmattarāghava*
UttaRāC	*Uttararāmacarita*
VāsiDS	*Vāsiṣṭhadharmaśāstra*
VāyuP	*Vāyupurāṇa*
Vikramo	*Vikramorvaśīya*
ViṣṇuP	*Viṣṇupurāṇa*
ViṣṇuSm	*Viṣṇusmṛti*
YājñaSm	*Yājñavalkyasmṛti*

Preface

A SENIOR FELLOWSHIP from the American Institute of Indian Studies enabled me to prepare the first version of the translation and commentary of the *Araṇyakāṇḍa* in India in 1979–1980. The research for the book and most of the writing were finished by summer, 1984.

Robert Goldman proved again to be a wonderful colleague and friend. I thank him for his patience with the delays caused by my other research commitments and for his many suggestions on ways to improve the work. Sally Sutherland expertly dealt with all our electronic communications and labored hard to ensure editorial consistency. I am grateful to the late V. W. Paranjpe, Professor Emeritus of Deccan College, Pune, for checking files of the *Encyclopedic Dictionary of Sanskrit* on my behalf, and to Pt. Srinivasa Sastri, with whom I discussed some of the problematic passages in the text.

Two-thirds of my way through this volume, my second and last of the Translation Project, I received much needed encouragement from my friends U. R. Ananthamurthy and A. K. Ramanujan, who not only taught me a great deal about the meaning of the *Rāmāyaṇa* but also reminded me how profoundly important this poem has been, and continues to be, to the social, religious, and literary life of India.

The last of countless passes through the translation was reading it aloud, commas and all, to the poet Judith Kroll. I appreciate her goodwill enormously and her many fine suggestions. My colleague at the University of Iowa, Paul Greenough, as ever was willing to read through my essays and share his learning and critical intelligence with me. Susan Oleksiw did a good job copy-editing a complicated work.

The Introduction brings together in abbreviated and revised form essays that have appeared elsewhere: "The Divine King in the Indian Epic," *Journal of the American Oriental Society* 104 (1984), pp. 505–28; "Rāma's Madness," *Wiener Zeitschrift für die Kunde Südasiens* 29 (1985), pp. 43–56; "Rākṣasas and Others," *Indologica Taurinensia* 13 (1985–86), pp. 152–67. I want to thank Ernest

Bender, Gerhard Oberhammer, and Oscar Botto for their suggestions.

My daughters were the greatest source of joy and support while I worked on this book. If it has any merit, it is mainly because I wanted them to like it.

Sheldon Pollock

Guide to Sanskrit Pronunciation

The pronunciation of Sanskrit is usually not very difficult for English speakers. A few guidelines will serve to clarify the basic pronunciation of the sounds. English examples are based on hypothetical "dictionary" pronunciaton.

Vowels

a	like the u in "but"
ā	like the o in "mom"
i	like the i in "bit"
ī	like the ee in "beet"
u	like the first u in "suture"
ū	like the oo in "pool"
ṛ	something like the ri in "rig"
e	like the a in "gate"
ai	somewhat like the i in "high"; this sound becomes a diphthong to glide slightly into an "i" vowel.
o	like the o in "rote"
au	somewhat like the ou of "loud" with a similar lip-rounding glide.

Consonants

k	like the k in "skate"
kh	like the k in "Kate"
g	like the g in "gate"
n̄	like the n in "sing"
c	like the ch in "eschew"
ch	like the ch in "chew"
j	like the j in "jew"
ñ	like the n in "cinch"
ṭ	like the first t in "start"
ṭh	like the first t in "tart"
ḍ	like the d in "dart"
ṇ	like the n in "tint"
t, th, d, dh, n	like the four preceding sounds, but with the tip of the tongue touching or extending slightly between the teeth

p like the p in "spin"
ph like the p in "pin"
b like the b in "bin"
m like the m's in "mumps"
y like the y in "yellow"
r like the r in "drama"
l like the l in "lug"
v produced generally with just the slightest contact between the upper teeth and the lower lip; slightly greater than that used for English w (as in "wile") but less than that used for English v (as in "vile")
ś like the sh in "shove"
ṣ produced with the tongue-tip further back than for ś, but giving a similar sound
s like the s in "so"
h like the h in "hope"
ṃ a nasalization of a preceding vowel
ḥ an aspiration of a preceding vowel pronounced, almost like an echo, as an "h" followed by the short form of the preceding vowel. For example: devaḥ, pronounced deva(ha)

INTRODUCTION

1. The Problem of the *Araṇyakāṇḍa*

CONTEMPORARY readers of the *Rāmāyaṇa*, when leaving behind "Ayodhyā" (Book Two) and entering the "Forest" (Book Three), are likely to have the impression that they have suddenly fallen down the rabbit hole into the world of Wonderland. Although this is not something traditional audiences seem to have felt (the commentators certainly give no hint of feeling discontinuity), from their first acquaintance with the *Rāmāyaṇa* westerners have always found something highly problematic about the transition between the two books and between the two major portions of the epic they represent.

We are certainly justified in believing that the perspective has changed dramatically and the emphasis shifted. The intensely didactic, even homiletic, discourse of the *Ayodhyākāṇḍa*—its almost obsessive concern with the foundations of correct sociopolitical behavior, with *dharma* ("righteousness") as the necessary condition of communal life, and its recognition of the human predicament before *dharma*'s often conflicting and always imperious demands—has given way in the *Araṇyakāṇḍa* to what seems the entertainment of a romance. In the "Forest" we no longer encounter the problems most humans must confront and solve, those so thoroughly explored in the prior book; we seem no longer to be in a human realm at all.

This may be overstating the case, for the *Araṇyakāṇḍa* maintains an interest in many of the central concerns of the previous volume. Yet the problem of what unifies these two very different sections of the poem remains a challenging one. The epic genre, at least as far as we are able to characterize it on the basis of those examples preserved for us (the *Mahābhārata*, *Vessantarajātaka*, *Nalopākhyāna*, *Harivaṃśa*), seems to have required such a transitional episode within the social, political, and ethical problematic they all share. But most scholars have paid little attention to this convention of the epic and so have not moved very far beyond highly subjective first impressions. In the case of the *Rāmāyaṇa*, consequently, the view persists that the poem is a fusion or amalgamation of two very different and in fact unrelated stories.

This idea was first expressed with conviction and force by the great nineteenth-century Indologist Hermann Jacobi. "One can recognize at first glance," he tells us, "that [the saga of the *Rāmāyaṇa*] is composed of two utterly different and distinct parts. [In the *Ayodhyākāṇḍa*] everything is human, natural, totally free from fantasy. . . . The case is quite otherwise in the second half of the saga, where everything is marvellous and 'fantastic.' "[1] Since Jacobi had determined, with an *a priori* certitude that is arresting, that the epic is essentially the reworking of an ancient "nature" myth, it is not surprising that in his interpretation of the poem he was compelled to leave the first half of it entirely out of consideration.

Most discussions of the problem of *Rāmāyaṇa* unity since Jacobi's time have taken as their point of departure what he had recognized "at first glance" and have only sought to provide additional evidence in support. A particularly tenacious argument of a literary-historical sort is that derived from the *Dasaratha Jātaka*. This text, found in the Pali collection of stories about the Buddha's former births, recounts a tale very similar to that of the *Ayodhyākāṇḍa*—and nothing further. By a mechanical logic it has come to be viewed as representing an archaic version of the poem, which accordingly "must have" ended, like the Buddhist text, with the prince's return directly from the forest and "must have" known nothing of the demon-king Rāvaṇa and his abduction of Sītā. According to this analysis, the *Araṇyakāṇḍa* stands revealed as exogenous to the "original" tale of Rāma.

How little cogency there is to this argument, which draws chronological inferences from what is merely thematic variation, should be apparent, although it has taken years for anyone to provide an adequate demonstration.[2] Yet the dichotomous view of the structure of the *Rāmāyaṇa* that is derived from arguments based on the *Dasaratha Jātaka*, along with highly subjective impressions of what counts as narrative coherence and a conviction that an archaic nature myth formed the original foundation, remains dominant in almost all critical discussion of Vālmīki's epic. The need to develop

[1] Jacobi 1893, pp. 126–27.

[2] Goldman 1984, pp. 32ff.; see also Gombrich 1985, who dismisses the notion that the *Dasaratha Jātaka* can be taken seriously as an early version of the Rāma legend.

a unitary understanding of the poem was eliminated by eliminating the perception of the poem as a unitary work.[3]

What is striking about this literary criticism, beyond the frailty of its arguments, is the cultural arrogance that underlies it. The presumption of the truth of a Western vision is coupled with an implicit dismissal of the entire tradition that produced and preserved the epic. What in this tradition has been considered the first and greatest poem, and venerated as such for two thousand years, is now declared to be, not a meaningful whole—as Indian audiences have invariably taken it to be—but a congeries of utterly distinct and unrelated materials.

Suppose we were to take seriously what generations of performers and audiences have felt, not to speak of the composer, that the monumental poem is not made up of two heterogeneous and uncombinable narratives, but forms a meaningful whole? One of our principal critical tasks would then be to ponder how the work functions as a unit, how its parts fit together to establish a large and coherent pattern of signification. A provisional readiness to posit meaningful unity of the work is at the very least a hermeneutical necessity. If we begin with the hypothesis of meaningless, irrational disunity, we cannot ask meaningful and rational questions. But we face more than a necessity. We face also a postulate authorized by the tradition itself, which has always regarded the poem as of a piece.

Another way to think of this shift in critical perspective is to distinguish between two kinds of history of the poem. If earlier criticism concentrated on the epic's "genetic history" and dismembered the work in the search for its primal components, we might now want to take its "receptive history" more centrally into consideration: Approaching the epic as a whole, in conformity with the tra-

[3] See for example Keith, who speaks of the *Rāmāyaṇa* as "the blending together of two distinct legends, the court intrigues of Ayodhyā and the legend of Rāma's war on Rāvaṇa for the rape of Sītā—in ultimate origin a nature myth." By an almost perverse logic, Keith then argues that the very skill with which the poet has blended together the two heterogeneous parts is evidence of his aesthetic genius (Keith 1920, p. 43). The opinion continues to be transmitted with vigor, by Miller (1974, pp. 132–33), Warder (1975, p. 176), and most recently Smith, who shows how far *Rāmāyaṇa* scholarship continues to be bedeviled by the *Dasaratha Jātaka* (Smith 1980, pp. 62, 73, 76 note 7).

ditional mode of reception, and seeing how it works as a whole can reveal a dimension of the poem's meaning easily as significant as any derived from considering the elements of its genesis. For understanding the work includes, and maybe principally so, understanding what it may have meant in Indian social, intellectual, and cultural history.[4]

[4] For one helpful statement on the distinction between genetic and receptive history (*Entstehungsgeschichte* and *Wirkungsgeschichte*) see Weimann 1978.

2. Summary of the *Araṇyakāṇḍa*

SOON AFTER ENTERING Daṇḍaka wilderness, Rāma is welcomed by the sages living in the forest. They entertain him and ask that, as king, he fulfill his obligation of ensuring their safety. Rāma pushes on deeper into the forest, on the way encountering and killing the monster Virādha, who had tried to abduct Sītā. He then makes his way to the sage Śarabhaṅga. The holy man directs Rāma to the sage Sutīkṣṇa, and before the prince sets out, he watches as Śarabhaṅga immolates himself in a ritual fire and thereupon attains the world of Brahmā. Rāma is then visited by a throng of ascetics, who again beg his protection against injury at the hands of the *rākṣasas*. After seeking out Sutīkṣṇa, Rāma visits the ashrams of the different sages who had been accompanying him and thus passes the first ten years of his fourteen-year forest exile (*sargas* 1–10).

Rāma then returns to Sutīkṣṇa and is directed by that sage to the ashram of the great seer Agastya. The prince is heartily welcomed by Agastya, who provides him with magical weapons and directs him to the lovely region of Pañcavaṭī, where he is advised to establish his ashram and live out the remaining years of banishment. En route to their new home, they encounter an old acquaintance of Rāma's father, Daśaratha, the vulture-king Jaṭāyus, and he is invited to come live in Pañcavaṭī as well (*sargas* 10–14).

One day, while Rāma, Lakṣmaṇa, and Sītā are living peacefully in Pañcavaṭī, they are approached by a *rākṣasa* woman named Śūrpaṇakhā, the sister of Rāvaṇa, king of *rākṣasas*. Śūrpaṇakhā is attracted to Rāma, who jokingly directs her to his brother, and he back to Rāma. Eventually, the *rākṣasa* woman becomes enraged and attacks Sītā. Rāma orders Lakṣmaṇa to cut off Śūrpaṇakhā's ears and nose as punishment. Seeking vengeance, Śūrpaṇakhā hastens to her brother Khara, who dispatches fourteen *rākṣasa* warriors against Rāma. After these are slain in combat, Khara himself leads an army of fourteen thousand to do battle. Rāma annihilates the entire demon force, Khara and his generals included (*sargas* 15–29).

Śūrpaṇakhā in despair makes her way to Laṅkā, the island-fortress of her brother Rāvaṇa. She first reproaches him for his dissolute ways and utter ignorance of the assaults made upon the *rākṣasas*. She then explains in detail what Rāma and Lakṣmaṇa did to her and Khara, tantalizingly describing Sītā to the demon-king. Devising a plan, Rāvaṇa sets off on a sky-going chariot to the mainland and the residence of the *rākṣasa* Mārīca, who is living the life of an ascetic. Mārīca has had two previous encounters with Rāma and both times barely escaped alive. He listens in terror, therefore, as Rāvaṇa reveals his plan: He asks that Mārīca turn himself into a bejeweled deer, explaining that when Sītā sees the deer, she will send Rāma and Lakṣmaṇa to capture it. In their absence the demon-king will abduct Sītā and ultimately be able to slay the two brokenhearted princes. Mārīca's attempt to dissuade Rāvaṇa proves fruitless, and he is compelled to cooperate (*sargas* 30–40).

Arriving at Rāma's ashram, Mārīca takes on the form of a jewel-studded deer and wanders around the grounds. At the sight of the magical deer Sītā begs Rāma to capture it, and the prince sets out after it. Mārīca leads Rāma far from the ashram until finally, exhausted, he is within range of the prince's arrow and is shot. As he lies dying, he cries out in Rāma's voice for Lakṣmaṇa to come to his aid. Sītā hears the cry and in panic insists that Lakṣmaṇa go to Rāma. When Lakṣmaṇa hesitates to leave her alone and unguarded, Sītā questions his motives. He then leaves in a rage. Waiting nearby, Rāvaṇa seizes this opportunity and approaches Sītā in the guise of a wandering mendicant. She welcomes him hospitably and tells him the story of Rāma's exile. The demon-king then reveals himself and begs Sītā to come away with him and be his queen; when she refuses, he carries her off (*sargas* 40–47).

The vulture-king Jaṭāyus, awakened by the commotion, rushes to Sītā's aid. He valiantly struggles with Rāvaṇa, only to be slain in the end. Rāvaṇa flies off with Sītā, who from midair lets fall her wreath of flowers, her golden silk shawl, and her lovely ornaments—the last retrieved by five monkeys on a mountain peak. Reaching Laṅkā, Rāvaṇa again asks Sītā to be his wife. At her stubborn refusal, he has her confined in a grove of *aśoka* trees, guarded by ferocious *rākṣasa* women (*sargas* 48–54).

Rāma, meanwhile, finally recognizing the trap into which he has fallen, is filled with worry. On the way back he sees Lakṣmaṇa coming toward him despondently, and so becomes even more fearful. When he reaches the ashram he finds it empty and spots the evidence of Sītā's struggle. He begins wildly to search the woodland for his wife, like a madman, asking the trees and animals if they know what happened to Sītā and threatening to destroy the world unless he is told. In due course he comes upon the flowers dropped by Sītā, sees the signs of the battle between Jaṭāyus and Rāvaṇa, and finally discovers the vulture-king himself. With his dying breath the bird tells him it was Rāvaṇa who abducted Sītā, but he can say nothing more. Out of filial piety Rāma cremates Jaṭāyus and then continues his search for Sītā (*sargas* 55–64).

In the course of their search the brothers encounter the colossal, headless Kabandha, a monster whose massive arms they sever in battle. When at his request they cremate him, Kabandha arises from the pyre in the wondrous form of a celestial being. He instructs them to go to Lake Pampā and Mount Ṛśyamūka, where the monkey-king Sugrīva is living in exile: He will help them find Sītā. The brothers accordingly set out. On the way, they encounter Śabarī, an old female ascetic who has long been awaiting Rāma's arrival and who shows them warm hospitality. After giving them a tour of the wondrous sights in the ashram of her long-dead spiritual masters, she performs a ritual self-immolation and enters the world of Brahmā. Rāma and Lakṣmaṇa, eager to find Sugrīva, push on and come at last to the shores of Lake Pampā (*sargas* 65–71).

3. The *Rāmāyaṇa*: Myth and Romance?

WHEN I ASSOCIATE the *Rāmāyaṇa* with the genre of romance, I use the term advisedly. Perhaps the dominant critical opinion concerning the section of the epic that begins with the *Araṇyakāṇḍa* holds it to be primarily a fabulous adventure tale, displaying many of the features we associate with the romance genre from its beginnings in the early Greek novel. Although not actually using the word *romance*, the German scholar Pax was the first to look at the work morphologically and identify motifs in this book and those that follow that suggest a generic similarity with European Märchen and ultimately with romance. These include, according to Pax, the abduction of a beautiful woman by a monstrous creature (often the woman's father), her imprisonment in a labyrinthine castle, and her rescue by a hero with the help of animals and by means of a sky-going conveyance.[5]

In fact, the inventory of techniques and motifs representative of European romance and present in the *Araṇyakāṇḍa* and later books could be substantially extended beyond what Pax noticed.[6] For example, in terms of narrative, the *Araṇyakāṇḍa* has the episodic quality of romance, making it quite unlike the narrative in the *Ayodhyākāṇḍa* with its unwavering attention to the storyline. The genre characteristics of the *tīrthayātra* or "tour of pilgrimage sites," which was to find such massive expression in the forest book of the *Mahābhārata*, may be present here only in embryonic form (the stories of the Pañcāpsaras Pond and of Vātāpi and Ilvala, *sarga* 10, for instance, or that of Matañga's forest, *sarga* 70). Yet the overall structure of the narrative, particularly in the first half of the book, reveals the fascination of all romance with the individual sensational episode, and thus employs a discontinuous, catenic way of storytelling markedly different from the previous volume.[7]

[5] Pax 1936 (the work is unfortunately vitiated by bizarre conclusions about the original homeland of the *Rāmāyaṇa* tale). Rāvaṇa becomes the father of Sītā in numerous South and Southeast Asian *Rāmāyaṇas* (Pax had in mind particularly the Kashmiri version). For further remarks on the almost constituent motif of father-daughter incest in European romance, see Frye 1976, p. 44.

[6] For a convenient catalog, on which the comparative observations here and in the following paragraph largely draw, see Dean 1979, pp. 3–13.

[7] A useful distinction between the "hence" narrative of realism, such as is found in

More strictly thematic features of the romance genre found in the *Araṇyakāṇḍa* include marvels and wonders encountered only in an alien environment (*sarga* 4, for example, or 70); the piety of the protagonist and the idealized love relationship between himself and the heroine (and the sexual aggressiveness and deviance of the "others," *sargas* 16ff., 44ff.); the loss of the beloved, the hero's wanderings and the dimension of quest, and the gods' role in the unfolding adventure (*sargas* 55ff.); tokens of recognition (Sītā's ornaments, 52.1ff. and 4.6.1ff.; Rāma's ring, 4.43.1ff. and 5.34.1ff.; Sītā's hair ornament, 5.36.1ff. and 5.64.1ff.); the hero's triumph and, what is most intriguing, his final experience of self-discovery (*sargas* 102–7), which in some respects forms the preeminent message of this category of literature.

So there are an appreciable number and provocative set of convergences between Books Three through Six of the *Rāmāyaṇa* and the European romance genre. And though they have not as yet been cataloged or analyzed, these shared characteristics have made themselves felt and have led many scholars to conclude that the *Rāmāyaṇa* as a whole is best understood as a form of romance.[8] Nevertheless thinking of Vālmīki's poem in this way, however justified it may appear to be by certain surface resemblances, has clear drawbacks. For one thing it stimulates inappropriate, if not false, expectations; for another, it makes some readers less receptive to the product of a very different literary culture, closing off instead of providing access to a whole range of topics in which Vālmīki seems to be deeply interested. Adventure, love, and service, staples of romance that have little broad social significance, are certainly part of his poem, but so are those patterns of "public behavior" that are the central concern of a very different species of literature.[9]

How may we conceptualize this different species of literature that stands in opposition to romance? Here the reflections of Northrop Frye on the distinction between romance ("folktale") and what is not romance—what he terms myth—are valuable:

---

the *Ayodhyākāṇḍa*, and the "and then" narrative of romance is drawn by Frye 1976, pp. 47ff.

[8] See for example van Buitenen 1974, p. 70.

[9] This contrast between romance and epic is well drawn in Jackson 1974, pp. 17–18.

> The difference between the mythical and the fabulous is a difference in authority and social function, not in structure. If we were concerned only with structural features we should hardly be able to distinguish them at all. . . . There are only so many effective ways of telling a story, and myths and folktales share them without dividing them. But as a distinctive tendency in the social development of literature, myths have two characteristics that folktales, at least in their earlier stages, do not show, or show much less clearly. First, myths stick together to form a mythology, a large interconnected body of narrative that covers all the religious and historical revelation that its society is concerned with, or concerned about. Second, as part of this sticking-together process, myths take root in a specific culture, and it is one of their functions to tell that culture what it is and how it came to be, in their own mythical terms.[10]

It is this characteristic quality of "authority and social function," of didactic interest in paradigmatic collective values (rather than idiosyncratic personal ones), that informs the *Rāmāyaṇa*. For all its fabulous diversions, the *Araṇyakāṇḍa* fully shares this interest, and we should review this briefly before turning to consider just what sort of myth Vālmīki's great poem embodies.

What most strongly suggests to us the element of romance in the *Araṇyakāṇḍa* is the situating of the action in the forest. This locale is almost emblematic of romance, supplying an "ancient symbol of uncertain fate," as one of the foremost contemporary scholars of romance puts it.[11] For the traditional India of Sanskrit literature, the forest has additional, more complex connotations. As we saw in the introduction to the *Ayodhyākāṇḍa*, the forest is viewed in stark opposition to the town or city; it is a place prior to, or at least exterior to, many of the claims and obligations of the social world. Life in the forest is not bounded by the confines of family existence; on the contrary, it is precisely where those escaping such confines come to find peace and transcendence—the renouncer, the ascetic, the seer—and, indeed, those who are forced out of collective existence, exiles like Rāma himself. There is in India an ancient link between the spiritual quest and the forest (perhaps crystallized in the name given texts of the later vedic corpus, the

[10] Frye 1976, pp. 8–9.
[11] Vinaver 1966, p. 8.

Āraṇyaka-s, "Forest Books," which pondered doctrines too holy or dangerously mysterious for village life).[12] In this place outside the socialized and the humanized, all that a human is not can be found—monstrous subhuman creatures as well as beings of an almost superhuman spirituality; it is a place where demons, men, *ṛṣis*, demigods, and gods all mingle. More than anything, it is these "interrelated layers of integral powers" that serve to create the "restless and imaginative world" of romance.[13]

Yet certain features of the forest that are almost archetypal in the West are noticeably absent from the *Rāmāyaṇa*. Meditating on the literary image of the wilderness, W. H. Auden speaks of it as "the place where there is no community, just or unjust, and no historical change for better or for worse. . . . Therefore the individual [in the wilderness] is free from both the evils and the responsibilities of communal life."[14] For the ancient Indian king, whether he is on the throne or in exile, there is no freedom from the "responsibilities of communal life." There remains incumbent upon Rāma the obligation of protecting the sages of the wilderness. The ascetics themselves declare this in the very first *sarga* and thereby set the tone for the rest of the book:

> We are residents of your realm and need your protection. Wherever you may find yourself, in city or forest, you are our king, the lord of the people. . . . You must always protect us ascetics, for we are as your children.[15]

From the very beginning of the "Forest" there is a continuous "intrusion" of the central problems of the "Ayodhyā," so resolutely antiromantic in their fundamental significance, so heavily laden with "authority and social function." This in part is what makes it difficult to agree that the *Araṇyakāṇḍa* and what follows is romance in any but a superficial sense.

Just as there is nothing intrusive about the appeal of the ascetics, so there is nothing intrusive about the *Araṇyakāṇḍa* in the epic as a whole. Far from signaling a departure from the previous narra-

[12] Oldenberg 1923, p. 128. See also Parpola 1981, p. 162 and note, who stresses the rites in the *āraṇyakas* that are associated with Śiva, "the dread god of the forest and death" (something pertinent to the discussion of Rāma's "madness" below).

[13] Dean 1979, p. 9.

[14] Auden 1967, p. 15.

[15] 3.1.19–20.

tive, let alone generic discontinuity, this book provides an essential complementarity that helps identify its function in the larger whole of the *Rāmāyaṇa*. One of the more productive ways to think of this unitary product—that is, one producing more interesting and denser layers of meaning—is as a sustained and elaborate "myth" exploring the nature of king, the character and quality of his powers, and every domain in which these powers are manifested. The forest was one such domain, where a fundamental dimension of the kingly function could be illuminated. To appreciate the vision of the king in the forest, however, we need to know how kingship was thought of in traditional Sanskrit culture. And this leads us to confront the basic question of the interpretation of the *Rāmāyaṇa*, the divinity of the hero. For the divinity of Rāma and the nature of the king are inseparably related problems, and together they reveal not only principal concerns of the *Araṇyakāṇḍa* but also a major structural feature of the *Rāmāyaṇa*.

4. The Divine King of the *Rāmāyaṇa*

THE PROBLEM OF RĀMA'S DIVINITY

THE TRADITIONAL readings of the *Rāmāyaṇa* of Vālmīki—including both the countless literary adaptations and the interpretations of the medieval commentators—never questioned the epic's fundamental "organic" unity. Consequently, there was never any doubt that the divinity of the hero formed an integral and authentic feature of the poem and, as such, a fundamental condition of its meaning. Although a wide range of other kinds of interpolations were identified, and a good deal of the narrative itself was felt to pose serious problems of exegesis, nowhere in the history of the indigenous artistic or scholarly appreciation of the poem are arguments ever raised against the divine status of the hero; never, for example, was the suspicion ever voiced that those portions of the epic explicitly positing Rāma's status as an incarnation of Viṣṇu were deliberate, and unassimilable, sectarian interpolations.

Such, however, were the arguments and suspicions of Western scholars from their earliest acquaintance with the poem. Wilson in 1840 noted quizzically, and with evident impatience at the inconsistency, that "Rāma, although an incarnation of Vishnu, commonly appears in his human character alone." The first editor of the epic in Europe, A. W. von Schlegel, questioned the authenticity of those passages that recount the *avatāra*, and his student Lassen argued the matter on far wider narrative grounds, commenting,

> In the epic poems Rāma and Krishna appear, it is true, as incarnations of Viṣṇu, but at the same time as human heroes. These two conceptions are so poorly combined that both generally behave merely like exceptionally gifted men: They act in accordance with human motives, and do not assert their divine superiority at all. It is only in a few sections, interpolated precisely to inculcate their divinity, that they appear as Viṣṇu. One cannot read either poem carefully without having one's attention called to these later interpolated sections of deification, often awk-

wardly inserted, loosely connected with the development of the story, and quite superfluous.[16]

Predictably, attention was soon directed to these interpolations, which Lassen had felt to be self-incriminating. Homeric analysts had already shown how much easier it is to drop a given passage without harm to the "story" than to demonstrate its legitimacy, not to say necessity (for little in the end is necessary).[17] In the same spirit, John Muir marshaled a host of examples that by their contrariety, narrative inconsequentiality, illogicality, or redundancy were thought to prove that the divinity of Rāma could not have formed part of the "original" poem.[18]

If Gorresio and Weber could still call the question an open one, with the publication of Jacobi's book on the *Rāmāyaṇa* in 1893 the issue was to be decided once and, apparently, for all.[19] The theme of Rāma's being a divine incarnation, we are told, was not an original part of the poem but a later addition restricted to the "attached" passages and in no way informing the entire work. Jacobi attributes the deification of Rāma to a process of euhemerization whereby the hero of a (quasi-historical) saga is merging with a popular local divinity, the resulting demigod finally coming to be reckoned an *avatāra* of Viṣṇu. But the divinity of the hero remains a conception that cannot be demonstrated for the five "real" books of the poem; "quite the contrary, there Rāma is thoroughly human."[20]

This in brief is the opinion that has been generally embraced in Western scholarship with respect to the central problem of inter-

[16] Lassen 1866, pp. 586–87 (1st ed.,1843 pp. 488–89). Lassen remarks on his teacher Schlegel's misgivings (apparently never expressed in writing) on p. 587 note of the 1866 edition. For Wilson's puzzlement, see 1840, p. ix.

[17] The medieval Indian scholiasts understood the problem here, cf. Ck cited in the note on 2.73.16.

[18] Muir 1872–1874, vol. 4, pp. 441–81. The traditional interpretation of a good part of this material, for example, the exemplary synthesis of the eighteenth-century scholar-commentator Tryambakarāya Makhi in his monumental *Dharmākūtam*, adequately responds to most of Muir's problems (see Pollock 1984a). The traditional interpretation is not, as a rule, reading alien material into the poem at all; on the contrary, it is reading out what is already there.

[19] Gorresio 1843–1848, vol. 5, pp. xliv–xlviii (soberly concluding, *sub judice lis*); Weber 1870, p. 6.

[20] Jacobi 1893, pp. 61, 65.

pretation bearing on Vālmīki's poem.[21] It is a notion of peculiar tenacity and prevalence, which now, through the operations of what is referred to rather darkly as *wirkungsgeschichtliche Bewusstsein* (that interpretive consciousness shaped by past interpretations), conditions the response many readers will have to the text.

There is no denying that portions of the *Rāmāyaṇa* as we find it in the medieval manuscripts upon which the critical edition is based are later interpolations. Perhaps as much as one-quarter of this vulgate did not form part of the monumental oral poem of "Vālmīki," from which all our recensions and versions derive.[22] For all that, it is striking that a substantial number of the passages long under suspicion have received text-historical vindication from the critical edition. Far from corroborating prevailing scholarly opinion, this edition raises questions about the development and interpretation of the poem that are more complex than earlier scholars realized and that cast serious doubt on the interpretations they offer.

Even though the critical edition reveals interpolations in Books Two through Six touching on the divinity of the hero, they are still

[21] Representative is the standard literary history of Winternitz 1904–1920, pp. 496, 501: "Only in Books 1 and 7 is Rāma throughout considered as a divine being, an incarnation of the god Viṣṇu. In Books 2–6, apart from a few passages which are doubtless interpolated, he is always only a mortal hero"; "in the genuine books Rāma is merely a human hero" (cf. p. 478), or the more recent statement of Botto, that Rāma, "a national hero, whose behavior in the course of the poem is essentially human, is at a certain moment [in the history of the transmission of the text] divinized" (1969, pp. 64–65; cf. p. 69); Goldman and Masson regard Rāma as a "great, but strictly human warrior-prince" (1969, p. 95). In the most recent discussion Brockington (1984) stubbornly reaffirms Jacobi's view: "Far from being a Vaiṣṇava epic, Vālmīki's Rāmāyaṇa is no religious epic at all. It is lamentable that misunderstanding of this point . . . should still persist so long after Jacobi's explicit declaration" (p. 13). Brockington employs an elaborate five-stage scheme of text evolution to demonstrate the developing conception of the hero (from one who is "thoroughly human" to a god, pp. 218–25). There have been dissenting voices, but few new counterarguments (for example, Whaling 1980, pp. 82–92). Whereas Smith seems to accept the received opinion that it is only in Books One and Seven that Rāma is identified with Viṣṇu (1980, p. 50), elsewhere he makes an important if terse counter-claim: "the later material . . . was added to satisfy a need, not to propose an aggrandisement of the hero; it really makes no sense to suggest that the composition of a few thousand lines of verse can, of itself, confer deity on a man, however heroic he may have been" (p. 72, and note 31, where he reasonably suggests that later sectarian revisionists would have done their job more thoroughly).

[22] I discuss the question in Pollock 1984b.

strikingly rare.[23] The complete textual history of the epic, therefore, tends only to strengthen an argument made by Walter Ruben more than fifty years ago (though wholly ignored thereafter): Since so many interpolations in Books Two through Six that are clearly later than the presumed late deification of Rāma say virtually nothing of his divine status, its absence from the five "authentic" books need not indicate its late date. A more cogent explanation might be that mention of it was suppressed in those books "for one reason or other."[24] Below I will discuss what some of these possible reasons might be. A number of them are already identified in the traditional interpretation of the epic. What this interpretation richly demonstrates is that the commentarial tradition—the closest thing we have to an original audience—was entirely aware of the necessity of eliminating explicit reference to the divine identity of Rāma.[25] This suggests that Ruben's hypothesis cannot be dismissed by assuming that "some unspoken but uniformly observed agreement among generations of *Rāmāyaṇa* scribes and reciters" is unwarranted or inherently implausible.[26]

If text criticism leaves open the question whether Rāma's divinity is original to the monumental poem, "higher criticism" as usually practiced has not brought us much closer to a solution. In the first place, the reasons for identifying as insertions materials authenticated by manuscript testimony have never been clearly spelled out. What seems detachable need not, of course, have been attached, for little of this or any other poem is not finally detachable. Anyway, who decides on the criteria for judging what is narratively essential and appropriate in a Sanskrit epic? Moreover, the nature of interpolation itself is complicated (though this has yet to be adequately theorized), and different kinds of motivations underlie it. Interpolation often serves, not to introduce altogether new narrative material, but instead to expand or make manifest the elliptical or latent; what at first sight might appear to be inno-

[23] See for instance 3.423*; 5.1048*.5ff., especially lines 14–21; 6.254*; 6. App. I, No. 32.

[24] Ruben 1936, p. 63.

[25] A representative example is Cg on *sarga* 4.183–19 below; see the note there.

[26] Thus Goldman 1984, p. 43 note. There certainly was "agreement," and it was not in the least unspoken. But why should this be conspiracy, rather than a function of the literary, mythological, and in fact theological sensitivity of artists participating more authentically in a work of art of their own culture?

vation may in reality be amplification or elucidation. The interpolations referring to Rāma's divinity might thus be elaborations of themes embedded in the text—perhaps deeply or structurally embedded, but there nonetheless—which we have been ignoring or doubting because of suspicion provoked by materials that are, admittedly, later insertions. This would provide one reasonable answer to a basic question, though one rarely raised, about the history of the poem: Why should it have proved so perfectly easy to "transform" fundamentally a "heroic epic" according to a later theological program, and to do this without a trace of resistance?[27] Perhaps it has not been transformed at all.

The meaning of a text, as we know, is not just a function of its most literal signification, of what is directly expressed in any given set of verses (unstable as they are). The meaning is also inscribed in higher-order (and more stable) narrative features, in the logic of the story, for example, or in larger motifs and themes. These can generate meaning by their implications, for instance (in the case of narrative logic), or (in the case of motifs) by their literary-historical associations. If there is any truth to this observation, then the divinity of the hero of the *Rāmāyaṇa* cannot be eliminated by the facile excision of any portions of the text. It pervades the tale and is constitutive of it.

Much of the argument against the divinity of Rāma, furthermore, is based on a sense of the "divine" that is unthinkingly ethnocentric. What is "contradictory" in the behavior of "human incarnations," as Lassen would have it, may be so only according to a narrow theological rationalism. What, again, are the standards for deciding whether behavior is reasonable and logical in the case of a being so resolutely unreasonable and illogical as a human embodiment of divinity? Even in passages that are widely held to be interpolations, such as Rāma's interview with his long-dead father, Daśaratha, a curiously ambivalent, "contradictory" attitude is entertained toward the hero: The old king, at the same time as he acknowledges that Rāma is in fact "the heart of the gods, their deepest secret" (6.107.31; cf. verse 30), can still speak to him as if

[27] The interpretive history of the Homeric poems offers an interesting contrast here. The attempts from Theagenes to the Stoics and Neoplatonists to reread the Greek epics as religious allegories not only left the text of the poems completely unaffected but also met with challenge or ridicule in their own times and were ignored thereafter.

he were nothing more than his human son, wishing him "long life" (107.23; similarly Śiva, 107.4–6).[28] Unless we are obstinate enough to postulate interpolations in our "interpolation" here, we must rethink our own sense of what constitutes contradiction and propriety in a text at times very foreign to a modern western reader. It is worth remembering, too, that it was precisely these "contradictory" aspects in the nature of Rāma that have so often been the source of religious mystery and the object of theological reflection.[29] In the Indian tradition, at least, the unity of the "divine savior" and the "ideal human" was easily accommodated.[30]

If the theme of the divine king is authentic to the monumental poem of Vālmīki, obviously it will fundamentally change the way we understand the work as a whole and the *Araṇyakāṇḍa* in particular. We may come closer to deciding the issue in question if we direct our attention to the poem's "structured" message residing in certain higher-order narrative features. One of these is the boon of Rāvaṇa, which is inextricably meshed with the divine status of the hero.[31] The logic of the terms of the boon necessitates the agency of a transcendent entity, one both god and man, for only such a being can confront the power of cosmic evil Rāvaṇa embodies. This is confirmed by the poem itself in various explicit references to the divine plan underpinning the whole action. It is also the conclusion we are compelled to draw by the morphology of the boon motif throughout the history of Indian mythology. The nature of the divine king in ancient India and its historical connection with early Vaiṣṇavism provide further evidence and suggest some new interpretations of the poem on a more global level.

The meaning of a literary text is admittedly not a set of brute

[28] This applies equally to what are evidently later insertions in the *Mahābhārata*, where Kṛṣṇa figures centrally as the supreme deity. He too displays an oddly "inconsistent" nature—now divine, now human—that is not easily explained as a result of interpolation (see for instance much of the earlier portion of Book Twelve, especially chapters 51ff., or a passage such as 6.102.59–70).

[29] We are told, for instance, that in the eyes of Rāmānanda, the important religious reformer of the fifteenth (or fourteenth) century, "History does not afford a better example of a great ruler, loyal husband, and merciful Lord than Rāma" (Srinivasachari 1970, pp. 545–46; cf. Gonda 1963, p. 169).

[30] Cf. Gonda 1963, p. 169.

[31] Although as "genuine" an element of the narrative as any that one could point to, the boon, like the divine status of the hero, has been widely (though mistakenly) believed to be a later insertion (see for example Miller 1974, pp. 132–33).

facts waiting to be assembled, but neither can it be said to be totally, let alone arbitrarily, constituted by the receiver. Texts make promptings and suggestions, have claims of logic and literary-historical associations, and all of this takes place within a finite and to a degree accessible cultural context. The text seems sometimes to be speaking to us on its own and to raise its own questions. Perhaps it is possible to discover these questions and listen to this speech rather than drowning it out with our own querulous presuppositions.

RĀVAṆA'S BOON IN THE *RĀMĀYAṆA*

The first mention of Rāvaṇa's boon in Books Two through Six of the *Rāmāyaṇa* occurs here in the *Araṇyakāṇḍa*, when the *rākṣasa* is introduced to us for the first time:

> It was he who long ago in the great forest had practiced austerities for ten thousand years and unflinchingly cut off his own heads as offering to the Self-existent Brahmā. It was he who had no longer to fear death in combat with any beings—gods, *dānavas, gandharvas, piśācas*, great birds, or serpents—any beings but men.[32]

The causal connection between these two verses will be obscure to the reader unfamiliar with the whole story. It remains so throughout the poem, illuminated elsewhere only dimly, as in the sixth book:

> Then the overlord of the *rākṣasas*, in a towering rage, spoke in the midst of the *rākṣasas*, to encourage them to battle: "For a thousand years I practiced the most intense asceticism, in one holy place and another, until the Self-existent Brahmā was propitiated. In reward for this asceticism Brahmā graciously granted that I need never fear gods or *asuras*."[33]

There may well have been aesthetic reasons for the partial, almost grudging revelation of Rāvaṇa's boon; nowhere in Books

[32] 3.30.17–18. See the notes on these verses concerning the variants in the northern recension and related matters. The commentator Cs here remarks, "Rāvaṇa neglected to include men [in his request], since he considered them nothing more than his food." On this see below, pp. 22–23.
[33] 6.80.22–24.

Two through Six is the whole story told consecutively and straightforwardly.[34] This is what has misled many scholars into doubting the authenticity of the theme. But in addition to manuscript testimony, which is unanimous in those places I have already cited, the boon is mentioned in passing at strategic junctures in the story. Indeed, we are never permitted to forget the conditions under which the hero is operating. Sītā, for example, says to Rāvaṇa in the dramatic moment after he has abducted her, "Even if *asuras* or gods cannot kill you, Rāvaṇa, you have now aroused the bitter enmity of someone you cannot escape alive."[35] In fact, Rāma himself knows of the boon, for prior to his battle with Rāvaṇa he sends him the following message: "Surely today, at last, your pride has been crushed that came from the gift of Brahmā's boon. For here I stand at the threshold of Laṅkā, bearing a staff to punish you who gave me such sorrow by carrying off my wife."[36]

The theme of the boon functions in part to elevate the narrative to the realm of mythic event. It does this by the structural affinity it bears to the many other epic boons that require a divine solution, and I shall come back to this. What I want to consider now are the terms of the boon itself, in isolation from its literary-historical associations. What do these terms imply?

By means of his ascetic mortifications Rāvaṇa has forced the hand of Brahmā and been awarded a boon that makes him invulnerable to all divine and semi-divine beings. The inference to be drawn from the terms of the boon, therefore, is that given by Rāvaṇa's general Prahasta in the *Yuddhakāṇḍa*: "Gods, *dānavas, gandharvas, piśācas*, divine birds, and serpents are utterly incapable of harming you in battle—what of monkeys!" (6.8.2): And what indeed of men? In Book Seven and elsewhere in the *Rāmāyaṇa* tradition it is stressed that Rāvaṇa did not bother to request invulnerability from men and other lower forms of life; it was superfluous.

[34] The only detailed account is in 1.14.12ff. and 7.10.10ff. Cf. also *MBh* 3.259.22ff.

[35] 3.54.8. Cf. 52.18, "mighty Rāvaṇa, deluded by the boon he had been granted, spoke."

[36] 6.31.53. In 6.28.28 Rāma speaks of Rāvaṇa as being "filled with power by reason of the gift of a boon," a line that might appear to be merely formulaic were it not for the passage just cited. See also 4.61.6, where Sampāti relates the prophecy he received from Niṣākara: "The demon [*nairṛta*] shall carry off his wife from Janasthāna—the lord of *rākṣasas*, whom neither gods nor *dānavas* can ever slay."

They were harmless in his eyes, nothing more than food.[37] But what is excluded from the boon is, of course, the only thing that could become the means of his destruction. Therefore Hanumān's inference is the very opposite of Prahasta's. He warns Rāvaṇa, "Because you are invulnerable to gods, *dānavas, gandharvas, yakṣas*, and *rākṣasas*, you could defeat them. Still, monkeys pose a danger to you."[38] Yet the true conclusion of the inference, already hinted at in the passage cited above (3.30.18), is drawn in the fifth book, when Hanumān again addresses Rāvaṇa:

> All the *dharma* [here "power"] you came to possess by your intense practice of austerities it would be most imprudent to destroy—and the life, too, that you possess. You rely on the invulnerability you secured by your ascetic practices, invulnerability with respect to gods and *asuras*. But there is one all-important consideration with respect to that:[39] Sugrīva is not a god or *asura* or *rākṣasa*, not a *dānava, gandharva, yakṣa*, or great serpent. Rāghava is a man, your majesty, and Sugrīva the king of monkeys. How, therefore, do you hope to save your life?[40]

In the end, with clear if futile insight, Rāvaṇa himself grasps this bitter fact:

> Seated upon his heavenly golden throne Rāvaṇa glanced at the *rākṣasas*, and then spoke: "In vain, all in vain were the intense austerities I practiced. The equal of Indra I may be, and yet a man has defeated me. Here, at last, those terrible words of Brahmā have come home to me: 'Know that men still pose a danger to you.' I had become invulnerable to gods, *dānavas, gan-*

[37] See for example *Yuddhakāṇḍa* App. I, No. 32.55; *MBh* 3.265.28. Note also Rāvaṇa's scarcely figurative threat to eat Sītā for breakfast, in 3.54.22.

[38] 6.47.53; compare the insertion of the southern recension, 6.547*.

[39] I substantially agree with Cg (*ayaṃ vakṣyamāṇo hetuḥ*, though he goes on to gloss *bhavadvadhahetuḥ*), against most of the other commentators in my interpretation of the verse.

[40] 5.49.23–26. There are several textual problems in verses 25–26, though none major. I read with the vulgate in verse 25, for as the northern recension serves to corroborate and one of the oldest commentators, Crā, affirms, the reading *mānuṣaḥ* in *pāda* b is false. Note too that although much of the southern recension (though not the vulgate) omits verse 26ab, the idea is attested in the parallel tradition preserved in 1045*. Its absence in part of the southern recension may have resulted from the belief that clarifying to Rāvaṇa the danger posed by Rāma (who, unlike Sugrīva, will indeed kill him) was unaesthetic or narratively improper.

dharvas, yakṣas, rākṣasas, great serpents; but I had never asked to be invulnerable to men."[41]

If for the moment we consider just the terms of Rāvaṇa's boon and the gradual revelation of its single yet critical flaw, only two interpretations seem possible: (a) Rāvaṇa with fatal hubris underestimated the power of man, and he learned this in the hardest way possible, by being killed by one; (b) Rāvaṇa's view of man's power was correct; such creatures, along with all other lower forms of animal life, had no possibility of slaying him: Men are weak and powerless by nature, but especially in the face of the magnitude of evil Rāvaṇa represents, and consequently, he who killed the overlord of *rākṣasas* could not have been a man at all.

It is worth stressing the importance of this central paradox, whichever interpretive option we choose, that runs like a red thread through the poem. Man was not included in the wish because he was judged too insignificant to count. His association with other animals only enhances this estimation. But by that very exclusion, man becomes the sole being who *might* destroy Rāvaṇa and, in that respect at least, becomes more powerful than the gods themselves.

Both explanations of the boon motif entail larger interpretations of the poem. The first one implies that the *Rāmāyaṇa* is offering us a celebration of human potentiality, a paean to man's endurance and triumph over superhuman adversity in an almost Sophoclean mode ("So many awful wonders, yet none more wonderful than man," etc.). This presupposes a man-centered cosmos, since it is exclusively to man that, in the poem's central, insistent question, all efficacy in the struggle against evil is ascribed. But there is no evidence elsewhere in the epic to support this supposition and nothing in traditional Indian culture that would make such an interpretation credible.

If Rāvaṇa's boon does not implicitly exalt the powers of man, then what is it telling us? To my mind it implies that we cannot be dealing with the simple story of a mortal hero, however powerful he may be, struggling with and overcoming a demonic creature (as a genetic literary history of "Indo-European epic," comparing the stories of Theseus, Beowulf, or Siegfried, might urge). If that had been the conception of the composer of the *Rāmāyaṇa*, there would

[41] 6.48.4–7; see also the lament of the *rākṣasa* women, 6.82.29, cited below, p. 27.

have been no reason whatever to build into the story the motif of the boon. This theme serves no other purpose than to "problematize" the human dimension of the hero. In addition to linking the narrative and its hero with the ancient mythic paradigm I describe below, the motif raises questions about the hero's nature that never would be raised were this nature not intended as matter for speculation, interrogation, and wonder in itself. Everywhere the poem indicates that Rāvaṇa's assessment was correct; we are continually reminded that a man can never slay Rāvaṇa and the other *rākṣasas*. What the events of the story are forcing us to conclude is that Rāma cannot, in fact, be a man.

In the *Rāmāyaṇa* allusion is constantly made to the presumed mortality of the hero. This is partly a function of the boon itself, but the effect of the repeated reference to Rāma's human limitations is to engender incredulity in the audience, as in the characters themselves, about his status as a human:

> (Śūrpaṇakhā to Khara:) You are no hero, but a braggart making false claims of valor if you cannot kill Rāma and Lakṣmaṇa, mere human beings the two of them. (3.20.16)
>
> (Khara:) Should the king of the gods himself come on his rutting elephant Airāvata and attack with thunderbolt in hand, in my rage I could kill him in battle. What then of two human beings! (3.22.24)
>
> Fighting all alone on foot, one man, Rāma, killed fourteen thousand awesome *rākṣasas*. (3.25.22; cf. 31.11, 34.8)
>
> (Rāvaṇa to Mārīca:) You cannot dissuade me from doing battle with Rāma—a man, after all, an evil, foolish man. (3.38.4–5)
>
> (Rāvaṇa to Sītā:) Enjoying not only the pleasures mortals enjoy [cf. 3.45.1], lovely lady, but divine pleasures, too, you shall soon forget that short-lived mortal, Rāma. (3.46.14; cf. 47.12 and *MBh* 3.265.28)
>
> (Vinatā to Sītā:) Give your love to Rāvaṇa . . . and give up Rāma, a wretched mortal. (5.22.18–19; cf. verses 3–4)
>
> (Rāvaṇa:) Rāma is a wretched mortal, all alone with only monkeys to aid him. How can you think him capable of doing any-

thing . . . ? And I am lord of *rākṣasas*, a source of terror to the gods themselves! (6.27.4–5)

(Rāvaṇa to Indrajit:) You defeated Indra in combat, one whose deeds have no peer. Shall you prove incapable of slaying two mortals when you face them in combat? (6.67.3)

(The wives of Rāvaṇa:) He who filled Śakra and Yama with terror, who stripped Vaiśravaṇa of the aerial chariot Puṣpaka, who struck wild terror into *gandharvas*, seers, and the great gods, here he lies slain in battle. He who knew no reason to fear *asuras*, gods, or great serpents had this to fear, and from a man. Gods could not kill him, nor could *dānavas* or *rākṣasas*, yet here he lies slain in battle by a mere man, fighting on foot. He whom gods could not slay, nor *yakṣas* or *asuras*, has found his death, like some impotent creature, at the hands of a mortal. (6.98.12ff.)

(Mandodarī laments Rāvaṇa's death:) But surely it was true, great-armed brother of Vaiśravaṇa, that even Indra himself, the breaker of fortresses, feared to stand face to face with you when angered. Surely the seers, veritable gods on earth, the glorious *gandharvas* and the *cāraṇas* took to the horizons in dread of you. And here you are, defeated in battle by Rāma, a mere man. Do you feel no shame, your majesty? What can this mean, greatest of *rākṣasas*? You bestrode the universe in all your royal majesty and might, no one could withstand you, and yet you have been slain by a man, a hermit of the forest. You could take on any form at will and moved beyond the realm of mortals. It makes no sense that Rāma should have destroyed you in combat. (6.99.3ff.)[42]

Gradually, from passages such as these, the mystery of Rāma's nature begins to emerge. "It makes no sense" that Rāma, "a mere

[42] In this category should be placed the repeated, and to my mind curious, epithets applied to Rāma: *gatāyuḥ* (for example, 3.46.14, 53.21; 5.22.21); *parimitāyuḥ* (for example, 3.47.13); *kṣīṇajīvitaḥ* (for example, 3.2.10, 21.3, 34.10). The paradox (that a "mere man, fighting on foot," a "hermit of the forest," should become the slayer of Rāvaṇa) is used with masterful effect in the *Harivaṃśa*, especially in Kaṃsa's frenzied monologue in chapter 65 ("On the one hand there is this wretched cowherd, this man whose powers are sapped by death; and on the other, those wonders performed in my pasturelands that only someone powerful as a god could perform," verse 34). It may be that like many of its other literary characteristics (see Ingalls 1968, p. 393), the *Harivaṃśa* borrowed here also from the *Rāmāyaṇa*.

mortal," should destroy Rāvaṇa in combat. Of course it makes no sense. This is the conclusion the characters gradually draw:

> (Aviddha to Rāvaṇa, as reported by Saramā to Sītā:) Restore Sītā to the lord of men, and show him high honor. The miraculous events at Janasthāna are surely sufficient evidence for you. . . . What man on earth could have slaughtered those *rākṣasas* in battle? (6.25.21–22)

> (Malyavān to Rāvaṇa:) We believe that Rāma is Viṣṇu in a human body.[43] Powerful Rāma cannot be a mere man, not he who bridged the ocean, a most miraculous accomplishment. Rāvaṇa, make peace with Rāma, the king of men. (6.26.31–32)[44]

> (The lament of the *rākṣasa* women:) It must be Rudra or Viṣṇu, or great Indra, god of the hundred rites, or Death himself who has taken on the form of Rāma and is killing us. . . . No god or *gandharva*, no *piśāca* or *rākṣasa* can save a creature attacked by Rāma in combat. (6.82.24ff.)

> (The lament of Mandodarī:) I cannot believe this deed was Rāma's that was done at the forefront of the army, that he should defeat you who were fully prepared for any challenge. Long ago you conquered, first, your senses, and then the three worlds: Your senses remembered that enmity, and it is they who must now have conquered you. Or no, it must be Vāsava come in person in the form of Rāma, exerting his magic powers without warning, to destroy you.[45] For the very day your brother Khara, accompanied by all those *rākṣasas*, was killed in Janasthāna, I knew Rāma could not be a man. (6.99.8–11)[46]

If such references as these served only to show that Rāma is in fact a god, then the terms of the boon come into play, and Rāvaṇa

[43] The northeast version reads "in the deceitful form of a man."

[44] Ck and, following him, Ct call the verse an interpolation. But it is only the Telugu tradition (to which Ck belongs) that does not transmit it.

[45] Cf. the insertion of the southern recension, 3114*: "But Indra is too weak: This must have been the great magician [*mahāyogin*] Viṣṇu."

[46] To encourage this doubt is certainly the effect of *sargas* 19–29 of the *Araṇyakāṇḍa* (the northern recension of the passage from the *Yuddhakāṇḍa* cited above adds similar verses about Rāma's slaying of Vālin and Mārīca, 6.3115*). Nīlakaṇṭha Dīkṣita, the learned seventeenth-century poet, makes this point in his *Rāmāyaṇasārasaṃgraharaghuvīrastava* 12.

need have had nothing to fear: A god cannot slay him. A mere man, pure and simple, could not possibly kill Rāvaṇa, but neither could a god, pure and simple—and yet Rāvaṇa lies dead. By the logic of the narrative we are encouraged if not compelled to conceive of some intermediate being that partakes of both existential realms, combining the nature derived from each into a new, superordinated power—to conceive, in fact, of a god-man.

There are explicit statements in the poem, in addition to its narrative logic, that foster this conception. When Śūrpaṇakhā describes Rāma and Lakṣmaṇa to her brother Khara, saying, "Two handsome young men have arrived, delicate yet powerful. . . . They are the image of the king of *gandharvas* and bear all the signs of royalty. Whether they are gods or men I cannot tell for certain" (3.18.11–12); when Sītā refers to Rāma as having "divine powers" (3.54.14) or Lakṣmaṇa speaks of him as "my brother, who has the powers of a god" (3.66.11), we might be inclined to dismiss it as so much epic hyperbole, like the many tags (*devopama-*, "godlike," and so on) that have been generally viewed as mere ornamental epithets. But it becomes increasingly difficult not to take these statements at face value when we encounter more pointed expressions of this idea, as for example Lakṣmaṇa's words to Rāma later in the *Araṇyakāṇḍa* when he is ready to destroy the worlds in a rage over the loss of Sītā: "Your thoughts are too profound for even the gods to fathom, wise brother. . . . Be aware of your powers, which are as much divine as human."[47]

To be sure, we encounter in other epic traditions frequent reference to what might be judged no more than a semi-divine status of the hero—*theoeikelos axilleus* ("godlike Achilles,"), for example, to go no further afield than the *Iliad*. Yet in such cases the descriptions are purely rhetorical, and this is made quite clear when Homer is compelled to explain, "The first of men [Achilles], but not a match for Gods" (*Iliad* 21.264, in Pope's epigrammatic version). It is precisely the asymmetry between the hero's aspiration to divinity and his irreducible humanity that lies at the core of Homeric and much other epic poetry. As one of the wisest of contem-

[47] 3.62.18–19. *Rām* 2.17.26 adds an intriguing detail. With the sole, and inconsistent, exception of northeast manuscripts (which misunderstood and revised, see Pollock 1986, pp. 358–59), the tradition unanimously makes Rāma twenty-five years old (3.45.10), "and that, they say," as Rāma himself explains for us, "is invariably the age of gods" (3.4.14).

porary Hellenists put it in describing just this contrariety (what he has termed "the heroic paradox"), allusions such as these epithets frame "imply a kind of absolute status which the hero strives to gain," although at the same time he possesses "a desperate self-knowledge" that he is ineluctably mortal.[48] The comparable passages in the *Rāmāyaṇa*, taken in the all-important context of Rāvaṇa's boon, which categorically debars gods and implicitly debars men, acquire a peculiarly mythic resonance absent from the Greek epic with its pervasive tragic humanism. And although there are moments when Rāma's human frailties are stressed, much of the narrative of the *Rāmāyaṇa* serves principally to amplify this mythic resonance till such point as Rāma's unique status as a being of a second order—part god, part man—forces itself unmistakably upon our awareness.

THE MORPHOLOGY OF THE BOON MOTIF

The theme of Rāvaṇa's boon, considered morphologically, opens a similar window, through which we see more than a simple human aspect in Rāma, more too than a "superhuman" aspect. He eludes both because, as the unfolding narrative itself urges us to recognize, he must be a new order of being.

Just as the thematic structure of the *Rāmāyaṇa* moves the narrative to the level of mythic struggle, so too does the very character of the antagonist. In no other respect does Vālmīki's poem so depart from the conventions of the epic as represented by the *Mahābhārata* as in the dimensions of the struggle in which the hero is engaged. The demonic power of the foe is formidable and vast, on an altogether unearthly scale:

> [Śūrpaṇakhā] found Rāvaṇa in his splendid palace, radiant in his power. . . . A hero invincible in combat with gods, *gandharvas*, spirits, or great seers, he looked like Death himself with jaws agape. He carried lightning-bolt wounds received in clashes with gods and *asuras*. His chest was seamed with scars where Airāvata's pointed tusks had gored him. He had twenty arms and ten necks. . . . In combat with gods his body had been wounded in hundreds of places, by blows from Viṣṇu's discus and all the other weapons of the gods. He could effortlessly perturb the im-

[48] Whitman 1982, p. 22.

perturbable seas, level mountaintops, and vanquish the gods. . . . It was he who had gone to the city of Bhogavatī, defeated Vāsuki and Takṣaka. . . . It was he who had gone to Mount Kailāsa and conquered the man-borne Kubera. . . . It was he who in a mighty rage would destroy the gardens of the gods. . . . It was he who, tall as a mountain peak, would extend his arms and prevent the glorious powers, the sun and moon, from rising. . . . He was Rāvaṇa, "he who makes all creatures wail," the terror of all the worlds.[49]

The scale of evil envisioned by the poet, spanning the universe from the nether regions to the heavens, is well beyond the familiar world of most epic literature, where the powers of the antagonist generally retain recognizably human dimensions. The lord of *rākṣasas* exceeds the human capacity for evil to an even greater degree than he exceeds, with his ten heads and twenty arms, the physical power of human beings:

> I am he who terrifies the worlds, with all their gods, *asuras*, and great serpents. I am Rāvaṇa, Sītā, supreme lord of the hosts of *rākṣasas*. . . . In fear of me the gods, *gandharvas, piśācas*, great birds, and serpents flee in terror, as all things born are put to flight by fear of Death. . . . At the mere sight of my face, Maithilī, once my anger has been provoked, the gods with Indra at their head flee in terror. In my presence the wind blows cautiously, and the sun's hot rays turn cold in fear. The leaves on the trees stop rustling, and the rivers slacken their current wherever I am, wherever I go. . . . I can lift the earth in my arms while standing in the sky; I can drink up the ocean, I can slay Death in battle. I can shatter the earth with my sharp arrows . . . or bring the sun to a halt.[50]

In Indian intellectual and cultural history, the question of evil seems generally to be conceived and represented as a mythic problem on a cosmic plane. The demonic is hardly formulated in hu-

[49] 3.30.4–20. On the name Rāvaṇa, see the note on 3.30.20; the popular etymology and its cosmic dimension are corroborated by so (relatively) early a text as the *Harivaṃśa, trailokyarāvaṇaṃ krūraṃ rākṣasaṃ rākṣaseśvaram* (31.123).

[50] 3.45.22; 46.3, 7–9; 47.3–4. Cf.3.60.8–9, and 5.21.16. It is instructive to compare the last verse cited above (3.47.4) with Sītā's description of Rāma later in the *Araṇyakāṇḍa*: "He who could destroy the moon in the sky, send it crashing down to earth, or dry up the ocean, shall come here and set Sītā free" (54.11).

man terms at all; it defines itself only against the divine, as the latter defines itself only against the demonic.[51] The struggle against such evil, in Indian mythology, lies as a rule outside the sphere of human participation. This is plainly the case with Rāvaṇa, whose existence imperils the universal no less than the terrestrial order of things, and whose extermination is therefore a matter of divine concern and intervention. This is something of which the poet takes pains to remind us at critical moments throughout the narrative.

The first intimation that Rāma's personal tragedy—his exclusion from succession to the kingship and his banishment—is part of a greater plan occurs in the second half of the *Ayodhyākāṇḍa*. En route to visit Rāma, Bharata meets the seer Bharadvāja, who admonishes the young prince, saying, "Bharata, you must not impute any fault to Kaikeyī. The banishment of Rāma will turn out to be a great blessing."[52] The notion that any "great blessing" could come about as a result of the tragic events in Ayodhyā—the death of the king, the bitter divisions in the palace, the disaffection of the entire populace—had to strike an "original" audience as paradoxical. Not until the end of the second book is some clarification offered, when for the first time in Books Two through Six Rāvaṇa's name is mentioned. Bharata has stubbornly refused to accede to Rāma's wishes to accept the kingship, in contrast to Rāma, who is prepared to accept his own lot. It is the intervention of semidivine beings that seems to turn the balance: "Then all at once the hosts of seers, eager for the destruction of ten-necked Rāvaṇa, spoke to Bharata, tiger among kings."[53]

What had appeared to be a localized, circumscribed, self-contained set of social and political problems in "Ayodhyā" is now seen to be part of a divine initiative made necessary by the periodic recrudescence of demonic evil. The *Ayodhyākāṇḍa*, given the peculiar focus of its social vision, was an inappropriate arena for anything more than fragmentary revelations. The present book, where Rāma finds himself in a realm that transcends the human world to the same degree that it descends to the demonic, is quite different.

[51] See further O'Flaherty 1976, pp. 9, 58.

[52] 2.86.28.

[53] 2.104.4. See my note on this verse. Although I still find the passage inferior on aesthetic grounds, I am now much less certain of the text-critical judgment I reached there.

The gods themselves acknowledge the heavenly plan that the hero's sufferings advance; and the demons present themselves to permit the plan's advancement.

While proceeding to the ashram of the sage Śarabhaṅga,

> Rāma beheld a great marvel. He beheld Indra himself, lord of the wise gods. His body was luminous as fire or the sun. . . . Seeing Rāma drawing near, Indra, lord of Śacī, took leave of Śarabhaṅga, then turned to the wise gods and said: "That man approaching is Rāma. Before he can address me, conduct me to my residence; hereafter he may see me. When he has accomplished his task and gained victory, I will see him without delay. For he has a great deed to do, impossible for anyone else to accomplish." So Indra spoke, wielder of the thunderbolt.[54]

Besides suggesting a crucial point that the traditional interpretation has always understood—the incarnate god is, or in this particular case must be, ignorant of his divinity—this passage increases our suspicion of a vaster, even cosmic, background of the action of the *Rāmāyaṇa*. This suspicion is finally confirmed by what happens when Sītā is abducted:

> When Vaidehī was assaulted, a blinding darkness enveloped the world, the whole world from end to end, all things that move and do not move. With his divine eye, the majestic Grandfather Brahmā saw the outrage upon poor Sītā, and murmured, "What had to be done has been done. . . ."[55] As [Rāvaṇa] carried Vaidehī over Varuṇa's abode, the waves heaved in agitation, and the

[54] 3.4.4–5, 17–20. Later on, in 3.29.29–32, after the defeat of Khara and the fourteen thousand *rākṣasas*, the "royal seers and supreme seers" will assemble and tell Rāma, "It was to this end that the great and mighty Indra . . . paid his visit to the holy ashram of Śarabhaṅga. The great seers contrived a means of bringing you to this place in order to slay these savage, evil *rākṣasas*." But Indra does not, as promised, appear to Rāma here and will not until after the death of Rāvaṇa (Book Six, *sarga* 105), when the seers virtually repeat what they have said ("You have done what we required, son of Daśaratha [champion of righteousness]," 3.29.32, cf. 6.105.26). The story of Khara prefigures that of Rāvaṇa, and the poet of *Araṇyakāṇḍa* 4 may, in fact, have had the latter rather than the former in mind when composing this Indra episode. For further remarks on this passage, especially the traditional interpretation of Indra's reluctance to converse with Rāma, see the annotations on these verses.

[55] It is typical of the unreflective impressionism ruling in *Rāmāyaṇa* criticism when the editor of the *Araṇyakāṇḍa* remarks that "reference to Brahman here disturbs the narration and therefore seems to be an interpolation" (Bhatt 1963, p. 409).

> fish and serpents were trapped deep below. Then, celestial musicians hovering in midair raised a clamor, and perfected beings cried out, "This is the end of Rāvaṇa!"[56]

Sītā herself will later tell Rāvaṇa, "I know for certain I could never have been stolen away from the wise Rāma, were it not that Fate had destined it—to bring about your death."[57]

In light of these passages it is worth reconsidering two others that, although unimpeachable on textual grounds, have often been called into question on the grounds of "higher" criticism, as being somehow out of keeping with the overall character and concerns of Books Two through Six.[58] The first occurs late in the sixth book: After the defeat of Rāvaṇa, Rāma's long-dead father appears before him on a celestial chariot and says, "Now at last I understand, dear son, how it was by the gods' doing that [you], supreme among men [*puruṣottama*],[59] were destined for this, for bringing about the death of Rāvaṇa. . . . You have completed your stay in the forest, and kept your promise; you have fulfilled the wishes of the gods by killing Rāvaṇa in battle."[60] The second forms part of the lament of the *rākṣasa* women, just before Rāvaṇa is slain:

> The Grandfather had once been won over by Rāvaṇa and granted that he should never suffer harm at the hands of gods, *dānavas, and rākṣasas.* But he had never asked for that with re-

[56] 3.50.9–10, 52.9–10. Malyavān, the venerable great-grandfather of Rāvaṇa, later urges the demon-king to restore Sītā to Rāma and make peace with him; since "the gods and seers and *gandharvas* wish him victory," it is useless to fight him (6.26.10).

[57] 5.20.21.

[58] The first from at least as early as Muir ("this chapter, as it now stands, could not have formed part of the original *Rāmāyaṇa*," 1874, p. 178), to most recently van Daalen ("In 6.105 the gods call Rāma the foremost of the gods. . . . Rāma's divinity is obviously inconsistent with the concept of Rāma as a truly human hero; we can safely assume that Rāma was utterly human in the original *Rāmāyaṇa*," 1980, p. 139; cf. p. 190). These are mere assertions. Both passages are fully represented in every recension and version of the poem; additionally they (or the environment in which they are embedded) show precisely those sorts of inter-recensional variants that speak in favor of their existence during the period of the oral transmission of the poem (see Pollock 1984b, pp. 85ff.; cf. 6.1864*, 1865*, 1866*, etc.; 6.3278*, 3298*, etc.).

[59] Or indeed, "Supreme [that is, Primal] Being"; on this see further below. Both Cm and Cg read the vocative here (not reported in the crit. ed.). The northern recension gives for the second half-verse "that you incarnated yourself in this world [or, on earth]."

[60] 6.107.17, 22.

spect to men, and now it is from a man that harm is coming, we are certain, terrible harm that shall take the life of Rāvaṇa and of every *rākṣasa*. . . . When the *rākṣasa* had got his boon, he began to oppress the gods with his power. They went and paid homage to the Grandfather where he sat blazing with ascetic splendor. The Grandfather was gratified, and for their welfare the great one spoke these great words to the deities: "Forevermore from this day forth all *dānavas* and *rākṣasas* shall eternally roam the universe overmastered with fear." . . . The gods then convened and under the lead of Indra they all propitiated the great god, the bull-bannered destroyer of the Triple City.[61] The great god was propitiated and said to the deities, "For your welfare there shall come into being a woman, to bring destruction upon the *rākṣasas*" [cf. 3.52.6, 11]. . . . And Sītā must be she, employed now by the gods to slay the *rākṣasas*—as once, long ago, Hunger slew the *dānavas*—and she shall devour us and Rāvaṇa as well.[62]

In the total context of Books Two through Six, there is clearly little that argues against the authenticity of these last two passages, and much that speaks in their favor. Viewed comprehensively, they show themselves to be, not afterthoughts or isolated allusions, but part of a design. The cumulative impact of such periodic revelations is to transform the perspective from which we view the story. Once more the assumption is encouraged that the human narrative is intricately meshed with, and finally subsidiary to, a divine plan in which Rāma (along with Sītā) has for some reason been appointed the principal actor.[63] The character of Rāvaṇa, as we have seen, reinforces this assumption, as does the boon motif. For the formula by which this motif is constituted posits this signification, and at the same time clarifies why this "mere man" should have become the instrument of a cosmic purpose.

The boon was granted to Rāvaṇa by Brahmā in consequence of

[61] Ct remarks that Brahmā had ordained only that the *dānavas* and *rākṣasas* live in terror; Rudra would provide for their annihilation.

[62] 6.82.29–36. Cf. 3.35.5, where Sītā is suspected of being "born to take [Rāvaṇa's] life." The theme probably contributed to the creation, or absorption, of the story of Vedavatī at *Uttarakāṇḍa* 17.

[63] As has long been maintained, on the basis of Sītā's birthstory (*Bālakāṇḍa* 65; *Ayodhyākāṇḍa* 110) and the radical signification of her name (literally, "furrow," or maybe even "crown land"), she would represent an earth goddess, perhaps specifically the Earth goddess joined by a *hieros gamos* to the sacral king.

the intense asceticism the *rākṣasa* had performed over thousands of years, and it provided that he could never be slain "by gods, *dānavas, gandharvas, piśācas*, great birds, or serpents." In Sanskrit epic and purāṇic literature the performance of austerities almost mechanically compels the gods to fulfill any demand of the claimant. They are invariably asked to grant the gift of immortality, but they themselves won this only with great effort when they churned the empyreal ocean, and it is the one gift they cannot bestow.[64] Yet like so many others, Rāvaṇa seeks to achieve the same result by a gambit widely familiar in folklore: attempting to frame the perfect wish. The sheer impossibility of an exhaustive catalog, however (in this case overdetermined by Rāvaṇa's scornful dismissal of man), immediately implies that a solution is assured; the very provisions of the boon make it inevitable that a proxy will be found. Not a god, since the gods have become, so to speak, contractually impotent; nor yet a man, men being constitutionally impotent, the "food" of *rākṣasas*. Instead it must be an unprecedented combination of the two.

These thematic implications are in part manifested in the divine plan sketched above. In addition, the way the boon is formulated—which turns out to be an ancient building block of Indian myth—necessarily entails this: The formulation ensures that the boon will be counteracted, and what will counteract it is a previously nonexistent being, either a purely deceptive being or, more usually, one entirely outside the catalog of natural possibility. Before tracing the roots of this "morpheme" into the vedic tradition and the special association it later comes to have with the corpus of Vaiṣṇava mythology, let us examine its function as a structural feature in epic myth-making.[65]

In *MBh* 1.201 is found the "old tale" (*itihāsa purātana*) of Sunda and Upasunda, brothers born in the line of the "great *asura*" Hi-

[64] As the *Mahābhārata* often tells us (1.201.20ff.; 8.24.6ff., etc.).

[65] The motif of the boon granted in recompense of asceticism has never been examined in detail, despite its prevalence in the literature. In fact, I am unable to find much outside Hopkins's observation that "the weakness of the gods mentally continually leads to their giving boons to their cunning foes" (1915, p. 43). Hopkins misunderstands the mechanistic dynamic that is of the very substance of *tapas* and yoga (for it is a commonplace in Indian texts that ascetic renunciation, if once undertaken, must inevitably bear fruit): The gods grant boons under a compulsion that is beyond their control, yet the terms by which they grant them demonstrate, precisely, their comprehensive foresight.

raṇyakaśipu. Inseparable companions and deeply devoted to one another, they resolve to conquer the universe, and set off for the Vindhya Mountains to practice austerities. The gods come to fear their growing ascetic power and try to disrupt their mortifications by tempting them with precious objects, women, and the like. But the gods are unsuccessful, and in the end the Grandfather must appear before the two and grant them a boon. In addition to magic powers, they seek immortality, the one thing Brahmā must withhold. "But," says Brahmā, "you may choose some way of dying that will make you as good as deathless."[66] They reply, "Let us have nothing to fear from anything existing [*bhūtam*] in the three worlds, anything that moves or does not move—anything, Grandfather, but ourselves."[67] There must of course be an omission in their request for invulnerability, otherwise they would indeed be immortal, and so they choose what alone seems to them unthinkable as a source of danger. Brahmā agrees, and in the possession of their boon the demons attack the gods, conquer heaven and the netherworld, and, coming to earth, slaughter kings and brahmans, on whose sacrifices the power of the gods depends. The seers appeal to Brahmā, who reveals the way to slay the demons. Viśvakarman is asked to create a woman, and gathering "every existing thing in the three worlds, everything that moves and does not move that was beautiful," the divine craftsman fashions a new creature whose beauty was unlike that of any female in the three worlds.[68] Sunda and Upasunda see her, fall to fighting over her, and so kill each other.

The cosmic dimension of the story is worth singling out first. The boon activates a power that throws the universe—the triple world of heaven, earth, and the underworld—into turmoil, making divine intervention unavoidable. The catalog of conditions in the boon requested by the *asuras* is familiar, as is the use of a ruse to obviate them. The demons had aimed at and nearly achieved the exhaustive list; what they neglected to include was a combination of already existing substances into some hitherto nonexistent being, emanating from the gods and yet not one of them. And it

[66] 1.201.20; on this often misunderstood line see Nīlakaṇṭha.
[67] 201.23.
[68] 203.14.

is this, and this alone, that is able to trigger the necessary yet seemingly unattainable event, the fratricidal conflict.

A second epic example of the motif is contained in the well-known story of the demon Tāraka and the birth of Skanda.[69] When after their marriage the divine couple Śiva and Ūmā begin their lovemaking, the gods grow fearful lest the offspring of such a union bring about universal destruction and therefore implore Śiva to withhold his seed. He agrees, but Ūmā, furious that the chance of her bearing children is ruined, curses the gods to be childless themselves. Agni, the god of fire, was absent at the time of the curse. A drop of Śiva's seed, moreover, had fallen from him and into Agni, where it grew great. Now, at this time, oppressed by the demon Tāraka, the gods and all other divine creatures seek the aid of Brahmā, explaining, "The Blessed One gave the *daitya* a boon, and he has become overweening in his power. The gods cannot kill him. How then is he to be quelled? For the boon he acquired from you, Grandfather, was this: 'Let me be invulnerable to gods, *asuras, rākṣasas*.' And the gods have now been cursed by Rudrāṇī when we ruined her chance of bearing children. She said, 'You shall never have offspring,' lord of the universe."[70] And Brahmā replies, "Agni was not there at the time of the curse, best of gods. He shall produce a child to slay this enemy of the gods. And that shall be a creature transcending the gods, *dānavas*, and *rākṣasas, gandharvas*, men, serpents, and birds" (84.8–9). Skanda is later born and slays Tāraka.

As before, in addition to the boon, the catalog of exclusions, and the cosmic peril, a being of an entirely new order is required, different from and greater than any existent divinity, since its origin is unique and in fact is antinomic: It is the seed of Śiva, borne by Fire (Agni), fertilizing Water (the Ganges), and brought forth simultaneously by six different mothers, whereupon its several parts miraculously merge.

Especially suggestive is the myth of the *asura* Hiraṇyakaśipu and his death at the hands of Viṣṇu in the form of a man-lion.[71]

[69] The version to which I refer here is found in *MBh* 13.83–86. See also *Bālakāṇḍa* 36.

[70] 13.84.5–7 (translated thus *pace* the unidentified commentary cited in the critical notes).

[71] The earliest version is contained in the *Mahābhārata* tradition, *MBh* 3.27*.53–62 (cf. Hacker 1959, pp. 25–26 and note 1.1). The story must already have been

> Long ago, in the Kṛta Age, the haughty enemy of the gods, the Primal Being of *daityas*, practiced austerities for ten thousand years, and ten hundred years, and five. . . . Brahmā was pleased with his asceticism and acts of self-denial, and appeared before him in person. . . . "Please choose a boon," he said, "and fulfill whatever desire you wish." Hiraṇyakaśipu replied, "O best of gods, let me never be slain by any gods, *gandharvas, yakṣas, rākṣasas, piśācas,* or men." The great-armed Viṣṇu then took on a form that had never before existed: The Lord made one-half of his body a man's, the other half a lion's, and rubbing his hands together he went to the assembly hall of the lord of *daityas*. The Primal Being [*ādipuruṣa*] of the *daityas*, the enemy of the gods, the delight of Diti, saw that form, one never seen before, and his eyes blazed red in anger. Hiraṇyakaśipu . . . closed with the man-lion, the far mightier lord of beasts . . . and with its razor-sharp claws the man-lion's body tore the demon to pieces.[72]

Demonic evil on a cosmic scale can be neutralized by none of the available divine powers.[73] The supreme god Viṣṇu must contrive "an embodiment that had never before existed," again a miraculous life form necessitated by the comprehensive exclusions of the boon.

We can now see that these narratives are offering us an established constellation of mythological components: a boon awarded as a result of ascetic practices; an ensuing threat of cosmic evil; the intervention of the divine and its transmutation into a preternatural form that circumvents the boon's apparent all-inclusiveness—

---

known in a fuller form given, first, the elliptical quality it has here; second, the need for an answer to the central question, why the form of a man-lion (the one question Hacker oddly does not ask, 1959, p. 26); and finally, that it supplies material for paradigmatic reference in the old battle books of the epic (see for example *MBh* 7.164.146, 168.21; cf. 3.100.20). I thus include in the synopsis that follows this necessary elaboration, the earliest version of which is found in the *HariVaṃ* tradition (especially 31.32–43).

[72] *HariVaṃ* 31.32–43. The text and interpolations here, as in later versions of the myth, extend the list to exclude death by any weapon, by anything wet or dry, neither by night nor by day, in the sky or on the ground, inside or outside (see also *MBh* 2.21*.194–99), which together result in the elaboration in later renditions that Viṣṇu slays the demon at sundown, emerging from a pillar in his palace, and so on.

[73] Cf. also *HariVaṃ* 31.63; the connection with the *rāmāvatāra*, 31.123, can hardly be missed.

implying above all how impossible it is to contain the divine within any ordinary category of life.

That this has to be seen as a very ancient and invariant pattern of expectation is made probable by the evidence of vedic mythology. One example attesting to the existence of the formula from earliest Indo-Aryan times, as well as an ancient association with Viṣṇu, will suffice.[74] The narrative of the dwarf incarnation of Viṣṇu is alluded to frequently in the earliest strata of vedic literature, although the first connected narrative is that of the *Maitrāyaṇī Saṃhitā*:[75]

> [The gods wanted to recover their realm from the demons.] They turned Viṣṇu into a dwarf and brought him [to the demons]. "Whatever he might cover in three strides shall belong to us [the rest to you]." He strode first over this, then this, then that [that is, earth, sky, heaven].[76]

The vedic texts are very spare in their narratives and do not tell how the demons had acquired the power to seize control of the universe. Early epic and purāṇic literature supplies the necessary background. Here the demon Bali replaces the anonymous horde of *asuras*, and the standard motif resurfaces:

> Bali, the great *asura*, had become invulnerable to all creatures, and you [Viṣṇu] took on the form of a dwarf and ousted him from the triple world.[77]

> Brahmā, the granter of boons, granted that you [Bali] attain the power of Indra, that you be deathless and unconquerable in battle.[78]

[74] The widespread and ancient myth of Indra and Namuci fits perfectly into this pattern: a cosmic struggle with soteriological meaning (cf. Gonda 1960, p. 58), a boon, a catalog of exclusions, a divine ruse that violates natural laws (soft foam becomes the weapon used to decapitate the demon, etc.). See *ṚV* 1.53.7 and 8.14.13, *MaiS* 4.3.4, *TaiBr* 1.7.1.6 (and cf. Bloomfield 1893, pp. 143–63).

[75] See Tripathi 1968, where most of the relevant data is collected.

[76] *MaiS* 3.7.9. Cf. Tripathi 1968, p. 35.

[77] *MBh* 3.100.21.

[78] *HariVaṃ* App. I, No. 42B, lines 2325–27 (vulgate 3.63.5–6). When Indra attacks Bali he hears a divine voice that tells him, "Desist, you cannot slay Bali in combat. . . . He is superior by reason of the gift of the boon. . . . Only the Blessed One [Viṣṇu] shall be able to slay him" (*HariVaṃ* 64.21–25). When the gods come to supplicate Viṣṇu, they explain, "By reason of the gift of the boon from Brahmā,

The motif is thereupon subject to a slight inversion; it is now the demon Bali who dispenses a boon to Viṣṇu. The dwarf is given as much land as he can cover in three steps, and as the *Mahābhārata* tradition puts it, "Hari took on a divine, utterly miraculous form as he strode out, and with three strides he took all the earth."[79]

From the beginning, this act of Viṣṇu's has been associated with his divine mission. Concomitantly, Bali—exactly like Hiraṇyakaśipu and Rāvaṇa—is regularly represented as a power of cosmic dimensions.[80] And the miraculous transformation, far from being a trickster's "stratagem to avert the suspicion of the asuras," fits squarely into the pattern I have been tracing.[81] In that environment the pattern recovers something of its centrality to ancient myth and to the understanding of the divine in early Indian thought: As in the case of the man-lion and all the others, an attempt is made to give expression to the incomprehensible character of the divine, whereby we can begin to understand that it does not exist within the world of nature, "the realm of necessity," that it is not constrained by the limits of the possible. No inventory of the physical world, however exhaustive, can subsume the capabilities of what transcends all natural categories. On the one hand, then, the divine may be what it certainly seems not to be (the dwarf, for example), and on the other, it can indeed be what has never been seen to be (the man-lion).[82]

[Bali] seized the whole world from us. . . . And it is said he is invulnerable to us all" (70.46–47; cf. also Tripathi 1968, pp. 81ff., especially p. 88).

[79] *MBh* 3.27*.79.

[80] Explicitly only from the epic period on (*MBh* 12.216.5–6; cf. *HariVaṃ* App. I, No. 42B, lines 2322–24 [vulgate 3.63.4]), but likely to derive from ancient material. On Viṣṇu's soteriological mission, see *ṚV* 6.49.13, "Three times did Viṣṇu measure out the terrestrial realms for the afflicted Manu," that is, again, man; cf. Tripathi 1968, p. 4.

[81] Macdonell 1897, p. 41; see also Gonda 1969, p. 146.

[82] Further consideration of the development of the *avatāra* doctrine, to which these theological reflections lead, is not possible here (preliminary speculations are offered by Hacker 1960, pp. 47–70). Nevertheless, it is worth noting that in Vaiṣṇava circles—along with notions of immanent divinity, of a present god whose *vibhūtis* empower the world and yet who remains a *deus absconditus*, a god hidden by the vast powers of his *māyā* and deceit—the motif was adopted as a major component in the mythic representation of Viṣṇu's salvationary purpose. In the cosmogony of *MBh* 12, for example, during Brahmā's demiurgic activity Viṣṇu reflects, " 'Brahmā has created all these creatures, *daityas, dānavas, gandharvas, rākṣasas*. . . . There are many of them on the earth, and they are powerful. They shall practice asceticism and

I suggest that the figure of Rāma, from the time the full narrative took shape in the monumental *Rāmāyaṇa*, has been conceived after the model furnished by these ancient morphemes of Indian myth.[83] Neither a man nor even a "simple" god, he incorporates the two and so, in a sense, transcends them both.

When I use the term "myth" here, I have in mind a patterned representation of the world, with continuing and vital relevance to the culture, which furnishes a sort of invariable conceptual grid upon which variable and multifarious experience can be plotted and comprehended. It is this essential power to interpret and explain reality—and I mean social reality in the first instance—that has gone largely unappreciated in previous mythic interpretations of the *Rāmāyaṇa*.[84] Having assembled the essential building blocks, we are in a position to explore the mythological map of experience charted by the *Rāmāyaṇa*, to discover what Frye might call the myth's "authoritative social function," how, that is, it "tells a culture what it is." A point of entry is provided in the last example of the theme I want to look at.

In the tale of Dhundhumāra the protagonist is an earthly king (in fact, like Rāma, a member of the Ikṣvāku dynasty) but stands in a special and intriguing relationship to divinity:[85] The aged

---

acquire ultimate boons, and driven mad by their boons all without fail shall harass the gods, the seers, the ascetics. . . .' So [Viṣṇu] reflected, and he created many forms in order to make himself manifest [*prādhurbhavabhavāya*]: the boar, the man-lion, the dwarf, and the man [that is, Rāma Dāśarathi]. 'With these I shall slay the evil enemies of the gods' " (verses 337.29–36).

[83] Although I am primarily concerned here with a structure of thought, not a matter of literary history, it should be mentioned that Vālmīki knew well both the Bali and Namuci myths (3.27.3, 29.28; see also my note on 2.12.8 and references there, and 6.47.119) and exploits them to telling effect in similes, as when Lakṣmaṇa says to Rāma, "My wise brother, you shall recover Janaka's daughter Maithilī as surely as great-armed Viṣṇu recovered the earth and left the demon Bali in chains" (3.59.22, recurring at 5.19.24; a later rhapsode reveals the paradigm fully when he has Mārīca attempt to dissuade Rāvaṇa by saying, "The delight of the Raghus could slay Bali, or Namuci," 3.738*).

[84] These for the most part have been either mechanical or completely reductive. (I am thinking less of Jacobi's own theory of the *Rāmāyaṇa* as a vedic myth *redivivus* [1893, pp. 126–39] than of its present-day reaffirmation from the Dumézilian perspective, for instance, Puhvel 1974, and the direct application to the *Rāmāyaṇa* of the *idéologie* in its pure, Procrustean form, [Dubuisson 1979, expanded in 1986]).

[85] The oldest version is contained in *HariVaṃ* 9.46–77. As is the case with the man-lion myth, this archaic version is at times so elliptical that it must presuppose a fuller

Ikṣvāku king Bṛhadaśva, having set his son Kuvalāśva on the throne, retires to the forest. The sage Uttañka tries to stop him, seeking the king's protection from the *rākṣasa* Dhundhu, who lies beneath the sands of the ocean Ujjanaka practicing austerities in order to destroy the worlds, the thirty gods, and Viṣṇu himself. "For the gods cannot slay him," Uttañka explains, "nor can *daityas* or *rākṣasas*, great serpents, *yakṣas*, or *gandharvas*—no one, for he once received a boon from the Grandfather of the world." The king is asked to slay the demon "for the good of the worlds," and Uttañka tells him further that Viṣṇu shall augment his power by means of his own divine might, thanks to a boon the god once granted the sage. But the aged king, having renounced all violence, declines to do the deed himself and directs the sage to his son. Kuvalāśva and Uttañka proceed to the ocean and then, "The Blessed One, Lord Viṣṇu, entered into Kuvalāśva with his fiery power at the direction of Uttañka, and for the good of the world." By drinking up the tidal wave caused by the demon's earthquake, and with the water putting out the fire within it, the king, "a great yogin by means of Viṣṇu's yoga," kills the volcanic Dhundhu (and so receives the name Dhundhumāra).

Once again a situation is contrived that points up the incapacity of the gods, or of any other divine or semi-divine being, to confront and master evil on their own (whether moral or natural evil makes no difference). Another creature—man—is required; but being naturally powerless man needs the infusion of Viṣṇu's power. Filled with the divine potency, this extraordinary new creature, the earthly king—and only he, no god or man—can protect the brahmanical world order (here represented by Uttañka) by destroying evil.[86]

Here as in other versions of the motif, the catalog of the boon

narrative. The derivative version of the *Mahābhārata* (3.192–95) provides necessary elaboration.

[86] Similar in structure and concept are the stories of Arjuna's defeat of the Nivātakavaca demons (*MBh* 3.169) and his destruction of the demon city Hiraṇyapura (*MBh* 3.170). Discussing the Nivātakavaca tale Scheuer refers to the "familiar schema of the king-*avatāra* delivering the gods and the worlds from the domination of *asuras*," and asserts that, "exactly like the *MBh* as a whole, or again, the *Rāmāyaṇa*, it is but another episode in the war of the gods and *asuras*, the reconquest of the gods" (Scheuer 1982, p. 227). If this is so, one wonders why it is not the gods themselves, *in propria persona*, who are fighting. What is above all significant about the tales is the modification they introduce in the ancient theme.

does not imply that the slayer can be merely a creature inadvertently omitted from the list. If explicitly excluded, he must then be charged with divine potency; if not, he must belong to a new order of being, in substance not comparable to any hitherto conceivable life forms. Dhundhumāra, like Rāma, is clearly not the sort of hero familiar to us from Western epic, for such heroes are men who do more than ordinary men, not more than gods. These two, by contrast, are men who do what, for some reason, gods cannot. Not merely more than human, they are in some way more than divine. Finally, what makes the adaptation of the ancient motif particularly suggestive, complex, and powerful in the *Rāmāyaṇa* is that this second-order being, this divine human or mortal god, is here coupled with a sociopolitical representation of everyday life in traditional India: Such intermediate beings, gods who walk the earth in the form of men, are kings.

THE ANCIENT INDIAN KING

The divine nature of the earthly king has been a matter of dispute among students of early Indian thought. Most contemporary scholars, however, agree that the conception was present from the time of the vedas and continuously gained in importance thereafter.[87]

There is no need to invoke the strong concomitance between authority and the supernatural in *pensée sauvage* in order to establish this, nor the sacred status of the king elsewhere in the Indo-European cultural domain.[88] In the vedic hymns kings, or better chiefs, share certain major activities with the gods, Indra in particular, and they play as well a role of cosmic significance; they are called not only "half gods" (*ṚV* 4.42.8–9) but also "gods among men" (*AV* 6.86.3).[89] Additional evidence is provided by the ritual prose texts discussed below. By the time of the epics, lawbooks, and, later, the first *purāṇas*, the documentary evidence becomes overwhelming. We can look at one representative epic text from

[87] See for example Spellman 1964, pp. 27, 37; Gonda 1969, p. 103.

[88] On the first see Gonda 1969, p. 9; the sacral king of Indo-European antiquity is discussed in Dumézil 1948, pp. 19ff.; a detailed and instructive recent study of a particular Indo-European tradition is that of Chaney on the "Woden-sprung kings" of Germanic paganism (Chaney 1970, especially pp. 7–42).

[89] See further in Gonda 1969, pp. 109, 54 and note 368.

our most important source of traditional Indian political theology, the *Rājadharma* section of the *Mahābhārata*. This offers a strikingly forthright expression of attitudes and beliefs about kingship, and in several respects seems almost a gloss on the story of the *Rāmāyaṇa*:

> If kings did not exist, no creatures anywhere could exist, and because kings exist, other creatures do. Who dares refuse them homage? Whoever bears the burdens imposed by the king, which bring happiness to all the world; whoever strives to please and benefit him, wins both this world and the next. But whoever even thinks of doing evil to the king assuredly finds affliction in this world, and at death goes to hell. Never should the king be scorned as being a mere mortal: He is great divinity existing in the form of a man. He can take on any of five different forms, as occasion demands: He may become Fire, the Sun, Death, Vaiśravaṇa, or Yama. One must be zealous and careful not to contradict the lord, nor grumble against him, if one hopes to acquire righteous merit. A man who acts in opposition to the king never gains happiness, neither he himself nor anyone close to him—son, brother, friend. Even when driven onward by the wind, its charioteer, fire might leave something in its wake; but to the one who thwarts the king nothing whatever will be left. All that the king owns is to be preserved as his; keep your distance from it. Taking something of his should be seen to be as fraught with terror as death itself; touch it and you perish. . . . The king is the very heart of hearts of his subjects, their foundation, refuge, and ultimate happiness. Putting their reliance in their king, people never fail to win this world and the world to come.[90]

Passages like this make it evident that kings—or more precisely, righteous kings—were invested with the status, the powers, all the ontological meaning and significance of divinity. But can we be certain the author of the *Rāmāyaṇa* shared this conception? For though the *Rājadharma* discourse seems representative for much

[90] *MBh* 12.68.37–59; cf. *MBh* 12.65.29, "A king of men is an eternal god; the gods themselves hold him in honor." That happiness depends on obedience to the king is stressed in the *Rām*, see 38.20 below, and note the close parallel in 38.12 regarding the functions of the several divine forms (explained in the *Rājadharma* passage, verses 41–47).

of the epic period, it has often been noted that stony silence if not outright contradiction with respect to the king's divinity can be found elsewhere; some early lawbooks, for example, seem indifferent or even hostile to the notion.[91]

The silence encountered in the early *dharmaśāstras* need not, of course, be interpreted negatively, and the denials of a king's divinity need not belong to the historical period of the monumental poet. And even if contemporary with him, denial of kingly divinity indirectly implies that for some it was an article of belief (a verse from the *Ayodhyākāṇḍa* discussed below makes this clear). In any case, the orientation of the *Rāmāyaṇa* is hardly in doubt. Whether or not this reflects widespread consciousness may be a matter of secondary importance. At times, Vālmīki's poem leaves the impression that the political theology is a doctrine in the making and that its consolidation is a principal objective of the poet.

Although we cannot expect to find in a poetic text like the *Rāmāyaṇa* the discursive plenitude of the *śāstra* portions of the *Mahābhārata*, we can still assemble sufficient evidence to determine its understanding of the divinity of kings. A passage strategically placed at the beginning of the *Araṇyakāṇḍa*, for example, setting the tone for all that follows, nicely expresses the bivalent nature of the earthly king. Here the seers are addressing Rāma: "As guardian of righteousness and glorious refuge of his people, a king is worthy of reverence and esteem. He is a guru who wields the staff of punishment. A king is a fourth part Indra himself and the protector of his subjects, Rāghava. Therefore he enjoys the choicest luxuries and is held in honor by the world" (3.1.17–18).

These verses imply a divinity of a "functional" sort, referring in particular to the king's protectorship through his exercise of legitimate force. Something similar occurs in the *Ayodhyākāṇḍa.* Here Bharata is urging Rāma to return to the city and take up the duties of kingship, which he sees himself incapable of shouldering. For, he argues, "some say a king is but a mortal; I esteem him a god. His conduct in matters of righteousness and statecraft, it is rightly said, is beyond that of mere mortals" (2.95.4). If the divine status of the king may have been subject to public questioning, its existence would by the same token be confirmed, and its truth, too, in

[91] Some of these are cited in Hopkins 1931, pp. 309–16 (his translation of *Rām* 2.95.4 [p. 313], however, follows the inferior text of the northern recension).

the eyes of the authorial arbiter whose voice is plain to hear in these lines. But there is more than just inferential evidence. In the *Kiṣkindhākāṇḍa* the poet flatly states his own view, through the character of Rāma himself: "It is kings—make no mistake about it—who confer righteous merit, something so hard to acquire, and precious life itself. One must never harm them, never criticize, insult, or oppose them. Kings are gods who walk the earth in the form of men"[92] (4.18.37–38).

What does it signify to make this claim of divinity? What does it mean that the king is a god? The few scholars who do not ignore it have been prone to minimize the importance of divine kingship in ancient India. For one thing, it is claimed that the element of divinity inheres in the office, not the person, of the king.[93] For another, kings were not the only such beings in existence. Brahmans, too, were "gods on earth." Thus in a way comparable to no other culture India was "prolific of human gods." In fact, as though we were in the grip of a market economy of the sacred, divinity in India is said to be "cheap."[94]

Neither of these claims has much force. First, the dichotomy between king and kingship finds little support in Indian epic texts. That distinction itself is a juristic concept belonging primarily to the European medieval period and derived ultimately from Christian symbolism.[95] Moreover, even though there is no suggestion whatever in Books Two through Six of the *Rāmāyaṇa* that the divine king has any competition from a divine brahman, who is simply ignored, I do not believe such a law of supply and demand is

[92] It may be that *naradeva-*, a common word for "king," carries in the *Rāmāyaṇa* a still-vital radical signification, and indeed perhaps as a *karmadhāraya* compound ("man-god," just like *narasiṃha-*, "man-lion"; this seems to be the interpretation in the *BhāgP*, for example, 1.3.22), rather than *tatpuruṣa* ("god among men"; cf. Gonda 1969, p. 63). Thus when Hanumān says to Rāvaṇa, "There is no one in the three worlds who, having once offended Rāghava, could ever find happiness. . . . Show proper respect to this man-god [*naradeva-*]; give back Jānakī" (5.49.19), it may be that we are to hear this subtle resonance in the compound and to understand that Rāvaṇa is being given one last chance to comprehend the inherent, and inevitably fatal, limitations of his boon.

[93] A representative paper is Basu 1959. See also Lingat 1973, p. 208 and note 7, and p. 211.

[94] The first quote is from Frazer (cited in O'Flaherty 1976, p. 9), the second, from Basham 1954, p. 86.

[95] Kantorowicz 1957 is a magisterial exposition of the concept.

applicable in the domain of political theology; the question of quantity need have no impact whatever on the value of the representation. This value is constituted by, and directly proportional to, the quality of being of the divine king, irrespective of its quantity. And the quality of his being is unique in two respects: the king's function and his origin.[96] The king is functionally a god because like a god he saves and protects; he is existentially or ontologically a god because he incorporates the divine essence.

The king, we are told in the *Rājadharma* section of the *Mahābhārata*, is the root of the three ends or needs of human life (the *trivarga*); *dharma* itself is "rooted" in the king. The exercise of kingship is thus the highest manifestation of *dharma* and the refuge of every living soul on earth. All beings depend on *dharma*, and *dharma* depends on the king. But what is the core of *rājadharma*? "The age-old *dharma* of kings consists of protection, and it is this that maintains the world itself." The king provides security, in particular to brahmans and ascetics, who are usually, as in the *Araṇyakāṇḍa*, represented as those most threatened with violence. This is a "gift of life" (cf. *Rām* 4.18.37, cited above, p. 46), equal to no other, and by means of it alone the entire brahmanical order and the sacrificial cult by which it sustains the universe are preserved.[97]

Although the king has other functions besides protecting his subjects (which his possession of other divine substances enables him to execute),[98] it is his providing welfare, in the widest sense of the term, that remains his special trait. The god who increasingly in Indian religious history comes to discharge this soteriological function and whose substance is later said to be fused with that of the earthly king is Viṣṇu. For although Viṣṇu does not himself occupy the position of king in the Indian pantheon—that is held by Indra—he has a unique role in the preservation of the cosmos that proved to be a far more compelling political-theological determinant. From the time of the earliest hymns of the *Ṛgveda* and with

[96] These were the principal categories later adopted by the authors of the *purāṇas* in their analysis of the sources of the king's authority. See Ghoshal 1966, p. 330.

[97] The verse quoted (*MBh* 12.57.42; cf. 32.2) may be by Bhārgava, that is, Vālmīki (cf. the variants noted in the critical apparatus on verse 40a). For the king as root of the *trivarga*, cf. 12.137.95; as the root of *dharma*, 12.68.8, with 56.2; and see further 63.21, 25, 64.20, 29, 56.3, and 91.5. Gonda argues that the semantic value "protect" is a radical signification of Indo-European *reg-* (Gonda 1956, pp. 151–67).

[98] See *MBh* 12.68.40 quoted above, p. 44, and the references noted there.

growing frequency thereafter, Viṣṇu's preeminent task is to aid suffering mankind by reestablishing the righteous brahmanical organization of society.[99]

This "parity of functions" at an early date entailed an equivalence of being. Suggestive testimony is to be found in a ritual textbook of the Taittirīyas (a branch of the vedic tradition with which Vālmīki may have had particular affinities).[100] During the royal consecration ceremony the king "takes the [three] strides of Viṣṇu, he becomes Viṣṇu himself and thereby triumphs over all these worlds."[101] In the epic period the texts become even more numerous and explicit. We have already seen how Dhundhumāra was able to execute his protective activities only by absorbing the power of Viṣṇu. Perhaps the best representation of the doctrine of substantive identity between king and divinity, and one of the most important expository texts in the epics on the origin of kingship, is the tale of the birth of Pṛthu, the first righteous king. Once created, the king vows righteousness and promises to protect "the earthly brahmans" and preserve the brahmanical social order. The gods perform his consecration, and thereupon,

> The eternal Viṣṇu himself established the law that no one was ever to transgress against the king. And by means of his ascetic power the Blessed Viṣṇu entered into the king, so that the world would bow in homage to these gods of men, like very gods. . . . For why otherwise would people stand at the bidding of a king—who is no different from them in his body or sense powers—were it not for this quality of divinity?[102] . . . When his merit has

[99] We have glimpsed this already in the myth of the dwarf incarnation. See also Tripathi 1968, pp. 1–26, and Gonda 1969, pp. 164ff., where much of the pertinent information is made available.

[100] Cf. Pollock 1986, p. 37 and note 3.

[101] *TaiBr* 1.7.4.4. Cf. also Gonda 1969, pp. 58–59, 164–65. It is irrelevant that, technically, Rāma is not yet a consecrated king, for his status is hardly ambiguous. Not only do Rāma's sandals occupy the throne of Kosala, but he is regarded as king throughout his forest exile, in fact, as "king" or "master" "of all the world" (cf. 3.11.27, 28.10, 35.13, 48.4, 5, 14; 5.32.27).

[102] Cf. 12.59.6–12: "His hands and head and neck, his intellect and senses, his sperm and bone and marrow, his flesh and blood, are like any other man's; like any other man he feels joy and sorrow . . . like any other man is born and dies. Why then does this one rule over all the earth? . . . It must be for no small reason that all the world bows before one man, as before a god" (a passage strikingly reminiscent of *Richard II* 3.ii.174ff.).

> been exhausted, a king comes from heaven to earth to be born. . . . Endowed then with the greatness of Viṣṇu on this earth, he becomes endowed with intelligence and attains greatness. No one transgresses against the law established by the gods. All stand at the bidding of one, and conform to his behavior.[103] Therefore, best of kings, wise men in this world have forever declared that gods and gods of men are equal.[104]

The identification of the earthly king and Viṣṇu becomes so thoroughgoing that by the time of the earliest *purāṇas* "every emperor, in every cosmic age both past and future, is born on earth with a portion of Viṣṇu within him."[105] The reality of the representation is brought home to the contemporary reader by, for example, the inscriptions of the imperial Guptas, particularly the description of King Samudragupta as the "Inscrutable Being" [that is, Viṣṇu], "a man only insofar as he conforms to social convention, but in reality a god who has taken up residence in the world."[106] Or by Viśākhadatta's great play, the *Mudrārākṣasa,* at the end of which the poet eulogizes his patron (possibly Candragupta) by asserting that Viṣṇu, who once took on the form of a boar to save the earth, has now assumed the form of this king.[107] In the epic and post-epic period texts proliferate that affirm and elaborate on the essential unity of the earthly king and Viṣṇu. Representative of the medieval view of the king as savior is the important Vaiṣṇava sectarian work, the *Ahirbudhnyasaṃhitā*:

> The king is the ultimate being, a lord consisting of [parts of] all the gods. He is the locus of the effective energy of Viṣṇu, he consists of the Blessed One Himself. The Lord God created the king long ago, emitting him from His own head; consecrated on the head, therefore, the king is placed far above all other creatures. The king is twice so great as a brahman, and his praises are sung in the *vedas* and *śāstras*. The fool who in delusion hates the king, hates Hari; the man who in delusion hates Hari, hates

[103] I read this line with the southern recension; the doctrine that all follow the actions of a king is an old one, see *Rām* 2.101.9 and note.

[104] *MBh.* 12.59, 129–41.

[105] *VāyuP* 57.72.

[106] The Allahabad Pillar Inscription c. A.D. 370 (Sircar 1965, pp. 266–67, lines 25–28).

[107] *MudrāRā* 7.19.

> Lakṣmī; and the foolish hater of Lakṣmī is lost to all *dharma*, is driven from all worlds, is excluded by all the gods, and exists forevermore in blinding, bottomless darkness. But the wise man who seeks earthly and heavenly prosperity will esteem the king, the supreme deity of all worlds.[108]

The divine king is a spiritual redeemer (not necessarily, as represented here, a function of his identification with Viṣṇu), who not as an intercessor with the gods but directly secures the spiritual welfare of his people. He is "guru of the world to come"; show him contempt and all one's religious works prove fruitless (*MBh* 12.65.28). He is, according to a passage already cited, "the very heart of hearts of his subjects. . . . Putting their reliance in their king people win this world and the world to come" (*MBh* 12.68.59, above, p. 44). This reflects not a cult of king worship in the strict sense—kings in India did not often usurp the position of the gods in the all-important sacrificial rites—but a spiritual function symmetrical with and finally indistinguishable from his social function, which the king exercises by reason of the divine substance he incorporates. It seems to be precisely this power to effect spiritual emancipation that underpins much of the action of the *Araṇyakāṇḍa*. What I have in mind is illustrated by the structurally comparable narratives of Śarabhañga and Śabarī, Virādha and Kabandha.

These episodes, which celebrate the liberating power of the king, frame Book Three of the epic. At the beginning and end of the volume Rāma encounters two evil monsters imprisoned in horrific forms as a result of curses, and immediately thereafter two people of extraordinary holiness. The king slays the monsters, thereby releasing them from their confinement and allowing them to recover their proper place in heaven. Both Śarabhañga the ascetic and the mendicant woman Śabarī commit ritual suicide after their encounter with Rāma. Śarabhañga had put off departing for the world of Brahmā, which he had won by his asceticism, until he had experienced Rāma; but "now that we have met," he tells the king, "I will go to the highest heaven, where the gods reside" (3.4.26), whereupon he immolates himself. Śabarī has also been waiting for Rāma, having been told by her gurus, "One day Rāma shall come to this holy ashram of yours. You are to receive him.

[108] *AhirbuS* 16.14–19; cf. *BhāgP* 1.18.42.

Once you have beheld him you shall go to the highest imperishable worlds" (3.70.11–12). After providing him hospitality she, too, destroys herself in the sacrificial fire.

By direct intervention, then, or by his mere presence, Rāma, "the one to whom all creatures pay homage,"[109] offers freedom from the miseries of this world. For the holy ascetic and mendicant, there is nothing further to live for having once experienced him; the *darśana* of the divine king functions as both the ratification of their holiness and the mechanism of their release. The evil monsters for their part are cleansed by the royal punishment exacted by Rāma, and so made fit again for heaven. Punishment as a divine institution and instrument of emancipation is standard doctrine not just for traditional Indian political theology but for Vālmīki himself: "When men who have done evil deeds are punished by the king, they are purified and go to heaven, just like men of virtue" (4.18.30).[110]

Thus, from the time of the *Rājadharma* discourse of the *Mahābhārata* and probably much earlier, the king was widely characterized as a "deity in the form of a man," a being in which "mankind and divinity actually meet and combine."[111] On these grounds

[109] *sarvabhūtanamaskṛtam* (3.69.20). The phrase, which is authenticated text-critically, is used elsewhere in epic literature almost exclusively of Brahmā and Śiva.

[110] Cf. *MBh* 12.56.7 (vulgate): "Just as the rising sun dispels the evil darkness, so the righteous acts of a king [that is, his exercise of punishment] save from lightless and evil hell." See also the unidentified *smṛti* text cited there by Nīlakaṇṭha: "People who have [committed crimes and so] become polluted are purified when punished by kings; they are thereby fulfilled and go to heaven, no less than the good." On the "divine institution" of punishment see Lingat 1973, p. 214 (cf. p. 67), who refers in particular to *VāsiDS* 19.48. One possible reason why the ancient legend of Indra and Ahalyā (cf. *ŚatBr* 3.3.4.18 etc.) was drawn into the *Rāmāyaṇa* corpus (1.48) was the opportunity it offered to demonstrate precisely this salvational capacity of Rāma's. This is, in fact, how the later tradition interpreted it, especially Tulsī Dās (cf. Whalen 1981, p. 242, also p. 18; the story remains a major spiritual moment in contemporary Rāmlīlā performances). That this particular episode was selected to illustrate the king's emancipatory power no doubt has to do with its content, the theme of adultery, which is one of the poem's obsessions. Rāma later will actively punish the adulterous Śūrpaṇakhā (here in *sarga* 17; see also pp. 78ff. below), a pivotal event of the story, and at the climax of the poem demand the purification of his queen (6.103ff.).

[111] Gonda 1969, p. 54. This political theology, according to Kauṭilya, was to be actively inculcated: Intelligence agents were to encourage the belief among the people that kings occupy the position of Indra and Yama; to scorn them is to invite divine punishment, and so on (*ArthŚā* 1.13.5ff.).

alone we might be justified in concluding that the divinity of the hero of the *Rāmāyaṇa* must have been a central feature of the poem from the beginning. The morphology of the boon motif also compels this conclusion (and at the same time accounts for the absence of any clear reference to Rāma's divine nature), since it invariably requires a transcendent fusion of existential categories.[112] Indeed, the extraordinary synthesis here of the numinous and the human—the divine man who is king of men, the human god—is a particularly brilliant contribution of the *Rāmāyaṇa* to an old and venerable mythopoetic tradition, which renews the force of this myth by tapping into a vital reservoir of everyday representations and beliefs concerning kingship.[113]

Gradually, however, the conception of the divine king basic to the story of Rāma was influenced by two factors already mentioned. First, the god Viṣṇu came to be associated—perhaps initially as a result of their functional identity—with the earthly king. Second, in Vaiṣṇava theological circles there developed the theory of the *avatāra*, a doctrine of vast absorptive, syncretistic force, which views every manifestation of divine power as testimony to the omnipotence and immanence of Viṣṇu.[114] These factors have so fundamentally conditioned the transmission of the poem that it cannot be proved on textual grounds that the composer of the monumental *Rāmāyaṇa*, from which all versions and recensions of the work derive, was ignorant of or indifferent to the equation of Rāma and Viṣṇu. And there are additional features, narratological

[112] The traditional interpretation understood this well. If it were emphatically expressed—if Rāma himself were shown to know—that he is a "divine mortal," the terms of the boon would not, in fact, be honored. I discuss this traditional exegesis in detail in Pollock 1984a (the translation of Tryambaka's commentary runs from the third paragraph on p. 232 through the first paragraph on p. 238).

[113] What these might have meant on the level of everyday life in traditional India is suggested, for instance, by the brief description of the Balinese divine king, the "Great God," found in Geertz 1983, p. 178.

[114] The first factor is captured in the old formula *nāviṣṇuḥ pṛthivīpatiḥ*, "No king exists without [or perhaps better, "is not"] Viṣṇu," which provided a sufficient condition for the identification; the second is captured in the statement of the *HariVaṃ*, *nāsty āścaryam avaiṣṇavam*, "No miraculous power but that it comes from Viṣṇu" (113.75), which provided a necessary condition. For the first formula cited, see Ck on *Rām* 2.5.1; Ḍhuṇḍhirāja on *MudrāRā* 7.19; cf. Kane 1962–1975, vol. 3, pp. 24–25. The second point is touched on by Hopkins 1931, pp. 313–14.

and aesthetic, which, far from challenging this equation, make it seem as "authentic" as any dimension of the poem.

Nevertheless, the hypothetical effects of the appropriation of the text by early Vaiṣṇavism has finally no bearing on the question of the divine status of Rāma as it was originally conceived, or on our interpretation of the monumental *Rāmāyaṇa*, which accordingly is obliged to view this status as a constitutive and determinative feature of the poem. How does such a perception affect our interpretation of the poem in a more global sense?

Let us review the passage in which, in order to convince Rāma to return to Ayodhyā, Bharata argues that even if some people think a king but a mortal, "I esteem him a god. His conduct in matters of righteousness and statecraft, it is rightly said, is beyond that of mere mortals." This verse distills what Book Two, the first "movement" of the poem, goes to such great lengths to exemplify. The *Ayodhyākāṇḍa* is a profound study in the righteousness of the king and his authority. Rāma possesses these attributes in a measure that only a divine being can.[115] This is also the case with his protective and punitive activities, the exercise of legitimate force, which forms the subject of Book Three and the rest of the poem.

Here we return to the problem that confronted us at the very beginning of our analysis of the *Araṇyakāṇḍa*: Are the two halves of the poem really genetically incompatible, one part epic myth, the other romance? Is there any unity to this work? I suggest that the nature of kingship itself provides the unifying theme and the impulse to explain the "divine" power of the king as comprehensively as possible. Whether we accept the speculative notion that the forest is the very source of royal authority, or regard it more as an "extrasocial sphere" where the violence of the kingly warrior could be exhibited, a realm of *artha* (or *daṇḍa*) complementing that of *dharma* (especially necessary in the idealized world of "Ayodhyā"), the world outside the settled town seems essential in the kingly narrative of power and legitimacy in premodern India.[116] Looking at the *Rāmāyaṇa* from this perspective, we can regain a sense of the work as a meaningful whole, which Indian audiences

[115] It is precisely his sense of righteousness, *dharma*, that makes it impossible for Rāma to go back to Ayodhyā, thereby demonstrating how naive is the younger brother's argument.

[116] See Falk 1973 and Heesterman 1985, pp. 108–27.

have always felt. What we may have been inclined to view as "romance" elements threatening to shatter this unity serve instead to enlarge the site of the narrative, so that the full range of the divine king's activities may be contemplated.

This perspective may also enable us to view in another and more revealing light one of the most startling episodes in the poem, one that seems to contradict everything we have so far learned about the hero's character.

5. Rāma's Madness

THE MOST POWERFUL scene of the *Araṇyakāṇḍa*—next to Rāvaṇa's abduction of Sītā—and one of the more problematic of the entire *Rāmāyaṇa* is Rāma's madness over the loss of his wife (*sargas* 58–62, with *sargas* 50–57 as prelude). The problem in this episode is that the hero contradicts virtually everything the poet, up to this point, has encouraged us to believe about him.

The whole force of the preceding narrative is directed to creating a character inhabiting an emotional and ethical realm far removed from that of normal mortals. If there is any single virtue that characterizes the hero's conduct through the first two and a half books of the poem, it is his equanimity, a trait deriving from his ability to eliminate all personal concerns from every social or ethical calculation. In the *Ayodhyākāṇḍa* Rāma is one who "never grows angry, whatever the insult" (2.36.3); one who would "ignore a hundred injuries, so great was his self-control" (2.1.16); it is said that "benevolence, compassion, learning, good character, restraint, and equanimity—these are the six virtues that adorn" Rāma (2.30.12).[117] Yet what we are presented with in this deeply moving passage of the third book negates this hitherto consistently drawn portrait. This seems less the exploration of another side of his character than a complete reversal.

The *Ayodhyākāṇḍa* seeks to establish an innovative definition of the *dharma*, the code of conduct, of kshatriyas: Violence as far as possible is to be eschewed in the realm of sociopolitical action.[118] The *Araṇyakāṇḍa* shows us a different domain of action where this new valuation of *kṣatradharma* is not always applicable (the shift in focus from the one book to the next is well illustrated by the exchange between Sītā and Rāma on the bearing of arms in a forest where ascetics make their home, *sargas* 8–9). In this realm, the ideal king is prepared to subordinate every consideration of personal welfare and safety to the duty of protecting the brahmanical order of society. In the mad scene, however, both the hero's earlier

[117] Cf. also 2.1.15 and 2.21.

[118] See for example 2.18.32ff., especially verse 36; *sarga* 101, in particular verses 19ff., and for a discussion, Pollock 1986, pp. 64ff.

convictions in "Ayodhyā" and his single-minded devotion to royal duty in the "Forest" seem to be not only displaced but inverted or rejected.

The descent into madness is described slowly and carefully. Rāma has been drawn away on a distant chase by the *rākṣasa* Mārīca in the form of a bejeweled deer. When finally slain, Mārīca cries out for help, imitating Rāma's voice. Lakṣmaṇa, who had been left behind to guard Sītā, is forced by her to go to Rāma's aid, and with the ashram now unprotected Rāvaṇa abducts the princess. Returning to find the hermitage empty, Rāma scours the surrounding forest for his wife, frantically searching, "wandering like a madman" (58.33), his grief giving him "the look of a madman" (58.10), questioning the trees of Janasthāna, the elephants, tigers, mountains, rivers. He then discovers the evidence of Jaṭāyus's fatal struggle against Rāvaṇa (*sarga* 60), and concludes that Sītā has been slain or stolen away. Our growing suspicion of profound transformation in the hero's character at this point becomes a certainty: Rāma now explicitly renounces the political ethics to which he has hitherto so tenaciously held, and implicitly rejects the principal duty incumbent upon him as king, at the same time crying out in maniacal fury and threatening cosmic destruction:

> Since Vaidehī has been devoured or carried off, who in this mortal world—or which god—has thought it possible to injure me? But then, any creature, Lakṣmaṇa, knowing no better, will despise the man of compassion, however heroic he may be, the very master of the worlds. The thirty gods themselves must surely think me powerless, because I have been mild, compassionate, and self-restrained, striving for the welfare of the world. Look how in my case, Lakṣmaṇa, a good has become an evil. But now I will efface it—as the great rising sun effaces the light of the hare-marked moon—in order to exterminate the *rākṣasas* and all living things. No *yakṣa, gandharva*, or *piśāca*, no *rākṣasa, kinnara*, or man shall be left in peace, Lakṣmaṇa. Watch now, Lakṣmaṇa, as I fill the sky with missiles and darts, leaving no space whatever for creatures that move about the three worlds. I will bring the host of planets to a standstill, darken the moon that brings the night, paralyze both fire and wind, blot out the light of the sun; I will grind the mountain peaks to dust, dry up every body of water, uproot every tree, vine, and shrub, annihi-

late the ocean. If the gods do not restore Sītā to me safe and sound this very instant, they shall witness the full extent of my power, Saumitri. Not a single creature, Lakṣmaṇa, shall escape into the sky: The darts shot from my bowstring will form a net without a gap. Behold now, Lakṣmaṇa, the devastation caused by my iron shafts, the birds and beasts driven wild and ravaged, the world plunged into chaos, from one end to the other. Because of what happened to Maithilī I will shoot my arrows from a full-drawn bow, arrows no one can withstand, and rid this mortal world of all *piśācas* and *rākṣasas*. Now the gods shall witness the power of my shafts when I ply them in anger; they shall see how far they carry when, my patience exhausted, I release them. No god or *daitya*, no *piśāca* or *rākṣasa* shall survive when in my rage I lay waste the universe. The worlds of the gods and *dānavas* and *yakṣas*, besides that of the *rākṣasas*, shall come crashing down one upon the other as my darts fly wave after wave, smashing them to pieces. I will obliterate the boundaries of all the worlds with my shafts. Like old age or death or time or fate, which no creature has ever defied, Lakṣmaṇa, so in my rage I cannot be withstood; let no one doubt it. Unless they show me Sītā, the bright-smiling, flawless princess of Mithilā, I will overturn this world, mountains and all, its great serpents and men, its *gandharvas* and gods." (60.36–52)

The profound sense of injury expressed here is attributed to precisely the ethical code that had marked the hero's character in the previous book. Not only does he seek to exact vengeance on the *rākṣasas*, but he is prepared to slay "all living things," from serpents to gods, including men; the whole cosmos is threatened with annihilation. Besides this startling negation of Rāma's emblematic self-possession, there is at the same time a terrible violence here—in fact, a terrible "unrighteousness" (*adharma*) in him who is the "champion of righteousness" (*dharmabhṛtāṃ varaḥ*). For the king's paramount duty is to offer protection, and this is an obligation articulated in Book Three no less than in the poem as a whole. At the very beginning of the *Araṇyakāṇḍa* we are told that the king is supposed to be "guardian of righteousness and glorious refuge of his people," "the protector of his subjects" (3.1.17, 18). Rāma himself is deeply conscious of this duty:

> I may repeat the words you yourself uttered, my lady: "Kshatriyas only bear bows lest any voice be raised in distress." (3.9.3)
>
> I come as king . . . to end the life of evildoers and all who wish the world ill. (3.28.10)

Lakṣmaṇa, in an interesting reversal of roles (contrast for instance 2.18–20), recognizes and tries to apprise his brother of the deviation in his behavior and its unrighteousness:

> Anguished and tormented by the abduction of Sītā, Rāma was prepared to annihilate the worlds, like the fire that comes on doomsday. He kept glancing at his taut-strung bow, racked incessantly with sighs, raging like Rudra himself. . . . At the sight of such rage in Rāma as he had never seen before, Lakṣmaṇa cupped his hands in reverence and addressed him through a mouth gone dry with fear: "You have always been mild in the past, self-restrained, and dedicated to the welfare of all creatures. Do not abandon your true nature, yielding to rage. The splendor of the moon, the radiance of the sun, the movement of the wind, the patience of the earth—all this is constant, so too your incomparable glory. . . . You must not destroy the worlds because of one single being. Lords of earth must be gentle and cool-headed, and must mete out just punishment. (3.61.1–9)[119]
>
> If in your sorrow you consume the worlds with your might, tiger among men, where are your subjects to find relief from their torment? . . . What good would it do you, bull among men, to cause universal destruction? (3.62.6, 20)

Rāma is calmed, for the time being at least, but the terrific vision of the apocalyptic destruction of which he is capable—as elemental as time, death, fate—is a stark revelation that remains fixed in the contemporary reader's consciousness.

This has also been true for traditional Indian audiences. One index of the power this scene (in particular Rāma's search for Sītā through the woods of Janasthāna, especially *sarga* 58) has exercised in Indian literary culture is its influence on later Sanskrit lit-

[119] Rāma has recovered his characteristic sense of equity by 6.67.37. When Lakṣmaṇa wishes to release the "weapon of Brahmā" in order to kill Rāvaṇa's son Indrajit, the elder brother dissuades the younger from slaying all the *rākṣasas* on earth because of the crimes of only one of them. See also Goldman 1980 for reflections on the complementarity of the two heroes' characters.

erature. The greatest poet of classical India, Kālidāsa, adapted it for his *Vikramorvaśīya* (where in act 4 the mad king Purūravas searches frantically through Kumāravana for his beloved, the *apsaras* Urvaśī), thus inaugurating a series of adaptations in court literature.[120] The most impressive of the popular adaptations is found in the cycle of Kṛṣṇa legends (the *gopīs*' wild quest for the lover who has abandoned them). The motif is introduced first in the *Viṣṇupurāṇa* (5.13.25–41) and then reworked, with brilliant amplification, in the *Bhāgavatapurāṇa* (10.30).[121]

In addition to helping us gauge the dramatic effect of the *Araṇyakāṇḍa* episode in court and popular culture, these later adaptations might appear to suggest an interpretation. For what they all emphasize is that irrational behavior such as Rāma's in the mad scene is a natural consequence of a deeply felt love that has been brutally denied. In pre-modern India, the scientific (śāstric) discourse on madness—that of medicine, for example, or law—generally views the phenomenon as physiological in origin (resulting from an imbalance of the humors) or as sheer demonic possession, without, however, denying that emotional disturbance can play a causal role.[122] It is this last, however, that comes to be regarded as the unique source in medieval literary contexts. For the rhetoricians, madness is "a mental confusion brought about by passion, grief, fear, and the like."[123] In fictional representations it is exclu-

120 The scene closely follows the *Araṇyakāṇḍa*, but it is palpably inferior to the epic in one crucial respect: The sense of overwhelming desperation is gone from the search; there is now something almost comedic about it all. And of course, before the fourth act itself is played out, the king has been reunited with the *apsaras*. Yet another extended treatment is found in Bhavabhūti, *Mālatimādhava* act 9, although by this time the effectiveness of the theme in belles-lettres has been virtually exhausted. The one Rāma play of later medieval times to deal specifically with the scene is Bhāskara Bhaṭṭa's *Unmattarāghava* (which is based, however, not on the *Rāmāyaṇa* passage itself but on Kālidāsa's adaptation of it). Rājaśekhara's *Bālarāmāyaṇa* (act 5) and Jayadeva's *Prasannarāghava* (act 6) appear to look to both predecessors.

121 The theme is absent from the *HariVaṃ*, and scarcely represented in the *BrahmP* (chapter 189).

122 See Bhishagratna 1907–1916, vol. 3, pp. 387–89. Cf. Jolly 1901, pp. 147–48. *Mitākṣarā* on *YājñaSm* 2.140 (where those excluded from inheritance are enumerated) neatly summarizes the traditional tripartite etiology of madness.

123 *SāhiD* 3.160; see also *RasGañ* p. 90, where madness is listed under the *vyabhicārabhāvas* and defined as follows: "Madness is miscognition [literally, "the appearance of something where it actually is absent"] brought about by separation [from the beloved], a terrible calamity, profound bliss, and the like. It is different from [mere erroneous] cognition, insofar as it is originated [by such external causes as those

sively correlated with the first of these emotions and, in fact, comes to be listed as an integral stage in the normal progression of thwarted love, which begins in infatuation and, if allowed to run its course, terminates in death.[124]

Yet there is considerable difficulty in understanding the scene in the *Araṇyakāṇḍa* primarily on the basis of the medieval etiology of madness in its literary environment. That is to say, it is hard to see the episode the way its later adapters appear to have done, as an automatic consequence or necessary component of a conventional aesthetic category, what in Indian aesthetic theory is termed the "dominant affective-aesthetic experience" (*rasa*) of "love-in-separation" (*vipralambhaśṛṅgāra*). (Nor is it simply that Rāma has been separated from the woman he loves, whom he has been willing on other occasions to abandon in favor of a higher good; compare for example 2.31.36.) The contrast here with his earlier behavior, indeed, the fundamental conflict with his paradigmatic social and moral authority, seems far too sharp to be accommodated by so facile an explanation.

The Indian tradition appears to have acknowledged that the episode was in serious need of interpretation. That offered by the *Bhāgavatapurāṇa* (c. tenth century) is viewed as authoritative by the majority of medieval commentators. Accepting as an authentic feature of the poem Rāma's status as an *avatāra* of Viṣṇu, the *purāṇa* explains, "God's incarnation as a mortal in this world is not simply for slaying *rākṣasas*, but is meant to instruct mortals. How else could it be that the Lord, the Self delighting in Himself, should have suffered so because of Sītā? The Blessed One, Vāsudeva, is the Self . . . without attachment to anything in the three worlds. He would not [except for the purpose of such instruction] have experienced that faintheartedness caused by [his attachment to] a woman."[125] Thus, according to one widespread understanding of

---

listed], whereas [false] knowledge is innate. Although properly one of the illnesses [cf. p. 85], it is here listed separately in order to emphasize its peculiar strangeness in comparison with other illnesses."

[124] The first appearance of the list seems to be *NāṭyaŚā* chapter 6 (1971–1983, p. 718), where the ten *kāmāvasthas* are inventoried (as enunciated by the "authors of the erotological textbooks"), and chapter 26, verses 168ff., where they are defined (*unmāda*, "madness," in verses 183–84).

[125] 5.19.5–6. The doctrine profoundly influenced the traditional commentaries on Vālmīki's epic. Cm cites this verse in his comment on vulgate 6.59.120. See also Cm's remarks in the note on 60.10 below.

the poem, Rāma's behavior throughout is to be taken as altogether "mimetic"; it is not real, but a representation with explicit didactic function.[126] The episode of his madness, consequently, is to be viewed as a cautionary tale, as the *Bhāgavata* itself elsewhere takes pains to spell out: "The basest of *rākṣasas* came into the woods stealthily, like a wolf, and abducted the princess of Videha. With his brother in the forest [Rāma] acted the part of a wretched man when separated from his beloved, thereby to illustrate what happens to all who are too much attached to women."[127]

The *Bhāgavata*'s analysis of this and comparable episodes in the *Rāmāyaṇa* (as for instance when Rāma is preparing to cross over to Laṅkā and in a rage threatens to dry up the ocean, 6.14) secured widespread approval in medieval India and is thus an index of at least one domain of indigenous understanding.[128] Far from exhausting the meaning of the scene, however, this interpretation, too, shows signs of expediency, deriving from an almost palpable puzzlement in the face of a symbolic structure for which nothing in the earlier part of the poem has prepared us.

If, then, Rāma's frenzied search, madness, and threats of holocaust present us with more questions than some traditional aesthetic or theological interpretations can answer, we might ask whether viewing the episode from a less localized cultural-literary perspective could disclose other, more interesting meanings. Such a wider vantage point is readily available, since the madness of the hero is a common motif in world literature.[129] In Shakespeare, for example, it is introduced with such remarkable regularity into the

[126] See further in Pollock 1984a and 1986, notes on 2.2.28; 16.57.

[127] 9.10.11.

[128] Nīlakaṇṭha Dikṣita, for example, echoes the sentiment of the *Bhāgavata* in his *Rāmāyaṇasārasaṃgraharaghuvīrastava* 17 (one of a series of reflections on particular episodes of the epic viewed as enigmatic in the medieval period).

[129] Two recent full-scale studies of the question are Felman 1978 and Feder 1980. This is not the place to go into detail on the representation of madness in ancient Indian literature. Whereas madness is as common in traditional India as elsewhere (this is indicated in part by the multiplicity of psychotherapies the culture has developed to deal with madness; cf. Kakar 1982), it is rarely explored in literary discourse. One is hard pressed to think of other examples than Rāma (and Śiva; see below); the attempted suicide of Vasiṣṭha, for instance (*MBh* 1.167), or the self-genocide of the Vṛṣṇis (*MBh* 16) seems very different. The contrast with, say, ancient Greek literature, which investigates madness in so many varieties (Dionysus, Orestes, Cassandra, Ajax, etc.), is instructive and might suggest psychic denial of the phenomenon in traditional India.

career of the protagonist as to appear almost an essential dramaturgical component.

Like Rāma, Shakespearean heroes pass through a "cycle of change," including a descent into madness whereby they turn into their own antithesis. Besides providing intense theatrical experience, madness in Shakespeare can symbolize the terrible dilemma of the tragic hero, as a mark of both the exceptional punishment to which he becomes liable and the exceptional insight he commands. It also makes available a voice—the speech of the madman—through which the more acute perception of life possessed by the poet himself, and the possibly dangerous truths to which he has privileged access, can be expressed with relative impunity.[130]

What we find happening in Shakespearean tragedy and in much of Western literature may also supply the expectations and "prejudgments" that westerners bring to Vālmīki's epic. But it should be evident that few of the symbolic features of Western literary madness are applicable to what takes place in the *Araṇyakāṇḍa*. The dramatic intensity of the scene is unquestioned, but Vālmīki has secured such intensity elsewhere and in less problematic ways. Rāma does seem to become his own antithesis here; the transformation does occur during the course of the "tragic journey" of the hero (at once a psychological journey of self-discovery and a geographical one).[131] But this is only to restate the problem, not answer it. Rāma's madness is certainly no punishment, and it affords him no opportunity to exercise deeper insight. The poet does not take advantage of the madman's clearer vision to enunciate any critique.

If comparison between literary cultures offers little help in understanding what Rāma's madness means in Vālmīki's epic, we do

[130] The above paragraph derives from the classic essay of Mack 1970, especially pp. 40–47. On the etiology of madness in the Renaissance West (which is strikingly similar to that in medieval India, originating in the same three ways of humoral dysfunction, possession, or intense love) see Feder 1980, pp. 98ff., especially pp. 114–16.

[131] On the traditional—and in my view the most forceful—interpretation of Rāma's self-discovery at the end of Book Six, whereby he gains knowledge far different from that attained by Aeneas or Dante, see Pollock 1984a. Clearly I am inclined to view the claim to antiquity of that scene far more favorably than other scholars. As an integral part of Vālmīki's text, it can be persuasively explained as a necessary conclusion; at the same time it explains much of the narrative itself. Far more awkward is the view that is it an interpolation.

best to remain as close as possible to Indian presuppositions. Yet the narrow presuppositions of the medieval interpretations do not take us very far, either. It is here, perhaps, that the central concerns of the epic should guide our interpretation of its parts. If, in the first instance, the *Rāmāyaṇa* is an imaginative inquiry into the nature of kingship and the peculiar, transcendent nature of the king, it may be useful to think of the apparent reversal of Rāma's character in response to the abduction of his wife as an extension of this concern.

The solution to Rāvaṇa's boon can be provided only by an intermediate, almost composite being, the "god who walks the earth in the form of a man." But if the powers of this being are divine, he nevertheless remains, "in some measure, a man."[132] The problem of the god-king's humanity is certainly at issue in one important theme of the poem, the limitation of Rāma's self-knowledge. The poet follows its ramifications throughout the text and employs it to great advantage in problematizing the motivation of the hero. At various points in the epic, as we have seen, evidence is given of a divine plan governing the action of the *Rāmāyaṇa*, and one very intriguing aspect of this plan is Rāma's ignorance of it. His conduct in protecting the sages of Daṇḍaka wilderness, which provokes the hostility of the *rākṣasas* and sets in motion the rest of the action of the tale, is presented as his own free choice, a righteous and heroic king's response to violence and evil, and one that he did not know could not fail in its purpose. Consequently, when Rāma asserts near the end of the sixth book, "I, a man, have overcome the adversity brought on by fate. . . . What a man could do, Sītā, all that he could do, I have done" (6.103.5, 13), the irony affecting much of the poem strains to the breaking point.

In the same way, this irreducible humanity of the king could impinge on Rāma's emotional response to life in general and be at work in the poet's creation of the episode of madness. Kings, we are perhaps being told, may participate in a divine realm by reason of their preternatural mode of being, and by what this directly entails, their transcendent knowledge of and power to maintain *dharma*. But they are not altogether alien to us; they feel desire and

[132] *Rām* 7. App. I, No. 10.28 (cited also by Hopkins 1931, p. 312). Recall also Lakṣmaṇa's words to Rāma in 3.62.19, "Be aware of your powers, which are as much divine as human."

need love, and when this is denied them they are hurt, grow wrathful and finally mad, like the most wretched of mortals. By this narrative argument kingship and the king recover a human face.[133]

There may be some validity to this interpretation, and indeed to some of the others, indigenous and comparative, that we have examined. We should be reluctant to dismiss any of them entirely, resisting all impulse to secure the single "correct" reading, since, as so much recent scholarship reminds us, no such thing really exists.[134] I am offering this interpretation only as a counterpoint to another one, also based on the central problem of the nature of the king, that I find to be more compelling.

We have observed that the unique nature of the earthly king is frequently explained by a doctrine well known to the *Rāmāyaṇa* tradition, too: The king is a synthesis of various divine powers. He not only is "a fourth part Indra himself" (3.1.18), but also incorporates the essential characteristics of each of the principal gods. "The power of kings is infinite," according to one formulation in the *Rāmāyaṇa* itself, "they are able to take on any of five different forms: They can be hot like Agni, god of fire, bold like Indra, or mild like the Moon; they can exact punishment like Yama, or be gracious like Varuṇa" (3.38.12). These are not to be thought of simply as shared characteristics, much less mere figures of speech, but as equivalences or, better, substantival identities. In the appropriate circumstances the terrestrial king literally *becomes* the one or the other god. This very prevalent tenet of Indian political theology offers another way of thinking about this problematic epi-

[133] Some of the commentators, interpreting the scene in accordance with the doctrine of the mimetic nature of Rāma's *avatāra*, reach a related conclusion. Ct, for example, argues that Rāma's display of grief (which Rāvaṇa would be informed of through spies) is meant to confirm to Rāvaṇa that his adversary is, in fact, a man, something necessary if the demon's death is to be secured in compliance with the terms of the boon; if the king were to show no anger at such a moment, Rāvaṇa would conclude that he is not a man. (It is not, however, at all clear that it is Rāvaṇa who must be convinced of Rāma's humanness rather than Rāma himself.) An alternative explanation for Ct is that Rāma's being afflicted with emotional distress is a result of his fleshly embodiment (a theological-philosophical doctrine other commentators use to explain Rāma's ignorance of his true nature). See further in the notes on 60.1 and 52 (and cf. 29.20 note).

[134] A point effectively reiterated in Rabkin 1982, pp. 1–32.

sode.[135] A passage again from that central text on kingship of the epic period, the *Rājadharma* section of the *Mahābhārata*, brings out the pertinence to our scene of the transformations of the god-king. One verse especially merits close attention:

> When evil beings commit egregious evil, then this god [that is, the king] becomes Rudra himself: By their evil acts, evil beings turn him into Rudra, and then he harms all, good and bad alike.[136]

Some portion of the meaning of our scene in the *Araṇyakāṇḍa* may be to suggest that, under the compulsion of Rāvaṇa's "egregious evil," Rāma has become Rudra-Śiva. Like his prototype, the dread god of the forest and death, Rāma has gone mad, and like him he is bent on, and capable of, cosmic destruction.[137] The specific catalyst of the god-man's madness may be that which affects normal mortals; it may be that the undifferentiated aggression arising from the frustration of his desire is like that of any mortal, as is the tendency of the victim of violence to commit violence himself.[138] But what I think brings us to the heart of the scene lies rather in the quality and dimension of the king's destructive power when his will is thwarted. We have seen the *Rājadharma* warn about this power and the larger causes that trigger it:

> A man who acts in opposition to the king never gains happiness, neither he himself nor anyone close to him—son, brother, friend. Even when driven onward by the wind, its charioteer, fire might leave something in its wake; but to the one who thwarts the king nothing whatever will be left. All that the king owns is to be preserved as his; keep your distance from it. Tak-

[135] For further references on this doctrine, see the note on 3.38.12. It is attested in the inscriptions of historical kings, too. Samudragupta, for instance, claims to possess the powers of the gods Kubera, Varuṇa, Indra, and Yama (Sircar 1965, p. 267, line 28). On the substantival identity between king and gods, cf. the text cited by Vallabha on *RaghuVa* 3.11: "A king's body is made by taking the power of Indra, the fire of Agni, *the anger of Hara* [Śiva], the wealth of Vaiśravaṇa, and the gentleness of the Moon.

[136] *MBh* 12.74.17.

[137] On the madness of Śiva see for example *BhāgP* 4.2.14; and cf. O'Flaherty 1976, pp. 65, 278, 307, and Kinsley 1974, pp. 274ff. For Śiva as god of the forest and of death, cf. Parpola 1981, p. 162.

[138] Cf. Feder 1980, p. 21.

ing something of his should be seen to be as fraught with terror as death itself; touch it and you perish.

Like a very god the king when gratified fulfills your every need, and when angered, like a very fire he destroys you, root and branch.[139]

From this perspective, Rāma's madness seems less an anomaly or deviation whereby the hero approaches his opposite than a "natural" manifestation of those violent and destructive capacities inherent in him as king, which have hitherto lain dormant and, in a sense, like fiery *pralaya* itself—final cosmic destruction—are above (or a part of a superordinated) *dharma*. "In the exercise of kingship," according to one recent study, "there is a dimension of violence, of destructiveness, and impurity, which in the *Mahābhārata* makes Śiva's intervention necessary. . . . Rudra-Śiva . . . expresses what one might call the dimension of terror (*raudra*) of the king or kingly *avatāra*."[140] In the *Rāmāyaṇa*, Śiva seems to be made manifest in the person of the divine king, who incorporates this particular god's essence no less than those of other, more benign, divine powers.

Much of the *Araṇyakāṇḍa* seems to be enacted under the very banner of Rudra. We have already noticed once how Rāma is compared to the terrifying divinity; this rhetorical signal, absent from the preceding volumes, now becomes frequent.[141] Moreover, throughout the book the *rasa* shifts repeatedly back to *raudra*, the "terrible," the presiding deity of which, as our earliest systematic work on aesthetics tells us, is Rudra.[142] And it is the terrible, de-

[139] *MBh* 12.68.39–52; *MBh* 12.83.31; cf. *ArthŚā* 5.4.17.

[140] Scheuer 1982, p. 241.

[141] Cf. the note on 3.15.39.

[142] See *NāṭyaŚā* 6.44. There may actually be a genetic literary link between the scene of Rāma's madness in the *Araṇyakāṇḍa* and Śiva's madness over the death of his wife Satī. Vālmīki encourages the parallel when he describes Rāma after the discovery of the loss of Sītā as "raging like Rudra himself when he sought to slay the victim at Dakṣa's sacrifice" (61.2). In the *KālikāP* version of the myth, Śiva is absent when Satī commits suicide, and on returning to his hermitage and finding his wife's body, he at first refuses to believe what he sees. After learning what had provoked Satī's act, he flies into a rage, destroys the sacrifice of Dakṣa, and, filled with grief, "like a common mortal" he bursts into tears. Taking up his wife's corpse he goes off—as another *purāṇa* puts it—"wandering like a madman" (*DevīBhāP* 7.30.45) and ready to destroy the universe (see *KālikāP* 18.1ff.; *BṛDharmaP* 2.40ff.; Zimmer

structive aspect of the god that will predominate in Rāma for the rest of the poem, until his purpose is achieved with the death of Rāvaṇa.

The interpretation of Rāma's madness as a manifestation of the transcendent cosmic violence of the earthly king reveals coherence in an otherwise incoherent image. On this analysis, too, the ideological interests of the "Forest" are again seen to construe broadly with those so insistently presented in the more familiar sociopolitical universe of "Ayodhyā."[143] They now appear to be indissolubly linked with a political theology sustained by the notion of a triune godhead to be fully developed in classical Hinduism: The power of a king is infinite indeed, and as easily as he can preserve the world, he can, if provoked, destroy it.

1948, pp. 296–306; O'Flaherty 1973, pp. 298–300). Like the medieval commentaries on the *Rāmāyaṇa*, Śaiva texts come to insist that the god is not in reality distraught by the death of Satī; it is simply his *līlā*, or divine play, to appear to be so. See O'Flaherty 1973, p. 147 and references cited there.

[143] Cf. Pollock 1986, pp. 9–24.

6. *Rākṣasas* and Others

THE *Araṇyakāṇḍa* presents interpretive problems that, so far, have been best addressed by a "mythic" reading of the narrative. This derives largely from the Indian tradition itself—from the political theology of pre-modern India—and from more general ideological functions of literary production. But Vālmīki is not only concerned with kingship and the king's mysterious nature and activity as a "consubstantial" god-man. The fantastic creatures, for example, the *rākṣasas* and others that we encounter for the first time in the *Araṇyakāṇḍa* and that occupy the center of attention for much of the rest of the poem, have little to do in themselves with the larger theme of kingship and seem less easily accommodated by the interpretive strategies used so far. Whereas conceptions of kingship are culture-specific and so require considerable effort on the part of outsiders to understand, the monstrous presences may seem more familiar to westerners. To some extent they do fit into a pattern of signification known to Western imaginative literature. But they also offer a specific vision of the Other in traditional India, and that is what makes them uniquely interesting to us.

The "city" books of both the *Rāmāyaṇa* and the *Mahābhārata* develop in strikingly similar ways.[144] And it is precisely these many similarities that make the particular divergences so intriguing. One of the salient differences between the two narratives concerns the outrage perpetrated against the heroine. In the *Mahābhārata*, Draupadī is dragged half naked into the assembly hall by her husbands' "brothers"; the outrage is virtually a public one, its location eloquently symbolic of the intense political struggle between the two sets of claimants to the throne; and the perpetrators are the kinsmen of the Pāṇḍavas and all too human as antagonists. Everything from context to antagonist serves to sharpen the political reference of the assault.

The parallel event in the *Rāmāyaṇa* is Rāvaṇa's abduction of Sītā. Here, however, the outrage is for all purposes a private one; it occurs in the forest with only the trees, streams, mountains, and animals of Janasthāna to witness it. As if by design it is empty of

[144] See Pollock 1986, pp. 33–36.

the localized political content that pervades the scene in the other epic. This narrative alteration seems in keeping with the focus of the poem—kingship as cosmically envisioned, as it were, *sub specie aeternitatis* and with none of the *Mahābhārata's* insistent specificity. Finally, and most important, the antagonist is not only not a political rival of Rāma's (the idealized world of Ayodhyā neither permits nor acknowledges the existence of any rival that could provoke the desperate, self-destructive political response of the *Mahābhārata*) but hardly belongs to the same biological order as the hero.

We have seen that, by the morphology of much of the story, it is easy and necessary to assimilate Rāvaṇa into a venerable line of demonic antagonists (Hiraṇyakaśipu and the rest), and that consequently he often seems to represent the power of cosmic evil incarnate. But this transcendence is far from constant, and certainly what Rāvaṇa signifies seems much richer and more complex than any such cosmic status would allow. This is true in general of the *rākṣasas* that so thickly inhabit the world of the "Forest" and the *Rāmāyaṇa* as a whole. They are such striking and enigmatic creatures that we cannot help asking who they can be and what meanings they might bear.

These questions have been posed often in the past, and Grierson's remark typifies the answer still usually given: "Most people admit that behind the mythical Rakṣasas and Asuras, there were memories of, or allusions to, very real personalities [that is, "human beings obnoxious to the authors of the passages in which their names occur"]. . . . Rakṣasas have often been identified with this or that aboriginal tribe, and no one has ever objected to this on principle."[145] The predilection for historicizing the monstrous beings of epic (and vedic) texts in this manner is widely shared, and if scholars have mostly been too circumspect to frame specific equations, a number of possible identifications have nonetheless been offered.[146] Thus *rākṣasas* have been viewed as cannibals, primitive

[145] Grierson 1912, pp. 67–69.

[146] With respect to pre-epic literature, Gonda has reiterated the long-held view that "it is not always possible to decide whether a definite name belongs to an aboriginal enemy or to a demon. Śambara, for instance, seems to be a demon in part of the corpus [the *ṚV*], but may elsewhere be a human chief" (Gonda 1975, p. 129; cf. Macdonell and Keith 1912, vol. 2, p. 355). Hillebrandt is also unsure; the *rakṣas* (as presumed, for example, to be referred to in *ṚV* 7.104) may be the gods or heroes

cave-dwellers, theriomorphic shamans, masked dancers in totemic rites of a sort still found among the Gond and other tribes, or historical ethnic groups whose descendants still bear cognate names (for instance, several subtribes and subcastes in modern Bihar).[147] They have even been identified—here we find a specific equivalence, which has secured a measure of Indological notoriety for the very disdain with which it was greeted—with the Sinhalese Buddhists, the opponents and finally victims of a hegemonic Brahmanism, represented in this rigid allegory by Rāma.[148]

Perhaps, as Grierson asserts, this mode of historicization is not in principle objectionable. After all, people do make their fictions out of their facts and treasure their stories because they help make comprehensible their own histories. There is also evidence that Indians like anyone else are prone to interpret their stories in historicizing ways. For the more xenophobic of the late medieval commentators on the *Rāmāyaṇa*, for instance, the *rākṣasas* of the Kali Age are Muslims; the representations of the epic miniaturists are largely demonizations of various tribal peoples.[149] The problem with this perspective, however, is that it obstructs any view of what the *rākṣasas* might signify in the imaginative world of the epic poem itself. To explore this, narrow historical constraints seem out of line; whether or not the *rākṣasas* ever had concrete, local identity, this is not what interested the composer of the monumental *Rāmāyaṇa*. Attempting to recover that sort of historical specificity,

---

of enemy tribes (1927–1929, vol. 2, pp. 413–14). Keith finds it impossible to determine the "precise nature" of vedic *rākṣasas* with any certainty (Rapson 1922, vol. 1, p. 106).

[147] So Ruben 1939, p. 299, summarizing the views of Hopkins (1915, pp. 38ff.) and of Macdonell (1897, pp. 162ff.), and citing the ethnography of Risley (1891, see particularly vol. 2, p. 194). Similar in spirit are the more recent observations of Thapar: "The concentration of the term *rākṣasa* in the Vindhyan region would perhaps identify them with the chalcolithic cultures and the Black-and-Red ware people of the second and early first millennium B.C." (Thapar 1978, p. 19).

[148] See Wheeler 1869, vol. 2, pp. 249ff. (cited in Weber 1870, pp. 4–5). Jacobi ridiculed Wheeler's allegorical equation first because of its historical improbability and second (a point made in part already by Weber) because it is essentially meaningless, having been for 2000 years inaccessible to all but a lone Victorian Englishman (Jacobi 1893, pp. 89–90). He does not himself, however, hazard any interpretation of the *rākṣasas*.

[149] See the note on 3.3.24 for Ck's, Ct's equating Muslims (Yavanas) with *rākṣasas* (an equation encouraged by the burial customs of the demons). The pictorial demonizations await study.

consequently, is one of the least interesting and productive of the critical operations we can undertake.

Though by abandoning the search for concrete referentiality beyond the text, we are not abandoning the task—the essential task, in my view—of historicization. What these creatures represent or refer to within the confines of the poem still has an irreducible portion of historicity—but it is the historicity of a mentality. It is as generalized imaginative representations, large symbolic responses to important human problems, that the *rākṣasas* may yield their richest signification. And what are these, after all, but the responses and representations of specific historical people, the traditional Indians who created and experienced the *Rāmāyaṇa*, as a way of interpreting their problematic historical world.

Rākṣasas are not the only fabulous creatures we confront in the "Forest"; the entire epic from the end of *Ayodhyākāṇḍa* through the *Yuddhakāṇḍa* takes place in regions inhabited by creatures fundamentally alien to the city of Ayodhyā. As if mapping out the boundaries of the expanded, extra-human domain of the narrative that begins with the *Araṇyakāṇḍa*, the poet frames the book with symmetrical episodes in which the hero confronts the monstrous, first in the person of Virādha (*sargas* 2–3) and later of Kabandha (65–69). These two incidents point up variations in the poet's representation of the fantastic that help us distinguish some instructive traits marking the *rākṣasas*.

Both Virādha and Kabandha are, with epic imprecision, called *rākṣasas*, but what among other things differentiates them from *rākṣasas* is that they live permanently in the forest, alone and without community.[150] Moreover, they are each locked into a physical form that provides a graphic objective correlative of their geographical and sociological marginalization. First Virādha:

> And there, in the heart of the forest that teemed with ferocious animals, Kākutstha beheld, towering before him like a mountain peak, a roaring, man-eating monster. Sunken-eyed, huge-mouthed, his belly deformed, he was massive, loathsome, deformed, gigantic, monstrous, a terror to behold; clad in a tiger

[150] The text is somewhat uncertain about what species of being Kabandha is. In 65.24, before his life history is made known to the audience, he is referred to as "foremost of *dānavas*" (a class of beings usually kept distinct from *rākṣasas* in the *Rāmāyaṇa*).

> skin dripping with grease and spattered with blood, as terrifying to all creatures as Death with jaws agape. On an iron pike he held impaled three lions, four tigers, two wolves, ten dappled antelopes, and the massive head of an elephant, complete with tusks, and smeared with gore. And he was roaring deafeningly. (3.2.4–8)

And then Kabandha:

> As they carried on their relentless search through the entire forest, a tremendous noise broke out that seemed to shatter the forest. The deep wood seemed altogether enveloped in wind; the noise coming from the forest seemed to fill the heavens. Seeking the source of the noise, Rāma and his younger brother came upon a mammoth, huge-chested *rākṣasa* in a thicket. The two of them drew near and there, facing them, stood the giant Kabandha, a creature without head or neck, his face set in his belly. The hair on his body was bushy and wiry, he towered before them like a mountain, a savage creature like a black storm cloud and with a voice like thunder. And in his chest, darting glances, thick-lashed, tawny, prodigious, wide, and terrible, was a single eye. Ravenously licking his massive lips and massive fangs, he was devouring tremendous apes and lions, elephants and deer. Contorting his two dreadful arms, each one of them a league in length, he would seize all sorts of animals in his hands—apes, deer, flocks of birds. He pulled in countless animals and pulled them apart limb from limb as he stood there blocking the path the two brothers were taking. (3.65.12-20)

The unchangeable physical deformity of these two creatures is an index of their moral deformity. The symbolic concomitance between physical and moral qualities has already made itself felt on several occasions in the *Ayodhyākāṇḍa* : in the malevolent servant Mantharā, who is wicked and ugly; in Sītā, who is good and beautiful; in Kaikeyī, who is beautiful and corruptible, and thus powerfully ambivalent. We shall encounter it again in the polymorphic ambiguity of the *rākṣasas* of Laṅkā.[151] The life histories of the two monsters make this relationship clear. Both are in reality celestial

[151] Cf. Pollock 1986, p. 50 and note 2, where I try to show that this formulation of concomitance is old and becomes a commonplace in classical literature. See also the note on 8.5 below.

(and relatively benign) beings who were cursed to enter monstrous bodies as a consequence of moral transgression.[152]

Virādha and Kabandha can easily be compared with other fantastic creatures familiar from *Weltmärchen*. Kabandha in particular recalls the first monster in European literature, the one-eyed cyclops Polyphemus, a devourer of men, who

> did not range with
> others, but stayed away by himself; his mind was lawless,
> and in truth he was a monstrous wonder made to behold, not
> like a man, an eater of bread, but more like a wooded
> peak of the high mountains seen standing away from the others.
> (*Odyssey* 9.188–92)[153]

Or consider the later monsters of Pliny, the Blemmyae, notably, that for millennia have fascinated westerners—Shakespeare, for example, whose Othello describes them as "men whose heads / Do grow beneath their shoulders" (1.iii.144–45). To a large extent creatures like Virādha and Kabandha seemed to have functioned for traditional Indians as the Plinian monsters for Romans and later Europeans. The Sanskrit epic poet tells of the monstrous races in the unexplored, exotic lands to the south precisely as Pliny writes of those in North Africa and "Ethiopia" (indeed, of the "Bragmanni" themselves). The fascination such creatures hold for both is evident. Their appeal is based on such things as "fantasy, escapism, delight in the exercise of the imagination, and—very important—fear of the unknown."[154] The religious-ethical dimension of the monsters of the European Middle Ages is also coded in the

[152] The *gandharva* Tumburu became Virādha as punishment for neglecting his duties toward Kubera (his negligence was itself a result of his sexual incontinence), and the *dānava* Danu became Kabandha after arrogantly attacking Indra, the king of gods. There is some textual uncertainty in the two stories. Kabandha's exposition of his history in 3.67 seems to be a fusion of two separate tales, one contained in verses 1–6, the other in verses 7–16; a situation also present, apparently, in the Virādha story, cf. 3.5–6 and 18ff. See further in the note on 67.1.

[153] What gives the cyclops his particularly inhuman and offensive quality in the eyes of the Greeks is precisely his asocial existence. Further interesting reflections on the cyclops are offered in Page 1966, pp. 1–20. The translation quoted is Lattimore 1967.

[154] Friedman 1981, p. 24 (for Pliny's Bragmanni, cf. pp. 164ff.). This interesting book helped to focus much of my thinking about the Indian version of Pliny's teratology.

Indian epic species: Their appearance and behavior result from transgressions committed in a previous embodiment; their existence is literally a curse. They are fallen creatures who, as I suggested earlier, can be liberated only by the spiritual sword wielded by the god-king Rāma.[155]

Several of these traits and a somewhat comparable "appeal" are possessed by Rāvaṇa and the other *rākṣasas*.[156] But they diverge in a number of crucial respects. The *rākṣasas* of Laṅkā may also inhabit a region at great remove from the human; their island-fortress is situated at the edge of the geographical—and moral—world of traditional Indians. But this is not exactly the antiworld usually associated with monsters.

The land of the *rākṣasas* is in many respects a carbon copy of Ayodhyā itself. The description of their city—its layout, architecture, palaces, and mansions—which is given in vivid and often luxuriant detail, could as easily be applied to Rāma's: Like Ayodhyā it is "as grand as Amarāvatī," the city of Indra, "equal to the city of the gods in heaven," a "happy and delighted city."[157] Admittedly cities in Sanskrit texts are regularly described in such ways.[158] What is noteworthy is that the poet felt no compulsion to deviate from the formula in the case of the *rākṣasas*. Similarly, their social organization seems indistinguishable from that of Ayodhyā. The same holds true in the political sphere, which has all the distinctive features of the traditional Indian polity, with monarchical sovereign, ministerial apparatus, and all the rest. Even the most pronounced aberration from the world of Ayodhyā, the tyranny of the king, seems a peculiarly human excess. In the domain of religious life, we find a close—if sometimes inverted—approximation to brahmanical society: There exist, for example, *brahma-rākṣasas*, who know the *vedas* and *vedāṅgas*, and who perform sacrifices.[159]

[155] Cf. Friedman 1981, pp. 89–103, 187, where he notes that the monstrous races are viewed as cursed and so may function as "theological warnings."

[156] The word *rākṣasa* itself is puzzling. Avestan cognates seem to authenticate the radical signification "an injurious being or thing," though little more than this is certain (Mayrhofer 1956–80, vol. 3. pp. 30–31; see also the earlier discussions in Macdonell 1897, p. 164, and Hopkins 1915, p. 38).

[157] Detailed descriptions of Laṅkā are found at 3.46.9–12, 53.7–12; 5.2.6ff., 48ff., 3.3ff. For the comparison with Ayodhyā (for instance, 1.5.15), cf. 3.46.10, 5.2.17, 6.3.9.

[158] Cf. Schlingloff 1969, especially pp. 5–9.

[159] For example, 5.16.2, though the sacrifices are often inverted, black-magic rites, like Indrajit's in the *Yuddhakāṇḍa*.

Unlike the monsters of the forest, then, the *rākṣasas* of Laṅkā inhabit a sociopolitical domain fully comparable to that of the human community of Ayodhyā and familiar to the poem's audiences at large.[160] The significance of this sociopolitical normality can be gauged when we try to be precise about what constitutes the "otherness" of the creatures. Among the key factors of this status—diet, speech, clothing, weapons, customs, and social organization—only the first shows deviation in the case of the *rākṣasas* (they eat human beings).[161] The large pool of signs of recognizability, in addition to the existence of several good *rākṣasas* capable of responsible moral choice (Vibhīṣaṇa, Trijaṭā, and others), serves almost to humanize these creatures. The consequence of this, however, is only to make them more threatening, and their deviations from the human all the more frightening and expressive, because all the more imaginable.

Among the more significant if obvious deviations is the violence of the *rākṣasas*. The ferocity of Virādha and Kabandha may first come to mind, but *rākṣasa* violence does not have the brute, blind, and feral quality of the two monsters. On the contrary, the violence of *rākṣasas* is in large part informed with elements of mind—with hatred. We find it directed specifically against those who in the traditional elite view represent the fundamental values of the ethical-religious domain and preserve this domain and the cosmic order that depends upon it by means of their sacred rites—namely, the brahmans.[162] The specter of this violence haunts the poem from the end of the *Ayodhyākāṇḍa*:[163]

> The *rākṣasas* have been molesting the ascetics. They show themselves in every form of deformation, loathsome, savage, and terrifying forms, a horror to behold. Enemies of all that is noble, they defile some ascetics with unspeakable impurities and strike terror into others by suddenly appearing before them. Stealthily they prowl the ashram sites, one after the other, and take a mad delight in harassing the ascetics. They scatter the ladles and the

[160] They would appear to inhabit such a domain from as early as the *Atharvaveda* (cf. Oldenberg 1917, p. 267; Macdonell 1897, p. 163 and references cited there).

[161] Cf. Friedman 1981, pp. 27ff. on the factors of "otherness."

[162] The association of the *rākṣasas* in particular with disturbances of the sacred rites is an ancient one, going back to the *ṚV* (as noted first, I believe, by Hillebrandt 1927–1929, vol. 2, p. 414).

[163] To be sure, we encounter this already in Book One, in the episodes of Mārīca/Subāhu and Tāṭakā.

other sacrificial implements; they douse the fires with water and break the vessels when the oblations are under way. (2.108.13–17)

In the "Forest" their depredations are described considerably more horrifically: We find brahman ascetics being brutally tormented by the *rākṣasas*, the many corpses of those whom they have killed in every way imaginable lying about, and so on (3.5.14ff.).[164] In the *Araṇyakāṇḍa* this violence is directed at the brahmans' protector, Rāma. The first third of the book is dominated by the attack of the "eaters of raw flesh" on the prince and his wife, and the image of the vengeful Śūrpaṇakhā lusting to drink their "foaming blood" as they lie dead on the field of battle.[165]

A second notable deviation from the humans they so closely resemble (and from Virādha and Kabandha, too) is the deeply ambiguous physical nature of the *rākṣasas*. They are the most labile creatures, formulaically described (curiously enough, like the monkeys that appear later in the poem) by the epithet *kāmarūpin*, "able to take on any form at will." Monsters like Virādha and Kabandha are trapped within their horrific bodies; only marginally less so are human beings, for it requires superhuman perseverance to tap the transformative power of asceticism and so transcend the embodied state (as only a rare sage like Śarabhaṅga can do, *sarga* 4). *Rākṣasas*, by contrast, have the natural ability to change their form whenever they wish: Vātāpi could become a sacrificial ram (3.10.53ff.; 41.39–42), Mārīca a golden deer dappled with brilliant gems (*sargas* 40–42), or Rāvaṇa a brahman (*sargas* 44–47). "Māyā is a power inherent in *rākṣasas*," says the *Mahābhārata*, "their age and form are whatever they want them to be" (6.86.60).

The metamorphic power of the *rākṣasas* no doubt introduces an important element of suspense and drama into the tale. The possibility that one's interlocutor may not be what one believes him to be is profoundly disturbing. But the mystery of metamorphosis is a substantial theme in the *Rāmāyaṇa* as a whole, reaching beyond the *rākṣasas* perhaps to the heart of the poem, if there is any truth to the suggestion that the peculiar nature of the god-king under-

[164] See also 3.37.4–6. One of the more graphic descriptions of slaughter is to be found in the *MBh* 3.100 (the demons described, called Kāl[ak]eyas, though technically not *rākṣasas*, are virtually identical with them).
[165] 3.18.15–16; 21.5, etc.

lies the narrative. For one thing, gods like demons have the natural ability to metamorphose.[166] For another, an *avatāra* (even in the relatively unelaborated form of the god-king) is by definition delusive; on top of this, the god-king consists of portions of many gods, any one of them—for instance, Rudra—able to become dominant at any time. It is probably appropriate and necessary, then, to include the hero himself as an essential component in this theme.

Vālmīki has substantially enriched the common epic motif of demonic transfiguration and intensified the features that make the *rākṣasas* the fascinating and terrifying beings they are. In the case of Rāvaṇa, the motif of the sham ascetic, which becomes common in later Hindu fiction, can sustain a variety of interpretations.[167] It can function, as it often does elsewhere, as little more than a banal ethical admonition ("evil can masquerade as good," for example, as Lakṣmaṇa says to Rāma in Book Two, "There are cunning people who wear the guise of righteousness," 2.20.8). Or, again, it may result from sheer dramaturgical necessity. The only way Sītā can readily converse with Rāvaṇa is if he appears as a character that, in the Indian context, will not compromise her: the guest who visits her is a brahman (not a handsome young kshatriya) who might curse her should she refuse him.[168] She therefore admits Rāvaṇa into the leaf hut and speaks with him—for it is in such dramatic artifice that fiction lives. And the transformation of the *rākṣasa* back into his "true" form is unquestionably spectacular drama:

> Then suddenly Rāvaṇa, younger brother to Vaiśravaṇa, abandoned the kindly form of beggar and assumed his true shape, one such as Doom itself must have. With eyes flaming bright red, with earrings of burnished gold, with bow and arrows, he became once more the majestic ten-faced stalker of the night. He had thrown off the guise of mendicant and assumed his own

[166] As Indra, who, in a way disturbingly similar to Rāvaṇa, seduces Ahalyā by adopting the form of a sage (1.47.15ff., after "waiting for an opening," verse 17; cf. 3.44.2, 8), or here in Book Three takes on the form of a soldier in order to destroy the austerities of an ascetic, 3.8.13–19.

[167] On the motif in general, see Bloomfield 1924. The thief regularly disguises himself as an ascetic, and so does the "ardent lover . . . in order to win or carry off his lady love" (p. 230). Both aspects seem to be present in the *Araṇyakāṇḍa* episode, which unfortunately Bloomfield does not mention.

[168] Cf. 3.44.33, 45.2.

> form again, the colossal shape of Rāvaṇa. . . . With his long arms and sharp fangs he resembled a mountain peak; seeing him advancing like Death himself, the spirits of the forest fled overpowered by fear. (3.47.6–8, 17)

But beyond the dramatic and ethical dimensions, there is a pronounced and significant strain of irony here. Not only are brahman ascetics the primary target of *rākṣasa* violence (3.5.20), which makes Rāvaṇa's adopting such a disguise especially despicable, but in addition, the renouncer with his rigorous sexual self-control embodies an ethos fundamentally antithetical to Rāvaṇa. For we shall find that in his "real" nature Rāvaṇa is not only the colossal many-limbed monster but also the exquisite lover.

The other *rākṣasas* of the *Rāmāyaṇa* exercise their transformative powers less frequently; they are generally pictured as embodiments of absolute terror, bearing only faint traces of physical likeness to humans (thus Triśiras the "Three-Headed" and other warriors in Khara's army, or the demons that guard Sītā in the *aśoka* grove, *sarga* 54). This is unremarkable except in the case of Śūrpaṇakhā. It is a nearly invariable motif in Sanskrit literature that female *rākṣasas* assume forms of stunning beauty to seduce men (as Hiḍimbā, to cite an instructive parallel, does in the *Mahābhārata* story recounted below). Śūrpaṇakhā tells us herself that as a *rākṣasa* woman she can take on any form at will (16.18), yet she appears before Rāma in her horrific shape:

> Rāma was handsome, the *rākṣasa* woman was ugly, he was shapely and slim of waist, she misshapen and potbellied; his eyes were large, hers were beady, his hair was jet black, and hers the color of copper; he always said just the right thing and in a sweet voice, her words were sinister and her voice struck terror; he was young, attractive, and well mannered, she ill mannered, repellent, an old hag. And yet, the god of love, who comes to life in our bodies, had taken possession of her. (3.16.8–10)

In view of the literary convention, it is puzzling that the *rākṣasa* woman should retain her real form here.[169] Although this provides

[169] Vālmīki's treatment is followed in few other *Rāmāyaṇa* traditions. In the Tamil adaptation of Kampan, for example, Śūrpaṇakhā comes before Rāma in a form beautiful as "soft ambrosia." In many folk versions, as in the Balalata theater of Karnataka, Śūrpaṇakhā also appears as a lovely woman; when she is subsequently

undeniable, albeit cruel, humor, it borders on the absurd. The poet has taken something of a risk, which the overall sexual-political orientation of the poem may help us understand.

The feature of *rākṣasa* otherness that, next to violence, most decidedly excludes them from the human universe of Vālmīki's poem is their intemperate and aggressive sexuality, something associated with them from the time of their earliest appearance in Indian literature.[170] This is a dominant characteristic of the *rākṣasas* from their first appearance in the *Araṇyakāṇḍa* and supplies the principal motivation for the book's two principal—and very symmetrical—events, Śūrpaṇakhā's attempted seduction of Rāma and Rāvaṇa's abduction of Sītā.

The unrestrained sexuality of the *rākṣasas* (to which their metamorphic powers are a useful adjunct) is repeatedly emphasized throughout the poem. The whole care of the *rākṣasas*, we are told, is "to master the sports of lovemaking" (3.36.20). Though Śūrpaṇakhā clearly needs considerable practice in these sports, her attempt to seduce first Rāma and then Lakṣmaṇa (*sargas* 16 and 17) discloses an assertive sexuality that recognizes no restraints of family ties ("I am prepared to defy them all [her brothers], Rāma, for I have never seen anyone like you," 16.21), or of shame in general, as is pointedly asserted later in the epic (6.82.6ff.). And she is punished by Rāma not so much in accordance with a primal urge toward "the unsexing of the bad mother," much less as "an act of apparently senseless violence," but because it is Rāma's duty as king to exact punishment in general, and specifically punishment for infringement of the sexual code.[171]

---

disfigured, she regains her natural form. The "comedy" of the scene is thus without actual violence.

[170] Cf. *ŚatBr* 3.2.1.40, "The *rakṣas* pursue women here on earth . . . and implant their seed therein." This aggressive libidinousness is coupled with transformative powers, as in *ṚV* 10.162.5, where the *rakṣas* are said to take on the form of brother, husband, lover, and thus approach women unsuspected. See the useful discussion and collection of citations in Oldenberg 1917, pp. 264ff.

[171] For the king's obligation to punish, cf. *MBh* 12.63.28, 70.31, etc.; the king is responsible for punishing sexual transgressions, too (cf. for example *ManuSm* 8.371). Facial mutilation is prescribed as a punishment for fornication/adultery in *ArthŚā* 4.10.10, the offending woman is to have her ears and nose cut off; cf. 4.12.33; and also Parāśara cited by Haradatta on *GautDŚ* 3.5.35: "As for she who commits fornication/adultery and out of a perverse nature does not do penance . . . she is to have her nose, etc., cut off.") Recognizing these cultural presuppositions

This is a harsh sexual-political message in itself, even more so when juxtaposed to other similar epic narratives. A parallel incident in the *Mahābhārata*, the *Hiḍimbavadhaparva* (1.139–43), for instance, affords a provocative contrast. The *rākṣasa* Hiḍimba catches the scent of the Pāṇḍavas while they are asleep in the wilderness during their forest exile. His sister Hiḍimbā is sent to bring back their flesh for him to eat, but she is smitten with love the moment she sees Bhīma, who is standing guard. She refuses to do her brother's bidding, takes on the seductive form of a beautiful woman, and forthrightly and unashamedly confesses to Bhīma her infatuation (" 'We shall dwell forevermore in the mountain fastnesses—be my husband,' she exclaimed, compelled by the bodiless god that moves within our bodies").[172] Hiḍimba comes to investigate and finds his sister, and in response to his reproaches, Bhīma argues in support of the *rākṣasa* woman's romantic love for him. After killing Hiḍimba, Bhīma is ready—or at least pretends he is ready—to slay the sister as well. She appeals to Kuntī and Yudhiṣṭhira, claiming that she has abandoned her loved ones, her people, and her *svadharma* for Bhīma. Yudhiṣṭhira allows the two to marry, although they are permitted to make love only during the day: Bhīma must return every night. The two share an idyllic love, until the narrative gently removes Hiḍimbā from the scene.

The basic plan of the episode is comparable with the Śūrpaṇakhā scene of the *Araṇyakāṇḍa*; the two narratives agree even in several verbal details. But the attitude toward the *rākṣasa* women is radically different: Hiḍimbā is not only regarded as a possible mate for Bhīma but, after what appears to be a blissful romance, actually bears him a son, whom he grows to love dearly (and who will die fighting on his father's side in the Bharata war).

The differences in the treatment of the theme reflect a deeper disagreement in the two epics about the social constraints on sex-

---

behind the incident saves us from the mistake of Smith (1980, pp. 66–67, ". . . senseless violence," since "there is no implicit compulsion . . . upon Rāma to act virtuously: [his] job is battle"), or of Kakar (1981, pp. 98–99, "unsexing the bad mother," though the micro-interpretation remains compelling, that through "the well-known unconscious device of the upward displacement of the genitals," this becomes "a fantasied clitoridectomy, designed to root out the cause and symbol of Śūrpaṇakhā's lust").

172 Compare *MBh* 1.139.25 with *Rām* 3.16.21, 24; *MBh* 1.141.4, 142.8 with *Rām* 3.16.10.

ual relations. The male fantasy of the fairy bride, as the *Mahābhārata* presents it, is stripped of all its gratification in the *Rāmāyaṇa*: here Śūrpaṇakhā is as if transmuted into the *churel*, the succubus of the Indian male's nightmare world, who threatens him with death through sexual depletion and must therefore be suppressed.[173] The details of an interpretation along these lines are certainly debatable, but it seems unlikely we can avoid the general conclusion that such narratives are aesthetically processing a fundamental male fantasy, and in very different ways.

Rāvaṇa's abduction of Sītā, too, fits into this category. It is allegedly undertaken in revenge for Khara's death.[174] But it is quickly shown to be devoid of any but sexual significance. The fires of lust are lit in the *rākṣasa* when Śūrpaṇakhā first describes Sītā to him:

> Rāma has a lawful wife named Sītā, princess of Videha. And what a glorious woman she is, with her large eyes, slender waist, and full hips. No goddess, no *gandharva* woman, no *yakṣa* or *kinnara* woman, no mortal woman so beautiful have I ever seen before on the face of this earth. He who claims Sītā as wife and receives her delighted embraces has more reason to live than anyone else in all the worlds, the breaker of fortresses, Indra himself, included. She is a woman of good character, with a form beyond all praise, a beauty unequaled on earth. She would make a perfect wife for you, and you a perfect husband for her. How broad her hips, how full and high her breasts, how lovely her face. Why, I all but brought her back to be your wife. The moment you saw Vaidehī's full-moon face, you would find yourself at the mercy of the arrows of Manmatha, god of love. (3.32.14–20)

Rāvaṇa resolves at once to abduct her, as he has abducted any number of women, human and divine (33.3; cf. 45.24, 7.24.1ff.).

Later in the poem, however, we are told that the women in Rāvaṇa's harem—the daughters of royal seers, of the *pitṛs*, *daityas*, *gandharvas*, *rākṣasas*—are present not just because they were phys-

[173] The *Rāmāyaṇa* may be expressing a wider anxiety: women in general are sometimes figured as female *rākṣasas*, as in the anonymous verse, "With a look she consumes your heart, with a touch she consumes your power, and in the act of love she consumes your every drop of manly strength—woman is a *rākṣasī* in her very person" (*SubhāRaBh* p. 348, no. 9).

[174] Cf. 3.34.20, 52.21–24; cf. 38.6.

ically abducted but also because they were enchanted by Rāvaṇa's charms and now love no one but him (5.7.66). Elsewhere in the same book the king of *rākṣasas* is discovered resting after making love with the women of his harem: he is lounging on a sheepskin-covered couch, strewn with flowers, perfumed with incense, fanned with rare yak-tail fans; he is dark, with flashing earrings, clothed in silvery clothing, anointed with precious sandalwood cream. "He is extraordinarily handsome, he who could take on any form at will" (*surūpaṃ kāmarūpinam*), so much so that Hanumān watching him says to himself, "What beauty, what fortitude, what strength and splendor. . . . Had the mighty lord of *rākṣasas* not been unrighteous, he would instead have justly been made protector [*rakṣitṛ*] of the world of the gods, Śakra included" (5.47.17).

Like Milton's Satan, Rāvaṇa has to be endowed with substantial "merit," since great evil presupposes the perversion of great virtues. But also like the representations of the devil in Western literature, with whom desire is ever present, Rāvaṇa's sexuality and seductiveness are a fundamentally dominant trait.[175] What the *rākṣasas* in general seem largely to signify is the very antithesis of the sexual canons—so strict, and at times so bloodless, with an almost strident insistence on monogamy—of the *Rāmāyaṇa*.[176] If this is not already perceptible in the *Araṇyakāṇḍa*, it becomes transparent later in the epic, especially in Book Five. There we are shown the private life of the *rākṣasas*, a continuous orgy of drink, food, and lovemaking. The poet dwells on the evidence of their luxurious dissipation with the evident satisfaction of a skillful artist manipulating the most illicit fantasies of his audience.[177]

When we ask who, then, the *rākṣasas* are and what they mean in the *Rāmāyaṇa*, we are presented with a number of possibilities. Certainly they have a dimension that is more or less universal. Beyond the sheer satanic, they seem to channel fear of the foreign—of what is different though shockingly recognizable—and specifically that "ancient fear that 'they' will take away 'our' women."[178]

[175] On the Western devil and desire, cf. Todorov 1973, pp. 127 and 143.

[176] For further discussion see Pollock 1986, pp. 53–57.

[177] See especially *sargas* 3–9. Friedman also has noted that the sexual license of the Plinian peoples was the primary focus of westerners' abhorrence of them (1981, pp. 203–4).

[178] The *ārya* or member of brahmanical society distinguished himself categorically

Sexual theft of the *rākṣasa* sort could be viewed, thus, as a metaphor for interracial strife (mixed with a deep anxiety about the limits of exogamy, for which a creature like Rāvaṇa represents an extreme). In Indian literary imagination, too, the foreign may easily have been transmuted into the monstrous.[179]

The objects of this transmutation resist localization and chronological fixity. Of any original racial, ethnic, or geographical specificity, none remains in the *Rāmāyaṇa.* Their one reality seems to be that of fantasized aliens, who are both feared and desired, threatening mortal danger at the same time that they attract with an extraordinary, unsocializable sexuality, and whose very otherness is the source of both the fascination and the repulsion.

Fascination and repulsion, however, are always responses to categories of our own construction, brought to bear on objects of our own construction. If the fantastic in literature concerns the relation of man with his desire, these remain historical men and women, with, so to speak, historical desires.[180] And it is herein that we encounter the cultural specificity and, in a general sense, historicality of the *rākṣasas.* They are the imaginative product of the confrontation of traditional Indians with their particular forms of desire—in its two primary forms, libidinal and aggresssive—representing all that traditional Indians most desired and most feared. *Rākṣasas* are creatures polluted by violence, blood, and carnivorous filth, who kill and eat those they kill and, what is maybe worse, threaten the very foundation of human life, the brahmans who maintain the cosmologically essential sacrifice (and perhaps by reason of their very privilege and power provide a focal point for aggression). At the same time, in their libidinized forms, they enact

---

from the outsider, the *anārya* (a word applied to Śūrpaṇakhā in 17.19), with whom he could in no way see himself as equal (cf. *ManuSm* 10.73).

[179] Here I am adopting ideas from a recent analysis of Dracula, with whom obviously Rāvaṇa has much in common (Protean mutability, for example, or the identity of food and sexual object; see Stevenson 1988 and p. 145 for the quote). But Dracula's social and political world is very different from that of the Englishmen, and to that degree the threat he poses seems far more distant than Rāvaṇa's. For a superb review of a specific historical instance of the sexual focus of interracial conflict, which provides striking parallels to the literary instance of the *Rāmāyaṇa,* see Jordan 1968, especially pp. 136ff.

[180] See Todorov 1973, pp. 124ff., particularly p. 139, who, however, ignores the historicality of the fantastic. For Stevenson, by contrast, the vampire, "a reflection—however uneasy and strange—of ourselves," is much more securely situated in time.

the deepest sexual urges—total abandonment to pleasure, as well as absolute autonomy and power in gratifying lust. Since they are broadly humanized in so many features, their deviance in others becomes not only a scandal but also a risk: Enacting the repressed desire, and perhaps rage, of the traditional Indian, they are what he might become were the barrier of conscience—or that of fear inspired by the dark shadow of royal punishment—eliminated.[181] From this perspective, we may see the *rākṣasa* as an index of traditional Indian primal terror and desire, objectified together in a single symbolic form.

[181] As Derrett points out, theft and adultery were viewed as the two most reprehensible crimes in traditional India, and it was felt that only the presence of political authority keeps all men from becoming thieves and fornicators (Derrett 1975, pp. 127, 139).

ARAṆYAKĀṆḌA

Sarga 1

1. Soon after entering the vast wilderness, the wilderness of Daṇḍaka, Rāma, the self-disciplined and invincible prince, saw a circle of ashrams where ascetics dwelt.

2. *Kuśa* grass and bark garments were strewn about it, and, flooded with brahmanical splendor, it was as luminous and blinding to the eye as the sun's circle in heaven.

3. It was a place of refuge for all creatures; its grounds were always kept immaculate, and troupes of *apsarases* ever paid homage there and danced.

4. Spacious fire-sanctuaries made it beautiful, so too the sacrificial implements, the ladles and all, hide garments and *kuśa* grass, bundles of kindling, pitchers of water, and roots and fruit.

5. Tall forest trees encircled it, holy trees that bore sweet fruit. It was a place of worship of offerings and oblations, a holy place echoing with the sounds of *brahma*, the sacred *vedas*.

6–7. Wildflowers carpeted it, and there was a lotus pond filled with lotuses. Ancient sages were present there, temperate men who ate only roots and fruit, wore bark garments and black hides, and shone like fire or the sun. Supreme seers, holy men given to rigorous fasting, deepened its beauty.

8. It resembled the abode of Brahmā; the sounds of *brahma*, the sacred *vedas*, echoed through it, and illustrious brahmans who knew the meaning of *brahma* deepened its beauty still further.

9. When powerful, majestic Rāghava saw the circle of ashrams, he unstrung his great bow and approached.

10. And when the great seers, who were endowed with divine knowledge, saw Rāma, they joyfully approached him and glorious Vaidehī.

11. They were men who followed the ways of righteousness, strict in their vows, and when they saw him, appearing like the rising moon, they received him with benedictions.

12. With astonished expressions the forest-dwellers beheld Rāma's handsome physique, his lovely attire, youthfulness, and splendor.

13. Vaidehī, Lakṣmaṇa, and Rāma were like marvelous appari-

tions, and the forest hermits all stared at them with unblinking eyes.

14. Thereupon the illustrious sages, dedicated to the welfare of all creatures, invited Rāghava into their leaf huts as their guest.

15. And showing Rāma honor in accordance with precept, they fetched him water, those illustrious, firelike sages who followed the ways of righteousness.

16. Knowing what was right, they offered the great prince roots, flowers, fruit of the forest, and their ashram as well. And then, with hands cupped in reverence, they spoke:

17. "As guardian of righteousness and glorious refuge of his people, a king is worthy of reverence and esteem. He is a guru who wields the staff of punishment.

18. "A king is a fourth part Indra himself and the protector of his subjects, Rāghava. Therefore he enjoys the choicest luxuries and is held in honor by the world.

19. "We are residents of your realm and need your protection. Wherever you may find yourself, in city or forest, you are our king, the lord of the people.

20. "We have renounced violence, your majesty, and learned to control our senses and anger. You must always protect us ascetics, for we are as your children."

21. So they spoke, and with fruit, roots, wildflowers, and other sorts of food they paid worship to Rāghava and Lakṣmaṇa.

22. And other firelike ascetics, perfected beings whose conduct accorded with custom, also gratified lord Rāma as custom required.

The end of the first *sarga* of the *Araṇyakāṇḍa* of the *Śrī Rāmāyaṇa*.

Sarga 2

1. Such was the hospitality the sages provided Rāma, and toward sunrise he took leave of them all and plunged back into the forest.

2–3. With Lakṣmaṇa following behind, Rāma soon beheld the heart of the forest, the haunt of wolves and tigers, crowded with herds of various other animals; a tangle of trees, vines, and shrubs, with murky pools; the different sorts of birds fallen silent, and the swarms of crickets chirping.

4. And there, in the heart of the forest that teemed with ferocious animals, Kākutstha beheld, towering before him like a mountain peak, a roaring, man-eating monster.

5–8ab. Sunken-eyed, huge-mouthed, his belly deformed, he was massive, loathsome, deformed, gigantic, monstrous, a terror to behold; clad in a tiger skin dripping with grease and spattered with blood, as terrifying to all creatures as Death with jaws agape. On an iron pike he held impaled three lions, four tigers, two wolves, ten dappled antelopes, and the massive head of an elephant, complete with tusks, and smeared with gore. And he was roaring deafeningly.

8cd–9ab. The moment he saw Rāma, Lakṣmaṇa, and Sītā, princess of Mithilā, he attacked them in a rage, like Death attacking people at their fated hour.

9cd–10ab. He let out a blood-chilling roar that seemed to shake the very earth. Then, seizing Vaidehī in his embrace, he strode off, crying:

10cd–11ab. "You there, short-lived creatures who wear matted hair and bark garments yet share a wife between you, who have entered Daṇḍaka wilderness bearing bows and arrows and swords:

11cd–12ab. "How is it two ascetics are living with a young woman? You are evil men impersonating sages and following the path of unrighteousness. Who are you two?

12cd–13ab. "I am Virādha the *rākṣasa*. Armed with weapons I eternally roam this impassable forest, feeding on the flesh of seers.

13cd–ef. "This shapely woman shall be my wife. And as for you evil men, I will drink your blood on the field of battle."

14. So the wicked Virādha insolently spoke, and as Janaka's daughter Sītā listened to his arrogant words, she was terror-struck and started trembling violently, like a plantain tree in a high wind.

15. When Rāghava saw the beautiful Sītā locked in Virādha's embrace, his mouth went dry, and he said to Lakṣmaṇa:

16. "Do you see, dear brother! The daughter of King Janaka, a

glorious princess raised in perfect comfort, my virtuous wife, is caught in Virādha's embrace.

17. "All that Kaikeyī planned for us, Lakṣmaṇa, and chose with her boon and desired in her heart has come true all at once.

18. "She who, not content with kingship, and farsighted on her son's behalf, drove me into the forest—I who wish all creatures well—my middle mother should now at last be pleased.

19. "That someone else should touch Vaidehī pains me as nothing ever has, not the theft of my kingdom, Saumitri, nor even Father's death."

20. So Kākutstha spoke, overwhelmed with tears and grief. But Lakṣmaṇa, enraged and hissing like a cornered snake, said:

21. "You are the equal of Vāsava and defender of all creatures, Kākutstha! And yet you stand there as if defenseless while I am here ready to serve you. What good is this complaining?

22. "In my rage I will kill the *rākṣasa* Virādha this instant with a single arrow, and when the breath of life has left him, the earth shall drink in his blood.

23. "The rage I felt toward Bharata in his lust for kingship I shall vent against Virādha, like Indra, wielder of the thunderbolt, unleashing his bolt upon a mountain.

24. "Set in motion by the forceful movement of my arm, my great arrow shall crash down upon his great chest, ripping the life from his body, and he will go crashing down sprawled upon the earth."

The end of the second *sarga* of the *Araṇyakāṇḍa* of the *Śrī Rāmāyaṇa*.

Sarga 3

1. Now, once again Virādha spoke, making the forest resound, "Identify yourselves to me, as I demanded: Who are you two, and where are you going?"

2. When the *rākṣasa*, his face ablaze, had put these questions to him, mighty Rāma told him of his family, the Ikṣvākus.

3. "Know that we are two virtuous kshatriyas residing in the forest.

But we want to know about you. Who are you who roam Daṇḍaka?"

4. Virādha then replied to the valorous Rāma, "Very well, I shall tell you, your majesty; hear me, Rāghava.

5. "I am, they say, the son of Jaya, and my mother is Śatahradā. All the *rākṣasas* on earth call me Virādha.

6. "By ascetic practices I won the favor of Brahmā, who granted that no weapon of this world could ever kill me, not even cut or pierce me.

7. "Relinquish this woman and, without so much as a backward glance, hurry and begone the way you came. Then I shall not take your life."

8. Eyes red with fury Rāma replied to Virādha, the hideous, evil-minded *rākṣasa*:

9. "Curse you, vile and wretched creature. You are surely courting death—and death you shall find now in battle. Do not move: You cannot escape me alive."

10. Rāma then strung his bow, quickly affixed one well-honed arrow after another, and shot them at the *rākṣasa*.

11. He fired seven arrows from his taut-strung bow, swift, gold-feathered arrows that flew like Suparṇa or the wind.

12. Trimmed with peacock feathers, the fiery arrows tore through Virādha's body and fell to the ground dripping with blood.

13. Seizing a pike like Indra's banner, he let out a tremendous roar, looking for all the world like Death with jaws agape.

14. The pike resembled a thunderbolt or some blazing object in the sky, but with two arrows Rāma, foremost of warriors, smashed it to pieces.

15. Then all at once Saumitri broke the left arm of the terrible *rākṣasa* while Rāma broke the right.

16. His arms broken, the *rākṣasa* Virādha, massive as a storm cloud, fell headlong in agony to the ground, like a mountain shattered by a thunderbolt. Then he spoke to Kākutstha, bull among men:

17. "Now I realize, my son, that you must be Rāma, the worthy son

of Kausalyā, and that this is illustrious Vaidehī, and this, glorious Lakṣmaṇa.

18. "I was cursed to take on this monstrous *rākṣasa* body. I am really the *gandharva* Tumburu, and it was Vaiśravaṇa who cursed me.

19–20ab. "But I begged his forgiveness, and the glorious god said to me, 'When Rāma, the son of Daśaratha, slays you in battle, then you shall recover your true form and go to heaven.'

20cd–21ab. "Such were King Vaiśravaṇa's words. Because of my passion for the *apsaras* Rambhā, I had grown careless in my attendance on the king, so he grew angry and cursed me.

21cd–ef. "By your grace, I have been freed from this dreadful curse and may now return to my true abode. I wish you well, slayer of foes.

22. "A league and a half from here, my son, lives righteous Śarabhañga, a great and powerful seer, radiant as the sun.

23. "Visit him at once; he will see to your welfare. But first consign me to a grave, Rāma, then go your way in safety.

24. "Such is the immemorial custom with respect to dead *rākṣasas*. Those that are buried in a grave gain worlds that are eternal."

25. So the mighty Virādha spoke to Kākutstha, and tormented by the arrows he left his body, ready to enter heaven.

26. As he was hauled away and cast into a pit, the pointed-eared Virādha let out a monstrous, deafening roar, howling at the top of his voice.

27. After they had killed the *rākṣasa* and recovered Maithilī, the two brothers, bearing their gold-worked bows, relaxed at their ease in the great forest like the sun and moon in heaven.

The end of the third *sarga* of the *Araṇyakāṇḍa* of the *Śrī Rāmāyaṇa*.

Sarga 4

1. After mighty Rāma had killed the awesomely powerful *rākṣasa* Virādha, he embraced Sītā and comforted her. Then turning to his splendid brother, Lakṣmaṇa, he said:

2. "This trackless forest is a dreadful place, and we are not forest-dwellers. Let us go at once to visit the ascetic Śarabhaṅga."

3. And so Rāghava set out for Śarabhaṅga's ashram.

4. Nearing the abode of the godlike Śarabhaṅga, a sage purified by asceticism, Rāma beheld a great marvel.

5–6. He beheld Indra himself, lord of the wise gods. His body was luminous as fire or the sun, he stood without touching the ground. His jewelry was sparkling bright, no speck of dust sullied the garment he wore, and many great beings resembling the god himself were worshiping him.

7–9. And near the god he saw a chariot hovering in midair, looking like the morning sun, with bay horses harnessed to it. There was an immaculate parasol, like a bank of silvery clouds or the disk of the moon, adorned with many-colored garlands; and a pair of splendid, priceless yak-tail fans with golden handles, held by two fair women who waved them over the god's head.

10. *Gandharvas*, deathless gods, perfected beings, and many supreme seers sang glorious hymns in praise of him as he hovered in midair.

11. At the sight of Indra, god of the hundred rites, Rāma said to Lakṣmaṇa, "Once, long ago, we heard that Śakra, the god invoked far and wide, possesses horses, divine horses that hover in midair. Those very bays are surely them.

12–13. "And the hundreds upon hundreds of young men who stand sword in hand around his chariot, wearing earrings and necklaces that flash like fire upon their chests—all of them, Saumitri, tiger among men, would appear to be twenty-five years old.

14. "And that, they say, is invariably the age of gods, the very age, it would seem, of these handsome tigers among men.

15. "Stay here a moment with Vaidehī, Lakṣmaṇa, while I find out for certain who this splendid being beside the chariot might be."

16. So Kākutstha spoke, bidding Saumitri to stay behind. Then he set out for the ashram of Śarabhaṅga.

17. Seeing Rāma drawing near, Indra, lord of Śacī, took leave of Śarabhaṅga, then turned to the wise gods and said:

18. "That man approaching is Rāma. Before he can address me, conduct me to my residence; hereafter he may see me.

19. "When he has accomplished his task and gained victory, I will see him without delay. For he has a great deed to do, impossible for anyone else to accomplish."

20. So Indra spoke, wielder of the thunderbolt, and bade the ascetic farewell. After showing him high honor, the tamer of foes went to heaven on his chariot harnessed with bays.

21. When thousand-eyed Indra had departed, Rāghava proceeded with his companions and came upon Śarabhaṅga as he was performing the fire sacrifice.

22. Rāma clasped his feet, and Sītā and Lakṣmaṇa did the same. The sage invited them in and procured them seats, and with his permission they sat down.

23. Rāghava then asked about Śakra's visit, and Śarabhaṅga explained everything to him.

24. "The granter of boons wishes to conduct me to the world of Brahmā. By severe ascetic practices have I won it, Rāma, a place impossible for impure men to reach.

25. "But I knew you were living nearby, tiger among men, and I would not go to the world of Brahmā without first having seen you here as my honored guest.

26. "Now that we have met, I will go to the highest heaven, where the gods reside. Blessed and imperishable are the worlds I have won, the worlds of Brahmā and of heaven's vault. Tiger among men, please accept the worlds that are now mine."

27. So the seer Śarabhaṅga spoke, and Rāghava, tiger among men and master of all sacred texts, made this reply:

28. "I hope to win all these worlds for myself, great sage. What I need now, however, is for you to advise me of some place to dwell in these woods."

29. So Rāghava spoke, Śakra's equal in power, and wise Śarabhaṅga addressed him once more:

30. "Make your way to the sacred region where the ascetic Sutīkṣṇa lives. He will arrange a dwelling place for you in a lovely part of the forest.

31. "Tiger among men, the path is there. But stay one moment, my son, and watch as I abandon my body, as a snake abandons its worn-out skin."

32. Then, having stoked the fire and made the oblation of clarified butter, mighty Śarabhaṅga, expert in vedic hymns, entered the fiery eater of oblations.

33. The fire consumed the hair on the great sage's body, the hair on his head, his worn-out skin, his bones, and whatever flesh and blood remained to him.

34. And Śarabhaṅga became a youth once more, brilliant as fire, and he rose radiant from the altar of fire.

35. Passing beyond the worlds of those who maintain the sacred fires, beyond those of the great seers and of the gods, he ascended to the world of Brahmā.

36. The bull among the twice-born, a man of holy deeds, beheld Grandfather Brahmā with his retinue in his abode, and when the Grandfather saw the brahman he rejoiced and said, "I bid you welcome."

The end of the fourth *sarga* of the *Araṇyakāṇḍa* of the *Śrī Rāmāyaṇa.*

Sarga 5

1. When Śarabhaṅga had gone to heaven, hosts of sages assembled and came to visit mighty Rāma Kākutstha.

2. There were *vaikhānasas* and *vālakhilyas, saṃprakṣālas* and *marīcipas.* There were many ascetics of the sort that pound their food with stones or subsist on leaves.

3. Some were sages who use their teeth as mortars, or keep themselves submerged; who subsist on water, or eat nothing but air.

4–5. There were those who make their abode in the open, who always sleep upon the ground, or dwell only in the heights. There were self-mastering men who clothe themselves in wet garments or ceaselessly intone their prayers; who are ever engaged in ascetic practices or subject themselves to the five ascetic fires. All of them were possessed of brahmanical majesty and intently concentrated in yoga, all the ascetics who came to visit Rāma in the ashram of Śarabhaṅga.

6. When the host of righteous seers had come before him, they spoke earnestly to Rāma, champion of righteousness and one most wise in the ways of righteousness.

7. "You are lord and master of the House of the Ikṣvākus and of this earth, great chariot-fighter, like Indra the munificent among the gods.

8. "You are famed throughout the three worlds for your greatness and valor. Your filial devotion is profound, no less your truthfulness and righteousness.

9. "We have come before you, great prince who know and cherish the ways of righteousness, and we must speak out because we are in need. Please forgive us for this, lord.

10. "It would be an act of great unrighteousness, dear Rāma, for a lord of the earth to take a sixth part in tax without providing protection as though to his sons.

11–12. "But he who strives constantly and energetically to protect all who live in his realm as though they were his very own life, or sons dearer to him than life, secures long-lasting fame, Rāma, for many years to come. He reaches the place of Brahmā and even there is exalted.

13. "A king who protects his subjects as he rightly should acquires a fourth part of the supreme righteousness amassed by a sage who lives on nothing but roots and fruit.

14. "Here a great throng of forest hermits has gathered, brahmans most of them. They are being horribly slaughtered by *rākṣasas*, undefended, Rāma, though you are present to defend them.

15. "Come see the bodies of the many purified sages slain in every imaginable way by dreaded *rākṣasas* in the forest.

16. "The sages who dwell by the Pampā river and along the Mandākinī and those living on Mount Citrakūṭa are being butchered.

17. "We can tolerate no longer these terrible outrages that ferocious *rākṣasas* are commiting against ascetics in the forest.

18. "So we have taken refuge with you, our one sure place of ref-

uge. Save us, Rāma, lest we be slaughtered by the stalkers of the night."

19. After hearing the distraught ascetics, the righteous prince Kākutstha said to them all, "You have no need to plead with me; I stand at the bidding of all those in distress.

20. "It must have been to accomplish your purpose that chance has brought me here: My sojourn in the forest shall bear great fruit. I am ready to slay in battle the *rākṣasas,* the enemies of ascetics."

21. When the mighty and noble prince, firmly keeping to the ways of righteousness, had bestowed this boon upon the ascetics, he set out with them and Lakṣmaṇa to visit Sutīkṣṇa.

The end of the fifth *sarga* of the *Araṇyakāṇḍa* of the *Srī Rāmāyaṇa.*

Sarga 6

1. So Rāma, slayer of enemies, set out for Sutīkṣṇa's ashram with his brother and Sītā and those twice-born men.

2. He traveled a long way, crossing deep rivers, until he saw a huge mountain towering before him like a thundercloud.

3. The two Rāghavas, best of the Ikṣvākus, then made their way with Sītā into a grove densely wooded with different kinds of trees.

4. And on his way he saw, deep in the gloomy forest with its many fruit-bearing and flowering trees, an ashram garlanded with bark-cloth garments.

5. There sat the ascetic Sutīkṣṇa, a man grown old in asceticism, his hair matted with dirt and mud. Rāma addressed him according to precept:

6. "Holy one, I am Rāma. I have come to see you. Will you address me, great seer, you who are wise in the ways of righteousness and strive for truth?"

7. The sage then turned his gaze upon mighty Rāma, champion of righteousness, and drawing him into his arms he said:

8. "You are most welcome here, mighty Rāma, champion of righteousness. With your arrival this ashram seems to have found its rightful protector at last.

9–10ab. "I have been waiting for you, mighty and glorious prince, and that is why I have not yet ascended hence to the world of the gods, leaving my body behind on the earth. I heard, about the time you reached Citrakūṭa, that you had been deposed from the kingship.

10cd–ef. "The king of gods, Indra of the hundred rites, has come here, Kākutstha, and told me I have won all worlds by my holy deeds.

11. "Come then, with your wife and Lakṣmaṇa, and by my grace enjoy yourself in the worlds won by my asceticism, worlds where gods and seers reside."

12. Like Vāsava addressing Brahmā the self-controlled Rāma replied to Sutīkṣṇa, a great and brilliant seer awesome in asceticism and truthful in speech:

13. "I hope to win those worlds for myself, great sage. What I need now, however, is for you to advise me of some place to dwell in these woods.

14. "You are knowledgeable in all matters and dedicated to the welfare of all creatures—that is what the great Śarabhañga Gautama said of you."

15. So Rāma spoke, and the great and famous seer, filled with deep joy, made this gentle reply:

16. "This very ashram, Rāma, has every possible virtue; you may pass your time here pleasantly. Seers in great numbers frequent the place, and roots and fruit are always plentiful.

17. "Herds of animals come and go at this ashram, glorious prince; how fetching they are wandering about without the least fear."

18. Hearing the great seer's words, Lakṣmaṇa's eldest brother drew forth his bow and arrow, and firmly replied:

19. "Most illustrious sage, I might chance to slay the herds of animals congregating here, with one of my sharp-edged arrows that flash like lightning bolts.

20. "You would be implicated in it, and what worse misfortune than that? No, I do not think it good for me to spend too much time in this ashram."

21. So Rāma spoke to the granter of boons and then went to per-

form the twilight worship. After the evening worship was over, he arranged to spend the night there.

22. When twilight was past and he saw night coming on, the great Sutīkṣṇa himself prepared pure food, such as is proper fare for ascetics, and offered it to the two bulls among men.

The end of the sixth *sarga* of the *Araṇyakāṇḍa* of the *Śrī Rāmāyaṇa*.

Sarga 7

1. Honored by Sutīkṣṇa, Rāma and Saumitri spent the night there, and at dawn they awoke.

2. Rāghava rose promptly and with Sītā bathed in ice-cold water fragrant with the scent of lotuses.

3–4. Next, at the proper hour and according to precept, Vaidehī, Rāma, and Lakṣmaṇa worshiped the fire and the gods in the forest, the refuge of ascetics. Thus purified and seeing the rising sun, the bringer of day, they approached Sutīkṣṇa and gently addressed him:

5. "We have passed the night comfortably, holy one. You have shown us honor, honorable sage. We now ask leave of you; we wish to set forth, for the sages are urging us to make haste.

6. "We are hastening to visit all the ashrams belonging to the holy seers who live in Daṇḍaka wilderness.

7. "We wish to take leave of you, we and these great sages, who are constant in righteousness and tempered by asceticism, men like smoldering fires.

8–9. "Before the sun shines too bright to endure—like a lowborn man getting rich in crooked ways—we wish to go," said Rāghava, bowing in veneration with Saumitri and Sītā at the feet of the sage.

10. As the two men touched his feet, the great sage raised them up, warmly embraced them, and said to them with affection:

11. "May you and Saumitri go your way in safety, Rāma, along with Sītā here, who follows like a shadow.

12. "Go, mighty prince, and visit the lovely ashrams of these sages living in Daṇḍaka wilderness, men purified by their ascetic practices.

13–15. "You will see forests all in flower, abounding in fruit and roots, with herds of tame animals and flocks of tame birds; ponds and lakes with clumps of blooming lotuses and sparkling clear water, teeming with waterfowl; mountain cascades that delight the eye, and delightful stretches of wilderness echoing with the cries of peacocks.

16. "Go then, my son, and you, too, Saumitri, and may you return once more to my ashram after your visit."

17. So he spoke, and Rāma replied with a word of assent. After reverently circling the sage, he and Saumitri prepared to set forth.

18. Large-eyed Sītā then gave the brothers their splendid pairs of quivers, their bows, and gleaming swords.

19. Strapping on the splendid quivers and taking up their twanging bows, Rāma and Lakṣmaṇa left the ashram to begin their journey.

The end of the seventh *sarga* of the *Araṇyakāṇḍa* of the *Śrī Rāmāyaṇa*.

Sarga 8

1. As her husband, the delight of the Rāghus, was setting forth with Sutīkṣṇa's leave, Vaidehī addressed him in an affectionate tone of voice:

2. "Acquiring great righteousness requires the greatest care, and only he who avoids deliberate misdeeds can gain it in this world.

3. "As for deliberate misdeeds, there are just three. Telling lies is bad enough, but the other two, sexual intercourse with another man's wife and unprovoked violence, are even worse.

4. "You have never been, nor will you ever be, guilty of telling lies, Rāghava. And how could you possibly lust after the wife of another man, an act that destroys righteousness?

5. "Both of these misdeeds can be avoided by those who have mastered their senses, and I know you control your senses, my handsome husband.

6. "But the third one, violence—the taking of life without provocation, and recklessly—to this you may be prone.

7. "You have promised to slay the *rākṣasas* in combat, my mighty husband, in order to protect the seers who live in Daṇḍaka wilderness.

8. "And to this end you have set forth to the forest known as Daṇḍaka, in company with your brother, armed with bow and arrows.

9. "As I watch you setting out, my mind grows sick with worry, though thinking about your deeds usually brings me the greatest happiness.

10. "For I disapprove, my mighty husband, of going to Daṇḍaka forest. I shall explain the reason why; just hear what I have to say.

11. "You and your brother are going to the forest bow and arrow in hand, and I fear the sight of any forest-dweller might cause you to shoot your arrows.

12. "For in this world a bow to a kshatriya is kindling to a fire: If it comes too close, his blazing power flares up wildly.

13. "Once upon a time, my great-armed husband, there was a truthful and pure ascetic who lived far off in a holy forest, where animals and birds delighted to come.

14. "To hinder his ascetic practices Indra, lord of Śacī, came to his ashram in the guise of a soldier, sword in hand.

15. "And in that ascetic's ashram he deposited the splendid sword, given by way of a pledge to him who practiced holy asceticism.

16. "After receiving the weapon, the sage grew obsessed with guarding the pledge, and even wandering the forest guarded the trust committed to him.

17. "Whenever he went out to gather fruit and roots, he would not go without the sword, so obsessed was he with guarding the pledge.

18. "From his constantly bearing the weapon, the ascetic's heart by degrees turned violent, and he forgot his ascetic vows.

19. "The sage took delight in wanton violence, became reckless, lured by unrighteousness, all because he lived with the weapon. Finally he went to hell.

20–21. "Only because I love and respect you am I reminding you—not teaching you—that on no account should you take up your bow and, unprovoked, turn your thoughts to killing the *rākṣasas* of Daṇḍaka. My mighty husband, I disapprove of your killing creatures that have done no wrong.

22. "Mighty kshatriyas, finding themselves in the forests inhabited by men who practice self-restraint, need bows only for protecting those in distress.

23. "How incongruous they are, weapons and the forest, the kshatriya order and the practice of asceticism—it is all so at odds. We must respect the customs of the place.

24. "Wicked thoughts, my noble husband, can come from handling weapons. When you are back in Ayodhyā, you may follow the kshatriya code.

25. "But my joy would be unending, like that of my mother-in-law and father-in-law, should you renounce the kingship altogether and become a contented sage.

26. "From righteousness comes material wealth, from righteousness comes happiness. Through righteousness one gains everything. The very essence of this world is righteousness.

27. "But righteousness belongs only to the vigilant, those who relentlessly control themselves by various acts of self-restraint. No, true happiness is not easily won.

28. "Remaining ever pure of heart, dear husband, follow the ways of righteousness appropriate to an ascetics' grove. But then, you already know all this, this and the whole universe as it is in truth.

29. "Only a woman's impulse made me speak this way, for who would presume to tell you what righteousness is? But still, give it careful thought, you and your younger brother, and do without delay whatever you think best."

The end of the eighth *sarga* of the *Araṇyakāṇḍa* of the *Śrī Rāmāyaṇa*.

Sarga 9

1. Rāma listened to the words that Vaidehī, princess of Mithilā, spoke in her devotion to her husband, and then he replied with firm adherence to righteousness.

2. "This is sound advice, my lady. What you have said in your affection is worthy of you and testifies to your high birth, righteous daughter of Janaka.

3. "And yet, I may repeat the words you yourself uttered, my lady: 'Kshatriyas only bear bows lest any voice be raised in distress.'

4. "And the sages undertaking strict vows in Daṇḍaka wilderness are indeed distressed, Sītā. They themselves, the refuge of others, have taken refuge with me.

5. "Engaged in the practice of righteousness, they have been dwelling in the forest, living on fruit and roots, but now they are terrified of the savage *rākṣasas* and can find no peace.

6. "Time and again, while they are engaged in various penances in the forest, the ferocious *rākṣasas* that live on human flesh come and devour them.

7. "So many were being devoured that the best of twice-born sages living in Daṇḍaka wilderness came to me, saying, 'Rescue us!'

8. "And when I heard those words that fell from their lips, I did obeisance at their feet and said this:

9. " 'Please forgive me, sirs! How boundless is my shame that when I should be seeking out seers like you, you have had instead to seek me out.' And in the presence of those twice-born men I spoke up and said, 'What is it I may do?'

10. "All the assembled host then spoke these words in a single voice: 'There are many *rākṣasas* in Daṇḍaka wilderness, who can take on any form at will. They are brutally oppressing us, Rāma, and you must save us.

11. " 'When the time of the oblation is come, faultless prince, and at the times of the lunar rites, *rākṣasas* who feed on raw flesh, who are all but immune from attack themselves, attack us.

12. " 'Under attack by the *rākṣasas*, the ascetics in their distress have sought some refuge, and you are our one sure refuge, sir.

13. " 'True, we could kill the nightstalkers with our ascetic powers, but we are reluctant to squander what took so long to amass.

14. " 'Ascetic practice is ever beset by obstacles, Rāghava, and so difficult to perform. That is why, although devoured by *rākṣasas*, we do not unleash our curse.

15. " 'You and your brother, therefore, must protect us from oppression by the *rākṣasas* who live in Daṇḍaka wilderness, for you are our sole defender in the forest.'

16. "When I heard their words, daughter of Janaka, I promised to do my utmost to safeguard the seers of Daṇḍaka wilderness.

17. "And having once promised I could never, so long as I live, violate my pledge to the sages. For truthfulness has always been the one thing I cherish.

18. "I would sooner give up my life, Sītā, or even you and Lakṣmaṇa, than break a promise I have made, especially to brahmans.

19. "Therefore I am bound to safeguard the seers. I would do this even unasked, Vaidehī; how much more so now I have given my word?

20. "Still, I am deeply gratified by what you have said, Sītā, in your affection for me and your goodness of heart. No woman offers guidance to a man she does not love. It was worthy of you, my lovely wife, and becoming to one of your House."

21. So the great Rāma spoke to his beloved Sītā, daughter of the king of Mithilā. Then, armed with his bow and in the company of Lakṣmaṇa, he traveled on to the lovely forests of austerities.

The end of the ninth *sarga* of the *Araṇyakāṇḍa* of the *Śrī Rāmāyaṇa.*

Sarga 10

1. Rāma went in front, fair-waisted Sītā in the middle, and behind followed Lakṣmaṇa, bow in hand.

2–4. As they traveled on with Sītā, they saw varied mountain landscapes, forests, lovely rivers with cranes and sheldrakes upon the sandbanks, ponds covered with lotuses and thronged with water birds, dappled antelopes massed in herds, rutting horned buffaloes and boars, and elephants butting at trees.

5–6. They had traveled a long distance and the sun was hanging low when all at once they spied a lovely pond one league across. It was blanketed with white lotuses and blue water lilies, adorned with herds of elephants, and filled with waterfowl, cranes, and white and gray geese.

7. From within the lovely clear pool could be heard the sound of singing and musical instruments, but there was no one to be seen.

8. Their curiosity aroused, Rāma and the great chariot-fighter Lakṣmaṇa proceeded to question a sage named Dharmabhṛt.

9. "We are all filled with curiosity, great sage, hearing this wonderful sound. What can it be? Please tell us."

10. So Rāghava spoke, and the righteous sage proceeded to recount in full the story of the lake.

11. "Rāma, this pond, brimful all year round, is called Pañcāpsaras, the Pond of the Five *Apsarases.* The sage Māṇḍakarṇi fashioned it by his ascetic power.

12. "Now, the great sage Māṇḍakarṇi practiced intense asceticism for tens of thousands of years, subsisting on air and ever immersed in water.

13. "All the gods grew anxious, and led by Agni, god of fire, they all assembled and said, 'This sage means to displace one of us.'

14. "Then all the gods directed the five chief *apsarases*, heavenly women dazzling as lightning, to disrupt his ascetic practices.

15. "In order to accomplish the purpose of the gods, these *apsarases* brought the sage under the spell of passion, in spite of his knowing right from wrong.

16. "These same five *apsarases* became the sage's wives, and he built a house for them hidden within this pond.

17. "And the five *apsarases* have lived there happily ever since, making love to the sage, who regained his youth by means of his ascetic power.

18. "As they play together one can hear, as now, the notes of musical instruments mingling with the tinkle of jewelry and the enchanting sound of singing."

19. "Wonderful!" said glorious Rāghava and his brother when they heard the account given by the purified sage.

20. While the sage was telling his tale, Rāma spied a circle of ashrams, with *kuśa* grass and bark garments strewn about, and surrounded by various trees.

21–25. With Vaidehī and Lakṣmaṇa, Rāghava Kākutstha then entered the majestic circle of ashrams, where he stayed for a while most comfortably, honored by the great seers. And then that expert in great weapons visited by turns the ashrams of the ascetics with whom he had previously been staying. In one place Rāghava lived comfortably for some ten months, in others a year, or four months, five, six, or more; here an extra month, there a month and a half, three months, or eight. And while he was living this agreeable life and enjoying himself in the ashrams of the ascetics, ten years went by.

26. At the end of his tour, majestic, righteous Rāghava returned with Sītā to the ashram of Sutīkṣṇa.

27. The sages honored Rāma on his return to the ashram, and there, too, the tamer of foes lived for some time.

28. Now once, as Kākutstha was staying in the ashram and waiting in attendance on the great sage Sutīkṣṇa, he politely addressed him with these words:

29. "Holy one, I have often heard, in the tales of storytellers, that Agastya, the best of sages, lives in this wilderness.

30. "But I do not know the place because this forest is so vast. Where is the holy ashram of the great and wise seer?

31. "By your grace, sir, I should like to pay a visit there with my younger brother and Sītā to do obeisance to the sage Agastya.

32. "For it is a wish most fondly cherished in my heart that I might personally serve that foremost of sages."

33. When the sage Sutīkṣṇa heard the words of righteous Rāma, son of Daśaratha, he joyfully replied to him:

34. "I myself, Rāghava, was about to suggest the very same thing: Take Lakṣmaṇa and Sītā and go pay a visit to Agastya.

35. "How fortunate that you should just bring this up with me yourself. I shall tell you, my child, where the great sage Agastya lives.

36. "Go four leagues south of this ashram, my son, and there you will come upon the great, majestic ashram of Agastya's brother.

37. "It is in a level forest clearing, adorned by a grove of pepper plants; a lovely place with many flowers and fruits, resounding with the cries of different birds.

38. "There are all kinds of pleasant lotus ponds there, brimming with clear water, abounding in geese and ducks, and adorned with sheldrakes.

39. "Spend one night there, Rāma, and early the next morning travel southward, skirting the dense forest.

40. "There, after traveling one league more, you will come upon Agastya's ashram in a delightful forest clearing surrounded by many trees. Vaidehī will enjoy herself there, and so will you and Lakṣmaṇa.

41. "For it is a lovely forest clearing encircled by many trees. If you are of a mind to see the great sage Agastya, why not set your mind on going this very day, glorious prince?"

42–43. After listening to the sage, Rāma and his brother did obeisance and set forth with Sītā to find Agastya, seeing on their way forests of brilliant color, cloudlike mountains, lakes, and rivers as the road presented them to view.

44. As he was proceeding at his ease along the way by which Sutīkṣṇa had directed him, he spoke these words to Lakṣmaṇa in deep delight:

45. "That is surely the ashram of the brother of the great and holy sage Agastya that I see.

46. "For here along the way one can make out the trees of the grove, thousands of them bending under the weight of their fruit and flowers.

47. "And from the grove, carried on the breeze, comes the smell of ripe peppers with its sudden rush of pungency.

48. "Here and there you can see piles of logs heaped up and, along the way, the sheaves of *darbha* grass the color of cat's-eye beryl.

49. "And there in the heart of the forest—like a mountain peak shrouded in black cloud—looms the column of smoke from the ashram fires.

50. "And at the secluded landing places on the river there are twice-born men; they have completed their ritual baths and make flower offerings with blossoms gathered by their own hands.

51. "Such was Sutīkṣṇa's description, dear brother, exactly as I heard him give it. This is surely the ashram of Agastya's brother.

52. "It was his virtuous brother, with the good of all at heart, who stamped out the threat of death and made this region a sure place of refuge.

53. "Once upon a time two brothers lived together here, the cruel Vātāpi and Ilvala, great *asuras* who killed brahmans.

54. "The pitiless Ilvala, disguised as a brahman and speaking the ritual language of Sanskrit, would invite sages to *śrāddha* feasts.

55. "His brother would take on the guise of a ram, and Ilvala would ritually prepare him and feed him to the twice-born men, in accordance with the rite prescribed for the *śrāddha*.

56. "Then, when the sages had eaten, Ilvala would exclaim in a loud voice, 'Vātāpi, come forth!'

57. "Hearing his brother's summons, Vātāpi, bleating like a ram, would burst forth splitting open the body of every single brahman present.

58. "In this way the eaters of raw flesh, who could take on any form at will, in league with one another killed thousands of brahmans time and again.

59. "The gods then sought the aid of the great seer Agastya, and he presented himself at the *śrāddha* feast, they say, and ate the great *asura*.

60. "Thereupon Ilvala, proclaiming the feast at an end and offering the sprinkling of the hands, called to his brother, 'Come forth!'

61. "But as he was calling his brahman-killing brother, the wise Agastya, best of sages, chuckled and said to him:

62. " 'How is your brother supposed to come forth? I have digested him; he has gone to the house of Yama, this *rākṣasa* disguised as a ram.'

63. "Now, hearing the words that told him his brother was dead, the nightstalker flew into a rage and prepared to attack the sage.

64. "He attacked the lord of the twice-born, but the sage, possessed of brilliant powers, incinerated him with his fiery eye, and he died.

65. "The ashram here, adorned with ponds and forests, must belong to the brother of that sage, who in compassion for brahmans did a deed no one else could do."

66. While Rāma was conversing in this fashion with Saumitri, the sun set and the moment of twilight arrived.

67. After performing the evening twilight worship with his brother according to precept, he entered the ashram and did obeisance to the seer.

68. Rāghava, suitably received by the sage, spent that one night there, making a meal of roots and fruit.

69. When night was passed and the sun's immaculate disk appeared, Rāghava asked leave of Agastya's brother.

70. "Holy one, I bid you farewell; I have passed the night comfortably. I now ask leave of you, for I am going to see your guru, your elder brother."

71. "You may go," he replied, and the delight of the Raghus set out on the road as directed, all the while observing the forest.

72–74. Soon Rāma came to a place where he saw woodland trees by the hundreds: *nīvāras, panasas, tālas, timiśas, vañjulas, dhavas, ciribilvas, madhūkas, bilvas*, and *tindukas*. They were all in flower and twined about by flower-topped vines; their bark was rubbed raw by elephants' trunks; they were crowded with monkeys and resounded with flocks of wild birds by the hundreds.

75. As mighty Lakṣmaṇa, bringer of glory, followed close behind, lotus-eyed Rāma spoke to him:

76. "Seeing that the leaves on these trees are so glossy and the birds and beasts so gentle, the ashram of the great, purified seer must not be far away.

77–78. "He who is known throughout the world as Agastya, 'Stopper of the Mountain,' by reason of his own deed—that must be his ashram we see, garlanded with bark garments, where the forest is wrapped in thick smoke and the cries of various birds are echoing; a place where wild beasts grow tame and the weary traveler finds rest.

79. "It was this virtuous man, with the good of all at heart, who stamped out the threat of death and made the southern region a sure place of refuge.

80. "This must be the ashram of that seer whose power made the

rākṣasas look on this southern region with terror and give up their hold on it.

81. "From the moment the virtuous sage set foot in this region, the nightstalkers ceased hostilities and grew peaceable.

82. "And so this southern region, now safe from attack by savage creatures, is known by the name of that holy man throughout the three worlds.

83. "The greatest of mountains, Mount Vindhya, heeds his command and no longer grows, as it once did, to obstruct the course of the sun.

84. "Yes, this must be the ashram of long-lived Agastya, whose deeds are renowned throughout the world, a majestic ashram where the beasts that inhabit it are tame.

85. "This goodly man, revered by the world and always eager that the good should prosper, will ensure our welfare now that we have sought him out.

86. "Here, my dear and lordly brother, I will propitiate the great sage Agastya and live out what time remains of my sojourn in the forest.

87. "Here gods and *gandharvas*, perfected beings and supreme seers constantly attend upon Agastya, a seer given to rigorous fasting.

88. "Here no untruthful man may live, no one cruel or guileful, malevolent or licentious; that is the sort of sage he is.

89. "Here dwell gods and *yakṣas*, great serpents and birds, they too given to rigorous fasting and eager to uphold the ways of righteousness.

90. "Here great perfected beings cast off their bodies and in new bodies ascended to heaven as supreme seers, in aerial chariots gleaming like the sun.

91. "Here gods will make one a *yakṣa* or offer immortality or various kingly offices to good creatures who propitiate them.

92. "We have come to his ashram. Enter first, Saumitri, and inform the seer that Sītā and I have arrived."

The end of the tenth *sarga* of the *Araṇyakāṇḍa* of the *Śrī Rāmāyaṇa*.

Sarga 11

1. Entering the ashram, Rāghava's younger brother Lakṣmaṇa came upon a student of Agastya's and addressed him with these words:

2. "The powerful Rāma, eldest son of King Daśaratha, has come with his wife, Sītā, to see the sage.

3. "I am Lakṣmaṇa, his younger brother, and his faithful and devoted helper. You may perhaps have heard of me.

4. "By order of our father we have entered the dreaded forest. We all wish to see the holy one. Please inform him."

5. On hearing Lakṣmaṇa's words, the ascetic replied with a word of assent and entered the fire-sanctuary to inform the sage.

6. He cupped his hands in reverence on entering and promptly told the greatest of sages, invulnerable in his ascetic power, about the arrival of Rāma.

7. "Two sons of Daśaratha are here, Rāma and Lakṣmaṇa. They have entered the ashram along with Rāma's wife, Sītā.

8. "The tamers of foes have come to see you, sir, in order to offer obedient service. Please direct me in what I should do next."

9. When he learned from his student that Rāma, Lakṣmaṇa, and illustrious Vaidehī had come, he spoke these words:

10. "How fortunate that now at long last Rāma has come to see me. I myself had been hoping with all my heart that he might come.

11. "Go and welcome Rāma, his wife, and Lakṣmaṇa and show them into my presence. Why has he not been shown in yet?"

12. So the great and righteous sage spoke, and the student did obeisance to him and replied with a word of assent, his hands still cupped in reverence.

13. Then, in a flurry of confusion, the student hurried out and said to Lakṣmaṇa, "Where is Rāma? He himself may enter and go see the sage."

14. Lakṣmaṇa then went to the ashram along with the student and directed him to Kākutstha and Sītā, daughter of Janaka.

15. The student, speaking deferentially in consequence of Aga-

stya's words, showed him in as custom demanded and with the cordial welcome he deserved.

16–18. Entering with Sītā and Lakṣmaṇa, Rāma looked around the ashram, at the tame gazelles that wandered about, at the shrines of Brahmā, Agni, Viṣṇu, great Indra, Vivasvān, Soma, Bhaga, Kubera, Dhātṛ and Vidhātṛ, and Vāyu.

19. Then the sage abruptly rose from where he sat encircled by his students, and Rāma saw him advancing at the head of the sages, ablaze with power. The mighty prince turned to Lakṣmaṇa, bringer of glory, and said:

20. "Here, he is coming out, Lakṣmaṇa, the holy seer Agastya. I can tell by his noble bearing that he must be that treasure-store of asceticism."

21. So the great-armed prince spoke of Agastya, and in deep joy the slayer of enemies clasped the feet of the sage who was radiant as the sun.

22. And after doing obeisance to him, righteous Rāma stood with hands cupped in reverence, and with him stood Lakṣmaṇa and Sītā of Videha.

23. Once the sage had received Kākutstha and honored him with a place to sit and water for his feet, he asked after his health and bade him be seated.

24. He poured an oblation into the fire, presented the welcome-offering, and paid homage to his guest; then he gave them food in accordance with the ways of forest hermits.

25. When the bull among sages, wise in the ways of righteousness, finally seated himself, he addressed righteous Rāma, who sat with hands cupped in reverence.

26. "To be sure, Kākutstha, an ascetic who mistreats a guest is destined to feed on his own flesh in the other world, like the man who bears false witness.

27. "And you who are now my dear guest are king of all the world, a great chariot-fighter, a man held in reverence and esteem, who keeps to the ways of righteousness."

28. So speaking, he paid reverence to Rāghava with fruit and roots, flowers and such, to his heart's content, and then addressed him further:

29. "Here is a heavenly, great bow, tiger among men, inlaid with gold and diamonds. It was fashioned by Viśvakarman and belongs to Viṣṇu.

30. "This supreme arrow that gleams like the sun and never misses its mark was given by Brahmā to great Indra, who gave it to me along with this pair of quivers that never run out of shafts.

31. "They are filled with razor-sharp darts glowing like fires. And here is a sword inlaid with gold, with a scabbard of pure gold.

32. "With this bow, Rāma, Viṣṇu long ago slew great *asuras* in battle and recovered the radiant royal splendor of the gods, who make their abode in heaven.

33. "Receive this bow for victory, giver of honor, this pair of quivers, this arrow and sword, as Indra, wielder of the thunderbolt, once received his bolt."

34. So the mighty and holy Agastya spoke, and having bestowed the entire collection of splendid weapons on Rāma, he addressed him further.

The end of the eleventh *sarga* of the *Araṇyakāṇḍa* of the *Śrī Rāmāyaṇa*.

Sarga 12

1. "My blessings on you, Rāma and Lakṣmaṇa. I am pleased and gratified that you have come with Sītā to do obeisance to me.

2. "You must be fatigued by your wearying journey, terribly wearied. It is evident that Maithilī, daughter of Janaka, is most disconsolate.

3. "For she is very delicate, and never before has sorrow heaped its scorn upon her. But driven by affection for her husband, she has come to the forest, where troubles abound.

4. "You must do all you can to ensure Sītā's comfort here, Rāma, since in following you into the forest she has done a most difficult thing.

5. "For from the hour of their creation, delight of the Raghus, such has been the nature of women: to love their man when things go smoothly, and when things get hard, to leave him.

6. "Unpredictable as lightning are women, sharp as swords, and quick to fly away as Garuḍa or the wind.

7. "But this wife of yours is free from all these faults. She is as worthy of praise and esteem as the goddess Arundhatī.

8. "You will be an ornament to this region, Rāma, tamer of foes, if you make your dwelling here with Saumitri and Sītā."

9. So the sage spoke, and Rāghava, his hands cupped in reverence, deferentially replied to the seer who blazed with the brilliance of fire.

10. "How fortunate I am, how favored, that I, my brother, and my wife have virtues enough to please the great sage and granter of boons.

11. "But could you now direct me to some well-watered and abundantly forested region where I can establish my ashram and live in comfort and happiness."

12. Hearing what Rāma said and thinking a moment, the righteous and wise Agastya, best of sages, spoke these words of wisdom:

13. "Two leagues from here, my son, is a majestic region known as Pañcavaṭī abounding in roots and fruit, water and animals.

14. "Go and establish your ashram there with Saumitri; you can enjoy yourself even as you are obeying your father's order to the letter.

15. "For I have come to know all that has happened to you, faultless prince, by means of my ascetic powers and in consequence of my affection for Daśaratha.

16. "And by these same powers I have also discovered your heart's true desire, despite your having promised to live with me here in this forest of austerities.

17. "And that is why I tell you to go to Pañcavaṭī. It is a lovely stretch of forest and Maithilī will be comfortable there.

18. "The region has everything to recommend it, Rāghava; it is not too far from here, and the Godāvarī river is close by as well. Maithilī will be comfortable there.

19. "It is a secluded, holy, and lovely place, great-armed prince, rich in fruit and roots, and all different kinds of birds come flocking there.

20. "Although accompanied by a wife, you are capable of protecting her. Then, too, Rāma, living there you can safeguard the ascetics.

21. "Yonder, mighty prince, one can just make out a large grove of *madhūka* trees. You must head north of it, toward the banyan.

22. "There, upon a rise of ground not far from a mountain range, is the region known as Pañcavaṭī, where the woodlands are always in flower."

23. So Agastya spoke, and Rāma and Saumitri honored the truthful seer and asked leave of him.

24. And when the two of them had been given leave and had fallen at his feet and done obeisance, they and Sītā left his ashram for Pañcavaṭī.

25. Taking up their bows and strapping on their quivers, the princes, fearless in battle, resolutely proceeded to Pañcavaṭī along the path by which the great seer had directed them.

The end of the twelfth *sarga* of the *Araṇyakāṇḍa* of the *Śrī Rāmāyaṇa*.

Sarga 13

1. As the delight of the Raghus was traveling to Pañcavaṭī, he encountered on the way a huge vulture of awesome strength.

2. Seeing that bird in the forest, the illustrious Rāma and Lakṣmaṇa took him for a *rākṣasa* and demanded, "Who are you?"

3. In a gentle and kindly voice that immediately won them over he replied, "My child, know that I was your father's friend."

4. On learning of his acquaintance with his father, Rāghava paid him homage and then intently inquired of his name and family.

5. When he heard Rāma's question, the bird proceeded to tell of himself and his family, starting with the origin of all creatures.

6. "Hear me, great-armed Rāghava, as I list from the very beginning all the lords of creatures who existed in ancient times.

7. "The first of them was Kardama, after whom came Vikṛta, then Śeṣa, Saṃśraya, and mighty Bahuputra.

8. "Then came Sthāṇu and Marīci, Atri and powerful Kratu, Pulastya, Aṅgiras, Pracetas, and Pulaha.

9. "Dakṣa and next Vivasvān, then Ariṣṭanemi and mighty Kaśyapa, who was the last of them, Rāghava.

10. "Now, the lord of creatures named Dakṣa, so we have heard, glorious Rāma, had sixty daughters, all endowed with glory.

11–13ab. "From their number Kaśyapa married eight of the loveliest: Aditi and Diti, Danū and Kālakā, Tāmrā and Krodhavaśā, Manu and Analā. And joyfully Kaśyapa then addressed the maidens, 'Bear sons who are my equal, to be masters of the three worlds.'

13cd–14ab. "Aditi was willing, great-armed Rāma, and so were Diti, Danū, and Kālakā, but the others were not.

14cd–15ab. "Of Aditi were born the thirty-three gods, tamer of foes: the Ādityas, Vasus, Rudras, and Aśvins, slayer of enemies.

15cd–16ab. "Diti bore glorious sons called the Daityas, my son. Long ago this treasure-laden earth and all the seas and forests belonged to them.

16cd–17ab. "Danū bore a son named Aśvagrīva, tamer of foes, and Kālakā bore Naraka and Kālaka.

17cd–18. "Krauñcī, Bhāsī, Śyenī, Dhṛtarāṣṭrī, and Śukī were the five daughters Tāmrā bore, all of them famed throughout the world. Krauñcī bore the owls, and Bhāsī the kites.

19. "Śyenī bore the hawks and mighty vultures, Dhṛtarāṣṭrī all the white geese and the gray geese.

20. "And, be pleased to know, dear Rāma, the same lovely creature bore the sheldrakes, whereas Śukī bore Natā, whose daughter was Vinatā.

21–22. "Krodhavaśā bore ten children, Rāma: Mṛgī, Mṛgamandā, Harī, Bhadramadā, Mātaṅgī, Śārdulī, Śvetā, Surabhī, Surasā, who was endowed with all auspicious marks, and Kadrukā.

23. "The offspring of Mṛgī were all the deer, Rāma, foremost of kings; those of Mṛgamandā were the apes, antelope, and yaks.

24. "Next, Bhadramadā bore a child named Irāvatī, whose son was Airāvata, the great world-protecting elephant.

25. "The offspring of Harī were the simians, the fleet monkeys and langurs, whereas the sons Śārdulī bore were the tigers.

26. "The offspring of Mātaṅgī were the elephants, bull among men, and the son Śvetā bore was named Śvetākṣa, one of the guardian elephants of the directions.

27. "Then, dear Rāma, the goddess Surabhi bore two daughters, one named Rohiṇī, the other, glorious Gandharvī.

28. "The children Rohiṇī bore were the cows, and Gandharvī's were the horses. Surasā bore the great serpents, Rāma, and Kadru the snakes.

29. "To the great Kaśyapa, Manu bore men, bull among men, the brahmans, kshatriyas, *vaiśyas*, and *śūdras*.

30. "From her mouth were born the brahmans, from her breast the kshatriyas; from her thighs were born the *vaiśyas* and from her feet the *śūdras*, as is set down in the holy texts.

31ab. "Analā brought forth all the holy fruit trees.

31cd–32. "Now, Vinatā was the granddaughter of Śukī, and Kadrū was Surasā's sister. Kadrū bore the thousand great serpents that hold up the earth, and Vinatā had two sons, Garuḍa and Aruṇa.

33. "By this Aruṇa was I begotten, tamer of foes, and my elder brother Sampāti. Know me to be Jaṭāyus, whose mother was Śyenī.

34. "I will live with you, if you wish, and keep watch over Sītā whenever you and Lakṣmaṇa are away."

35. Rāghava once more paid homage to Jaṭāyus, embraced him warmly, and bowed before him. For he had heard about Jaṭāyus's friendship with his father, who had often spoken of it.

36. And so, committing Sītā, princess of Mithilā, to the care of the powerful bird, he went with him and Lakṣmaṇa to Pañcavaṭī, ready to destroy his enemies as a flame destroys moths.

The end of the thirteenth *sarga* of the *Araṇyakāṇḍa* of the *Śrī Rāmāyaṇa*.

Sarga 14

1. On reaching Pañcavaṭī, a place teeming with all kinds of wild animals, Rāma addressed his mighty brother Lakṣmaṇa:

2. "We have come to the place to which the great seer directed us. This must be Pañcavaṭī, dear brother, the place where 'the woodlands are all in flower.'

3. "Survey the woodland all about. You are clever at such things: Which place would you recommend for our ashram?

4–5. "Look for some place with a source of water nearby, the sort of spot where Vaidehī, you, and I may be comfortable, Lakṣmaṇa: where there are forests and water to delight us, where fuel and flowers, *kuśa* grass and fresh water are nearby."

6. So Rāma spoke, and Lakṣmaṇa cupped his hands in reverence and made this reply to Kākutstha as Sītā looked on:

7. "I shall always be subject to your will, Kākutstha, should you live a hundred years. You need only tell me to build in the place you choose yourself."

8. The splendid prince was well pleased with Lakṣmaṇa's words, and after some reflection, he chose a place endowed with all the qualities he sought.

9. Coming to the place he had chosen, Rāma took Saumitri's hand in his and spoke to him about building the ashram.

10. "This is a splendid place, flat and lined by flowering trees. Here, dear brother, is where you should build us a proper ashram.

11. "Nearby I can see a lovely lotus pond adorned with lotuses radiant as the sun and charged with a fragrant scent.

12. "Over there is the lovely Godāvarī lined by flowering trees, just as the purified Agastya had described it.

13. "It is neither too far nor too near, and teems with geese and ducks and lovely sheldrakes, and is thronged with herds of animals.

14. "One can see the grand, majestic mountains, dotted with grottoes, thick with blooming trees, and echoing with the cries of peacocks.

15. "With veins of gold, silver, and copper threaded here and there, the mountains resemble elephants painted with a latticework of brilliant stripes.

16–18. "There are lovely trees on the mountains, *sāla*, *tālas*, *tamālas*, *kharjūras*, *panasas*, *āmrakas*, *nīvāras*, *timiśas*, and *puṃnāgas*; thick groves of various other trees—mangoes, *aśokas*, *tilakas*, *campakas*, and *ketakas*, and flowers, vines, and shrubs; sandalwood trees, too, and *syandanas*, *nīpas*, *panasas*, *lakucas*, *dhavas*, *aśvakarṇas*, *khadiras*, *śamīs*, *kiṃśukas*, and *pāṭalas*.

19. "This is a pure and holy spot teeming with birds and beasts, and here is where we will live, Saumitri, in the company of this bird."

20. So Rāma spoke, and before long Lakṣmaṇa, the powerful slayer of brave enemies, had built an ashram for his brother.

21. He built a leaf hut there, spacious and very lovely, with walls of clay and crossbeams fashioned of long bamboo, making it very sturdy.

22. Majestic Lakṣmaṇa then went down to the Godāvarī river and, after bathing, returned bearing lotuses and fruit.

23. Making an offering of flowers and, in accordance with precept, performing the rite to appease the spirits, he showed Rāma the ashram he had built.

24. Rāghava together with Sītā saw the pleasant ashram he had built and was greatly delighted by the leaf hut.

25. Then, in deep delight he drew Lakṣmaṇa into his arms, and embracing him tightly and affectionately, he said:

26. "I am pleased with you, my lordly brother, this is a great deed you have done. But the embrace I now give you is all the compensation I can offer for it.

27. "You have shown yourself to be wise in both thought and deed, Lakṣmaṇa, and one who knows the true meaning of righteousness. With such a son as you my righteous father has not passed away."

28. So Rāghava spoke to Lakṣmaṇa, and in that fertile place the bringer of glory gladly settled down to a happy life.

29. Constantly attended by Lakṣmaṇa and Sītā, the righteous prince lived there like a deathless god in heaven, for a time.

The end of the fourteenth *sarga* of the *Araṇyakāṇḍa* of the *Śrī Rāmāyaṇa*.

Sarga 15

1. While the great Rāghava was living a happy life there, autumn passed and winter, the welcome season, arrived.

2–3. Once, when night was brightening into dawn and the delight of the Raghus went down to the lovely Godāvarī river to bathe, his mighty brother Saumitri, humbly bearing the water pot and following behind with Sītā, addressed him with these words:

4. "The season you love has come, beloved brother, the most beautiful ornament of the year.

5. "The world crackles with frost and the earth is bedecked with a garland of crops; water is uninviting, and instead fire, the bearer of oblations, is what appeals most.

6. "Now is the time for pious men to worship the ancestral spirits and gods with offerings of first fruits, whereupon they are freed from sin.

7. "The countryfolk have all they desire; their cows give milk more richly than ever. And kings march forth on expedition with hopes of conquest.

8. "The sun keeps steadfastly to the region where the god of death holds sway, and so the north has lost its ruddy glow, like a woman without her auspicious forehead rouge.

9. "Himālaya, the 'Snowy Mountain,' by nature a treasure store of snow, now with the sun so far away is even deeper in snow and all the more deserves its name.

10. "The skin is pleasantly warmed at noon, now the most pleasant time to stroll. Sunshine appeals on days like this, and shade and water lose any appeal.

11. "Mornings are frosty now, powdered with snow, bitterly cold and windy; the sun is weak, and the wilderness seems empty.

12. "No longer can one sleep outdoors. Led by the Puṣya star the nights pass cold and gray with snow and last far longer than their three watches.

13. "As for the moon, all its appeal has passed to the sun. Its disk is misty gray and its glow has vanished, like that of a mirror clouded over by breath.

14. "Mist has sullied the moonlight, and even when the moon is full, it does not really shine. You mark it, but miss its beauty, as with Sītā when she is flushed with sun.

15. "The west wind's touch is cold by nature, but doubly so now when it blows at dawn, shot through with snow.

16. "Mist covers the fields and their stands of wheat and barley. How beautiful they look at sunrise, with the cranes and *krauñca* birds calling there.

17. "How beautiful the golden rice plants look. Their heads, the color of wild date palm blossoms, are so heavy with grain that the stalks are gently bowed.

18. "With its rays drawing near in a cloak of snow and frost, the sun, even at its zenith, resembles the moon.

19. "The morning sunshine is too weak even to be felt, but it grows pleasantly warm to the skin by noon. How beautifully it glows, a faint pale red upon the earth.

20. "How beautiful the floor of the forest appears, with the early morning sunlight playing upon it and the meadows slightly dampened by a fall of hoarfrost.

21. "The expanses of forest seem fast asleep, wrapped up in the darkness of hoarfrost, blanketed by the darkness of snow, with not a blossom open.

22. "The sand on the riverbanks is wet with snow, the water thickly covered with mist, and only their cry reveals the presence of cranes.

23. "Because of the falling sleet, the sun's weakness, the cold, the water even on the mountaintops has the bitter taste of poison.

24. "The lotus ponds have lost their beauty, ravaged by the snow: The leaves have aged and withered, the filaments and cups shriveled, and nothing but stalk remains.

25. "Tiger among men, at this hour back in the city, righteous Bharata, lost in sorrow, is practicing mortifications in devotion to you.

26. "He has given up the pride and pomp of kingship, its many and various luxuries, to be an ascetic who rigorously fasts and sleeps on the cold ground.

27. "At this moment, he too is probably getting ready to bathe, going down to the Sarayū with his subjects, who constantly attend on him.

28. "He is a delicate young man, who was raised in perfect comfort. How can he endure the cold, plunging into the Sarayū in the last watch of the night?

29. "He is lotus-eyed, swarthy, regal, slim, and tall, wise in the ways of righteousness, truthful in speech, controlled by shame, and self-restrained.

30. "He is kind-spoken and gentle, long-armed, a tamer of foes; he has given up every comfort, devoting himself heart and soul to his noble brother.

31. "Great Bharata, your brother, shall win a place in heaven by emulating your every act of asceticism in the forest.

32. "Bharata disproves the well-known saying that men conform to their mother's nature rather than their father's.

33. "How could our mother Kaikeyī, with a husband like Daśaratha and a son like good Bharata, have ever turned so cruel?"

34. So righteous Lakṣmaṇa spoke in his affection, but Rāghava would not hear his mother maligned and said:

35. "You must never criticize our middle mother, dear brother. Continue instead to speak as you were of Bharata, the leader of the Ikṣvāku dynasty.

36. "But no, do not: For determined though I am to keep my vow and live in the forest, you would pain my heart, in my love for Bharata, and make me waver again like a child."

37. And lamenting in this fashion, he reached the Godāvarī river, where he bathed with his younger brother and Sītā.

38. They satisfied the ancestral spirits and deities with water-offerings, and then in concentration intoned the hymn to the rising sun and the gods.

39. After bathing, while he stood in the company of Lakṣmaṇa and Sītā, Rāma resembled the blessed lord Rudra after his bath, attended by Nandi and the daughter of the mountain king.

The end of the fifteenth *sarga* of the *Araṇyakāṇḍa* of the *Śrī Rāmāyaṇa*.

Sarga 16

1. After their bath Rāma, Sītā, and Lakṣmaṇa left the bank of the Godāvarī for their ashram.

2. Returning to the ashram, Rāghava and Lakṣmaṇa performed the morning rites and then returned to the leaf hut.

3. Great-armed Rāma sat with Sītā before the leaf hut, shining like the moon beside the sparkling star Citrā, and began to converse with his brother Lakṣmaṇa about one thing and another.

4. As Rāma was sitting there engrossed in conversation, a certain *rākṣasa* woman chanced to come that way.

5. She was the sister of Rāvaṇa, the ten-necked *rākṣasa*, and her name was Śūrpaṇakhā. Coming upon Rāma, she stared at him as if he were one of the thirty gods.

6–7. Rāma had long arms, the chest of a lion, eyes like lotus petals. Though delicate, he was very strong and bore all the signs of royalty. He was swarthy as the blue lotus, radiant as the love-god Kandarpa, the very image of Indra—and when the *rākṣasa* woman saw him, she grew wild with desire.

8–10. Rāma was handsome, the *rākṣasa* woman was ugly, he was shapely and slim of waist, she misshapen and potbellied; his eyes were large, hers were beady, his hair was jet black, and hers the color of copper; he always said just the right thing and in a sweet voice, her words were sinister and her voice struck terror; he was young, attractive, and well mannered, she ill mannered, repellent, an old hag. And yet, the god of love, who comes to life in our bodies, had taken possession of her, and so she addressed Rāma:

11. "Your hair is matted in the manner of ascetics, yet you have a wife with you and bear bow and arrows. How is it you have come into this region, the haunt of *rākṣasas*?"

12. Questioned in this fashion by the *rākṣasa* woman Śūrpaṇakhā, the slayer of enemies in his open manner proceeded to tell her everything.

13. "There was a king named Daśaratha, courageous as one of the thirty gods. I am his eldest son, named Rāma, known to people far and wide.

14. "This is Lakṣmaṇa, my devoted younger brother, and this my wife, the princess of Videha, known as Sītā.

15. "I was compelled to come to live in the forest by command of my mother and my father, the lord of men, and I wanted to do what is right, for doing right has always been my chief concern.

16. "But I should like to know about you. Tell me, who are you? To whom do you belong? For what purpose have you come here? Tell me truthfully."

17. Hearing his words and consumed with passion, the *rākṣasa* woman replied, "Listen, then, Rāma, I shall tell you, and my words will be truthful.

18. "My name is Śūrpaṇakhā. I am a *rākṣasa* woman, who can take on any form at will, and I roam this wilderness all alone, striking terror into every living thing.

19. "The *rākṣasa* named Rāvaṇa, the lord of all *rākṣasas*, is my brother, so too the powerful Kumbhakarṇa, who lies ever fast asleep.

20. "So is Vibhīṣaṇa, but he is righteous and does not behave like a *rākṣasa*. My other brothers are Khara and Dūṣaṇa, famed for their might in battle.

21. "But I am prepared to defy them all, Rāma, for I have never seen anyone like you. I approach you as I would a husband, with true love, best of men. Be my husband forevermore; what do you want with Sītā?

22. "She is ugly and misshapen and unworthy of you. I alone am suited to you; look upon me as your wife.

23. "I will devour this misshapen slut, this hideous human female with her pinched waist, along with this brother of yours.

24. "And then, my beloved, you shall roam Daṇḍaka with me, viewing all the different mountain peaks and forests."

25. Thus addressed by the wild-eyed creature, Kākutstha burst out laughing but then went on to reply with customary eloquence.

The end of the sixteenth *sarga* of the *Araṇyakāṇḍa* of the *Śrī Rāmāyaṇa*.

Sarga 17

1. As Śūrpaṇakhā stood there bound tight in the bonds of desire, Rāma smiled and, humoring her, replied in jest:

2. "I am already married, my lady, and I love my wife. And for women such as you, to have a rival wife is a source of bitter sorrow.

3. "But my younger brother here is of good character, handsome, powerful, majestic, and still unmarried. His name is Lakṣmaṇa.

4. "He has never had a woman before and is in need of a wife. He is young and handsome and will make a good husband, one suited to such beauty as yours.

5. "Accept my brother as your husband, large-eyed, shapely lady. With no rival wife the two of you will be inseparable as sunlight and Mount Meru."

6. When the *rākṣasa* woman, wild with desire, heard Rāma address her in this way, she promptly forsook him and said to Lakṣmaṇa:

7. "I shall make you a lovely wife, one befitting your beauty. And together we shall roam so pleasantly all through Daṇḍaka."

8. Lakṣmaṇa smiled at the words of the *rākṣasa* woman Śūrpaṇakhā and with customary eloquence made this fitting reply:

9. "Why would you want to be my wife, lotuslike beauty? I am completely subject to the will of my noble brother; I am a slave, and she who is my wife must be a slave as well.

10. "Become instead the junior wife of my noble brother, large-eyed lady of unblemished beauty. He is prosperous, and with him your fortunes, too, will prosper and you will be happy.

11. "Soon enough he will turn away from this misshapen slut, this hideous old wife with her pinched waist, and give his love to you alone.

12. "What man with any sense would reject this singular beauty of yours, my fair and shapely lady, and bestow his affections on a human female?"

13. So Lakṣmaṇa spoke, and the potbellied, hideous creature, unused to teasing, thought he was in earnest.

14. Then as Rāma, the invincible slayer of enemies, sat with Sītā before the leaf hut, the *rākṣasa* woman addressed him once more, wild with desire.

15. "It is on account of this misshapen slut, this hideous old wife with her pinched waist, that you care so little for me.

16. "I am going to devour this human female at once, before your very eyes; then, free of any rival, I shall live happily with you."

17. And with this, she flew into a rage, and with eyes flashing like firebrands she shot toward the fawn-eyed princess, like a giant meteor toward the star Rohiṇī.

18. But as she was about to fall upon Sītā, like the very noose of Death, mighty Rāma angrily restrained her and said to Lakṣmaṇa:

19. "Never tease savage, ignoble creatures, Saumitri. Look at Vaidehī, dear brother; she is frightened half to death.

20. "Now, tiger among men, mutilate this misshapen slut, this potbellied, lustful *rākṣasa* woman."

21. So Rāma spoke, and powerful Lakṣmaṇa, in full view of his brother, drew his sword and in a rage cut off the creature's ears and nose.

22. The dreadful Śūrpaṇakhā, her ears and nose hacked off, gave out an earsplitting roar as she fled back into the forest the way she had come.

23. Mutilated, spattered with blood, and all the more dreadful now, the *rākṣasa* woman roared incessantly, like a storm cloud when the rains come.

24. Gushing blood all over, a terror to behold, she disappeared into the deep forest, howling, her arms outstretched.

25. She made her way then to her brother, the awesome Khara, who was in Janasthāna together with a troop of *rākṣasas*. Mutilated, she fell before him to the ground, like a bolt of lightning from the sky.

26. Spattered with blood, wild with fear and confusion, Khara's sister told him the whole story—how Rāma had come into the for-

est with his wife and Lakṣmaṇa, and how she herself had been mutilated.

The end of the seventeenth *sarga* of the *Araṇyakāṇḍa* of the *Śrī Rāmāyaṇa*.

Sarga 18

1. At the sight of his sister fallen before him, mutilated and spattered with blood, the *rākṣasa* Khara was consumed with rage and began to question her:

2. "You possess great power and daring, you go your way like Death himself, going where you please, taking on any form you please. Who has brought you to this state?

3. "Which one of the gods, *gandharvas*, spirits, or great seers could it have been? Who was the mighty creature that mutilated you?

4. "For I know of no one in the world who would dare offend me, unless it be the thousand-eyed god, great Indra, chastiser of Pāka.

5. "Today I will take someone's life with my deadly arrows, like the crane that drinks the milk and leaves the water mixed with it.

6. "Who must I kill in combat, ripping into his vitals with my arrows? Whose bright-red foaming blood shall the earth drink in?

7. "From whose corpse shall the swarming carrion birds tear the flesh—gorging on it in delight—once I have slain him in battle?

8. "The gods and *gandharvas*, the *piśācas* and *rākṣasas* will not save that wretch once drawn into deadly battle with me.

9. "When you have come to your senses, you must tell me the name of that savage creature who attacked and overwhelmed you in the forest."

10. Hearing what her brother said in his rage, Śūrpaṇakhā tearfully replied:

11. "Two handsome young men have arrived, delicate yet powerful; their eyes are large as lotus petals, and they dress in barkcloth and black hides.

12. "They are the image of the king of *gandharvas* and bear all the signs of royalty. Whether they are gods or men I cannot tell for certain.

13. "And in their midst I saw a young woman, beautiful and fair-waisted, and all adorned in jewelry.

14. "It was those two together, all on account of that woman, who brought me to this state, like some defenseless slut.

15. "Now I long to drink their foaming blood when they lie dead on the battlefield—her blood, that whore, and theirs.

16. "Dear brother, grant me this, my one and only wish: after the battle to drink her blood and theirs."

17. When she finished speaking, Khara, in a rage, gave orders to fourteen powerful *rākṣasas*, the likes of Death himself.

18. "Two men bearing arms, dressed in barkcloth and black hides, have entered the dreaded wilderness of Daṇḍaka in the company of a woman.

19. "Kill the two of them and that harlot, and then return. My sister here shall drink their blood.

20. "This is my sister's most deeply cherished wish. Go at once, *rākṣasas*, and fulfill it, crushing the two of them with your might."

21. Thus instructed, the fourteen *rākṣasas* set out with her to that place, like clouds driven before the wind.

The end of the eighteenth *sarga* of the *Araṇyakāṇḍa* of the *Śrī Rāmāyaṇa*.

Sarga 19

1. When the dreaded Śūrpaṇakhā reached Rāghava's ashram, she showed the *rākṣasas* the two brothers and Sītā.

2. They saw powerful Rāma seated before the leaf hut, with Lakṣmaṇa and Sītā, princess of Videha.

3. Majestic Rāma Rāghava, seeing the *rākṣasa* woman come back bringing others with her, spoke to his splendid brother Lakṣmaṇa:

4. "Look to Sītā for a moment, Saumitri, while I slay these creatures here that have come to the aid of the *rākṣasa* woman."

5. Such were the words of the celebrated Rāma, and Lakṣmaṇa heard and acknowledged them with a word of assent.

6. Righteous Rāghava then strung his great bow inlaid with gold and addressed the *rākṣasas*:

7. "We are two sons of Daśaratha, the brothers Rāma and Lakṣmaṇa. Together with Sītā we have entered the trackless Daṇḍaka forest.

8. "We are self-controlled ascetics who subsist on fruit and roots and follow the ways of righteousness as we live in Daṇḍaka wilderness. Why do you threaten us with violence?

9. "You are the evil creatures that have wrought havoc in the great forest. And at the direction of the seers I have come, bow in hand, to kill you.

10. "Stay where you are, wicked creatures, come no closer. And if you value your lives at all withdraw completely, stalkers of the night."

11–12. The fourteen *rākṣasas*, brahman-slayers armed with pikes, flew into a rage when they heard his words. With eyes blazing bright red, the dreaded creatures made a harsh reply to Rāma, the soft-spoken, bright-eyed prince, and they shivered with delight, unacquainted as they were with his prowess.

13. "It is you who, having provoked the anger of our master, the great Khara, shall lose your life today, killed by us in battle.

14. "For you are all alone, too weak even to face our multitude on the field of battle, much less fight in combat.

15. "These clubs and pikes and spears wielded by our arms shall rob you of the bow clutched in your hand, rob you of strength and life."

16. With this, the fourteen *rākṣasas*, brandishing their swords and weapons, furiously attacked the invincible Rāma Rāghava, hurling their pikes at him.

17. But Kākutstha splintered all these fourteen pikes at once with as many arrows adorned with gold.

18. Then, in a towering rage, the mighty prince grasped fourteen iron shafts, arrows sharpened on stone, and brilliant as sunlight.

19. Holding them in his grasp Rāghava drew his bow, took aim at his targets, the *rākṣasas*, and shot the arrows like Indra, god of the hundred rites, shooting his thunderbolts.

20. They were gold-feathered and razor-sharp, adorned with gleaming gold, and they shed light like huge comets as they flew through the sky.

21. Swiftly the arrows pierced the chests of the *rākṣasas*, then emerged dripping with blood and sank into the ground with the crash of lightning bolts.

22. The *rākṣasas*, shot through the heart, their bodies butchered, drenched with blood, fell to the ground like trees uprooted, and the breath of life left them.

23. Seeing them fall to the ground, the *rākṣasa* woman, terrified, blind with rage, again let out a ghastly shriek.

24. Howling shrilly Śūrpaṇakhā sped off and again made her way to Khara. With the blood scarcely dry on her she fell before him in agony, as a broken vine might fall, its sap oozing out.

25. Having seen the *rākṣasas* fall in battle, Khara's sister Śūrpaṇakhā ran off and told him all that had happened, how the *rākṣasas* had been slain, every last one.

The end of the nineteenth *sarga* of the *Araṇyakāṇḍa* of the *Śrī Rāmāyaṇa*.

Sarga 20

1. Thus, to Khara's ill luck, Śūrpaṇakhā returned, and at the sight of her collapsed before him in a rage, he addressed her in a clear and steady voice:

2. "Why are you still weeping when just now I issued orders on your behalf to heroic, blood-drinking *rākṣasas*?

3. "They are devoted and loyal to me and have always served my interests. They kill but cannot themselves be killed, nor would they ever fail to do my bidding.

4. "What is this, then? I want to know why you are still wailing 'Help me!' and writhing like a snake upon the ground.

5. "Why are you helplessly lamenting when I am present to help

you? Come now, get up, do not be afraid. Here, have done with this faintheartedness."

6. Addressed in this comforting manner by Khara, the unassailable *rākṣasa* woman wiped her teary eyes and answered her brother:

7–8. "All fourteen heroic and dreaded *rākṣasas* you sent on my behalf to kill Rāghava and Lakṣmaṇa—merciless though they were, and armed with pikes and spears—have been killed in battle by Rāma with arrows that pierced them to the quick.

9. "When I saw that great deed of Rāma's, how those powerful *rākṣasas* dropped instantly to the ground, I was seized with great terror.

10. "In fear, alarm, and desperation, I again took refuge with you, nightstalker. For I see danger everywhere I look.

11. "I am drowning in a vast ocean of grief—an ocean where the waves are waves of terror, where a sea monster lurks, despair itself. Can you not save me?

12. "All the *rākṣasas*, eaters of raw flesh, who came to my aid now lie dead on the ground, killed by Rāma's sharp arrows.

13. "If you are at all moved to compassion for me or those *rākṣasas*, nightstalker, if you are daring and mighty enough to fight Rāma, then pluck out this thorn in the side of the *rākṣasas*, who has made Daṇḍaka wilderness his home.

14. "If you do not slay my enemy Rāma today, then I shall not hesitate to take my life before your very eyes.

15. "I really think you do not dare to stand face to face with Rāma in combat when he is armed for battle with his bow.

16. "You are no hero, but a braggart making false claims of valor if you cannot kill Rāma and Lakṣmaṇa, mere human beings the two of them.

17. "Better hurry and leave Janasthāna with your kinsmen. This is no place to live for one with little power and less courage.

18. "You shall be overwhelmed by Rāma's might and instantly perish, for how mighty Rāma is, the son of Daśaratha. And his brother is powerful as well, the one who mutilated me."

The end of the twentieth *sarga* of the *Araṇyakāṇḍa* of the *Śrī Rāmāyaṇa*.

Sarga 21

1. Thus Śūrpaṇakhā insulted the heroic Khara, and in the midst of the *rākṣasas* he spoke with great harshness:

2. "The contempt shown you fills me with such rage as I have never felt, rage as irrepressible as the heaving salt sea water.

3. "I care nothing for the power of Rāma, that short-lived mortal. Because of those evil acts of his, he is doomed to lose his life.

4. "Stop your tears, do not be distraught. I intend to send Rāma and his brother to the abode of Yama.

5. "And as Rāma lies upon the ground cut down by my battle-ax, as his life is ebbing away, *rākṣasa* woman, you shall drink his hot red blood."

6. She was delighted to hear the words coming from Khara's mouth, and then foolishly she began to praise her brother as the best of *rākṣasas*.

7. After Khara had received first her abuse and then her praise, he addressed Dūṣaṇa, his general.

8–10. "There are fourteen thousand dreaded *rākṣasas* who bow to my will and do not turn their back in battle. Blue-black as storm clouds, awesome in their onslaught and savage in their deeds, they are endowed with power and dreadful might, and take pleasure in acts of violence against the world. Their mouths are huge, their strength is great, their pride like that of the tiger. Dear friend, assemble these proud *rākṣasas*, every last one.

11. "Make ready my chariot at once, dear friend, my bows and brilliant arrows, my swords and various sharp lances.

12. "I intend to march out at the head of the great offspring of Pulastya and use all my battle skills to slay that savage Rāma."

13. So he spoke, and Dūṣaṇa then brought before him his great sun-colored chariot, with purebred dappled horses harnessed to it.

14–16. Impatiently, then, Khara mounted his chariot. It resembled the peak of Mount Meru, ornamented with burnished gold, with golden wheels and yoke poles of cat's-eye beryl; it was spacious and decorated with auspicious designs worked in gold: fish and flowers, trees and rocks, flocks of birds, the sun and moon and stars. It was furnished with standards and swords, and adorned with bells, and harnessed to it were purebred horses.

17. Observing him mounted on his chariot, the awesome *rākṣasas* took up their positions around him and powerful Dūṣaṇa.

18. Now, when Khara saw all the great *rākṣasa* bowmen with their terrible shields, arms, and standards, he cried out to them from his chariot, "Onward!"

19. Then, with their terrible shields, arms, and standards, the *rākṣasa* army set forth at lightning speed and with a deafening roar from Janasthāna.

20–22. With hammers, spears, pikes, and keen battle-axes, with swords and gleaming javelins and discuses in hand, with lances and terrible clubs and massive bows, with cudgels, swords, bludgeons, and harpoons held high, awesome to behold, the fourteen thousand dreaded *rākṣasas* marched out from Janasthāna, obedient to the will of Khara.

23. Khara watched as the awesome *rākṣasas* went racing ahead, and a moment afterward his own chariot set forth as well.

24. The charioteer, reading Khara's thoughts, urged on the dappled horses all ornamented with burnished gold.

25. And as the chariot of Khara, destroyer of enemies, was urged swiftly forward, it gave out a noise that extended to every quarter of heaven and to all points in between.

26. In a towering rage, harshly clamoring, Khara hastened onward like Death to slay his enemy, and time and again he urged on his charioteer, roaring like a swollen cloud bursting with a shower of hailstones.

The end of the twenty-first *sarga* of the *Araṇyakāṇḍa* of the *Śrī Rāmāyaṇa*.

Sarga 22

1. As that dreaded troop set forth, a rumbling, mule-gray storm cloud ominously showered down water red as blood.

2. The swift horses harnessed to Khara's chariot unaccountably stumbled on a flat, flower-strewn stretch of the royal highway.

3. A dark, blood-rimmed disk, like the ring of a twirling firebrand, began to cover the sun, bringer of day.

4. Then a huge vulture, inauspicious bird, flew near and began attacking the standard high atop its golden shaft.

5. In the environs of Janasthāna, flesh-eating birds and beasts attacked and sent up their different raucous cries, harshly clamoring.

6. In an unpropitious quarter, dreaded jackals raised loud, ghastly howls, boding ill for the demons.

7. Awesome clouds resembling crumbled mountains and pouring down blood-red water filled all the space in space.

8. A dreadful pall of darkness descended and made them shiver with fear, so dense it obscured every quarter of heaven and all points in between.

9. Twilight, red as fresh blood, came on before its time, and dreadful birds and beasts turned toward Khara and began to screech.

10. Jackals dreadful to look at and always ominous portents in battle, turned toward the army and began to scream, spitting flames.

11. A cloud like a barrier-omen appeared beside the shining sun, and suddenly, before its appointed time, a total solar eclipse occurred.

12. The wind blew wildly, the sun that brings the day went dark, and though it was not yet nighttime the stars came out, like fireflies.

13. Birds and fish went into hiding, lotuses withered on the ponds, and in an instant trees were stripped of their fruit and flowers.

14. Cloud-gray dust swirled up even with no breeze blowing, and myna birds began crying, "*vīcīkūcī!*"

15. Meteors dreadful to behold came crashing down, and a tremor passed through the earth, mountains, forests, and groves.

16. Khara bellowed from his chariot, fully comprehending; his left arm throbbed and his voice caught in his throat.

17. As he gazed about, tears came to his eyes, and pain was etched in his forehead. But in his madness he would not turn back.

18. Then, as he watched these evil portents appear that would horrify anyone else, Khara laughed and addressed the *rākṣasas*:

19. "These are all great portents and terrible to see, but why should I in my power give them any thought, any more than the strong man gives the weak?

20. "With my keen arrows I could bring down even the stars from heaven. In my rage I could throw the fear of death into Death himself.

21. "Rāghava is arrogant in his power, so is his brother Lakṣmaṇa, and I will not return until I kill them with my sharp arrows.

22. "My sister shall have her heart's desire and drink their blood. Because of what they did to her, Rāma and Lakṣmaṇa are doomed.

23. "Never before have I met defeat in combat. You all know this for a fact; I am not telling a lie.

24. "Should the king of the gods himself come on his rutting elephant Airāvata and attack with thunderbolt in hand, in my rage I could kill him in battle. What then of two human beings!"

25. The great legion listened as the *rākṣasa* roared out his boast, and bound up as they were in the bonds of death, they delighted in it no end.

26. The great seers, gods, and *gandharvas,* the perfected beings and celestial bards assembled, anxious to watch the battle.

27. And having assembled in a body, the holy ones said to one another, "May cows and brahmans fare well, and all whom the worlds hold in esteem!

28. "May Rāghava conquer in battle the stalkers of the night, the sons of Pulastya, as once the god who bears the discus conquered in battle all the mighty *asuras.*"

29. With these and many like remarks the supreme seers watched the army of *rākṣasas,* whose lives were soon to end.

30. Aboard his chariot Khara sallied forth from the vanguard of the army, and at the sight of this other *rākṣasas* did the same.

31–32. Śyenagāmi, Pṛthugrīva, Yajñaśatru, Vihaṃgama, Durjaya, Karavīrākṣa, Paruṣa, Kālakārmuka, Meghamāli, Mahāmāli, Sarpāsya, Rudhirāśana—these twelve mighty warriors marched forward flanking Khara.

33. Mahākapāla, Sthūlākṣa, Pramāthin, Triśiras as well—these four generals followed Dūṣaṇa at the rear.

34. With an awesome surge, lusting for battle, the ferocious army of *rākṣasa* warriors advanced rapidly against the two princes, like a string of eclipsing planets against the sun and moon.

The end of the twenty-second *sarga* of the *Araṇyakāṇḍa* of the *Śrī Rāmāyaṇa*.

Sarga 23

1. While the harsh and brutal Khara was making his way to the ashram, Rāma and his brother saw the very same portents.

2. The appearance of the dreadful portents, boding ill for creatures, was enough to horrify anyone. At the sight of them Rāma addressed Lakṣmaṇa with these words:

3. "Look at those great portents of mass destruction, great-armed brother, how they appear to foretell the annihilation of all *rākṣasas*.

4. "There in the sky, ragged, mule-gray clouds are swirling, raining blood and rumbling harshly.

5. "All my arrows are smoldering in eager anticipation of battle, Lakṣmaṇa, and my gold-backed bows are writhing.

6. "Forest birds are screeching nearby, the sort that lead me to believe we may soon find ourselves in danger and our very lives in jeopardy.

7. "There will no doubt be a great clash of arms: The constant twitching of my arm tells me so.

8. "But your face looks bright and clear, my heroic brother. This means victory is at hand for us, and defeat for our enemy.

9. "For when the face of a man preparing for battle darkens over, Lakṣmaṇa, it means his life is at an end.

10. "Still, for his own good a wise man should take steps against any trouble he foresees before it arrives.

11. "Therefore you must take Vaidehī and, arrows in hand and bearing your bow, seek refuge in a mountain cave, one overgrown with trees and hard to attack.

12. "I do not want you to question this command of mine. I implore you by these feet to which you bow. Go, dear brother, without delay."

13. So Rāma spoke, and Lakṣmaṇa gathered up his bow and arrows and sought refuge with Sītā in an inaccessible cave.

14. When Lakṣmaṇa and Sītā had entered the cave, Rāma said to himself, "Good, it is all arranged," and then he donned his armor.

15. Adorned in his firelike armor, Rāma had the appearance of a smokeless flame flaring up in the dark.

16. Gathering up his arrows and brandishing his great bow, the mighty prince took up his position there, filling the quarters of heaven with the sound of his twanging bowstring.

17. Then the gods and *gandharvas*, the perfected beings, celestial bards, and *guhyakas* turned to one another in utter terror and said:

18. "There are fourteen thousand awesome *rākṣasas*, and righteous Rāma is all alone. How will the battle come out?"

19. Just then, with a deep rumble, the army of the demons appeared on every side with their terrible armor, weapons, and standards.

20–21. They let out roars like lions, shouted at one another, and twanged their bows; without letup they stormed about, raising a wild clamor and beating their drums, so that the tumultuous noise filled all the forest.

22. The noise terrified the animals that ranged the forest, and without a backward glance they ran off to where it was quiet.

23. Deep as the ocean, bristling with weapons of every sort, the army advanced against Rāma in a wild surge.

24. Expert as he was in combat, Rāma took in the scene with a glance, scanning Khara's army as it came on ready for battle.

25. He strung his awesome bow, drew shafts from his quiver, and filled himself with a violent rage to slay all the *rākṣasas*.

26. It was all but impossible to gaze at him then, enraged as he was and blazing like the fire at the end of a cosmic age. The spirits of the forest shuddered to see him possessed with might.

27. In his rage Rāma had the very look of the god who wields the *pināka* bow when about to destroy the sacrifice of Dakṣa.

The end of the twenty-third *sarga* of the *Araṇyakāṇḍa* of the *Śrī Rāmāyaṇa.*

Sarga 24

1. Approaching the ashram with his escort, Khara saw Rāma, destroyer of enemies, standing there enraged, his bow held steady.

2. At the sight of Rāma he raised his taut-strung, harshly twanging bow, and urged the charioteer to drive on toward him.

3. On Khara's command the charioteer drove the horses to where great-armed Rāma stood alone, brandishing his bow.

4. Seeing Khara dart forward, all his companion nightstalkers surrounded him, bellowing loudly.

5. Aboard his chariot in the midst of the demons, Khara resembled Lohitāñga, the red planet, rising amid the stars.

6. Then, in a rage, all the nightstalkers began to shower their various weapons upon the awesome bowman, invincible Rāma.

7. Blind with fury, the *rākṣasas* sought to kill Rāma in combat with iron hammers and pikes, missiles, swords, and axes.

8. Like mighty, roaring storm clouds they attacked Rāma Kākutstha, eager to kill him in battle.

9. The hordes of *rākṣasas* let loose a shower of arrows upon Rāma, like massive clouds showering the king of mountains with torrents of rain.

10. Surrounded by hordes of dreaded *rākṣasas*, Rāghava resembled Śiva, the great god, surrounded by his hordes of attendants on a moonless night.

11. With his darts Rāghava met the weapons shot by the demons just as the ocean meets the rivers' floods.

12. When the terrible weapons pierced his body, Rāma did not waver any more than a great mountain wavers beneath the blows of many flaming thunderbolts.

13. Rāma Rāghava was wounded, his whole body smeared with

blood, so that he looked like the sun at twilight enveloped by clouds.

14. The gods, *gandharvas*, perfected beings, and great seers as well sank down in despair to see him all alone, encircled by so many thousands.

15. But then Rāma flew into a rage, and bending his bow into an arc, he unleashed sharp arrows by the hundreds and thousands.

16. Inescapable, unendurable, like the very noose of Doom, were the true-flying, heron-feathered arrows Rāma shot in battle as if for sport.

17. As if for sport Rāma shot his arrows at the enemy soldiers, and like the noose of Doom, each arrow claimed a *rākṣasa*'s life.

18. After piercing the bodies of the *rākṣasas* the arrows, drenched in blood, continued their flight through the sky, gleaming with the splendor of blazing fires.

19. Deadly shafts beyond number went flying from the arc of Rāma's bow, taking the lives of the *rākṣasas*.

20. In the battle Rāma with his arrows shattered their bows by the hundreds and thousands, shattered their lofty standards and armor, cut off their heads, their braceleted arms, and their legs firm and muscular as elephants' trunks.

21. Pierced by reed darts, iron shafts, and sharp-tipped barbed arrows, the nightstalkers raised an awful cry of agony.

22. There was no respite for the army from the moment Rāma began to ravage them—like fire in a dry forest—with his sharp darts that pierced them to the quick.

23. Some of the nightstalkers, heroes of awesome power, continued to hurl pikes and swords and battle-axes at Rāma in a towering rage.

24. But great-armed Rāghava, warding off the weapons with his arrows in battle, took their lives and cut their throats.

25. The surviving nightstalkers ran in despair to Khara, seeking refuge from the arrows that ravaged them.

26. Dūṣaṇa met them, rallied them all, and then attacked Kākutstha in a rage, like Death attacking Rudra.

27. Reinforced by Dūṣaṇa, those who fell back took courage, and armed with boulders and *sāla* and *tāla* trees, they attacked Rāma again.

28. It was amazing, the battle that once more broke out between Rāma and the *rākṣasas*, a tumultuous, terrible battle that would horrify anyone.

The end of the twenty-fourth *sarga* of the *Araṇyakāṇḍa* of the *Śrī Rāmāyaṇa*.

Sarga 25

1. With his keen shafts, righteous Rāghava countered the intense, deadly shower of trees and boulders.

2. And as he countered that shower of weapons, Rāma narrowed his eyes like a bull and flew into a towering rage to slay all the *rākṣasas*.

3. Possessed with rage and almost ablaze with might, he sprayed his arrows in every direction over Dūṣaṇa and the army.

4. This enraged the lord of the army, Dūṣaṇa, the spoiler of enemies, who seized a horrible cudgel that looked like a mountain peak.

5–6. The cudgel was encircled with hoops of gold, studded with sharp iron barbs, and smeared with the greasy flesh of his foes; like a lightning bolt to the touch, strong enough to break enemy citadels or to crush the army of the gods. Seizing this serpentlike cudgel, the savage nightstalker Dūṣaṇa attacked Rāma in battle.

7. But even as Dūṣaṇa attacked, Rāghava drew two arrows and cut off his braceleted arms.

8. The massive cudgel dropped from his severed hand and fell upon the battlefield, like a banner of Śakra falling from on high.

9. And Dūṣaṇa, his arms lying scattered about him, fell to the ground like a spirited elephant with shattered tusks.

10. At the sight of Dūṣaṇa falling to the ground, slain in battle, all the creatures acclaimed Kākutstha with cries of "Well done!"

11. At this juncture, three soldiers of the vanguard, Mahākapāla, Sthūlākṣa, and powerful Pramāthin, flew into a rage and in a body attacked Rāma, bound as they were in the bonds of death.

12. The *rākṣasa* Mahākapāla took up a huge pike, Sthūlākṣa seized a lance, and Pramāthin a battle-ax.

13. When they hurled themselves against Rāghava, he received them as welcome guests, with his sharp, pointed shafts.

14. The delight of the Raghus severed the head of Mahākapāla and, with a flood of countless arrows, crushed Pramāthin.

15. And he so filled Sthūlākṣa's eyes with sharp arrows that he fell down dead upon the ground, like a lofty tree newly sprouting with twigs.

16. Then mighty Rāma set about killing the remnants of the army with fiery shafts ornamented with diamond and gold.

17. His gold-feathered arrows, like smoky tongues of fire, cut down the *rākṣasas* as lightning bolts fell massive trees.

18. With one hundred barbed arrows Rāma killed a hundred *rākṣasas*, and with a thousand he killed a thousand of them on the field of battle.

19. As the arrows pierced their armor and ornaments, pierced and splintered their bows, the nightstalkers fell to the earth besmeared with blood.

20. Spattered with blood and their hair streaming wild, they fell in combat, strewn upon the treasure-laden earth like *kuśa* grass upon a broad altar.

21. The forest was filled with dead *rākṣasas* and made muddy with their blood and torn flesh; in an instant it had become a place of utter terror, a vision of hell itself.

22. Fighting all alone on foot, one man, Rāma, killed fourteen thousand awesome *rākṣasas*.

23. From out of that whole army were left only the great chariot-fighter Khara, the *rākṣasa* Triśiras, and Rāma himself, crusher of enemies.

24. When Khara saw his awesome force destroyed by powerful Rāma in the great battle, he drove toward Rāma on his huge chariot, like Indra brandishing his lightning bolt.

The end of the twenty-fifth *sarga* of the *Araṇyakāṇḍa* of the *Śrī Rāmāyaṇa*.

Sarga 26

1. As Khara drove toward Rāma, the lord of the *rākṣasa* army named Triśiras fell in with him and spoke these words:

2. "Give me a chance, bold Khara, and restrain this sudden impulse of yours. You shall see great-armed Rāma cut down in combat.

3. "I give you my solemn promise—I touch my weapon as proof—that I shall slay Rāma, whom all the *rākṣasas* should have slain.

4. "I shall be his death in battle—or he mine. Restrain your lust for battle and for a moment be a judge.

5. "Either you will return to Janasthāna delighted that Rāma has been killed, or, if I am killed, you will meet Rāma yourself in combat."

6. So Triśiras begged him in his eagerness to die, and when Khara had given permission, saying, "Go, then, and fight," he set out toward Rāghava.

7. On a brilliant chariot harnessed with swift horses Triśiras—a triple-peaked mountain he seemed—attacked Rāma in battle.

8. Like a storm cloud he let loose a vast torrent of arrows, and he let out a roar as loud as a bass drum when its skin has been dampened with water.

9. When Rāghava spotted the *rākṣasa* Triśiras approaching, he received him with his bow, brandishing his sharp shafts.

10. It was a great, tumultuous battle that took place between Rāma and Triśiras, supremely powerful both of them, as they clashed like lion and elephant.

11. At last, when Triśiras grazed his forehead with three darts, Rāma, filled with fury and tolerating no more, said in a passion:

12. "Ha! So this is the power of the bold, heroic *rākṣasa*, who scratches me on the forehead with arrows soft as flowers. Now you receive my arrows as they fly from my bowstring."

13. Such were his impassioned words, and in a rage he sank fourteen arrows, like poisonous snakes, into the chest of Triśiras.

14. Mighty Rāma cut down his four swift horses with four strong-jointed arrows.

15. With eight shafts Rāma cut down the driver in the chariot box and with one more splintered the lofty standard.

16. As Triśiras leaped from his disabled chariot, Rāma pierced his heart with darts, and the nightstalker stood there, stunned.

17. In his boundless power the prince would tolerate no more and, taking three sharp shafts, sent them flying and cut off the *rākṣasa*'s three heads.

18. Spurting blood and tormented by Rāma's darts, the nightstalker fell to the ground where but a moment before his own heads had fallen.

19. The surviving *rākṣasas*, attendants of Khara, broke ranks, and like deer frightened by a tiger, they fled and would not halt.

20. Khara watched them flee, then angrily turned away and on his own attacked Rāma, just as Rāhu the Eclipse attacks the moon.

The end of the twenty-sixth *sarga* of the *Araṇyakāṇḍa* of the *Śrī Rāmāyaṇa*.

Sarga 27

1. Having seen Dūṣaṇa killed in battle along with Triśiras, having witnessed Rāma's prowess, Khara himself was seized with terror.

2. He had seen the *rākṣasa* army, a great, irresistible force, destroyed by one man, Rāma; he had seen Dūṣaṇa and Triśiras killed.

3. Observing with a sinking heart his force all but destroyed, the *rākṣasa* Khara attacked Rāma as once Namuci attacked Vāsava.

4. Forcefully he drew his bow and shot his arrows at Rāma, blood-drinking iron shafts darting like raging, poisonous snakes.

5. From aboard his chariot Khara repeatedly twanged his bowstring and displayed his missiles, his skillful use of the different maneuvers with arrows employed in combat.

6. Catching sight of him Rāma, the great chariot-fighter, drew his huge bow and filled with arrows every quarter of heaven and all points in between.

7. His unendurable shafts gave off sparks like fires, filling every opening in the sky, as the showers of the rain god do.

8. In all of space there was no more space because of the sharp darts Khara and Rāma shot; it was all one mass of arrows.

9. Covered by webs of arrows, the sun was blotted out as the two struggled together in their fury to slay each other.

10. With reed darts, iron shafts, and sharp-tipped barbed arrows, he struck Rāma in battle like a great elephant with goads.

11. All creatures watched as the *rākṣasa* kept his position in the chariot, bow in hand, looking like Death with noose held ready.

12. Bold as a lion, Khara advanced with a lion's bold strides, but at the sight of him Rāma shuddered no more than a lion in the presence of a feeble deer.

13. Upon his great sunlike chariot Khara hurtled toward Rāma in battle, like a moth nearing a flame.

14. Displaying his agility Khara shattered great Rāma's bow and arrow right at the grip.

15. In his fury he took up seven more arrows, like Śakra's lightning bolts, and there in battle sank them into Rāma's armor.

16. Struck by the firm-jointed darts unleashed by Khara, Rāma's corselet fell to the ground from his body radiant as the sun.

17. As arrows plunged into every limb, Rāghava in his rage took on the look of a blazing, smokeless fire.

18. To put an end to his foe, Rāma, destroyer of enemies, then strung another bow, a great one that gave off a booming sound.

19. This was the best of bows, the mighty bow of Viṣṇu that the great seer had bestowed on him, and brandishing it he attacked Khara.

20. Then Rāma, enraged in combat, took up strong-jointed arrows fletched with golden feathers and splintered Khara's standard.

21. The gorgeous golden standard fell to the ground in countless splinters, like the sun falling by order of the gods.

22. Knowing the vital spots, Khara, enraged, took aim at his heart and wounded Rāma's body with four arrows, as if wounding an elephant with prods.

23. Many darts were sent flying from Khara's bow, and Rāma, his

body drenched with blood from his wounds, was seized with a wild fury.

24. The best of bowmen grasped his bow in the face of this supreme challenge and, supreme archer that he was, shot six arrows, all well aimed.

25. He sank one dart into Khara's head, two into his arms, and with three crescent-headed arrows struck him in the chest.

26. Enraged and eager to kill the *rākṣasa*, the mighty prince then shot thirteen iron shafts, arrows sharpened on stone, and brilliant as sunlight.

27–28. With one arrow, powerful Rāma demolished Khara's chariot yoke in combat; with four, his four horses; with the sixth, the head of his charioteer; with three more he demolished the main yoke pole, with two, the axle; with the twelfth, Khara's bow and arrows. And after wreaking this destruction in battle, Rāghava, the equal of Indra, laughed as he took up the thirteenth arrow like a thunderbolt and pierced Khara.

29. His bow shattered, chariot lost, horses and charioteer dead, Khara jumped to the ground, club in hand, and took his stand.

30. The gods and great seers then assembled in their grand aerial chariots, and with hands cupped in reverence the whole assembly joyfully praised the deed of the great chariot-fighter, Rāma.

The end of the twenty-seventh *sarga* of the *Araṇyakāṇḍa* of the *Śrī Rāmāyaṇa*.

Sarga 28

1. When Khara, having lost his chariot, took his stand with his club at the ready, mighty Rāma addressed him—and if his tone of voice was mild, the words he used were harsh:

2. "Standing at the head of a great force, a host of elephants, horses, and chariots, you have done utterly ruthless deeds that all the world finds repugnant.

3. "No one who is cruel, does evil deeds, makes creatures tremble, can long survive, not the lord of the three worlds himself.

4. "For all unite to destroy one whose deeds are brutal and per-

verse, nightstalker, just as when a vicious snake comes among them.

5. "A person may give no thought to the evil he does from greed or lust, but like a lizard that feeds on hailstones he will surely see its end result—when he comes to grief.

6. "What then must be the fruit you reap, *rākṣasa*, for slaying the illustrious ascetics who live in Daṇḍaka wilderness, following the ways of righteousness?

7. "Savage creatures who do evil and are held in repugnance by the world do not long retain their power, like trees cut off at the root.

8. "Inevitably in the course of time, the agent harvests the bitter fruit of his evil act, just as trees come into flower with the passing of the seasons.

9. "Like eating poisoned food, nightstalker, evil deeds in due course bear their fruit in this very world.

10. "I come as king, nightstalker, to end the life of evildoers and all who wish the world ill.

11. "The arrows adorned with gold I unleash upon you shall rend your flesh, piercing you as snakes will pierce an anthill.

12. "And slain in battle you and your army shall hasten after those righteous men you devoured in Daṇḍaka wilderness.

13. "The supreme seers you killed in the past shall now look down upon you, they in their aerial chariots and you, slain by my arrows, in hell.

14. "Fight all you will, try as hard as you can, lowest of your kind. I will now strike off your head like a toddy palm fruit."

15. So Rāma spoke, and Khara flew into a rage, his eyes blazing red. Laughing but blind with rage he replied to Rāma:

16. "How can you sing your own praises, son of Daśaratha, and when so unpraiseworthy at that, on the strength of killing some common *rākṣasas* in battle?

17. "The bold and powerful, those who are truly bulls among men, never speak of themselves in the pride of their own might.

18. "Only the crude and common man, Rāma, held as scum of the

kshatriya order in the eyes of all the world, makes such empty boasts as you have made.

19. "Would anyone truly brave in battle bring up his family and praise himself—and so inopportunely, when the hour of his death is at hand?

20. "Your boasting has only shown how worthless you really are, like false gold smelted down in a grass fire.

21. "Can you not see me standing before you holding my club, unshakable as a rich-veined mountain that holds the earth in place?

22. "With club in hand like Death with his noose, I could easily take your life in battle—all life in the three worlds.

23. "Though I have much to say to you, I will say no more, lest the sun go down and our battle be suspended.

24. "By killing you now I shall stop the tears for the fourteen thousand *rākṣasas* you have slain."

25. So Khara spoke, and in a violent rage he hurled his club at Rāma, a superbly banded club that blazed like a lightning bolt.

26. The huge club shot forth in a blaze from Khara's hand, incinerating trees and shrubs as it passed in onward flight.

27. But even as the flaming club came flying toward him, like the very noose of Death, Rāma's arrows splintered it in midair.

28. Broken to bits by the arrows, the club fell to the ground, like a serpent felled by the power of spells and magic herbs.

The end of the twenty-eighth *sarga* of the *Araṇyakāṇḍa* of the *Śrī Rāmāyaṇa*.

Sarga 29

1. After breaking the club with his darts, Rāghava, who cherished righteousness, spoke to Khara in a passion but with a smile on his lips:

2. "Is this all the power you can show me, lowest of *rākṣasas*? How inferior you are in strength to me, how hollow your boast!

3. "Your club lies here on the ground, broken by my darts, and with it any trust in your arrogant vaunting lies destroyed.

4. "Your words were empty, too, when you said, 'I shall herewith stop the tears for the slain *rākṣasas*.'

5. "For I will take your life, *rākṣasa*, as Garutmant took the drink of immortality, you low, treacherous brute.

6. "Now I will cut your throat with my darts and from the gaping wound the ground will drink your blood with its frothing, bubbling ornaments.

7. "And all caked with dirt you shall lay your arms limply upon the earth and sleep with her in a close embrace, as if she were some hard-won woman.

8. "And when you lie in that deep slumber, scum of the *rākṣasas*, this Daṇḍaka forest shall become a place of refuge for all in need of refuge.

9. "No more shall the sages fear to wander the forest of Janasthāna, *rākṣasa*, after my arrows have made your dwelling place your resting place.

10. "Today the *rākṣasa* women who used to terrify others shall flee in terror and utter desolation, their kinsmen dead, their faces bathed in tears.

11. "Today all shall learn the taste of grief, stalker of the night, all those equally baseborn women who have for husband the likes of you.

12. "Vicious brute, ever a thorn in the side of brahmans! Because of you the sages cast their oblations into the fire with fear."

13. So in the midst of battle Rāghava spoke with passion, and Khara replied furiously, insulting him in the harshest tone:

14. "Only your brash arrogance makes you fearless in the very face of danger. You have lost all sense of what to say and not to say, because Death has you in his power.

15. "For once the noose of Doom is wound around his neck, a man no longer knows what is or is not to be done, and all six senses fail him."

16–17. So he spoke to Rāma, and knitting his brow into a frown, the nightstalker glanced around for a weapon to use in battle. He spotted a huge *sāla* not far away, and biting his lip, he tore the tree up by the roots.

18. As he raised it in his arms, the powerful *rākṣasa* bellowed, and hurling it at Rāma he cried out, "You are slain!"

19. As the tree hurtled toward him mighty Rāma splintered it with a flood of darts, and then he filled himself with a violent fury to kill Khara in battle.

20. Breaking out in sweat, his eyes blazing red in the fury of battle, Rāma pierced Khara with thousands of darts.

21. His blood flowed in a foaming torrent from the gashes made by the darts, like a stream cascading down Mount Prasravaṇa.

22. Khara reeled from the arrows Rāma shot in combat, but then he grew drunk on the smell of his own blood and attacked him at breakneck speed.

23. Drenched with blood he threw himself upon him in a wild frenzy, but the seasoned warrior sidestepped him with one quick move.

24. Rāma then took up a fiery arrow, like a second staff of Brahmā, to slay Khara in battle.

25. It was the arrow given by the wise king of gods, Indra the munificent. The righteous prince fixed and shot it at Khara.

26. Raising his bow, Rāma shot the great arrow, and with a crash like a bolt of lightning it struck Khara in the chest.

27. Khara fell to the ground as the arrow's fire burned him up the way Andhaka once fell burned to ashes by Rudra in the White Forest.

28. Struck, Khara fell like Vṛtra cut down by the thunderbolt, or Namuci by the foam of the sea, or Bala by Indra's lightning bolt.

29. All the royal seers and supreme seers then assembled, and jubilantly lauding Rāma they spoke these words:

30. "It was to this end that the great and mighty Indra, chastiser of Pāka and breaker of fortresses, paid his visit to the holy ashram of Śarabhaṅga.

31. "The great seers contrived a means of bringing you to this place to slay these savage, evil *rākṣasas*.

32. "You have done what we required, son of Daśaratha, and now the great seers can follow the ways of righteousness at peace in Daṇḍaka."

33. Meanwhile mighty Lakṣmaṇa and Sītā, having made their way out of the mountain fastness, happily entered the ashram together.

34. After Lakṣmaṇa did obeisance to him, mighty Rāma entered the ashram victorious amid the acclaim of the great seers.

35. Vaidehī warmly embraced her husband, pleased to see that he had killed the enemy and brought peace to the great seers.

The end of the twenty-ninth *sarga* of the *Araṇyakāṇḍa* of the *Śrī Rāmāyaṇa*.

Sarga 30

1–2. Now, when Śūrpaṇakhā saw how Rāma all alone had killed the fourteen thousand awesome *rākṣasas* in battle, and Dūṣaṇa, Triśiras, and Khara as well, once more like a storm cloud she let out a deafening roar.

3. When she saw the feat accomplished by Rāma, impossible for anyone else to do, she set out in wild panic for Laṅkā, where Rāvaṇa held sway.

4. She found Rāvaṇa in his splendid palace, radiant in his power, his advisers sitting beside him like the Maruts next to Vāsava.

5. He was seated upon a golden throne radiant as the sun, and he looked like a fire on a golden altar blazing with rich oblations.

6. A hero invincible in combat with gods, *gandharvas*, spirits, or great seers, he looked like Death himself with jaws agape.

7. He carried lightning-bolt wounds received in clashes with gods and *asuras*. His chest was seamed with scars where Airāvata's pointed tusks had gored him.

8. He had twenty arms and ten necks. His regalia was a wonder to behold. A broad-chested, mighty king, he was marked with all the marks of royalty.

9. He sparkled with earrings of burnished gold and the glossy beryl he wore. His arms were handsome, his teeth bright white, his mouth huge, and he was as tall as a mountain.

10. In combat with gods his body had been wounded in hundreds of places, by blows from Viṣṇu's discus and all the other weapons of the gods.

11. He could effortlessly perturb the imperturbable seas, level mountaintops, and vanquish the gods.

12. A breaker of laws he would violate the wives of other men, and use any unearthly weapon to obstruct the sacrifice.

13. It was he who had gone to the city of Bhogavatī, defeated Vāsuki and Takṣaka, and abducted Takṣaka's wife.

14. It was he who had gone to Mount Kailāsa and conquered the man-borne Kubera, stealing his aerial chariot, Puṣpaka, that flies where one desires.

15. It was he who in a mighty rage would destroy the gardens of the gods, the heavenly forest Caitraratha with its lotus pond, and Nandana forest.

16. It was he who, tall as a mountain peak, would extend his arms and prevent the glorious powers, the sun and moon, from rising.

17. It was he who long ago in the great forest had practiced austerities for ten thousand years and unflinchingly cut off his own heads as offering to the Self-existent Brahmā.

18. It was he who had no longer to fear death in combat with any beings—gods, *dānavas*, *gandharvas*, *piśācas*, great birds, or serpents—any beings but men.

19. It was he who in overweening pride of power would pollute the holy *soma* at the seats of the oblation, when in the course of their rites the brahmans consecrated it with vedic hymns.

20. He would disrupt sacrifices at their climax, then murder the brahmans. He was savage and wicked, cruel and ruthless, delighting in the misfortune of others. He was Rāvaṇa, "he who makes all creatures wail," the terror of all the worlds.

21. The *rākṣasa* woman beheld this savage and powerful brother of hers, clad in heavenly garments and jewels, adorned with heavenly garlands, the illustrious lord of *rākṣasas*, delight of the House of the Paulastyas.

22. Śūrpaṇakhā, who once lived free from fear, now wild with fear and confusion, told him the dreadful story of how the great prince

had mutilated her. As she displayed herself, his eyes grew wide and blazed.

The end of the thirtieth *sarga* of the *Araṇyakāṇḍa* of the *Śrī Rāmāyaṇa*.

Sarga 31

1. As Rāvaṇa, who made the worlds wail, sat among his ministers, Śūrpaṇakhā in her rage and desolation addressed him with harsh words:

2. "Drunk as you are on sensual pleasures, so licentious and unbridled, you overlook the one thing you must not, the presence of terrible danger.

3. "When a lord of the earth is lustful, addicted to vulgar pleasures, a slave to his passions, his subjects see him as no better than a cremation fire.

4. "If a king fails to attend to affairs himself and in timely fashion, those affairs come to grief, so too his kingdom and the king himself.

5. "The ruler of men who is not his own master, grants no audience, or makes no use of spies is shunned by men as elephants shun a muddy riverbank.

6. "If rulers of men are not their own masters and fail to protect their realm, their grandeur disappears, like mountains sunk beneath the sea.

7. "How can you stay king when, though staunchly opposed by gods, *gandharvas*, and *dānavas*, you do not even bother to use spies?

8. "Rulers of men who do not master espionage, diplomacy, or their treasuries, your highness, are no more than common men.

9. "Kings are called farsighted precisely because, through their spies, they can see anything, however far away.

10. "Surrounded by worthless advisers, you have made no use of spies, I am sure, and thus are unaware that your people, and Janasthāna, have been destroyed.

11. "Fourteen thousand awesome *rākṣasas* killed by a single man—Rāma—and with them Khara and Dūṣaṇa.

12. "Tireless Rāma attacked Janasthāna, and he has made Daṇḍaka safe and won security for the seers.

13. "But, consumed with lust, negligent, and no longer your own master, Rāvaṇa, you are unaware of the danger present in your realm.

14. "In times of trouble no one runs to aid a king who has been cruel and ungenerous, negligent, haughty, and treacherous.

15. "When a ruler of men is arrogant and aloof, conceited and quick to anger, in times of trouble even his own people will slay him.

16. "A king who ignores his affairs, blind to dangers, is quickly toppled from his kingship—and the wretch is then not worth a straw.

17. "Dry logs have some use, even clods of dirt or dust, but not a ruler of the earth fallen from power.

18. "For no matter how able, a king deposed is as useless as a worn-out garment or crushed garland.

19. "But a king who is alert, well informed, and self-controlled, knowing what must be done and acting in keeping with righteousness, enjoys a long reign.

20. "The king who, though his eyes be closed in sleep, watches with the eye of diplomacy, who shows his grace no less than anger, is honored by his people.

21. "But you are a fool, Rāvaṇa, and devoid of such virtues, and so lack spies to tell you of the massacre of the *rākṣasas*.

22. "A king who misjudges his enemy, is addicted to sensual pleasures, fails to recognize the proper time and place for things, gives no thought to weighing the pros and cons of an issue—such a king soon ruins his kingdom and himself."

23. Rāvaṇa paid heed as she recited his failings in this fashion, and for some time afterward the lord of nightstalkers, with all his wealth and pride and power, sat lost in thought.

The end of the thirty-first *sarga* of the *Araṇyakāṇḍa* of the *Śrī Rāmāyaṇa*.

Sarga 32

1. When the raging Śūrpaṇakhā had finished her harsh speech, Rāvaṇa, too, was filled with rage and from where he sat among his ministers he began to question her:

2. "Who is this Rāma? What does he look like? How powerful is he, how bold? And for what reason has he entered the impassable Daṇḍaka wilderness?

3. "What weapon could Rāma possibly have used to kill the *rākṣasas* in combat, to kill Khara, Dūṣaṇa, and Triśiras?"

4. Questioned in this fashion by the lord of the *rākṣasas*, the *rākṣasa* woman, blind with rage, proceeded to tell all she knew of Rāma.

5. "Rāma is the son of Daśaratha. He has long arms and large eyes and resembles Kandarpa, god of love, though clad in barkcloth and black hides.

6. "He has a bow like Śakra's, banded with gold, and drawing it to its fullest he shoots flaming iron shafts that, like snakes, carry deadly poison.

7. "I could not even see powerful Rāma take up his terrible arrows in combat, draw his bow, or shoot.

8. "But I could see the army cut down by the shower of arrows, like a tall stand of grain cut down by Indra with a shower of hailstones.

9–10. "Fighting on foot, all alone, with those sharp arrows he killed fourteen thousand awesome *rākṣasas* in a split second, and a second later killed Khara and Dūṣaṇa as well. He has made Daṇḍaka safe and won security for the seers.

11. "I alone just barely escaped from the great and celebrated Rāma: Although he treated me with contempt, he shrank from killing a woman.

12. "He has a mighty brother, of equal prowess and virtue, who is loyal and devoted to him, the brave Lakṣmaṇa.

13. "Implacable and invincible, sure of victory with his boldness, power, and intelligence, he is always there, Rāma's right arm, a veritable second self.

14. "Rāma has a lawful wife named Sītā, princess of Videha. And

what a glorious woman she is, with her large eyes, slender waist, and full hips.

15. "No goddess, no *gandharva* woman, no *yakṣa* or *kinnara* woman, no mortal woman so beautiful have I ever seen before on the face of this earth.

16. "He who claims Sītā as wife and receives her delighted embraces has more reason to live than anyone else in all the worlds, the breaker of fortresses, Indra himself, included.

17. "She is a woman of good character, with a form beyond all praise, a beauty unequaled on earth. She would make a perfect wife for you, and you a perfect husband for her.

18. "How broad her hips, how full and high her breasts, how lovely her face. Why, I all but brought her back to be your wife.

19. "The moment you saw Vaidehī's full-moon face, you would find yourself at the mercy of the arrows of Manmatha, god of love.

20. "If you have any interest in taking her to wife, put your best foot forward at once to win her.

21. "At the same time, lord of *rākṣasas*, do one last act of kindness for the *rākṣasas*, and slay that cruel Rāma, who is living a hermit's life.

22. "When you have killed him and Lakṣmaṇa, the great chariot-fighter, with your sharp arrows, you will then enjoy the widowed Sītā to your heart's content.

23. "If what I am saying meets with your approval, Rāvaṇa, lord of *rākṣasas*, do as I say without a moment's hesitation.

24. "Now that you have heard how the nightstalkers of Janasthāna were killed by the unerring arrows of Rāma, and how Khara and Dūṣaṇa were killed, you must act at once."

The end of the thirty-second *sarga* of the *Araṇyakāṇḍa* of the *Śrī Rāmāyaṇa*.

Sarga 33

1. When Rāvaṇa had heard Śūrpaṇakhā's horrifying tale, he dismissed his advisers and turned his thoughts to the question at hand.

2–3. After pondering the question, examining it carefully, and weighing the pros and cons, the strengths and weaknesses, he decided exactly what to do, and firmly resolved made his way to the lovely carriage house.

4. The overlord of *rākṣasas* went secretly to the carriage house and urgently told his driver to make ready the chariot.

5. At this, the charioteer stepped lively and at once made ready the chariot, a splendid one prized by his master.

6–7. It was a golden, jewel-encrusted chariot that flew where one desires. Harnessed to it were asses decked out with trappings of gold, their faces like those of *piśācas*. The majestic overlord of *rākṣasas*, younger brother of Kubera, bestower of riches, ascended the chariot; with the rumble of a storm cloud he set out for the ocean, lord of streams and rivers.

8. Ten-faced Rāvaṇa carried with him a white yak-tail fan and white parasol, and he sparkled with jewelry of burnished gold and the glossy beryl he wore.

9. Dressed in regalia a wonder to behold, with his ten heads he resembled the ten-peaked king of mountains; he had twenty arms, this enemy of the thirty gods, this slayer of lordly sages.

10. Aboard his chariot that flew where one desires, the overlord of *rākṣasas* appeared like a thundercloud in the sky ringed with lightning and a flight of cranes.

11. Powerful Rāvaṇa gazed down upon the rocky coast, dotted with thousands of different fruit-bearing and flowering trees;

12. Lotus ponds with cool clear water, and sprawling ashrams with sacrificial altars;

13. Plantain trees and *āḍhikas* growing densely, and coconut palms lending their beauty, along with *sālas*, *tālas*, *tamālas*, and other flowering trees.

14–15. Supreme seers given to rigorous fasting graced it; great serpents and birds, *gandharvas* and *kinnaras* by the thousand; perfected beings who had mastered desire, celestial bards, *ājas*, *vaikhānasas*, *māṣas*, *vālakhilyas*, and *marīcipas*.

16. There were *apsarases* by the thousands, all expert in the sports of lovemaking. Their jewelry and garlands were heavenly, heavenly too their beauty.

17. It was a place the majestic wives of the gods would visit and touch with majesty, where hosts of *dānavas* wandered, and gods, who drink the nectar of immortality.

18. It was full of geese, *krauñca* birds, and cormorants, and the call of cranes set it ringing. There were lovely carpets of cat's-eye beryl, made smooth and glossy by the ocean's force.

19–20. Hastening onward, the younger brother of Kubera, bestower of riches, saw on all sides spacious white chariots that could fly where one desires. They belonged to those who had conquered higher worlds by their acts of asceticism; all were decked with heavenly garlands and gave forth the sound of pipes and singing. There were *gandharvas* and *apsarases* to be seen as well.

21–25ab. He saw pleasant forests of sandalwood, thousands of trees with gratifying redolence and roots juicy with resin; forests and orchards of fine aloe, noble *takkolas* and fragrant fruit-trees, *tamāla* flowers and pepper-plant shrubs; heaps of pearls drying on the shore, carpets of conch shells, mounds of coral, mountains of gold and silver everywhere; enchanting cascades and pools of clear water.

25cd–26ab. His gaze fell on cities crowded with elephants, horses, and chariots, filled with grain and riches, adorned with women like perfect jewels.

26cd–27ab. Such was the shore of the ocean, king of rivers, everywhere level and smooth, with breezes gently caressing. It was as if the very summit of heaven had come into view.

27cd–28ab. And there he saw a banyan tree where seers were gathered. Massive as a storm cloud, its branches extended a hundred leagues in every direction.

28cd–ef. To one of these branches, once upon a time, mighty Garuḍa had come, carrying a huge tortoise and elephant on which to feed.

29. But the leafy branch suddenly gave way under the weight of mighty Suparṇa, greatest of birds.

30. Upon it supreme seers had gathered together: *vaikhānasas*, *māṣas*, *vālakhilyas*, *marīcipas*, *ajas*, and *dhūmras*.

31–32. In compassion for them, righteous Garuḍa rushed up and caught the branch—a hundred leagues long—in a single claw, both elephant and tortoise clinging to it still. After devouring their flesh, the greatest of birds used the branch to lay waste the realm of the Niṣādas. He had freed the great sages and felt delight beyond compare.

33. And this delight made him twice as bold and resolute: He resolved to go in quest of the nectar of immortality.

34. Shattering the iron latticework and breaking into the supernal treasure house, he stole the nectar from its hiding place in the palace of great Indra.

35. This was the banyan called Subhadra that Rāvaṇa, younger brother of Kubera, bestower of riches, now beheld. Hosts of great seers still frequented it, and the claw marks left by Suparṇa were still to be seen.

36. Reaching the further shore of the ocean, lord of rivers, he saw an ashram in a secluded, holy, and lovely stretch of forest.

37. And there he saw the *rākṣasa* Mārīca, who wore black hides, matted hair, and barkcloth, and practiced rigorous fasting.

38. Rāvaṇa met with him according to custom, and thereafter, clever speaker that he was, addressed these words to the *rākṣasa*.

The end of the thirty-third *sarga* of the *Araṇyakāṇḍa* of the *Śrī Rāmāyaṇa*.

Sarga 34

1. "Mārīca, my friend, hear what I have to tell you. I am troubled, and my sole refuge from these troubles is you.

2–3. "You know Janasthāna, where once lived my brother Khara, great-armed Dūṣaṇa, my sister Śūrpaṇakhā, the mighty *rākṣasa* Triśiras, an eater of raw flesh, and many another heroic night-stalker who was tried and tested.

4–5. "On my orders the *rākṣasas* had made their dwelling there, oppressing the sages who followed the ways of righteousness in the great wilderness—fourteen thousand awesome *rākṣasas*, heroes tried and tested, who bowed to the will of Khara.

6. "But recently these *rākṣasas* of Janasthāna, powerful and ever vigilant, met in combat with Rāma.

7. "Rāma, in a fury, but without one harsh word, set his bow and arrows to work on the field of battle.

8. "And with his keen arrows this mere man, fighting on foot, killed fourteen thousand ferocious *rākṣasas*.

9. "He killed Khara and cut down Dūṣaṇa in combat, he killed Triśiras as well and has made Daṇḍaka safe.

10. "This Rāma who destroyed the army is a short-lived mortal, scum of the kshatriya, a man whose father cast him out in anger, him and his wife.

11. "A man of no character, a cruel, vicious, greedy, intemperate fool, he has forsaken righteousness and in his unrighteousness takes pleasure in others' misery.

12. "It was him who, without provocation, in an act of brute force mutilated my sister in the wilderness, cutting off her ears and nose.

13. "He has a wife named Sītā, a woman like the daughter of the gods. I mean to abduct her by force from Janasthāna, and you must help me.

14. "For with you at my side to help me, powerful Mārīca, you and my brothers, I would think nothing of facing all the gods united in battle.

15. "So you have to help me, *rākṣasa*, as I know you can, for you have no equal in might, in battle, and in pride.

16. "This is the reason I come to you, nightstalker. Now listen, and I shall tell you what you can do to help me.

17. "Turn yourself into a golden deer dappled with silver spots and go grazing near Rāma's ashram within view of Sītā.

18. "When Sītā sees you transformed as this deer, she will surely tell her husband and Lakṣmaṇa to capture you.

19. "Then, with the two of them gone and the place deserted, nothing can stop me from carrying Sītā off, as Rāhu the Eclipse makes off with the moonlight.

20. "Afterward, with Rāma in agony over the theft of his wife, I know I can easily slay him and so gain my innermost heart's desire."

21. But the moment great Mārīca heard talk of Rāma, his mouth went dry and he was seized with utter terror.

22. Acquainted as he was with Rāma's prowess in great battles, he grew terrified, and his heart sank in despair. Cupping his hands in reverence, he made a forthright reply for both Rāvaṇa's good and his own.

The end of the thirty-fourth *sarga* of the *Araṇyakāṇḍa* of the *Śrī Rāmāyaṇa*.

Sarga 35

1. After listening to the words of the lord of *rākṣasas*, the wise Mārīca, a clever speaker himself, replied:

2. "How easy to find those who say what you want to hear, your majesty; how difficult to find one who gives—or heeds—unpleasant but sound advice.

3. "Clearly you know nothing of Rāma, since you are too careless to make use of spies—not how great his might, how distinguished his virtues, how much like great Indra or Varuṇa he is.

4. "I fear no *rākṣasa* on earth will be safe from harm, my friend; I fear that Rāma in his rage will empty the world of them.

5. "I fear the daughter of Janaka was born to take your life. I fear some awful doom will strike because of Sītā.

6. "I fear the city of Laṅkā, ruled by a lord like you—dissolute and a slave to his passions—will perish, and with it you and all the *rākṣasas*.

7. "A king like you, of poor judgment and poor character, a slave to his passions, takes bad advice and ends up destroying his kingdom, his people, and himself.

8–9. "Rāma, the delight of Kausalyā, was not disowned by his father. It is absolutely false to say he knows no bounds, is greedy, of bad character, or the 'scum of the kshatriyas.' He is not lacking in virtue or righteousness, nor is he vicious; on the contrary, he is devoted to the welfare of all creatures.

10. "When the righteous prince saw how Kaikeyī tricked his father, he accepted forest exile to preserve the truth of his father's word.

11. "To please Kaikeyī and his father, Daśaratha, he gave up the luxuries of kingship and entered Daṇḍaka forest.

12. "Rāma is not cruel, my friend, or stupid or intemperate. You must not say such things; they are groundless lies.

13. "Rāma is righteousness incarnate, a just man who strives for truth. He is king of all this world, like Vāsava of all the gods.

14. "His might it is that protects Vaidehī; how then can you dream of taking her by force? Easier to take the sunlight from the sun.

15. "In battle, this Rāma suddenly ignites, an all-consuming fire, whose bow and sword are kindling, whose arrows licking tongues: Do not walk right into it.

16–17. "Armed with his bow and arrows, this hero implacably destroys the armies of his foes. When the mouth of his bow gapes wide and blazes and the fiery tongues of his arrows dart out, Rāma becomes Death himself. Do not get too near him, my friend, lest you lose every pleasure, your kingship, and the life you hold so dear.

18. "Janaka's daughter belongs to one of immeasurable might. You will not carry her off in the forest, not when she can rely on Rāma's bow.

19. "He loves fair-waisted Sītā more than life itself, and she has always been a faithful wife. He is a blazing fire, and she the flame that leaps from it.

20. "What can you possibly gain, overlord of *rākṣasas*, by this futile adventure? For the moment you face him in battle your life is finished—your life, your every pleasure, your hard-won kingship.

21. "Consult with all those advisers of yours who are righteous, Vibhīṣaṇa first and foremost, and only then decide.

22. "Weigh the pros and cons, the strengths and weaknesses, and honestly compare your power and Rāghava's; then decide where your true interests lie and do what is best.

23. "As for me, I am sure it is not best for you to meet the prince of Kosala in battle. Listen to me a moment longer, overlord of nightstalkers, and I shall tell you what is best and prudent."

The end of the thirty-fifth *sarga* of the *Araṇyakāṇḍa* of the *Śrī Rāmāyaṇa*.

Sarga 36

1. "Once upon a time I, too, wandered this earth in pride of power, tall as a mountain and possessing the strength of a thousand elephants.

2. "Looking like a blue-black cloud, wearing a crest jewel and earrings of burnished gold and armed with an iron cudgel, I would roam Daṇḍaka wilderness, feeding on the flesh of seers and striking fear into all the world.

3. "But then the great sage, righteous Viśvāmitra, who was terrified of me, came in person to Daśaratha and addressed the lord of men as follows:

4. " 'Let Rāma come and vigilantly protect me at the time of the lunar sacrifice, lord of men, for I am terribly afraid of Mārīca.'

5. "So the great and illustrious sage Viśvāmitra spoke, and righteous King Daśaratha replied to him:

6. " 'Rāghava is a mere twelve years old and unpracticed in arms. I, on the other hand, am prepared to go with all the army at my command and slay your enemy, best of sages, just as you desire.'

7. "Thus the king spoke, and the sage once again addressed him: 'No one on earth but Rāma has the power it takes to defeat that *rākṣasa*.

8. " 'A mere boy he may be, but he is mighty and capable of subduing him. I will take Rāma and go. My blessings on you, slayer of foes.'

9. "Thus the sage Viśvāmitra spoke, and taking the prince he returned in high spirits to his own ashram.

10. "When the sage was consecrated for sacrifice in Daṇḍaka wilderness, Rāma took up his position nearby, brandishing his shining bow.

11. "He was just a beardless youth, standing bow in hand, clad only in a loincloth—yet majestic and swarthy, with lovely eyes, a topknot, and a garland of gold.

12. "Rāma shed the radiance of his might over Daṇḍaka wilderness, looking like the newly risen crescent moon.

13. "It was then I came, resembling a storm cloud, wearing ear-

rings of burnished gold. Powerful in my possession of a boon, I arrogantly approached the ashram.

14. "He saw me as I entered, and instantly I raised my weapon, but all he did on seeing me was calmly string his bow.

15. "In my folly I was contemptuous of Rāghava—'He is just a boy,' I thought—and so I charged headlong at Viśvāmitra's altar.

16. "Then he shot a dart, sharp and murderous, and its impact hurled me into the ocean, a hundred leagues away.

17. "The force of Rāma's arrow carried me far away and dropped me insensible in the bottomless waters of the ocean. When much later I regained consciousness, my friend, I made my way back to the city of Lañkā.

18. "Thus did I escape on that occasion, but my companions were cut down by this 'mere boy, unpracticed in arms,' the tireless Rāma.

19. "So if, despite my warning, you quarrel with Rāma, it will not be long before terrible misfortune befalls you and you perish.

20. "And upon the *rākṣasas*—all of whose care it is to master the sports of lovemaking and hold crowded fairs and festivals—you shall bring down misery and disaster.

21. "On account of Maithilī you shall see Lañkā laid to waste, with its array of mansions and palaces, and all the precious objects that adorn it.

22. "For though they may commit no evil themselves the innocent perish through the evils of their allies, like fish in a pool of snakes.

23. "You shall see the *rākṣasas*, who anoint their bodies with heavenly sandalwood cream and adorn themselves, with heavenly jewelry—you shall see them lying dead upon the ground through no one's fault but your own.

24. "And you shall see the surviving nightstalkers fleeing in the ten directions with their wives—if their wives have not been carried off—and seeking refuge in vain.

25. "Yes, you shall surely see Lañkā enmeshed in a net of arrows, engulfed in fiery flames, its dwellings burnt to cinders.

26. "You have thousands of lovely women in your harem, your

majesty; be content with your own wives, *rākṣasa*, and thus preserve your House.

27. "If you want to continue enjoying your prestige, prosperity, kingship, and your own precious life, give no offense to Rāma.

28. "But if—despite this urgent warning from me, your friend—you still lay violent hands on Sītā, your forces shall be crushed, Rāma's arrows shall take your life, and you and all your kin shall go down to the house of Yama."

The end of the thirty-sixth *sarga* of the *Araṇyakāṇḍa* of the *Śrī Rāmāyaṇa*.

Sarga 37

1. "Thus did I barely escape that day we met in combat. But now hear what happened next.

2. "Although dealt with like this I persisted and returned to Daṇḍaka forest accompanied by two *rākṣasas* in the shape of animals.

3. "I roamed the wilderness of Daṇḍaka as a huge, powerful animal with sharp horns and a flaming tongue, feeding on human flesh.

4. "I roamed among sacrificial sites, places of pilgrimage, and sacred trees, a most dreaded creature, Rāvaṇa, assaulting the ascetics.

5. "Slaughtering the ascetics who followed the ways of righteousness in Daṇḍaka wilderness, I would drink their blood and devour their flesh.

6. "And so, feeding on the flesh of seers, terrifying all who lived in the forest, I roamed through Daṇḍaka, a savage creature drunk on blood.

7–8. "Now once, as I was roaming through Daṇḍaka wilderness, desecrating the ways of righteousness, I again encountered Rāma. He had adopted the life of an ascetic, given to rigorous fasting and devoted to the welfare of all creatures. The beautiful Vaidehī was present, too, and the great chariot-fighter, Lakṣmaṇa.

9. "I felt contempt for mighty Rāma, who was living in the forest: 'He's just an ascetic now,' I thought, remembering our former enmity.

10. "I lowered my sharp horns—I had taken the shape of a beast—and attacked him in a towering rage. I remembered that earlier blow and, fool that I was, sought to kill him.

11. "But he drew his powerful bow and shot three darts, sharp and murderous, and swift as Suparṇa or the wind.

12. "The strong-jointed darts looked like thunderbolts, utterly terrible, blood-drinking things they were, and all three of them came at once.

13. "But knowing Rāma's prowess, having encountered the danger once before, I cunningly dodged them and so escaped. But the other two *rākṣasas* were killed.

14. "Escaping Rāma's arrow, barely saving my life, I wandered off as an ascetic and came to this place, to practice yoga and meditation.

15. "But now behind every tree I seem to see Rāma clad in barkcloth and black hides, wielding his bow like Death himself with noose in hand.

16. "Or rather, thousands of Rāmas do I see in my fear; this whole wilderness, Rāvaṇa, has become nothing but Rāma to me.

17. "It is Rāma I see, lord of *rākṣasas*, even when no one is near; I see him in my dreams and start up, half out of my mind.

18. "I am so terrified of Rāma that even a word beginning with an R—riches, for instance, or roads—fills me with terror, Rāvaṇa.

19. "I know what power Rāma has: It is best not to fight him, *rākṣasa*. But go ahead, do battle or make your peace with him; only do not mention him if you hope to see me anymore.

20. "I say this only for my kinsman's good, for if you fail to heed my words, you and all your kin will surely lose your lives in battle, killed by Rāma's unerring arrows."

The end of the thirty-seventh *sarga* of the *Araṇyakāṇḍa* of the *Śrī Rāmāyaṇa*.

Sarga 38

1. Mārīca had advised him what was best and prudent, but Rāvaṇa rejected it as a man ripe to die rejects his medicine.

2. Mārīca's words were to Rāvaṇa's advantage and benefit, but driven as he was by doom, the reply of the overlord of *rākṣasas* was imprudent and harsh:

3. "What utter nonsense you are telling me, Mārīca; like seed sown in a desert, nothing at all will come of it.

4–5. "You cannot dissuade me from doing battle with Rāma—a man, after all, an evil, foolish man who abandoned his loved ones, his kingship, his mother and father, and went off to the forest at a moment's notice on orders of a mere woman.

6. "No, he killed Khara in battle and come what may I will carry off Sītā, the woman he loves more than life itself. And you shall be present.

7. "My heart is set on it, Mārīca, my mind is made up, and all the gods and *asuras*, Indra included, cannot stop me.

8. "You are to speak thus only when asked to give arguments for and against, or to say what might or might not work, in the course of my deliberations on this matter.

9. "A wise counselor speaks only when asked, raising his hands cupped in reverence—if, that is, he seeks to prosper in the king's regard.

10. "One does not speak in opposition to a king who rules the earth. One offers beneficial advice gently, earnestly, and with courtesy.

11. "But a king does not gladly hear even beneficial advice if it is insulting and disrespectful, for he deserves respect.

12. "The power of kings is infinite, they are able to take on any of five different forms: They can be hot like Agni, god of fire, bold like Indra, or mild like the Moon; they can exact punishment like Yama, or be gracious like Varuṇa.

13. "As a result, kings must be shown respect and honor in all circumstances. But you are ignorant of such usages and bent on a course of sheer madness.

14. "What effrontery, *rākṣasa*, when I am paying a visit, to speak to me so harshly. I did not ask to hear arguments for or against, or to be told what is 'best' for me. In this task you must, and shall, give me your help.

15. "You must become a golden deer dappled with silver spots and entice Vaidehī. Then you are free to do as you please.

16. "When Maithilī sees your magical golden deer form, she will be wonder-struck and at once tell Rāma to capture it.

17. "Then, when Kākutstha and Lakṣmaṇa are gone, I shall abduct Vaidehī at my leisure, just as thousand-eyed Indra once abducted Śacī.

18. "After you have done what I require of you, *rākṣasa*, you are free to do as you please. I shall even bestow half my kingdom upon you, faithful Mārīca.

19. "A safe journey to you, dear friend, and may it lead to the success of our undertaking. When I have tricked Rāghava and gained possession of Sītā without a fight, I shall return with you to Laṅkā, my purpose achieved.

20. "You have no choice but to do what I require; I will force you if I must. He who stands in opposition to a king is forever barred from happiness.

21. "If you encounter Rāma, there is a chance you will lose your life; but if you oppose me, you will die that very instant. Think it over carefully and do what is for your good."

The end of the thirty-eighth *sarga* of the *Araṇyakāṇḍa* of the *Śrī Rāmāyaṇa*.

Sarga 39

1. When the nightstalker Mārīca had been given his orders, royal orders however perverse, he made this harsh reply to the overlord of *rākṣasas*:

2. "Who could have been so wicked, nightstalker, as to counsel the destruction of your sons and kingdom, your ministers and yourself?

3. "Who could have been so wicked as to resent your happiness? Who has treacherously advised you to open wide the doors of death?

4. "It is only too clear that your rivals, powerless themselves, hope

you will perish, nightstalker, before the onslaught of one far mightier.

5. "Who has been so low as to give you this bad advice, nightstalker, in hopes that you might perish by your own doing?

6. "How can you not put to death those advisers, Rāvaṇa, who are guilty of not doing all they could to prevent your veering from the proper course?

7. "Good ministers must at all costs prevent a wayward king from taking an evil course. Yet you were not prevented, as you should have been.

8. "It is through their master's grace, your highness, that advisers acquire what righteousness, profit, pleasure, and glory they may have.

9. "But all this counts for nothing, Rāvaṇa, should their master go astray; and if he loses his sense of virtue, all the people come to grief.

10. "For kings are the source of both righteousness and victory, your highness. Therefore, he who is lord of men must be protected in all circumstances.

11. "But the brutal man will not safeguard a king's position, nightstalker, nor will the perverse or undisciplined man.

12. "For the king and with him all those advisers who counsel brutal measures are quickly overthrown, like a chariot driven down a rough road by a reckless charioteer.

13. "And as so often happens in the world, the good, who mind their own business, perish with all that is theirs through the faults of others.

14. "Subjects benefit from the protection of a perverse and brutal master, Rāvaṇa, as little as sheep from that of a jackal.

15. "The *rākṣasas* shall inevitably perish, Rāvaṇa, all who follow you as king, their cruel, imprudent, intemperate king.

16. "You are bringing down upon your head dreadful, unfathomable disaster. What good is there in perishing with your army?

17. "For soon after killing me, Rāma will slay you, though I at least will find fulfillment in dying at the hand of my enemy.

18. "Consider me dead the instant Rāma sets eyes on me, and know that you yourself and all your kin are dead the moment you carry off Sītā.

19. "If with my help you abduct Sītā from the ashram, you are doomed, we both are doomed, and Laṅkā and all the *rākṣasas*.

20. "I have your best interests at heart, nightstalker, in giving you this warning, yet you ignore my words. But then, no man on the point of death will heed his friends' advice."

The end of the thirty-ninth *sarga* of the *Araṇyakāṇḍa* of the *Śrī Rāmāyaṇa*.

Sarga 40

1. So Mārīca spoke, but for all his harsh talk he stood in dread of the lord of nightstalkers. Wretchedly, then, he said to Rāvaṇa, "Well, let us go.

2. "The instant Rāma sets eyes on me again, raises his sword, his bow and arrow, or some other weapon to slay me, my life is at an end.

3. "But what can I do in the face of such perversity as yours? So here, I am coming, my friend. I wish you well, nightstalker."

4. The *rākṣasa* was delighted by his words, and embracing him warmly, he said:

5. "There are the brave words I had hoped to hear from you. You were some other nightstalker a moment ago; now you are Mārīca.

6. "Here stands my flying chariot, studded with jewels and harnessed with asses, their faces like those of *piśācas*. Come aboard with me at once."

7. Rāvaṇa and Mārīca then boarded the palatial chariot and at once left the circle of ashrams behind.

8–9. And so, viewing the towns far below, the expanses of forest, the mountains, streams, kingdoms, and cities, they arrived in due course in Daṇḍaka wilderness. And then Mārīca and Rāvaṇa, overlord of *rākṣasas*, beheld the ashram of Rāghava.

10. Alighting from the gilded chariot, Rāvaṇa took Mārīca by the hand and said:

11. "What you see here, surrounded by plantain trees, is the site of Rāma's ashram. Quickly now, my friend, do what we came here to do."

12. Hearing Rāvaṇa's words, the *rākṣasa* Mārīca turned himself into a deer and began to graze near the entrance to Rāma's ashram.

13–16. The deer's horns were tipped with rare gems, his face mottled dark and light, one part like pink lotuses and the other like blue. His ears were like sapphires or blue lotuses, his neck gently elongated, his belly gleaming sapphire. His flanks were like the pale, velvety *madhūka* flower, the rest golden lotus shoots, and his hooves glowed cat's-eye beryl. He was slim and slender of leg, and brilliantly crowned with a tail tinged with every color of the rainbow. He was studded with all sorts of precious stones that lent him a glossy and captivating hue. In an instant the *rākṣasa* had changed himself into this magnificent deer.

17–18. It was a lovely and captivating form, sparkling with all its precious metals, that the *rākṣasa* assumed to entice Vaidehī. And shedding a brilliant radiance over the forest and Rāma's ashram, he duly went grazing in the meadows all around.

19. Dappled with hundreds of silver spots, a lovely sight to see, he grazed among the trees, breaking off and nibbling the tender shoots.

20. Back and forth he went to the plantain grove and among the *karṇikāra* trees, at a slow pace, trying to catch Sītā's eye.

21. What a brilliant spectacle the great deer made, with his back the hue of blue lilies, as he leisurely grazed in the vicinity of Rāma's ashram.

22. Going back and forth, appearing suddenly here and suddenly there, the splendid deer went grazing.

23. One moment he would frisk about, then lie upon the ground; he would approach the ashram's entrance and then withdraw amid a herd of deer.

24. And once more he would return with the other deer following behind, hoping Sītā would notice him, this *rākṣasa* become a deer.

25–26ab. He gamboled about, meandering in graceful circles.

Other forest animals stared at him, came close and sniffed, and then all scampered off in every direction.

26cd–27ab. For he was still a *rākṣasa*, of course, who liked nothing more than killing animals. But to hide his true nature he did not eat these forest animals, though they were close enough to touch.

27cd–28ab. At this very moment, lovely eyed Vaidehī, busily picking flowers, came out beyond the trees.

28cd–29ab. The fair-faced woman with flashing eyes wandered about picking flowers, *karṇikāra*, *aśoka*, and mango flowers.

29cd–ef. The beautiful lady, not meant for life in the wilderness, caught sight of the jewel-studded deer, his limbs sparkling with gems and pearls.

30. She with her sparkling teeth and ruby lips stood there, eyes blossoming with wonder, staring longingly at the deer and his hide of silvery metal.

31. And the magical deer saw Rāma's beloved, too, and stopped to graze there, illuminating, it seemed, all the forest.

32. And when Sītā, daughter of Janaka, saw that jewel-studded deer, the likes of which no one had ever seen before, she stood lost in sheer wonder.

The end of the fortieth *sarga* of the *Araṇyakāṇḍa* of the *Śrī Rāmāyaṇa*.

Sarga 41

1–2. The flawless beauty with full hips and a complexion of polished gold was picking flowers when she spotted the deer with his beautiful flanks of gold and silver hue. In delight she cried out to her husband and to Lakṣmaṇa, who stood armed and ready.

3. Rāma and Lakṣmaṇa, those tigers among men, glanced up in Vaidehī's direction at her call, and saw the deer.

4. Seeing him Lakṣmaṇa at once became suspicious and said to Rāma, "I am sure that deer is none other than the *rākṣasa* Mārīca.

5. "When kings who delight in the hunt enter the forest, Rāma, this evil creature, who can take on any form at will, assumes this or that disguise and kills them.

6. "He knows magic, tiger among men, and this is the magic form of a deer he has taken on, as dazzling to the eye as a mirage.

7. "For nowhere in all the world, Rāghava, master of the world, does there exist such a deer, sparkling with gems. I am certain this is magic."

8. But even as Kākutstha was speaking thus, bright-smiling Sītā interrupted—the deception had taken her reason away—and said in great delight:

9. "Dear husband, what an exquisite deer! He has stolen my heart away. Please catch him for me, my great-armed husband. He shall be our plaything.

10–11. "Here at our ashram many beautiful animals come wandering in droves: yaks and antelope, apes, herds of spotted gazelle, monkeys, and *kinnaras*. Lovely and powerful animals are always grazing here, my great-armed husband.

12. "But never before have we seen an animal such as this, your majesty, none so brilliant, tame, and radiant as this magnificent deer.

13. "His body sparkles with different colors and is speckled with chips of precious stones; he illuminates the entire forest, shining like the hare-marked moon.

14. "What coloring, what beauty, what sweet sounds he makes. He has utterly stolen my heart away, this amazing, sparkling deer.

15. "If you can catch him alive the deer will be a thing to marvel at, a source of wonder.

16. "And when our sojourn in the forest has ended and we are back in the kingdom once again, this deer will adorn the women's quarters.

17. "The heavenly form of this deer will be a source of wonder for Bharata, my brother-in-law, and for my mothers-in-law as well, my lord.

18. "But if you cannot catch the splendid deer alive, tiger among men, then his hide would be a source of great pleasure to me.

19. "Were the creature to be killed, I should like his golden skin to be stretched over a cushion of straw, to make a seat.

20. "You might think it willful, heartless, or unladylike of me, but I am so filled with wonder at the beauty of this creature.

21. "Even the mind of Rāghava is lost in wonder at the sight of him; with his golden hide and horns of precious gems, he shows all the brilliance of the morning sun, all the luster of the starry heavens."

22. When Rāghava heard these words of Sītā's and looked at the amazing deer, he addressed his brother Lakṣmaṇa in delight:

23. "Just see how Vaidehī longs to have this deer, Lakṣmaṇa. Because of his surpassing beauty he shall die today.

24. "Not in the renowned forest of Nandana, nor in famous Caitraratha, let alone on earth, Saumitri, is any such deer to be found.

25. "The lovely patterns on the deer's pelt, both with the nap and against it, are brilliantly flecked with chips of gold.

26. "Look how when he yawns his gleaming, flamelike tongue darts from his mouth like lightning from a cloud.

27. "His face gleams with sapphire and crystal, his belly glows with conch shell and pearl. Indeed, this indescribable deer could beguile the heart of anyone.

28. "Anyone would be lost in wonder to see this heavenly form fashioned of every precious stone, glittering like gold.

29. "Both for meat and sport, Lakṣmaṇa, kings armed with bows go hunting and kill animals in the deep forest.

30. "In the deep forests they gather riches with determination, precious metals of all sorts, veined with gems and gold.

31. "But here is all the wealth a man could ask for, Lakṣmaṇa, riches enough to swell his coffers, just as Śukra's coffers come to be swelled with all the wealth men dream of.

32. "Those who know the theory behind material success and those who achieve it, Lakṣmaṇa, say a man in want of something should go and get it without hesitation.

33. "Yes, fair-waisted Vaidehī shall seat herself next to me upon the precious golden hide of this rare deer.

34. "There is no hide, I should think—antelope's or gazelle's, goat's or ewe's—that could be so soft to the touch.

35. "This majestic deer and the heavenly deer that roams the sky are both of them heavenly—that deer of the stars and this deer of the earth.

36. "Then again, if it turns out to be 'the magic of that *rākṣasa*,' as you tell me, Lakṣmaṇa, then it is my duty to slay him.

37. "For the savage, impious Mārīca used to roam the forests injuring the bulls among sages.

38. "He has killed many a king and expert bowman out hunting, and so this deer, if it be he, must be slain.

39. "Once upon a time Vātāpi lived in this place. He had utter contempt for ascetic brahmans and would kill them from within their stomachs, as her foal will kill a she-mule when it comes to be born.

40. "But finally one day he met up with the greatest sage in the world, the mighty Agastya. As usual he had himself served up to him as food.

41. "At the conclusion of the feast the holy one perceived that Vātāpi was about to assume his true form again. Smiling slyly he said to him:

42. " 'It was reckless of you, Vātāpi, to show such mighty contempt to the best twice-born in this mortal world. And for that you are now to be digested.'

43. "Just as happened with Vātāpi, Lakṣmaṇa, no *rākṣasa* can hope to live that treats with scorn someone like me, who is constant in righteousness and self-controlled.

44ab. "Now that he has fallen into my hands I will slay him, just as Agastya slew Vātāpi.

44cd–45ab. "But you must remain here to protect Maithilī, armed and on your guard, delight of the Raghus. For our first responsibility is to her.

45cd–46ab. "I intend to go at once, Saumitri, and bring back the deer dead or alive.

46cd–47ab. "Just see how Vaidehī longs for the hide of this deer, Lakṣmaṇa. And because of his splendid hide the deer shall die today.

47cd–48. "Stay in the ashram with Sītā, Lakṣmaṇa, and be on your guard. I intend to kill the dappled deer with my first shot, and afterward skin him and come straight back.

49. "With the aid of wise Jaṭāyus, the capable and all-powerful bird, take care of Maithilī. Be on your guard every moment, Lakṣmaṇa, and suspicious of everything."

The end of the forty-first *sarga* of the *Araṇyakāṇḍa* of the *Śrī Rāmāyaṇa*.

Sarga 42

1. After instructing his brother the mighty prince, delight of the Raghus, strapped on his gold-hilted sword.

2. He then strapped on a pair of quivers and took up his proper ornament—the bow with triple curve—and set off at a rapid pace.

3. The deer spied the lord of kings rushing toward him and he led him on, now timorously hiding, now showing himself again.

4. With sword strapped on and taking up his bow, Rāma ran toward the deer, imagining he saw his form shimmering before him.

5–6. At one moment he would spot him running through the deep forest, temptingly near, and would take his bow in hand, only to look once more and find the deer beyond the range of his arrow. In one stretch of forest he came into sight leaping through the air in frightful panic, and then he passed into another stretch and out of sight.

7. Like the disk of the autumn moon veiled in tatters of cloud, he was seen one instant and gone the next.

8. Now appearing, now disappearing, he drew Rāghava far away, and helplessly deluded by him Kākutstha flew into a rage.

9. Then the deer halted in exhaustion and withdrew to a shady spot in the meadow, not far away, where Rāma spotted him surrounded by other animals of the forest.

10. Seeing the deer mighty Rāma was determined to kill him. The powerful prince nocked his sturdy bow and drew it back with power.

11. Aiming at the deer he shot a gleaming, flaming arrow fashioned by Brahmā that glared like a snake as it darted forth.

12. The supreme arrow penetrated the illusory deer form and like a bolt of lightning pierced the heart, Mārīca's heart.

13. The deer leaped high as a palm tree and with a ghastly shriek fell to the ground, tormented by the arrow, his life ebbing away. And as Mārīca lay there dying, the shape he had assumed began to disappear.

14. Knowing the time had come, in Rāghava's own voice he cried out, "Oh Sītā! Oh Lakṣmaṇa!"

15. Pierced to the quick by an arrow unlike any other, Mārīca once more took on the form of a massive *rākṣasa*, giving up the deer form and his life.

16. Struck by the arrow, he became a *rākṣasa* once more, with huge fangs, a necklace of gold, sparkling earrings, and every other ornament to adorn him.

17. Seeing that dreadful sight, the *rākṣasa* fallen on the ground, Rāma thought suddenly of Sītā and recalled what Lakṣmaṇa had said.

18. "With his dying breath this *rākṣasa* cried out at the top of his voice, 'Oh Sītā! Oh Lakṣmaṇa!' How will Sītā react to hearing this?

19. "And great-armed Lakṣmaṇa, what will be his state of mind?" As these thoughts came to righteous Rāma, the hair on his body bristled with dread.

20. Then Rāma's consternation gave way to a feeling of fear that shot through him with sharp pangs: The deer he had slain was in fact a *rākṣasa*, the voice it had used was his own.

21. He killed another dappled deer and taking the meat hurriedly retraced his steps to Janasthāna.

The end of the forty-second *sarga* of the *Araṇyakāṇḍa* of the *Śrī Rāmāyaṇa.*

Sarga 43

1. Now, when Sītā heard that cry of distress, in her husband's own voice, coming from the forest, she said to Lakṣmaṇa, "Go and find out what has happened to Rāghava.

2. "My heart—my very life—is jarred from its place by the sound of his crying in deep distress that I heard so clearly.

3–4. "You must rescue your brother, who cries out in the forest. Run to your brother at once, for he needs help! The *rākṣasas* have him in their power, like a bull fallen among lions." So she spoke, but Lakṣmaṇa, heeding his brother's command, did not go.

5–6. Then the daughter of Janaka angrily said to him, "You wear the guise of a friend to your brother, Saumitri, but act like his foe, refusing to aid him in his extremity. You hope Rāma perishes, Lakṣmaṇa, isn't that so? And it is all because of me.

7. "I think you would be happy should some disaster befall your brother. You have no real affection for him, so you stand there calmly with the splendid prince gone from sight.

8. "For with him in danger and me here, how could I prevent what you came here with the sole intention of doing?"

9. So Sītā, princess of Videha, spoke, overwhelmed with tears and grief, and Lakṣmaṇa replied to her as she stood there frightened as a doe.

10–11. "My lady, there is no one, god or man, *gandharva*, great bird, or *rākṣasa*, *piśāca*, *kinnara*, beast, or dreaded *dānava*—no one, fair lady, who could match Rāma, the peer of Vāsava, in battle.

12. "Rāma cannot be killed in battle. You must not talk this way, for I dare not leave you in the forest with Rāghava gone.

13. "His power cannot be withstood, not by any powers however vast, not by all three worlds up in arms, or the deathless gods themselves, their lord included.

14. "Let your heart rest easy, do not be alarmed. Your husband will soon return, after killing that splendid deer.

15. "That was clearly not his voice, or any belonging to a god. It was the magic of that *rākṣasa*, unreal as a mirage.

16. "You were entrusted to my safekeeping, shapely Vaidehī, by the great Rāma. I dare not leave you here alone.

17. "Then too, dear lady, because of the slaughter at Janasthāna, where Khara perished, we have earned the hostility of the night-stalkers.

18. "*Rākṣasas* delight in causing trouble, Vaidehī, they make all kinds of noises in the deep forest. You need not worry."

19. Though what he said was true, Sītā was enraged by Lakṣmaṇa's words. Her eyes blazed bright red as she made this harsh reply:

20. "Ignoble, cruel man, disgrace to your House! How pitiful this attempt of yours. I feel certain you are pleased with all this, and that is why you can talk the way you do.

21. "It is nothing new, Lakṣmaṇa, for rivals to be so evil, cruel rivals like you always plotting in secret.

22. "You treacherously followed Rāma to the forest, the two of you alone: You are either in the employ of Bharata or secretly plotting to get me.

23. "I am married to Rāma, a husband dark as a lotus, with eyes like lotus petals. How could I ever give my love to some ordinary man?

24. "I would not hesitate to take my life before your very eyes, Saumitri, for I could not live upon this earth one moment without Rāma."

25. Such were the words Sītā spoke to Lakṣmaṇa, so harsh they made his hair bristle with horror. But he controlled himself, and with hands cupped in reverence he addressed her:

26. "I dare not answer, Maithilī, for you are a deity in my eyes. And yet inappropriate words from a woman come as nothing new.

27. "This is the nature of women the whole world over: Women care nothing for righteousness, they are flighty, sharp-tongued, and divisive.

28. "May all the inhabitants of the forest give ear and bear me witness how my words of reason met so harsh a reply from you.

29. "Curse you and be damned, that you could so suspect me, when I am only following the orders of my guru. How like a woman to be so perverse!

30. "I am going to Kākutstha. I wish you well, fair woman. May the spirits of the forest, each and every one, protect you, large-eyed lady.

31. "How ominous the portents that manifest themselves to me! I pray I find you here when I return with Rāma."

32. Now, when Lakṣmaṇa addressed her in this fashion, Janaka's daughter began to weep. Overwhelmed with tears she hotly replied:

33. "Parted from Rāma I will drown myself in the Godāvarī, Lakṣmaṇa, I will hang myself or hurl my body upon some rocky place.

34. "Or I will drink deadly poison or throw myself into a blazing fire. I would never touch any man but Rāghava, not even with my foot!"

35. Such were the insults Sītā hurled at Lakṣmaṇa in her sorrow, and sorrowfully she wept and struck her belly with her fists.

36. At the sight of large-eyed Sītā so deeply anguished and weeping, Saumitri was beside himself and tried to comfort her, but she would say nothing more to her husband's brother.

37. Then, cupping his hands in reverence and bowing slightly, Lakṣmaṇa, the self-respecting prince, said goodbye to Sītā. And as he set forth to find Rāma, he turned around again and again and looked back at Maithilī.

The end of the forty-third *sarga* of the *Araṇyakāṇḍa* of the *Śrī Rāmāyaṇa*.

Sarga 44

1. Rāghava's younger brother, angered by her harsh words and sorely longing for Rāma, set forth without further delay.

2. This was the opening ten-necked Rāvaṇa had been waiting for, and he took advantage of it at once. Assuming the guise of a wandering mendicant, he turned his steps toward Vaidehī.

3. Clad in a soft saffron robe, with topknot, parasol, and sandals, and goodly staff and water pitcher hanging at his left shoulder—disguised like this, as a mendicant—he approached Vaidehī.

4. Both brothers had left her, and in his pride of power he advanced upon her, like total darkness advancing upon the twilight, when both sun and moon have left.

5. He gazed at the glorious young princess as ominously as a planet might gaze upon the star Rohiṇī when the hare-marked moon is absent.

6. At the appearance of the dreaded, evil creature, the trees that grew in Janasthāna stopped rustling and the wind died down.

7. At the sight of him peering around with his blood-red eyes, the swift current of the Godāvarī river began to slacken in fear.

8. Ten-necked Rāvaṇa had waited for an opening, and Rāma had given him one. In the guise of a beggar he drew near to Vaidehī.

9. As Vaidehī sat grieving for her husband, the unholy Rāvaṇa in the guise of a holy man edged closer to her, like the sluggish planet, Saturn, closing in on Citrā, the sparkling star.

10–11. Like a deep well concealed by grass, the evil one in the guise of a holy man stood watching Vaidehī, illustrious wife of Rāma—the beautiful woman with lovely teeth and lips, and a face like the full moon—as she sat in the leaf hut tormented with grief and tears.

12. The blackhearted stalker of the night stole ever closer to Vaidehī, the woman dressed in garments of yellow silk, and with eyes like lotus petals.

13. With arrows of Manmatha, god of love, lodged deep within his heart, and the sounds of the *vedas* on his lips, the overlord of *rākṣasas* appeared before the deserted hut and courteously spoke.

14. Rāvaṇa began singing her praises, that loveliest of women in the three worlds, a radiant beauty, like the goddess Śrī herself without the lotus.

15. "Who are you, golden woman dressed in garments of yellow silk, wearing a lovely lotus garland, and like a lotus pond yourself?

16. "Are you the goddess Modesty or Fame? Are you Śrī or lovely Lakṣmī or perhaps an *apsaras*, lovely lady? Could you be Prosperity, shapely woman, or easygoing Pleasure?

17. "Your teeth are bright white, tapered, and even; your eyes are large and clear, rosy at the corner, black in the center.

18–19. "Your hips are full and broad, your thighs smooth as an elephant's trunk. And these, your delightful breasts, how round they are, so firm and gently heaving; how full and lovely, smooth as two palm fruits, with their nipples standing stiff and the rarest gems to adorn them.

20. "Graceful lady with your lovely smile, lovely teeth, and lovely

eyes, you have swept my heart away like a river in flood that sweeps away its banks.

21. "Your waist I could compass with my fingers; how fine is your hair, how firm your breasts. No goddess, no *gandharva* woman, no *yakṣa* or *kinnara* woman, no mortal woman so beautiful have I ever seen before on the face of this earth.

22. "Your beauty, unrivaled in all the worlds, your delicacy and youth, and the fact of your living here in the woods stir the deepest feelings in me.

23. "I urge you to go home, this is no place for you to be living. For this is the lair of dreaded *rākṣasas*, who can change their form at will.

24. "In the most delightful palaces, in luxuriant, fragrant city gardens is where you should be strolling.

25. "To my mind you deserve the finest garlands and beverages and raiment, and the finest husband, lovely black-eyed lady.

26. "Could you be one of the Rudras or Maruts, sweet-smiling, shapely woman, or one of the Vasus, perhaps? You look like a goddess to me.

27. "But *gandharvas* do not pass this way, nor do gods or *kinnaras*, for this is the lair of *rākṣasas*. How is it you have come here?

28. "There are monkeys here, lions, panthers, and tigers, apes, hyenas, and flesh-eating birds. How is it you do not fear them?

29. "And the dreaded elephants that go running wild, maddened by rut—how is it you do not fear them, lovely lady, all alone in the deep wilderness?

30. "Who are you, to whom do you belong, where do you come from, my precious, and why are you wandering all alone through Daṇḍaka, the haunt of dreaded *rākṣasas*?"

31. Such was the praise evil Rāvaṇa lavished on Vaidehī. But seeing he had come in the garb of a brahman, Maithilī honored him with all the acts of hospitality due a guest.

32. First she brought forward a cushion and offered water for his feet, and then she called him when food was ready, for he looked kindly enough.

33. When Maithilī observed that he had come in the garb of a twice-born—a brahman with a begging bowl and saffron robe; when she saw these accoutrements, it was impossible to refuse him, and so she extended him an invitation befitting a brahman.

34. "Here is a cushion, brahman, please be seated and accept this water for your feet. Here I have made ready for you the best fare the forest has to offer. You may partake of it freely."

35. So Maithilī extended him a cordial invitation, and as Rāvaṇa gazed at her, the wife of the lord of men, he confirmed his resolve to take her by force, and with that, consigned himself to death.

36. Her husband in his honest garb had gone to hunt the magic deer, and she waited for him and Lakṣmaṇa, scanning the horizon. But she saw neither Rāma nor Lakṣmaṇa—only the deep, green forest.

The end of the forty-fourth *sarga* of the *Araṇyakāṇḍa* of the *Śrī Rāmāyaṇa*.

Sarga 45

1. When Rāvaṇa came in the guise of a mendicant to carry off Vaidehī, he had first put some questions to her. Of her own accord she now began to tell her story.

2. For Sītā had thought a moment: "He is a brahman and my guest. If I do not reply he will curse me." She then spoke these words:

3. "I am the daughter of Janaka, the great king of Mithilā. My name is Sītā, may it please the best of twice-born, and I am the wife of Rāma.

4. "For twelve years I lived in the house of Rāghava, enjoying such pleasures as mortals enjoy. I had all I could desire.

5. "Then, in the thirteenth year, the king in concert with his kingly counselors approved the royal consecration of my husband.

6. "But just as the preparations for Rāghava's consecration were under way, a mother-in-law of mine named Kaikeyī asked her husband for a boon.

7. "You see, Kaikeyī had already married my father-in-law for a

consideration. So she had two things she now could ask of her husband, the best of kings and a man who always kept his word: One was the consecration of Bharata, the other, my husband's banishment.

8. " 'From this day forth I will not eat, or drink, or sleep, I will put an end to my life if Rāma is consecrated.'

9. "Such were Kaikeyī's words, and though my father-in-law, who had always shown her respect, begged her with offers of commensurate riches, she would not do what he begged of her.

10ab–874*. "Rāma, my mighty husband, was then twenty-five years old, and I had just passed my eighteenth birthday.

10cd–ef. "His name is renowned throughout the world, his eyes are large, his arms strong. He is virtuous, honest, truthful, and devoted to the welfare of all people.

11. "When Rāma came into his father's presence for the consecration to begin, it was Kaikeyī who addressed my husband, in a rush of words:

12. " 'Listen to me, Rāghava, and hear what your father has decreed. The kingship is to be given to Bharata uncontested.

13. " 'As for you, you are to live in the forest for nine years and five. Go into banishment, Kākutstha, and save your father from falsehood.'

14. "Without a trace of fear my husband Rāma answered Kaikeyī, 'So be it,' and in firm compliance with his vow did just as she had told him.

15. "For Rāma has taken a solemn vow, brahman, one never to be broken: always to give and not receive, to tell the truth and not lie.

16. "Rāma has a constant companion, his half brother Lakṣmaṇa, a tiger among men and mighty slayer of enemies in battle.

17. "This brother Lakṣmaṇa, who keeps to the ways of righteousness, firm in his vows, followed bow in hand when Rāma went into banishment with me.

18. "And so the three of us were driven from the kingdom for the sake of Kaikeyī. Thus it is under compulsion, best of twice-born, that we now wander the dense forest.

19. "Rest a moment; or you can even pass the night here if you like. My husband will soon return bringing an abundance of food from the forest.

20. "But can you just tell me your name, your clan, and family? How is it that you, a brahman, wander all alone in Daṇḍaka wilderness?"

21. So Sītā, wife of Rāma, spoke, and powerful Rāvaṇa, overlord of *rākṣasas*, made a reply that froze her blood:

22. "I am he who terrifies the worlds, with all their gods, *asuras*, and great serpents. I am Rāvaṇa, Sītā, supreme lord of the hosts of *rākṣasas*.

23. "Now that I have set eyes on you, flawless, golden lady dressed in silk, I shall no longer take any pleasure in my own wives.

24. "From one place and another I have carried off many splendid women. May it please you to become chief queen over every one of them.

25. "In the middle of the ocean lies my vast city Laṅkā, perched upon a mountain peak and ringed by the sea.

26. "There, my radiant Sītā, you shall stroll with me through the forests, never longing for this life you are leading in the wilderness.

27. "Five thousand slave women all adorned with ornaments shall wait upon you hand and foot, Sītā, if you become my wife."

28. So Rāvaṇa spoke, but Janaka's daughter, that faultless beauty, angrily and with utter contempt for the *rākṣasa* replied:

29. "I am faithful to Rāma, my husband, the equal of great Indra, unshakable as a great mountain, imperturbable as the great sea.

30. "I am faithful to Rāma, the great-armed, great-chested prince, who moves with the boldness of a lion, a lionlike man, a lion among men.

31. "I am faithful to Rāma, the king's most cherished son, a great-armed, mighty prince of wide renown and strict self-control, whose face is like the full moon.

32. "As for you, you are a jackal in the presence of a lioness, to come here seeking me, whom you can never have. You could no more touch me than touch the radiance of the sun.

33. "You must be seeing many a golden tree of death, ill-fated Rāvaṇa, if you seek to gain the beloved wife of Rāghava.

34. "You are seeking to pluck the fang from the mouth of a poisonous snake, the tooth from the mouth of a hungry lion in pursuit, the foe to all beasts.

35. "You are seeking to carry off Mandara, greatest of mountains, in your hand, to drink the *kālakūṭa* poison and take no harm of it.

36. "You are rubbing your eye with a needle, licking a razor with your tongue, if you seek to violate the beloved wife of Rāghava.

37. "You are seeking to cross the ocean with a boulder tied around your neck, to take into your hands the very sun and moon, if you seek to assault the beloved wife of Rāghava.

38. "You have seen a blazing fire and seek to carry it away in a cloth, if you seek to carry off the virtuous wife of Rāma.

39. "You are seeking to walk atop a row of iron-headed spears, if you seek to violate the proper wife of Rāma.

40. "As different as a lion and a jackal in the forest, the ocean and a ditch, rare wine and gruel, so different are Dāśarathi and you.

41. "As different as gold and lead, sandalwood paste and slime, a bull elephant and a cat in the forest, so different are Dāśarathi and you.

42. "As different as Garuḍa, the son of Vinatā, and a crow, a peacock and a gull, a vulture and a crane in the forest, so different are Dāśarathi and you.

43. "As long as Rāma walks the earth, mighty as thousand-eyed Indra, armed with his bow and arrow, you may take me but could never enjoy me, no more than a fly the diamond chip it swallows."

44. Such were the words the good woman addressed to the evil nightstalker, but a shudder passed through her body, and she began to quiver like a slender plantain tree tossed by the wind.

45. And when Rāvaṇa, mighty as Death himself, observed how Sītā was trembling, he thought to frighten her still further by telling of his House, his power, the name he had won for himself, and the deeds he had done.

The end of the forty-fifth *sarga* of the *Araṇyakāṇḍa* of the *Śrī Rāmāyaṇa*.

Sarga 46

1. Even as Sītā was speaking in this manner, Rāvaṇa flew into a passion, and knitting his brow into a frown he harshly replied:

2. "I am half brother to Vaiśravaṇa, lovely lady. My name is Rāvaṇa, if you please, the mighty ten-necked one.

3. "In fear of me the gods, *gandharvas*, *piśācas*, great birds, and serpents flee in terror, as all things born are put to flight by fear of Death.

4. "In connection with some issue between us Vaiśravaṇa, my half brother, and I came into conflict. In a rage I attacked and defeated him in battle.

5. "Tormented by fear of me he left his own prosperous realm and now dwells on Kailāsa, highest of mountains, with only men to convey him.

6. "For the aerial chariot that flies where one desires, the lovely Puṣpaka, once belonged to him. But I took it by force of arms, my beauty, and now ride upon it through the sky.

7. "At the mere sight of my face, Maithilī, once my anger has been provoked, the gods with Indra at their head flee in terror.

8. "In my presence the wind blows cautiously, and the sun's hot rays turn cold in fear.

9. "The leaves on the trees stop rustling, and the rivers slacken their current wherever I am, wherever I go.

10. "On the further shore of the ocean lies my lovely city, Laṅkā, grand as Indra's Amarāvatī, thronged with dreaded *rākṣasas*.

11. "It is a lovely, dazzling city ringed by a white rampart, with gateways made of gold and towers of cat's-eye beryl.

12. "It is crowded with elephants, horses, and chariots, the sound of pipes resounds there, and its gardens are beautiful, filled with trees bearing any fruit one wants.

13. "Living there with me, proud princess Sītā, you shall forget what it was like to have been a mortal woman.

14. "Enjoying not only the pleasures mortals enjoy, lovely lady, but divine pleasures, too, you shall soon forget that short-lived mortal, Rāma.

15. "So meager is his power that King Daśaratha, in order to enthrone a favored son, was able to drive him into the forest, firstborn though he was.

16. "What use is this witless Rāma to you, large-eyed woman, a miserable ascetic who lets himself be deposed from the kingship?

17. "The lord of all *rākṣasas* has come here in person, of his own accord. Do not reject him, whom the arrows of Manmatha, god of love, have so badly wounded.

18. "For if you do reject me, timid lady, you shall live to regret it, just like Urvaśī after she spurned Purūravas."

19. So he spoke, but Vaidehī was overcome with rage—her eyes grew red, and though all alone in that deserted spot, she made this harsh reply to the lord of *rākṣasas*:

20. "How can you want to commit such an outrage, you who claim Vaiśravaṇa as brother, a god to whom all beings pay homage?

21. "The *rākṣasas* shall inevitably perish, Rāvaṇa, all who have you for their king, a cruel, imprudent, intemperate king.

22. "A man might abduct Indra's wife, Śacī herself, and still hope to save his life, but he who carries me off, the wife of Rāma, has no life left to save.

23. "One might steal the incomparable Śacī from the hand that wields the thunderbolt and long remain alive. But violate a woman like me, *rākṣasa*, and even drinking the nectar of immortality will be no escape for you."

The end of the forty-sixth *sarga* of the *Araṇyakāṇḍa* of the *Śrī Rāmāyaṇa*.

Sarga 47

1. Hearing Sītā's words the awesome ten-necked Rāvaṇa struck his hands together and made ready to assume his massive form.

2. Again he addressed Maithilī, and far more severely than before: "It seems you did not hear, madwoman, when I spoke of my strength and valor.

3. "I can lift the earth in my arms while standing in the sky; I can drink up the ocean, I can slay Death in battle.

4. "I can shatter the earth with my sharp arrows, madwoman, or bring the sun to a halt. I can take on any form at will. You see before you a husband ready to grant your every wish."

5. And as Rāvaṇa spoke thus in his wild rage, his yellow-rimmed eyes turned fiery red.

6. Then suddenly Rāvaṇa, younger brother to Vaiśravaṇa, abandoned the kindly form of beggar and assumed his true shape, one such as Doom itself must have.

7. With eyes flaming bright red, with earrings of burnished gold, with bow and arrows, he became once more the majestic ten-faced stalker of the night.

8. He had thrown off the guise of mendicant and assumed his own form again, the colossal shape of Rāvaṇa, overlord of *rākṣasas*.

9–10. With eyes flaming bright red in his rage, lowering like a bank of storm clouds, clad in a red garment Rāvaṇa stood before Maithilī, staring at her, perfect jewel of a woman, with her jet-black hair, her sunlike radiance, and the fine clothes and ornaments that she wore. And he said:

11. "If you seek a husband whose fame has spread throughout the three worlds, shapely woman, be mine. I am a lord worthy of you.

12. "Love me forever. I shall be a lover to win your praise, and never, my beauty, will I do anything to displease you. Give up this love for a mortal being, and bestow your love on me.

13. "What possible virtues could make you love this short-lived Rāma, a failure, stripped of kingship? You think you are so smart, but what a fool you really are!

14. "He is a simpleton, who at the bidding of a woman abandoned his kingdom and loved ones to come and live in this forest, the haunt of wild beasts."

15. And so speaking to Sītā, princess of Mithilā, who deserved the same kindness she always showed others, Rāvaṇa seized her as the planet Budha might seize the star Rohiṇī in the sky.

16. With his left hand he seized lotus-eyed Sītā by her hair and with his right hand by her thighs.

17. With his long arms and sharp fangs he resembled a mountain

peak; seeing him advancing like Death himself, the spirits of the forest fled overpowered by fear.

18. Then with a dreadful rumble Rāvaṇa's great chariot came into view, that unearthly chariot fashioned by magic, with wheels of gold, and harnessed with asses.

19. With loud, harsh threats he then clutched Vaidehī to his breast and boarded the chariot.

20. Caught in Rāvaṇa's grip and wild with despair, the glorious Sītā screamed at the top of her voice, crying, "Rāma!" But Rāma was far away in the forest.

21. Filled with desire for one who was filled with loathing for him, Rāvaṇa flew up holding her writhing like a serpent queen.

22. As the lord of *rākṣasas* carried her off through the sky, she screamed shrilly like a woman gone mad, in agony, or delirious:

23. "Oh great-armed Lakṣmaṇa, you have always sought favor with your guru. Don't you know that I am being carried off by a *rākṣasa,* who can change his form at will?

24. "And you, Rāghava, you renounced all life's pleasures, everything of value, for the sake of righteousness. Don't you see me being carried off in defiance of all that is right?

25. "And surely, slayer of enemies, you are the one to discipline wrongdoers. Why then don't you punish so evil a creature as Rāvaṇa?

26. "But no, the result of wrongdoing is not seen right away. Time is a factor in this, as in the ripening of grain.

27. "And as for you, Doom must have robbed you of your senses to do what you have done. Disaster shall befall you at the hands of Rāma, a terrible disaster that will end your life.

28. "Ah, now Kaikeyī and all her family must be satisfied. Rāma's lawful wife has been taken from him, that glorious prince whom nothing but righteousness could satisfy.

29. "Janasthāna, I call on you and you *karṇikāra* trees in full blossom: Tell Rāma at once that Rāvaṇa is carrying off Sītā.

30. "I greet you, Mount Prasravaṇa, with your flower garlands and massive peaks: Quickly tell Rāma that Rāvaṇa is carrying off Sītā.

31. "I greet you, Godāvarī river, alive with the call of geese and cranes: Tell Rāma at once that Rāvaṇa is carrying off Sītā.

32. "And you spirits that inhabit the different trees of this forest, I salute you all: Tell my husband that I have been carried off.

33–34. "All creatures that live in this place, I appeal to you for help, all you flocks of birds and herds of beasts: Tell my husband that the woman he loves more than life itself is being carried off, that Sītā has been carried away, helpless, by Rāvaṇa.

35. "Once the powerful, great-armed prince discovers where I am—albeit in the other world—he shall come in all his valor and bring me home, were it Vaivasvata himself, god of death, who had carried me off.

36. "Jaṭāyus, tell Rāma and Lakṣmaṇa just how I was carried off, tell the whole story, from beginning to end!"

The end of the forty-seventh *sarga* of the *Araṇyakāṇḍa* of the *Śrī Rāmāyaṇa*.

Sarga 48

1. From deep in sleep Jaṭāyus heard her cry. He glanced up and all at once saw them, Rāvaṇa and Vaidehī.

2. The great, majestic bird, tall as a mountaintop, his beak sharp as a razor, then called out these wise words from his tree:

3. "Ten-necked Rāvaṇa, I am Jaṭāyus, the powerful king of vultures who keeps to the ancient ways of righteousness and puts his trust in truth.

4. "Rāma, son of Daśaratha, is king of all the world, the equal of great Indra and Varuṇa, and dedicated to the welfare of all creatures in the world.

5. "The shapely woman you now seek to carry off belongs to him, the master of the world. Her name is Sītā, and she is his glorious, lawful wife.

6. "How could any king who keeps to the ways of righteousness defile the wife of another man, and a king's wife at that, who is inviolable above all? It is a despicable thing, powerful Rāvaṇa, to defile the wife of another. Put the thought out of your mind.

7. "A wise man should not do what others would censure. One must look upon the wives of other men as no less inviolable than one's own.

8. "It is according to how kings behave, delight of the Paulastyas, that the learned decide questions of profit, pleasure, or righteousness not settled in the sacred texts.

9. "For a king is righteousness, pleasure, and the ultimate repository of wealth; the king is the root from which all conduct springs, be it good or evil.

10. "You are evil and reckless by nature, foremost of *rākṣasas*. How could you possibly have secured your lofty position of power? It is as though a sinner had acquired a celestial chariot.

11. "Indeed, one can never change one's true nature. The noble do not linger long in the dwelling of the wicked.

12. "Mighty Rāma is a righteous prince and has never wronged you in your city or realm. Why is it you are wronging him now?

13–14. "If Khara, coming to Janasthāna on Śūrpaṇakhā's account, overstepped all bounds and so was slain by tireless Rāma, tell me now in all honesty, what crime is Rāma guilty of that you should go and carry off this woman, the wife of the master of the world?

15. "Release Vaidehī at once or he shall consume you with his terrible eye, as fiery as the lightning bolt of Indra that consumed the demon Vṛtra.

16. "A poisonous snake is caught in the hem of your cloak and you do not know it; the noose of Doom is wound around your neck and you do not see it.

17. "A man should only bear a load, my friend, that does not bring him to his knees; he should only eat the food he can safely digest.

18. "Who would attempt a deed that can bring him no righteous merit, no worldly fame or glory, nothing but physical pain?

19. "It was sixty thousand years ago I was born, Rāvaṇa, and all that time I have justly reigned in the kingship of my fathers and forefathers.

20. "I am old and you are young; you are mounted, clad in armor, and bear a bow and arrows. Still, you shall not take Vaidehī and go your way unscathed.

21. "You cannot carry off Vaidehī by force before my very eyes, no more than one can rob the *vedas* of their plain sense by arguments tricked out with logic.

22. "Stand a moment and fight, Rāvaṇa, if you are brave enough. You shall soon be lying upon the ground, slain like Khara before you.

23. "For Rāma, who has often killed *daityas* and *dānavas* in battle, this man clad in barkcloth, shall soon slay you in combat.

24. "But I myself must do what I can: Both princes are far away and no doubt your hasty departure, coward, is from your fear of them.

25. "As long as there is life in me you shall not abduct the lovely, lotus-eyed Sītā, beloved queen of Rāma.

26. "Come what may, I will serve the great prince Rāma, and Daśaratha, too, even if it costs me my life.

27. "Stop, ten-necked Rāvaṇa, stop but a moment. Look, I offer you hospitality, the warm hospitality of battle to the death. I will hurl you from your splendid chariot, nightstalker, like ripe fruit from its stem."

The end of the forty-eighth *sarga* of the *Araṇyakāṇḍa* of the *Śrī Rāmāyaṇa*.

Sarga 49

1. So Jaṭāyus spoke, with good sense. But Rāvaṇa flew into a rage, and all his twenty eyes began to blaze like fire.

2. Eyes flaming bright red in anger, wearing earrings of burnished gold, the implacable lord of *rākṣasas* attacked the lord of birds.

3. The clash between them there in the deep forest was tumultuous, like two clouds clashing in the sky, driven before the wind.

4. It was an amazing battle that took place between vulture and *rākṣasa*, such as two lofty, garlanded mountains might have fought when they still had wings.

5. The powerful nightstalker showered the vulture-king with terrible reed darts, iron shafts, and sharp-tipped barbed arrows.

6–7. But the vulture Jaṭāyus, powerful lord of birds, endured the shower of arrows, Rāvaṇa's missiles, as they came falling in combat, and with the sharp claws of his feet tore at his body again and again.

8. Then in a rage ten-necked Rāvaṇa, aiming to crush his enemy once and for all, took up ten terrible arrows, each one of them like the staff of Death.

9. These keenly honed, terrible, crescent-headed darts mighty Rāvaṇa shot with bow full-drawn. They went flying straight and pierced the vulture.

10. And yet Jaṭāyus, seeing Jānakī weeping in the *rākṣasa*'s chariot, ignored the arrows and attacked again.

11–12. With his claws the mighty lord of birds shattered Rāvaṇa's pearl-studded bow and all his arrows, and with his wings battered his shield that blazed like fire.

13. Unleashing all his power in combat, Jaṭāyus then killed Rāvaṇa's team, those unearthly fleet asses with the faces of *piśācas* and breastplates made of gold.

14. Next came the great splendid chariot that could fly where one desires. He shattered it altogether, the yoke pole rigged to it, the sparkling wheels of gems and gold that made it gleam like fire; then the fly whisks and the parasol radiant as the full moon.

15. Rāvaṇa, bow shattered, chariot lost, charioteer and team all dead, clutched Vaidehī to his breast and leaped to the ground.

16. Seeing Rāvaṇa leap down to the ground from his shattered vehicle, the creatures of the forest acclaimed the vulture-king with shouts of commendation.

17. But the aged king of birds had exhausted himself, and seeing this, Rāvaṇa sprang up again in delight, still holding Maithilī.

18. And yet, as he set off in delight clasping Janaka's daughter to his breast, the vulture-king Jaṭāyus flew up to him and spoke these words:

19. "This is the wife of Rāma, whose arrows strike like thunderbolts. Can you not see, foolish Rāvaṇa, that carrying her off will lead to the slaughter of the *rākṣasas*?

20. "You, your allies and kinsmen, your ministers, forces, and retainers are drinking poison as a thirsty man gulps water.

21. "Those who recklessly ignore the consequences of their acts quickly perish, and so will you.

22. "You are caught fast in the noose of Doom. Where can you go to free yourself from it—where can a fish go once it has swallowed the bait and hook that must destroy it?

23. "For the invincible Kākutstha Rāghavas shall never forgive your assault upon their ashram, Rāvaṇa.

24. "You have done a thing condemned the whole world over, and how like a coward you did it, taking the route of a thief, not a hero.

25. "Stand a moment and fight, Rāvaṇa, if you are brave enough. You shall soon be lying upon the ground, slain like your brother Khara.

26. "When a man's end is near, he hazards some act of unrighteousness that seals his fate, and this is just what you have done.

27. "What man, after all, would do a deed whose consequences are sure to be evil? No one, not the lord of the world himself, the blessed Self-existent Brahmā."

28. With these wise words the mighty Jaṭāyus hurled himself violently upon the back of the *rākṣasa*, ten-necked Rāvaṇa.

29. Seizing him with his sharp claws he began to tear at him all over, flailing him like a driver riding an unruly elephant.

30. He tore at him with his claws, sank his beak into his back and ripped out his hair, using the only weapons he had, his claws, wings, and beak.

31. Relentlessly the vulture-king tormented him, until the *rākṣasa* began to shake and his lips to tremble with fury.

32. Harried and blind with rage, Rāvaṇa struck at Jaṭāyus with open hand, all the while clutching Vaidehī tightly to his left side.

33. But Jaṭāyus, the foe-taming lord of birds, got clear and with his beak tried to wrench apart those ten left arms.

34. In a rage ten-necked Rāvaṇa cast Sītā aside and pummeled the vulture-king with fists and feet.

35. For a short while the two of them grappled, the chief of *rākṣasas* and the foremost of birds, both incomparable in strength.

36. But as the bird persevered in his struggle on Rāma's behalf, Rāvaṇa drew his sword and cut off his wings, feet, and flanks.

37. The moment the savage *rākṣasa* cut off his wings, the vulture fell stricken to the ground, barely alive.

38. At the sight of Jaṭāyus fallen upon the earth, drenched with blood, Vaidehī ran to him in sorrow as if he were a kinsman.

39. The lord of Laṅkā stood watching as Jaṭāyus fell back upon the ground, his body blue-black as a storm cloud, his chest milk white, his noble power like a forest fire suddenly put out.

40. But as the bird lay fallen on the earth, crushed before Rāvaṇa's onslaught, moon-faced Sītā, daughter of Janaka, took him in her arms and wept.

The end of the forty-ninth *sarga* of the *Araṇyakāṇḍa* of the *Śrī Rāmāyaṇa*.

Sarga 50

1. The overlord of *rākṣasas* watched as the vulture, barely alive, fell writhing to the ground not far from Rāghava's ashram.

2. But the woman whose face was like the moon, overlord of stars, began to lament bitterly when she saw the vulture-king cut down by Rāvaṇa.

3. "Whenever good or evil is about to befall a person, aren't portents shown to him? Aren't signs perceived and birds of omen seen or heard?

4. "Rāma, don't you know—surely you must know what terrible disaster threatens you? Surely, Kākutstha, it is because of me that birds and beasts are in flight.

5. "Kākutstha! Come quickly with Lakṣmaṇa and save me!" the woman cried in wild terror, as if they were nearby and could hear.

6. While Vaidehī was lost in helpless lamentation, her garlands crushed and jewelry in disarray, Rāvaṇa, overlord of *rākṣasas*, came running up to her.

7. She clung to a massive tree, twining herself around it like a vine while the overlord of *rākṣasas* shouted over and over again, "Let go!"

8. "Rāma, Rāma!" she cried, the woman Rāma had left all alone in the forest, until like Death himself Rāvaṇa seized her by the hair—and thereby condemned himself to death.

9. When Vaidehī was assaulted, a blinding darkness enveloped the world, the whole world from end to end, all things that move and do not move.

10. With his divine eye, the majestic Grandfather Brahmā saw the outrage upon poor Sītā and murmured, "What had to be done has been done."

11. All the supreme seers living in Daṇḍaka wilderness shuddered and trembled to see the outrage upon Sītā.

12. As the woman cried "Rāma, Rāma! Lakṣmaṇa!" Rāvaṇa, overlord of *rākṣasas*, took her and flew up into the sky.

13. All adorned in ornaments of burnished gold and dressed in garments of yellow silk, the princess looked like a streak of lightning flashing from a storm cloud.

14. Her yellow garment billowed out and made Rāvaṇa look all the more lurid, like a mountain engulfed in flames.

15. The lotus petals worn by beautiful Vaidehī, coppery and fragrant, were scattered over Rāvaṇa.

16. Her golden silks, billowing out way up in the sky, resembled a cloud stained copper by the rosy rays of the midday sun.

17. As she was held fast in Rāvaṇa's embrace way up in the sky, her pure radiant face, without Rāma, began to fade like a lotus ripped from its stalk.

18ab. It looked like the moon peeping out through the tatters of a blue-black cloud.

18cd–20. Her flawless face, the color of a lotus cup, that smooth forehead and silky hair, faultless nose and soft ruby lips, and those sparkling white jewels, her perfect teeth, a weeping face now and streaked with tears, but still as lovely as the moon—her beautiful golden face was quivering before the lord of *rākṣasas*, and like the moon appearing by day it shone but faintly, without Rāma.

21. Maithilī was golden skinned, the *rākṣasa* deep blue-black, and folded within his arms she looked like the star that glitters within a sapphire.

22. Fair as a lotus, golden hued, with ornaments of burnished gold, the daughter of Janaka in Rāvaṇa's embrace looked like a streak of lightning caught within a storm cloud.

23. The sound of Vaidehī's ornaments made the overlord of *rākṣasas* still more like a rain cloud, pure blue-black and now sounding as well.

24. A shower of blossoms fell all over the ground, dropping from the crown of Sītā's head as she was carried off.

25. And driven by the force of his onrush, it went swirling back all over ten-necked Rāvaṇa.

26. The cascade of blossoms came swirling back around Vaiśravaṇa's younger brother, like the brilliant wreath of stars that swirls around high Mount Meru.

27. Vaidehī's jewel-studded anklet was shaken from her foot, and gently tinkling it fell like an arc of lightning.

28. Vaidehī's coloring, fair as a tree's new shoot, lent a glow to the *rākṣasa*'s blue-black limbs, like a golden girth upon an elephant.

29. In the natural radiance of her beauty, Sītā resembled a comet in the sky as Vaiśravaṇa's younger brother shot skyward, carrying her off.

30. Her flame-colored ornaments were scattered noisily upon the ground, falling like stars from the firmament when their store of merit has been exhausted.

31. Shining like the moon, the overlord of stars, Vaidehī's pearl necklace slipped from between her breasts and fell like the white Ganges descending from heaven.

32. It was only a gust of wind as Rāvaṇa flew up that shook the trees with their flocks of different birds, but it seemed they were waving their arms and crying, "Do not be afraid!"

33. With lotuses overturned, fish and water creatures frightened, sighs rising from their vaporous waters, the lotus ponds seemed to be grieving for Maithilī as for a friend.

34 From every side lions, tigers, deer, and birds swarmed together and went running after them in a fury, following Sītā's shadow.

35. As Sītā was being carried off, the mountains also seemed to wail, their craggy arms outstretched and waterfalls staining their faces with tears.

36. At the sight of Vaidehī being carried off the majestic sun that brings the day was overcome with gloom, and his glowing disk faded to pale white.

37–38ab. "There is no such thing as righteousness, much less truth, uprightness, or kindliness, if Rāvaṇa can carry off Vaidehī, the wife of Rāma." So all the animals seemed to grieve, and the grieving spread from group to group.

38cd–39ab. Their young looked desolate and began to weep, and though their eyes were clouded by falling tears, the frightened little creatures kept looking up.

39cd–40ab. The spirits of the forest were seized with violent trembling in every limb, to see the wretched plight of Sītā, to hear her wild screams.

40cd–41. "Lakṣmaṇa! Rāma!" Vaidehī cried in a voice still sweet as ever, time and again glancing down at the earth. Her hair was disheveled, her auspicious forehead rouge was smeared, and yet she remained defiant as ten-necked Rāvaṇa carried her off, to his certain destruction.

42. Maithilī had always been a woman of bright flashing smile. But now that she was separated from all her family, now that both Rāghava and Lakṣmaṇa were nowhere to be seen, her face was drained of color under a crushing weight of fear.

The end of the fiftieth *sarga* of the *Araṇyakāṇḍa* of the *Śrī Rāmāyaṇa*.

Sarga 51

1. When Janaka's daughter Maithilī saw Rāvaṇa flying up into the sky, she was stricken with misery and filled with wild terror at the grave danger facing her.

2. Her eyes red with rage and weeping, Sītā addressed the fierce-eyed overlord of *rākṣasas* as he carried her off, weeping pitifully.

3. "Do you feel no shame at what you are doing, base Rāvaṇa, to steal me away when you knew I was alone and then to run off?

4. "It was you, wasn't it, you vicious coward, who, seeking to carry me off, got my husband out of the way by magically taking the form of a deer? You struck him down, too, the one who tried to rescue me.

5. "Oh yes, you have shown how very brave you are, lowest of *rākṣasas*. For didn't you proclaim your name and conquer me in battle?

6. "Aren't you ashamed to have done so contemptible a thing as this, carrying off a woman left all alone, one who belongs to another man?

7. "Men the world over will talk of the despicable thing you have done, the height of brutality and unrighteousness. And you pride yourself on being brave.

8. "A curse upon that courage and strength you bragged about. A curse upon such behavior as yours, which will disgrace your House in the eyes of all the world.

9. "What can be done when you are fleeing so fast? Stop but a moment and you would not leave here alive.

10. "For were you only to come within sight of those two princes, you would not live a moment longer, not if all your army were with you.

11. "You could no more withstand the touch of their arrows than a bird can withstand the touch of a raging forest fire.

12. "Please let me go, Rāvaṇa, for your own good, please! For my husband will be furious with you for assaulting me, and he and his brother will send you to your destruction, if you do not let me go.

13. "The very object you have in mind in carrying me off by force, base *rākṣasa*, will be vain.

14. "For being at the mercy of my enemies and denied the sight of my godlike husband, I could not long survive.

15. "Surely you are heedless of your own welfare and safety. How

true that at the hour of death a mortal keeps to the very course he should abandon.

16. "All people on the point of death reject just what can save them. And I can almost see the noose of Doom wound around your neck.

17. "If you can feel no fear in your dangerous position, ten-faced Rāvaṇa, clearly you must be seeing those trees of gold.

18. "And soon, Rāvaṇa, you shall see the dreadful river Vaitaraṇī running in torrents of blood and the awful forest leafed with sword blades.

19. "You shall see the prickly silk-cotton tree and its flowers of burnished gold, its foliage of precious beryl, its clusters of iron thorns.

20. "For having so wronged the great prince, pitiless Rāvaṇa, you shall survive no longer than if you had swallowed poison.

21. "You are hopelessly caught in the noose of Doom, Rāvaṇa. Where can you go to be safe from my great husband?

22. "Without help from his brother and in the twinkling of an eye, Rāghava killed fourteen thousand *rākṣasas* in battle.

23. "How then could that powerful hero, expert in all weapons, fail to kill you with his keen arrows when you have stolen his cherished wife?"

24. Such and more were the bitter words Vaidehī cried out in pitiful lamentation, overpowered by grief and fear in Rāvaṇa's tight embrace.

25. But even as the radiant young princess uttered those many anguished and pitiful words of lamentation, evil Rāvaṇa carried her off struggling and trembling in her every limb.

The end of the fifty-first *sarga* of the *Araṇyakāṇḍa* of the *Śrī Rāmāyaṇa*.

Sarga 52

1. As Vaidehī was being carried off, she saw no one who might help her until she caught sight of five great monkeys on a mountain peak.

2. The large-eyed, shapely Maithilī dropped her golden silk shawl among them, and her lovely ornaments, in hopes they might tell Rāma.

3. She unfastened her garment and let it fall with her jewelry among them, but ten-necked Rāvaṇa was too wild with excitement to notice she had done so.

4. The great, tawny-eyed monkeys looked up unblinking at large-eyed Sītā crying out.

5. Across Lake Pampā the lord of *rākṣasas* made his way, heading toward the city of Laṅkā with Sītā weeping in his arms.

6. Rāvaṇa shivered with delight as he carried her off, though it was his own death he was embracing, a sharp-fanged, poisonous viper.

7. Over forests and rivers, mountains and lakes he crossed, speeding through the sky like an arrow shot from a bow.

8. Reaching the ocean, the dwelling place of whales and crocodiles, the everlasting adode of Varuṇa, and the final refuge of rivers, he set out across it.

9. As he carried Vaidehī over Varuṇa's abode, the waves heaved in agitation, and the fish and serpents were trapped deep below.

10. Then, celestial musicians hovering in midair raised a clamor, and perfected beings cried out, "This is the end of Rāvaṇa!"

11. With Sītā struggling in his embrace—his own death in bodily form—Rāvaṇa entered the city of Laṅkā.

12. Making his way through the well-arranged streets of the city, he entered his inner chamber through the maze of closely guarded gates.

13. There Rāvaṇa deposited her, as the magician Maya might deposit his demon magic, and black-eyed Sītā sat lost in grief and utter confusion.

14. Ten-necked Rāvaṇa then turned and spoke to some *piśāca* women, a terror to behold: "See that no one, male or female, visits Sītā without my consent.

15. "Pearls and gold, raiment and jewelry, whatever she may want is to be given her, for such is my will.

16. "And let none of you speak one unkind word to Vaidehī, intentionally or not, if you value your lives at all."

17. So the mighty lord of *rākṣasas* addressed the *rākṣasa* women. As he left the inner chamber, wondering what to do next, he encountered eight powerful *rākṣasas*, eaters of raw flesh.

18. Seeing them, mighty Rāvaṇa, deluded by the boon he had been granted, addressed them, flattering their might and power:

19. "Hurry now, take every kind of weapon and leave at once for Janasthāna, once Khara's dwelling place but now his resting place.

20. "You must live there in Janasthāna, for it is empty now that the *rākṣasas* have all been killed. Trust in your virile power and lay all your fears aside.

21. "The vast forces I had stationed in Janasthāna have been destroyed in battle—Dūṣaṇa and Khara among them—by the arrows of Rāma.

22. "Because of this, I feel rage surging uncontrollably within me, such rage as I have never felt before. Rāma has aroused in me deep, ferocious enmity.

23. "And for the hatred this enemy of mine has provoked I want revenge. I shall find no rest until I kill him in combat.

24. "Only when I have killed Rāma, the murderer of Khara and Dūṣaṇa, shall I find contentment, like a poor man finding treasure.

25. "While you are living in Janasthāna, you shall report on Rāma's activities and tell me precisely what he is doing.

26. "You must all proceed with caution, nightstalkers, at the same time making every effort to bring about Rāghava's death.

27. "I have witnessed your power on the field of battle many times, and that is why I am assigning you to Janasthāna."

28. Such were the generous compliments the eight *rākṣasas* received, and doing obeisance to Rāvaṇa they left Laṅkā unmarked by the eye, and set forth all together for Janasthāna.

29. Rāvaṇa shivered with delight to have obtained Sītā, to be holding the princess of Mithilā in his possession, to have incited the implacable enmity of Rāma. In his delusion, the *rākṣasa* rejoiced.

The end of the fifty-second *sarga* of the *Araṇyakāṇḍa* of the *Śrī Rāmāyaṇa*.

Sarga 53

1. After giving orders to the eight powerful and dreaded *rākṣasas*, Rāvaṇa in his folly believed his goal accomplished.

2. Tortured as he was by the arrows of Kāma, god of love, his thoughts turned to Vaidehī, and he hurriedly reentered his lovely dwelling to see her.

3. On entering his residence Rāvaṇa, overlord of *rākṣasas*, saw Sītā lost in grief in the midst of the *rākṣasa* women.

4–5. Her face was drenched with tears, she was wretched and crushed under a heavy weight of grief. She was like a boat upon the open sea buffeted by gusting winds and about to sink; like a doe that has strayed from the herd and been brought to bay by hounds. Wretchedly she hung her head as the nightstalker advanced.

6. Overpowered by grief, wretched, and powerless though she was, the overlord of *rākṣasas* forced her to come and see his dwelling, and a heavenly dwelling it was.

7–9. It consisted of an array of palaces and mansions with thousands of women in attendance; it was home to all kinds of birds, and all kinds of precious objects embellished it. There were pillars that ravished the eye, elaborately worked in burnished gold, crystal, silver, diamond, and beryl. Drums like those in heaven echoed through archways of burnished gold as he climbed with her up an elaborate golden staircase.

10. There magnificent windows were found made of ivory and silver, screened in by latticework of gold, and looking out onto row upon row of palaces.

11. Ten-necked Rāvaṇa pointed out to Maithilī the different quarters of his residence all brilliantly whitewashed and sparkling with precious stones.

12. Sītā stood lost in grief as Rāvaṇa showed her the pools and ponds blanketed with flowers of every variety.

13. After evil Rāvaṇa had shown her all his splendid abode, he said to Vaidehī, daughter of Janaka:

14–15. "There are three hundred and twenty million nightstalking *rākṣasas*, not even including the aged and children, Sītā, and of all these awesome creatures I am master. Myriads stand at the bidding of one alone—me.

16. "The reins of all my royal power are in your hands, and my life, too, large-eyed lady. For you are more precious than the very breath within me.

17. "In my entourage are many thousands of women. Be mistress of them all, beloved Sītā: Be my wife.

18. "There is no need for further thought; please, just accept my offer and be gracious to one in such torment. Give me your love.

19. "Laṅkā is surrounded by the sea, as far as a hundred leagues. Not the *asuras* and gods with Indra himself could assault it.

20. "Nor do I know of anyone in all the worlds, god or *yakṣa*, *gandharva* or seer, whose might equals mine.

21. "What use have you for Rāma—that weakling deposed from his kingship, that miserable, short-lived ascetic, a mere man?

22. "Give your heart to me alone; I would be a perfect husband. Think, too, how soon youth passes, bashful Sītā; come make love with me.

23. "Dismiss the thought of ever seeing Rāghava again. He cannot possibly come here, lovely Sītā, not in his wildest dreams.

24. "One could sooner bind with ropes the wind that races through the sky, or grasp the brilliant flame of a blazing fire.

25. "In all three worlds, my beauty, I know no one strong enough to take you away when mine are the arms that hold you tight.

26. "Let the waters of the royal consecration pour down upon you; reign in power over this great kingdom of Laṅkā. And in perfect contentment make love with me.

27. "Through your sojourn in the forest you have paid for any misdeeds of former lives. Here you shall enjoy the rewards of the righteousness you practiced.

28. "Here every garland is charged with heavenly fragrance, Maithilī, and the ornaments are the finest. Come enjoy it all with me.

29–30. "Puṣpaka, the sunlike aerial chariot I took by force from my brother Vaiśravaṇa, is spacious, lovely, and swift as thought. Use it to your heart's content, shapely Sītā, in my company.

31. "But your clear lotuslike face, a vision of delight—how pale it looks and sad, my fair-hipped beauty.

32. "Don't be ashamed, Vaidehī, as if this were a lapse from righteousness. The feeling I have for you, my lady, is sanctioned by the *vedas*.

33. "See, I touch my heads to your smooth feet. Be gracious to me; I am your slave, to use as you will.

34. "Not in vain, however, are the words I speak through parched lips, not in vain does Rāvaṇa bow down his head to any woman."

35. So ten-necked Rāvaṇa spoke to Maithilī, daughter of Janaka; for having fallen under the power of doom, he thought of her as his own.

The end of the fifty-third *sarga* of the *Araṇyakāṇḍa* of the *Śrī Rāmāyaṇa*.

Sarga 54

1. Though sick with grief, Vaidehī was unafraid for all of Rāvaṇa's talk, and placing a straw between them she answered back:

2–3. "There once was a king named Daśaratha, a steadfast bulwark of righteousness, known far and wide as a man true to his promises. He had a son named Rāma Rāghava, who is famed for his righteousness throughout the three worlds. His arms are long and his eyes are large, he is my husband and my god.

4. "He was born into the House of the Ikṣvākus, a prince with the shoulders of a lion and radiant splendor. And he is the one, together with his brother Lakṣmaṇa, who shall take your life.

5. "If he had been there to see your violent attack on me, you would now be lying in Janasthāna, killed in battle like Khara.

6. "They are dreaded and powerful, all the *rākṣasas* you have sent forth against Rāma, yet they shall find themselves impotent, like the venom of snakes against Suparṇa.

7. "Their bodies shall crumble before the golden arrows shot from his bow as the bank of the Ganges crumbles before the waves.

8. "Even if *asuras* or gods cannot kill you, Rāvaṇa, you have now aroused the bitter enmity of someone you cannot escape alive.

9. "Some life is still left you before powerful Rāghava makes an end of it, but how precious little you have, like a victim bound to the sacrificial post.

10. "If Rāma were only to turn the blazing anger of his eyes upon you, *rākṣasa*, you would succumb in an instant, burned to ashes.

11. "He who could destroy the moon in the sky, send it crashing to earth, or dry up the ocean, shall come here and set Sītā free.

12. "You shall lose your senses, your strength, your majesty, and your life. Because of what you have done, Laṅkā shall become a city of widows.

13. "This evil deed of yours, taking me from the forest and away from my proper place beside my husband, will not bring you any pleasure.

14. "For my splendid husband has divine powers, and all the time he has been living in the desolate wilderness of Daṇḍaka, he has trusted in his own might and feared nothing.

15. "With his arrows showering down in combat, he shall wash your body clean of your power, your might, and this brash arrogance of yours.

16. "When a man's destruction, ordained by doom, is near at hand, he grows reckless in his actions, and it is this that dooms him.

17. "The moment you assaulted me, scum of the *rākṣasas*, doom overtook you, and it can only end in the slaughter of the *rākṣasas*, your women, and yourself.

18. "A pariah cannot desecrate an altar in the place of sacrifice, equipped with the ladles and other utensils, and sanctified by the hymns of brahmans.

19. "This body of mine has no more feeling; throw it in chains or have it killed. I care nothing about preserving it, or my life either, *rākṣasa*. I will not disgrace myself in the eyes of all the world."

20. Such were the harsh words of Vaidehī, and not another word would she speak to Rāvaṇa.

21. After listening to Sītā's words, he replied with a harsh threat that made her shudder with horror:

22. "Listen to what I have to say, my lovely Maithilī: If within the

space of twelve months you do not yield to me with a sweet smile, the cooks shall chop you into minced meat for my breakfast."

23. Such were the harsh words of Rāvaṇa, who made his enemies wail, and then in a rage he spoke to the *rākṣasa* women:

24. "Send me the most monstrous *rākṣasa* women, flesh-eating, blood-drinking creatures, a terror to behold. Have them humble her pride at once."

25. Women then appeared as he had commanded, monstrous and terrible to behold. They cupped their hands in reverence to him and then surrounded Maithilī.

26. Springing forward and nearly shattering the earth with his wild stamping, terrible King Rāvaṇa addressed them:

27. "Take Maithilī into the grove of *aśoka* trees. Keep her surrounded there and guard her closely.

28. "There, using terrible threats and gentle coaxing, break the will of Maithilī, as one does with a wild cow elephant."

29. So under orders from Rāvaṇa, the *rākṣasa* women took Maithilī and went to the *aśoka* grove.

30. It was overgrown with all kinds of flowering and fruit-bearing trees, the sort that produce whatever one wishes; birds flocked there, too, singing sweetly at every season.

31. But Maithilī, daughter of Janaka, finding herself at the mercy of the *rākṣasa* women, was engulfed in grief like a doe in the midst of tigresses.

32. They glared at her through misshapen eyes and made brutal threats till she could find no peace; and when she thought back on her husband and beloved brother-in-law, she nearly lost her mind under a crushing weight of grief and fear.

The end of the fifty-fourth *sarga* of the *Araṇyakāṇḍa* of the *Śrī Rāmāyaṇa*.

Sarga 55

1. After killing the *rākṣasa* Mārīca, who had been ranging about in the form of a deer—he could take any form at will—Rāma quickly headed back on his path.

2. He hurried on, eager to see Maithilī, when from behind him a cry rang out, the ghastly cry of a jackal.

3. The ominous cry made him shudder; he was filled with dread to hear a jackal cry and thought to himself in fear:

4. "It bodes ill, I know, when a jackal howls. I only hope Vaidehī is safe from *rākṣasas* who might devour her.

5. "But what if Lakṣmaṇa heard the scream that Mārīca, in his deer form, cried out in imitation of my voice?

6. "The moment he heard the cry, Saumitri would leave Maithilī—she would send him herself—and come racing after me.

7–8. "The *rākṣasas* must have joined forces in plotting Sītā's death: Mārīca became a golden deer to draw me from the ashram; once he had led me away and been struck by my arrow, he turned back into a *rākṣasa* and then called out the words, 'Oh Lakṣmaṇa, I have been hit!'

9. "I only hope the two of them are safe without me to protect them in the forest. For I have aroused the *rākṣasas'* enmity by the events in Janasthāna. And now I see many terrible portents."

10. Such were Rāma's fearful thoughts on hearing the jackal's cry and thinking how he had been lured away by the *rākṣasa* in the form of a deer. Filled with dread he made his way back to Janasthāna.

11. The great prince, sick at heart already, was still more heartsick when birds and beasts approached and passed him on the left, uttering terrible cries.

12. Soon after seeing these most terrible portents Rāghava caught sight of Lakṣmaṇa gloomily coming his way.

13. They neared each other and met, the distraught and sorrowing Lakṣmaṇa, the distraught and sorrowful Rāma.

14. But then Lakṣmaṇa's eldest brother began to rebuke him for coming and leaving Sītā alone in the desolate, *rākṣasa*-haunted forest.

15. The delight of the Raghus took hold of Lakṣmaṇa's left hand, and though his voice was sweet as ever, he spoke words that were harsh and full of pain:

16. "Oh Lakṣmaṇa, what a damnable thing you have done, to leave Sītā and come here! Dear brother, I only hope she is safe.

17. "But I have little doubt, mighty brother, that the daughter of Janaka has vanished completely or been devoured by the *rākṣasas* who roam the forest.

18. "So many omens have shown themselves to me, and all bode ill. Ah Lakṣmaṇa, are we going to find Sītā safe and sound?

19. "It was a *rākṣasa* in the guise of a deer that lured me off on a long chase. After much effort I managed to hit my mark—and as he lay dying he turned back into a *rākṣasa*.

20. "I am sick at heart and wretched at what has happened, Lakṣmaṇa; my left eye is throbbing fitfully. Sītā no doubt is gone—she has been carried off, or has set out on her own, or is dead."

The end of the fifty-fifth *sarga* of the *Araṇyakāṇḍa* of the *Śrī Rāmāyaṇa*.

Sarga 56

1. When the righteous son of Daśaratha saw how wretched Lakṣmaṇa was, how he had come into the desolate forest without Vaidehī, he began to question him closely.

2. "Where is Vaidehī, Lakṣmaṇa? Could you have left her behind to come here, the woman who accompanied me when I set forth to Daṇḍaka wilderness?

3. "Where is fair-waisted Vaidehī, the woman who shares my sorrow as I run wretchedly through Daṇḍaka, driven from my kingdom?

4. "Where is Sītā, a woman like a daughter of the gods, the woman who shares my life? I cannot bear to be without her, mighty Lakṣmaṇa, not for a moment.

5. "Without the golden daughter of Janaka, I would spurn lordship over the whole earth, Lakṣmaṇa, over the deathless gods themselves.

6. "Is Vaidehī still alive, the woman I love more than life itself? Dear brother, will banishment prove to be for nothing?

7. "Will Kaikeyī finally be happy, Saumitri, getting what she wants when you are out of the way and I am dead because of Sītā?

8. "Will Kaikeyī achieve every goal, dear brother, having both the kingship and her son? Will poor Kausalyā lose her only son and be forced to wait on Kaikeyī hand and foot?

9. "I am returning to the ashram to see if Vaidehī is still alive. If I find that good woman is gone, Lakṣmaṇa, I will end my life.

10. "If I come back to the ashram and Vaidehī cannot speak to me, my Sītā smiling the way she used to, I shall die, Lakṣmaṇa.

11. "Tell me, Lakṣmaṇa, whether Vaidehī is still alive or not. Or have *rākṣasas* devoured the poor woman because of your carelessness?

12. "Vaidehī is young and delicate and has never known sorrow before. The grief of being parted from me is sure to break her heart.

13. "It must truly have frightened even you when that cunning, evil *rākṣasa* cried out 'Lakṣmaṇa!' at the top of his voice.

14. "I suspect Vaidehī must have heard that voice so like my own and in her panic sent you off at once to find me.

15. "And you did the worst possible thing: By abandoning Sītā in the forest you have given the cruel *rākṣasas* an opening for wreaking their vengeance.

16. "The flesh-eating *rākṣasas* are aggrieved over Khara's death; those dreaded creatures have killed Sītā, I am certain of it.

17. "Ah, I am truly drowning in disaster! What am I to do now, destroyer of enemies? I fear what I am sure to find."

18. With these thoughts about the beautiful Sītā preying on his mind, Rāghava hurried back to Janasthāna with Lakṣmaṇa.

19. Rebuking his anguished brother, feeling hungry, tired, and thirsty, distraught and sighing till his mouth was parched, he reached the grounds of his ashram and found them empty.

20. The mighty prince rushed into the ashram, searching everywhere they used to while away their time. "It is so, then," he thought as he stood in their dwelling. He shuddered, and his flesh began to crawl.

The end of the fifty-sixth *sarga* of the *Araṇyakāṇḍa* of the *Śrī Rāmāyaṇa*.

Sarga 57

1. When Saumitri had arrived from the ashram and the two of them were making their way back, Rāma, the delight of the Raghus, in the anguish of his sorrow had questioned him at length.

2. "Why did you come without Maithilī," he asked, "when I left her alone in the forest only because I trusted you?

3. "As soon as I saw you coming without Maithilī, Lakṣmaṇa, my heart sank knowing that the great evil it feared was true.

4. "My left eye has been throbbing, my arm and heart as well, from the moment I saw you in the distance, Lakṣmaṇa, coming down the path without Sītā."

5. So he spoke, and good Lakṣmaṇa Saumitri, plunged even deeper into sorrow, made this reply to the sorrowful Rāma:

6. "It was not on my own initiative that I left her to come here; it was Sītā herself who insisted I go to you.

7. "The words that sounded just like her husband's cry—'Oh Sītā! Oh Lakṣmaṇa! Save me!'—reached Maithilī's ears.

8. "And when she heard that cry of pain, in her love for you Maithilī, weeping and wild with fear, said to me, 'Go, I beg you, go!'

9. "Again and again Maithilī urged me to go, but I had full confidence in you and replied:

10. " 'I know of no *rākṣasa* that could frighten him. Rest easy, it is not as it seems; someone else has made that cry.

11. " 'How could your husband, Sītā, ever utter such base and contemptible words—"Save me!"—when he himself could save the thirty gods?

12. " 'No, someone else, for some reason, must have imitated my brother's voice and raised that strident cry, "Save me, Lakṣmaṇa!" Do not be alarmed the way some common woman might.

13. " 'No more yielding now to weakness, get a hold of yourself, don't be anxious. In all three worlds there exists no man—and there never will—who could defeat Rāghava in battle.'

14. "So I spoke to Vaidehī. But she was frantic and through streaming tears made this dreadful reply:

15. " 'You have your wicked heart set wholly on me. But even if you bring about your brother's death, you shall never have me.

16. " 'You are in league with Bharata, that is why you followed Rāma here and why you now refuse to help him when he is crying in agony.

17. " 'Secretly you are an enemy who followed along because of me. You have been waiting for Rāghava to give you an opening, so now you won't go to help him.'

18. "When Vaidehī addressed me in this fashion, I flew into a rage, and with eyes blood red and lips quivering in anger, I left the ashram."

19. So Saumitri spoke, and wild with anguish Rāma said, "Dear brother, you did wrong to come without her.

20. "You know full well I am capable of defending myself against *rākṣasas*, and yet you left Maithilī just because of words spoken in anger.

21. "I am most displeased with you for deserting Maithilī, for coming here just because of some harsh things heard from an angry woman.

22. "It truly shows poor judgment that under pressure from Sītā you succumbed to anger and did not do as I had ordered.

23. "The *rākṣasa* who took the form of a deer and drew me from the ashram lies slain by my arrow.

24. "I fixed an arrow in the bow, drew it, and struck him as if in sport. He let out a broken cry, the shape of the deer vanished, and he turned back into a *rākṣasa* adorned with bracelets.

25. "But no sooner did my arrow strike than he assumed my voice and, with an anguished cry, uttered those dreadful words that carried far, making you leave Maithilī and come."

The end of the fifty-seventh *sarga* of the *Araṇyakāṇḍa* of the *Śrī Rāmāyaṇa*.

Sarga 58

1. As Rāma started back he felt a fitful throbbing below his left eye; he stumbled, too, and a fit of trembling seized him.

2. He saw one ominous portent after another and each time would murmur, "Can all be well with Sītā?"

3. He hurried on, yearning for the sight of Sītā, and when he saw their dwelling empty, his heart stood still.

4. Then, as if suddenly startled, the delight of the Raghus lurched forward and began searching everywhere, the length and breadth of the cottage grounds.

5. The leaf hut with Sītā gone looked to him like a lotus pond when Śrī, goddess of beauty, is gone and winter has ravaged it.

6–7. The cottage grounds were empty and, with the trees rustling, almost seemed to weep. The flowers had faded, the birds and beasts had fallen still, and the spirits of the forest had departed. The place had lost its beauty and looked ravaged, with the bark clothes and holy *kuśa* grass scattered about, and the cushions in disarray. At the sight of all this Rāma began to lament and could not stop.

8. "She is lost or dead, carried off or devoured! Or no, perhaps she is afraid and hiding, or has taken to the forest.

9. "Could she have gone to pick flowers or fruit? Maybe she went to the lotus pond or down to the river for water."

10. He hunted through the forest tirelessly but could not find his beloved. Grief turned his eyes blood red, grief gave him the look of a madman.

11. Rāma dashed from tree to tree, from river to river, up and down the mountains, lost in lamentation and sinking ever deeper into the muddy waters of grief.

12. "Have you seen my beloved, *kadamba* tree? She loved you so much. Tell me if you know what happened to my beautiful Sītā.

13. "Tell me if you have seen her, *bilva* tree. Her breasts are as large as your fruits, her limbs as smooth as your young shoots, and she wears as silky yellow a dress.

14. "Perhaps you, *arjuna* tree—she loved you, too—perhaps you can tell me about my beloved, whether or not the shy daughter of Janaka is still alive.

15. "The *kakubha* tree—so like it are her velvety thighs—plainly knows something of Maithilī, for how lush its vines appear, its shoots and blossoms.

16. "Since bees are buzzing about this splendid *tilaka* here, it plainly has some knowledge of her who loved the tree so well.

17. "*Aśoka*, 'dispeller of grief'! Grief is tearing at my heart. Let me be called *aśoka*, too, by quickly showing me my beloved.

18. "Palmyra palm, if you have seen a shapely woman with breasts like your ripe fruits, tell me about her if you feel any pity for me.

19. "If you have seen Sītā, rose-apple tree, a woman with a rosy-golden glow, if you have any knowledge of my beloved, do not hesitate to tell me.

20. "Or you there, deer, do you know anything of fawn-eyed Maithilī? My beloved might be among the does: Her flashing glances are so like theirs.

21. "Elephant, I am sure you would know if you had seen her. Her thighs are just as smooth as your trunk. Tell me, best of elephants.

22. "Tiger, if you have seen Maithilī, my moon-faced love, speak out in full confidence; you have nothing to fear.

23. "Why are you running away, my lotus-eyed love? I'm sure I saw you hiding behind that tree. Why won't you speak to me?

24. "Stop, please stop, my lovely! Have you no pity for me? You never used to play such pranks. How can you ignore me?

25. "Your yellow silk clothes have given you away, my beauty. Run all you like, I have spotted you. But stop, if you have any feeling for me.

26. "No, I am sure that is not her. The sweet-smiling girl must have come to harm—surely that is the only reason she would ignore me in my plight.

27. "Plainly the child has been devoured by flesh-eating *rākṣasas* who tore my beloved apart, limb from limb, when I left her alone.

28. "That full-moon face of hers with flashing earrings, that per-

fect nose, those lovely teeth and lips, have all been eclipsed, I am sure of it, swallowed up in darkness.

29. "Even as she was lamenting, my beloved's soft, lovely throat, pale as the *campaka* flower, was devoured along with the lovely necklace she wore.

30. "And as she flailed about, her arms, soft as a spray of leaves, were devoured, I am sure of it—bracelets, armlets, trembling hands, and all.

31. "I abandoned the child to be devoured by *rākṣasas*, like a woman left behind by a caravan, beyond the help of all her kinsmen.

32. "Oh great-armed Lakṣmaṇa, do you see my beloved anywhere? Oh my beloved, my beautiful Sītā, where can you have gone?"

33. So Rāma lamented on and on as he ran from wood to wood—rushing on impulse from one place to scour another compulsively, or wandering like a madman—obsessed with the search for his beloved.

34. Through forests and thickets, over rivers and hills and mountain cascades, he rushed about, wandering without rest.

35. After he had traversed the vast, deep forest and explored the whole of it, his hopes of finding Maithilī remained unfulfilled, and so he redoubled his efforts in searching for his love.

The end of the fifty-eighth *sarga* of the *Araṇyakāṇḍa* of the *Śrī Rāmāyaṇa*.

Sarga 59

1–2. When Rāma, son of Daśaratha, found the ashram empty, the leaf hut vacant, the seats in disarray; when he found Vaidehī missing and had looked everywhere for her, he stretched out his noble arms and wailed.

3. "Where is Vaidehī, Lakṣmaṇa? Where on earth could she have gone? Has someone carried off my beloved, or devoured her, Saumitri?

4. "Sītā, if you are hiding behind a tree to play a joke on me, enough of your joking. Come to me now, in my bitter sorrow.

5. "The fawns that used to play with you so trustingly, dear Sītā, are lost in worry, teary-eyed at your absence.

6. "I know I shall die from the crushing grief of Sītā's abduction, and soon the great king, my father, will see me in the other world.

7–8. " 'How dare you—when I gave you an order and you made a promise—come into my presence before the appointed time?' That is plainly what my father will say in the other world, and he will curse me for my wayward, ignoble conduct, and failing to keep my word.

9–10. "Where have you gone, my fair-waisted wife, leaving me here helplessly stricken with grief, miserable, and pitiful? You have shattered all my dreams, vanishing as his good reputation leaves a dishonest man. Without you I shall die."

11. So Rāma Rāghava lamented in the bitter anguish of his sorrow, yearning for the sight of Sītā, but Janaka's daughter was nowhere to be seen.

12. Failing to find Sītā, the son of Daśaratha sank down in despair like an elephant in deep mud. Then Lakṣmaṇa, with Rāma's best interests at heart, earnestly addressed him:

13. "Do not despair, my great-armed, valiant brother. Together we shall try again. There are many lovely caverns in this forest.

14. "Maithilī loves to roam the woods and is enchanted by the forest. She probably went into the forest or down to the flowering lotus pond.

15. "Perhaps Vaidehī is at the river, where fish abound and the rushes grow thick. Or maybe she is hiding somewhere in the woods, aiming to frighten us, bull among men, or put us to a test.

16. "If you will, majestic Kākutstha, let us at once attempt another search for Janaka's daughter and explore the whole forest: She is sure to be there. Only do not let your mind give way to grief."

17. Hearing these heartfelt words of Lakṣmaṇa's, Rāma composed himself and began to search with Saumitri.

18–19. The sons of Daśaratha looked everywhere for Sītā, thoroughly searching the forests and mountains, the rivers and lakes, the slopes of the mountain, its caves and peaks. But for all their thorough searching they could not find her.

20. After searching all over the mountain, Rāma said to Lakṣmaṇa, "Saumitri, I have seen not a trace of Vaidehī anywhere on the lovely mountain."

21. And as Lakṣmaṇa, consumed with sorrow, wandered back through Daṇḍaka wilderness, he answered his mighty brother:

22. "My wise brother, you shall recover Janaka's daughter Maithilī as surely as great-armed Viṣṇu recovered the earth and left the demon Bali in chains."

23. So heroic Lakṣmaṇa spoke, but Rāghava, numb with sorrow and in a wretched voice, only replied:

24. "The whole forest has been searched inch by inch, wise brother, the flowering lotus ponds and this mountain as well, with all of its many caverns and streams. But I have seen not a trace of Vaidehī, who is dearer to me than life itself."

25. So Rāma wretchedly lamented, and overpowered for the moment by the agonizing grief of Sītā's abduction, he fainted.

26. Becoming faint in every limb he sank down insensible, unconscious in the misery of his anguish, and heaving deep and burning sighs.

27. Lotus-eyed Rāma sighed again and again and, in a voice choked with sobs, again and again cried out, "Oh my beloved!"

28. Righteous Lakṣmaṇa, humbly and with hands cupped in reverence, tried every way he knew to comfort the brother he so deeply loved.

29. But Rāma was deaf to the words that fell from Lakṣmaṇa's lips and cried out over and over for his beloved Sītā who had disappeared.

The end of the fifty-ninth *sarga* of the *Araṇyakāṇḍa* of the *Śrī Rāmāyaṇa*.

Sarga 60

1. Rāma was desolate and addressed Lakṣmaṇa in a tone of utter desolation: "Go down at once to the Godāvarī and look around. Perhaps Sītā went to the river to fetch lotuses."

2. So Rāma spoke, and Lakṣmaṇa set off again at a quick pace for the pleasant Godāvarī river.

3. After searching its many landing places Lakṣmaṇa reported back to Rāma: "I cannot find her at the landings, and she does not answer when I call.

4. "I cannot imagine, Rāma, where fair-waisted Vaidehī, the one relief of all our cares, could possibly be."

5. Hearing Lakṣmaṇa's words Rāma, desolate and wild with anguish, went down to the Godāvarī river to see for himself.

6. He stood at the shore and cried, "Oh, where is Sītā?"

7. But the animals would not tell Rāma, nor would the Godāvarī river, that it was the lord of *rākṣasas* who had taken her and thereby condemned himself to death.

8. The animals then urged the river, "Tell him about his love." But she refused to reveal Sītā's fate, no matter how piteously Rāma asked.

9. For the river was thinking about the evil Rāvaṇa—how he looked, what he could do—and was too afraid to tell what had happened to Vaidehī.

10. So the river held out no hope to him of seeing Sītā again, and in the agony of his loss Rāma said to Saumitri:

11. "What shall I say, Lakṣmaṇa, when I meet Janaka and Vaidehī's mother and she is not with me? How shall I break the news?

12. "Where has Vaidehī gone, she who relieved all the grief I suffered while living in the wilderness on things of the wild, stripped of my kingship?

13. "How long the nights will seem to me as I lie awake, the princess gone from my sight, the support of all my kinsmen stripped from me.

14. "I will roam through Janasthāna, by the Godāvarī, over Mount Prasravaṇa here; I will continue roaming far and wide on the chance of finding Sītā."

15. As the brothers were speaking together in this fashion, they saw a trail of flowers that had fallen upon the earth.

16. At the sight of the shower of blossoms that had fallen on the

ground, mighty Rāma was overcome with sorrow and said to Lakṣmaṇa sorrowfully:

17. "I recognize these flowers here, Lakṣmaṇa: I gave them to Vaidehī in the woods and she entwined them in her hair."

18. So great-armed Rāma spoke to Lakṣmaṇa, bull among men, but then he flew into a rage and cried out to the mountain in the distance, like a lion roaring at a puny deer:

19. "Mountain! Show me the gold-hued, golden Sītā, before I bring all your slopes crashing down.

20. "The fire of my arrows shall burn you to ashes, no grass, no trees, not one twig left, and then you shall be shunned forevermore.

21. "Or this river here, I will dry it up this instant, Lakṣmaṇa, if it does not tell me instantly about my moon-faced Sītā."

22. So Rāma spoke in a fury, as if ready to unleash fire from his eye, but just then he saw the huge footprints of a *rākṣasa* impressed upon the earth.

23. What Rāma spotted were the winding tracks left by Sītā and the *rākṣasa*. His heart began to pound wildly, and he said to his dear brother:

24. "Look, Lakṣmaṇa, here are bits of gold broken off the ornaments belonging to Vaidehī, and here are her various garlands, Saumitri.

25. "And look, Saumitri, the ground is spattered everywhere with drops of blood sparkling like those bits of burnished gold.

26. "Lakṣmaṇa, I fear that *rākṣasas*, who can take on any form at will, have wantonly butchered Vaidehī, have torn her limb from limb, or devoured her.

27. "Or could it be that two *rākṣasas* quarreled over Vaidehī and had a terrible fight here, Saumitri?

28. "Whose bow is this lying broken on the ground, dear brother? It is huge, studded with pearls and backed with burnished gold.

29. "Whose golden armor is this lying shattered on the earth, shining like the morning sun, studded with bosses of cat's-eye beryl?

30. "Whose parasol is this dropped on the earth with its handle

broken, dear brother, a hundred-ribbed parasol festooned with heavenly wreaths?

31. "Whose asses are these that have been killed in battle, huge, awesome creatures with golden breastplates and the faces of *piśācas*?

32. "Whose war chariot is this overturned and broken, shining like a blazing fire and fitted out with a battle standard?

33. "Whose arrows are these splintered and scattered about, all adorned with gold, their shafts made long as a chariot axle to do their terrible work?

34. "Just see, dear brother, my hatred of the *rākṣasas* has grown a hundred times more deadly than before, for they may change their outward forms at will but never their savage hearts.

35. "Poor Sītā is dead, or has been devoured or carried off into the deep forest, her righteousness no defense at all.

36. "Since Vaidehī has been devoured or carried off, who in this mortal world—or which god—has thought it possible to injure me?

37. "But then, any creature, Lakṣmaṇa, knowing no better, will despise the man of compassion, however heroic he may be, the very master of the worlds.

38. "The thirty gods themselves must surely think me powerless, because I have been mild, compassionate, and self-restrained, striving for the welfare of the world.

39. "Look how in my case, Lakṣmaṇa, a good has become an evil. But now I will efface it—as the great rising sun effaces the light of the hare-marked moon—in order to exterminate the *rākṣasas* and all living things.

40. "No *yakṣa*, *gandharva*, or *piśāca*, no *rākṣasa*, *kinnara*, or man shall be left in peace, Lakṣmaṇa.

41. "Watch now, Lakṣmaṇa, as I fill the sky with missiles and darts, leaving no space whatever for creatures that move about the three worlds.

42–43. "I will bring the host of planets to a standstill, darken the moon that brings the night, paralyze both fire and wind, blot out the light of the sun; I will grind the mountain peaks to dust, dry up every body of water, uproot every tree, vine, and shrub, annihilate the ocean.

44. "If the gods do not restore Sītā to me safe and sound this very instant, they shall witness the full extent of my power, Saumitri.

45. "Not a single creature, Lakṣmaṇa, shall escape into the sky: The darts shot from my bowstring will form a net without a gap.

46. "Behold now, Lakṣmaṇa, the devastation caused by my iron shafts, the birds and beasts driven wild and ravaged, the world plunged into chaos, from one end to the other.

47. "Because of what happened to Maithilī, I will shoot my arrows from a full-drawn bow, arrows no one can withstand, and rid this mortal world of all *piśācas* and *rākṣasas*.

48. "Now the gods shall witness the power of my shafts when I ply them in anger; they shall see how far they carry when, my patience exhausted, I release them.

49. "No god or *daitya*, no *piśāca* or *rākṣasa* shall survive when in my rage I lay waste the universe.

50. "The worlds of the gods and *dānavas* and *yakṣas*, besides that of the *rākṣasas*, shall come crashing down one upon the other as my darts fly wave after wave, smashing them to pieces. I will obliterate the boundaries of all the worlds with my shafts.

51. "Like old age or death or time or fate, which no creature has ever defied, Lakṣmaṇa, so in my rage I cannot be withstood; let no one doubt it.

52. "Unless they show me Sītā, the bright-smiling, flawless princess of Mithilā, I will overturn this world, mountains and all, its great serpents and men, its *gandharvas* and gods."

The end of the sixtieth *sarga* of the *Araṇyakāṇḍa* of the *Śrī Rāmāyaṇa*.

Sarga 61

1. Anguished and tormented by the abduction of Sītā, Rāma was prepared to annihilate the worlds, like the fire that comes on doomsday.

2. He kept glancing at his taut-strung bow, racked incessantly with

sighs, raging like Rudra himself when he sought to slay the victim at Dakṣa's sacrifice.

3. At the sight of such rage in Rāma as he had never seen before, Lakṣmaṇa cupped his hands in reverence and addressed him through a mouth gone dry with fear:

4. "You have always been mild in the past, self-restrained, and dedicated to the welfare of all creatures. Do not abandon your true nature, yielding to rage.

5. "The splendor of the moon, the radiance of the sun, the movement of the wind, the patience of the earth—all this is constant, so too your incomparable glory.

6. "I do not know whose war chariot this could be, with all its weapons and accoutrements, or who broke it and why.

7. "A battle must indeed have just ended here, prince; the place looks so dreadful, torn up by hooves and wheels, and spattered with drops of blood.

8. "But only one *rākṣasa* seems to have engaged in this fight, not two, my clever brother, for I find no footprints left by a great army.

9. "And you must not destroy the worlds because of one single being. Lords of the earth must be gentle and cool-headed, and must mete out just punishment.

10. "You have always been the refuge of all creatures, Rāghava, their ultimate resort. Which of them would ever look with approval upon the loss of your wife?

11. "The rivers, oceans, and mountains, the gods, *gandharvas*, and *dānavas* would no more do you an injury than the pious would harm a man consecrated for a rite.

12. "What you must do, your majesty, is search for the one who carried off Sītā, with me at your side, your bow in hand, and the supreme seers to help us.

13. "We shall search the seas, mountains, and forests, all the dreadful caverns, the lotus ponds, and mountain streams.

14. "We shall search relentlessly through the worlds of gods and *gandharvas*, until we track down the one who carried off your wife.

15. "And afterward, if through conciliation the thirty gods do not restore your wife, lord of Kosala, then you shall do what the hour demands.

16. "If you cannot recover Sītā by peaceful means, by conciliation, tact, or diplomacy, lord of men, then unleash the flood of your gold-feathered arrows, as devastating as great Indra's thunderbolts."

The end of the sixty-first *sarga* of the *Araṇyakāṇḍa* of the *Śrī Rāmāyaṇa*.

Sarga 62

1. Consumed with grief, helplessly lamenting, Rāma was numb with shock, insensible in the grip of profound stupor.

2. But having calmed him momentarily, Lakṣmaṇa Saumitri bowed down and pressed his head to his brother's feet, trying to rouse him.

3. "King Daśaratha brought about your birth only by performing great mortifications and a great sacrificial rite, like the immortal gods obtaining the drink of immortality.

4. "Your virtues had so won his heart that when he was separated from you, the king and lord of the earth became a god, as we heard from Bharata.

5. "If you do not endure the sorrow that has befallen you, Kākutstha, what other person, lesser and weaker as he must be, will ever endure?

6. "If in your sorrow you consume the worlds with your might, tiger among men, where are your subjects to find relief from their torment?

7. "This is the way of the world. Yayāti, son of Nahuṣa, won the right to live in Indra's heaven, and then misfortune touched him.

8. "Or consider the great seer Vasiṣṭha, our father's family priest: A hundred sons were born to him in a single day, but all of them were later killed.

9. "And the mother of the world, the goddess to whom all people

pay homage, the earth herself—as we see, my truthful brother—is sometimes shaken.

10. "The mighty sun and moon, the two eyes of the universe, upon which everything is founded, are sometimes eclipsed.

11. "The greatest beings, the gods themselves, cannot escape destiny; how then could any other beings, men of flesh and blood?

12. "They say that even among the gods, Śakra and the rest, misfortune no less than good fortune is to be found. You should not agonize, then, tiger among men.

13. "Whether Vaidehī is simply lost or has, in fact, been carried off, you must not grieve, faultless hero, like a lesser man.

14. "Men like you do not grieve, Rāma, for they always see things as they truly are. However great their difficulties, their sight remains unclouded.

15. "Think the matter through clearly in your mind, best of men. For it is by applying their minds that the wise distinguish right from wrong.

16. "Without doing this, without carefully weighing an action and examining the arguments for and against it, the desired result is never attained.

17. "In the past, my mighty brother, it was always you who advised me; indeed, who would presume to advise you, were Bṛhaspati himself, preceptor of the gods, to come in person?

18. "Your thoughts are too profound for even the gods to fathom, wise brother. All I mean to do is rouse your reason, which grief has lulled to sleep.

19. "Be aware of your powers, which are as much divine as human, bull of the Ikṣvākus. Direct your efforts to slaying those who have shown their hatred of you.

20. "What good would it do you, bull among men, to cause universal destruction? No, instead you must identify that one evil enemy and destroy him."

The end of the sixty-second *sarga* of the *Araṇyakāṇḍa* of the *Śrī Rāmāyaṇa*.

Sarga 63

1. Rāghava, elder brother though he was, no sooner heard the wise words Lakṣmaṇa spoke than he recognized their great worth, as he was always ready to do.

2. Great-armed Rāma restrained his towering wrath, and leaning on his shining bow he said to Lakṣmaṇa:

3. "What are we to do, dear Lakṣmaṇa, where are we to go? Think of some way that Sītā may be restored to my sight."

4. So Rāma spoke, racked with anguish, and Lakṣmaṇa replied, "You must search here, through Janasthāna. The place is infested with *rākṣasas* and densely covered with trees and vines.

5. "There are mountain fastnesses here, gorges, ravines, and dreadful caverns everywhere that harbor herds of different kinds of beasts.

6. "Together we must carefully search the abodes of the *gandharvas* and the places where the *kinnaras* dwell.

7. "Great and wise men like you, bull among men, are no more shaken in times of trouble than mountains are shaken by gusts of wind."

8. So Lakṣmaṇa spoke, and Rāma set out with him to traverse the entire forest, still enraged and holding a terrible razor-headed arrow affixed to his bow.

9. It was then he saw the bird huge as a mountain peak, illustrious Jaṭāyus, where he lay fallen on the ground drenched with the blood of his wounds.

10. At the sight of this creature the size of a mountain peak, Rāma said to Lakṣmaṇa, "Here is the one, I am certain, who devoured Sītā, princess of Videha.

11. "This is plainly a *rākṣasa* who roams the woods in a vulture's guise. And there he sits at his ease, having devoured large-eyed Sītā. I intend to slay him with my darts, my terrible, flame-tipped, unerring darts."

12. With this, Rāma fell upon the vulture in a rage, holding the razor-headed arrow affixed to his bow and shaking the earth, it seemed, all the way to the ocean's edge.

13. But then, in a desolate, most desolate voice, and spitting up foaming blood, the bird addressed Rāma, son of Daśaratha:

14. "She for whom you search the deep forest as though for a healing herb—and long may you live, Rāma—your queen, and my life as well, have both been taken by Rāvaṇa.

15. "I saw your queen as powerful Rāvaṇa was carrying her off, Rāghava, when you and Lakṣmaṇa had left her all alone.

16. "I rushed to Sītā's aid and gave battle, destroying Rāvaṇa's chariot and royal parasol, and bringing him to the ground.

17. "This broken bow is his, this is his shield, and this his war chariot, Rāma, broken in the battle.

18. "But I had exhausted myself, and then Rāvaṇa drew his sword and cut off my wings, and taking Sītā, princess of Videha, he flew up into the sky. You have no need to kill me; the *rākṣasa* has already done so."

19. When Rāma heard his tale—a tale he cherished, since it touched on Sītā—he embraced the vulture-king and then, with Lakṣmaṇa, burst into tears.

20. Rāma was overcome with sorrow as he gazed at him gasping for breath all alone in that trackless, inaccessible place, and he said to Saumitri:

21. "Expulsion from the kingdom, living in the forest, Sītā lost, this bird slain—the misfortunes that I have suffered are fierce enough to consume fire itself.

22. "Were I to try to sail across the brimful ocean, I am convinced that with my luck even the lord of rivers would run dry.

23. "In all this world of things that move and do not move, there exists no one more luckless than I, no one entangled in a net of disaster so vast as mine.

24. "Here my father's friend, the aged vulture-king, lies upon the ground, struck down because of my own inimical fate."

25. So Rāghava spoke, all the while caressing Jaṭāyus and, with Lakṣmaṇa, showing him all the affection of a son for his father.

26. As the vulture-king lay spattered with blood from his severed wings, Rāma embraced him. "Where is Maithilī, my very life?" he cried out and sank to the ground.

The end of the sixty-third *sarga* of the *Araṇyakāṇḍa* of the *Śrī Rāmāyaṇa*.

Sarga 64

1. As the vulture lay on the ground where he was brought down by the savage Rāvaṇa, Rāma gazed at him and addressed Saumitri, his staunchest friend:

2. "This bird was struggling on my behalf, I am sure, and that is why the *rākṣasa* struck him down in combat. Now he is about to lose his life, the hardest loss of all.

3. "But look, Lakṣmaṇa, some breath still remains in his body. He is gazing up, though the gaze is vacant and his voice has failed.

4. "Jaṭāyus, if you can still speak, please, tell me about Sītā, and how you yourself met your end.

5. "What reason had Rāvaṇa to carry off Sītā? What wrong have I ever done Rāvaṇa, that he should carry off my beloved?

6. "And Sītā's lovely moonlike face, what did it look like at that hour, noblest of birds? Was there anything that she said?

7. "What powers does this *rākṣasa* possess, what does he look like, what feats has he accomplished, and where does he live? Dear friend, answer my questions!"

8. While Rāma lamented without respite, Jaṭāyus gazed up at him in desolation and replied in the faintest voice:

9. "It was Rāvaṇa who carried her off, the lord of *rākṣasas*, and as he shot through the sky he worked a prodigious magic of winds and storms.

10. "When I had tired myself out, my son, the nightstalker cut off my wings, and taking Sītā, princess of Videha, he set forth heading south.

11. "My breath is coming harder, Rāghava, everything is swimming before my eyes. I see the golden trees now and their streaming hair of spikenard!

12–13. "Rāvaṇa left with Sītā at the hour called Vinda: Wealth lost at this hour is soon recovered by the owner. But he was unaware of it, Kākutstha, and like a fish that takes the hook, he shall soon perish.

14. "Do not agonize over the daughter of Janaka. You shall soon kill the *rākṣasa* in battle and once again rejoice in Vaidehī's company."

15. The vulture had been lucid while replying to Rāma, but he was nearing death; blood mixed with bits of flesh had begun to dribble from his beak.

16. "It was Viśravas's son himself, the brother of Vaiśravaṇa . . ." but with this, the lord of birds let go the breath of life and could capture it no more.

17. "Tell me, tell me!" Rāma cried, cupping his hands in supplication, but the breath of life had left the vulture's body and passed into the sky.

18. The vulture's head dropped to the earth, his legs stretched out rigidly, his body was convulsed and then fell back to the ground.

19. Rāma gazed at the vulture, at his tawny eyes and lifeless mountain of a corpse, and then, in the desolation of his many sorrows, he said to Saumitri:

20. "This bird had dwelled in peace for many years in this dwelling place of *rākṣasas*, roaming here through Daṇḍaka wilderness.

21. "He was born a long time ago and had lived for many years, and now he lies here slain—how inescapable is doom.

22. "Look at him, Lakṣmaṇa, this vulture who went to the aid of Sītā and was killed in my service by the powerful Rāvaṇa.

23. "On my account the lord of birds relinquished the great kingship of vultures, that of his fathers and forefathers, and gave up his life as well.

24. "You see, Saumitri, everywhere, even among the animals, can be found good creatures that follow the ways of righteousness, that are brave and provide a sure place of refuge.

25. "Dear brother, slayer of enemies, my sorrow over Sītā's abduction has not been so hard to bear as the death of this vulture in my cause.

26. "The lord of birds was no less worthy of reverence and esteem in my eyes than majestic, glorious King Daśaratha.

27. "Saumitri, fetch wood. I intend to build a fire and cremate the king of vultures, who died for my sake.

28. "I will place him on the pyre, Saumitri, and cremate him, the lord of the world of birds, killed by the savage *rākṣasa*.

29–30. "Courageous king of vultures, may you go to the state attained by sacrificers, the state attained by those who keep the sacred fires, who do not turn their back in battle, who make gifts of land. May you go to that very state on taking leave of me; when I have purified you, may you proceed to the highest of worlds."

31. So righteous Rāma spoke, and placing the lord of birds upon the pyre, he lit it and cremated him, with all the sorrow one feels for a kinsman.

32. Powerful Rāma and Saumitri then went into the forest, killed several large, plump stags, and spread their parts about the bird.

33. Glorious Rāma carved off the flesh of the stags, cut it into chunks, and laid it on the lovely grass as an offering to the bird.

34. Rāma quickly intoned for him the prayer for reaching heaven, the one brahmans recite for men who have died.

35. Both princes then went down to the Godāvarī river and poured the funeral libation for the king of vultures.

36. Struck down in battle after accomplishing a glorious and most difficult feat, the king of vultures was purified according to the custom of the great seers and attained the holy state, which brings felicity.

The end of the sixty-fourth *sarga* of the *Araṇyakāṇḍa* of the *Śrī Rāmāyaṇa*.

Sarga 65

1. After making the funeral libation for Jaṭāyus, the Rāghavas set forth and went westward, scouring the forest for Sītā.

2. Armed with bows and arrows and swords, the Aikṣvākas then turned south, striking out on an unbeaten path.

3. It was nearly impassable, so densely overgrown, everywhere choked with shrubs and trees and vines, dreadful to see.

4. But the mighty princes forced their way along it, bearing southward, and soon they had traversed that vast and awesome wilderness.

5. Some six miles beyond Janasthāna the mighty Rāghavas entered the dense Krauñca forest.

6. It looked like a vast bank of clouds, and everywhere it seemed to bristle with life. Lovely flowers of all colors could be found there, and flocks of birds and herds of beasts.

7. Tormented by the loss of Sītā, the brothers began to search the woods in hopes of finding her; only now and then would they stop to rest.

8. But soon mighty Lakṣmaṇa, a man of courage, character, and honesty, cupped his hands in reverence and addressed his even mightier brother:

9. "My arm has started throbbing fitfully. I feel strangely uneasy and have been noticing portents, most unfavorable portents.

10. "So be on your guard, my noble brother, and heed my sound advice. For to me, at least, the portents foretell some peril soon to come.

11. "That bird there is a *vañculaka*, 'the deceiver,' most ominous of birds. His cries would seem to foretell our defeat in battle."

12. As they carried on their relentless search through the entire forest, a tremendous noise broke out that seemed to shatter the forest.

13. The deep wood seemed altogether enveloped in wind; the noise coming from the forest seemed to fill the heavens.

14. Seeking the source of the noise, Rāma and his younger brother came upon a mammoth, huge-chested *rākṣasa* in a thicket.

15. The two of them drew near and there, facing them, stood the giant Kabandha, a creature without head or neck, his face set in his belly.

16. The hair on his body was bushy and wiry; he towered before them like a mountain, a savage creature like a black storm cloud and with a voice like thunder.

17. And in his chest, darting glances, thick-lashed, tawny, prodigious, wide, and terrible, was a single eye.

18. Ravenously licking his massive lips and massive fangs, he was devouring tremendous apes and lions, elephants and deer.

19. Contorting his two dreadful arms, each one of them a league in length, he would seize all sorts of animals in his hands—apes, deer, flocks of birds.

20. He pulled in countless animals and pulled them apart limb from limb as he stood there blocking the path the two brothers were taking.

21. They withdrew then to the distance of a league and beheld the huge, ferocious, awesome Kabandha wrapped up in his own arms.

22. But then, stretching out these prodigious arms to their full extent, he seized the Rāghavas both at once, squeezing them with all his might.

23. Despite their own great arms and blazing power, despite their swords and sturdy bows, the mighty brothers were caught and helplessly drawn in.

24. Great-armed Kabandha, foremost of *dānavas*, then spoke to them: "Who are you two bull-shouldered men, bearing such great swords and bows?

25. "By entering this dreadful region you have offered yourselves to me as prey. State your business here and your reason for coming.

26. "With your bows and arrows and swords, looking like two sharp-horned bulls, you have entered the region where I dwell tormented by hunger—indeed, you have entered my very mouth, and your lives are lost."

27. When Rāma heard what the evil Kabandha said, his mouth went suddenly dry, and he spoke to Lakṣmaṇa:

28. "We go from bad to worse, my valiant brother. We have found, not my beloved, but a dreadful calamity that may cost us our lives.

29. "How great the power that doom exerts against all creatures, Lakṣmaṇa! Look at you and me, tiger among men, the two of us stunned by one calamity after another. Is not fate far too much for any creature to endure, Lakṣmaṇa?

30. "Powerful heroes expert in arms can be overcome by doom and collapse on the field of battle like dikes made of sand."

31. So he spoke, the glorious, valiant son of Daśaratha, whose courage was true and firm, but observing the stubborn courage of Saumitri, he steadied his heart by an act of will.

The end of the sixty-fifth *sarga* of the *Araṇyakāṇḍa* of the *Śrī Rāmāyaṇa*.

Sarga 66

1. Seeing the brothers Rāma and Lakṣmaṇa now entangled in the snare of his arms, Kabandha spoke:

2. "Why did you linger, mighty kshatriyas, when you could plainly see I was tormented by hunger? Fools, you must have been destined as my prey."

3. At this, Lakṣmaṇa, filled with pain yet resolved to resist courageously, said what the moment and their safety demanded:

4. "Any minute this foul *rākṣasa* will bolt us down. Come, let us cut off his massive arms at once with our swords."

5. Aware of what the time and place required, the Rāghavas took their swords and cut off his horribly bristling arms at the shoulder.

6. With a stroke the skillful Rāma cut off his right arm—the sword passed cleanly through—and mighty Lakṣmaṇa the left.

7. His arms cut off, the great-armed *rākṣasa* collapsed roaring like a thundercloud, making heaven and earth resound in every direction.

8. The *dānava* looked at his severed arms, at the sea of blood engulfing him, and, wretchedly now, asked the mighty princes, "Whoever can you be?"

9. So Kabandha spoke, and the good prince, powerful Lakṣmaṇa, told him about Kākutstha.

10. "This is the heir of the Ikṣvāku dynasty. His name is Rāma, and all people have heard of him. As for me, know that I am Lakṣmaṇa, his younger brother.

11. "My brother, who has the powers of a god, was living in the desolate forest when a *rākṣasa* carried off his wife. It is in search of her that we have come this way.

12. "And you, who are you, and how do you come to be hobbling about in the forest, with your legs broken, your flaming mouth in your chest, no more than a headless trunk?"

13. So Lakṣmaṇa spoke, and Kabandha, remembering what Indra had once told him, was overjoyed and replied:

14. "Welcome, tigers among men! How fortunate at last to see you, how fortunate to have you sever my arms from their sockets.

15. "Listen, tiger among men, I shall tell you exactly how it was, through an act of folly, that I came to suffer such deformity."

The end of the sixty-sixth *sarga* of the *Araṇyakāṇḍa* of the *Śrī Rāmāyaṇa*.

Sarga 67

1. "Once upon a time, great-armed prince, powerful and valiant Rāma, I was as handsome as the sun, or moon, or Śakra; I was endowed with an unbelievably beautiful form, which made me famous throughout the three worlds.

2. "But I would take on this other colossal form, Rāma, to terrify the worlds. I would go from place to place striking terror into seers who lived in the forest.

3. "One time I incurred the wrath of a great seer named Sthūlaśiras. I had attacked him in this form when he was busy gathering different foods of the forest.

4. "Looking me in the eye he called down a dreadful curse, saying, 'This form, ferocious and repulsive as it is, you shall have forever!'

5. "But I begged the enraged seer to set a limit to the curse provoked by my insulting him. And these were the words he spoke:

6. " 'When Rāma cuts off your arms and cremates you in the desolate forest, then you shall regain the grand and lovely form that is properly yours.'

7. "I would have you know, Lakṣmaṇa, that I am the son of Danu and was once radiantly handsome. It was in consequence of Indra's wrath that I acquired this form, on the field of battle.

8. "I had propitiated Grandfather Brahmā through intense austerities. He granted me long life, but then madness took hold of me.

9. "The thought occurred to me: I have secured long life. What can Śakra do to me? I acted on it and attacked Indra in battle.

10. "The hundred-jointed thunderbolt that came hurtling from his hand drove my head and lower limbs right into my trunk.

11. "I begged him to send me to the house of Yama, but he refused, saying to me, 'The Grandfather has spoken; his words must prove true.'

12–13. "I said to him, 'But I cannot eat, the blow of your thunderbolt has broken my lower limbs, my head, and mouth. How then am I to live at all, let alone for all that time?' Śakra then provided me with those arms, a league in length, and fashioned a sharp-fanged mouth set within my paunch.

14. "With those long arms I would be able to pull in creatures of the forest—lions, tigers, elephants, deer—from all around me and devour them.

15. "And Indra added, 'When Rāma and Lakṣmaṇa cut off your arms in combat, then you shall go to heaven.'

16. "You must surely be that same Rāma, bless you, for no one else could ever kill me, Rāghava, just as the great seer said.

17. "Now, I will give you some good advice, bull among men, and make known to you an ally, once the two of you have purified me with fire."

18. So Danu spoke, and righteous Rāghava answered him as Lakṣmaṇa listened:

19. "Rāvaṇa carried off my glorious wife, Sītā, at his leisure when my brother and I were absent from Janasthāna.

20. "But all I know is the *rākṣasa*'s name; we have no idea what he looks like, where he lives, or the full extent of his power.

21. "It is only right to take pity on men who have been running in circles like this, helpless and sick with grief, and who are ready to be of service.

22. "We will fetch dry branches broken off over time by elephants, prepare a huge pit, and cremate you, mighty Kabandha.

23. "But first you must tell us about Sītā, if in truth you know: By what route was she carried off, to what destination? Oh, do me this one great kindness!"

24. So Rāma spoke, and Danu, as one clever speaker to another, made his final reply:

25. "I do not possess divine knowledge, and I know nothing of Maithilī. But I will tell you who does know, once I have been cremated and have regained my proper form.

26. "For you see, my lord, until I am cremated, I can know nothing of the mighty *rākṣasa* who carried off Sītā.

27. "My knowledge was completely destroyed by the curse I brought upon myself when I acquired this form so repulsive to all the world.

28. "But come, before the sun drives his weary horses home, cast me into a pit, Rāma, and cremate me in accordance with precept.

29. "Just cremate me in a pit according to established usage, mighty prince, delight of the Raghus, and I shall tell you of one who will know about the *rākṣasa*.

30. "You will do well to form a friendship with him, Rāghava. He adheres to established usage, and will be pleased and straightway render you assistance.

31. "There is nothing in the three worlds of which he is ignorant, Rāghava; he once had occasion, for some reason or other, to wend his way through all the worlds."

The end of the sixty-seventh *sarga* of the *Araṇyakāṇḍa* of the *Śrī Rāmāyaṇa*.

Sarga 68

1. When Kabandha had finished addressing them, the two mighty lords of men went to find a cleft in the mountain and build a fire.

2. With huge flaming brands Lakṣmaṇa lit the pyre all around, till it was completely engulfed in flames.

3. The fire burned slowly as the body of Kabandha melted, for it was solid fat, like a lump of butter.

4. But then suddenly, jolting the pyre, he ascended like a smokeless flame, a mighty creature wearing a pair of spotless garments and a heavenly garland.

5. With a sudden rush he flew up in delight from the pyre, luminous and dressed in immaculate raiment, adorned with jewelry on every limb.

6. Upon a luminous, glorious aerial chariot harnessed with geese he stood in all his brilliance, shedding luster in the ten directions.

7. And from midair Kabandha said to Rāma, "Rāghava, listen carefully how to recover Sītā.

8. "There are six measures to bring to bear on every question, Rāma. But when the wick runs out on a man, he is hounded by adversity.

9. "Adversity threatens you. You and Lakṣmaṇa are all alone, and as a result this calamity, the attack upon your wife, has befallen you.

10. "Therefore, best of friends, you must at all costs find a friend, for unless you do—I foresee it in my thoughts—you shall not succeed.

11. "Listen to what I am about to tell you, Rāma. There is a monkey named Sugrīva. His brother Vālin, a son of Indra, has driven him from his country in a fit of rage.

12. "On the lofty mountain Ṛśyamūka, in the beautiful environs of Lake Pampā, the steadfast, mighty Sugrīva has taken up residence with four other monkeys.

13. "You must go there at once, Rāghava, and forthwith secure him as your comrade, sealing your compact in the presence of blazing fire to shun all treachery.

14. "Do not be disdainful of the lord of monkeys. Sugrīva is very powerful and can take on any form at will. He now finds himself in need of help and always honors claims of gratitude.

15. "The two of you could do at once what he wants done. But whether or not his needs are met, he shall do what you require.

16. "He is the son of Ṛkṣarajas but the natural offspring of the Sun. He has been wandering along Lake Pampā in dread of Vālin ever since he wronged him.

17. "At Mount Ṛśyamūka, where the forest-dweller is residing, lay down your arms and secure the monkey as your comrade at once, pledging your word.

18. "For the clever monkey-chief has discovered every single hiding place in the world of those creatures that feed upon the flesh of men.

19. "Nothing happens without his knowing of it, Rāghava, tamer of foes, nothing in all the world, to the farthest reaches of the sun's thousand shining rays.

20. "With the help of the monkeys he will search the rivers and wide hills, the mountain fastnesses and caverns until he finds your wife.

21. "He will dispatch giant monkeys, Rāghava, in every direction to hunt for Sītā, who must be sick with grief separated from you.

22. "Whether your flawless beloved is on the very summit of Mount Meru, or has gone down to the depths of the underworld, the best of monkeys will find his way there, kill the *rākṣasas*, and restore her to you."

The end of the sixty-eighth *sarga* of the *Araṇyakāṇḍa* of the *Śrī Rāmāyaṇa*.

Sarga 69

1. Now, after making known to Rāma the way to recover Sītā, Kabandha addressed him again, to answer the one essential question he knew remained.

2–3. "Here is a safe path, Rāma, along the western horizon there, where those pleasant flowering trees can be seen, rose-apples and *priyālas*, *panasas*, *plakṣas*, banyans, *tindukas*, fig trees, *karṇikāras*, mangoes, and so on.

4. "Climb them or bend them by force to the ground, but you simply must taste their ambrosial fruit before you go.

5. "Continue your journey through those lovely regions, from mountain to mountain, forest to forest, mighty princes, and you will come to the lotus-covered lake known as Pampā.

6. "It is free from pebbles, weeds, and pitfalls, Rāma, its landing places are level, its bed soft sand, and beautiful lotuses and water lilies cover it.

7. "Geese and cormorants, *krauñca* birds and ospreys flock to the waters of Lake Pampā, Rāghava, sending up their clear calls.

8. "The birds are not alarmed by the sight of men, so blessed are they in their ignorance of slaughter. And just wait until you taste them; they are plump as balls of butter.

9–10. "And there are fish in Lake Pampā, Rāma, redfish and crooked-snouts and reedfish—choice, fleshy ones, and not too bony. Lakṣmaṇa, in his constant devotion to you, will kill them with his arrows and bring them to you—scaling them, stripping off their fins, and roasting them on iron spits.

11–12. "And while you are eating your fill of fish on a bed of flowers from Lake Pampā, Lakṣmaṇa can easily draw some water and give you a drink from a lotus petal. It is silvery, crystal clear water, deliciously cool, safe and healthful, and charged with the scent of lotuses.

13. "There are handsome, plump wild boars that roam the forest, making their lairs in mountain caves. You will get to see them at Lake Pampā, best of men, when they come thirsting for water and begin to bellow like bulls.

14–15. "And when you take a stroll at dusk you will forget your grief, Rāma Rāghava, viewing the cool waters of Lake Pampā, the flowers massed on the *tilaka* trees, the night-blooming jasmine, blossoming water lilies and lotuses, the trees festooned with garlands.

16. "But those are garlands no man shall ever wear: In that place the students of Matañga once lived, seers who practiced deep meditation.

17–18. "They groaned under the heavy burden of fetching their guru food from the forest, so that drops of sweat dripped steadily from their bodies to the ground. And these were turned into garlands by the ascetic power of the sages; they sprang up from the drops of sweat and can never perish, Rāghava.

19. "Even today in that very place their servant can still be found, Kākutstha. She is an ascetic named Śabarī, who has survived all these years.

20. "She has always been devoted to righteousness, and when at

last she sees you, godlike Rāma, the one to whom all creatures pay homage, she shall go to the world of heaven.

21. "There, Rāma, situated on the western shore of Lake Pampā, you will find the site of that incomparable ashram, though it will be well concealed.

22. "Elephants cannot come there and attack that ashram or surrounding woodland because of the provisions of the seer Matañga.

23. "It is a forest like Nandana, the parkland of the gods themselves; you will enjoy yourself heartily there, where birds of every description congregate.

24. "Now, Ṛśyamūka with its flowering trees is just to the east of Lake Pampā. It is a noble mountain fashioned long ago by Brahmā, very difficult indeed to scale, and with elephant calves standing guard around it.

25. "When a man goes to sleep on the peak of that mountain, Rāma, whatever treasure he lights upon in his dreams, he is sure to discover when he wakes.

26. "But no wrongdoer or evil man may ascend it: *Rākṣasas* would seize him in his sleep and kill him on the spot.

27. "From there, Rāma, you can hear the loud trumpeting of the elephant calves that live in Matañga's wilderness and come to play in Lake Pampā.

28. "And there are furious bull elephants, too, their hides dark as storm clouds, which wander in herds or all alone, running with streams of ichor.

29. "They come to drink the clear, cool, healthful water there, and then they withdraw, plunging back into the forests where they make their homes.

30. "Now, in this mountain, Rāma, a large cave is visible. Its mouth is blocked by a boulder, which makes it all but impossible to enter.

31. "At the front entrance to the cave is a large and pleasant pool of cool water; abundant roots and fruit can be found nearby, and trees of every sort surround it.

32. "There Sugrīva lives with four other monkeys, though he sometimes takes up his position on the summit of the mountain."

33. So the mighty Kabandha instructed Rāma and Lakṣmaṇa as he blazed there in the sky in all his garlands and sunlike radiance.

34. Rāma and Lakṣmaṇa, ready to set forth, called out "Farewell!" to illustrious Kabandha hovering nearby in the sky.

35. "May you achieve success," Kabandha replied as he took leave of the joyful princes, ready to set forth himself.

36. Cloaked in the majesty of a sunlike body, his true form that he had now regained, and gazing down at Rāma from the sky, Kabandha spoke one last word of advice: "Secure that alliance!"

The end of the sixty-ninth *sarga* of the *Araṇyakāṇḍa* of the *Śrī Rāmāyaṇa*.

Sarga 70

1. Heading west the princes set out on the road Kabandha had shown them, which led through the forest to Lake Pampā.

2. Rāma and Lakṣmaṇa noticed the honey-sweet fruit trees densely clustered on the hillsides, but they pressed on, eager to find Sugrīva.

3. After spending the night on a mountain slope, the Rāghavas, delights of their House, arrived at the western shore of Lake Pampā.

4. On reaching the western shore of lotus-covered Pampā, they saw nearby the pleasant ashram of Śabarī.

5. When they reached the ashram, a pleasant spot encircled by trees, they glanced about and then made their way to Śabarī.

6. At the sight of the princes the perfected woman sprang up with hands cupped in reverence, and then she bowed to clasp the feet of Rāma and of wise Lakṣmaṇa.

7. Rāma then addressed the woman, an ascetic of austere vows: "I trust your holy practices thrive and that all obstacles to them have been overcome.

8. "I trust you fast and control your anger, great ascetic, that your vows of self-denial have been fulfilled. I trust the obedience you have shown your guru has been justly rewarded, soft-spoken lady, and that you have found peace of mind."

9. So Rāma questioned the aged ascetic Śabarī, whose perfection had won her the esteem of perfected beings, and she stood before him, and replied:

10. "The day you reached Mount Citrakūṭa, those I had been serving departed and ascended to heaven upon aerial chariots of incomparable radiance.

11. "And those great and illustrious seers, wise in the ways of righteousness, told me, 'One day Rāma shall come to this holy ashram of yours.

12. " 'You are to receive him and Saumitri, too, as guests. Once you have beheld him you shall go to the highest imperishable worlds.'

13. "On your behalf, bull among men, I have collected different sorts of forest food from where it grows on the banks of Lake Pampā, tiger among men."

14. So Śabarī spoke, and righteous Rāghava replied to the woman, who clearly had never been kept in ignorance:

15. "From Danu I have heard all about the power of those great ascetics. With your consent I would like to witness it with my own eyes."

16. When Śabarī heard the words that issued from Rāma's mouth, she went with the two princes and showed them around the great forest.

17. "The place you see here, delight of the Raghus, like a bank of clouds, where birds and beasts congregate, is known as the Forest of Matañga.

18. "Here, splendid prince, is where those purified sages, my gurus, would pay homage to the lakeside shrine with vedic hymns and offer it sacrifice to the accompaniment of hymns.

19. "To this altar sloping westward my honored gurus would bring flowers in hands trembling with weariness and make their offerings.

20. "You can see how, by the power of their asceticism, best of the Raghus, the altars have remained incomparably luminous till today, shedding splendor in every direction.

21. "Since they could not go there themselves—the weariness

brought on by fasting had enfeebled them—they used the power of thought to bring the seven seas here all together. You can see them still.

22. "After bathing they would hang their barkclothes here on the trees, and even today they remain moist in places.

23. "You have seen the entire forest and heard all there is to hear. I should like now to take leave of you and give up this body of mine.

24. "I wish to enter the presence of those purified sages to whom this ashram once belonged and whom I used to serve."

25. When Rāghava heard these words, so perfect in their righteousness, his face beamed with delight, and, seconded by Lakṣmaṇa, he replied, "You have my leave to go."

26. With Rāma's leave she immolated herself in fire, and looking like a blazing fire herself, she went straight to heaven.

27. It was to the holy place where those accomplished great seers rejoice that Śabarī went, by virtue of her meditation on the Self.

The end of the seventieth *sarga* of the *Araṇyakāṇḍa* of the *Śrī Rāmāyaṇa*.

Sarga 71

1. When Śabarī had gone to heaven by her own act, Rāghava paused to reflect in the company of his brother Lakṣmaṇa.

2. And reflecting on the power of those great sages, righteous Rāghava addressed Lakṣmaṇa, who stood at his service with single-minded devotion.

3. "We have seen the ashram, dear brother, that belonged to those accomplished seers, a place of many wonders, where deer and tiger live at peace and birds of every species make their home.

4. "At the landing places of the seven seas, we have bathed as custom requires and made offerings to the spirits of our ancestors.

5. "The misfortune that has hounded us has vanished, Lakṣmaṇa, and good fortune is at hand—it must be, since now my mind is once again filled with joy.

6. "I know in my heart, tiger among men, that soon good fortune will reveal itself. So come, let us go down to lovely Lake Pampā.

7. "Not far from there looms Mount Ṛśyamūka, the place where righteous Sugrīva, offspring of the beaming Sun, has been living with four other monkeys in constant fear of Vālin.

8. "I am impatient to meet the monkey-chief Sugrīva, dear brother, since the search for my Sītā now depends on him."

9. So Rāma spoke, and Saumitri replied, "Let us hurry then and go, for my own heart is no less impatient."

10. The supreme lord of the people then left the ashram with Lakṣmaṇa and went down to Lake Pampā.

11. They gazed over the vast forest, everywhere luxuriant with flowers and tall trees, alive with the calls of lapwing, peacock, woodpecker, parrot, and all kinds of other birds.

12–13. Rāma felt a pang of desire at the sight of the different kinds of trees and ponds as he made his way to the last and finest of the pools of Lake Pampā. It was called the Pond of Mataṅga and was fed by water from far away. On reaching the pool Rāma entered it to bathe.

14. Rāma, son of Daśaratha, was sick with grief as he entered Lake Pampā through its covering of lotuses.

15–17. There were pleasant groves clustered around the lake, brilliant with *tilakas*, *aśokas*, *puṃnāgas*, *bakulas*, and *uddālas*. Its water was choked with lotuses but brimming and crystal clear, with turtles and schools of fish. The beaches were of soft sand, and there were beautiful trees upon the banks, with vines growing twined about them like fast friends. It was the haunt of *kinnaras*, great serpents, *gandharvas*, *yakṣas*, and *rākṣasas*, a lovely treasure house of cool water surrounded by all kinds of trees and vines.

18–19. The pool was thickly covered with lilies, water flowers, and lotuses; and with the coppery red of the day lotuses, the white circles of the night water lilies, and the blue clusters of sky lotuses, it looked like a many-colored blanket. It was bordered by a grove of flowering mangoes, where the cries of peacocks echoed.

20. As mighty Rāma, son of Daśaratha, looked at Lake Pampā with Saumitri, he began to lament from the keen desire he felt.

21–22. Like a graceful woman Lake Pampā seemed, adorned in its different kinds of trees: *tilakas* and *bījapūras*, *vaṭas* and *śukladrumas*, flowering *karavīras* and *puṃnāgas*; shrubs of *mālatī* and *kunda*, *bhaṇḍīras* and *niculas*, *aśokas* and *saptaparṇas*, *ketakas* and *atimuktakas*.

23. Now, near its bank could be seen the mountain mentioned before, the one known as Ṛśyamūka, ornamented with veins of ore and many-colored flowering groves.

24. That was the dwelling place of the powerful monkey named Sugrīva, the son of great Ṛkṣarajas.

25. "Go now, bull among men," he said to the valiant Lakṣmaṇa, "and find Sugrīva, king of monkeys."

26. So, with his gaze fixed on the forest, Rāma had gradually traversed the long road and reached his distant goal; now at last he beheld the flocks of countless birds and lovely groves of Lake Pampā.

The end of the seventy-first *sarga* of the *Araṇyakāṇḍa* of the *Śrī Rāmāyaṇa*.

The end of the *Araṇyakāṇḍa*.

NOTES

Sarga 1

1. "of Daṇḍaka": "The king of that name whose country [Ck, Ct, "Maharashtra"] had become a wilderness in consequence of Indra's curse" (Cm, Cg, Ck, Ct; see note on 2.16.51).

"a circle of ashrams" *āśramamaṇḍalam*: Cm, Cg, Ck, Ct, Cr understand "circle" in the sense of "mass" ("so called because many dwellings [? read *vasti*] are placed together in one area in close proximity," Ck). This is to be distinguished from *āśramapada*, which signifies the site of a particular ashram.

2. "bark garments" *-cīra-*: The clothes would have been set out to dry in the sun after the ascetics' ritual bath (Cg). On the "bark garments" themselves that are traditionally worn by ascetics, see Emeneau 1962 (suggesting cloth woven of bast fiber).

"brahmanical splendor" *brāhmyā lakṣmyā*: Either the splendor that derives from asceticism (Cm), or from the study of the *vedas* and the performance of its precepts (Cg), or from "the study of the wisdom of *brahma*" (Ck, Ct).

4. "*kuśa* grass" *kuśaiḥ*: An essential component in a variety of vedic sacrifices.

5. "offerings and oblations" *balihoma-*: I agree with Cg, Cr in taking this as a *dvandva*; Cm, Ck, Ct understand it as a *tatpuruṣa*, "the oblating of offerings."

8. "who knew the meaning of *brahma*" *brahmavidbhiḥ*: Perhaps here *brahma* in the sense of "holy power."

Note the dignity lent to the verse by the repetition of *brahma-*. For an informative discussion of the semantic field of the word, the complexity of which is reflected in the different glosses of our commentators here and on verse 2 above, see Biardeau 1972, pp. 24–35.

9. "he unstrung his great bow" *vijyaṃ kṛtvā mahad dhanuḥ*: Once again Rāma does not entirely lay aside his weapon, as is customary on entering an ashram. See the note on 2.48.8, and below, 6.18ff. and note. Curiously, most of the NR here reads "stringing his bow" (though Ck should not be included among them, as the crit. ed. has it; he reads *vijyam*).

10. "divine knowledge" *divyajñāna-*: "They knew the secret of Rāma's *avatāra*, namely, that he was Viṣṇu descended in order to kill Rāvaṇa; that Sītā was Lakṣmī, and Lakṣmaṇa a portion [of Viṣṇu]," Cg; "They had knowledge of the past, present, and future: that Rāma was an *avatāra* of . . . the primeval guru *brahma*, who had descended in order to purify his own *śakti*; that it was he now coming, and that he would slay Rāvaṇa," Ck.

11. "like the rising moon" *somam ivodyantam*: "Because like the moon he removes darkness, or like the new moon is particularly worshipful; or again, because appearing in the wilderness he is like the moon surrounded by clouds," Cg; "They looked upon him as King Moon—note the scriptural statement, 'The moon is king of us brahmans' [*TaiS* 1.8.10 (d), *TaiBr* 1.7.4.2]; this would go to explain the request for protection they will soon make [verses 17–20, below]," Ck (so Ct, Cs, who adds, "Thus they were as happy as if they had seen their own king").

12. "handsome physique" *rūpasaṃhananam*: The compound is odd, being apparently redundant, and it gives the commentators trouble (is it here to be taken as a *dvandva*?). I agree with Ct, though the reading of Cm (*rūpaṃ sam-*) is attractive. The epic formula is in fact *siṃhasaṃhanana-*, "with the physique of a lion" ("handsome and well built" according to *AmaK* 3.1.12; see 6.21.30 with Cg there, *MBh* 1.68.4

and repeatedly in that epic), whereas *rūpasaṃhanana-* occurs nowhere else in epic Sanskrit.

"his lovely attire" *suveṣatām*: It is curious that the sages should admire Rāma's clothing (so Cr, who alone glosses the word reasonably), since he is supposed to be dressed just as they are (see 2.10.28, 16.28, 33.7). There is a related problem in 44.36 below; see the note there. Were *suveṣ-* instead to connote "simple clothing," the sages' astonishment would then be occasioned by the incongruity between Rāma's princely bearing and weapons and his hermit's clothes (as in 2.10cd–11ab, 16.11, 18.11 below).

13. "forest hermits" *vanacāriṇaḥ*: Cm wants to interpret this literally, "wanderers of the forest": "The birds, beasts, and so on are meant. And this is the significance of the passage: Blessed Rāma, Sītā, and Lakṣmaṇa are beyond the ken even of Brahmā and the other gods. But like the current of the Ganges, which flows over the halt and the lame alike, he had manifested himself before these forest creatures; and they, fearful of losing this blissful vision . . . will not even blink their eyes."

14. "their leaf huts" *parṇaśālāyām*: Literally, "their leaf hut." The singular implies that each seer invites Rāma into his own hut (Cg, Ck, Ct).

16. "they offered . . . flowers" *puṣpaṃ . . . nivedayitvā*: Apparently for Rāma to eat; see verse 21 below and 2.101.26 note.

"with hands cupped in reverence" *prāñjalayaḥ*: These brahmans, as Ck, Ct, and Cs observe, may bow before this kshatriya because they know his true nature; otherwise such deference would be improper (compare the note on 2.40.25).

17. This verse offers a general description of a king, without specific reference to Rāma. There is no need to read, or understand, "you are" with Cm, Ck (Ct), who accordingly refer the sages' knowledge of Rāma as god and king (which they say is implied by "worthy of reverence and esteem," respectively) back to verse 10.

"his people" *janasyāsya*: Less likely, "this people," that is, the ascetics (Cg).

18. "(A king is) a fourth part Indra himself" *indrasyaiva caturbhāgaḥ*: See the Introduction, Chapter 4d, for a discussion of the divinity of kings in traditional India. Cg takes the genitive *indrasya* as implying (*upalakṣaṇa*) the other world protectors, citing the statement, "A king is fashioned out of eight measures of the world protectors" (compare *ManuSm* 7.4, *LiṅgaP purvārdha* 35.5, and *SūktiRa* 39.18); thus also Cm. See further below, 38.12 and note.

19. "your realm" *bhavadviṣaya-*: "Even though the Daṇḍaka forest is not part of Rāma's realm, it can generally be considered such, since he is a universal emperor," Ck (but see the note on 2.43.11); "the deeper meaning, however, is that because he is an *avatāra* of Viṣṇu, all regions are his," Ct (so too Ck).

20. In the first half of the verse there is a causal sequence: violence or punishment depends on anger, which in turn is rooted in (unfulfilled) sensual desire (so Cg).

"we are as your children" *garbhabhūtāḥ*: So Cg. The subjects of a king are considered his *prajāḥ*, "offspring" or "children" (see Pollock 1986, pp. 21–24). The use of the word *garbha-*, "embryo," however, is unusual enough to lead Cm, Ck, Ct to remark that the king should protect his subjects "as a mother protects the unborn child in her womb."

22. "lord Rāma" *rāmam . . . īśvaram*: The first time in the epic the word is applied thus, as a bald epithet, to Rāma.

Sarga 2

1–9. According to Cg, this *sarga* is meant to demonstrate the abilities Rāma possesses that qualify him as a place of secure refuge, in anticipation of the sages' request that he destroy Khara (*sarga* 5).

2–3. The commentators take the qualifications (at least 2cd–3ab) as intimating the presence of the demon Virādha, though they give no convincing explanation of why the crickets are chirping. Evidently this is supposed to be an ominous portent, as in 1.23.12 (the dark forest of Tāṭakā).

9cd–10ab. "strode off" *apakramya*: The demon's threats make his "retreating" here seem out of place, but it is difficult to assign the verb any other meaning. Much of the NR reads instead *parikramya*, "strode about."

10cd–11ab. "short-lived creatures" *kṣīṇajīvitau*: A word that, like *gatāyuḥ* (46.14, 53.21; 5.22.21) and *parimitāyuḥ* (47.13), appears to carry an ironic overtone. Like Khara and Rāvaṇa later on, Virādha makes the fatal if understandable mistake of judging Rāma to be a "mere" mortal. See the Introduction, Chapter 4.

"share a wife between you" *sabharyau*: According to Cg, some commentators suggest that the word for wife here may be used merely in the sense of "woman" (that is, "who have come in the company of a woman," so Cm, Ck), or that the dual may be more syntactically than semantically conditioned (although only one is married, the adjective is made to agree with the dual subject). Cg himself argues that Virādha means to insult the two men with the reproach that they hold one wife in common, and this seems to me to be correct (Cs adds that Virādha is suggesting that she should thus be his wife, too). On the fundamental tensions in Rāma's way of life in the forest, see also the note on 16.11.

11cd–12ab. "impersonating sages" *munidūṣakau*: Or is it "desecrators [of the ways] of sages"? Compare *dharmadūṣakaḥ* in 37.7 below.

18. "farsighted" *dīrghadarśinī*: See the note on 2.69.2 for the semantic range of this word.

"middle" *madhyamā*: This despite the fact that Kaikeyī is usually considered the youngest of Daśaratha's three wives (though not by Ct here). Cg, "Kaikeyī is the youngest of the three chief queens, but the middlemost in age of the 350 other wives of the king" (Cm is similar; see the note on 2.19.22). The NE recension reads "youngest mother."

21. "the equal of Vāsava" *vāsavopamaḥ*: "Unlike the seers [*sarga* 1], Lakṣmaṇa does not possess knowledge of the true essence of *brahma* [that is, Rāma], who is the helper of all creatures, and to whom Vāsava could never be compared. Rāma himself has hidden this knowledge from his brother," Ck (other commentators also attempt to reestablish what they believe to be the proper subordination of Indra, glossing the compound, "to whom Vāsava might be compared" [Cg, Cr]).

23. "The rage I felt toward Bharata" *krodho bharate yo babhūva*: Lakṣmaṇa could not appease his anger at Bharata because the latter had come to Rāma seeking refuge (Cg), or because he did not show any desire for the kingship (Ck). Cg enlarges: "An objection might be raised: Bharata and Kaikeyī had Rāma exiled without thinking, and they did beg his forgiveness and ask him to return. Why then do Rāma and Lakṣmaṇa keep calling to mind their usurpation of the kingship? . . . Because in times of trouble [even good] people forget what may and may not be spoken, and it is to intimate this notion that these statements are made here." As

Venkatanathacharya suggests (1965, p. 14 note), the past tense of the verb may be significant: Lakṣmaṇa's anger was in fact placated after Bharata's arrival in Citrakūṭa (*Ayodhyākāṇḍa* 93ff.), though presumably a residue remained.

Sarga 3

5."Virādha": That is, "Insatiable," Cg remarking on the propriety of the name (*anvarthanāma*).

6. "no weapon of this world could ever kill me" *śastreṇāvadhyatā loke*: No doubt we are to keep this provision in mind when we come to verse 15 below.

8. In most of the NR here (and elsewhere in the *sarga*) it is, interestingly, Lakṣmaṇa who confronts the demon, as in *sargas* 65–66.

11. "taut-strung" *jyāguṇavatā*: The commentators are not helpful on this apparently tautologous item ("a cord in the form of a bowstring," Cg, Ck, Ct, Cr; "a twanging string," Cm, which is a guess). The compound is unattested elsewhere.

12. "dripping with blood" *śoṇitādigdhāḥ*: Perhaps overly clever Cg, "only 'partly [-*ā*-]' so, because the arrows emerged from his body before the blood could spurt," and Ck, " 'not at all' [-*a*-], because they flew so fast." I agree with Crā, Cm, Ct, Cr.

13. "like Death with jaws agape" *vyāttānana ivāntakaḥ*: According to Cg, with tongue protruding, which establishes a more elaborate comparison with Virādha and his pike, though see the use of the figure elsewhere, such as 30.6 below.

In his comment on an interpolated verse before verse 13 (41*), Ck notes that Rāma's arrows had little effect on the demon because of his boon (so Ct). This is explicitly stated in a following interpolation (43*): "He preserved his life by reason of his possession of the boon granted him" (line 5).

15. The NR reads instead that Rāma "implants" an arrow in Virādha's heart (45*).

Cg observes, "In the subjugation of both Virādha and Kabandha [below, 66.6], Lakṣmaṇa [breaks or] cuts off the left arm, Rāma the right. What necessitates this restriction? Because Lakṣmaṇa always takes up his position at Rāma's right side, and so [each] demon, in seizing Rāma with its right arm, seizes Lakṣmaṇa with its left."

Ck (so Ct) are demonstrably wrong to suggest that "the demon has still not lost his life, so the boon has not been contradicted." Virādha is clearly dying (see verse 23); compare also above, note 13.

16. The SR (46*) prolongs the attack on Virādha, after which "he still did not die" (46*.4), whereupon Rāma decides to bury him, stepping on his neck to hold him down while Lakṣmaṇa digs. Virādha then speaks, saying he had not known his assailant was Rāma (an interpolation no doubt motivated by the same anxiety as that felt by Ck; see verse 15 note).

17. "worthy son of Kausalyā" *kausalyāsuprajāḥ*: For the crit. ed.'s *kausalyā suprajāḥ* I read the phrase as a *tatpuruṣa* compound, in agreement with Cg, Ck, Ct, Cr (see the note on 2.14.11).

18. "Tumburu": According to Cg on 2.85.15, a singing instructor of the *apsarases*.

"Vaiśravaṇa": Another name for Kubera, king of *gandharvas* and *yakṣas*.

Are we being given two different stories explaining the identity of the monster, one in verses 5-6 (he is a *rākṣasa* who through asceticism won the grace of Brahmā), and another in verses 18ff. (he is a *gandharva* who was cursed)? Text-critically considered, both stories appear authentic, however incompatible. The gemination (if it is that) is oddly similar to what appears to be present in the Kabandha episode (see *sarga* 67 and note on verse 1).

20cd–21ab. "Rambhā": According to the commentator Rāmacandra on *RāmāCam* p. 162, she was the daughter-in-law of Vaiśravaṇa.

24. "Such is the immemorial custom with respect to dead *rākṣasas*" *rakṣasāṃ gatasattvānām eṣa dharmaḥ sanātanaḥ*: "The Yavanas [literally, "Ionians" (that is, Greeks), though the reference here is doubtless to Muslims], who are the *rākṣasas* of the Kali age, thus still follow this custom," Ck, Ct. According to Kālidāsa, *RaghuVa* 12.30; they bury Virādha lest the stench (of his burning corpse) pollute the groves of austerities.

25. "ready to enter heaven" *svargasaṃprāptaḥ*: The compound must have an inchoative aspect, as Cm, Cg, Ct perceive, for the demon could not actually reach heaven before the burial had taken place (for the verbal aspect, see the note on 2.3.5).

26. "at the top of his voice" *muktakaṇṭham*: The commentators all understand "having his throat freed," that is, from Rāma's foot (see the interpolation noted on verse 16 above), though the adverbial use of the compound is not infrequent.

27. "like the sun and moon in heaven" *divi sthitau candradivākarāv iva*: Cg attempts to explain the simile: The forest is comparable to heaven because it is both vast and dark; Rāma to the moon because he has his wife with him (corresponding to the constellation Rohiṇī; see the note on 2.106.3); and Lakṣmaṇa to the sun in being without his wife, and lacking full autonomy (though why the sun lacks autonomy is unclear). Cm and Ct offer similar fanciful explanations. For the figure compare 2.93.40.

Sarga 4

5–6. Many of these characteristics are standard traits of divine beings.

12–13. Most of the SR adds that the young men are cloaked in red (66*). On the troop of Indra's companions, normally considered to be the Maruts or stormgods—young, handsome men ornamented with gold, who are the same age, accompany Indra at the battle against the demon Vṛtra, and sing the victorious god's praises—see the convenient summary in Gonda 1960–64, vol. 1, pp. 61–62.

14. "tigers among men" *puruṣavyāghrāḥ*: Much of the NW and SR reads the vocative singular (referring to Lakṣmaṇa), and indeed it seems rather odd to apply this particular epithet to gods, an instance apparently without parallel in the *Rām* (but note the v.l.'s in the SR and NR on verse 12 above).

18–19. "conduct me to my residence" *niṣṭhāṃ nayata*: Crā, Cm, Cg (all S manuscripts read the third person here) have *nayatu* "Let him achieve (his end before he addresses me)." Cg cites *AmaK* (3.3.41) as authority for *niṣṭhā-* in the sense of "end," "goal," and indeed it is the common one (though the phrase *niṣṭhāṃ nī* seems to be attested only here in Sanskrit literature). But as Ck (who with Ct and Cr reads as per the crit. ed.) comments, "What Indra wants to do is avoid seeing Rāma at this time, and that is all he should say. . . ." Why should Indra wish to avoid any meeting with Rāma? Cg: "Were Indra to speak with him he would thereby reveal Rāma's divine nature . . . and [on verse 19] Rāma must do his great deed—the slaying of Rāvaṇa and so on—in the guise of a man" (so basically Ck; Cr, "The verse [19] suggests that Indra is afraid Rāvaṇa might be angry were he to speak with Rāma"; Ct, "It is inappropriate for one in such narrow straits [as Rāma] to behold such magnificence [as Indra's]").

This episode is further explicated in 29.30ff. below, but one must wonder whether that later "interpretation" is the one intended by the monumental poet here. For Indra does not meet with Rāma after the death of Khara, but only after the death of Rāvaṇa (*Yuddhakāṇḍa* 105ff.).

Cg's comment touches on an essential theme of the poem; see the Introduction, Chapter 4.

21. "with his companions" *saparicchadaḥ*: So Cg, Ck, Ct, Cr (see verse 22); Cs, perhaps to avoid any inconsistency with verse 15, glosses, "with his accoutrements, bows, arrows, etc."

24. "wishes to conduct me" *māṃ . . . ninīṣati*: "That is, under orders from Brahmā," Cg, Ck (Ct, "Or, it may have been Brahmā himself in the guise of Indra").

25. "the world of Brahmā" *brahmalokam*: The highest of the several heavens of classical cosmology, the others including the world of the fathers, that of the seers, and that of the gods (cf. also note 35 below). (Cg here cites *BhagGī* 8.16, which says that though the highest of heavens, even the world of Brahmā is perishable.)

"honored guest" *priyātithim*: "This signifies that in comparison even with the world of Brahmā the sight of Rāma is more efficacious in providing imperishable happiness," Cs; Cm glosses the compound as a *bahuvrīhi*, " 'to whom guests,' that is, devotees, 'are dear.' "

26. "please accept the worlds that are now mine" *pratigṛhṇīṣva māmakān*: Venkatanathacharya suggests that because Rāma has been banished from his own kingdom, the sage offers him an even grander residence, and he refers to Sutīkṣṇa's words and Rāma's reply in 6.10–13 below (1965, p. 36 notes). Cg, however, argues that the surface meaning here may relate to the hospitality shown to a guest (expressed by transferring one's *puṇya*, or merit, to him), but more deeply the verse concerns what is called the "delivering up" of all deeds to the Blessed One, that is, unattached action (so also Cm; Ct cites a verse of similar import from the *KūrmaP* [see 1.3.16 in the crit. ed.], and remarks, "It is clear from the *Gītā* and other works that acts of righteousness delivered up to the Blessed One give infinite rewards, insofar as they issue in liberation").

28. "I hope to win . . . for myself" *aham evāhariṣyāmi*: Rāma refuses because a kshatriya may not accept gifts (Cm; see for instance the note on 2.81.15). Moreover, as the *MBh* informs us, the kshatriya is able, by the proper execution of his own code of conduct, to win himself "infinite worlds" (see 12.64.19, 72.30).

30. "Make your way" *abhigaccha*: Some S manuscripts add that the direction is upstream, along the Mandākinī (76*).

31. "as I abandon my body" *yāvaj jahāmi gātrāṇi*: Cm justifies Śarabhaṅga's self-immolation (suicide being generally prohibited) by the following citation: "An old man who can no longer perform the rites of purification, and for whom medical treatment is no longer indicated, may destroy himself by [throwing himself from] a cliff, by fire, fasting, or drowning" (*AtriSm* 218; see also Kane 1962–1975, vol. 2, part 2, p. 926). Cg and Ck are no doubt closer to the truth when (on verse 32) they

describe this as the *brahmamedha*, a self-sacrifice for attaining divine existence (they adduce as proof-text an unidentified *upaniṣad*).

35. "the world of Brahmā" *brahmalokam*: The path to the world of Brahmā—through the flame of the cremation fire, and thence, ultimately, to the world of the gods, the sun, lightning, and finally *brahmaloka*—is described in the most ancient upaniṣads (*BṛĀraU* 6.3.15, *ChāndoU* 4.15.5–6), which Cg cites here.

Ck comments, "According to *śruti*, 'By works the world of the ancestors . . .' [compare *BṛĀraU* 1.5.16, the worlds of those who maintain the sacred fires are reached via the moon; the worlds of the 'seers,' that is, devotees, *upāsaka*] is reached via the sun; again according to *śruti*, 'By knowledge the world of the gods . . .' [see ibid.]; the gods are the thirty-three gods existing at the time of creation . . . and their worlds are reached via the north star. . . . The world of Brahmā is the fourth state."

36. "in his abode" *bhavane*: So I read for the crit. ed.'s *bhuvane* (compare, for example, 1.8 above).

Ck observes, "Since [Śarabhaṅga] waited for Rāma to arrive before performing his *brahma* sacrifice [that is, his self-immolation], it should be clear even to a child that Rāma is *brahma*" (so too Cg).

Sarga 5

1. "hosts of sages . . . came to visit . . . Rāma" *munisaṃghāḥ . . . abhyagacchanta . . . rāmam*: "The sages come to take refuge with Rāma, now that Śarabhaṅga, who had been powerful enough to protect them, went to heaven," Cg (though contrast the sages' own statement in 8.14).

2. "*vaikhānasas*": According to the traditional interpretation, "those sages born from the nails [*nakha-*] of Brahmā" (so Cm, Cg, Ck, Ct, Cs, Cr; Cm, Cs, alternatively, "those who follow the path of the sage Vikhanasa on the basis of the *sūtras* he promulgated").

"*vālakhilyas*": Again, traditionally "those sages born from the hair [*vāla-*] of Brahmā" (Cm, Cg, Ck, Ct, Cr; Cm also, "those who relinquish the previous stores of food when new food is acquired"). Vālakhilyas are mythological creatures, said to be the size of a thumb (see *MBh* 1.27.6ff.).

"*saṃprakṣālas*": "Those born from the water used to wash the feet of the Blessed One [so Ck, Ct, Cr]; or, those who live by consuming (on the same day) the means of subsistence that they collect every day, that is, *aśvastanikāḥ* [thus Cv reads and comments]," Cm; "those who are constantly washing their bodies," Cg; "those who live only on water in which food has been washed," Cs.

"*marīcipas*": "drinkers of moonbeams," according to the traditional interpretation, and Cm, Cg, Ck, Ct.

"that pound their food with stones" *aśmakuṭṭāḥ*: So Cm, Ck, though the commentators are more uncertain here: "those who eat raw food that has been pounded," Ct (similarly Cr); "who eat pulverized stones," Cs; "who strike themselves with stones," Cg (compare *ManuSm* 6.17 and *YājñaSm* 3.49).

3. "who use their teeth as mortars" *dantolūkhalinaḥ*: "That is, who husk rice and the like with their teeth only, and then eat it," Cm, Cg; so Ck, Ct.

"keep themselves submerged" *unmajjakāḥ*: "That is, in water up to their heads, as an act of self-mortification," Cm, Cg, Ck, Ct, Cr.

4–5. "who make their abode in the open" *ākāśanilayāḥ*: So Ck, Ct, Cr understand the compound; Cg glosses, " 'in the sky,' that is, in treetops"; Cm, " 'in the sky,' by the power of their meditations on the wind."

"ever engaged in ascetic practices" *taponityāḥ*: The commentators explain "asceticism" here as "the daily repetition of the *veda*," on the basis of an ancient equivalence (cf. for example *ŚatBr* 11.5.7).

"the five ascetic fires" *pañcatapaḥ*: In the "mortification of the five fires," the ascetic stands in the midst of four fires that he has built around him in a circle, while the summer sun shines above him as the fifth.

The NR considerably extends the list of ascetics (84*, 85*). We find comparable catalogs in *BaudhDS* 3.3.1–15; *MBh* 9.36.45, 12.17.10, 12.236.8ff., and *BuddhaC* 7.14ff.

7. "lord and master" *pradhānaś ca . . . nāthaḥ*: That is, of his House and of the earth, respectively (with Cg, Ck; see 2.23.31). This is the primary construction of the verse, and the nominative *mahārathaḥ* accepted by the crit. ed. is disruptive and most improbable. I read the vocative with T1,2, and M.

8. "greatness" *yaśasā*: For this sense of the word see 61.5 below (though the tautology "[famous . . . for] glory" is not unknown to the epics; compare *MBh* 3.50.10).

"Your filial devotion is profound, no less your truthfulness" *pitṛvratatvaṃ satyaṃ ca . . . puṣkalaḥ*: I agree with Cg in construing the adjective with *pāda* c also (against Cm, Cr). Alternatively: "Your devotion to your father is true [sincere], and your righteousness profound."

9. "Please forgive us" *naḥ kṣantum arhasi*: Cm comments, "Although, according to the maxim 'It is enough for those in need simply to present themselves before good men,' their purposes would be served merely by taking refuge with him; still, because of their extreme distress they must speak, and for this they beg his pardon" (so Cg, Ct; Cr, "This implies that people in need lose all sense of what they may and may not say").

11–12. "long-lasting . . . for many years to come" *śāśvatīm . . . bahuvārṣikīm*: Many manuscripts seek to remove what looks like a restriction or afterthought in the second phrase (though compare such phrases as *dīrghakālam anantakam*, "for a long time, endlessly," *MBh* 2.68.5).

13. On the doctrine that by protecting his subjects—which is his particular form of *dharma*—a king not only shares in the fruits of their agricultural produce but also acquires great merit, see the note on 2.4.44, *ManuSm* 9.306; Kane 1962–1975, vol. 3, pp. 56ff.; Spellman 1964, pp. 179–83. I understand the reference here to the sage to mean, not that the king takes a quarter of the holy man's merit (although it is elsewhere frequently said that a good king acquires one-quarter of his subjects' righteous merit, and a bad king one-quarter of their demerit; see for example *MBh* 12.66.26, 73.20, 76.6-8), but that the merit he acquires is comparable to that amount; see for example *MBh* 12.66.35, "By his protecting his subjects a king acquires a hundred times more righteous merit than he who follows the way of righteousness in the forest. . . ." Rather differently the commentators. According to Cg, Ck (so Cr), the verse is meant to answer the question, why should a king protect sages, who are unable to pay any tax ("subjects" then would refer to sages). But if the king is paid by them in righteous merit, why does he take one-quarter instead of the normal one-sixth? Cm responds to this: "The king takes a sixth of the merit acquired by people who fast or live on alms; a quarter from those who

eat the produce from the area protected by the king, and a half from those who grow fat on the king's own food and drink, this last in accord with the traditional statement, 'One gets half the merit performed by a man who grows fat on one's food and drink, while the performer himself gets the other half" [untraced] (so Ct).

14. "brahmans most of them" *brāhmaṇabhūyiṣṭhaḥ*: The rest would be kshatriyas and *vaiśyas* (Cm, Cg, Ck, Ct, Ctś); or, "knowers of *brahma* for the most part" (Cg, Ctś).

16. "Pampā river" *pampānadī-*: The reading is marked as uncertain (other manuscripts give "the woodlands by [or, "the banks of"] the Pampā"). The Pampā is called a river elsewhere (see 4.3.6, though there are variants), but more often a lotus pond (3.69.5; 6.111.17).

19. "the distraught ascetics" *tāpasānāṃ tapasvinām*: On *tapasvin* in the sense of "distraught, wretched" see 46.16 below, and notes on 2.23.3, 58.25, 102.2. Though the word is used in its other sense, "ascetic," in the very next verse, the tautology here would be most awkward. The least implausible of the commentators suggestions here (and on the similar problem in verse 9.12, see Cs and Cr there) is Cg's "superior ascetics" (*praśaṃsāyāṃ ini*, see *KāśiVṛ* 5.2.94).

Hereafter the SR adds,

> For this purpose pure and simple would I have had to enter the forest—to eliminate this outrage against you at the hand of the *rākṣasas*. Instead, doing my father's bidding have I entered the forest. (93*)

This passage renders a bit more intelligible the use of *yadṛcchayā* in verse 20: "[Thus] . . . chance has brought me here."

21. "had bestowed this boon" *dattvā varam*: Why should Rāma's pledge be called a "boon"? It is rather his duty to protect the sages, as they pointed out to him (above, verses 10ff.). The reading *(a)bhayam*, "(had bestowed, granted) security . . ." is supported by the entire NR as well as by several important S manuscripts (and note the later references, *ṛṣīṇām abhayaṃ dattam* in 31.12 and *abhayaṃ dattvā* in 32.10). I hesitate to emend the crit. ed. only because of the very peculiarity of the reading.

Sarga 6

3. "densely" *saṃtatam*: This reading (for the meaningless *satatam* of the crit. ed.) is corroborated by 5.2.13, 11.24.

4. "garlanded with barkcloth garments" *cīramālāpariṣkṛtam*: See the note on 1.2 above.

"gloomy" *ghoram*: The adjective is almost never used in reference to ashrams; on the contrary, it almost always connotes foreboding. Much of the NR and some S manuscripts variously remove it.

5. "hair matted with dirt and mud" *malapaṅkajaṭādharam*: Ck asserts that the "most widely accepted reading" here is *malapaṅkajadhāriṇam* (either "meditating in the lotus position [for the cleansing] of sin," or, "meditating on the lotus [of the heart for the cleansing . . .]").

6. "strive for truth" *satyavikrama*: See the note on 2.19.7, and Pollock 1983, pp.

276–79 (to which this example should have been added, as well as *MBh* 6.103.21 and 14.66.16). Many manuscripts show an uneasiness at having this epithet apply to a sage; clearly the original meaning of the compound was no longer grasped.

9–10ab. "and that is why I have not yet ascended" *nārohe 'ham*: As Venkatanathacharya points out (1965, p. 49 note), this is a more or less general statement, for unlike Śarabhaṅga, Sutīkṣṇa will not destroy himself after Rāma's departure; see below, 10.26, 33, etc.

"about the time you reached Citrakūṭa" *citrakūṭam upādāya*: The construction adopted here agrees with Cg. The NR transposes verses 9 and 10ab, which further suggests that the three half-lines are to be construed as I have done.

12. "self-controlled" *ātmavān*: Or, "self-respecting." The epithet is not often used in contexts allowing a precise determination of meaning. See the note on 2.27.27, and below, 43.37 note.

14. "in all matters" *sarvatra*: "In the means for attaining all the ends of man," Ck; " 'everywhere,' that is, in this world and in the next," Ct; "in the *vedas* and the *śāstras*," Cr.

17ff. Sutīkṣṇa's mentioning the tame animals that visit the ashram is unremarkable, a commonplace in such descriptions. Rāma's response, however, in verses 19–20 is peculiar. Presumably it is related to, and meant to emphasize, his love of hunting (see the note on 2.43.13–14), and the violent behavior that going armed can induce, something Sītā will caution him against later (*sarga* 8, especially verse 11). Mention of Rāma's predilection for hunting at this point in the narrative may be designed to prepare us for his rash decision in the Mārīca episode (41.21, 23–33). The commentators naturally are puzzled, and the SR reflects this puzzlement in interpolating after verse 17 the silly line "There is no other shortcoming in this ashram than the animals" (104*). Cm, Cg, Ck, Ct observe, " 'enticing,' that is, they disturb one's meditations with their dazzling coats," to which Ct adds, "as for example Mārīca will do later in the book"; —*lobhayati* is in fact the word used of Mārīca in 38.15, 40.18. Venkatanathacharya (1965, p. 52 note) seems to suggest that Rāma fabricates this reason in order to accommodate the sages with whom he has come (above, 5.21, 6.1), and who will urge him quickly to depart (7.5 below).

20. "You would be implicated in it" *bhavāṃs tatrābhiṣajyeta*: Or, with Cr, "You would be pained on their account," which is equivalent to the Ś1 gloss *(a)bhisaṃtapyet*. Cs, citing *Viśva*(*locanakośa*), might be closer to the truth in glossing "You might curse me," or, "rebuke me."

21. "granter of boons" *varadam*: Cg tries to give the ornamental epithet some contextual significance: "We gather from this that Sutīkṣṇa has assented."

"went to perform" *upāgamat*: See the note on 2.6.1 for this rare sense of the verb (Cg, " 'betook himself' to the twilight, that is, he went to the lakeside on account of ["in order to worship," Cm, Ck, Ct] the twilight").

22. "offered it to the two . . . men" *tābhyāṃ . . . dadau*: "As for Sītā, she eats only the remnants of Rāma's dinner," Cg.

Sarga 7

3–4. "fire" *agnim*: The tradition is much exercised over the question of what *āśrama* or life stage Rāma is in before and during his exile; this would be indicated in part by the number of ritual fires he maintains when in the forest. Since the singular is used in the present verse, Cg remarks, we must suppose that, at the time of his exile, Rāma had not yet instituted the three sacred fires of the householder; see further the note on 2.93.11. The NE recensions here reads *'gnitrayasya*, "the three fires."

"(in the forest,) the refuge of ascetics" *tapasviśaraṇe* (*vane*): This qualification in reference to the forest I find awkward, and it seems not to be attested elsewhere in epic literature. Weakly Cg, "It is used to indicate that the *pūjā* [worship] was of a sort appropriate to the place" (all other commentators are silent). Could the form be a dual ("[the two of them, who were] places of refuge for ascetics")? Note the use of the compound in 4.11.12 and 17, where as grammatically appropriate for this sort of compound, the inherent gender of the second member is retained with masculine antecedents. Still, the plurals in verse 4 seem to speak against this analysis.

"and seeing the rising sun" *udayantaṃ dinakaraṃ dṛṣṭvā*: Ritual texts are in disagreement on when precisely the morning ritual offering is to be made (see Bodewitz 1976, pp. 41–50). Cg remarks, "By the mention of the appearance of the sun after the offering of the oblation, there is suggested the doctrine that oblations are to be offered before sunrise, and therefore that the ritual activities of the Rāghavas conform to the sequence enunciated in the *Kātyāyana Sūtras* [see *KātyŚS* 4.12]."

7. "smoldering fires" *viśikhair iva pāvakaiḥ*: Literally, "flameless fires." The phrase is rather odd, and in fact appears to be attested nowhere else in epic literature. Perhaps it approximates the more common "smokeless fires," as Cm, Ct, Cr gloss it (Cg, "That is, whose greatness is kept hidden"; Ck, "fires contained in coals"). It is less likely meant to suggest that the ascetics' powers are diminished because of their fear of the *rākṣasas*.

8–9. "like a lowborn man getting rich" *lakṣmīṃ prāpyevānvayavarjitaḥ*: That is, the high splendor of the nouveau riche, who is without good breeding, is insufferable.

12. "ashrams" *āśramapadam*: I take this as a collective singular, as do Cm, Ct.

18. Cg speculates: "When they entered the ashram, Sītā, thinking there to be no need for weapons in such a place, deposited them somewhere in the sage's abode. During Rāma's talk with the sage [verses 8–16], recognizing the brothers' intention she retrieved the weapons and returned them. This occasions the thoughts she speaks in the following *sarga*."

Sarga 8

2. This verse is far likelier to be a reflection on *dharma* in general (note the NR's version, 120*), rather than specifically on the *dharma* of sages (so Cg).

"greatest care" *susūkṣmeṇa vidhinā*: "Subtle is the way of *dharma*" (*sukṣmā gatir hi dharmasya*) we are told repeatedly in the *MBh* (3.200.2 etc.), not "imperceptible" (whereby Roussel 1910–1912, pp. 36–7 is set adrift).

3. "even worse" *tasmād gurutarau*: *tasmād* is to be construed thus as ablative of comparison (*pace* Ck, Cg, and Venkatanathacharya 1965, p. 58 note). Sītā's point, of course, is that wanton violence would be a far greater sin in Rāma than his breaking his word. The verse unobtrusively frames three main themes of the poem in

general, and of the *Araṇyakāṇḍa* in particular: Rāma's truthfulness in keeping his father's word, Rāvaṇa's sexual outrage, and the violence that accompanies it.

4. "that destroys righteousness" *dharmanāśanam*: "This explains the preponderance of the sins expressed by "even worse" [verse 3 and note]; lying speech produces *adharma*, this sin both [produces *adharma* and destroys *dharma*]," Cg.

5. "my handsome husband" *śubhadarśana*: Cg explains, "That is, his beauty itself is proof [namely, of his virtue]; compare the statement in *śruti*, 'His beauty told of his greatness' [*TaiS* 5.1.2.1]." On the concomitance traditionally held in Sanskrit literature to exist between beauty and virtue, see Pollock 1986, p. 50 and note 2.

6. "without provocation" *nirvairam*: That is, "because the *rākṣasas* have not committed any offense against Rāma himself," Ct.

8. "Daṇḍaka": There may be an etymological pun here, *daṇḍaka-* also meaning "(where there are) those who punish (wrongdoing)."

Sītā is not quite correct here. Rāma is going to Daṇḍaka because of his promise, not to the seers, but rather to Kaikeyī (see 2.16.30, 37). In any case, it is odd that she should imply he is only now setting out to Daṇḍaka (see also verse 10), which he is said to enter in 1.1 above.

9. Cm, Cg, Ck, Ct all agree on what to my mind is an impossible construction here ("As I watch you setting out, and these deeds of yours, thinking about your happiness and welfare, my mind grows [*bhavet*] sick with worry"). Many N manuscripts read, rather more easily, "(the mind of me) who on every occasion thinks about your ultimate happiness."

11. "any forest-dweller" *vanacarān sarvān*: This reference should be kept nonspecific, in order to capture the irony present: "Might you not mistakenly slay some innocent forest-dweller," that is, perhaps, "as your father once did" (see *Ayodhyākāṇḍa* 57–58, although strictly speaking Sītā should be ignorant of the story recalled by Daśaratha on his deathbed, and made known to no one). Cm, Ct, Cr take Sītā to mean, "mistakenly slay any *rākṣasa*, even one who has done no harm."

14. Indra seeks to obstruct the austerities of any ascetic whose power threatens to grow great enough to challenge his own position as king of the gods (see also 10.12ff. below).

20–21. "creatures that have done no wrong" *aparādhaṃ vinā . . . lokān*: When asking Rāma's protection, the sages had already described the "outrages" committed by the *rākṣasas*. In view of this, Sītā's claim that the *rākṣasas* are innocent seems curious. It may be simply that the whole point of the passage is not so much to throw Rāma's resolve into doubt (or rather, to highlight it, as we shall see in the next *sarga*), but instead merely to emphasize Sītā's kindliness, and thus to intensify our sense of outrage at (or the irony of) the *rākṣasas*' mistreatment of one who spoke so earnestly in their favor.

22. "in the forests inhabited by men who practice self-restraint" *vaneṣu niyatātmanām*: I agree with Venkatanathacharya (1965, p. 65 note) in thus construing the two items; Cm, Cg, Ck, Ct, impossibly in my view, coordinate as an adjectival phrase with *pāda* d. Much of the NR plausibly offers, "(kshatriyas) who are intent on their own code of conduct."

23. Compare the very similar admonition of Bharata to Rāma (2.98.56), which is intended to urge just the opposite course of action. Note that *vyāviddham idam* here ("it is all so at odds") corresponds to *idṛśaṃ vyāhataṃ karma* in the *Ayodhyākāṇḍa* passage.

25. "mother-in-law" *śvaśrū-*: No doubt Kausalyā is meant ("she would rejoice that her son was forever free from the trouble of war," Cm), and not Kaikeyī (Cg).

27. "No, true happiness is not easily won" *na sukhāl labhyate sukham*: Literally, "Not through happiness is happiness won." On the charged sense of the repeated *sukham* see 2.98.30 and note. Although such anaphoric emphasis is not uncommon in Sanskrit, a more significant distinction may be intended here. The Jains, for example, distinguished between bliss, *sukham*, and the ordinary "feeling of happiness" *sukhā vedanā* (Jaini 1979, p. 104 note 35, and Jaini 1977). At the same time, in contrast to such ascetic programs as that of the Jains, the Buddha claimed "to attain happiness by happiness" (*sukhaṃ sukhena adhigantabbam*; compare Rhys Davids 1950, vol. 5, pp. xii-xiii; *Theragāthā* 63 and 220; *Aṅguttara* 2.3; *Majjhima* 1.93).

28. "the ways of righteousness appropriate to an ascetics' grove" *dharmaṃ tapovane*: As Cr rightly sees, some specification of the *kind* of *dharma* is required (see *deśadharma-*, "the customs of the place," in verse 23 and *kṣatradharma-*, "the kshatriya code," in verse 24). Thus the locative must in some sense be restrictive.

"But then" *hi*: On the adversative force of this particle, see the note on 2.98.50; *tu* is, in fact, read by several manuscripts here.

Sarga 9

1. "with firm adherence to righteousness" *dharme sthitaḥ*: " 'Righteousness' here has the sense of his duty to protect the sages," Cm; Cg adds, "This signifies that to Rāma the most important thing is fulfilling his promise [to the sages], even if it means suffering the torments of Sītā's absence [the ultimate result of his killing the demons]." Ck reads instead *saṃvardhitaḥ*, "increased," "that is, his knowledge of righteousness thus amplified" (Venkatanathacharya, "with renewed determination," 1965, p. 68 note), calling it the accepted reading, though as is often the case with Ck, no other manuscript offers it.

2. "testifies to your high birth" *kulaṃ vyapadiśantyā*: In agreement with Cg (cf. verse 20 below); Cm, Ck, Cr, " 'enunciating the proper code of conduct of our family,' namely, in 8.22."

3. " 'Kshatriyas only bear bows' " *kṣatriyair dhāryate cāpaḥ*: Rāma here reformulates Sītā's words in 8.22. Many manuscripts give, "What shall I say [or, "What need I say," or, "I do have something to say"]? You yourself spoke these words."

4. "the refuge of others" *śaraṇyāḥ*: See verse 9 below; less probably, "who are so in need of refuge."

7. "Rescue" *abhyavapadya*: For this verb in the sense of "save, rescue, succor," see 6.50.16 (*contra* Cg) and 6.51.26.

8. "did obeisance at their feet" *kṛtvā caraṇaśuśruṣām*: Literally, "showed obedience to"; this agrees with Cm, Cg, though the phrase is unusual. Ck attributes it to "dull-witted *paurāṇikas*" unable to construe "the ancient and widely accepted reading" *vacanaśuśruṣām*, "showed [that is, "resolved on," Cm, Ck, Ct] obedience to their words."

11. "at the times of the lunar rites" *parvakāleṣu*: The sacrifices on the full and new moon days.

12. "the ascetics in their distress" *tāpasānāṃ tapasvinām*: See 5.19 and note.

14. "although" *ca*: The concessive force of the particle is not usual, but may be

related to its more common adversative function (see for instance 35.2 below and Speijer 1886, p. 341).

An ascetic's curse is powered by, and so depletes, the spiritual energy derived from his penances.

16. With respect to Rāma's promise, Ck notes that as universal emperor Rāma is qualified to promise protection irrespective of the country in which he may find himself. In addition, though he may be living as an ascetic, Rāma remains a kshatriya and so still has the authority to protect those who take refuge with him (cf. Venkatanathacharya 1965, p. 71 note; the intricate problem of Rāma's sociological status—as a king who has adopted the life of an ascetic—is a matter of concern to the commentators throughout the epic, see for instance 2.46.58 note). Ct claims that "insofar as Rāma's enthronement will necessarily take place later, he may now execute the function of royal protector; anyway, the authority to protect belongs to the kshatriya caste [*jāti*] as a whole, not just to him on the throne." According to Ck, it is on these grounds that Rāma is justified in slaying Vālin (in *Kiṣkindhākāṇḍa*). But that Rāma is considered a virtual king is made clear elsewhere in the text (see below, 28.10 and note).

18. "I would sooner give up" *apy ahaṃ . . . jahyām*: "This Rāma proclaims despite the following express commandments: 'One must always protect oneself, even at the cost of one's own wife, or one's wealth'; 'A brother is one's very own image'; 'A wife is half of oneself' " (*TaiS* 6.1.8.5), Cg.

20. *pādas* cd, as Cr alone perceives, are parenthetical.

"worthy" *sadṛśam*: For this sense (rather than "similar to") cf. 2.3.22 and note. Cg (who reads *cātmanaḥ* at the end of *pāda* d) understands "characteristic of you," citing as another instance of Sītā's mercifulness the famous verse "The noble man must take pity on the good and evil alike, and on those who stand condemned to death: For there is no one who never errs" (6.101.36).

Sarga 10

1. "fair-waisted Sītā in the middle" *sītā madhye sumadhyamā*: Such light puns (this one is technically called a *pādānta yamaka*) are typical of the poet's style; cf. 18.13, 19.23, 21.1, and, for related varieties, 2.12.20, 13.20, 68.15.

Venkatanathacharya (1965, p. 73 note) points out that in the *Ayodhyākāṇḍa* when entering the wilderness, it is Lakṣmaṇa who goes first, and Rāma last (2.46.76–77). The reason for the change, he says, is that the seers who had gathered at Śarabhaṅga's hermitage are now accompanying Rāma and showing the way, whereas previously they were alone and passing through an unfamiliar forest. That even such apparently trivial details in the *Rāmāyaṇa* were held to be significant is richly exemplified by the detailed comment of Ctś, who reports that traditionally the verse is taken phonemically to contain, and in a complicated way to illustrate the meaning of, the sacred syllable *aum* (again according to tradition the next verse is held to illustrate the meaning of another word in the *mūlamantra* sacred to south Indian Vaiṣṇavas, namely, *nārāyaṇa*). The most detailed exegesis is found in Vedāntadeśika's *RahaTrSā*, chapter 3.

10. "the story (of the lake)" *prabhavaṃ* (*sarasaḥ*): So I read (with Cg, Ck, and most

other S manuscripts) for the crit. ed.'s *prabhāvam*, for what Dharmabhṛt goes on to recount is the "origin (of the name)," that is, the story, of the lake, not its "power."

11. "brimful all year round" *sārvakālikam*: In essential agreement with Ck, Ct, Cr ("always brimful with water"; Cg, "It brought forth sounds all the time").

"Māṇḍakarṇi": The only mention of Māṇḍakarṇi in Sanskrit literature seems to be the charming tale of him told here. The manuscripts disagree about the name, the NR reading Manda- or Madakarṇi, several G codices Māṃḍukarṇi. On the story cf. *RaghuVa* 13.38–40.

15. "knowing right from wrong" *dṛṣṭaparāvaraḥ*: Comparable to *dṛṣṭalokaparāvara-*, (2.56.5 with note there), and *śrutadharmaparāvara-* (2.34.27). All seem to mean pretty much "knowing right from wrong, good from bad." Rather differently the commentators: "knowing the individual and universal soul," Cm, Cg; "knowing the higher and lower knowledge, which is learned from the upaniṣads," Cr; "knowing *dharma* and *adharma*, pertaining both to this world and the world to come," Ct.

21–25. "with whom he had previously been staying" *yeṣām uṣitavān pūrvaṃ sakāśe*: Possibly this refers to the ascetics encountered at Śarabhaṅga's ashram (5.1ff.) who had been traveling with Rāma (so the *ṭīkā* in VSP, p. 68 note; Venkatanathacharya 1965, p. 77 note), or equally well to those who left him at the end of Book Two (2.108, especially verse 20).

"for some ten (months)" *paridaśān (māsān)*: I agree with Cr.

"an extra month" *adhikaṃ māsam*: So I read with a variety of NE, D, and S manuscripts (for the crit. ed.'s *adhikān māsān*), in view of the evident ascending scale of time in verses 24d–25a.

Cg tries valorously to compute the ten years here from the poet's figures, but obviously they are meant to be illustrative only.

26. "At the end of his tour" *parisṛtya*: Ck reads instead *pratiśrutya*, "having promised," referring back to 7.16–17.

29. "Agastya": The story cycle of this sage, who is traditionally credited with bringing brahmanism to south India, is found also, and in much greater detail, in the forest book of the *MBh*, 3.94–108.

36. "Agastya's brother" *agastyabhrātuḥ*: Ct, Cs identify the (younger) brother as Idhmavāha on the basis of *BhāgP* 4.28.32.

40. "surrounded by many trees" *bahupādapasaṃvṛte*: The epithet makes little sense in connection with a forest. N manuscripts variously improve matters ("with different kinds of trees gently bent over," etc.).

41. "why not set your mind on going this very day" *adyaiva gamane buddhiṃ rocayasva*: According to Venkatanathacharya (1965, p. 82 note), Sutīkṣṇa urges Rāma to go in the knowledge that Agastya will provide him with magical weapons with which to slay the demons (see 11.29 below).

48. "*darbha* grass" *darbhāḥ*: This grass is used in sacrificial ceremonies, and so would lead to the inference that an ascetic's hermitage is nearby.

49. "like a mountain peak shrouded in black cloud" *kṛṣṇābhraśikharopamam*: For the analysis of the compound see 2.5.21 note. Cm, Ck, Ct, Cr, "like a black cloud and a mountain peak"; Cg, "like the top of a black cloud."

50. "secluded" *vivikteṣu*: Or, "purified, clean" (Cm, Cg, Ck, Ct, Cr).

"make flower offerings" *puṣpopahāraṃ kurvanti*: The reference appears to be to the offering of *pūjā*, otherwise rare in the *Rām* (though see the note on 2.17.6).

"gathered by their own hands" *svayam ārjitaiḥ*: Cg, Ctr cite *smṛti*, "A brahman must himself gather fuel sticks, flowers, *kuśa* grass, water, and the like" (untraced).

52. "his . . . brother" *yasya bhrātrā*: Agastya himself.

"death" *mṛtyum*: The murders committed by the demons.

"this region" *iyaṃ dik*: The south.

53ff. The story is also told, in a somewhat longer and more folktalelike form, in the *MBh* 3.94–97.

54. "*śrāddha*": A commemorative feast in honor of the ancestral spirits, consisting of offerings of balls of cooked rice, and gifts to and the feeding of brahmans.

55. "ram" *meṣa-*: For the serving of meat (though generally goat meat) at *śrāddhas*, see 2.71.1 and note, and 2.69.22.

57. "bleating like a ram" *meṣavan nadan*: "He would begin to bleat like a ram while still within their stomachs, by the power of the revivification spell [possessed by his brother]," Crā, Ck, Ct.

58. "the eaters of raw flesh" *tair . . . piśitāśanaiḥ*: The plural, according to Cm, Cg, is meant to include the attendants of the two demons; there are, however, other instances where the plural seems to take the place of the dual, cf. 67.20 below and note.

"in league with one another" *saṃhatya*: A good v.l., though offered only by a few D manuscripts and Cr, is *saṃhṛtya*, "having gathered [the thousands of brahmans] together [in one place]."

60. "the sprinkling of the hands" *hastāvasecanam*: The ceremony, especially sensible in a culture where food is eaten with the hands, marks the formal end of the ritual meal.

The NR in part explicitly states that Agastya consumed the demon-ram all by himself (171*.8ff., as in the *MBh* version of the story, 3.97.4-6), and thereby extirpates the evil totally.

70. Cg, Ct notice the hypermetric *pāda*, calling it archaic; Ck remarks, "There was no other way to employ these two words, *abhivādaye tvā*, without a hypermetric *pāda* resulting." Compare 2.95.31 and note, for the only other such instance in Books Two to Six.

76. "glossy" *snigdha-*: The leaves are "glossy" because the inhabitants of the ashram take special care of the trees (Cg).

"gentle" *kṣāntāḥ*: Bhatt (1963, p. 402) came to prefer *śāntāḥ*, though there is little to choose between the two words.

77–78. "Agastya, 'Stopper of the Mountain' ": I agree with Cm, Cg, Ck, Ct on the poet's intention of suggesting the etymology *agaṃ* [*syati* or] *stambhayati*, "he who paralyzed the mountain." See verse 83 and note below.

"thick smoke" *prājyadhūma-*: A widespread variant is *ājyadhūma-*, "the smoke of the [offerings of] clarified butter."

80. "look on . . . with terror" *trāsād dṛśyate*: I agree with Cg in construing the adverbial *trāsāt* thus, rather than with *nopabhujyate* (as do Cm, Ct, "because of fear they only look at it, but do not take possession of it"; the NE's *tāta* [for *trāsād*] speaks in their favor).

82. "is known by the name of that holy man" *nāmnā . . . bhagavataḥ . . . prathitā*: That is, the south is renowned as "Agastya's quarter" (Cm, Cg; *pace* the construction of Ck, Ct, Cr, Cs). In view of the earlier attack of Virādha, some of the commentators wonder whether it is not in fact just the region near Agastya's ashram rather

than the entire south that is safe from attack by demons. But their explanations are more unacceptable than this slight contradiction.

83. The story of Mount Vindhya's attempt (out of jealousy toward Mount Meru) to expand so as to block the course of the sun is narrated in *MBh* 3.101. Cr gives a slightly different account: (Mount) Vindhya was a student of Agastya's, who sought to overreach the sun. At the time when Vindhya was performing the "eight-limb bow" (a full prostration) before his guru, the gods begged the aid of Agastya, who ordered Vindhya, insofar as he was his student, to remain bowed upon the earth until his return. And from that time on Agastya has remained in the south.

Several N manuscripts hereafter insert a verse describing Agastya's other great feat, drinking up the ocean (185*; cf. *MBh* 3.101.15ff.).

86. "I will . . . live out what time remains" *śeṣaṃ . . . vatsyāmy aham*: Rāma's intentions are not wholly clear. He has promised to extirpate the *rākṣasas*, and so could not actually reside for the remainder of the period in Agastya's ashram, where we have just been told *rākṣasas* never come. Moreover, later he will ask Agastya to recommend some other site for his ashram (12.11), but see Agastya's words in 12.16 and the note there.

89. "eager to uphold the ways of righteousness" *dharmam ārādhayiṣṇavaḥ*: Literally, "eager to propitiate righteousness," a somewhat odd phrase (though occurring elsewhere, cf. *MBh* 12.76.17; Cr glosses, "that is, to accomplish *dharma*"), unless we are to think of *dharma* as personified (see also the note on 2.54.6). The variant in NE manuscripts, *munim*, gives the very reasonable (perhaps too reasonable) "eager to propitiate the sage."

90. "ascended to heaven . . . in aerial chariots" *vimānaiḥ . . . svar yātāḥ*: As in 2.58.40–42, the ascension of the ascetic boy slain by Daśaratha.

91. "good creatures" *bhūtaiḥ . . . śubhaiḥ*: Cm, Ct understand *śubhaiḥ* substantivally, "by their good deeds"; I agree with Cg.

Since the gods have the power to grant such rewards anywhere, the commentators specify that here at Agastya's ashram the rewards are bestowed in a very short time.

Sarga 11

1. Cg appears to hold that the purpose of this *sarga* is to demonstrate that Rudra is not to be worshiped (cf. below verses 17–18).

4. In this verse the presence of the syllable *yam* (*vayam*), which is the eighth syllable in the *Gāyatrīmantra*, indicates that at this point 7,000 verses of the (vulgate) *Rāmāyaṇa* have now been completed (Cm, Cg). This is the traditional method of counting the text; see the note on 2.39.5.

7. "with Rāma's wife, Sītā" *sītayā saha bhāryayā*: Strictly speaking, this prepositional phrase is syntactically governed by the dual subject of the clause, a semantic problem that the NR sought to eliminate (200*).

8. "what I should do next" *yad . . . anantaraṃ tattvam*: For *tattva* in the sense of what one should do, what is proper, see 2.18.17 and note, and 34.22 below (*tattvam vākyam*).

14. "ashram" *-āśramapadam*: A widespread variant here, and probably the correct

reading, is *-āśramadvāram*, "to the door, entrance, of the ashram" (so read by Cm, Cg, Ck).

15. "in consequence of . . . words" *-vacanāt*: So I read, with the NR and M2,3, for the crit. ed.'s (*vākyam* . . .) *-vacanam*, from which I derive little sense.

16–18. "Vivasvān, Soma, Bhaga . . . Dhātṛ and Vidhātṛ": These are, respectively, the sun, the moon, an obscure vedic god who offers "shares" (of good fortune), and two other deities connected with fate.

Verses 17–18 are omitted in NE manuscripts, and the NW reads "Śiva" for "Agni" in 17b (Ck [Ct, Cr] glosses "Agni" as "Four-faced Rudra"; Dhātṛ he takes as referring to Prajāpati, Vidhātṛ as referring to Viśvakarman); after verse 18 the SR adds, "the shrines of Yama, Varuṇa, Gāyatrī, the Vasus, Nāgarāja [that is, Ananta], Garuḍa, Kārtikeya, and Dharma." Cg calls these "shrines" temples for the worship of the different gods, who were (indirectly) referred to in the previous *sarga* (10.89, 91) as rewarding piety. "Insofar as Rudra is not mentioned among the gods worthy of receiving worship," Cg adds, "it is implied that he is not worthy. Those people who nowadays do worship him are following the dark *śāstras*."

25. "finally" *prathamam*: Against Ck, Cr, I agree with Ct (though only partly, for he construes the adverb with verse 24cd) that the sage does not sit down till this point (Rāma already being seated), because he has been so busy with their meal.

26. "mistreats" *anyathā . . . samudācaran*: Literally, "treats . . . otherwise" (sc., "than I have treated you"), though the line is elliptical. The NR simplifies here, "Having failed to honor an ascetic come to visit one"; Cg, Ck read an extra line at the beginning, "One should pour an oblation . . . and pay homage" (virtually repeating verse 24ab; this is not recorded in the crit. ed.). Some manuscripts add hereafter the oft-repeated verse, "When a man fails to honor to the best of his ability the guest who comes to his house, the guest goes taking all his [the host's] merit, and leaving behind all his own demerit" (209*; cf. *BrahmP* 114.36).

"is destined to feed on his own flesh" *svāni māṃsāni bhakṣayet*: In the *Uttarakāṇḍa* 68ff. Agastya tells Rāma the story of Śveta, King of the Vidarbhas: He renounces his kingship to practice asceticism, and finally reaches heaven, but because of earlier acts of inhospitality (see 1157*, 1158*.1–2; *PadmaP* 5.33.99–100) he is doomed to suffer hunger there and to feed on his own flesh, until Agastya releases him from his karmic punishment. None of the commentators except Ctr mentions this story; the allusion to it here is certainly recondite, and perhaps all that is meant is something proverbial, such as the verse Ctr cites from Yama, "One who does not feed an ascetic when he comes to visit . . . and then eats [later], must feed on his own flesh in the other world" (vol. 3, p. 83).

Cg notes further, "This statement is in fact directed principally to Sītā under the guise of an address to Rāma (for Rāma, who is called 'expert in the ways of righteousness,' hardly needs such instruction). Sītā, as a result of this, will readily show hospitality to Rāvaṇa" (*sarga* 44, especially verses 31–33).

27. "you . . . are king of all the world" *rājā sarvasya lokasya . . . bhavān*: For a discussion of the significance of this claim frequently made in the *Araṇyakāṇḍa* see the Introduction, Chapter 4.

29. "belongs to Viṣṇu" *vaiṣṇavam*: Because there are not two bows of Viṣṇu made by Viśvakarman, this must be the bow Rāma took from Paraśurāma and gave to Varuṇa [GPP 1.77.1], who then either himself or via Indra gave it to Agastya, aware that the time for killing the demon Khara was near (Cm, Cg, Ck, Ct). Rāma has an

overabundance of magical weapons, but this is not an unusual inconsistency in epic narrative (see Pollock 1986, p. 25 and note 2 [read there GPP *Yuddhakāṇḍa* 106, that is, crit. ed. 94], and 2.28.12–13). The bow Agastya gives him here will be used to kill Khara (3.27.19ff.).

30. "was given by Brahmā to great Indra, who gave it to me" *brahmadattaḥ . . . datto mama mahendreṇa*: This is the arrow that will be used to kill both Khara (3.29.25) and Rāvaṇa (6.97.4ff.). As the latter passage makes clear, the arrow was made by Brahmā and given by him to Indra, who subsequently gave it to Agastya. Cm, Ck, Ct take *brahmadattaḥ* as a proper name, too. Although this appears to be the case in 6.97.4, it is the radical signification of the compound that was more prominent, as verses 5ff. of the same passage demonstrate. The pair of quivers was also given by Indra, as *RāmāCam* p. 168 testifies (*sautrāmaṇaṃ tūṇīrayugmam*); Cv (reading *dattau*) in *pāda* c and the NR (reading *dattā*, taking *tūṇī* as feminine singular) sought to elucidate the construction.

33. "as Indra . . . once received his bolt" *vajraṃ vajradharo yathā*: Cg, Ck, Ct further exploit the simile: "Just as Indra took the thunderbolt because it was his, so you should take Viṣṇu's weapons, because you are Viṣṇu."

Hereafter several N and S manuscripts add,

> Maghavan gave me this impenetrable armor, which is like nothing else on earth to the touch, and gleams like fire or the sun; and whenever you are in danger think about the vehicle, the heavenly chariot yoked with bays, and Mātali [Indra's charioteer] will bring it to you. (213*; see *Yuddhakāṇḍa* 90 for the arrival of Mātali)

Some N manuscripts add, "Long ago, thousand-eyed Indra told me, Rāghava, 'When Rāma comes here give him this bow' " (214*).

34. At the conclusion of this *sarga*, or within the following, most S manuscripts and (in an unanticipated agreement) the NW recension insert the following passage (App. I, No. 3): Rāma retires for the night, and in the morning asks Agastya for the story of how the region was settled. Agastya relates that he came by chance to the region south of the Vindhyas, finding it a desert. He invoked the rain god, exiled death and disease, brought trees from the Himalayas by the power of thought, and performed other comparable miracles until gradually the area became habitable. The *rākṣasas*, however, began their hostile behavior from the time Rāma reached Citrakūṭa, and Agastya has not stopped them, knowing that Rāma himself has the power to do so. Agastya finally beseeches him to save the sages and the land that his ancestor had once destroyed (the Daṇḍaka wilderness [cf. above 1.1 note and reference]).

Sarga 12

1. The *sarga* division is problematic, as Cg remarks. See also the insertion noted on 11.34.

2. "terribly wearied" *pracuraśramaḥ*: I take this as modifying *khedaḥ* in *pāda* a. There is no reason, with Venkatanathacharya, to assume two separate sentences (1965, p. 102 note).

"is most disconsolate" *utkaṇṭhate*: According to the commentators, "yearning," that is, for a place to rest. But it would then be somewhat odd that they push on directly to Pañcavaṭī at the end of the *sarga*.

3. "and never before has sorrow heaped its scorn upon her" *duḥkhaiś ca na vimānitā*: This analysis agrees with Ct, Cr.

5. Compare the conversation between Sītā and her mother-in-law Kausalyā in 2.34.19ff.

6. "sharp as swords" *śastrāṇāṃ tīkṣṇatām*: That is, in respect of their readiness to sever the bonds of even long-held affection, according to Cm, Cg; they also suggest that the similarity between women and the wind or Garuḍa resides in their rash, inconsiderate behavior rather than in their quickness to run from a husband fallen on bad times. Ck remarks that Kaikeyī may be intended as paradigm here.

A similar gnomic depreciation of women is found in 6.10.9: "Wealth and cows invariably go together, self-control and brahmans, fickleness and women."

7. "the goddess Arundhatī" *devī hy arundhatī*: Or, "the lady Arundhatī," inasmuch as she is generally not considered a goddess (though see 2.110.10 and note; the NR largely eliminates the reference). She is the wife of Vasiṣṭha, family priest of the Ikṣvākus, but in fact is absent from the actual narrative of the *Rām*. The story is told in the *MBh* (3.214, especially verses 13–14) how the Goddess of the Sacrifice could imitate the form of all the wives of the seven seers, save that of Arundhatī, because of her fidelity and obedience to her husband (so also Ctr, vol. 3, pp. 84–85).

8. "this region" *ayaṃ deśaḥ*: Because of the deictic pronoun, the region referred to must be Agastya's ashram (Cm, Cg, Ct).

11. "direct me to some . . . region" *vyādiśa me deśam*: It is unclear why Rāma should ask for advice about some other place to live, considering the intention he expressed in 10.86 above; but compare Agastya's remarks in verse 16 below, with note there.

15. "by means of my . . . powers and in consequence of my affection" *prabhāvena snehād . . . ca*: The sage's affection for Daśaratha was the reason he bothered to discover the events through his ascetic powers, according to Cg. Quite improbably Cm, Cs, " '. . . all that has happened to you in consequence of Daśaratha's affection,' that is, for Kaikeyī"; Cm (second interpretation), Ck, Ct, " '. . . in consequence of my affection,' namely, for Rāma (Ct, "for one does not bother to learn by ascetic powers the history of one for whom no affection is felt"); and he also learned the history of what happened to Daśaratha."

16. The thought is elliptical; only Ct (and Cr) explain in a manner that honors the syntax: "Even though Rāma had promised to dwell with Agastya [10.86; though this is before Rāma's arrival, Agastya could have known of it by his ascetic powers], his inquiring in verse 11 here for information about some other dwelling place has led the sage to discover his real intention. For if he were indeed to dwell in Agastya's ashram, Rāma could not slay the *rākṣasas* as he had vowed [5.20], since *rākṣasas* do not come there [or rather, those that do are peaceful; see verse 10.81]." But why then did Rāma promise in the first place?

As many manuscripts demonstrate, there was difficulty in perceiving the connection between verses 16 and 17; some N texts insert, "But if you do not desire to dwell here" (227*), and some S versions, "[But] all the people will find out that you are dwelling [here]" (228*).

18. "it is not too far from here, and the Godāvarī river is close by as well" *nātidūre*

ca . . . godāvaryāḥ samīpe ca: So the commentators; but why should the region's being "not too far" be of any importance? It is possible the true meaning is, "not too far from the Godāvarī, yet [not too] near it" (see 14.13).

The *Mahābhārata* places Agastya's ashram at Prayāga (Allahabad) (vulg. 3.87.19–20, crit. ed. 85.14–15; compare Bhatt 1963, p. 402). This is obviously impossible, since the Godāvarī river, to which Rāma must be close, flows 500 miles south of Prayāga (it is Bharadvāja's ashram that the *Rāmāyaṇa* places at Prayāga, 2.48.1ff.; Agastya's is apparently near the Godāvarī itself in *Rām* 6.111.22).

20. "Although accompanied by a wife, you" *bhavān api sadāraḥ*": The only way I can understand the first half of this verse is to construe *api . . . ca* as a concessive collocation with *sadāraḥ*, and the second *ca* adversatively (cf. Speijer 1886, pp. 340ff.). To supply *tāpasānām* with *parirakṣaṇe* (so Cm, Cg, Ck, Ct, though the last two read *sadācāraḥ* for *sadāraś ca*) makes little sense.

"there" *atra*: In agreement with Cm, Cg, Ck, Ct.

21. "the banyan" *nyagrodham*: *nyagrodha* and *vaṭa* are synonymous, and Pañcavaṭī literally means "The place of the five fig trees." The singular in this verse should be taken as *jātyekavacanam* (collective singular).

22. "upon a rise of ground" *sthalam upāruhya*: I take *pañcavaṭī* as governing the gerundial phrase, *contra* Cg (and PW s.v. *sthala-*, which is, however, right in its definition of *sthala*—against Cm, Cg, Ck, Ct, "treeless"; Cr, "level ground").

"mountain" *parvatasya*: Or perhaps again a collective singular, "mountain range" (cf. *girayaḥ* in 14.14 below).

Sarga 13

1. "he encountered . . . a . . . vulture" *āsasāda . . . gṛdhram*: Internal evidence suggests that Rāma's meeting with the vulture Jaṭāyus at this point in the story is an interpolation introduced after the work of the monumental poet (see the notes on 48.1 and 63.10). Bhoja, however, knows of their meeting at this juncture of the narrative (*RāmāCam* p. 168).

2. "in the forest" *vanastham*: The majority of S manuscripts read for this insipid adjective *vaṭastham*, "in the fig tree" (cf. 12.21–22 and note). The true reading, however, may be *vanasthau* with the NW recension (see *vanastham . . . [rāmam]* in 15.31 below).

3. "that immediately won them over" *prīṇayann iva*: *iva* functions here as a metrically shortened form of *eva*, as often in the epics and in the *Rām* in particular (so Cg, Cr; cf. the notes on 2.4.42, 12.2, 108.6).

6. "lords of creatures": According to Ck, Ct, there are seventeen "lords of creation" (Prajāpatis); we must then (with Cr) understand *bahuputraḥ* as a proper name, to make out the full number (note, however, that Cm, Cg construe Ariṣṭanemi and Kaśyapa as referring to a single individual).

10. An "insertion" represented in both the NR and the SR describes the marriages and offspring of the remaining daughters of Dakṣa (233*).

11. Cm here notices, and tries in various ways to resolve, a contradiction with what he cites as a scriptural passage [untraced], in which Kaśyapa is said to marry thirteen of the daughters.

13cd–14ab. "willing" *tanmanā*: That is, to bear sons; the others bear only daughters.

Cg eliminates Danu from *pādas* cd, and includes Manu in verse 14ab by implication (see verse 29 below). Cm claims that only three obeyed their husband: Aditi, Diti, and Kālakā.

14cd–15ab. "the thirty-three gods" *devās trayastriṃśad*: The number is made out thus: twelve Ādityas, eight Vasus, eleven Rudras, and the two Aśvins.

17cd–18. The animal genealogy here and in the following verses is found also in the *MBh* (1.60.54ff.) in virtually identical form. Its southern manuscripts show some influence from the *Rām* tradition.

In the following list, the name of the mother generally is that of the species of bird (or animal) she bears; for instance, *śyenī* (verse 19) means "female hawk," *śārdūlī* (verse 25), "tigress."

"Krauñcī bore the owls" *ulūkān janayat krauñcī*: The NR reasonably reads "*krauñcas* (*sārasa* cranes)" for "owls," a reading supported by some S manuscripts in *MBh* 1.60.55.

20. The NR again persuasively has Śukī bear the parrots (*śukān*) (242*), which is certified by *MBh* 1.60.57. It was perhaps in view of the reference in verse 31cd–32 below that the SR revised here.

"be pleased to know" *bhadraṃ te*: This (to the translator often troublesome) interjection is typically used with an imperative in the epics, in the sense of "please." Here it is explained by Cg "as an attempt to secure Rāma's attention to the somewhat irrelevant history" ("the usage is characteristic of the poet, as part of a direct address, that is, 'Rāma, please listen,' " Ck [so Ct, Cr]).

23. "antelope, and yaks" *sṛmarāś camarās tathā*: According to Cm, Cg, Ct, the first are black-tailed yaks ("whose tails are used as hairpieces for women"), the latter, white-tailed ("their tails are used for royal fly whisks").

25. "simians" *harayaḥ*: Not just good sense suggests these are not "lions" (so Cg, Ck, Ct, Cr); see also *MBh* 1.60.62–63.

"fleet (monkeys)" (*vānarāś ca*) *tarasvinaḥ*: This is probably the correct reading of the passage (transmitted, if sparsely, by NE, NW, and S manuscripts [Cg, Ck], and supported by *MBh* 1.60.62; see also *Rām* 5.44.31; 13.39 v.l.), for the crit. ed.'s unparalleled and improbable *tapasvinaḥ* ("miserable," or "ascetic," monkeys). I also read *golāṅgulāś ca* in *pāda* c, confirmed by the *MBh* (1.60.62cd) and by common sense.

26. "Śvetākṣa": The reading of the *MBh* (1.60.64) is *śvetākhyam*, "called Śveta," and is supported here by several N manuscripts (whereas the SR of the *MBh* reads as the SR manuscripts here).

27. In 2.68.15ff. Surabhī is said to be the mother of cows (so some N manuscripts here; see App. I, No. 4.22), rather than, as here, the grandmother.

28. "great serpents . . . snakes" *nāgān . . . pannagān*: The commentators attempt to differentiate between the two: "The former are snakes with multiple hoods; the latter are ordinary snakes" (Cg, "or, the former have the features of humans, but with hoods and tails"); "*Nāgas* are kinds of nonvenomous snakes; *pannagas* are the [mythological] serpents Vāsuki and the rest," Ck.

30. "as is set down in the holy texts" *iti śrutiḥ*: See *ṚV* 10.90.12, where the four orders of brahmanical society are born from the Primal Being.

This verse is omitted in four S manuscripts (as well as by Cm, Cg [not noted in the crit. ed.], and atheticized in one manuscript of Ck), in the corresponding passage in the *MBh* (along with verse 29), and has all the signs of a clumsy (if old) interpolation. It is certainly odd to find it in the context of this cosmic (and in some ways comic) pedigree, given the theological importance of the vedic hymn.

31cd–32. "the thousand great serpents that hold up the earth" *nāgasahasraṃ . . . dharaṇīdharam*: One of the offspring of Kadrū is Śeṣa, on whom the world is said principally to rest.

33. "Śyenī": Cm suggets that this Śyenī must either be different from the one previously mentioned (verse 19); or, since there are no laws among animals, Aruṇa may have married his great-aunt Śyeṇī (so Cg, Ck, Ct).

35. "Jaṭāyus's (friendship)" (*sakhitvam . . .*) *ātmano*: Literally, "his (friendship)." I read *ātmano*, with the NR and M1, in place of the crit. ed.'s irrelevant *ātmavān*. For the use of *ātma-* reflexive to a subordinate noun rather than to the subject of the sentence, see 2.64.24 and note.

Sarga 14

1ff. Cg remarks that this *sarga* will show how Lakṣmaṇa serves Rāma, in accordance with his mother's words (2.35.8).

1. "wild animals" *-vyālamṛga-*: See the notes on 2.50.21, 53.5. (Cg glosses *vyāla-* as "vicious snakes"; Ck, Ct take *mṛga-* as "gazelles, etc.").

2. " 'the woodlands are all in flower' " *puṣpitakānanaḥ*: See 12.22 above.

3. "Which (place)" *katarasmin. . .* (*deśe*): The expected *katamasmin* is offered by only one manuscript.

4–5. "where there are forests and water to delight us" *vanarāmaṇyakaṃ yatra jalarāmaṇayakam*: *-rāmaṇyaka-* is read only by the SR; it appears to be *hapax*.

Cg's *sthala-* ("place," for *jala-*, "water," in *pāda* b) is supported by much of the NR (263*). He apportions the qualifications as follows: the forest's beauty will satisfy Sītā's desire for flowers, the beauty of the place, Rāma's desire for rest, and the fuel, etc., Lakṣmaṇa's desire to serve.

7. "you choose yourself" *svayaṃ . . . rucire*: I interpret *svayam* as equal to *tavaiva*, and take it closely with *rucire*.

15. "with a latticework of brilliant stripes" *gavākṣitāḥ . . . paramabhaktibhiḥ*: Cg rightly construes the two qualifications together and remarks, "People paint the sides of elephants with stripes in the shape of windows." On this sense of *bhakti-* see 5.47.4, and compare Mallinātha on *MeghDū* 19. For *gavākṣita-* in this sense see 6.87.26, 109.24.

21. "with walls of clay" *saṃghātamṛttikām*: Translated in agreement with Ck, Cr (so too Cm, Cg, though they read *saṃkhāta-*).

"crossbeams" *vaṃśa-*: Thus Cg, on the authority of the *Vaijayantī* lexicon (Cm adds, "They were used for supporting the thatch").

Virtually all manuscripts (save M3?) add or substitute "A house for Rāma, lovely and wonderful to behold" (268*.2, 269*, 270*.4).

23. It looks here as if Lakṣmaṇa is performing the *vāstuśānti* (or apotropaic rite at the construction of a new dwelling) with an offering of flowers. At the construction of the ashram on Mount Citrakūṭa, Rāma performed the ceremony by immo-

lating whole a black buck (see 2.50.15–18 and notes there). Observe, too, that Lakṣmaṇa builds only one hut (see 2.50.13).

25. "tightly and affectionately" *atisnigdhaṃ ca gāḍhaṃ ca*: I agree with Cg in taking *pāda* c adverbially with *pāda* a (Cm, Cr join *atisnigdham* with *vacanam*, "[and spoke these] affectionate words").

27. "wise in both thought and deed" *bhāvajñena kṛtajñena*: I understand these two adjectives as essentially complementary, as in the case of *śāstrajña* and *kṛtajña* in 2.1.20 (see the note there for this translation of *kṛtajña-* [supported by Cm, " 'Knowing the making,' that is, the constructing of houses"]), instead of the more common "grateful" (Ct, Cr; it is not clear what benefit Lakṣmaṇa would be repaying). The commentators have little idea what, otherwise, to do with *bhāvajña-* (" 'knowing the feelings of others,' that is, Lakṣmaṇa recognized that Rāma wanted a place to be alone with Sītā without his having to say it," Cg).

"With such a son as you" *tvayā putreṇa*: The same sentiment is expressed, on a weightier occasion, in 2.105.17. Cm here reads, "With you as [my] protector," explaining "You care for me just as my father did" (thus do Ct, Cr understand the reading of the crit. ed.); Cg, " 'My father is not dead but rather is fulfilling, as he always did, all my desires by way of you.' " The sense is certainly the same as in the earlier occurrence, namely, that Daśaratha has not been annihilated but is instead rejoicing in heaven, saved (*trāyate*) from hell (*put*) by his virtuous son (*putra*— so in part Cg; for the etymology, cf. 2.99.2 and note).

28. "bringer of glory" *lakṣmivardhanaḥ*: It is doubtful that this reading, in the nominative and construing with Rāghava (rather than in the accusative and construing with Lakṣmaṇa), is correct. The epithet is one of those most commonly used of Lakṣmaṇa (see 3.10.75, 11.19; 4.31.12; 6.89.9, etc.), and is nowhere, I think, found in reference to Rāma (though it is, once, applied to Daśaratha, 5.29.3). Moreover, none of the NR supports the reading of the crit. ed. But the almost unanimous testimony of the SR may mean more than the sheer conservation of an ancient corruption. Perhaps when used in reference to Rāma, as in reference to Daśaratha, the epithet has the more specific sense "successor to royalty."

"gladly" *vaśī*: See the note on 2.10.2. Less probable here is the meaning "self-controlled."

Sarga 15

2–3. "to bathe" *abhiṣekārtham*: There is a poignant shift in the meaning of *abhiṣeka* between Books Two and Three of the poem, from the sense of "rite of royal consecration" to that of "rite of ascetic ablution."

4. "the most beautiful ornament" *alaṃkṛtaḥ . . . śubhaḥ*: "That is, because of the ripe crops and the like," Ct, Cr.

5. "The world crackles with frost" *nīhāraparuṣo lokaḥ*: Or, according to Cm, Cg, " 'the world,' that is, people; their skin is 'rough' to the touch 'because of the frost' " (so Ct, Cr).

6. Cg cites Āpastamba: "One who has laid the sacred fires may not eat of the first fruits without performing the first-fruits sacrifice. When the rice, barley, and *syāmāka* have ripened, one must sacrifice" (cf. *ĀpaŚS* 6.29–31). Autumn is the time for the first-fruit offering of rice, whereas the offering of barley is done in the spring.

7. "kings march forth on expedition" *vicaranti mahīpālā yātrārtham*: The *topos* of classical poetry is that autumn, after the rainy season has ended, is the season for military expeditions (see for instance *RaghuVa* 4.24). But Kauṭilya (*ArthŚā* 9.1.24ff.) allows much more latitude, as does the *MBh* (crit. ed. 12.101.9–10, cited by Ctr), "In the month of Caitra [March–April] or Mārgaśīrṣya [November–December] are military expeditions recommended. All the crops are ripe then, and the earth is full of food; the temperature is neither too hot nor too cold."

8. After the autumnal equinox the sun's vertical rays start moving south of the equator, the region of Yama (see 2.57.11 and note).

10. "the most pleasant time to stroll" *atyantasukhasaṃcārāḥ*: The reading of two V and B manuscripts is appealing: *ādyantaduḥkhasaṃcārāḥ*, "at the beginnings and ends (of these days) is it most painful to stroll (while at noon . . .)." This would preserve *pāda* b from the redundancy that now affects it, and at the same time would more gracefully introduce verses 11–12.

11. "Mornings" *divasāḥ*: We must either read *pratyūṣāḥ* with NE manuscripts for the *divasāḥ* of the crit. ed. (an old dittography from verse 10?), or interpret that NE variant as a gloss on the reading of the crit. ed. (as I have done) and understand it in the sense of "daybreaks." Neither solution is very attractive, but as the verse stands, it is in stark contradiction with verse 10. Furthermore, verses 10, 11, and 12 appear designed to account for the days, dawns, and nights, for which either of the above solutions would provide.

"the wilderness seems empty" *śūnyāraṇyāḥ*: "Because the animals stay in their lairs because of the cold" (Cm, Cg; "That is, the forest has lost its beauty, the snow having made the foliage ugly," Ck, Ct, Cr).

12. "Led by the Puṣya star" *puṣyanītāḥ*: The reading found in Ś1, D1–3, *puṣyanetrāḥ*, "[nights] that have Puṣya as their leader, ruler [*netā*]," that is, nights when the earth is in alignment with the the asterism Puṣya (see Kirfel 1920, p. 36), gives us certainly the intended meaning, and is probably original (unless it is a learned correction); see *MahāBh* on *Pā* 5.4.116, *vārt.* 2. (Cm, Ct, Cr, "The length of the nighttime is indicated by the presence of the Puṣya asterism"; according to the editors of the Mylapore ed., the close of night in winter is signaled by Puṣya.)

"gray" *-aruṇāḥ*: So Ck, Ct ("the word also means the color of doves, and is so used throughout this entire passage"), *contra* Cg on verse 13; cf. also 22.1 below.

"their three watches" *triyāmāḥ*: Night consists of three "watches," each about three hours long.

13. "all [its] appeal has passed to the sun" *ravisaṃkrāntasaubhāgyaḥ*: The cool-rayed moon no longer has the power to attract people, as it can in the summer; it is the sun that now does so.

"clouded over" *-andhaḥ*: The entire verse is cited by Ānandavardhana in his great work of literary criticism, the *Dhanvyāloka* (p. 180, with the otherwise unattested reading in *pāda* b, *-āvṛta-* for *-aruṇa-*), in the course of his discussion of the instance of "suggestion" when the literal meaning of a word (here *andha-*, literally "blind") is not only unintended but completely "lost" in the signification of the verse.

14. "You mark it, but miss its beauty, as with Sītā when she is flushed with sun" *sīteva cātapaśyāmā lakṣyate na tu śobhate*: Cm, Cg understand, as if to eliminate any possible criticism of Sītā, "It looks like Sītā when she is flushed with sun—but does not have her beauty" (a rhetorical figure known as *vyatireka*, whereby a simple simile

is transformed so as to emphasize the excellence of the tenor at the expense of the vehicle). The NR reads "haggard by asceticism" for "flushed with sun."

16. "Mist" *bāṣpa-*: The word is rare in this sense, but cf. *RaghuVa* 13.29. (So also basically the commentators; Ct, citing *anye*, "frosty dewdrops"; Cm, Cg, Ck, Cr, "vapors, as from a well.")

17. "color" *-ākṛtibhiḥ*: Though the word normally means "shape," Cm, Cg, Ck are probably correct to take it in the sense of "color" here (that is, tawny; Ct, Cr are undecided, "They are like date palm blossoms because they are both bowed and yellow").

20. Hereafter the SR adds a charming verse, in which "a thirsty elephant touches the cold clear water . . . but then withdraws its trunk" (280*).

21. "wrapped up in the darkness" *-tamonaddhāḥ*: To Cg, the three qualifications indicate, respectively, that the trees are motionless, covered in a blanket, and with their eyes closed (thus producing a figure of speech called *utprekṣā*, or poetic fancy). Cm, attempting to explain the repetition of the word "darkness," suggests that in the first instance, the interior darkness of closed eyes is meant; in the second, the external darkness (Ck, Ct, Cr, similarly seeking to eliminate the tautology, take the first compound with *tamaḥ* as a *dvandva* ["darkness and hoarfrost"], the second as a *karmadhāraya* ["darkness that is snow, i.e., a blinding snow"], restricting the first to the evening, the second to the morning).

23. "has the bitter taste of poison" *rasavat*: I see no other way to understand the verse than with Cg: though the water is the purest possible—that found on the clean mountaintops—its icy coldness makes it impossible to drink, and so almost like poison (see verse 5 above; *rasa-* in the sense of "poison" is rare; Cg cites as authority the lexicographer Bāṇa).

24. "the filaments and cups shriveled" *śīrṇakesarakarṇikaiḥ*: The compound is a *karmadhāraya*, functioning (like *patraiḥ*) as *upalakṣaṇe tṛtīyā* with *kamalākarāḥ* (the *kesaras* and *karṇikas* surely do not belong to the leaves, as per Cr). But the syntax is admittedly awkward, and I suspect the correct reading in *pāda* a to be *padmaiḥ* with many S manuscripts and commentators.

25. "in the city" *pure*: Actually, in the nearby village Nandigrāma (cf. 2.107.2 and note).

Lakṣmaṇa's attitude toward Bharata as expressed here is a significant departure from his previous statements (see 2.90.13ff., 3.2.23), one for which the poet has not adequately prepared the reader.

27. "At this moment" *velām imām*: Accusative of time at which (cf. 2.37.26 and note, and 5.65.26).

28. "in the last watch of the night" *apararātreṣu*: "Like a woman newly widowed who goes out before people begin to stir about, so as not to have to look at them, Bharata is afraid of meeting people and hearing them say that, as Kaikeyī's son, he is responsible for the tragedy," Cg. A likelier interpretation is that since Bharata is now living as an ascetic (see 2.107.20–21, 6.112.6–7, 113.26ff.), he performs his morning ablutions at the hour appropriate to ascetics.

30. "devoting himself" *āśritaḥ*: "That is, he has taken up activities similar to Rāma's" (Ct, see 2.107.20–21).

34. Cg rather suspiciously: "As Lakṣmaṇa observed the travails of Rāma and Sītā in the early morning—bathing in the cold lake and so on—he was overcome with grief and as a result made ready to reproach Kaikeyī. But realizing that Rāma

would immediately grow angry if such reproaches were made, he first described the winter scene, incidentally as it were mentioning Bharata and so finding a chance to denounce Kaikeyī." Despite Rāma's advice here, note that he has already denounced his stepmother himself (above, 2.17–18), and will do so again (3.56.7–8 [so also Sītā, 46.28 and note]). The seventeenth-century poet Nīlakaṇṭha Dīkṣita cites this particular inconsistency as an almost essential component of Rāma's human *avatāra* (in his *Nalacaritranāṭaka*, prologue 3 [cited by Filliozat 1967, p. 48]).

35. "our middle mother" *ambā madhyamā*: See above, 2.18 note.

36. "But no, do not: For determined though I am" *niścitāpi hi*: A strong adversative force must be extracted from this clause, and it may well reside once again in the particle *hi* (see above, note on 8.28).

38. "They . . . intoned the hymn" *stuvanti*: The plural verb makes Cg anxious, and he hastens to point out that Sītā's hymn does not include any vedic *mantras* (which women were, later at least, prohibited from using). Whether or not the poet himself shares this anxiety is uncertain (cf. the note on 2.17.7, and on the plural as occasionally representing a dual, the note on 2.31.17, and below, 67.20 and note).

39. "resembled the blessed lord Rudra" *rudraḥ . . . bhagavān iveśaḥ*: Ct is without question correct, in my view, when he remarks, "By using this simile of Rudra the poet signals that Rāma's mind is now bent on the destruction [of the *rākṣasas*]." The references to Rudra (Śiva) will become more frequent over the coming *sargas* (see 23.27, 24.10, 24.26, 29.27) as the aesthetic mood (*rasa*) of the poem turns to *raudra*, "the ferocious" (the "presiding deity" of which is Rudra, cf. *NāṭyaŚā* 6.44), and the hero's terrible slaughter of the demons. See also the Introduction, Chapter 5.

"Nandi": Śiva's attendant, iconographically represented as a snow-white bull.

"the daughter of the mountain king" *agarājaputryā*: Pārvatī (also known as Ūmā, Gaurī, etc.), the wife of Śiva.

Sarga 16

1. Since the events of the *Rāmāyaṇa* are uniquely important to the cultural calendar of traditional India, determining them precisely preoccupies the commentators throughout the poem; each significant event has to fit into a sound chronology. Here, Cg argues that the events about to occur take place in the spring three years after Rāma's arrival in Pañcavaṭī, that is, at the beginning of the fourteenth (and last) year of his exile (the preceding description is that of his first winter in Pañcavaṭī, recounting the new hardships of his life there). The calculation behind this is complex, but is based on the following key points: Rāma had spent ten years visiting the different sages of the forest (10.25); after Rāvaṇa's abduction of Sītā, he gives her one year to submit to him (54.22 below); this period is nearly over by the time Rāma arrives in Laṅkā (5.35.7–8; 5.56.89); the victorious hero returns to Ayodhyā directly after slaying Rāvaṇa, fourteen years to the day since his departure (6.112.1, 14). (A complete chronology of the events of the poem is given by Cg on GPP 6.124.1, and is discussed at great length by Ct on GPP 6.108.35; see also Ct on 17.26 below).

2. After this verse the SR adds, "And he stayed there happily, honored by the great seers" (285*), providing the interval required by the chronological interpretation as instanced in Cg on verse 1 above.

3. Hereafter much of the NR inserts a passage in which Jaṭāyus comes and asks leave to return to his own dwelling, since Rāma is himself skillful (enough to provide protection); he promises to return after seeing his friends. Rāma dismisses him (286*; cf. 41.49, 48.1, 63.10 and notes; the insertion is motivated principally by the problem raised in 48.1 note).

5. "Śūrpaṇakhā": Literally, "Whose nails (claws) are (the size and shape of) winnowing fans."

"thirty gods" *tridaśa-*: A standard rounding-off of the "thirty-three gods," whose number is made up as at 13.14cd–15ab above.

8–10. The rhetorical figure here is known as the *viṣamālaṃkāra*, defined in the *SāhiDa* (10.71) as among other things "the juxtaposition of the incongruous" (so noted by Ct).

Śūrpaṇakhā, as a *rākṣasa* woman, can take on any form at will (cf. verse 18), something *rākṣasīs* often do in order to seduce anchorites or kshatriyas (cf. *MBh* 1.139.15ff., Hiḍimbā's seduction of Bhīma), something in fact Rāvaṇa himself will do (below, *sargas* 44ff.). It is therefore odd that she retains her natural hideous appearance here. Several N manuscripts seek to correct this by having her reflect (in an insertion hereafter, 289*) on assuming a heavenly form. But this obviously is contradicted by the sequel, despite the NR's attempts to alter it (e.g., 295*, 305*); see further in the Introduction, Chapter 6.

Śūrpaṇakhā's behavior in this scene will later be censured by the *rākṣasa* women of Laṅkā (cf. 6.82.6ff., especially verse 9, "an utterly absurd deed, one that she never should have done"). Her conduct is not only ridiculous (and that the passage is meant to be humorous to some degree is certain, however cruel a humor we may find it; cf. the note on 2.29.24 for a similar instance) but also sinful: She is behaving as an adulteress, and for that she will be appropriately punished by Rāma the king (see below, 17.20–21 and note on verse 21). The incident as a whole fits in with the pervasive deviant sexuality of the book, recapitulated in Rāvaṇa's rape of Sītā.

11. "Rāma has matted hair like a hermit, female companionship like a lover, and armaments like a kshatriya," Cg. On the antinomy of Rāma's nature, cf. Virādha's statements above, 2.10cd–12ab (and see Pollock 1986, p. 70 and note 11).

16. The SR adds, "For with your charming body you do not look like a *rākṣasa* woman to me" (296*), a verse the commentators find difficult to explain (Venkatanathacharya 1965, p. 134 note may be right to think the statement sarcastic).

19. "who lies ever fast asleep" *pravṛddhanidraś ca sadā*: Not really "ever." Kumbhakarṇa was given a boon by Brahmā allowing him to sleep for long (usually six-month) stretches, waking then for only a day to have a bite to eat (see 6.48.11ff.; 7.10.39)—until, as the poet Kālidāsa puts it, "Rāma's arrows lulled him into the long sleep" (*RaghuVa* 12.81).

20. Ck, Ct claim that another brother, Triśiras, is omitted here because, like Vibhīṣaṇa, he behaves in ways inappropriate to a *rākṣasa* (see below, 22.33, 25.23ff. and note on verse 23; there are two individuals named Triśiras, one a general in Khara's army, the other a son of Rāvaṇa).

21. "But I am prepared to defy them" *tān ahaṃ samatikrāntā*: On the immediate futurity of the past passive participle, see the note and reference on 3.25 above. "Transgress, defy," seems to be the normal semantic range of the verb in the *Rām*. (cf. 2.18.26, 27.29, 61.24). I interpret Śūrpaṇakhā's remarks to mean: I do not care what my brothers think about my loving a human being (or, about my entering into

a marriage without their consent or knowledge). This is not too distant from the commentators ("I am 'beyond them,' that is, I do what I like," Cg; "that is, I fear nothing they might do to me for pursuing you," Cm, Ck, Ct; the last two also suggest, " 'I excell them' in power," as substantiating their first explanation).

22. "worthy" *sadṛśī*: Generally indicating that the two parties share a commensurate rank and status (see 2.3.23 and note).

"I alone am suited to you; look upon me as your wife" *aham evānurūpā te bhāryārūpeṇa paśya mām*: I translate the *pādas* in agreement with Cr. Venkatanathacharya (1965, p. 136 note) suggests instead, "I alone, by reason of my beauty, am a wife [*bhāryā rūpeṇa*] deserving of you; look at me."

23. "slut" *asatīm*: It may perhaps be that Śūrpaṇakhā thinks, like Virādha earlier (cf. 2.11), that Sītā is being shared by Rāma and Lakṣmaṇa (see also Khara's words in 18.19 below). As the sequel seems to emphasize, however, the only one guilty of unchastity is Śūrpaṇakhā herself (compare the reappearance of the phrase in 17.20, carrying with it a tone of rectification).

"with her pinched waist" *nirṇatodarīm*: So essentially Cg, Ck, Ct, Cr, but Cm's "potbellied" points to a problem in the tradition's understanding of the meaning of the word (when the adjective reappears in 5.22.15 in reference to the "hideous" *rākṣasa* woman Vinatā, the commentators gloss "high waisted" [? *unnatodarī*], Cv, Cg; "narrow waisted," Cm; "deep" or "very deep waisted," Ck, Ct). See 17.13 note.

25. "wild-eyed" *madirekṣaṇām*: Less likely, "lovely-eyed," Cg (cf. 2.14.14; Cm, "red-eyed").

Sarga 17

1. "in jest" *svecchayā*: The reading should be marked as uncertain, insofar as the Northern Recension has nothing of the sort (it merely expands what I have translated as the causal phrase). Cm glosses, "having fun mocking his brother"; Cg, Ck read *svacchayā*, "lucid" (sc., "words"); and Ct believes the correct reading (cf. 303*) to be *svacchandām*, "the self-willed female" (if the word can mean that; contrast 6.104.22). The problem is by no means trivial—and perhaps for that very reason has the passage been subjected to such considerable revision—for the correct reading would give us some sense of the moral quality of Rāma's behavior. He is either intending to teach the immoral (*svacchandā*) creature a lesson, or exhibiting a self-indulgent, and to some extent cruel, levity (*svecchayā*). We should remember that the events about to take place here provide the impetus to the major event in the epic—Rāvaṇa's abduction of Sītā.

3. "still unmarried" *akṛtadāraḥ*: Lakṣmaṇa is of course married, according to both the *Bālakāṇḍa* (72.18ff.) and the *Ayodhyākāṇḍa* (2.110.51 and note). Since "Rāma never lies," the commentators attempt to explain away the remark. Cg, Cr argue that the statement really means "Lakṣmaṇa does not have his wife with him." Ct reasonably suggests taking the words at face value, on the grounds that "when one is joking a lie is not considered reprehensible." For a discussion of the issue of Lakṣmaṇa's marital status and its text-historical significance, see Goldman 1984, pp. 64ff.

5. "inseparable as sunlight and Mount Meru" *merum arkaprabhā yathā*: The sunlight (feminine gender in Sanskrit) is said to be always in contact with Mount Meru

(masculine), the center point of the world, around which the sun revolves. The simile is used of Rāma and Sītā in 2.35.21.

9. "lotuslike beauty" *kamalavarṇini*: I read the vocative with several S manuscripts and most of the commentators.

13. "potbellied" *(a)nirṇatodarī*: *nirṇatodarī* is used only of Sītā (cf. 16.23 and note, 17.11, 15), whereas Śūrpaṇakhā is called *mahodarī* (16.8, 17.20). Since there are no persuasive variants, I feel compelled to understand the adjective with the negative prefix. The adjective recurs in 5.22.15 and 6.82.6, but in the very same phrase, *karālā nirṇatodarī*, where presumably the same *sandhi* is present. See also the note on 16.23 above.

17. In the retelling of the incident by the later poet Kālidāsa, Śūrpaṇakhā, after her second solicitation of Rāma, flies into a rage when Sītā laughs at her (*RaghuVa* 12.36).

"Rohiṇī": See below, note on 44.5.

20. "mutilate this misshapen (slut)" *imāṃ virūpām . . . virūpayitum arhasi*: Kālidāsa had these words in mind when describing Lakṣmaṇa's act as a "tautology" (*vairūpyapaunaruktyena, RaghuVa* 12.40).

21. "cut off the . . . ears and nose" *ciccheda karṇanāsam*: This type of mutilation is prescribed in the lawbooks as punishment for adultery and fornication; see the Introduction, Chapter 6, and below, 18.14 (in the *MBh* [3.261.44] her nose and lips are cut, but not her ears). Note that in the *Bālakāṇḍa* (25.11), Rāma threatens Tāṭakā with a similar punishment.

25. "Khara": Literally, the "Harsh One." It is less likely that Vālmīki intends the pun "ass," though in some folk *Rāmāyaṇa* traditions, as in the Rāmlīlā of Banaras, Khara is represented as a donkey. (*AmaK* 1.3.36 and 2.9.77 allows both meanings.)

There is some uncertainty about the kinship relationship of Śūrpaṇakhā and Khara. According to the *MBh* version of the *Rām*, Khara is Śūrpaṇakhā's twin brother (3.259.8); in *Rām* 7.24.30, he is her "brother" insofar as he is the son of Śūrpaṇakhā's maternal aunt (in 7.9.21–27, in the story of the birth of the siblings Rāvaṇa, Kumbhakarṇa, Śūrpaṇakhā, and Vibhīṣaṇa, Khara is not mentioned).

"Janasthāna": Khara has been stationed in this region under orders from Rāvaṇa (see 34.4–5 below, and 7.24.29ff.), but the narrative does not make clear just where this is. Although it seems here as if Śūrpaṇakhā is leaving Pañcavaṭī and entering Janasthāna (cf. also 26.5), in 42.21 Rāma's ashram appears to be situated in Janasthāna itself (note additionally 44.6). Perhaps we have two names for the same area.

26. "told" *śaśaṃsa*: As often in the *Rām*, the lyric verse at the close of a *sarga* provides a synoptic preview of the coming action (so Cg, "The poet summarizes in this one verse the matter of the following *sarga*"; see the note on 18.21, 19.25 and, for a particularly dramatic example, 56.20 and note). We must thus temper our surprise, on reading *sarga* 18, to learn that Khara knows nothing of the events that have occurred.

Ct appends a learned note on chronology here, arguing that, since two additional months have to be intercalated in the calendar every five years (he cites *MBh* 4.47.3), there is some controversy over exactly when the thirteenth year began and thus when the events surrounding Rāvaṇa's abduction of Sītā take place. (He adduces the *PadmP* [probably the Bengali recension (cf. note on 2.51.4) but *PadmP* 4.36.21–22 is similar] but notes that there are variant readings of that passage, too.) See further on 16.1 above.

Sarga 18

2. "(you) go your way (like Death himself)" *(antakasamā) gatā*: The reading of the crit. ed. is improbable (I more or less follow Cg, Ct; Cm understands *āgatā*, "returned"). The NR offers the plausible *yudhi*, "(you are like Death himself) in battle."

3. "Which one of the gods, *gandharvas*, spirits . . ." *devagandharvabhūtānām . . . ko 'yam*: Despite the formulaic appearance of the list, we can infer that, like Rāvaṇa (30.18, Introduction, Chapter 4b), Khara disdainfully dismisses the power of humans. Much of the Khara episode in fact prefigures the story of Rāvaṇa.

4. "chastiser of Pāka" *pākaśāsanam*: The rather obscure epithet was interpreted in the epics and later as referring to an *asura* named Pāka (brother of Vṛtra, according to Cm); cf. for example *BhāgP* 8.11.19ff.

5. "Today I will take someone's life" *adyāhaṃ . . . prāṇān ādāsye*: The indefinite pronoun has, awkwardly, to be supplied; the NE seeks to remedy matters with the attractive reading *kasya* ("whose?" for *adya*).

"the crane" *sārasaḥ*: Cm, Cg, Ck, Ct, Cr gloss "goose," the feat being normally attributed to the royal goose. The precise significance of the simile, however, escapes me. Khara may mean, "I will not cause universal destruction (or rather, the destruction of all those divine and semi-divine creatures previously mentioned—though I could easily do it), but only take the life of that one malefactor." But this seems vaguely out of character. Perhaps the simile refers simply to his separating the life breaths from the body. NE manuscripts in any case replace the figure with another, "As the sun takes off the scanty water of a pool [*sarasaḥ*] with its beams" (327*), which has the appearance of a literate revision of the original, and no longer understood, *topos*.

8. The verse will be repeated nearly verbatim by the *rākṣasa* widows during their lamentations for their dead and their expressions of fear for their king, Rāvaṇa, whom "No god . . . could save" once he is joined in combat with Rāma (6.82.27; the reading in this latter verse, *upasṛṣṭam*, is offered by the NR here for the improbable *apakṛṣṭam*).

11. The commentators here address the fact that even though Śūrpaṇakhā was injured by Rāma, she can still speak positively of him. Cm, citing 2.18.5, remarks, "The virtues of Śrī Rāma's heavenly beauty bring blessings to friend and foe alike, and therefore Śūrpaṇakhā, though mutilated by him, describes his beauty in the conviction that by so doing she will come to experience the supreme [spiritual] happiness." Rather similarly Cg, "(All she had to do at present was identify Rāma, yet she describes his beauty) because, though she was mutilated, her passion has not abated and she feels herself forced to speak what is in her heart. This is what happens to people—adversary or partisan—who have once seen Rāma. This is comparable to the case of Hanumān's describing Rāma to Sītā [5.33.8] (when all he had to do was mention Rāma's distinguishing marks)."

After this or the following verse most S manuscripts insert,

> Living on fruit and roots, temperate men, ascetics who follow the ways of righteousness, they are two sons of Daśaratha, the brothers Rāma and Lakṣmaṇa. (330*)

12. "Whether they are gods or men" *devau vā mānuṣau vā tau*: On the possibility that such a statement may be more than a rhetorical flourish, see the Introduction, Chapter 4.

15. "whore" *anṛjuvṛttāyāḥ*: See above, the note on 16.23. Cg remarks, "The implication is that Śūrpaṇakhā thinks the princes mutilated her at Sītā's instigation."

17ff. Cm reports a story (said by him to be found in the *MBh*, although I have not been able to locate it) that in a previous existence Khara was Candrakānta, wise son of Yājñavalkya (both Dūṣaṇa and Triśiras were thought to have been his sons, too, in an earlier birth), who, by reason of Śiva's curse, was reborn in a demon's body. The curse was set to terminate when Viṣṇu, incarnated as Rāma, should slay him. In accordance with his usual interpretation, Cm argues that on hearing the story of Rāma from Śūrpaṇakhā, Khara comes to understand that Rāma is Viṣṇu, and, longing for death at Rāma's hands, he instructs the demons to engage him in battle under the pretext of pleasing his sister. Thus although Khara's words might at first seem harsh, they are in fact kindly. (Ct objects to this analysis: Khara and the others who became *rākṣasas* by reason of Śiva's curse had, from the very beginning of the curse, no knowledge of the Blessed One's form [that is, his having taken the form of Rāma]; only at the moment of death would they remember the limit to the curse, and regain their true forms by recognizing His form.)

Jacobi (1897, pp. 605–6) may have been correct in arguing that the following account of the attack of the fourteen *rākṣasas* is a copy (*Abklatsch*) of the fight with the fourteen thousand *rākṣasas* (*sargas* 21ff.). It is absent from both tables of contents (1.1.47, GPP 1.3.20); neither the *Rāmopākhyāna* nor Kālidāsa knows anything of the incident.

21. Hereafter a verse appears that, according to manuscript distribution, ought to have been included in the text:

> But the *rākṣasas*, armed with sharp arrows though they were, found themselves incapable of quelling that man of supreme power; they were like elephants in the midst of a raging forest fire. (344*)

As with 17.26 (see the note there), this would supply a brief summary of the subsequent action.

Sarga 19

4. "come to the aid" *padavīm āgatān*: Here and in 20.12 I am inclined to see an idiom of sorts (see also pw, s.v. *padavī*). This also agrees with Cm, Cr.

7. "Daṇḍaka forest" *daṇḍakāvanam*: The lengthening (presumably *metri causa*) is, I believe, unique to this passage.

9. "that have wrought havoc" *viprakārān*: Ct, Cr understand the form as an ablative, "because of your crimes"; I agree with Cm, Cg, Ck.

10. "wicked creatures" *saṃduṣṭāḥ*: So I read against the crit. ed. For *saṃtuṣṭa-* can hardly bear the meaning with which the commentators feel compelled to laden it (" 'content,' that is, unafraid," Cg; " 'content with' [that is, prepared for giving] battle," Cr). As we have seen elsewhere (2.78.8 and note there; see also the variants recorded at 3.43.22), this is a very common corruption for *saṃduṣṭa-*, which is attested here in both the NW and S recensions.

"come no closer" *nopasarpitum arhatha*: *upasarpitum* ("to come forward [to meet]," compare *MBh* 5.193.342–35), accepted by the crit. ed., is apparently the reading of the NE version. But this actually makes sense only if at the same time we accept the

NE version of *pāda* ("withdraw from here"). For when one commands "Stay, stand" in Sanskrit battle poetry, it usually means "Do not run from me, stand and fight" (see 3.9 above, 49.25; 6.91.20, etc.). The likelier reading may therefore be *nāpasarpitum* (with D3, corroborated by the reading *nopāvartitum* of Cg, Ck, Ct), "(stay where you are . . .) do not retreat."

11–12. "shivered . . . unacquainted" *hṛṣṭādṛṣṭa-*: Double sandhi (noticed also by Ct and questioned, unnecessarily, by Cr).

18. "sharpened on stone" *śilāśitān*: In agreement with Cm, Ck, Ct, Cr; improbably Cg, " 'sharp even against stones,' that is, able to split rocks."

"iron shafts" *nārācān*: Adducing literary sources Pant 1978, p. 162, describes the *nārāca* as made wholly of iron, and used only by the strongest and most skilled archers. (Apparently no *nārāca* of the ancient period has been found.)

22. Most of the NR has the arrows return to the quiver of their own accord (352*).

23. "ghastly shriek" *bhairavaṃ ravam*: A light pun (technically a *pādānta yamaka*).

25. Again the final verse summarizes the substance of the following *sarga* (so noted by Cm, Cg, Ct).

Sarga 20

1. "to (Khara's) ill luck" *anarthārtham*: Or, " 'to the misfortune,' namely, of the *rākṣasa* tribe," Cm, Ck, Ct, Cr; " 'for the destruction,' that is, of the *rākṣasas*," Cg.

"her collapsed . . . in a rage" *patitāṃ . . . krodhāt*: My construction is against that of Cr ("he addressed her in a rage"), who alone remarks on the adverb.

3. "They kill" *ghnanto 'pi*: Here, as Cm notes, *api* is not concessive, but emphatic.

6. "unassailable" *durdharṣā*: An ornamental epithet tenaciously holding its place despite the narrative impropriety (cf. note on 27.6 below).

14. "I shall not hesitate" *nirapatrapā*: That is, "shall have no qualms, shall not scruple," though this is not absolutely certain. The NR reads the vocative ("O shameless" [Khara]), whereas the explanation of the commentators ("She is said to be 'shameless' because her nose and ears have been cut off," Cg, Ck, Ct) sheds little light.

15. "armed . . . with his bow" *sacāpasya*: The NE version omits the reference, and much of the SR substitutes, "even attended by your forces" (*sabalo 'pi* or *sabalaś ca*), eliminating what might appear to be a vacuous detail. Yet there is a peculiar sanctity that seems always to have attached to the image of "Rāma with his bow" (the bow often referred to by the odd word *kodaṇḍa*; see further in Ghurye 1979, especially pp. 47ff.), perhaps partly in recognition that the bow is the one professedly Vaiṣṇava attribute that he bears (see 11.29 above). This seems to me to lend a certain authenticity to the reading of the crit. ed.

Sarga 21

1. "Khara . . . (spoke) with great harshness" *kharaḥ kharataraṃ vacaḥ*: A light pun (technically a *pādādi yamaka*), of which the poet seems particularly enamored (cf. for instance 21.26, 23.1).

2. "The contempt shown you" *tavāpamāna-*: I understand the genitive as objective (so also Venkatanathacharya 1965, p. 156 note), rather than subjective ("The contempt you have shown" [of me], thus Ct).

"as irrepressible as the heaving salt sea water" *na śakyate dhārayituṃ lavaṇāmbha ivotthitam*: My interpretation of the simile is that of Cg, Ck, and the NW recension; otherwise Cm, " '(as unbearable as) an . . . infusion of salt water,' that is, upon a wound," but this is hardly indicated by the language of the verse.

3. "I care nothing for the power of Rāma" *na rāmaṃ gaṇaye viryāt*: Thus the parallel version of the NR, 378*. Alternatively, "I care nothing for Rāma because of (my own) power" (thus it seems Ct, Cr); cf. 22.19.

"Because of those evil acts of his, he is doomed to lose his life" *ātmaduścaritaiḥ prāṇān hato yo 'dya vimokṣyati*: Rather differently the commentators: "Already struck down by his own evil acts . . ." (Ct, essentially Cg, Ck; Cm is silent). But what would this imply in the present context, except that the retribution is somehow inherent in the crime, as if Khara saw himself as an instrument of cosmic justice? But that is hardly likely. We do best to take the instrumental, not as means or agent, but as cause (*Pā* 2.3.23), and construe *hataḥ* closely with *vimokṣyati*. (Note that the NE recension, reading *hato yuddhe*, could not have understood the line as Ct does.)

5. The NE version graphically expands: Khara will dismember Rāma and his sister will eat the limbs, and he will have Sītā's flesh prepared in sauce for himself (379*).

6. Hereafter NE manuscripts add eight verses supplying the praise spoken by Śūrpaṇakhā (380*).

14–16. "Impatiently" *amarṣāt*: Cm glosses "angrily," citing the *Śakunaśāstra* ("Textbook on Augury"), "Anger presages [or, leads to] the failure of the enterprise."

"auspicious designs worked in gold" *kāñcanaiḥ māṅgalyaiḥ*: I agree with Cg, Ck in construing these qualifications with all the substantives in verse 15.

20–22. "harpoons" *vajraiḥ*: For this identification, see Rau 1973 (and cf. Das Gupta 1975).

Sarga 22

1. "showered down" *abhyavarṣat*: The double accusative with this verb is awkward. Many manuscripts read a locative absolute in *pāda* a.

"water red as blood" *śoṇitodakam*: I understand the compound as an *upamāsamāsa* with Cg; Ct, "water mixed with blood" (which is supported to some extent by 6.83.33, *vavarṣa rudhiraṃ devaḥ*).

3. "like the ring of a twirling firebrand" *alātacakrapratimam*: The circle described by a torch when whirled. This may be the first occurrence (see also 4.45.12) of a favorite image of illusionist philosophy (in addition to the epic references cited by Bhatt 1963, p. 404, cf. *MūlaMāKā* 17.33 and *LaṅkāSū* 9.3).

The verse is describing the beginning of the eclipse mentioned in verse 11 (here the reference is to the projection of the moon's disk, with its red edge, onto the sun with its pale white corona).

4. "inauspicious" *sudāruṇaḥ*: The word appears to be a technical term of augury (cf. 55.3, 65.11 below; 6.91.4, 94.25, 27).

6. "In an unpropitious quarter" *pradīptāyāṃ diśi*: Certain acts, sounds, and the like made by a bird or beast may be reckoned inauspicious, and so by extension is the quarter of space in which the animal is located. See *BṛhSaṃ* 85.15 (D. Pingree, personal communication).

"jackals . . . boding ill" *aśivāḥ* . . . *śivāḥ*: Again a light pun (*yamaka*, but I find no traditional category for this particular sort).

7. "crumbled mountains" *prabhinnagiri-*: The commentators try to make sense of the feeble simile: "that is, whose wings have been cut off by Indra," Cg, alluding to an ancient myth (cf. note on 2.83.19); "massed mountains," Cm; "running with minerals," Ct. Several S manuscripts, Crā, and Ck read instead "rutting elephants" (*prabhinnagaja-*), whereby the red madder would construe very effectively with the blood-red water of the clouds. Unfortunately the lection has no support from the NR.

9. "fresh blood" *kṣatajārdra-*: I take the compound as *paranipāta* (for *ārdrakṣataja-*; Cg instead, "['the color of,' that is, a cloth for example] 'wet with blood' "; so Cm, Ck, Ct). On the frequency of such inverted compounds in the epics see the note on 2.41.27.

10. "dreadful to look at" *ghoranidarśanāḥ*: Taken as synonymous with the more common *ghoradarśana*, against Cm, Cr, "being examples of bad omens," and Ct, "indicating danger," since both explanations appear tautologous in view of *pāda* c.

11. "A cloud like a barrier-omen" *kabandhaḥ parighābhāsaḥ*: My translation derives from the definition of *parigha-* in *BṛSaṃ* 85.51–52: *parigha-* is an unfavorable omen appearing before and behind an army (D. Pingree, personal communication). On this interpretation, the two half verses are not narratively related. But I remain uncertain because parallels in the epics point to a more logical connection between the two events. It is thus possible also to translate, "[Rāhu's] headless corpse, resembling a streak of cloud." That *kabandha-* (on the word itself see Renou 1939, pp. 390ff.) may mean, not "cloud" (so Cg), but "the headless corpse" of Svarbhānu is made probable by *MBh* 5.108.111 (*kabandhaḥ pratidṛśyate svarbhānoḥ*), and by the NR variant here (*sakabandhaḥ* . . . *svarbhānuḥ*, 395*, a reading interestingly reported by the SR of the *MBh* elsewhere in that epic, e.g., 6.108.9). For its part, *parigha-* in the sense of "(streak of) cloud" is corroborated by the parallel in *MBh* 8.31.41 (*kabandhaṃ meghasaṃkāśaṃ bhānum āvṛtya saṃsthitam*). (Cm [repeated by Ct], Cg gloss "appearing like an iron club"; cf. also Belvalkar 1947, p. 756.)

Cg cites *NītiSā* [17.27] for the portentousness of the sight of a corpse near the sun (a warning against encamping an army).

15. "(Meteors . . .) crashing" (*ulkāḥ* . . .) *sanirghoṣāḥ*: All but one D manuscript (and Ct, Cr) read instead *sanirghātāḥ* (corroborated to some extent by 2.4.17 and 6.94.18; the *pāda* as constituted occurs nowhere else in the epics). Although this seems to mean much the same thing as the reading of the crit. ed. (see for example Kullūka on *ManuSm* 4.105 or Mitākṣarā on *YājñaSm* 1.145), Cg here glosses it as "(meteors) along with whirlwinds" (he cites from Varāhamihira [*BṛSaṃ* 33.8]: "When a meteor . . . struck by the wind falls from the sky to the earth, it becomes a *nirghāta*," but this seems to mean "lightning flash," which is not what Cg intends).

22. "(are) doom(ed)" *viparyayaḥ*: I agree with Cm on the sense of the noun; Ct implausibly, "[Because of whom (that is, my sister) they suffered this 'transformation,' that is,] in the form of their savage intention [to mutilate her]" (so too Cr).

26. "gods, and *gandharvas*" *devagandharvāḥ*: See 23.17; or, "divine *gāndharvas*" (see the note on 2.85.14).

27. "in a body" *sahitāḥ*: Not "benignly" (Cg, Cr).

28. "the god who bears the discus" *cakrahastaḥ*: That is, Viṣṇu. In place of the Vaiṣṇava simile (rare for the *Rām*), the NR offers "Indra, Slayer of Pāka."

Sarga 23

3. "of mass destruction" *sarvabhūtāpahāriṇaḥ*: The variants of the NR confirm this meaning for the compound (Cr most improbably construes with *sarvarākṣasān* in *pāda* d), though this sets up a contrast with the second half of the verse that some adversative particle would be expected to signal (the NR reads in *pādas* cd, "[obliteration] of all human beings").

"to foretell the annihilation" *saṃhartum*: Thus we must assess the force of the infinitive, with Ck, Ct.

7. "my arm" *me bāhuḥ*: The NR makes it explicit that it is Rāma's right (auspicious) arm.

8. "looks bright" *suprabhaṃ . . . lakṣyate*: Contrast Rāvaṇa in 6.83.33, *vivarṇavadana-*, "his face was drained of color," just prior to his final battle with Rāma. See also 21.14–16 note above. This appears to be a common omen in epic battles; see *MBh* 6.20.2, Sukthankar 1929, pp. 171ff.

12. "you to question" *pratikūlayitum . . . tvayā*: The infinitive has a definite passive aspect, a rare usage (though cf. 5.33.59).

"by these feet" *pādābhyām*: That is, in essence, "upon my life" (*prāṇaiḥ* is in fact read by M3; cf. 2.18.38, *śāpitāsi mama prāṇaiḥ)*. Cg is referring to what appears to be a later usage when he comments, " 'You are implored by my feet': Rāma is using [in the third person] the mode of address that Lakṣmaṇa would himself use toward him" (that is, Rāmapāda).

The SR adds hereafter,

> "You are a mighty hero and certainly able to kill them, but I myself wish to kill all the *rākṣasas*." [That is, because of his personal promise to the sages to safeguard them (9.16).] (418*)

18. In a passage inserted by the NR after this verse the following lines are found: "We know who Rāma is, and how it happened he came to earth; but at the thought that he is now a man, our minds are shaken with pity" (423*.1–2). For some comments on the idea here, see the Introduction, Chapter 4.

20. "stormed about" *jṛmbhatām*: Ck, Ct remark, "By *jṛmbhaṇam* is signified the effect of taking an intoxicating substance in order to commence a battle without a thought for one's life."

25. "filled himself with . . . rage" *krodham āhārayat*: Cg makes it appear as if the verb has an actual causative sense, as if, that is, Rāma had to generate or work himself into a rage: "Though of a benign aspect he 'excited his own anger' in order to pluck out this irritating thorn [the *rākṣasas*]." Such instances of the verb phrase as *MBh* 7.165.125 and *HariVaṃ* 89.33, of the verb itself in similar contexts (see 14.24 above), and of the parallel expression *krodhaṃ bheje* (see 25.20 below) tell against the traditional explanation.

26. The parallel with *Iliad* 18, where Achilles appears in his divine armor radiating firelike flames, is striking. For perceptive comments on the "elemental vision" of the Greek epic poet, which are in some ways easily transferable to Vālmīki, see Whitman 1958, pp. 137ff.

27. "the god who wields the *pināka* bow" *pinākinaḥ*: Śiva.

"the sacrifice of Dakṣa" *dakṣasya . . . kratum*: Śiva was excluded from the sacrificial rite undertaken by his "father-in-law," Dakṣa, which he in a fit of rage proceeded to disrupt (a story told often in Sanskrit literature, beginning with *ŚatBr* 3.5.1.13ff.).

For the significance of the Saiva simile, compare above, 15.39 note.

NR insertions hereafter show the *rākṣasa* army as being literally stunned by the appearance of Rāma, until Khara resolves to attack him (App. I, Nos. 5, 6).

Sarga 24

7. "sought to kill" *nijaghnuḥ*: I give the perfect a conative aspect, as it appears to have elsewhere (see note on 2.12.18, but compare 43.36 note below); otherwise, simply though less plausibly, "they struck" (they do not actually reach Rāma until the next verse).

9. "king of mountains" *śailendram*: Himālaya.

10. "Śiva, the great god" *mahādevaḥ*: The half verse is absent in the recension of Cm, Cg (on what grounds the editor suspects haplography I do not know).

"his hordes" *gaṇaiḥ*: Śiva is often depicted in the company of ghastly, deformed attendants (his *gaṇas*).

"on a moonless night" *tithiṣu*: So basically Ct, Cr (who gloss with *pradoṣa-*); this is largely eliminated in the NR.

11. "Rāghava met the weapons" *śastrāṇi . . . rāghavaḥ pratijagrāha*: Indian epic heroes universally have the wonderful ability to arrest (and usually split) enemy weapons in midflight with their own arrows.

15. "bending his bow into an arc" *maṇḍalīkṛtakārmukaḥ*: "Rāma keeps his bow arced, the more swiftly to place and discharge arrows," Ck, Ct.

20. "lofty standards" *dhvajāgrāṇi*: Literally, "tops of standards," rather than "the best of standards" (as required by Sukthankar 1942, p. 1103, and 30.4 below; cf. 2.24.7 and note).

21. "reed darts" *nālīka-*: So Cg (Cm, Ck, Ct, Cr add that these arrows are tipped with iron).

"barbed arrows" *vikarṇibhiḥ*: "An arrow tipped with a barb that rips out the intestines when it is drawn out," Cm (so Ck, Ct, Cr).

24. "took their lives and cut their throats" *jahāra . . . prāṇāṃś ciccheda ca śirodharān*: Note the hysteron proteron (to which Cg also calls attention).

25. "seeking refuge from the arrows" *śaraṇārtham śara-*: The Sanskrit contains a pun (*pādādi yamaka*); on the poet's verbal playfulness at moments of high drama see 2.20.32 note.

26. "like Death . . . Rudra" *rudram ivāntakaḥ*: The simile of Śiva killing, not Death (*antaka*), but the demon Andhaka is found frequently in the battle books of the epics, although the full story is not reported until the *purāṇas* (cf. for example *MatsyaP* 179.2-40: the demon Andhaka, empowered by a boon, attempts to steal Devī and is defeated by Śiva). In both epics the two major recensions invariably

disagree on the correct spelling of the name, southern manuscripts always offering Antaka, northern manuscripts generally Andhaka (see *Rām* 3.29.27 below, and 6.33.6; *MBh* 7.48.10, 130.38; 8.15.8, etc.; what appears to be the first reference to the myth, *AV* 11.2.7, gives the name as Ardhaka). But Ct on 29.27 below is able to locate a myth in which Śiva is said to slay *Death*, and Cg alludes to it here ("Yama was conquered by Rudra"). I should still be inclined to alter the reading of the critical text here, except that no manuscript supports *-andhakaḥ*, the NR for the most part having an altogether different *pāda* ("as Namuci . . . Vāsava"), whereas the Lahore edition does in fact read *antakam*, supported to a degree by NW manuscripts.

28. The NR hereafter inserts a passage in which Rāma shoots a *gāndharva* arrow that confuses the *rākṣasas*, who begin to slay each other in the belief they are slaying Rāma (463*; in an SR insertion Rāma similarly employs a *gāndharva* arrow, but without the same results, App. I No. 7.5ff.; the NR receives some corroboration from Kālidāsa, *RaghuVa* 12.45). Identical is 6.81.22ff., when during the final battle with Rāma, the *rākṣasas* are "confused by a *gāndharva* weapon shot by the great one, and see thousands of Rāmas on the battlefield" and so begin to slay one another. This is something of an epic *topos*: in the *Mahābhārata*, Bhīma, at the height of his prowess, is viewed as being multiplied a hundred-thousand-fold (6.55.22); so too Abhimanyu, who makes use of the *gandharva* weapon (7.44.21–23), and Arjuna, who uses the *tvāṣṭra* weapon (7.18.11–12).

Sarga 25

2. "narrowed his eyes like a bull" *nimīlita ivarṣabhaḥ*: This suggests to Cg that "despite the shower of arrows, Rāma is unruffled and untroubled" (Ck, Ct believe him to close his eyes from the rain of weapons).

4. "Dūṣaṇa, the 'spoiler of enemies' " *dūṣaṇaḥ śatrudūṣaṇaḥ*: Again a pun (*yamaka* or *lāṭānuprāsa*) in the original.

5–6."lightning bolt" *vajrāśani-*: Not "diamond or lightning bolt" (see below, *vajrāśanikṛtavraṇam*, 30.7).

8. "banner of Śakra" *śakradhvajaḥ*: See note on 2.68.29.

10. "all the creatures" *sarvabhūtāni*: Presumably those mentioned in 22.26.

11. "Mahākapāla, Sthūlākṣa, and . . . Pramāthin": The names signify, respectively, "Big-skull" or "Fat-head," "Goggle-eyed," and "Crusher" or "Bruiser."

15. "like a lofty tree newly sprouting with twigs" *viṭapīva mahādrumaḥ*: Obviously the arrows protruding from the demon's eyes are meant to be likened to the sprouts of the tree (*contra* Cg and Cr).

17. "smoky" *sadhūmāḥ*: "That is, ready to burn, not like a coal [whose fire is encased within]," Cg.

23. "From out of that whole army" *tasya sainyasya sarvasya*: Cg glosses *sainya-* as "combatants" in order more logically to include Rāma; but the inconsistency (or better, the poet's changing his thought in midverse) is not unusual in the epics. Since other *rākṣasa* warriors are later shown to be still alive (cf. 26.19), Ct takes the opportunity to note that "each of the *rākṣasas* still had his private retinue left" (the *ṭīkā* on Cm notes that the poet in this verse is referring only to the principal fighters).

"Triśiras": This *rākṣasa* should be distinguished from the son of Rāvaṇa who bears the same name (6.56.3ff.; he is killed by Hanumān in 6.58.42). The incident of his death here, referred to elsewhere (see below, 30.1–2, 34.2–3, 9), is too prominent to warrant Hopkins's view (1915, p. 43) that "like a Homeric combatant," it is one and the same Triśiras who is slain twice. See also the note on 16.20.

Sarga 26

3. "I touch my weapon as proof" *āyuddhaṃ cāham ālabhe*: For touching one's weapons as a solemn corroboration of an oath (so Cr here) see note on 2.18.13.

"whom all the *rākṣasas* should have slain" *vadhārhaṃ sarvarākṣasām*: Thus in agreement with Ct, Cr (so Cg, Ck, who gloss the genitive as instrumental). Cm, Cs suggest, "who [has been] able to slay all the *rākṣasas*," which is preferable in sense but grammatically dubious. Or it may well be, "who deserves to be slain because of, for the sake of, all [these] *rākṣasas* [whom he has killed]"; cf. 28.24 (though this signification of the genitive would be nonstandard, cf. *Pā* 2.3.26).

5. "return to Janasthāna" *janasthānaṃ prayāsyasi*: According to 42.21, Rāma (and thus his assailants) are at present *in* Janasthāna (see also 17.25 note above).

6. "So" *tena*: Note the glossarial variants of the NR for this adverbial signification (*evam*).

"in his eagerness to die" *mṛtyulobhāt*: The commentators for some reason wish to weaken the phrase: " 'eagerness' for battle induced by 'Death' [Doom]" (Cg, Ck; Ct adding, "There is a deeper meaning: He is 'eager for death' at the hands of the Blessed One, having recognized his true nature now that, at the moment of death, his *rākṣasa* character has been transformed").

7. "a triple-peaked mountain" *triśṛṅga iva parvataḥ*: The name Triśiras means "Three-headed."

8. "a bass drum when its skin has been dampened with water" *jalārdrasyeva dundubheḥ*: Ck is no doubt correct to suggest that "treating a drum with water prepared with herbs increases its resonance," a practice continuing to the present day. (Cg is in error when he explains the simile to mean that the demon's voice was lost [cf. *MBh* 1.142.29 for an instructive parallel]; Ct claims that his roar was the opposite of what was expected, and thus augurs his coming death).

9. "with his bow" *dhanuṣā*: Cg, Cr construe this with the final phrase, " 'brandishing,' that is, shooting 'his . . . shafts with his bow' " (a redundancy uncharacteristic of the poet).

14. "strong-jointed" *saṃnataparvabhiḥ*: I am not altogether certain this translation is correct, but the commentators do not help here. Nīlakaṇṭha on *MBh* 6.45.44 vulgate glosses, "whose junctures are imperceptible."

18. "his own heads" *svaśirobhiḥ*: I understand the instrumental here as *upalakṣaṇe* (as for example in 25.9 above; thus also Ct), rather than, with Cm, Cg, as *hetau* (that is, "insofar as his own heads had fallen").

19. "the surviving *rākṣasas*" *hataśeṣāḥ . . . rākṣasāḥ*: See note on 25.23.

20. "turned away" *nivartya*: The causative aspect seems to be otiose (as in 47.19, 70.18 below; see note on 2.17.8). Cs takes it literally ("as they ran he 'turned them back' "), but as far as the poet is concerned, these *rākṣasas* are no longer part of the story.

Sarga 27

2. "Dūṣaṇa and Triśiras": The reading *dūṣaṇas triśirā* (the latter also as nominative), though having apparently some manuscript support, is syntactically impossible here. Taking a hint from the SR's *triśirodūṣaṇau* I read accusative dual with archaic *lopa* of the semivowel /v/ (and *triśirāḥ* declined *metri causa* as an a-stem).

3. "as once Namuci attacked Vāsava" *namucir vāsavaṃ yathā*: One of Indra's great feats as recounted in the *Ṛgveda* is the slaying of the *asura* Namuci; the story, insofar as it shares certain thematic elements with the *Rām*, is considered in the Introduction, Chapter 4.

5. "use of (. . . maneuvers with arrows)" *cacāra* (. . . *mārgān śaraiḥ*): Although the reading *cakāra* is supported by the oldest commentators and most of the SR, the choice of the crit. ed. (offered by several S manuscripts, Ct, and the NE recension) is corroborated by *MBh* 7.63.5, *carantas tv asimārgāṃś ca dhanurmārgāṃś ca śikṣayā*, and elsewhere in that epic (6.50.45; 7.13.51, 65).

6. "Rāma, the great chariot-fighter" *mahārathaḥ . . . rāmaḥ*: So called here and in verse 30 below, despite the absence of a chariot (see 25.22, "fighting . . . on foot")—a sort of *virodhābhāsa* or "apparent contradiction"—either because of the well-known conservatism on the part of epic poets with respect to standing epithets (the "sweet-smiling Damayantī" while she is heaving with sobs, the "swift-footed Achilles" while he is sitting in his tent; cf. 20.6 and note above), or according to the traditional view because of his prowess in battle (the Mylapore edition cites the śāstric definition of the term, "He who all alone can fight with ten thousand . . . is called *mahāratha*"); thus Cg, *contra* Cm, Cr, who take *sa* to refer to Khara (which appears to have been the understanding of the NE version; note its variant in *pāda* d).

"drew his huge bow and filled . . . every quarter" *diśaḥ . . . pūrayām āsa . . . sumahad dhanuḥ*: Without great confidence I explain the verbal construction here as a zeugma (see below verse 22 note, and the notes on 2.74.8 and 90.10; for this verb in the sense of "span, draw" see PW, s.v. 1. *par* 2. causative). There are two alternatives to this: taking the verb as a true causative ("caused his bow to fill"), or reading *sumahādhanuḥ* (that is, as a *bahuvrīhi* compound, as is faintly indicated by M2).

16. "his body radiant as the sun" *ādityavarcasaḥ*: Cg understands the adjectival phrase proleptically, "(Rāma) who (after his corselet fell) had the radiance of the sun."

19. "that the great seer had bestowed" *yat tad atisṛṣṭaṃ maharṣiṇā*: Agastya had given the bow to Rāma at 11.29.

21. "like the sun falling by order of the gods" *sūryo devatānām ivājñayā*: Cg calls the rhetorical figure an *utprekṣā* ("poetic fancy," and he takes *ājñā* "order" to mean "curse"), Ck, Cr call it an *abhūtopamā* ("similitude with something nonexisting or nonoccurring"), since the sun does not fall to the earth. Cs plausibly assumes that merely the sun's setting is meant.

22. "took aim at his heart . . . wounded . . . body" *gātreṣu . . . vivyādha hṛdi*: The reading *hṛdi* found in a few S manuscripts and accepted by the crit. ed. (for the *lectio facilior yudhi*) is certified by the NE's *urasi* (533*). But the two locatives then pose something of a problem, and once again a zeugma may be present.

23. "Rāma, his body drenched with blood" *sa rāmaḥ . . . rudhirasiktāṅgaḥ*: Cr, reluctant to admit that the blood is Rāma's, claims it to be that of the many *rākṣasas* he has slain. The problem is whether Rāma can bleed, or rather the higher-order

question of the god's humanness. The dominant theological position is articulated by Cg later in the poem: Rāma has to appear thoroughly mortal, for his incarnation is in part to instruct people; "if they believed He was immortal, they would think that they could never adhere to righteousness the way He does. But if they were to think him mortal, they would feel themselves able to imitate his ways."

24. "well aimed" *abhilakṣitān*: So Ck, Ct; Cm, "excellent," Cg, "famous."

26. "shot": Two of the oldest commentators, Cv and Cm, remark that the verb has to be supplied from a previous verse, and although this is rare in Vālmīki, no manuscript convincingly testifies to the contrary.

27–28. "with three . . . the main yoke pole" *tribhis triveṇum*: This component of the chariot appears to consist of a threefold piece of bamboo (hence the name *triveṇu-*); cf. Sparreboom 1985, p. 91.

"with two, the axle" *dvābhyām akṣam*: One manuscript amends, "the two axles."

Sarga 28

1. "his tone of voice was mild" *mṛdupūrvam*: "Because he was trying to be reasonable," Ck (so essentially Cg, Ct). Rāma never raises his voice; see 55.15 below and 2.1.15.

2. This should not be taken as a general remark (so Ck and apparently Ct), like verses 3-5, but one directed specifically at Khara (Cm, Cs, Cr) in reference to his crimes of slaying the seers (see verse 6).

5. "like a lizard that feeds on hailstones" *brāhmaṇī karakād iva*: I agree with the commentators in analyzing *karakād* as an (*upapada*) compound, *karakān atti*. "The red lizard dies from eating hailstones [not poison, as Satya Vrat would have it, 1964, p. 6] as quickly as if it were poison; just as the lizard itself commits an act that kills it, so does Khara" (Cg; Cm, "It is well known that hailstones are poisonous to the red lizard [and that it dies the very moment it eats them, Ct]"). This convention may be well known, but I have not seen it mentioned elsewhere in Sanskrit literature. The sentiment of the simile, however—that one who acts without considering the consequences learns his bitter lesson when it is too late—is voiced frequently in the *Ayodhyākāṇḍa*; compare for example 2.57.5, 60.6.

"its end result" *tasyāntam*: The pronoun refers back to a substantive (e.g., *karmaṇaḥ*) implied by *kurvāṇaḥ*.

8–9. The theme of karmic retribution formulated by Rāma here, as by Daśaratha in 2.57.4–9, is examined in the Introduction to the *Ayodhyākāṇḍa*, Chapter 5.

Cg (on verse 7) remarks on the immediacy of retribution for heinous crimes: "Those who commit minor sins experience the consequences of their deeds in another birth; but the cruel . . . perish quickly [that is, in this very world]" (compare his comment on 2.57.7).

10. "I come as king" *aham āsādito rājā*: Cm, Cg (not Ck as per the crit. ed.) read *rājñā*, "(I was appointed) by the king"; Ck, " 'I was brought,' namely, by the seers"; cf. 29.31 (but of course Rāma is supposed to be unaware of this at present). The entire NR supports the reading of the crit. ed. (see Gorresio ed. 3.35.11 and Lahore ed. 3.34.10). Rāma's calling himself king "suggests he possesses the authority to suppress the wicked" (Ck, Ct). On Rāma's being regarded (and regarding himself) as king throughout the *Araṇyakāṇḍa* (despite such later statements as 4.18.9, 11, 23ff.) see the Introduction, Chapter 4d.

12. "shall hasten after" *anugamiṣyasi*: Circumlocution for "shall die" (so Ct, who rightly refers to verse 13; not, with Cg, "because evil though they may be, men who fall in battle have the chance to gain heaven"; nor, with Cm, "men who are slain by Rāma attain the highest world," a theological position echoed in the *SkandaP*: "The *rākṣasas* who met Rāma in battle and were slain . . . took the path of absorption [into God]," cited in VSP ed., p. 170).

13. "and you, slain by my arrows, in hell" *tvāṃ nihataṃ bāṇaiḥ . . . nirayastham*: Ct, continuing the theological speculations here of the commentators on the previous verse, asks how one slain by God can go to hell. He explains that one who has committed a heinous crime such as brahman murder must necessarily first suffer the consequences of it. After suffering the torments of hell, one may then attain the highest state, but only if the Blessed One wills it.

14. "lowest of your kind" *kulādhama*: Or, with Ck, Ct, "low by reason of your kind, breed."

19. "bring up his family" *kulaṃ vyapadiśan*: Ck and Ct believe Khara is referring to Rāma's words in verse 10. But there Rāma can hardly be said to boast of his lineage (or could Khara mean make a slur against his own, Khara's, lineage, as in verse 14?).

20. "like false gold smelted down in a grass fire" *suvarṇapratirūpeṇa tapteneva kuśāgninā*: The force of the simile would have been more direct had we the genitive ([*laghutvaṃ*] *suvarṇapratirūpasya taptasya*): Rāma's vain boast (since brave men do not boast) shows his worthlessness, as a grass fire shows that imitation gold (Cg, "brass") is worthless. Such is Cm's explanation; however, I do not see that the grass fire is similar to the boast in point of "impropriety" (Ck); Ct elaborates, "Prior to the heating one may believe the vessel to be gold, but that belief vanishes after the heating; similarly the prima facie belief [on Khara's part] in Rāma's heroism is dispelled by his boasting."

21–22. Observe of course Khara's own vaunting.

23. "lest the sun go down" *astaṃ gacched dhi savitā*: "Although night would in fact augment the *rākṣasa*'s strength [cf. Hopkins 1915, p. 39], he would win no glory in killing a human being, who grows powerless at night. Such is Khara's meaning," Cg (so Cr). As Bhatt also notes (1963, p. 405), battles in epic India (as in Homeric Greece) were conventionally suspended during the hours of darkness.

24. "(tears) for the . . . *rākṣasas*" *rākṣasānām* (. . . *aśru-*): I analyze the genitive as objective, according to the *sūtra* cited above, 26.3 note. It is less likely that we are supposed to understand it subjectively (the tears they are weeping now, in their death), despite the later recurrence of the phrase in this sense (6.83.17).

25. "a superbly banded club" *gadāṃ paramāṅgadām*: Presumably Khara's club is wound about with golden straps, like that of Dūṣaṇa (cf. 25.5).

26. The NR adds hereafter a passage explaining that the club was given to Khara by Kubera, and that Rāma realizes he must use a divine weapon against it, the Āgneya arrow (the arrow "of the god of fire") (549*).

Sarga 29

1. "Rāghava, who cherished righteousness" *rāghavo dharmavatsalaḥ*: Although this is usually an ornamental epithet, Cg takes the reference to *dharma* here as signifying

Rāma's appreciation of the wrong that would be committed in slaying an unarmed combatant.

"in a passion (. . . with a smile)" (*smayamānaḥ* . . .) *saṃrabdham*: Troubled perhaps by the apparent contradiction, Cg takes the adverb as an adjective with *kharam* (understood); I agree with Cr (cf. verse 13).

3. "trust in your arrogant vaunting" *abhidhānapragalbhasya tava pratyaya-*: The genitive seems definitely to be objective, though Ck, Ct, Cr take it subjectively: "The club, by its own destruction, has destroyed your confidence (in it), namely, that you would slay your enemy with it."

5. "as Garutmant": For Garuḍa's theft of the *soma*, see below, 33.33ff. (and *MBh* 1.24ff.), and compare 2.22.14 note. I find the simile in this context to be odd; it is unlikely that the poet merely wishes to emphasize the decisiveness of the act. At all events, there is an interesting contrariety in using the figure, which expresses the attaining of immortality, in a context where death is threatened.

9. "your dwelling place your resting place" *janasthāne hatasthāne*: Literally, "people's place" and "place of the dead."

12. Ct observes, "Although it is inappropriate for the Blessed One to address [even] low creatures in this manner, he does so in order to produce the necessary excess of the anger-inducing *guṇa tamaḥ*, which will provide for the *tāmasa* destiny [of Khara]. This is required to make good his threat that Khara will go to hell" (cf. 28.13).

15. "all six senses" *-ṣaḍindriyāḥ*: The standard five, along with the mind as the seat of concept formation.

Ct interprets this verse as Khara's reflection on himself: "At the moment of death the form of the Blessed One has appeared to him; and by implication he begs forgiveness for his own bad conduct."

16–17. I interpret in accordance with the NR, which quite reasonably transposes the clauses "glanced around" and "spotted a huge *sāla*."

20. "fury" *roṣāt*: Cm, Cg, Ck, Ct connect the adverb with *pāda* a ("He broke out in sweat 'because of his fury,' not because of fatigue"). In accordance with his theological position Ct notes, "Here, too, anger is only assumed by the Blessed One, as an actor might do; it is not real, but only meant to sustain belief in his humanness."

21. "Mount Prasravaṇa": This mountain is located in Janasthāna (cf. 59.20, 60.10 below, *UttaRāC* 1.25.3).

22. "drunk on the smell of his own blood" *matto rudhiragandhena*: Fastidiously Cm and Cg take the instrumental as *upalakṣaṇe* ("drunk [and, sc., pervaded] with the smell of blood"); I agree with Cr.

23. "sidestepped" *apāsarpat pratipadaṃ kiṃcit*: So essentially Cm. Cv explains, "He went the opposite way, avoiding Khara as he fell upon him; he moved behind Khara by the way the demon had taken" (Cg, incorrectly I believe, takes *pratipadam* as adjective to Khara, explaining, "Rāma moves away to get the necessary room to shoot his arrows," that is, Rāma is not retreating [so Cm, Ck, Ct, Ctś]). Rāma's apparent retreat here is made a subject for a taunt in *UttaRāC* 5.34c.

24. "a fiery arrow" *pāvakasaṃkāśaṃ* . . . *śaram*: Pant (1978, p. 180) has collected evidence suggesting that the practice was known in ancient India of using arrows with flammable materials in the tip. From the *Rājataraṅgiṇī* the author cites what may be "the actual instance of the use of 'burning arrows smeared over with vege-

table oil, struck by which the enemies caught fire.'" Perhaps, however, the "burning" in the present passage is the sensation of poison (see 32.6 below).

The word order of the verse is quite dislocated (schematically a C A c B a), signaling I think the climactic moment (see 2.24.16, 2.96.4 and notes).

25. "given by the . . . king of gods" *dattaṃ . . . surarājena*: See 11.30 above.

27. "the way Andhaka once": See above, 24.26 and note. Ct here remarks, "The killing of Andhaka the *asura* is well known from the *purāṇas*. A widespread variant here is *antakaḥ* ["Death"]. It is known from the *Māhātmya* [of Śiva] that the god destroyed Death in the White Forest ["on the banks of the river Kāverī," according to Cm], in order to prolong the life of Mārkaṇḍeya. In *sarga* 36 of the *Uttarakāṇḍa* of the *Kūrmapurāṇa*, we are told of a royal seer named Śveta, a great devotee of Śiva's, who practiced asceticism on Mount Kālañjara. When Death came to kill him, Śiva destroyed Death with a blow from his left foot" (see *sarga* 35 of the crit. ed. of the *KūrmaP*; at the end of that narrative, Brahmā reminds Śiva that Death had done nothing wrong in coming to take away King Śveta—it was his appointed hour—and the god consequently consents to his revivification).

28. The three supreme deeds of Indra: for the killing of the demon Vṛtra by means of the thunderbolt, see *ṚV* 1.52; for the killing of Namuci with the foam of the sea, see 27.3 note and Introduction, Chapter 4c; for the killing of the demon Bala (or Vala) by the same bolt, see *ṚV* 10.67 and elsewhere. Cg here observes, "The first simile is employed to indicate that the killing was done by an unfailing weapon; the second, that it was done effortlessly; the third, that [the victim] was endowed with great capability"; Ck (Ct), "By means of the four similes concerning the destruction of Andhaka and the others [which could be achieved by no one other than] Rudra and Indra, the poet reveals the indestructability of the *rākṣasa* Khara in any way and by anyone other than Rāma or Brahmā." Note that Rāma's glorious deed of slaying Khara is used as a simile already in the battle books of the *MBh* (e.g., 7.82.28, "Having killed [Durmukha], Sahadeva was as brilliant as Rāma, son of Daśaratha, after he killed mighty Khara").

29. "supreme seers" *paramarṣayaḥ*: Brahman seers, according to Cg.

30. See *sarga* 4 above, especially verses 18-19 note. The *HariVaṃ* (31.118) appears to support the argument made here: "While dwelling in Janasthāna he (Rāma) did what was required by the thirty gods."

31. "The great seers contrived a means" *upāyena maharṣibhiḥ*: Śarabhaṅga (presumably under orders from Indra) instructed Rāma to go to Sutīkṣṇa (4.30); Sutīkṣṇa sent him to Agastya (10.34); Agastya gave Rāma the divine weapons and instructed him to go to Pañcavaṭī (12.13ff.) (cf. also Venkatanathacharya 1965, p. 214 note).

35. Cg provides a detailed allegorical interpretation of the *sarga* based on Teṅgalai soteriology: "Sītā's going into the cave without Rāma, and then coming out and embracing him after he had destroyed all the enemies, suggests the individual soul's going into the cavity of the heart, and being totally dependent; thereupon, under the guidance of a teacher, it 'sees' the supreme Lord, after He [or, the teacher?] has removed all the obstacles. The soul then 'comes out' and meets with the Lord, around whom the assemblies of the wise ever sit, and experiences the stream of His delights" (cf. Cg's comment on 2.47.22).

After *sarga* 29, the SR inserts (and without doubt it is an interpolation, and a clumsy one) an entire *sarga* (App. I, No. 10):

Akampana (a spy of Rāvaṇa's, according to Cg), returns to Laṅkā and reports on the slaughter of the *rākṣasas* in Janasthāna. When Rāvaṇa in a rage asks who is responsible, Akampana replies that it was Rāma. Rāvaṇa supposes that Rāma is in league with Indra and the other gods, on which Akampana corrects him. Rāvaṇa asserts that he will go to Janasthāna and slay Rāma and his brother. Akampana then expounds on Rāma's prowess, praising him with attributes suggesting Viṣṇu, and telling Rāvaṇa he will be unable to conquer him. Akampana then goes on to suggest a plan: He urges Rāvaṇa to abduct Sītā—he describes her in detail—explaining that, left without his wife, Rāma will die. Rāvaṇa assents, and the next [day?] departs on his flying chariot to visit the demon Mārīca. When Rāvaṇa demands his aid in abducting Sītā, Mārīca tries to dissuade him. He succeeds, and Rāvaṇa returns to Laṅkā.

The plot of the interpolation is impossible in view of what follows, and is aesthetically mediocre.

Cg here takes the opportunity to set forth in abundant detail the allegorical construction of the *Rāmāyaṇa* as a whole, as a complex exposition of the *śaraṇāgatimantra* (or "sacred formula on taking refuge [with the Blessed One]").

Sarga 30

4. "splendid palace" *vimānāgre*: See 2.24.7 note. Cm, Cg take *vimāna-* in the sense of the Puṣpakavimāna, Rāvaṇa's aerial chariot. This is probably correct. For although Puṣpaka is generally represented as a conveyance, Rāvaṇa's palace is called Puṣpa in 5.6.11 (which Cg there and on 5.7.1 equates with Puṣpaka), and in 5.7.9–15 it is clearly identified as a structure within which there is a kind of inner chamber (see Cv and Cg there, though contrast Ck on 5.7.18).

5. "a golden altar" *rukmavedi-*: The image is not sheer fantasy. Sacrificial altars made of golden bricks are mentioned by Āpastamba, according to the citation of Cg, Ck (see *ĀpaŚS* 19.11.1).

6. "invincible in combat with gods, *gandharvas*, spirits . . ." *devagandharvabhūtānām . . . ajeyam*: A reference to the boon bestowed on Rāvaṇa, clarified to some degree in verses 17-18 below. See also the Introduction, Chapter 4b.

7. "wounds" *-vraṇam*: Rāvaṇa's being only "wounded" by the thunderbolt shows he is not subject to death (at the hands of the gods), as Cg, Ck, Ct observe.

"gored" *utkṛṣṭa-*: In agreement with Ct, Cr.

8. "marks of royalty" *rājalakṣaṇa-*: This probably refers simply to his royal bearing, less likely to specific markings on the soles of the feet of universal monarchs (see note on 2.92.6).

9. "sparkled with . . . beryl" *-vaidūryasaṃkāśam*: *vaidūrya-* almost certainly signifies "beryl" ("cat's-eye" or "golden" beryl); see Mayrhofer 1956–1980, vol. 3, pp. 267–68 (interestingly, Śrī Laṅkā has traditionally been a major source for this semi-precious stone). This rules out Ct's gloss, "looked like," for Rāvaṇa is deep blue-black (see 50.18, 21 below).

11. "He could . . . perturb" *kṣobhaṇaṃ . . . -kāriṇam*: I understand the *pāda* as forming a single phrase, with the noun exceptionally dependent on the verbal adjective. Cg, Ck, Ct (so Cr) take *kṣobhaṇam* as an agential noun (*kartari lyuṭ, Pā* 3.3.113), "a perturber (. . . acting effortlessly)," which I find less meaningful.

13. "Vāsuki and Takṣaka": Two principal *nāgas* or mythological serpents, dwelling in the subterranean city Bhogavatī. The only other reference to this incident that I have discovered in the *Rām* (or elsewhere in the *Rām* tradition, for that matter) is 6.7.8.

14. "had gone to Mount Kailāsa" *kailāsaṃ parvataṃ gatvā*: Both the poem and the associated traditions are confused about the encounter between Rāvaṇa and his brother Kubera (Vaiśravaṇa). Whereas according to 6.7.3ff. (so in 7.14–15), Kubera is clearly defeated while on Mount Kailāsa, according to 46.5 below, it seems, Kubera is defeated in Laṅkā and driven off to the mountain (thus in the *Rāmopākhyāna, MBh* 3.259.32–33, Rāvaṇa defeats Kubera and ousts him from Laṅkā, though in this version Kubera takes up residence on Mount Gandhamādana).

"the man-borne Kubera" *naravāhanam*: This comes to be the normal ornamental epithet of the god. Although it is applied, in some epic texts, prior to Kubera's loss of his aerial chariot (see for example *MBh* 3.259.3; the author of 3.221.5 curiously finds no contradiction in having Naravāhana ride the Puṣpaka), here and in 46.5, which may be the first occurrences of the term in Sanskrit literature, it seems to have a more immediate narrative relevance (that is, "he who had nothing but men to convey him," after Rāvaṇa expropriated the chariot), as the epexegetical verse 46.6 demonstrates.

15. "would destroy" *vināśayati*: Most of the NR reads the past tense here. The incident is recounted in 7.13.8ff.

16. "powers" *paraṃtapau*: A strange epithet to apply to the sun and the moon, too strange for us to accept the easy solution offered by the NR (and G2, M2), which reads the singular (modifying Rāvaṇa). Note that in 62.10 the sun and moon are called *mahābalau*, "powerful."

17. "in the great forest" *mahāvane*: Identified only as the "ashram of Gokarṇa" (7.9.37, so also in an NR insertion below, 591*.1); according to the *Rāmopākhyāna* a Śaivite pilgrimage site and the residence of Mārīca (cf. *MBh* 3.261.54–55). Rāvaṇa's austerities are described in *Uttarakāṇḍa* 10.

18. The logical relationship of the boon (granted by Brahmā) mentioned in this verse and the austerities in the former is left implicit, perhaps as self-evident. In 7.10.17, the list of adversaries in battle with whom Rāvaṇa would be invulnerable is given as: Suparṇa, *nāgas, yakṣas* [so read in the present verse, for *gandharvas*, by the NR], *daityas, dānavas, rākṣasas*. "As for all other creatures," he says, "men and the like, I do not care a straw" (7.10.18, see further, Introduction, Chapter 4b); "Rāvaṇa neglected to include men, for he considered them only as food," Cs. The NR adds that Brahmā granted him the ability to go anywhere in a moment, and to take on any form at will [though most *rākṣasas* possess this power by nature], and "teeth white as the moon and bright as the sun" (591*).

19. "at the seats of the oblation" *havirdhāneṣu*: That is, in the sacred enclosures where the rites were performed ("the enclosures where the *soma* is pressed," Cm, Cg, Ck, Ct; Cg [so Ck, or possibly this is misprinted in Venkatanathacharya 1965, p. 230] appears to have *abhiṣutam*, "pressed," for *abhiṣṭutam*, "consecrated").

20. "sacrifices at their climax" *āptayajña-*: According to the commentators, when the rites reached the point at which the sacrificial stipends are given to the priests (Crā, Cg, Ck, Ct).

"Rāvaṇa, 'he who makes all creatures wail'" *rāvaṇaṃ sarvabhūtānām*: The standard (folk) etymology of the name (so Ct, Cs); a fuller explanation along the same lines is given in the *Uttarakāṇḍa*, though the account there is somewhat confused: When Rāvaṇa lifts up Mount Kailāsa, Śiva presses down on the mountain with his foot, causing the *rākṣasa* to wail; the god then bestows upon him the name Rāvaṇa, though he explains that it is because "the three worlds were made to wail, overcome with terror" [presumably by Rāvaṇa's own roar] (7.16.21–27). According to the literature examined by Mayrhofer (1956–1980, vol. 3, pp. 55–56), the word originally was "perhaps a pre-Aryan bird name."

21. "Paulastyas": Descendants of Pulastya, a son of Brahmā, the father of Viśravas, the grandfather of Rāvaṇa, and eponymous ancestor of all *rākṣasas* and *yakṣas*.

22. "lived free from fear . . . dreadful story" *sudāruṇaṃ vākyam abhītacāriṇī*: Thus the commentators seem generally to understand; Cg calls the verse a recapitulation of what has already been told. But it is possible the line refers ahead, "She fearlessly spoke the harsh words," that is, her criticism of Rāvaṇa in the next *sarga* (thus Ck).

Sarga 31

3. "cremation fire" *śmaśānāgnim*: The simile is curious, but none of the commentators remarks on it, which suggests they felt it had only a general application. Or are we to understand that such a king destroys his subjects' lives through, for example, excessive taxation?

5. "grants no audience, or makes no use of spies" *ayuktacāraṃ durdarśam*: So essentially the majority of the commentators. With regard to the second compound, however (used in a quite different sense in 2.35.19), Cr may well be right: "(Because he makes no use of spies his 'vision is bad,' that is) he is unable to see what is taking place far away" (and therefore is "not his own master"?). The need for a king to employ spies will be mentioned frequently in the book (see below, verses 7ff., 21; 35.3), and forms an almost obsessive theme in the *rājadharma* section of the *MBh* (for example, 12.69.6ff.).

Cg attempts to construe the qualifications with the simile as well: the mud at the riverside is *ayuktacāra-*, "through which it is unwise to move," and *asvādhīna-*, "not dependent on [not obedient to the will of] the creature moving through it."

7. "staunchly" *ātmavadbhiḥ*: In accordance with Cg's gloss, " 'striving,' that is, with all their attention given to counteracting Rāvaṇa."

19. "well informed" *sarvajñaḥ*: See 2.60.13 note; Cm, Ck, Ct explain, "knowing what is occurring in his own and in his enemies' realms."

"knowing what must be done" *kṛtajñaḥ*: Not "grateful"; see notes on 14.27 above and 2.1.20.

"acting in keeping with righteousness" *dharmaśīlaḥ*: There is obviously little dramatic propriety in putting such sentiments in the mouth of Śūrpaṇakhā. Here, as often, verisimilitude is sacrificed to the didactic and homiletic demands of the genre.

22. "who misjudges his enemy" *parāvamantā*: So Cg, Ck, Cr; Ct suggests, " 'who only scorns his enemy,' that is, but gives no thought to destroying them." Or, "who shows no respect for his enemy."

"addicted" *saṃgataḥ*: The reading of the crit. ed. seems to be unattested elsewhere in the sense required; an attractive variant is *saṃgavān* of NE and S manuscripts.

Sarga 32

1. "from where he sat among his ministers" *amātyamadhye*: Perhaps to enhance the sense of Rāvaṇa's reckless autocracy, the *Rāmopākhyāna* has Rāvaṇa dismiss all his advisers and question Śūrpaṇakhā in private (*MBh* 3.261.47).

3. "Triśiras": A slight inconsistency: Rāvaṇa has not yet been told that Triśiras is dead (cf. 31.11).

7. She never saw these actions of Rāma's because they were executed with extreme speed (Cg).

12. "of equal prowess and virtue" *guṇataḥ tulyavikramaḥ*: Literally, "of equal prowess [and equal] with respect to virtues," an awkward construction that part of the NR sought to simplify (reading *guṇavān*).

13. "a veritable second self" *prāṇo bahiścaraḥ*: Literally, "life breath external (to him)."

18. "I all but brought her back" *ānetum udyatāham*: The SR tries to clarify this by adding, "but I was disfigured by that cruel Lakṣmaṇa" (613*). "Śūrpaṇakhā lies here," says Ck (Ct), "in order to ingratiate herself with Rāvaṇa" (and from embarrassment, according to Cr [lest she have to admit her unseemly behavior]). The NR offers a substitute verse in place of the SR reading accepted by the crit. ed.:

> Her hips are broad, the corners of her eyes are rosy as a lotus. Even my heart, as I looked at her, was violently disturbed. (612*)

(See 2.3.12 note for a comparable verse.)

23. Apparently Rāvaṇa is supposed to approve of the advice she gives in verse 20, and to do what she says in verse 21. But the lines are elliptical, and the SR attempts to clarify by adding hereafter 618* (which I translate in the version of Cg, in part supported by NW manuscripts; see the variants on verse 23d): "Recognizing their impotence, steal away the woman by force to be your wife."

24. "act" *kṛtyaṃ pratipattum*: Literally, "resolve, decide on action," so Cr; compare the sense of *pratipatti-* in 2.19.14 and 20.10.

Sarga 33

1. "turned his thoughts" *buddhyā jagāma*: Thus I read, with several S and NE manuscripts, for the crit. ed.'s (and commentators') *buddhvā*. Rāvaṇa does not go anywhere physically until verse 3; the commentators are forced to understand either " 'went,' namely, to the inner chamber" (Cm), or "to Mārīca's ashram" (Ck, Ct, Cr).

4. "went secretly" *gatvā pracchannam*: Cg speculates on the possible significance of the phrase: "He goes thus lest, if he should proceed openly, Mandodarī and others [kindly *rākṣasas*] might prevent him [so Cm, Ct]; or because it was a shameful thing to renounce manliness [an open fight with Rāma] and resort to the ways of a thief [cf. the charge of Jaṭāyus, 49.24]; or again, in the sense that he decided on this course of action by himself, after dismissing his companions (see verse 1), who thus had no opportunity for considering the plan; compare the view expressed later by Kumbhakarṇa and others, that it is difficult to remedy something undertaken without consultation with one's ministers" (cf. 6. App. I, No. 3.196ff.; GPP 6.12.27ff.).

5ff. This chariot cannot be the Puṣpakavimāna, the aerial chariot expropriated from Kubera (see above, 30.14, 46.6), for this one will be left broken in Janasthāna (49.14, 60.32), and the Puṣpaka will be found still in Laṅkā (53.29–30; in 6.109.9ff., Rāma and Sītā ride back to Ayodhyā upon it). Yet the later *Rāmāyaṇa* tradition occasionally made the erroneous identification (cf. GPP 6.126.29 [crit. ed. Book Six 3518*], *NaraP* 49.56ff., and Raghavan 1973, p. 61). See also 46.6 note.

9. This verse is suspect, for it separates verses 8 and 10, thereby undermining the force of the simile: the dark cloud in the sky with its lightning and white cranes corresponding to Rāvaṇa on his chariot, with golden jewelry and yellowish cat's-eye beryl, and the white paraphernalia of royalty (thus too Cm, Cg, Ck, except that they coordinate the cranes with the ornamented chariot, which strikes me as wrong, an impression Ct, Cr confirm). If the present verse is an interpolation (virtually the entire NE version omits it), it may be a consequence of the same kind of numerological interest that motivated the insertion noted on 45.27 below.

15. "*ājas*": "Sons of the Unborn, that is, Brahmā," Cm, Ct, Cr, Cs; "sons of Brahmā not born from a womb," Ck; "not born from human wombs," Cg (reading *ajaiḥ*).

"*vaikhānasas*": See 5.2–5 note.

"*māṣas*": "Born in the Māṣa lineage," Cg; "a proper name," Cm, Ct, Cr, Cs (cf. verse 30 note below).

"*vālakhilyas*, and *marīcipas*": See 5.2–5 note.

16. "sports of lovemaking" *krīḍārati-*: By *paranipāta* for *ratikrīḍā-*.

18. "cormorants" *plava-*: For the identification, see Dave 1985, p. 299.

"carpets of cat's-eye beryl" *vaidūryaprastaram*: Uncertain; the concrete use of *prastara-* in verse 24 below favors the explanation of Cm, Cg ("on which there were rocks of beryl").

19–20. "They belonged to those who had conquered higher worlds" *jitalokānām*: As in 2.58.40–42.

21–25ab. "(sandalwood . . .) roots juicy with resin" *niryāsarasamūlānāṃ* (*candanānām*): I take the compound thus adjectivally, with Ct, Cr, though normally it is the wood, not the roots, of the sandalwood tree from which the precious oils are extracted. The alternatives are not appealing: Cg (understanding the compound as a *tatpuruṣa*) remarks, "From the roots of the plants called *mūla* [e.g., long-pepper plants?] comes the exudation of asafoetida"; Ck, "trees, the *guggada* and the like, which are a source of fragrant gum resins."

"carpets . . . mounds" *prastaram . . . -nicayam*: I understand these items as *jātyekavacanam*.

"coral" *pravāla-*: See note on 2.13.25.

26cd–27ab. Cg observes here, "This long description of the coastline is meant to suggest that, after taking the trouble to come so far, Rāvaṇa is all the more determined not to be dissuaded in his exhortation of Mārīca."

27cd–28ab. "there" *tatra*: The *MBh* (1.25.27) locates the tree at a place called Alambatīrtha, otherwise unknown.

28cd–ef.ff. The legend of Garuḍa is more fully recounted in *MBh* 1.24ff. Again Cg speculates on its narrative function: "The poet here is mocking Rāvaṇa, showing how foolish he is to oppose Rāma [that is, Viṣṇu], when even His mount [Garuḍa] has such illimitable power." This passage (like that recounting the appearance of Garuḍa in 6.40.33ff.) has full manuscript support, and if we are unwilling to accept the traditional explanation it becomes hard indeed to account for this seemingly gratuitous digression.

29. "leafy . . . Suparṇa" *suparṇaḥ . . . parṇabahulām*: For the rhetorical figure see 19.23 note.

30. "*māṣas*": "Born in the lineage Pūtimāṣa; or, being the size of a bean [*māṣa*]," Cm.

"*ajas*": The spelling (contrast above, verse 15) has preponderant manuscript support.

"*dhūmras*": Drinkers of smoke, according to Cm, Cg.

The NR adds that, worn out from their ascetic practices the seers, many thousands of them, were hanging from the branch (634*).

31–32. "caught . . . in a single claw" *ādāya . . . ekapādena*: I believe Cm, Cg, Cr are correct to construe these items together (the alternative, *ekapādena . . . bhakṣayitvā*, makes little sense).

"used the branch to lay waste" *hatvā śākhayā*: Ck, Ct, Cr imply that Garuḍa slays the Niṣādas merely by dropping the branch upon them (in *MBh* 1.26.17ff., the bird lets the branch fall on an uninhabited mountain in the north). According to Cg, Garuḍa eats the Niṣādas, and this is the case in the *MBh* version as well (cf. 1.25.9, though here he eats them prior to eating the elephants and the tortoise).

"He had freed the great sages" *mokṣayitvā mahāmunīn*: How the sages were oppressed by the Niṣādas (as the verse implies, so Cg; Cm, Ck, Ct, " 'he freed them,' that is, from confinement") we do not know. Venkatanathacarya (1965, p. 246 note) suggests that the bird "frees" the sages merely from the branch, that is, saved them from death by falling (grammatically sound and in harmony with the *MBh* version, 1.26.14).

34. "the iron latticework" *ayojālāni*: The treasure house is constructed so as to prevent anyone from entering into the area containing the *soma*. In the *MBh* the stronghold is described as follows: "In front of the drink of immortality Garuḍa saw a wheel made of iron. It had keen blades and a sharp rim, and incessantly it twirled . . . a lethal edge to dismember any who sought to steal the drink" (1.29.2).

Hereafter D3 adds, "He liberated his mother from slavery . . ." (640*; cf. *MBh* 1.30.16).

35. "Subhadra": On the naming of sacred trees, which function as shrines, compare 2.49.4 and note, 62.12; in the *MBh* the tree appears to be called Rohiṇapādapa (1.25.31; 337*).

37. "who wore black hides" *kṛṣṇājinadharam*: "This describes the marks betokening worldly indifference on the part of Mārīca, because he is now a devotee of Rāma's," Cg. In the *MBh* (3.261.55) Mārīca is called a "former adviser" of Rāvaṇa's, one who had become an ascetic in fear of Rāma.

Sarga 34

2–3. "who was tried and tested" *labdhalakṣāḥ*: Literally, "who had won the prize" or "hit the mark" (see Nīlakaṇṭha on *MBh* 4.61.46 vulg., "who does not swerve from the target"; Medhātithi on *ManuSm* 7.54, "successful in what they undertake"; Nīlakaṇṭha on *MBh* 8.10.5 vulg., "gaining victory". Differently Cm, Ct, Cr, " 'who had found an opportunity,' that is, who were filled with zeal for battle."

7. "without one harsh word" *anuktvā paruṣaṃ kiṃcit*: See above, 28.1 note.

11. These are, in large measure, the terms by which the poet has described Rāvaṇa himself (30.20). Perhaps thinking that Mārīca is now a "follower of righteousness," Rāvaṇa hopes to enlist his aid by representing his attack on Rāma as just retribution against a criminal.

12. "in an act of brute force" *sattvam āśritya kevalam*: Uncertain; the Mylapore editors felt the wording unable to bear this sense, the one apparently required, and proposed emendation (*'sattvam*, "ignominious conduct"). Implausibly the medieval commentators, " 'trusting merely in his strength,' that is, and not in righteousness," Cg, Ck, Ct.

13. The NR adds herein, "(Sītā . . .) who is like Śrī without her lotus" (654*).

14. "and my brothers" *bhrātṛbhiś ca*: "The surviving ones, that is, Kumbhakarṇa and the others," Cg, Ck, Ct.

22. "in great battles" *mahāhave*: I take this reading (it is the NR's, cf. 663*) to be more probable than that accepted by the crit. ed., *mahāvane*. The corruption is a common one (see note on 2.90.25).

Sarga 35

1. "the wise (Mārīca)" *mahāprājño* (*mārīcaḥ*): The NR reads instead, "wild-eyed and numb [with fear]" (664*).

2. The sentiment is repeated in 6.10.16 and explicitly taken up for comment by Kauṭilya in *ArthŚā* 5.4.12.

4. "I fear" *api*: Cg explains, "*api* has the sense of supposition, and would be accompanied by a change in tone of voice." This could instead be an optative of wish, "Oh that"; see 2.82.26 note (and cf. 2.66.5 and 43.31 below).

5. "born to take your life" *te jīvitāntāya notpannā*: No doubt passages like this (cf. also 6.82.29–36 and others that testify to the divine plan undergirding the narrative, discussed in the Introduction, Chapter 4c) encouraged the development of the story of Vedavatī recounted in *Uttarakāṇḍa* 17 (especially verses 22ff., and cf. 47.15–16 below and note). In some Jain and other *Rāmāyaṇas* we find the same motif of the predestined destruction of Rāvaṇa by Sītā, who is often represented as his daughter.

12. "groundless" *na śrutam*: The strong variant *duḥśrutam*, attested widely in the NR and SR, points to a comparable interpretation, "lies, infamous lies." Ct reads *naivam* in *pāda* d, understanding *pāda* c as, "(Rāma) has never even heard about lying [let alone speaks lies]. (You ought not to speak) thus" (not dissimilarly Cr). Possibly we should read *naśrutam*, though such compounds are rare in the poem. (Contrary to the report of the crit. ed., Ck reads *na śrutam*.)

14. "His might it is" *svena tejasā*: My interpretation finds some support in Ck, Ct. Cm, Cg, however, construe the possessive adjective as reflexive to *vaidehīm*, " '(guarded) by her own might,' that is, by the power conferred by her marital fidelity." Despite the suggestive parallel in 6.106.15, this explanation makes little sense here. The verse is located in a series of *ślokas* praising the might of Rāma, with Mārīca everywhere suggesting—to his own doom, as it turns out—that Rāvaṇa cannot steal Sītā with Rāma *present*; his own might protects her (not someone else's,

that of an army, for example). And indeed, as events show, Vaidehī's "might" proves ineffectual in stopping the demon.

15. "whose bow and sword are kindling" *cāpakhaḍgendhanam*: To secure a somewhat higher degree of intelligibility for the figure Cm offers the interpretation, " '[to whom] those holding bows and swords' [by *Pā* 5.2.127], that is, his enemies, ['are kindling']," his enemies being the objects that are burned; so Ct, though he analyzes, "those struck by his bow and arrows" (Cr, " 'the bows,' namely, of his enemies").

16–17. "fiery (tongues)" *-arciṣam*: Attractive variants are "fangs" in NW manuscripts; "tongues" in S and NE (680*) manuscripts.

18. "Janaka's daughter belongs to one of immeasurable might" *aprameyaṃ hi tattejaḥ yasya sā janakātmajā*: In conformity with his theology, Cg rearranges the emphasis here ("His might cannot be measured, to whom Janaka's daughter belongs"), commenting, "This expresses the superiority Rāma derives from his relationship with Sītā; compare the statement, 'God possesses divinity by reason of Śraddhā' [Faith personified as a female entity]" (the quotation is from *TaiBr* 3.12.3.1).

20. "hard-won kingship" *rājyaṃ caiva sudurlabham*: Comparing the use of *durlabhām* in 29.7 above, I understand the adjective as a simple qualification, rather than as a predicate with the whole line ("your life and all your happiness and your kingship will [then] be hard to get," so Cm, Ck).

The story of Rāvaṇa's usurpation of the kingship from his elder brother Kubera (see 30.14 above and note, 46.4–5 below) is narrated in detail in *Uttarakāṇḍa* 11.

21. The NR hereafter adds that Rāvaṇa should also consult "Trijaṭā, a great ascetic, a perfected being, free from all faults" (692*), the one female *rākṣasa* who will comfort Sītā during her captivity (*Sundarakāṇḍa* 25).

22. "what is best" *kṣamam*: Here as elsewhere (cf. 38.1) the word can be hard to translate, since it connotes both practicability and rectitude (so basically Cg).

Sarga 36

2. "Daṇḍaka wilderness" *daṇḍakāraṇyam*: In the *Bālakāṇḍa* (28–29) the site of Rāma's first encounter with Mārīca is not identified as the Daṇḍaka forest.

After this verse some N manuscripts add a passage recounting how Mārīca attacked the sages of Viśvāmitra's ashram, who refrained from avenging themselves on him lest they thereby diminish their store of ascetic power (697*; cf. above 9.13ff.).

4. "at the time of the lunar sacrifice" *parvakāle*: See note on 2.102.19; Ck, Ct, "at the time of sacrifice"; Cg, "at the time of the sacrificial extraction of the *soma*."

6. "a mere twelve years old" *bālo dvādaśavarṣo 'yam*: So I read with the SR (endorsed by Ñ1), for the crit. ed.'s "still short of sixteen." See the arguments adduced in the note on 2.17.26. The early commentators were sensitive to the (apparent) contradiction with 1.19.2, Cv asserting (erroneously), "Mārīca diminishes Rāma's age in order to frighten Rāvaṇa; in actual fact he was at that time just under sixteen" (so Crā, repeated by Cg).

11. "clad only in a loincloth" *ekavastradharaḥ*: "Rāma wore only the one garment because he was observing the vow of *brahmacarya* [religious studentship and thus celibacy]," Cm, Cg, Ct.

12. "like the newly risen crescent moon" *bālacandra ivoditaḥ*: Alternatively read *'bāla-* ("full moon"; cf. 2.54.10 note).

Although the simile refers merely to Rāma's youth and has no direct narrative function, Cg tries to find one: "By the simile of the rising moon we are to understand Rāma's being prepared to counteract hostile adversaries" (because the light of the moon hinders thieves; Ctś and the *ṭīkā* on Cm suggest that although ablaze with might, Rāma had a kindly aspect, like the newly risen moon). Cg further remarks, "Rāma's physical beauty is described by Mārīca because, enemy though he was, he found him very handsome."

13. "Powerful in my possession of a boon" *balī dattavaraḥ*: What boon Mārīca possessed is unknown; Ck (like Ct) is merely guessing when he says, "a boon given by Brahmā that he could be slain neither by gods nor by *asuras*."

16. "(the ocean,) a hundred leagues away" *(samudre) śatayojane*: Less likely, with Ct, " '(into the ocean) to a distance of a hundred leagues,' that is, from the shore."

20. "whose care it is to master the sports of lovemaking" *krīḍāratividhijñānām*: See 33.16 for the *paranipāta*. The libidinal appetites of the *rākṣasas* are frequently stressed in the poem—and figure significantly in this particular book. See the Introduction, Chapter 6.

22. "perish . . . like fish in a pool of snakes" *vinaśyanti matsyā nāgahrade yathā*: "The fish who live with the snakes perish when someone [Cm, "Garuḍa"; Ck, "a fisherman sent in by a king who wishes to bathe there"] takes steps to destroy the latter," Cg.

24. "if their wives have not been carried off" *hṛtadārān*: The commentators oddly gloss, "those who have abandoned their wives" (Cm, Cg, Ck, Ct).

Sarga 37

1. "next" *yad uttaram*: Unacceptably the commentators, "[. . . what happened, a thing] 'beyond,' that is, beyond this world, achievable by no one but him," Cg, Ck, Ct, Cr.

3. "human flesh" *māṃsa-*: Literally, simply "flesh." The NR (supported by several S manuscripts) makes the reference clear, "feeding on the flesh of seers." See verse 6.

7–8. "the life of an ascetic" *tāpasaṃ dharmam*: I take the first word as an adjective, with Ct.

"an ascetic, given to rigorous fasting" *tāpasaṃ niyatāhāram*: *pādas* cd of verse 8 construe with *rāmam* in verse 7.

9. "felt contempt for" *paribhūya*: Thus also in 41.39, 42 (so Cr). As Cg rightly notes, Mārīca assumes that, like all ascetics, Rāma would be devoted to non-violence (as are those mentioned in 1.20 above).

12. "strong-jointed" *saṃnataparvanaḥ*: *Metri causa* for *saṃnataparvāṇaḥ*; a similar case is 60.33 below; see note there.

13. "escaped" *muktaḥ*: "Only because Rāma's arrows do not pursue those who turn and flee," Cg, Cr.

15. "But now" *hi*: See note on 8.28 above for the adversative force in this particle.

Cg observes that when engrossed in thoughts of Rāma, whether out of love or fear, one can come visibly to behold Him (*sākṣātkāra-*). He cites two verses: "You depart not from the heart; in every direction are You seen" [cf. *MahāN* 3.26]; "When Rāma ruled the kingdom, the whole world became just Rāma" [cf. *MBh* 2. App., I 21.574, part of a *gāthā* sung by "those who know the ancient legends," cf. 568-81]. Fear being a comparatively more intense emotion, says Cg, the frightened man's vision of Rāma will accordingly be more intense.

18. "an R" *rakāra-*: Very rarely is this word used to refer to the phoneme /r/. The normal word, from the time of the early grammarians at least, has been *repha* (cf. *Pā* 3.3.108 *vart.* 4).

"roads": The crit. ed. actually reads *rathāḥ*, "chariots," for which no appropriate English equivalent could be found. But why indeed "chariots" when evidently what is wanted is a word, like "riches," connoting pleasure. This is provided by the NE and NW versions, which both support some variant signifying "women" (*ramaṇyaḥ* and *rāmāḥ*, respectively). An air of authenticity, however, caused by its very banality, lingers with the SR reading, which makes one hesitate to alter the text.

20. "my kinsman's good" *bandhuhita-*: Or, "my kinsmen's good."

Sarga 38

1. "ripe to die" *martukāmaḥ*: This compound, like the desiderative form of the verb *mṛ* (cf. 51.16 and note), can signify immediate futurity as well as desire (exactly which depends on the context). When a man is on the point of death, at least according to the convention of Sanskrit literature, his mind fails him and he cannot tell what will or will not benefit him (cf. 39.20 below, and 2.98.51 and note).

4–5. "(dissuade me from) doing battle" (*-vākyaṃ . . . mām . . . bhettuṃ . . .*) *saṃyuge*: Literally, "with respect to battle," though the locative is somewhat awkward, and later Rāvaṇa will say that by this plan he will avoid battle with Rāma altogether (verse 19). Cg accordingly interprets: to dissuade him from abducting Sītā (and instead persuading him) to battle with Rāma. "Rāvaṇa considers Rāma unworthy to fight for three reasons: because he is 'wicked,' a 'fool,' and a 'man'; the only proper recompense for his outrages is the abduction of his wife." Cg presumably has 37.19 in mind here, though that verse hardly suggests that Mārīca is persuading Rāvaṇa to fight rather than kidnap Sītā. (Ct, "Rāma is said to be 'wicked' because he slew a woman, Tāṭakā," see *Bālakāṇḍa* 25).

I agree with Ct (so Cg) in assessing verse 5 as corroboration of Rāma's foolishness (and consequently I de-emphasize its correlation with verse 6, against Cr).

"on orders of a mere woman" *strīvākyaṃ prākṛtam*: I explain the phrase as a kind of hypallage, for *prākṛtastrī-*; cf. 2.19.17.

12. More literally, "(five different forms): of Fire, Indra, [Soma, that is,] the Moon [see note on 2.85.17], Yama, and Varuṇa, the hotness, boldness, mildness, punishment, and graciousness" (for the figure of speech, technically *yathāsaṃkhya*, see note on 2.20.28). The politico-theological doctrine that the earthly king consists of essential parts of the *lokapālas* or "world protectors" is widespread (cf. note on 2.104.16, and 7. App. I, No. 12; see also Introduction, Chapter 4d).

14. "when I am paying a visit" *abhyāgataṃ mām*: The verb connotes the status of a guest, as Ct also perceives, and therefore Rāvaṇa is all the more to be honored.

16. The SR inserts after this verse:

> When Kākutstha has departed, go further away and call out like this, 'Oh Sītā! Oh Lakṣmaṇa!' imitating Rāma's voice. When he hears this, at Sītā's urging

Saumitri too in confusion will hurry off following Rāma's tracks, out of affection. (749*)

17. "as . . . Indra . . . Śacī": The story is unknown to me, and I suspect to the commentators, too, who are silent (the NE recension replaces the reference with "as Suparṇa [Viṣṇu's eagle] [might abduct] a she-serpent"). Perhaps a sort of "contrary-to-fact simile" (*viṣamā upamā*), since Śacī is Indra's wife.

18. NE manuscripts interpolate after this verse some lines in which Rāvaṇa asserts that neither Rāma nor any other mortal could pursue him (and Mārīca) to where he will take Vaidehī (750*).

19. "A safe journey to you" *gaccha . . . śivaṃ mārgam*: The standard idiom for "bon voyage"; the commentators implausibly see a pun: "(May you assume) a lovely deer form" (*taddhita* derivative from *mṛga-*).

20. "He who stands in opposition to a king is forever barred from happiness" *rājño hi pratikūlastho na jātu sukham edhate*: Not a personal conviction of Rāvaṇa's but a tenet frequently repeated in the epics; for one particularly close parallel, see *MBh* 12.68.49.

21. "there is a chance you will lose your life" *jīvitasaṃśayas te*: "That is, he might die or he might survive, as on the occasion of his two previous encounters with Rāma," Ck, Ct.

Sarga 39

1. "royal" *rājavad*: Translated thus following Cv, Crā, Cm, Cg (second interpretation; Ck reads *rājñā*; Cr, " '(he made this . . . reply)' like a king"). For a comparable problem brought on by this word, see 2.85.35 and note.

"perverse" *pratikūlam*: Ct understands the "perversity" to refer, not to the order to deceive Rāma, but to Rāvaṇa's threat to kill Mārīca unless he obeys (Ck takes the word adverbially with the main clause, remarking that Mārīca, now certain to die whether he agrees or refuses, speaks fearlessly).

8–15. The sense connection among these verses is, depending on one's viewpoint, very complex or very weak. This problem occasionally arises in the epics when proverbial verses (such as here, verse 10, which appears also in *MBh* 12.68.7 vulg., cf. also Bhatt 1963, p. 406) are strung together. I understand it thus: All a minister's life goals are attained by favor of the king (cf. 2.45.5); but even if he should win the king's approval it proves meaningless if the king himself is not virtuous; whereas if he is actually evil, his subjects suffer calamitously (verses 8–9; cf. following note); the king is thus the source of righteousness and must therefore be protected [by good counsel] (verse 10); only a good king can preserve the kingship (verse 11); bad ministers destroy the kingship (the king) and themselves (verse 12), for an innocent man can suffer from the evil deeds of others (verse 13, cf. 38.22); an evil king only appears to protect his subjects—in fact, he destroys them, as Rāvaṇa is destroying his own (verses 14–15).

9. "should their master go astray" *viparyaye*: This cannot, I think, have its more usual epic sense ("that failing," "in the absence of that," as, for example, in *MBh* 12.65.3), because the only referent would then be the king's "grace" in the previous verse (with which the second half of the present verse cannot intelligibly construe). Thus, though somewhat hesitantly, I follow Cg in assuming an abbreviated expression (for *guṇaviparyaye*, "[should there be] a reversal in his virtue"). (It is going too

far, however, to gloss *-prasādāt* in verse 8 ["grace," so rightly Cm, Cr there] as "virtue," a meaning that it cannot bear, in order to secure a tighter construction between the two halves of verse 9.)

10. "he who is lord of men must be protected" *rakṣitavyo narādhipaḥ*: And the only way truly to protect him is by good counsel (verses 11–12).

11. "the brutal man" *tīkṣṇena*: That is, the adviser who counsels brutal measures.

12. "with him" *tena*: Strictly, "with it," "the king's position," "the kingship" (verse 11), with which the *upamāna* of the simile, the chariot, would more properly construe.

16. "unfathomable" *kākatālīyam*: I defer here to the opinion of Cv, who, citing one Bhāguri, defines the word as meaning "something unexpected, signifying the same thing as 'a white crow' " (cf. also *KāśiVṛ* 5.3.106, "something unexpected and startling" [cited by Jacob 1907, p. 17]). Usually, however, this word relates to the *nyāya* (maxim) to which it literally refers, the "crow and the palm fruit," that is, to the coincidental fall of the fruit on the head of a crow the moment it lands on the tree (but without the crow's actually causing it to fall; essentially the same thing as *post hoc, non propter hoc*; see Nīlakaṇṭha on *MBh* 12.177.11, *MBh* 5.3.106, Mallinātha on *Kirātā* 3.31, *MālaMā* 84.7). But this common sense cannot, I think, fit here, because whether verse 16 goes with verse 15 or verse 17, Rāvaṇa has direct, not fortuitous, responsibility.

17. "I at least will find fulfillment in dying at the hand of my enemy" *anena kṛtakṛtyo 'smi mriye yad ariṇā hataḥ*: It is not clear what the poet means. The distinction, if one is actually being drawn, would seem to be between Mārīca's mode of dying and Rāvaṇa's (though so far as we know, and as Mārīca here affirms, both of them are sure to be slain by Rāma in battle), not between Mārīca's dying at the hand of Rāma or at the hand of Rāvaṇa, which appears to be the point of Ct's comment: "Death in battle at the hand of the enemy gives heaven as its reward; in comparison with this, death at the hand of a king [here, presumably, Rāvaṇa] is an evil death, and *śāstra* declares that one who so dies is denied the purification water and other rites. . . . Mārīca's mind, having been purified by asceticism and yoga, has acquired this knowledge [otherwise unavailable to *rākṣasas*]." The other commentators are of little help, interpreting for the most part according to apparently extraneous theological considerations, as Cm, Cg: "Mārīca has had a vision of Rāma's true, unparalleled greatness by his continually calling to mind Rāma's superhuman deeds, from his protecting Viśvāmitra's sacrifice to his slaying of Khara; and determining that Rāma is the Primal Being, he understands that death at his hand would fulfill the highest human goal. Thus is it formulated in the *Narasiṃhapurāṇa*: 'Death must be met at the hands of Rāma or Rāvaṇa; since in either case one must die, better at the hand of Rāma than of Rāvaṇa.' " (I do not find this verse in *NaraP*, though in 49.64 of that text Mārīca is reported as saying to Rāvaṇa, "Better to die at Rāma's hands than at yours"; some N manuscripts interpolate the verse cited by Cm, Cg in 762*.) Ck argues against the "stupid piety" of this theological interpretation by asking how Mārīca knows that Rāma is the Supreme Soul, and that death at his hand would be an act of grace to him (an objection Cg has anticipated, see above); and if he does know, why he tries to avoid experiencing it (an objection not anticipated by Cg). It may be that Mārīca means nothing more than that death at the hands of a great man is in itself something of a blessing (see 40.3 note below), and is thinking principally about himself, without intending to make any differentiation.

19. "you are doomed" *naiva tvam asi*: See 6.92.11 for corroboration of this pregnant sense of the verb.

20. "on the point of death" *paretakalpāḥ*: The reading here is doubtful. The verse recurs in 6.10.21, where the majority of N and S manuscripts, along with Crā and Cm, read *parītakālāḥ* ("[whose] time [of death] is at hand" [so the commentators there]), the reading offered here by NW manuscripts. Cf. 49.26 note below.

Sarga 40

1. Between *sargas* 39 and 40 the NR inserts a long (and dull) passage (App. I, No. 11), in which Mārīca tries further to dissuade Rāvaṇa, though finally consenting to assist (line 43); Rāvaṇa attempts to encourage him by minimizing Rāma's powers and glorifying his own (recounting his great deeds, including his lifting of Śiva's mountain [see 7.16], lines 72–73), and by asserting the inaccessibility of his island kingdom.

2. "The instant" *ca . . . ca:* The conjunctions express the simultaneity of the two actions, Rāma's seeing Mārīca and killing him; the second does not indicate "and your life, too, Rāvaṇa" (as per Ck, Ct, Cr).

3. "But what" *kiṃ tu*: To be understood as interrogative and adversative, respectively; Ck's *kiṃ nu* is attractive.

In the *Rāmopākhyāna* Mārīca decides that if one must die, it is better to die at the hand of a distinguished adversary [rather than at the hand of Rāvaṇa] (*MBh* 3.262.9, and above, 39.17 and note there).

6. The *MBh* version adds a nice touch here: Before his departure Mārīca performs for himself the water libation to the dead (3.262.14).

8–9. "towns . . . cities" *pattanāni . . . nagarāṇi*: According to Cg, the latter are provided with trees (*nagas*) (and therefore gardens), this distinguishing them from the former (he cites at length from the *Vāstuśāstra*, which, however, does not seem to corroborate his distinction); to Ck, Ct, the latter are political capitals.

13–16. "rare gems" *maṇipravara-*: Glossed "sapphire" by Cm, Cg, Ck (who remarks that it is poetic convention to use *maṇi-* only in this sense), Ct.

The commentators here and elsewhere in the *sarga* are oddly reluctant to believe that the deer is literally bejeweled, but that is clearly what the poet says (see verses 16, 18, 29, 32).

"pale, velvety *madhūka* flower" *madhūkanibha-*: See Ingalls 1965, p. 495.

19. "trees" *viṭapīnām*: Instead of *viṭapinām*, see Böhtlingk 1887, p. 215.

20. "plantain grove" *kadalīgṛhakam*: Thus Cm, Ct, Cr. I suppose this is the border of trees (perhaps a natural arbor) mentioned in verse 11, rather than "a man-made house constructed of plantain trees" (Cg, Ck). The word *gṛhaka-* seems not to be attested elsewhere.

26cd–27ab. "though they were close enough to touch" *saṃspṛśan*: Ck, Ct, Cr persuade me to treat this concessively; Cg takes it positively ("he would only touch them").

28cd–29ab. "picking flowers, *karṇikāra* . . . flowers" *karṇikārān . . . kusumāny apacinvantī*: Probably not double accusative with the root *ci* (Speijer 1886, pp. 34–5), but tree names used in the sense of their flowers, perhaps by *vart.* on *Pā* 4.3.166.

In accordance with its overall concern to establish a precise chronology for all the events in the poem (cf. 16.1 note above; the design of the poem itself gives substantial impetus to this concern; see for instance Pollock 1986, pp. 45–46), traditional exegesis seeks to determine here the exact time at which Sītā is abducted. Ct accordingly cites the evidence of the *aśoka* and mango flowers here (along with Rāma's two statements later, 4.1.6 and 4.1.16, and Rāvaṇa's threat in 54.22 coupled with 5.35.8) to show that the season is early spring.

29cd–ef. "not meant" *anarhā*: Cg tries to find a reason for the qualification: "This refers to the fact that the day of the completion of her vow [to live in the wilderness] is near at hand, and is meant to explain her excessive haste to have the deer captured"; Ct more cleverly, "The phrase implies that she will soon be living in a city" (that is, Rāvaṇa's). Perhaps it simply suggests that her fascination with the bejeweled deer betrays her ignorance of forest life.

30. "sparkling teeth and ruby lips" *ruciradantoṣṭhī*: On manuscript evidence and by reason of the feminine of the compound being applied to Sītā in 44.11, this is a more probable reading than that of the crit. ed., which applies the adjective to the deer. Such too is the reading of Cg, who supposes it to suggest her sensation of eager curiosity. More likely it is meant to call special attention to the woman's rare beauty: the poet underscores this repeatedly in the present passage (see verses 27, 28, 29; 41.1,2), as if to remind us that other eyes are seeing her for the first time—Rāvaṇa's.

Sarga 41

6. "the magic form of a deer" *māyāmṛgarūpam*: The crit. ed. is correct to print *māyā-* in compound with *mṛgarūpam*. Cm, Ct, Ct, Cr all read it separately ("it is his magic that has been turned into this deer form"). Perhaps they felt that the compound straddling the *pāda* boundary was unacceptable. Although this is rare, instances are found, for example in the next verse, *ratna-* (see also 2.54.10 note).

"mirage" *gandharvapura-*: Literally, "city of the *gandharvas*."

8. "But even as Kākutstha was speaking thus . . . Sītā interrupted" *evaṃ bruvāṇaṃ kākutsthaṃ prativārya . . . sītā*: "Kākutstha" refers to Lakṣmaṇa, as Cm, Ct see, and the gerund construes with Sītā (correctly Cg, Ck, Ct, Cr; incorrect is Speijer 1886, p. 298, "Laxmana thus speaking and dissuading her").

10–11. "yaks and antelope" *camarāḥ sṛmarāḥ*: See above, note on 13.23.

"powerful" *mahābalāḥ*: The adjective is decidedly inappropriate, but since the NR differs altogether here, it is not possible to decide among the variants (including also the probable *mahābala*, "my powerful [husband]," emphasizing Rāma's ability to capture the deer; *manoharāḥ*, "enchanting [animals]," is a mediocre revision).

12. "never before . . . seen" *na . . . dṛṣṭapūrvo . . . purā*: Literally, "never before . . . seen previously." Cg would eliminate the tautology by understanding "(and will not be seen) in the future [*purā*]."

15. "will be" *bhavati*: The verb seems to function as a future here. Possible too: "(this marvelous thing will be a source of wonder) about you," that is, it will be a feather in Rāma's cap to have captured so marvelous a creature alive.

20. "willful" *kāmavṛttam*: The reading is questionable, since the NR replaces it

with *kāmam uktaṃ mayā* (cf. 789*.22, 790*.21), "Although this is a (heartless) request I make." Cg, reading like the crit. ed., believes her horrible willfulness rests in her ordering her husband to fetch the deer (verse 9 above), for which she is now asking forgiveness (so Ck, Ct).

21."all the brilliance of the morning sun, all the luster of the starry heavens" *taruṇādityavarṇena nakṣtrapathavarcasā*: The deer's golden hide makes him like the newly risen sun, his silver spots like the starry sky (Cm, Cg, Ck, Ct, Cr).

23. "shall die" *na bhaviṣyati*: An idiom, as in verse 47ab below (see also 60.49, and 6.23.27, Nīlakaṇṭha on *MBh* 6.43.99 vulgate, and *BhagGī* 11.32). Rāma is declaring that he will kill the deer, something he proceeds to justify in verse 29. The commentators correctly understand the idiomatic sense of the phrase in verse 47ab, but are curiously reluctant to allow that meaning here ("[this] cannot possibly be [a deer]," Ck; "[this] cannot be alive," Ct; " '[this deer] will not be,' that is, such a deer as this will be impossible [ever] to find again," Cg).

24. "famous" *-saṃśrave*: Thus I conjecture, for the crit. ed.'s *-saṃśraye*. Although no manuscript reports it (at least according to the critical apparatus), it is inferable from the unanimous gloss of the commentators (*tadākhya-*), and would effectively parallel *-uddeśe* in *pāda* a. *-saṃśraya* must mean "located in," but it is meaningless to say the forest is located in Caitraratha when Caitraratha itself is the forest.

27. "sapphire and crystal" *masāragalvarka-*: This notoriously obscure compound is, I believe, to be taken as a *dvandva* (note especially verse 40.13 above, "its face mottled dark and light"). See Mayrhofer 1956–1980, vol. 2, p. 604; Nīlakaṇṭha on *MBh* 12.46.33 vulgate takes it as a *dvandva* too, but consisting of three items, "emerald" (*masāra-*), "moonstone" (*galu* glossed as *candrakānta-*), and "sunstone" (*arka*). Contrast Edgerton 1953, p. 436, where the compound is "said to mean sapphire or emerald"; Cm, Cg, Cr understand it as a *tatpuruṣa*, "a goblet of sapphire."

29–32. The train of thought here is difficult to follow. The following may be close to the truth: Both out of necessity and in sport, kings kill animals (verse 29), so I am justified in slaying this deer; they also search the woods for riches (verse 30), but this (deer form, verse 28) could give all the wealth one ever dreamed of (verse 31); and even if neither of these two reasons were valid, my behavior is warranted by the definition of *artha* given in the *śāstras* (verse 32).

Rāma's eagerness to go out hunting, despite Lakṣmaṇa's sound arguments, is something for which the audience has been prepared (see note on 2.43.14, and 6.17ff. and notes above). Is it considered by the poet, in the end, to be a vice, which leads even Rāma into trouble, as it had led his father Daśaratha (see 2.57-58)? Note also that, like Daśaratha, Rāma gives in to the wishes of the woman he loves, and in so doing brings disaster upon his own head.

31. "here is all the wealth a man could ask for" *tat sāram akhilaṃ nṛṇām*: The pronoun refers to the deer, and is attracted into the neuter of the predicate. (Wrongly the commentators, " 'Therefore excellent [*sāram*] wealth'—wealth amassed in accordance with the *śāstra*—'swells,' " Cm; " 'That wealth which swells,' that wealth from the forest, is 'excellent' [*sāram*], that is, better than the wealth that comes from the [agriculture of the] countryside," Cg, so Ck, Ct).

"just as Śukra's coffers come to be swelled with all the wealth men dream of" *manasā cintitaṃ sarvaṃ yathā śukrasya*: I take my cue for translating this cryptic line from a parallel adduced by Cg from the *MBh*, *manuṣebhyaḥ samādatte śukraś cittārjitaṃ dhanam*, "Śukra takes from men all the wealth they come by in their dreams" [or "their imagination," Arjunamiśra] (5.112.3; Nīlakaṇṭha on 5.114.3 vulg. interprets quite differently, and implausibly). The only references, however, that I can locate suggesting that Śukra has such vast wealth are here in *Rām* 4.50.12 (where the demon Maya is granted a boon, whereby he receives "all the wealth belonging to Uśanas" [that is, Śukra]), and in *MBh* 12.278.9 (where Śukra steals the wealth of Kubera).

32. "a man in want of something should go and get it" *arthī yenārthakṛtyena saṃvrajati*: The original is actually framing a definition: "(That is *artha*, here 'just gain') (with, i.e.,) to the accomplishment of which a man in want of the thing proceeds (without a second thought)." The mode of expression is obscure, and for this broad definition of *artha* I find no corroboration in the literature. Similarly, the place of the verse in the overall logic of the argument is difficult to determine. The commentators suppose the verse to be a reply to the objection, "Nonetheless one must never act without deliberation," which is to say, even if the other reasons are accepted, careful consideration in this instance will show that it is unwise to hunt the deer (Cm, Cg, Ct, Cr). Rāma seems to be stressing one of two things: either, "Given the traditional understanding of *artha*, there is no need for further deliberation"; or, "Since I am impelled to proceed to attain this object without further reflection, it must conform to the traditional notions regarding *artha*."

34. "goat's" *praveṇī*: So Ck, Ct, though the word is, so far as I can tell, unattested in this sense (Cm, Cg, "a type of blanket").

35. "the heavenly deer that roams the sky" *yaś ca divyo nabhaścaraḥ*: The constellation usually called Mṛgaśiras, "Deer's Head" (three stars of the constellation Orion, according to Kirfel 1920, p. 36).

37. "impious" *akṛtātmanā*: Compare the opposition *akṛtātma-* and *viśuddhātma-* in *MBh* 12.205.27.

38. "out hunting" *utthāya . . . mṛgayāyām*: I join the two items; see the NR's "gloss" *mṛgayāṃ gatāḥ* (790*.88). The commentators understand the gerund absolutely with *yena*, "(who), coming forth, or, springing forth (killed)," Cm, Cg, Ck, Ct.

39. For the full narrative of Vātāpi, see 10.53ff. above. Interestingly the NW version (789*) omits this (to my mind irrelevant) recapitulation of the story.

"as her foal will kill a she-mule when it comes to be born" *svagarbho 'śvatarīm iva*: Since mules—unless *aśvatarī* can mean the still-surviving wild Asiatic ass—are generally (if erroneously, cf. Rau 1980–1981, p. 188) regarded as barren by ancient Indians, it is unclear what the simile means, though Ct, Cr aver, "It is well known that only by bursting its mother's womb is the offspring of a mule born from her" (thus Arjunamiśra and Nīlakaṇṭha on *MBh* 12.138.30, where the same simile occurs). In the *ṢaḍviBr* 6.7.2 (cited by Rau) a mule's giving birth is considered a prodigy. Another (though almost equally puzzling) clue to the meaning of the *topos* may be contained in the statement in the *TaiS* that "Agni burns the birthplace" of the mule's foal (5.1.5.4). Cg, Ck, Ct mention other commentators who gloss the word *aśvatarī* as "crab" (or, scorpion), but I find no corroboration of this.

40. "the greatest sage in the world" *loke . . . mahāmunim*: Construing the two words together, though it is awkward, seems to be indicated by verse 42c below.

Two interesting variants: *caran* (for *cirāt*), "while wandering (through the world)"; and *lobhāt* (for *loke*; *sic* vulgate), "(But finally . . .) through his greed (he met up . . .)" (that is, his greed finally led to his confrontation with Agastya). NE manuscripts eliminate the problem altogether, reading *cirāt kālād*, "after a long time" (790*.92).

42. "to be digested" *jarāṃ gataḥ*: Thus Cg, Ct, Cr. The sense of the substantive (which normally means "old age"; the semantic bridge may be supplied by such idioms as *kālaḥ pacati bhūtāni* [*MBh* 17.1.3], "Time cooks creatures," i.e., digests them with its digestive "fire") is that of the verbal root *jṝ* from which it is derived; the usage is rare outside of medical texts, though it occurs also in 45.43 below.

43. "treats with scorn" *atimanyeta*: A vedic locution (cf. PW, s.v.), unattested in the epics (for which *ava* + *man* is substituted, as in 790*.98, the NE version). The commentators incorrectly gloss "transgress against" (Cm, Cg, Ct, Cr).

44cd–45ab. "our first responsibility" *yat kṛtyam*: Literally, "What(ever) we have to do"; the phrase is abbreviated from *yat kiṃcit kṛtyam* (see 2.20.26 and note).

45cd–46ab. "I intend to go" *yāvad gacchāmi*: Particularly with the first person singular *yāvat* can (as in verse 48) connote intention (see PW, s.v. 2c); the editor of the crit. ed. evidently mistook its function and consequently departed from the vulgate's correct articulation of lines 44cd–47ab (*paśya* in verse 46cd does not in itself mean, and cannot in the present context mean, "keep an eye on" [thus, however, Cr]; Cm suggests the difficult construction of joining 46ab with 44cd, with *tāvat* understood).

47cd–48. "with Sītā" *sītayā*: The preposition is omitted, as often (cf. verse 49 below), and as Ct perceives. The other commentators erroneously take the instrumental as *hetau* ("because of, on behalf of, Sītā").

After this verse (not after verse 44cd as per the crit. ed.), the NE recension adds, "You are not to budge until I return. *Rākṣasas* are wicked creatures, and will try all kinds of tricks" (790*.104–5).

49. "Jaṭāyus": See 13.36 above. Both the NE and the NW versions include this reference to Jaṭāyus (see 789*.69–70, 790*.106–7), even though earlier they showed the vulture to have departed (see 16.3 note). The SR is not altogether consistent, either, for the bird at present is supposed to be sleeping in a tree at some distance from the ashram (see 48.1 and note).

Sarga 42

2. "a pair of quivers" *kalāpau dvau*: Indian epic heroes often wear two quivers, one at either side of the back, because they are able to shoot ambidextrously.

"the bow with triple curve" *trivinataṃ cāpam*: "That is, [Viṣṇu's bow,] the *śārṅga*," Cm, Cg (cf. note on 20.15 above).

3. "timorously" *trāsāt*: Cr cleverly takes the adverb with both *pādas* c and d: For fear of Rāma, Mārīca disappeared; for fear of Rāvaṇa, he showed himself again.

7. "autumn" *śāradam*: This particular adjective is used "because [it is then, after the rains, that] tatters of cloud are present," Cg.

"and gone the next" *muhūrtān na prakāśate*: I follow the reading of the NE recension (supported in sense by the NW, 802*). The crit. ed. follows the SR, which offers "the next he appeared far away," construing *pādas* ab with verse 6, and leaving cd hanging in the air (so Cm, Cg, Ck).

8. "helplessly (deluded)" *vivaśaḥ* (. . . *mohitaḥ*): Cg, Ct seek to eliminate the unintentional criticism: "That is to say, under the sway of his curiosity, or, of his desire for the hide."

10. "nocked his . . . bow" *saṃdhāya . . cāpe*: The reading of the crit. ed. is dubious, especially insofar as not a single manuscript leaves the gerund without a direct object (cf. 807*, SR; 808*, NR), and also considering that it is Brahmā's arrow at issue.

12. "illusory (deer form)" *sadṛśam* (*mṛgarūpasya*): More literally, "the simulacrum (of the deer form)." The reading accepted by the crit. ed., *sa bhṛśam*, is based on very scanty and weak manuscript evidence (T3, G1, Dt, and some southern D codices), and worse, makes little sense. Ct's attempt to explain the *pāda* so constituted (*mṛgarūpasya*, sc., *mārīcarūpasya*) will not do, since we need two objects for the two verbs. The reading adopted for the translation is that of the oldest commentators, Cv and Crā, for which the variant presented by Cm, Cg, Ck (*śarīram*) appears to be a *lectio facilior*. Curiously, the NR omits the hemistich.

13. "leaped" *utpatya*: That is, he was launched upward by the force of the arrow (Ck, Ct).

14. The sequence of verses for this *sarga* in N manuscripts is confused enough to suggest that this verse is out of place (and in fact it would more properly appear after verse 16, or even 13cd).

19. "bristled with dread" *hṛṣṭatanūruhaḥ*: "In reality Rāma thrills with pleasure [not dread] at the realization that in consequence of these events all his purposes will be achieved," Ct (cf. the remarks of the commentators below, 50.11; for the question of the "divine plan," see the Introduction, Chapter 4c).

20. "(Rāma's) consternation gave way to a feeling of fear" *bhayaṃ . . . viṣādajam*: Cg believes Rāma's fear (with respect to Sītā) to come, not on the heels of his own consternation, but as a result of his anticipating consternation on the part of Sītā herself.

21. "He killed another dappled deer" *nihatya pṛṣataṃ cānyam*: Why does Rāma slay another deer? The commentators are puzzled, too, and none offers a convincing explanation. Cr argues that "another" here really connotes "unusual," the "unique" deer, Mārīca (but Rāma would hardly have taken the *rākṣasa*'s meat), and Ct maintains (if I understand him correctly, compare his remarks on GPP 46.1) that the poet has Rāma slay another deer only in order to occasion sufficient delay for the events of the following *sarga* to happen (though the fact that Mārīca had drawn Rāma "far away," 42.8, should suffice). Venkatanathacharya (1965, p. 303 note) supposes him simply to be bringing home dinner, something that Lakṣmaṇa, now otherwise employed, would normally have done. This was clearly the understanding of the NW version ("He killed other deer for their meat," 820*), and in 45.19 below Sītā informs Rāvaṇa that her husband will soon come "bringing an abundance of food from the forest" (explained by an SR insertion there as "the flesh of black deer, buffalo, and wild boar," 881*). The indecision among the manuscripts reflected in the critical text here as elsewhere may result from the discomfort later felt regarding Rāma's meat eating (see notes on 2.17.15, 48.15); still the narrative here seems inept.

"retraced his steps to Janasthāna" *janasthānaṃ sasārābhimukhaḥ*: On the question of the location of this area see 17.25 note above.

Sarga 43

8. "what you came here with the sole intention of doing" *yatpradhānas tvam āgataḥ*: That is, with the intention of violating Sītā himself. I agree with Ck in my analysis of the compound, which fits nicely in the context of verse 7—and of course produces one of the finer ironies of the book: Sītā's attack on Lakṣmaṇa opens the way for Rāvaṇa to do precisely what she falsely suspects of her brother-in-law. (The other interpretations, though they are basically attempts to palliate the insult and the sexual innuendo, deserve brief notice: " '[What use is there in (protecting) me when he,] bent on [whose protection] you have come here, is in danger,' because in such circumstances Sītā would not be expected to live a moment anyway," Cm, Ct; similarly but more simply Cg: " 'You came bent on him,' that is, on protecting him [and so you must do it]; 'what can I do here?' ")

10–11. "there is . . . could match" *vidyeta . . . pratiyudhyeta*: Apparently troubled by the first optative, and this somewhat uncommon sense of *prati* + *yudh*, Ct explains, "[none] would survive . . . who would fight against."

13. "their lord included" *seśvaraiḥ*: Indra, most probably, as Cg suggests (or, "their lords," that is, Brahmā, Viṣṇu, Śiva, in the opinion of Cr).

15. "or any belonging to a god" *na kaścid api daivataḥ*: Although based on only one manuscript (D6; M3, however, is close) and one commentary (Ck [followed by Ct and Cr]), the reading is unusual enough to lay some claim to authenticity. Presumably the distinction being drawn is between a god's real voice, which fortuitously sounds like that of the "godlike Rāma," and the absolutely counterfeit voice of the *rākṣasa* (the most widely attested reading, and an old one [Cv's], is *māyayā kenacit kṛtaḥ*, "Someone produced it by magic"; cf. NR 832*.2, "For even in the worst of circumstances Rāma would not call out in so cowardly a fashion"). Nonetheless, I wonder if the commentators preserving the reading failed to understand it, and that it means "or any that came about by chance" (*daiva-tas*). This at least sets up an intelligible opposition between Rāma's real voice and an accidental approximation of it—both of which Lakṣmaṇa would want to exclude before drawing the conclusion that it belonged to the *rākṣasa*.

16. "shapely" *varārohe*: A stock epithet of Sītā, but strikingly inappropriate in the present context. The commentators' silence, however, shows they were untroubled (cf. notes on 20.6 and 27.6).

20. "How pitiful this attempt of yours" *karuṇārambha*: Presumably referring back to the idea expressed in verse 8. Cs interestingly joins the whole *pāda* in compound, *anāryakaruṇārambha*, "You who take no pity on your brother" (a similar syntax in Ck, Ct, but with the nonsensical explanation "acting with ignoble pity"). Cg has some NE support for his *'karuṇārambha*, "how pitiless your venture."

"you are pleased with all this" *tava priyam*: I translate the crit. ed. here, which is the reading of the SR, but it is somewhat vague without the SR's following interpolation ("[I think you are pleased] with Rāma's great calamity," 835*), from which I borrow in recollection of verse 7 above. It is likely, however, that the true reading is preserved in the NE version, *priyā*, "(I believe you are) in love (with me)."

23. "I am married . . . a husband" *upasaṃśritya bhartāram*: Literally, "Having betaken myself [to him] as husband." Ś1 more straightforwardly reads *upasaṃgamya*, "Having [once] had sexual relations with" (on this sense of the word cf., for example, *MBh* 1.173.8).

27. "sharp-tongued" *tīkṣṇāḥ*: Cm, Cg gloss, "hardhearted."

28. "the inhabitants of the forest" *vanecarāḥ*: The sylvan deities (Cm, Ck, Ct, Cr); see verse 30 below. It certainly appears as if this verse interrupts the argument of verses 27 and 29, but no manuscript casts doubt upon its authenticity.

31. "I pray I find" *api . . . paśyeyam*: Such absolute constructions of the optative with *api* express a wish; see 2.82.26 note, and 35.4 above. Ck interprets as a question.

33. Sītā protests one last time apparently in order to neutralize the remaining trace of hesitation she senses in Lakṣmaṇa's words in verse 31 (thus Venkatanathacharya 1965, p. 309 note; Ck [so Ct] improbably supposes that Sītā wishes to assert her firmness of resolve lest Lakṣmaṇa suspect she might have relations with some other man in his absence).

34. "I would never touch any man" *na tv ahaṃ . . . puruṣaṃ spṛśe*: A claim made elsewhere by Sītā; see for instance 5.35.62–63. In his long commentary on this verse, Ct argues that by the threat, " '(I shall) throw myself into a blazing fire,' " Sītā is referring to what she will at all events actually do ("that is why no 'or' is used in this clause"). The implication for Ct is that Sītā will not go in her real form to Rāvaṇa's palace, but instead, committing her real body to the fire, she will go in a magical form (Ct here cites *KūrmaP* [*adhyāya* 2.33.112ff.], "Fire took Rāma's beloved and disappeared"; after the death of Rāvaṇa, Fire restores the real Sītā to Rāma in *Rām* 6.106; cf. also Raghavan 1973, pp. 37–38). If Rāvaṇa had touched the *real* Blessed Lady, claims Ct, he would have perished instantly, and the slaughter of all the *rākṣasas* would never have taken place. That is the reason Sītā produces a magical form of herself. The burning of Laṅkā by the fire on Hanumān's tail [*Sundarakāṇḍa* 52] is an additional consequence of [Sītā's entering into the fire]: Agni, god of fire, had fallen under the power of Rāvaṇa and so could not burn his city, but by the entrance of Her *śakti* into Fire it regained the capacity to do so. (See also Pollock 1986, p. 28 and note 6, as well as Cg on 6.106.6, who scoffs at the belief in the *māyā* Sītā.)

35. "struck her belly with her fists" *pāṇibhyāṃ . . . udaraṃ prajaghāna*: "By this phrase what must be suggested is the thought that 'My belly can only be filled by the death of all the *rākṣasas*'; otherwise the poet would have conformed with the well-known fact that women strike their breasts in moments of grief" (Ct; *uraḥ* is in fact read in the NE version).

36. "tried to comfort" *āśvāsayām āsa*: Note the clear conative aspect of the perfect here (see also 59.28 below, and note on 2.12.18).

"but" *ca*: See above, 9.14 note.

"she would say nothing more" *na . . . uvāca*: She refuses to say anything out of anger at what she supposes to be Lakṣmaṇa's attempt to delay his departure by comforting her (Cg, Ck, Ct).

"husband's brother" *bhartuḥ . . . bhrātaram*: The circumlocution (instead of using simply *devara*, "brother-in-law," or the like) serves to suggest the alienation that has entered Sītā's relationship with Lakṣmaṇa. The proper kinship term, *devara-*, will be employed when Sītā has cause to regret what she did (54.32; note, however, that in the *MBh* version, *devara-* is used at this junction in the story, 3.262.25).

37. "self-respecting" *ātmavān*: Surely here the correct—if an unrecorded—sense (contrast above, note on 6.12). The common meaning "self-controlled, self-possessed" is hardly apposite; what Lakṣmaṇa is doing is wholly impulsive, and a function of his wounded pride, as Rāma will point out (57.19–22).

"turned . . . and looked back" *avekṣamāṇaḥ*: Used as in 2.80.25.

Sarga 44

1. "longing" *vikāṅkṣan*: Cg is alone in understanding "unwilling[ly he set forth toward Rāma]."

2. "opening (. . . [and he took advantage of] it)" *antaram* [*āsthitaḥ*]: The noun is to be taken with both *pādas* a and b (so Cg; Cr interprets *āsthitaḥ* absolutely, " 'intent,' that is, on abducting Sītā").

"Assuming the guise of a wandering mendicant" *parivrājakarūpadhṛk*: Rāvaṇa's disguise as an ascetic is perhaps the first occurrence of what was to become a standard narrative motif of classical Sanskrit literature, the false ascetic (see Bloomfield 1924). Note that Hanumān, too, will approach Rāma and Lakṣmaṇa in the form of a mendicant (*Kiṣkindhākāṇḍa* 14).

"he turned his steps toward" *abhicakrāma*: In each of verses 3, 4, 8, 9, 12 a different verb expressing "motion toward" is employed, producing a crescendo of dramatic intensity. Cm believes that the verbs connote gradually higher degrees of propinquity.

3. "a . . . staff" *yaṣṭi-*: Taken by Cg, Ck, Ct, Cr to be the "triple staff" (*tridaṇḍa*), which indicates complete ascetic renunciation (cf. Kane 1962–1975, vol. 2, part 2, pp. 937ff.); Ct cites the *Rāmopākhyāna* description of Rāvaṇa as *tridaṇḍadhṛk* (*MBh* 3.262.16); for Cg, Cr, this status is implied by the attribution of the topknot, which he claims only the *tridaṇḍin* may wear.

4. "like total darkness advancing upon the twilight" *saṃdhyām iva mahat tamaḥ*: Cg remarks that "Here we have a 'simile with the nonexistent' [*abhūtopamā*], since the darkness cannot possibly exist so long as the twilight lasts," but this seems hypercritical; the darkness can still be said to "advance on" the glow of twilight.

5. "as a planet" *grahavad*: The planet is Mercury, as 47.15 below shows (not a comet or meteor, with Ct, Cr, who are remembering 17.17 above). The asterism Rohiṇī (five stars in the constellation Taurus, according to Kirfel 1920, p. 36) is represented in Sanskrit literature as the beloved of the moon (see 2.106.3 note), and the NW version enhances the simile by employing in its variant here the common sobriquet of Rāma, Rāmacandra ("[looked at] her left without Rāma [the prince who was pleasing as] the moon"). Cg attempts to explicate the meaning of the figure: "Just as a hostile planet's gazing at [that is, conjunction with] [the asterism] Rohiṇī works evil for the world, precisely so does Rāvaṇa's gaze at Sītā."

Although we may derive little satisfaction from such astronomical similes, they evidently possess deep aesthetic power for a traditional audience (they are used in the poem at moments of high drama, see for example verse 9 below, and especially 47.15 and note). We might be less impatient with them if we reflect on the centrality of astrology in traditional Indian life.

6. "the dreaded, evil creature" *ugraṃ pāpakarmāṇam*: The reading is marked as uncertain. A widespread variant is *ugratejaḥkarmāṇam*, "doer [of deeds] of fierce heat, brilliance," something perhaps more to be feared by trees than "evil."

12. "garments of yellow silk" *pītakauśeyavāsinīm*: Unlike Rāma and Lakṣmaṇa, Sītā has retained her courtly garments during the forest exile, at the insistence of King Daśaratha (see *Ayodhyākāṇḍa* 33).

13. "the sounds of the *vedas* on his lips" *brahmaghoṣam udīrayan*: Cg cites the prescription, "[A mendicant] should [daily] recite the upaniṣads" (*ĀruU* 2).

14. "like the goddess Śrī herself without the lotus" *padmahīnām iva śriyam*: The goddess is represented as residing in a lotus. It is unlikely that the poet would have felt there to be any contradiction with the following verse.

15. "like a lotus pond yourself" *padminīva*: "Because her face, eyes, hands, and feet are [soft or tapered] like lotuses," Cg.

16. "Modesty" *hrī*: Otherwise the commentators (Cg, for instance, cites *śruti* to support his gloss "Earth, the wife of Viṣṇu"; Cm, "Hrī and the rest are particular *śaktis* of Viṣṇu"), but with little plausibility.

17ff. In the classical period Sanskrit poets generally take care to present an orderly description of female beauty. Normally they begin with the head and end with the feet (similar is the medieval *ordo effictionis*; see also *DaśkuC* pp. 3–4 [though contrast p. 50, a description that proceeds from foot to head], and Vallabhadeva on *KumāSaṃ* 1.32). An interpolation of the NR attempts to approximate this schema (858* [+ verse 18], 860*: brows, cheeks, ears, breasts, hands, waist, the line of hair below it, the pubes, thighs, toes, soles, and feet).

18–19. "firm" *saṃhatau*: So I read, with half of the SR and the entire NR (cf. 861*) for the crit. ed.'s *sahitau*; see also below, verse 21, *saṃhatastanī*, and in 6.5.14, *saṃhatau . . . stanau*. The adjective is virtually obligatory in such passages.

"gently heaving" *saṃpravalgitau*: I adopt this variant, found in several S manuscripts, for the crit. ed.'s *saṃpragalbhitau*, a non-epic word, it appears, and one that is also short on sense (" 'that grow bold,' namely, in embraces," Ck, Ct). This choice is further corroborated by the use of the verb in 6.4.88, *pravalgantam ivormibhiḥ*, "(the ocean) gently heaving, it seemed, with its waves," precisely the image the present verse, I think, wishes to convey (see also the description of Urvaśī in the *MBh* [3. App. I, No. 6.51], *stanau tasyā vavalgatuḥ*).

21. "compass with my fingers" *karāntamita-*: Within the circle of thumb and forefinger (Cg, Ck, Ct, Cr).

"No goddess, no *gandharva* woman" *naiva devī na gandharvī*: Repeated from Śūrpaṇakhā's report, 32.15 above.

26. Hanumān will address the same words to Sītā in 5.31.5.

27. "*gandharvas*": The NE version attempts to make this reference intelligible by an insertion before the verse (865*, ". . . Are you perhaps a *gandharva* woman . . . ?").

28. "panthers, and tigers" *dvīpivyāghramṛgāḥ*: The final element, given the context, can hardly be taken to mean "deer"; in fact it looks as if it is functioning almost as an otiose suffix. But the reading is disputed in the manuscripts, and perhaps "wolves" (with several southern codices) is the correct one.

"flesh-eating birds" *kaṅkāḥ*: Thus in agreement with Cg (normally the word means simply "heron").

32. "when food was ready" *siddham*: See verse 34 below.

33ff. The verses are recapitulatory, as Cg observes (see note on 2.57.38–39).

33. "saffron robe" *kusumbha-*: So Cm, Cg, Ck, Ct; Cg and Ct offer as alternative glosses, "water pot."

"(impossible) to refuse" (*aśakyam*) *uddveṣṭum*: Cm, Cg presumably read *udveṣṭum* ("who was not to be fed [because his intention (*-darśanāt*) was to harm her (*apāya-*)"], the latter definitely a reading inferior to *upāya-*, "accoutrements" [it is this that Ct criticizes, *pace* Bhatt 1963, p. 407]), though this is not reported in the crit. ed. Neither *ud* + *dviṣ* nor *ud* + *viṣ* appears to be lexicographically recorded.

"she . . . him . . . befitting a brahman" *brāhmaṇavat tam aṅganā*: (Literally, "the woman. . . .") For the reading see the emendation of the editor (Bhatt 1963, p. 407). The text as printed would give, "(she honored him) as he had come, like a brahman," still preferable perhaps, despite the repetition of *āgatam*.

Cg cites here, "Merely on account of his saffron robe and staff is an ascetic to be honored, without fail," this presumably despite what must strike us as the unascetic words Rāvaṇa has spoken.

36. "in his honest garb" *suveṣam*: Again the odd epithet for Rāma (if we read it straightforwardly, "well dressed," so Cr; Crā, Cg, Ck, Ct all gloss it merely "handsome," which is still irrelevant here), since he is dressed in barkcloth and hides (see 1.12 and note above). It gains some narrative relevance if we take the prefix *su-* as connoting "true, honest": Rāma's clothes truly declare the man and his good intentions—Rāma is a real ascetic, at least for the present—in stark contrast to the deceptive mendicant guise of Rāvaṇa.

Sarga 45

4. "For twelve years I lived" *uṣitvā dvādaśa samāḥ*: I read with the SR (supported by the NW version) for the reasons of chronology outlined in the note on 2.17.26 (the crit. ed.'s reading is, "For one year I lived"). For the finite use of the continuative here (thus, too, understood by Cg), see the note on 2.18.32.

5. "in the thirteenth year" *trayodaśe varṣe*: Again I accept the reading of the vulgate, see above (the crit. ed. has "a year later"). The emendations here and in the previous verse are those required in any case by the text-critical principles of the crit. ed.; if those principles are "wrong here" (van Daalen 1980, p. 214), then they are wrong everywhere, a claim that I have tried to show cannot be sustained (Pollock 1984b).

"the king" *rājā*: In place of *rāmam* as printed (an emendation made by the editor of the crit. ed., see Bhatt 1963, p. 407; the same manuscript evidence would of course require the slight alteration of *pāda* d).

6. "mother-in-law" *āryā*: The word is used in the epics to refer in a respectful way to a broad range of kinship relationships.

7. "had already married . . . for a consideration" *pratigṛhya . . . sukṛtena*: This translation, wholly at odds with the commentators, is supported by this signification of *pratigṛhya* elsewhere in the *Rām* (cf., for example, 13.11 above); *sukṛtena* I understand as instrumental of price, "at the price, cost, of a benefit, favor," that is, the promise to her of the succession of her own son, Bharata (cf. 2.99.3, 9.10ff. and notes, 10.25, and Introduction to the *Ayodhyākāṇḍa* in Pollock 1986, pp. 27ff.). The singular "boon" mentioned in the previous verse, and the quite emphatic "two

things" in the present one, make this analysis unavoidable. Cg, Ct gloss, "Having caused him to swear by his righteous merit" (thus Cm; cf. 2.10.25, but there we read the form *parigṛhya* [which in fact is what the *Rāmopākhyāna* presents in its version of the story, *MBh* 3.261.24], offered here only by some undistinguished S manuscripts); "or, 'Having got him under her power by her good service,' reminding him, that is, how she had saved his life" (see 2.10.25 and note); Ck, Ct, " '[Having gotten him under her power (Ct)] by his favor,' in the form of the boon he granted."

8. On this verse, which is absent from the crit. ed. of the *Ayodhyākāṇḍa*, see the note on 2.9.45.

In a NE insertion hereafter the attempt is made to account for her *two* requests (when only one boon was granted) by repeating the story of the boon given at the war of the gods and *asuras* (cf. 2.9.9ff.)

9. "with offers of commensurate riches" *arthair anvarthaiḥ*: "Useful riches," Cm, Cg, Ct; " 'sensible, purposeful,' sc., words," Ck.

10. "twenty-five years old" *pañcaviṃśakaḥ*: For a detailed analysis of the problem of Rāma's age, see the note on 2.17.26. Ck here remarks, "There is some [crow's tooth, that is] mare's nest of a discussion about Rāma's age centering on this verse. I ignore it. Then again, let me simply report," and he goes on to transcribe a traditional verse, which makes Rāma twelve at the time of his marriage, twenty-five at the time of his departure from Ayodhyā, and just under forty when Sītā is abducted. These are the figures given also by Cg here, and what scrutiny of the manuscript tradition reveals.

"and I had just passed my eighteenth birthday" *aṣṭādaśa hi varṣāṇi mama janmani gaṇyate*: 874* must be added to the text, for the only important manuscript that omits it, Ñ1, omits also the narratively essential verse 9, which shows that there was a lacuna in its exemplar.

"passed" *gaṇyate*: (Literally, "[eighteen years] were counted.") A rare case of singular for plural *metri causa*.

Cm, Cg note that by the */bh/* in verse 10a, the ninth syllable of the *Gāyatrīmantra*, 8,000 verses of the [traditional] *Rām* have been completed (see note on 2.39.5).

Nearly all manuscripts (Ś, T3 are lacking here) add hereafter, "But my glorious father Daśaratha was tormented by passion, and to do what Kaikeyī wanted he did not have Rāma consecrated as king" (875*, 876*).

13. "in the forest" *vane*: The single word enjambment over hemistich boundary is rare in the *Rām*, and thus has dramatic force in the present instance (cf. note on 2.21.14).

15. With respect to Rāma's vow see 2.81.16 and note, and 5.31.21.

18. "under compulsion" *ojasā*: In the sense of *balāt*, a usage I have not encountered elsewhere (though 5.49.22 may provide a possible parallel). Cg, Cr seem to understand, "by our own power," which makes little sense.

19. Most of the SR adds hereafter, "Bringing the flesh of black deer, buffalo, and wild boar he has slain" (818*), on which see 42.21 note above.

20. "clan, and family" *gotraṃ ca kulam*: Cm, Ct distinguish them, claiming the former to be the paternal, the latter the maternal kin group (though usually both are reckoned paternal groups, the latter being a smaller division within the lineage).

"How is it that you . . . wander all alone in Daṇḍaka wilderness" *ekaś ca daṇḍakāraṇye kimarthaṃ carasi*: According to *śruti*, says Cg, "A mendicant should enter a village to beg," and so should live in a forest near a village; Sītā thus reasonably wishes to know why he is wandering about in an area far away from the people who could give him alms.

21. "that froze her blood" *tīvram*: Cg glosses "hurriedly," explaining that "Rāvaṇa had been impatiently awaiting the chance to reveal his own power [and so accomplish his abduction]."

It is surprising that Rāvaṇa, after all the care he took in his disguise, should so straightforwardly reveal himself. Perhaps the disguise was merely a way to gain the confidence of Sītā (or, not straightway to frighten her off, so Rāmacandra on *RāmāCam* p. 192), draw her into telling him her story, and so reveal unequivocally who she is, though it is improbable Rāvaṇa had any doubts; or likelier, a safety measure to confirm that his stratagem had worked, and that Rāma and Lakṣmaṇa are in fact gone.

22. The NE version adds a few more particulars hereafter: that he is brother to Kubera, son of Viśravas, grandson of Pulastya, who was himself son of Brahmā; and that Brahmā had granted him a boon (885*).

27. After this the NE version adds the interesting verse, "I am familiar with the fourteen [branches of science], I am adorned by the sixty-four [fine arts], I know the twenty-five principles [of Sāṃkhya], I am Rāvaṇa, give me your love" (cf. Ct on GPP 48.25, who dismisses this as an interpolation on text-critical and narrative grounds).

In a long note here Ct is at pains to refute the theological position of Cm, which attempts to show that Rāvaṇa is really a devotee of Sītā's (albeit a *tāmasabhakta*), and that therefore all his remarks here can be interpreted as promises of self-abandoning devotion to his *iṣṭadevatā*, toward whom he is in reality behaving like a son (Cm does in fact attempt to maintain this interpretation throughout much of the *Araṇyakāṇḍa* and later; see for example the remarks on 46.16 below). Ct asserts there is nothing to indicate that Rāvaṇa has any knowledge of the ultimate truth; furthermore, to believe that he knows Rāma and Sītā to be the supreme Lords would stand in flat contradiction with the *ViṣṇuP* (Ct goes on then to cite at length the interesting passage from this text, 4.15.1ff., where Rāvaṇa's failure to secure final liberation even though slain by the Blessed One is reckoned a consequence of his believing Rāma to be a mere human being; he looks upon Sītā, too, with a profane eye, he abducts her thinking her a mere woman and not the Mother Goddess, and for that the Blessed One slays him). "The efforts of [Maheśvara]tīrtha and others to construe otherwise such statements as Rāvaṇa makes here are totally fruitless."

29ff. "I am faithful to Rāma" *rāmam anuvratā*: On the refrain style from here to the end of the *sarga* (29–31; 32–39; 40–42), see the remarks in 2.25.5 note.

30–31. The NE version and two NW manuscripts transpose these two verses, which makes sense in view of the metaphor used in verse 32.

30. "a lionlike man" *nṛsiṃham*: By this, according to Ct, is suggested Viṣṇu's *avatāra* as the man-lion.

In an NE insertion here, Sītā compares Rāma to Viṣṇu and herself to Śrī (892*.12).

32. "You could no more touch me" *nāhaṃ śakyā tvayā spraṣṭum*: It is not clear what Sītā really means by this claim—Rāvaṇa will have no trouble in carrying her off. Perhaps simply "touch and yet survive"? Or does the locution connote sexual union?

33. "many a golden tree" *pādapān kāñcanān . . . bahūn*: I am unable to find any

information concerning this sign of imminent death, to which Vālmīki refers elsewhere (cf. 51.17, 64.11). The commentators merely remark, "It is well known [from the *purāṇas*, Cr; from the *jyotiḥśāstra*, according to Cm on 64.11] that a person on the point of death sees golden trees, or, that seeing golden trees is a sign of imminent death" (Cm, Ck, Ct). The convention is known to the *MBh*, too (cf. 6.94.12).

34. The two halves of this verse construe only if forced. NE and NW manuscripts (in part) felt similarly and read, "You are [madly] seeking to seize the meat from the mouth of a starving rampant lion" (894*, 895*; note particularly the agreement of Ñ1 and D1, 3). This may have been original and, later viewed as an unsuitable image for Sītā to use however allusively of herself, awkwardly altered.

Cg, Ct, Cr identify the figure in this and the following verses as *nidarśanā* "(negative) illustration" (see Gerow 1971, p. 202).

35. "to carry off Mandara . . . in your hand" *mandaraṃ . . . pāṇinā hartum*: According to the *Uttarakāṇḍa* at least (the incident does not, however, appear to be mentioned in Books Two through Six), Rāvaṇa is in fact said to have lifted Mount Kailāsa from its foundations (cf. 7.16).

"*kālakūṭa* poison" *kālakūṭaṃ viṣam*: A byproduct generated when the gods and demons churned the Milk Ocean for the drink of immortality (the legend, curiously, is excluded from the accounts of the myth in the crit. eds. of both the *Bālakāṇḍa* [see notes on 1.44.17 and 24] and the *MBh* [1.274*], though it is clear from *Rām* 5.16.20, 20.26 that Vālmīki knows it).

36. "licking" *leḍhi*: Ct reminds us that the correct form for the second person singular of this verb (that printed is third singular) is *lekṣi*, a variant given by the NE version (900*).

37. "the very sun and moon" *sūryācandramasau cobhau*: Note the vedic dual (*devatādvandva*), "de type solennel" as Renou puts it (1968, p. 103, though he incorrectly repeats Michelson's error [1904, p. 95] that the *Rām* presents no examples of the form; see also note on 2.85.14). Perhaps, consequently, the NE's *devau* ("gods") for *ubhau* ("both," "the very") is to be preferred. Recall that Rāma and Lakṣmaṇa are compared to the sun and moon earlier (see 3.27, 22.34, and note also 30.16).

38. "You have seen" *dṛṣṭvā*: The reading strikes me as weak. The NE offers *baddhvā*, "You have tied up (a blazing fire in a cloth)"; cf. *MBh* 11.1.32, *agniṃ vastreṇa pariveṣṭayet*, "[as] one who would try to wrap up fire in a cloth."

40. "rare wine" *surāgrya-*: My translation is based on Cg (thus too Ck, Ct, Cr).

41. "lead" *sīsaloha-*: Literally, "lead metal." Cg would join the second element with "gold" as well, "since gold is counted one of the nine metals" (I agree with Ct, Cr).

"in the forest" *vane*: The nuance of this qualification, used in the next verse also, escapes me as it escaped the NE version, which on both occasions eliminates it.

43. "no more than a fly the diamond chip it swallows" *vajraṃ yathā makṣikayāvagīrṇam*: No doubt a bizarre image at first sight, but finally not impossible, and, given the tone of verses 32–42, rather appropriate. The commentators, with the exception of Cv, try to simplify matters by citing *śruti* to show that *vajra-* ("diamond") can mean "clarified butter" (thus, "as ghee eaten along with a fly in it cannot be digested," Cm, Cg, Ck—a simile with little propriety in the present context; somewhat better are Ct, Cr, "as ghee eaten by a fly cannot be digested"; the reading "*ājyam* [ghee]" has actually made its way into several inferior manuscripts); however, I find no authority for this signification. Can the NW version have preserved the correct reading in *vajraḥ*, "like the glue eaten by a fly"?

The image of "digesting" Sītā, which appears also in 5.49.22 (and cf. below, 48.17), has perhaps more than metaphorical significance: *rākṣasas* looked upon humans as objects not just of sexual but also of gustatory pleasure; see Rāvaṇa's threat in 54.22 below, and note on 21.5 above.

Hereafter the NE version adds,

> Śacī might be taken from Indra, who bears the thunderbolt; the flame might be taken from the flaming fire, or Umā from Sthāṇu [Śiva], the lord of the world, but you, Rāvaṇa, can never take me from Rāghava. (910*)

Sarga 46

1. "(he) harshly (replied)" *paruṣākṣaram* (. . . *pratyuvāca*): The adverb can as well be taken with *pāda* a ("[was speaking] in this harsh manner"), as Venkatanathacharya suggests (1965, p. 328 note).

2. "half brother" *sāpatnyaḥ*: Literally, "son of a co-wife," similarly *vaimātraḥ* in verse 4 (cf. 45.16). It is interesting that despite Rāvaṇa's own distinguished lineage (cf. 45.22 note), he should derive particular pride from his kinship with Kubera. Sītā will accordingly challenge him on this (see verse 20 below).

4. "(half) brother" *bhrātā* (*vaimātraḥ*): Many manuscripts, of both recensions, read *rājā*, "king." Rāvaṇa's usurpation of his elder brother's throne is related in Book Seven, *sarga* 11. What is here expressed by the vague phrase *kāraṇāntare*, "in connection with some issue between us" (cf. 67.31 and note, and 4.10.23, in reference to Sugrīva and Vālin), appears in the *Uttarakāṇḍa* to have been nothing less than Rāvaṇa's lust for power, in which he was encouraged by his maternal grandfather Sumālin and others. (Cs suggests the compound refers to "the keeping of his mother's command," that is, Rāvaṇa's promise to his jealous mother that he would someday equal or outshine his brother, 7.9.32ff.)

5. "his own . . . realm" *svam adhiṣṭhānam*: Laṅkā, according to Cm, Ct, Cr. It certainly does look as if it is there that Rāvaṇa defeats Kubera, who then quits his home for Mount Kailāsa, though this is at odds with other versions of the incident (see 30.14 note).

"with only men to convey him" *naravāhanaḥ*: The following verse, describing the expropriation of Kubera's (Vaiśravaṇa's) sky-going chariot, seems intended to clarify this obscure epithet—in later literature it is applied to Kubera in an altogether ornamental manner—which I therefore invest with a more immediate narrative relevance in the translation. See also 30.14 note.

6. The story is related in *Uttarakāṇḍa* 15. Note that the Puṣpaka must still be in Laṅkā (see 33.5ff. note), and therefore I translate "the lovely," not "this. . . ." It is noteworthy that the verse is so explicit about Rāvaṇa's riding in the sky-going chariot, for in the *Rāmopākhyāna* Kubera curses him that he shall never do so (*MBh* 3.259.34–35).

7. After this verse some N manuscripts insert eight lines in which Rāvaṇa claims to have defeated the (other) world protectors Śakra, Varuṇa, and Yama (911*; on the last see 47.3, 6.7.13 and 7.20–22).

9–10. Compare 1.14.9–10, where the elements are said to moderate their force in the presence of Rāvaṇa, and, as in verse 7 above, the gods to stand in fear of him.

9. "wherever" *yatra tatra*: See PW, s.v. *yatra* 1b. A number of manuscripts seem to have mistaken the usage, and so transpose the two adverbs in order to eliminate the apparent inversion of the reasoning.

10. "On the further shore of the ocean" *pāre samudrasya*: "That is, on Mount Trikūṭa in the middle of the ocean, which may be said to resemble a further shore," Cg.

11. "a white rampart" *prākāreṇa . . . pāṇḍureṇa*: It is white because it is either whitewashed (Ck, Ct) or made of silver (Cm, Cg, Ct, Cr; in 6.3.13 it is said to be golden).

12. "gardens . . . filled with" *saṃkulodyāna-*: I agree with Cr in taking this as a compound, even though it occasions an unpaninian syntax with the external items in *pāda* c; Venkatanathacharya 1965, p. 331 note, takes the two words in the compound separately.

14. "Rāvaṇa here answers the criticism implicit in Sītā's earlier statement [45.4]," Cg.

"that short-lived mortal" *gatāyuṣaḥ*: On this emphatic reference to the presumed mortality of the hero, see 2.10 note above. (Ct comments: "The sense is either that his life is delimited in actual number of years—that is, 11,000 [cf. e.g., 6.116.90]—or that Rāvaṇa intends to slay him.")

16. "miserable ascetic" *tāpasena tapasvinā*: See 5.19 note above. I find no authority for taking either *tāpasa-* (Cg) or *tapasvin* (Ck, Ct) in the sense of "coward."

In a paroxysm of pious horror at these criticisms of Rāma even in the mouth of Rāvaṇa, Cm reinterprets this passage (verses 13–18, and verse 16 in particular) as containing a glorification of Rāma as Nārāyaṇa, "in reality" (though the surface or literal meaning [*prātītikārtha*] may signify something quite different). (Cf. Ct's arguments noticed above on 45.27.)

17. "(lord of) all (*rākṣasas* has come here in person), of his own accord" *sarva* (*rākṣasabhartāraṃ*) *kāmāt* (*svayam ihāgatam*): Ct reads instead, *rakṣa . . . kāmaya*, "Save (the master of *rākṣasas*), make love (to me who have come here in person)" (recorded only partially in the crit. ed.).

"of his own accord" *kāmāt*: See note on 2.86.1; here probably also with some resonance of "out of desire."

18. "timid lady" *bhīru*: "The epithet is used to intimate that Rāvaṇa believes the only reason Sītā might reject him is her fear of Rāma," Cg.

"just like Urvaśī after she spurned Purūravas" *caraṇenābhihatyeva purūravasam urvaśī*: Literally, ". . . kicked . . . with her foot." The love story of the lunar king Purūravas and the *apsaras* Urvaśī is told in many different texts, starting with the *ṚV* (10.95; see Kosambi 1951, and Wright 1967). No version represents Urvaśī as "kicking" the king; in the vedic poem (verse 13), and only there, she may be said to reject him scornfully, and it is to this that I believe the words here figuratively refer (a dead metaphor, thus, exactly comparable to the English word spurn).

Most of the SR adds hereafter,

> That man, Rāma, is not equal to my little finger in battle! To your good fortune am I come; love me, fairest woman. (913*)

19. "in that deserted spot" *rahite*: Cg notes that although solitude is usually a spur to passion, the poet shows Sītā here speaking harshly in solitude and thereby underscores her chastity and fidelity.

20. "This verse implies that Sītā believes Rāvaṇa fraudulently represented his lineage," Ct.

22. Cf. the words of Mārīca above, 39.15.

23. "a woman like me" *mādṛśīm*: The circumlocution (for "me," simply) is used, according to Cg, to "to avoid the vulgar."

Ct here cites the verse discussed in 45.27 note.

Sarga 47

1. "made ready to assume" *cakāra*: The verb probably has an inchoative aspect (cf. note on 2.70.3), since Rāvaṇa's form is not changed until verse 6. The NE version found this awkward, and read verses 8 and 6 directly after verse 1.

Rāvaṇa takes on his true form, in the opinion of Ct, either for fear that Sītā might turn violent at the moment of abduction, or because the mendicant's garb might prove an impediment to him, since "even worn as a disguise it induces a certain tranquillity of temperament."

2. "did . . . hear" *śrutau*: Thus in agreement with Cg, Ck. Ct's alternative is possible, however: "(I suppose you) have (not) heard (about . . .)."

3. "I can slay Death" *mṛtyuṃ hanyām*: See note on 46.7 above; though often given separate names, Death and Yama are in the epics usually considered virtually identical (see for example Hopkins 1915, p. 108).

6. "younger brother to Vaiśravaṇa" *vaiśravaṇānujaḥ*: The point of the epithet is to suggest, according to Cg, "despite the identical conditions of their birth, how cruel one of the two became."

9–10. "a red garment" *raktāmbara-*: According to the traditional color associations reported by Bharatamuni, red is indicative of the emotional atmosphere, not of eroticism (that would be dark blue), but of violence (cf. *NāṭyaŚā* 6.42, [*śyāmo bhavati śṛṅgāraḥ* . . .] *rakto raudraḥ prakīrtitaḥ*).

"her jet-black hair, her sunlike radiance" *asitakeśāntāṃ bhāskarasya prabhām iva*: The two statements have no intrinsic connection (though Ct and Cs construe them so, on the basis of the statement in the *ChāndoU* [8.6.1], "The sun is yellow . . . deep blue-black"), but are juxtaposed merely to establish a contrast, characteristic of Vālmīki's style (see also note on 2.35.21).

15. "as . . . Budha . . . Rohiṇī in the sky" *budhaḥ khe rohiṇīm iva*: Budha is the planet Mercury; on Rohiṇī see above, 44.5 note.

As previously observed (44.5), it is hard to feel the aesthetic force of the vapid simile, which seems particularly unhappy coming at the climax of so extraordinary a crescendo of dread over Rāvaṇa's desecration of Sītā. The commentators appear to have felt this, too, in the present instance, for they take pains to justify the simile. Cg (similarly Ck) claims a likeness is being made to something hypothetical (*abhūtopamā*): Rāvaṇa's act was as evil as it would be if Budha were ever to lay hold of Rohiṇī, who is his own mother (according to such passages as *MBh* 7.119.4). Ck finds deep theological significance in the simile, and claims that the meaning of the verse is accessible to the understanding of *yogins* alone, and cannot be the subject of open inquiry.

The *ṭīkā* on Cm (GPP p. 284) reports the traditional interpretation (citing the *SkandaP*) which explains that Rāvaṇa does not actually touch Sītā herself, but only seizes her shadow (as *rākṣasas* are able to do). He avoids actually touching her, since twice before when he had outraged women, he had been cursed (by Vedavatī, 7.17.22ff., and by Nalakūbara, 7.26.42ff.).

18. "wheels" *-aṅgaḥ*: So correctly glossed by Cg (cf. *hemacakra* in reference to Khara's chariot, 21.14).

19. "to his breast" *aṅkena*: See note on 2.66.4 for this often misunderstood word (Cg, "at the thighs"; Ck, "at the hips, that is, with his other arms").

"boarded" *āropayat*: I take the causative here as *svārthe* (see note on 26.20 above), insofar as Sītā is still in his arms in the next verse (the commentators are silent).

Hereafter the NE version inserts the following verse:

> It was at the hour when it is half day and half night, when the sun is half set and the moon half risen that the *rākṣasa* seized Vaidehī, like a *śūdra* seizing the revelation of the *veda*. (926*)

20. "Sītā screamed at the top of her voice" *aticukrośa . . . sītā*: "Sītā's magical shadow [see above, 43.34 note] also has the power to mimic human behavior," Ct.

23. "Lakṣmaṇa": That Sītā should summon Lakṣmaṇa at this juncture is inconsistent unless we assume a degree of remorse on her part for which we have not been prepared (cf. 54.32 and note); it is additionally odd coming between verses 24 and 26, which are clearly addressed to Rāma. But there are no variants in the manuscripts.

"who can change his form at will" *kāmarūpiṇā*: The reading, adopted by the crit. ed., is supported principally by D6, several B manuscripts, and G2,3 along with Ct. Most of the SR (the NR diverges here) offers *mām amarṣiṇā*, "(is carrying) me off in implacable anger," "that is, over the death of Khara," says Cg implausibly, for how is Sītā to know this? We must have the pronoun *mām* ("me") here somewhere, although the reading of the line as transmitted in the S version is weak. One conjecture that suggests itself is *amarṣiṇīm* ("against my will," which seems to be the meaning of the adjective in 5.29.8, *amarṣāpahṛtā jānakī rāvaneṇa*).

24. "life's pleasures" *jīvitaṃ sukham*: The hendiadys is paralleled elsewhere in the *Rām*; see note on 2.18.22.

26. "But no" *na tu*: So I read, for the *nanu* of the crit. ed., with Crā, Cg (misreported by the crit. ed.), Ck, and most S manuscripts. The verse supplies the reason why Rāma (or Lakṣmaṇa) cannot immediately punish Rāvaṇa (so Cg, Ck). Contrast the view of retribution articulated in 28.9 above.

27. The verse is addressed to Rāvaṇa; the NE version tries to ease the transition by identifying him as the subject. For other cases of sudden change in addressee see 2.11.6, 52.22 and note, 53.24. Such shifts sometimes certainly result from manuscript confusion; in the present instance, however, it may serve to indicate a dramatic disorientation in Sītā's thinking, as suggested by verse 22 above.

28. "Kaikeyī . . . must be satisfied" *sakāmā . . . kaikeyī*: Despite Rāma's prohibition against doing so (15.34–35), Sītā blames her mother-in-law for her troubles both here and later in the epic (6.23.4ff.).

"has been taken" *hriyeyam*: Apparently a passive with active termination, though there is little call for the optative (see also Böhtlingk 1887, p. 220), unless we have a case of double sandhi (*hriye iyam* > *hriya iyam* > *hriyeyam*). The NR offers the reasonable *hriye 'ham*.

30. "tell" *śaṃsadhvam*: The plural verb, here and in verse 31, is explained by Cr as referring to the different animate parts of the mountain (or river). The NE ver-

sion reads the singular in both places. Ck considers the two verses to be interpolations, and they are in fact missing from several manuscripts of the NE, NW, and S versions (though the editor unjustifiably assumes haplography).

35. In an SR insertion hereafter Sītā sees Jaṭāyus, but warns that Rāvaṇa is too powerful for the vulture to attempt to stop by force (937*).

Sarga 48

1. Cg remarks, "The story of Jaṭāyus is presented in these two *sargas* [48, 49] in order to reaffirm for people the ideal that a servant must subordinate his own interests as far as he is able to those of his master." According to 41.49 Jaṭāyus was to help guard Sītā, and that he did not immediately come to her aid but was off sleeping in a tree is something the NR attempted to explain by the insertion noted on 16.3 (and to some extent again here in interpolation 939*, which shows the vulture to be on a "lovely mountain outcropping"), though see 41.49 note. The *Rāmopākhyāna* does not introduce Jaṭāyus at all until this point in the narrative (*MBh* 3.263.1), and this together with the narrative problems does suggest that the previous encounter (13.1ff.) is a later addition (though how Sītā would know to address him by name here would remain unexplained; there is no evidence, however, that the entire Jaṭāyus episode is "a clumsy interpolation in honor of Rāma," as Hopkins asserted, 1915, p. 211). Jaṭāyus's afternoon napping—he is some 60,000 years old, after all (verse 19)—might be taken as justifying his dilatoriness to some extent. And the poet certainly does seem to wish to enhance this image of the aged grandfather by lending a kind of homiletic, Nestorian quality to his discourse.

3. "puts his trust in truth" *satyasaṃśrayaḥ*: Ck, Ct, and several manuscripts read instead *satyasaṃśravaḥ*, "whose promise is true," that is, his promise to protect Sītā (13.34).

It is noteworthy that Jaṭāyus knows Rāvaṇa—he recognizes him immediately (see also verse 10 and note below)—sharing in this respect the knowledge possessed by his brother Sampāti, who will later inform the monkeys of the whereabouts of Sītā (4.57.19ff.). On this see Goldman and Masson 1969.

6. "and a king's wife at that" *viśeṣeṇa rājadārā*: Sexual intercourse with a king's wife is, according to the commentators, comparable to incest (Cm, Ct, Ctr [who cites one Vyāghra]).

7. "what others would censure" *yat paro 'sya vigarhayet*: I translate the reading of the crit. ed. (thus Cm, Cg, Ck, Ct, Cr), although it seems unusually vacuous even for a simple homiletic on consensual morality (as well as tautologous, amounting to little more than "a wise man should not do what he should not do"). Nor does it construe at all well with *pādas* cd, which suggest that the intended sense is: the wise man is to treat others as he would be treated. The conjectural *parasya* (or, *pareṣu*), or the reading attested in NE manuscripts, *pareṣām* (though the intention here is somewhat different), would offer the more intelligible, "[A wise man should not do] what he would censure in someone else."

8. "according to how kings behave" *anu rājānam*: The classical doctrine of the *dharmaśāstras* is that questions not treated in the *śāstras* themselves are to be determined in accordance with "the conduct of the good" (*sadācāra*) or, sometimes, "the learned" (*śiṣṭa*). Insofar as the king may be both, he could be said to establish the standard. But I believe we have here a somewhat earlier stage of development in

the doctrine of the foundations of moral conduct, that typified in the *Mahābhārata*, which repeatedly claims that the king is the source of all *dharma* (see, for example, 12.63.25ff., 12.68.8). See the Introduction, Chapter 4, and for the idea itself, *Rām* 2.101.9 and note, and above, 39.10.

"righteousness" *dharmam*: The location of the word in the verse is unusual. There seems to be no metrical exigency for it; perhaps it is a position of emphasis. Various manuscripts attempt emendation.

9. "the ultimate repository of wealth" *dravyāṇāṃ cottamo nidhiḥ*: A periphrasis for *artha*. Cg notes, "People behave in accordance with righteousness, or contrary to it, depending on how the king himself behaves."

"conduct" *dharmaḥ*: Here the word clearly must have a much broader sense than normally: a way of being, or acting.

10. "How could you possibly have secured your lofty position of power" *kathaṃ tvam . . . aiśvaryam abhisaṃprāptaḥ*: If kings are the standard of morality, then obviously only the good should be kings, hence Jaṭāyus's amazement. Again the vulture-king seems to be rather well acquainted with Rāvaṇa.

"a celestial chariot" *vimānam*: These appear to be awarded, in the first instance, to the dead in recognition of their beneficent life on earth (cf. 2.58.42). Perhaps here we have also the implicit criticism that Rāvaṇa has no right to the Puṣpaka chariot.

11. "Indeed" *kāmam*: The adversative particle has decisive manuscript support, whereas *kāmasvabhāvaḥ* not only does not occur in the *Rām* but also introduces an unnecessary restriction in the verse, against which the generalizing *yo yasya* also argues. (Perhaps it originates in a scribal reminiscence of *pāpasvabhāvaḥ* in the previous verse.) For this restrictive use of *kāmam* in the emphatic initial position see 2.4.26.

"The noble . . . linger" *ārya āvasati*: Such or the plural (*āryā āvasanti*, or, *nivasanti*) is probably the correct reading here (for the misprinted critical text, and mistaken editorial emendation, Bhatt 1963, p. 408; Cg does read *āryam*, glossing it "the instruction of the good" [which "does not dwell long in the 'abode,' that is, the heart, of the wicked"], but I find no attestation of the neuter *āryam* as substantive). The line is problematic, but the point of the rhetorical figure of "substantiation" (*arthāntaranyāsa*) seems to be that the evil man may "entertain" or try to cultivate a beneficent character, but it can never become a permanent trait of his personality (the whole verse answering the implicit objection: Once evil, always evil? Might Rāvaṇa not perhaps have changed [and so become worthy of kingship, verse 10]?).

13–14. Like Jaṭāyus, Rāvaṇa's younger brother Vibhīṣaṇa will later assert that Rāma has done no wrong to Rāvaṇa, since Khara merely got what he deserved; and like the vulture-king he, too, will ignore what was done to Śūrpaṇakhā (6.9.13–15).

15. "with his . . . eye" *cakṣuṣā*: Presumably with his evil eye (cf. for example *MBh* 2.71.3), rather than with the fiery ascetic power emanating from a "third" eye. Cg notes, "The implication is that Rāma could slay him with a mere glance," and this hardly seems to be a dead metaphor (for "wrathful glance" or something of the sort).

"as . . . Vṛtra": See 29.28 note above.

19. "the kingship of my fathers and forefathers" *pitṛpaitāmahaṃ rājyam*: Jaṭāyus succeeded to the kingship of the vultures even though his brother, Sampāti, was the elder of the two (cf. 4.56ff. and vulgate 3.58.2, 11); another example of the pervasive theme of the "disqualified elder" (cf. Pollock 1986, pp. 13ff. and note 12).

20ff. Jaṭāyus's reflections seem complicated by the fact that he may be thinking of two things at once: Rāma's returning and fighting (verses 22, 23) and his own fighting in the event Rāma does not return (verses 20, 21, 24ff.).

21. "rob the *vedas* of their plain sense by arguments tricked out with logic" *hetubhir nyāyasaṃyuktair dhruvāṃ vedaśrutīṃ*: For the sin of trying to interpret away the clear sense of the *vedas* by means of logic see note on 2.94.33. Ctr (p. 185) appositely cites the *KāṭhU* (1.2.9): "Not by reasoning is this thought to be attained." Cg extends the simile even further: "Just as the man who would alter the sense of the *vedas* perishes while the *vedas* themselves remain unharmed, so by stealing away Sītā will Rāvaṇa perish while no harm will come to Sītā. Such is the deeper meaning." Cm observes, "The power with which Rāvaṇa is endowed is as illusory as the force of logical argumentation. He cannot steal away Sītā, who will herself destroy him, just as the *veda* in the course of time overrules logical reasoning."

22. "fight" *yuddhyasva*: (More properly *yudhyasva.*) Fight, that is with Rāma (thus, also, Cg's third interpretation); see verse 23d.

23. "who has often killed *daityas* and *dānavas*" *asakṛt . . . yena nihatā daityadānavāḥ*: Although the verse is missing in NE manuscripts, the editor may be correct in inferring haplographic omission there, rather than interpolation elsewhere. For all that, the verse is still unusual, since Rāma nowhere is said to have accomplished such feats (see, however, Sumitrā's words in 2.39.11). The implication of the lines, for Ct, is that "Rāma is the supreme Lord," which is the significance of the citation adduced by Cg, "He is therefore said to be 'the deity that stands above both gods and *dānavas*' " [cf. *ParaS* 23.47], and how it was understood by Hopkins, who took it as another sign that the whole episode of Jaṭāyus is a later insertion (1915, p. 211).

24. Jaṭāyus here realizes that his challenge to Rāvaṇa to wait and fight Rāma is absurd: It is precisely for fear of Rāma that Rāvaṇa is hurrying off. This convinces him that he must take matters into his own hands (verses 25ff.).

Sarga 49

2. "wearing earrings" *-kuṇḍalaḥ*: It is remarkable how frequently attention is called to the jewelry worn by the *rākṣasas* (in the *Araṇyakāṇḍa* alone, cf. 24.20, 25.7, 30.9, 33.8, 36.2, 36.13, 42.16, 47.7, 57.24). What is unclear, however, is the significance we should attribute to this detail.

4. "garlanded" *mālyavatoḥ*: Cm, Cg, Ck, Ct understand this instead as a proper name, "the two Mount Mālyavans," one in the Daṇḍaka forest, one in Kiṣkindhā (or, according to Cm, Ct, on the flank of Meru). I agree with Cr; cf. 47.30, where the word is glossed as an adjective by Cg and the *ṭīkā* on Cm, and 5.56.14.

"when they still had wings" *sapakṣayoḥ*: Mountains are supposed to have had wings until Indra chopped them off (see the note on 2.83.19).

6–7. "(shower of arrows,) Rāvaṇa's missiles" (*śarajālāni*) . . . *rāvaṇāstrāṇi*: The appositive is out of style; the emendation *rāvaṇāstāni* ("shot by Rāvaṇa") easily suggests itself (see also Ct), but is not reported by the crit. ed. to have any manuscript support.

11. Hereafter the NW version (963*, so the NE [968*] and the SR [969*] after verse 14) adds that Jaṭāyus slays Rāvaṇa's charioteer (cf. verse 15 and note below).

11–12. "shield" *śarāvaram*: See De 1958, p. 1145; less likely "quiver" (suggested by some commentators on 63.17 below).

15. "charioteer and team all dead" *hatāśvo hatasārathiḥ*: The quarter verse is strictly formulaic (see, for example, 27.29 above, 6.34.28; *MBh* 6.49.28, 109.16, etc.; note here *-aśva-*, "horses," though only asses have been referred to), and so we need not be too troubled that no charioteer has previously been mentioned (see above 11 note, though also 33.4ff.); the SR, however, feels it has to add a verse later to account for him (see 60.33 note). Or perhaps the charioteer would simply be assumed to be present, insofar as heroes as a rule do not drive their own chariots.

23. "upon their ashram" *āśramasyāsya*: "By the word 'ashram' is meant the woman in the ashram, as in the [metonymical] locution, 'the stands cheered,' " Cg. The larger term is used apparently to underscore the heinousness of the attack, made against men not on the field of battle.

24. "taking the route of a thief" *taskarācarito mārgaḥ*: The charge will be repeated by Rāma when he faces Rāvaṇa in combat (6.92.17).

26. "When a man's end is near" *paretakāle*: The verse may seem self-contradictory, since it combines two notions: (a) at the hour of his death a man behaves irrationally (see, for example, 2.98.51, and below, 51.15; so Venkatanathacharya here, "Only if one's death were near would one do such a deed," 1965, p. 351 note); (b) irrational behavior brings about one's death, or perhaps better, seals one's fate (Cg, "from doing this type of deed he will necessarily and without delay meet death"). And yet one wonders whether the SR, whose reading was accepted by the crit. ed., did not actually misunderstand (falsely harking back to *paretakalpān* in 39.20) an original preserved in the NR, *parītakālaḥ* (which I take as *pūrvanipāta* for the metrically more awkward *kālaparīta-*, "harried, beset, by Doom"), which finds some support in the *MBh*: *parītakālān iva naṣṭasaṃjñān*, "like men beset by Doom, and [so] driven mad" (6.73.43; cf. *parītāḥ kāladharmaṇā*, 14.53.21).

27. "not the lord of the world himself, the . . . Self-existent Brahmā" *lokādhipatiḥ svayaṃbhūḥ*: That is, not even he (or they, according to Ck, Ct, who understand the first epithet to refer to Indra) who apportions the fruit of good and evil deeds.

28. "upon the back" *pṛṣṭhe*: "By this specification we gather that Rāvaṇa has ignored Jaṭāyus and is fleeing," Cg.

34. "with fists and feet" *muṣṭibhyāṃ caraṇābhyām*: Note the dual, which the poet generally uses in reference to Rāvaṇa (for eyes, hands, arms; thus consistently in 5.8.13–20), unless he means particularly to emphasize the *rākṣasa*'s multilimbed physical form.

35. "incomparable in strength" *atulavīryayoḥ*: Or, very possibly, "whose powers were not equal."

40. "bird" *patraratham*: Literally, "with wings for chariot," a not-uncommon kenning but here used with pathetic irony now that Jaṭāyus's wings have been severed.

Sarga 50

3. "Whenever good or evil is about to befall" *sukhaduḥkheṣu*: I agree with Cr in taking this compound independently; Cm, Cg, Ck, Ct construe it closely with *nimittam* ("a portent of good or evil"), which I find improbably awkward.

"signs perceived" *lakṣaṇajñānam*: Such as twitches and the like (Ck adds such things as seeing oneself crooked-headed or headless in a mirror or water), which are considered to be portents (and which Rāma will in fact perceive, though not in time, *sarga* 55), so Cm, Cg, Ct. The reading is disputed, however, and some manuscripts or commentaries or both understand *jñānam* separately, "a sudden premonition" (so Cv; Ck, Ct read instead [*lakṣaṇaṃ*] *svapnam*, "[signs and] dreams," but of course Rāma is not at present asleep).

"birds of omen seen or heard" *śakunisvaradarśanam*: Less likely Cm, Cg, who analyze the second element as a *tatpuruṣa*, " 'the sight,' that is, perception 'of the sounds of birds' "; I am supported in part by Ct, Cr.

5. "could hear" *śṛṇvatām*: Expect the dual (cf. 67.20 note below for further examples of the epicism). Cm explains, "(she cried as one might if people 'were nearby and) could hear' " (Ct, " 'so that only those in the vicinity might hear': that is, lest Rāma come too soon [and the divine plan of slaying all the *rākṣasas* be frustrated]").

7. "a massive tree" *mahādrumān*: I do not understand the use of the well-attested plural: one cannot simultaneously cling to many large trees. Or are we to take it distributively, "one tree after another"? Uncertain, I translate as singular.

9. "from end to end" *amaryādam*: Literally, "without limits." The commentators, perhaps rightly, all interpret figuratively ("the world became 'without limits,' " the natural limits, or better, specific natures, of things had been overstepped), but this makes little sense without the interpolation that follows ("The wind did not blow, the sun did not shine," 996*), unless the insertion was made precisely to explain the function of the qualification. (The usage in 60.46 may be thought to support this.)

10. " 'What had to be done' " *kāryam*: The necessary outrage on the part of Rāvaṇa that would provoke the implacable enmity of Rāma. On the issue of the "divine plan" and its central (and authentic) presence in the *Rām*, see above, 4.19 note.

11. "shuddered (and trembled)" *prahṛṣṭā* (*vyathitāḥ*): Many S manuscripts (including the vulgate) seem to mistake the meaning of *prahṛṣṭa-* here and, taking it in its more usual sense ("shivered," that is, with joy), are forced to interpolate "knowing that Rāvaṇa was now doomed to meet with destruction" (997*; see also the NW variants for the end of the *pāda*, *muditāḥ*, *paramapritāḥ*, "delighted," "overjoyed"), and this is how Cm, Cg, Ck, Ct, Cr interpret also. There is no need to assume joy on the part of the seers; *prahṛṣṭa-* in a negative sense (which its collocation with *vyathita-*, "trembled," seems to necessitate) is attested elsewhere in the *Rām* (see above, 42.19, and 56.20 and note below), and cf. *MBh* 14.65.10.

12. "flew up into the sky" *jagāmākāśam*: Obviously there is a fundamental uncertainty, if not inconsistency, in the poet's conception of the *rākṣasa*. He has emphasized the wonders of his aerial chariot repeatedly (cf. for instance 40.6, 49.14), and yet here Rāvaṇa is able to fly without it (Jaṭāyus has destroyed it [49.15] and Rāma is shortly to find it [60.32]; Bhoja has Rāvaṇa mount a second flying chariot, which just happens to be at hand, *RāmāCam* p. 195).

13ff. Cg explains the various implications of these verses: Sītā will remain in Rāvaṇa's grasp only so long as lightning in a cloud (verse 13); Rāvaṇa will suffer for his taking hold of Sītā (verse 14); Rāvaṇa's power will quickly crumble (verse 15); the copper cloud is like an omen presaging the death of Rāvaṇa [like the red clouds that appear at the end of a cosmic age].

13. "flashing from a storm cloud" *saudāmanī*: The phrase *vidyut saudāmanī* is for-

mulaic; the second element is obscure. My translation derives from the lexicographically attested definition of *sudāman* as "cloud."

15. With an insertion hereafter (1001*) the NE version recalls the garment, cream, and wreaths given Sītā by Anasūyā, remarking how they shone in the sky (see 2.110.17 and note).

16. "midday" *ātape*: So Cg. Cm, Ck, Ct, Cr gloss instead " 'half light' [*ā* in the sense of *iṣat*], that is, twilight, for it is then that clouds take on a coppery color" (a meaning that is unattested).

18cd–20. "streaked with tears" *vyapamṛṣṭāsram*: Literally, "in which the tears have been (partly) wiped away" (so basically Cm, Ct, Cr; Cg, "with unceasing tears"; Ck, "with tears not wiped away").

"quivering before" *-samādhūtam*: So Cg, Cr; contrast the more literal use of the verb in verse 25 below.

21. "star" *kāñcī*: Literally, "gleaming line, or, band." Although the word is nowhere attested in this sense, the *Dhātupāṭha* (1.182–83) glosses *kaci, kāci dīptibandhanayoḥ*, and this is partially reflected in the D1 variant *lekhā*, "shining streak." For a fuller analysis of the problem, and the impossibility of the traditional interpretation, see Pollock 1983.

22. "Fair as a lotus, golden hued" *padmagaurī hemābhā*: Cg attempts to distinguish the two epithets: "The first suggests her delicacy, the second the permanence of the hue of her complexion."

23. "pure" *vimalaḥ*: Cg, Ck read instead *sacapalaḥ*, "flashing (with lightning)."

24. "A shower of blossoms" *puṣpavṛṣṭiḥ*: Ct here criticizes Ck, whom he reports (it is not found in the edition of Ck) as offering the interpretation that these flowers are rained down by the gods, in thanks that the Mother (Sītā) has fulfilled their wish (of allowing herself to be the catalyst for the destruction of the demons). Ct claims the gods could have no such power in the presence of Rāvaṇa, and that on the contrary these are the flowers Sītā is wearing, which Rāma will recognize later (60.17).

28. This verse appears to be out of place; several S manuscripts and commentators (Cm, Cg, Ck) read it after verse 22.

"fair" *-raktā*: Thus Cg ("the word is used simply in the sense of 'colored'), not, as usually, 'red' " (so Ck and Ct, who adds "red because of her deep anger").

29. "Vaiśravaṇa's younger brother" *vaiśravaṇānujaḥ*: "The repeated use of the phrase [see verse 26] is meant to suggest the utter impropriety of the deed and thereby intimate that retribution for it will be swift in coming," Ct (heinous crimes must be paid for in this very life, see note on 28.8–9 above). For the poet's skillful use of kinship terms, which encourages us to recognize a fundamental continuity (or discontinuity) of behavior in the people linked by the term, cf. the note on 2.72.1.

30. "when their . . . merit has been exhausted" *kṣīṇāḥ*: Abbreviated for *kṣīṇapuṇyāḥ*, as in 5.15.20 (similarly explained by Ck, Ct). After death, beings may attain the rank of stars by reason of the meritorious conduct (cf. 6.23.19); when their store of merit is exhausted, they must reenter the cycle of rebirth (apparently the popular explanation of shooting stars, see 2.106.11 and note).

31. "descending from heaven" *gaganāc cyutā*: The Ganges was brought down from heaven by Rāma's ancestor Bhagīratha, see *Bālakāṇḍa* 41–42.

32. For an image similar to the one found here and in verse 35 see 2.40.28 and note (Rāma's departure from Ayodhyā).

33. "sighs rising from their vaporous waters" *jalocchvāsāḥ*: I believe the crit. ed.'s *gatotsāhām* ("whose energy [to resist] is gone," that is, "yielding") to be an incorrect reading both on textual grounds (it is based only on the undistinguished manuscripts T1 and D6, and on Ct) and because of the contextual indications offered by verses 32 and 35. D4, whose reading I adopt, appears to preserve the truth, or something very like the truth; *-ucchvāsa-* itself, furthermore, is widely represented in the manuscripts. The commentators are divided: Cm is close to me, reading *gatocchvāsāḥ*, "(the rivers) 'sighing' from their seeing Sītā in such a plight"; so Ck, who glosses "whose life breaths have departed" (absurdly Ct, "because in fear of Rāvaṇa their waters have dried up"); Cg reads *gatocchvāsām*, "(Maithilī who had) fainted."

38–39ab. "frightened little creatures" *vitrastakāḥ*: Not, I think, an otiose *ka-* suffix (so Cg, Ck, Ct), or a frequentive (Roussel 1910–1912, p. 45), but one signifying pity (by *Pā* 5.3.76).

40cd–41. "defiant" *manasvinīm*: *Manasvin* is one of the more indeterminate epithets among the poet's vast store. The signification I give it here (deriving from the radical sense "spirited") gains support from 6.74.10 (see also 5.50.15, 16). Cg glosses "firm-hearted," that is, faithful to her husband.

Sarga 51

5. "For didn't you proclaim your name and conquer me in battle" *viśrāvya nāmadheyaṃ hi yuddhe nāsmi jitā tvayā*: An example of pure sarcasm such as this is rare in the *Rām* (Sītā repeats it, however, in 5.20.22). Rāvaṇa "proclaims his name" in 45.22 above (but not, of course, as a hero on the field of combat) and "conquers" Sītā "in battle," but only against an old bird. The commentators do not carry the sarcasm into the second half of the verse (and so understand, "You did not proclaim . . .").

8. "you bragged about" *tvayā kathitam*: See 47.3ff. (so Cg).

9. "What can be done when you are fleeing so fast" *kiṃ śakyaṃ kartum evaṃ hi yaj javenaiva dhāvasi*: The hemistich refers back to verse 8: Rāvaṇa's (claim to) courage is meaningless if he runs from a fight. (Such is essentially Cm's second explanation).

12. "will send you to your destruction" *vidhāsyati vināśāya*: *Contra* Cm, Cg, Ck, Ct, " 'will make,' namely, an effort, 'to kill you' " (Cr, "will find a way").

13. "object" *vyavasāyena*: "That is, to enjoy her sexually. The poet's expression shows delicacy," Cg.

15. "mortal" *martyaḥ*: The general sentiment of the line is formualic and proverbial, and so we might not want to make too much of the use of "mortal" here. It may be, however, that it is precisely to the marginal defect in Rāvaṇa's boon-won immortality that the poet wishes to draw our attention.

16. "on the point of death" *mumūrṣūṇām*: Compare note on 38.1. That simple futurity can in fact be the significance of the *kṛt* suffix *u* (cf. *Pā* 3.2.168) is shown by 6.36.34 (this semantic aspect is covered by *vārt.* 1 [*āśaṅkāyām*] on *Pā* 3.1.7).

17. "you must be seeing" *sampaśyasi*: The tense of the verb is probably truly present (cf. 45.33), in contrast to verse 18, where it is future (see verse 19). On seeing golden trees as a sign of imminent death, compare note on 45.33.

18. "Vaitaraṇī": A river in hell.

"forest leafed with sword blades" *khaḍgapatravanam*: Cg takes this as a proper name of a particular hell.

19. "the prickly silk-çotton tree" *śālmalīṃ tīkṣṇām*: From the various descriptions of it, the tree seems like our common honey-locust. Cm, Ck, Ct call it a "torture tree," and Cg remarks that one of the tortures to which Rāvaṇa shall be subjected in hell will be having to embrace such a tree, as a punishment for having embraced another man's wife. In his tour of hell, the *Mahābhārata* hero Yudhiṣṭhira beholds, in addition to the sword forest and the river running with blood, the silk-çotton tree, which is called a "torture device for evildoers" (*MBh* 18.2.25).

Sarga 52

1. "five great monkeys" *pañca vānarapuṃgavān*: The exiled monkey-prince Sugrīva and his four companions (cf. 4.6.7ff.). Very deftly the poet here introduces the principal characters of the coming book.

5. "Lake Pampā": This seems to be a lake, rather than a river or pond (cf. 69.5 below, and note on 5.16 above).

6. "shivered with delight" *susaṃhṛṣṭaḥ*: According to Cg, only after he was making for Laṅkā was Rāvaṇa "happy," for up until then he traveled with one eye on Rāma's ashram. Ct remarks, "Some commentators [e.g., Cm, see verse 29 below] explain that Rāvaṇa was 'happy' because he had [hereby] attained a means of death at the hands of Rāma; that without some egregious act of evil and, consequent upon it, the diminution of his merit, he could not bring about his death; and that, recognizing this, and being of a *tāmasa* behavior, he acted and spoke obscenely to Sītā, Mother though she is. But this interpretation does not accord with the poet's words in verse 29, 'In his delusion, the *rākṣasa* rejoiced,' or with those in 53.1."

9. "heaved" *parivṛtta-*: I agree with Cm; Ck, Ct, Cr understand, more or less, "ceased."

11. "death in bodily form" *rūpiṇīṃ mṛtyum*: It is rare that *mṛtyu* is feminine in gender, but see PW, s.v. 2 end.

12. "closely guarded" *saṃrūḍha-*: The commentators understand "crowded"; I suspect some confusion with *saṃruddha-*, as in *HariVaṃ* 96.62, *saṃruddhau rakṣibhiḥ*.

13. "as . . . Maya might deposit his demon magic" *mayo māyām ivāsurīm*: Maya is the preeminent *asura* architect and worker in magic (see 4.50.10ff.). The simile itself is odd in sense, but the alliterative wordplay and the apposite genders of the words (*maya-* being masculine, *māyā* feminine) mitigate this to some degree. (Cg, seeking to connect the simile with the story of Maya narrated in 4.50.9ff., explains, "Just as Maya, lord of the Triple City [to be distinguished, he tells us, from the architect of the *asuras*; see his comment on GPP 4.52.10–13], deposited the magically endowed woman [reading *striyam* for *āsurīm*] Svayamprabhā [an *apsaras*] in the cave," although neither in the *Rām* version of the story nor in the purāṇic account mentioned by Cg [*MatsyaP* 140.80ff.] does Maya appear to do this.) Ct observes, "By this is suggested that it was the magical, illusory form of Sītā that went to Laṅkā, the real Mother having entered fire, as implied before" (43.34 and note).

14. "*piśāca* women" *piśācīḥ*: The poet nowhere indicates that these creatures (which usually seem to be something akin to goblins) are in any way different from *rākṣasas*. The latter term is applied to them in verse 17 below.

15. "for such is my will" *macchandato yathā*: The *-tas* morpheme and *yathā* are

tautologous (cf. 40.5, *macchandād iva [bhāṣitam]*). The commentators differ: Cm, "by virtue of my permission" (*madanujñābalāt*; or should we perhaps read *madājñā-*, "of my order"?); Cg, " 'as' would be given to me 'according to my will, desire' "; Ck, " 'in order that' [*yathā*] she might be brought 'under my will, control.' "

18. "the boon" *vara-*: See above, 30.17–18, and Introduction, Chapter 4b.

28. "unmarked by the eye" *alakṣyadarśanāḥ*: Either because of their speed (Cg), or their powers of invisibility (Ct). No further mention of these *rākṣasas* will be made in the *Rām.* (The episode is otherwise suspect; Bhoja has the demons sent prior to the abduction of Sītā, *RāmāCam* p. 187, where the commentator notes the discrepancy).

29. "to have obtained" *upalabhya*: So in agreement with Cm, Ck, Ct, Cr, since the slight redundancy with what follows ("to be holding," literally, "having gotten") is not uncharacteristic of the poet (Cg glosses, "to have seen," a possible but unnecessary remedy).

"[and] to have incited" *prasajjya . . . ca*: Cg (endorsed by Venkatanathacharya 1965, p. 375 note) wants to interpret the conjunction, which I have left untranslated, concessively, "although (thereby) provoking." But see Rāvaṇa's words in verses 21–24, and above in *sarga* 34, especially verse 20 (and cf. verse 38.6): He wants not only to have Sītā in his possession but also to avenge Khara by killing Rāma.

Sarga 53

2. "Tortured . . . by the arrows of Kāma" *kāmabāṇasamarpitaḥ*: Possibly *paranipāta* (for *samarpitakāmabāṇaḥ*, though cf. 2.17.30), hence the many variants.

3. "his residence" *tadveṣma*: The women's quarters, according to Cg.

4–5. "open sea . . . gusting winds" *vāyuvegaiḥ . . . arṇave*: "The winds are meant to represent her grief, the sea [water] her tears," Ct.

7ff. According to Pax (1936, pp. 619, 621; cf. Liebich 1936, p. 33, who argues on the basis of Alberuni's image of Rāvaṇa's stronghold), the castle of Laṅkā was constructed like a maze or labyrinth (a point he invokes to tie in the tale with a variety of European romance). But I see little evidence in the poem itself for this judgment, beyond the more or less concentric construction of royal palaces in general (see 2.5.4 note).

7–9. "Drums . . . echoed" *-dundubhinirhrādam*: Cg wants the staircase itself to echo "like" a drum as they ascend it. But drums resounding in royal palaces is a commonplace of Sanskrit poetry (see, in the *Rām*, 2.34.36, 5.5.11).

14–15. "Myriads" *sahasram*: More often than not the word denotes merely a large number, "countless" as Ck sees (see also 2.2.6 and note). The other commentators predictably attempt various explanations for why this "thousand" does not stand in contradiction with the "thirty-two million."

22. "perfect" *sadṛśaḥ*: See note on 16.22.

"how soon youth passes" *yauvanaṃ hy adhruvam*: Similar is the sentiment later expressed by Rāma: "I feel so sad, not that my love is far away, or because I am brooding on how she was taken from me. The one reason I am grieving is that her youth is slipping away" (6.5.5).

24. I agree with Cg, Ct in seeing this verse as a substantiation, an elaboration of

the impossibility mentioned in the previous verse. Cr wants to link it to what follows.

26. "Let the waters of the royal consecration pour down upon you; reign in power" *anupālaya/abhiṣekodakaklinnā*: Rāvaṇa's offer to consecrate Sītā as ruler of Laṅkā is peculiar enough to have motivated a variety of artificial interpretations on the part of the commentators (for example, Ck, Ct, " 'Let the waters' of a pleasure bath 'pour down upon you,' " to be construed with the last quarter verse; according to Cg, Sītā would share in the consecration ceremony only in the sense that she would be chief consort of the consecrated king). Although the queen's participation in the rite of royal unction is nowhere indicated in the description of the ritual in the *Ayodhyākāṇḍa*, where Sītā plays no role, or in the vedic texts studied by Heesterman (1957), it is suggested by other passages in the *Rām* (6.38.6 and 14), and by the definition of "queen" given in *AmaK* 1.6.13 (*devī kṛtābhiṣekāyām,* " 'queen' is defined as one who has been consecrated"). But it may be that Rāvaṇa is in fact offering her sovereignty. There are numerous historical precedents in ancient India for women holding royal power, and literary examples, as in the Solar Dynasty itself (see *RaghuVa* 19.55–57, though here it may actually be the unborn child carried by the queen whom it is intended to consecrate). Note also the interpolation discussed in note on 2.33.12.

27. All demerit acquired from past misdeeds must be expiated by suffering in some future life; once that demerit has been consumed, one may proceed to enjoy the pleasure earned from one's past good deeds. (The parallel verse in the *MBh* [3.265.16] seems to be an imperfect recollection of the present passage.)

29–30. See note on 33.5ff.

32. "The feeling I have for you, my lady" *devi niṣyando yas tvām abhigamiṣyati*: In the main I follow the interpretation of Ck (Ct), and accordingly read *devi* (it has overwhelming manuscript support), for the crit. ed.'s *daiva-* (*niṣyandaḥ*), which seems pointlessly reiterative ("He who is coming to you is an offspring of the gods, of a seer" [thus the editors of the Mylapore edition], is implausible despite the parallel in *MBh* 3.265.14). Problems, however, remain. *niṣyanda-* in the transferred sense ("outpouring" of emotion, "feeling,") appears not to be attested elsewhere in the *Rām*, and indeed the one parallel I am able to find is contained only in the eastern recension of the *HariVaṃ*, *bhāvaniṣyandaḥ* (cf. the variants on 63.29). The force of the future also remains unexplained (although Rāvaṇa may merely be thinking of the long duration of his amorous feelings; Ck construes *abhi* closely with *tvām* ["affection for you"], and reads as the main verb *bhaviṣyati*, "will be [in accordance with the teachings of the *vedas*]").

"sanctioned by the *vedas*" *ārṣaḥ*: One of the forms of marriage mentioned in the *dharmaśāstras* is the *rākṣasa* marriage, taking a woman by force (cf. *ManuSm* 3.33). This, Rāvaṇa seems to be asserting, is appropriate to him and so in accordance with *dharma* (see also 5.18.5; Ck, Ct are quick to point out that the śāstric precept applies to unmarried girls only, and Rāvaṇa's defending his actions on such grounds only demonstrates all the more clearly how blinding is his lust). A different passage is cited by Cg, which lists the seven types of women who are permitted second marriages (see *NāraSm* 15.45), but this is less to the point.

33. This scene harks back to Book Two (10.40–41) when the lovesick and heartbroken Daśaratha bows down to touch his head to the feet of Kaikeyī. And as the

abasement of Daśaratha before a woman (that is, his sexual immoderation) was rewarded with death, so too will Rāvaṇa's.

"heads" *śirobhiḥ*: Contrast the singular in the next verse, and see note on 49.34 above.

34. "not (in vain does Rāvaṇa)" *na cāpi* (*rāvaṇaḥ*): The particles require us to carry over *śūnya-* as adverb from the previous line.

Sarga 54

1. "placing a straw between them" *tṛṇam antarataḥ kṛtvā*: It might not at first appear that the commentators' concrete explanation is compelling, namely, that she interposed an actual straw between herself and Rāvaṇa, chaste woman that she was, in order to avoid speaking face to face with another man (Cm, Cg, Ck, Ct, Cs, Cr). But this is supported by Ctr on 5.19.3 with the following citation from the *SkandaP*, "A woman should never even hear the name of another man; and if she must unavoidably do such a thing as speak with him, she should interpose a straw between them," and in his note on the parallel passage in *Rām* 5.19.3, Jhala (1966, p. 481) appositely adduces Bhāsa's *DūtVā* 35.3, *tṛṇāntarābhibhāṣyo bhavān*, "You are a person to be addressed only through an interposed straw." Alternatively we have an idiom, "without caring a straw" (that is, either for what he just said, or for the consequences of what she is about to say), perhaps literally, "putting a straw within" (that is, in the scales), for *tṛṇa-* is so often used elsewhere as signifying "worthless" (cf. *Rām* 5.56.71, *tṛṇavat bhāṣitaṃ tāsāṃ gaṇayām āsa*, "didn't care a straw what they said," or *MBh* 6.109.32. PW, s.v. *antara-* suggests "in her heart looking on him as a straw."

Why does Rāvaṇa not simply force Vaidehī to make love to him, as he forced her to come to Laṅkā? Ck argues that Rāvaṇa is mindful of the curse upon him of his nephew Nalakūbara (in consequence of Rāvaṇa's rape of the *apsaras* Rambhā, *Uttarakāṇḍa* 26, especially 43ff.; cf. note on 47.15 above) that Rāvaṇa would die if he ever again made love to a woman against her will (Ct notes, "and that is why Sītā here is said to be 'unafraid' "). Ck continues, "And so Sītā was completely untouched, and after being upheld as such by all the gods, was in the end taken back by Rāma. Mother Vaidehī cannot be suspected of any breach whatever."

7. "Their bodies" *śarīram*: The singular (as Cr also sees) has collective force (*jātyekavacanam*).

11. Sītā's boasting of Rāma's powers reminds one of nothing so much as Rāvaṇa's boasting of his own (47.3 above).

12. "You shall lose" *gata-*: The past participle has again an aspect of immediate futurity (see note on 16.21 above).

Cg cites from *smṛti*: "One's life, strength, fame, and wealth instantly perish when one molests another man's wife" (untraced; cf. *ManuSm* 4.134).

14. "has divine powers" *daivatasaṃyuktaḥ*: I agree with Cg on this somewhat unusual phrase (Cm implausibly, "The fates are favorable to him"; many S manuscripts and Ck, Ct, Cr read *devarasaṃyuktaḥ*, "has my brother-in-law with him," see verse 32); see also below, 66.11, *devaprabhāva-*, "who has the powers of a god." See also the Introduction, Chapter 4d.

21. "harsh . . . that made her shudder with horror" *paruṣaṃ romaharṣaṇam*: The *pāda* is best taken with what follows rather than what precedes (so Cr); if Sītā spoke

harshly (verse 20), so does Rāvaṇa (verse 23), and his speech is called "horrific" with more propriety than Sītā's. (For a comparable construction see above, 46.1 and note there.)

22. Cg notes, "Sītā was abducted in the month of Caitra, since at the end of one year [to the month] Rāvaṇa is slain. Thus we conclude that Rāma stayed for three years in Pañcavaṭī. The description of late winter (*sarga* 15) must therefore be meant to indicate the particularly high degree of Rāma's asceticism and does not signify [the time at which] Śūrpaṇakhā comes upon him." Cf. above, note on 40.28cd-29ab.

31. "in grief" *śoka-*: In punning contrast to the *aśoka* ("griefless") grove.

32. "beloved brother-in-law" *dayitaṃ . . . devaram*: Here there is no question that the poet is suggesting remorse on Sītā's part (see 43.36, 47.23 and notes there).

Sarga 55

1. The NR inserts before this a *sarga* in which Brahmā explains to Indra that Sītā has entered Laṅkā for the good of the world; but lest she die in despair at Rāma's not being able to find her, Brahmā dispatches Indra to her. Indra arrives in Laṅkā with Sleep, who overpowers the *rākṣasa* guards. Indra assures Sītā that Rāma will come with an army of apes and monkeys, and slay Rāvaṇa, and that he himself will offer aid. Indra gives her celestial ghee supplied by Brahmā, by which she will maintain her health. She asks Indra for assurances of his identity, and he reveals his divine characteristics to her. Sītā praises the god, and consumes the proffered ghee (App. I, No. 12).

4. "from *rākṣasas* who might devour her" *rākṣasaiḥ bhakṣaṇaṃ vinā*: The syntax was too obscure for the NR, which reads, "from the *rākṣasas*, without Lakṣmaṇa" (*rakṣobhyo lakṣmaṇaṃ vinā*).

5. "But what if Lakṣmaṇa" *lakṣmaṇaḥ . . . yadi*: On conditional clauses without apodosis, see Speijer 1886, p. 371.

"in imitation (of my voice)" (*svaram*) *ālambya* (*māmakam*): The reading of the crit. ed., *ālakṣya*, seems to me a clearly inferior variant, and one that is unconstruable, as the commentaries of Cm, Ct, Cr show. I accept the text of the NW, NE, and several S manuscripts (including Cg); see also 57.12, *ālambya . . . svaram*, and 57.25, *svaram . . . ālambya*.

7–8. The syntactical structure here is somewhat loose, perhaps designedly so, to mirror Rāma's distraught and worried thoughts; one senses a kind of breathless rushing together of Rāma's ideas. The NR sought to normalize matters by rearranging the sequences of half verses.

"he turned back into a *rākṣasa*" *rākṣaso 'bhūt*: I agree with Cg, Ck, Ct in taking the noun predicatively. A possible alternative: "(only when he had led me far off) was the *rākṣasa* (struck)," for the fact that primarily confirms Rāma's suspicions seems to be that he could only slay the deer when he had been led far away (this despite verse 19 below, the point of which is different).

10. "hearing . . . and thinking" *śrutvā*: The continuative construes by zeugma also with *pāda* c, as Venkatanathacharya also perceives (1965, p. 396 note; *cintayan* refers back to verses 4ff., and can hardly govern *pādas* cd here).

11. The verse describes some of the omens that are appearing (and that Sītā had wondered about earlier, 50.3-4).

15. "sweet as ever . . . harsh" *madhurodarkam . . . paruṣam*: My analysis agrees with Cm's second explanation ("sweet in sound, but bitter in sense"); see also 50.40cd.

20. "has set out on her own" *pathi vartate*: That is, to look for Rāma herself (or perhaps, "has fled along the forest path"); *contra* Ck, Ct, " 'is on the road,' that is, is in the process of being stolen away."

Sarga 56

6. "for nothing" *mithyā*: Because without Sītā he will die there and never return (as is stated in the next verse). Possibly also, "(prove to be) false," that is, unfulfilled, because he will have died in grief for Sītā before the completion of the term of his exile (so Cm and, essentially, Ck, Ct; see also 59.7).

7. "when you are out of the way" *gate tvayi*: Literally, "with you gone" (though surely not "dead"). There is no license to interpret "with you returned to Ayodhyā" with Cm, Cg, Ck, Ct (for Kaikeyī is well aware of Lakṣmaṇa's close relationship with Rāma—compare 2.8.20, for example—as Venkatanathacharya points out, 1965, p. 400 note).

Cg comments, "Rāma had always felt that Kaikeyī sent him to the wilderness so that he would die, and this he reveals now, in light of the maxim, 'We learn what people really feel by what they say when they are asleep, drunk, or angry' " (see 2.47.7 note and 2.52.17, and contrast above, 15.34–35 and notes there).

8. "dear brother" *saumya* [*na*]: The editor of the crit. ed. points out in an addendum that the reading *saumyena* "([wait on her] carefully, politely," so Cm, Ck, Ct, "in the attitude of a slave") is perhaps to be preferred (Bhatt 1963, p. 410).

17. "I fear what I am sure to find" *śaṅke prāptavyam īdṛśam*: That is, the loss of Sītā. Ck understands something like " 'I am aware that such sorrow must be experienced,' in consequence of *karma*," and like Ct interprets the utterance, erroneously I believe, as an expression of Rāma's fortitude in suffering.

19. "hungry, tired, and thirsty" *kṣudhā śramāc caiva pipāsayā ca*: The instrumentals are *upalakṣaṇe*, as is the ablative, by attraction (Ct emends to instrumental).

This verse and the next anticipate and summarize the narrative of the next two *sargas* (so remarked also by Cm, Cg, Ck, Ct), a type of synoptic prefiguration of coming action (cf. 30.22 note). See further note on 57.1.

20. " 'It is so, then' " *etad tad*: Cv alone (citing "Others," none of whom is extant) reports this (to my mind obvious) signification. The other commentators seem to have been misled by the presence of *prahṛṣṭa(romā)* ("his flesh began to crawl"), which again has a negative sense (cf. 50.11 and note); impossibly, thus, Cg, Ck, Ct, "his hair bristled (with delight when he recalled) 'this and that' (joy they shared) in their pleasure spots."

"as he stood in their dwelling" *nivāsabhūmau*: Some verbal needs to be supplied; one alternative to the translation adopted, "he sank down upon the floor of their dwelling."

Sarga 57

1. The story here recommences back in the forest, on the return journey toward the ashram (which the brothers will not reach until *sarga* 58). Although the type of

prefiguration noted on 56.19 is not uncommon, this example is extreme, the chronology of the narrative being so emphatically violated. Nor are there any text-critical indications that this is not part of the authentic design of the work. It thus seems almost as if the poet so commiserated with the reader that he was reluctant to prolong the painful revelation of Rāma's loss. In any case the speedy resolution of the drama does allow him to deal in a more detailed (and leisurely) fashion with the attitudes of the characters.

"from the ashram . . . their way back" *āśramāt . . . antarā*: Thus I translate the crit. ed. in accordance with the interpretation of Cm, Cg, Ck, Ct. Perhaps, however, the reading of the NR (+M1), *āśramam*, is the correct one and to be explained as governed by *antarā*: "before [literally, between (the time they set out and)] the ashram was returned to."

3. "(sank knowing) that the . . . evil (it feared) was true" (*śaṅkamānam*) . . . *pāpaṃ yat satyaṃ (vyathitam)*: The clause is elliptical; it is presumably reduced from *yat pāpaṃ . . . tat satyam iti vyathitam*. This interpretation agrees basically with Cm (second gloss), but in general the commentators' analysis here requires a far too complex and improbable syntax.

4. "My left eye has been throbbing" *sphurate nayanaṃ savyam*: A bad omen.

5. "good Lakṣmaṇa" *lakṣmaṇaḥ śubhalakṣaṇaḥ*: A standard alliterative epithet of the prince (see Pollock 1986, p. 50), it here exhibits a more pointed narrative character, reinforcing the impression of Lakṣmaṇa's unimpeachable ethical behavior (Vālmīki often enlivens ornamental epithets into narrative significance, cf., for instance, 2.2.34 and note).

12. "for some reason" *kiṃnimittam*: Abbreviated *metri causa* for *kiṃcinnimittam* (so too in the opinion of Cm, Cg, Ct, Cr).

The immediate succession of two six-*pāda ślokas* is improbable; 12cd and 13ab should have been printed as a single verse.

15. "even if you bring about your brother's death" *vinaṣṭe bhrātari prāpte*: The syntagma is equivalent to *vināśe bhrātuḥ prāpte*.

17. "waiting for Rāghava to give you an opening" *rāghavasyāntaraprepsuḥ*: Although the words do not actually appear in *sarga* 43, where Sītā rebukes Lakṣmaṇa, they provide retrospectively a moment of fine narrative artistry. These are the words used of Rāvaṇa (44.8), and thereby bitterly ironic: Sītā is ensuring the very disaster she seeks to avoid. This is an irony the poet strives for elsewhere in the scene (see note on 43.8).

25. "words that carried far" *sudūrasaṃśravam . . . vacanam*: I agree with Cr in construing the adjective thus, rather than with *svaram* ("voice"), as do Cm, Cg, Ck, Ct.

Sarga 58

1. Cg here notes, "The composition has up to this point treated of [the aesthetic topic] love-in-union; now begins the treatment of love-in-separation, which will continue up to the point when Rāma climbs Mount Suvela [*Yuddhakāṇḍa* 20ff., where presumably the aesthetic sentiment *vīra*, "heroism," begins]. The other aesthetic sentiments dealt with in literature [wrath, terror, pity, etc.] are [also] depicted insofar as they are supplemental to love-in-separation. . . . Among the ten mental states of love-in-separation the eighth in particular, 'madness,' is what the poet will

deal with in the next three *sargas*." On the interpretation of Rāma's madness see the Introduction, Chapter 5.

Twitching in any part of the left side of the body, and tripping at the beginning of a journey, are evil portents.

4. "startled" *udbhraman*: Compare the use of the word in 37.17 and verse 33 below (Cm, Cg, "flying up"; Ct, "going about").

"lurched forward" *vikṣipan*: The intransitive use of the verb appears not to be elsewhere attested.

6–7. "with the trees rustling, almost seemed to weep" *rudantam iva vṛkṣaiḥ*: Presumably it is the rustling of the trees that gives the ashram the sound of weeping. (Confusingly the commentators: Cg, "[it seemed to weep because] the bees [in the trees] had lost their voices" [?]; Ck, "the trees seemed to be weeping because they had lost their beauty, and so the cottage seemed to be weeping, too").

"The flowers had faded, the birds and beasts had fallen still" *mlānapuṣpamṛgadvijam*: The zeugma is a rather hard one, but of a sort not without parallel (see notes on 27.6 and 55.10).

8. "afraid and hiding" *nilīnā . . . bhīruḥ*: As the adjective shows, the verbal cannot suggest playful hiding (as Cm, Cg wish it), in contrast to verse 23.

10ff. Here begins the mad search for Sītā, a magnificent scene that has inspired many great poets, notably Kālidāsa (*Vikramorvaśīya* Act 4), Bhavabhūti (*Mālatimādhava* Act 9), the composers of the *Viṣṇupurāṇa* (5.13.24ff., a significant improvement over the folktale treatment of the scene as preserved for us in the *Brahmapurāṇa* 189.22ff.), and—perhaps the finest adaptation of all—the *Bhāgavatapurāṇa* (10.30). It was presumably to such scenes as this that Hopkins was referring when he spoke of the "childish laments" of Rāma (1922, p. 264); the Indian tradition obviously did not see the matter that way. Besides the compliment paid by the adaptations already referred to, perhaps the most characteristic explicit evaluation of the emotional intensity the scene has had for Indian audiences is that made by the great playwright Bhavabhūti when he makes Lakṣmaṇa say, "The way my brother behaved, out of his senses when Janasthāna was left empty—it was enough to make a rock weep, to split a heart of adamant" (*UttaRāC* 1.28). See further remarks in the Introduction, Chapter 5.

10. "the look of a madman" *unmatta iva lakṣyate*: Cm remarks, "The particle expressing similitude is to be construed in every clause in this verse, as in the following, for in actual fact this is not a description of what really happens to Śrī Rāma. The lamentation for Sītā and all the rest is simply acting on the part of Rāma, in order to instruct people; and it is precisely to demonstrate this that the omniscient blessed Vālmīki here and there has employed words expressing similitude, in verse 4, for example, as well as here." To corroborate his position Cm quotes from the *Bhāgavatapurāṇa* (9.10.11ff.), on the didactic dimension of the scene of Rāma's madness (see Introduction, Chapter 5). Ct cites the same passage, but in support of the view that the point of the present scene is to suggest "that of all things in the world one's wife is the most beloved. That is why Rāma does not grieve as much when he is separated from his mother and father." (Ck seeks to refute Cm's interpretation, see notes on 59.1 and 60.38, and his editor asks the logically consequent question, why should people be taught to rave like a madman in such circumstances, rather than ~~show~~ firmness and calmness [Venkatanathacharya 1965, p. 412 note]). Cm adduces also the *Umāsamhitā* of the *Skandapurāṇa*, where Viṣṇu says, "'I

became the son of Daśaratha and slew Rāvaṇa in battle; and in my *avatāra* as Rāma I acted as if I were ignorant. Even the wise should not, because of *māyā*, entertain doubts about this. For I wanted to delude the *rākṣasa* with my *māyā* so that he would think me a man.' Otherwise that [*māyā*] could never affect him [Viṣṇu] in any way." Cm continues, "Furthermore, lamentation over diverse sorrows is a function of the belief that the body and so on constitute one's Self, and such a belief is founded upon ignorance. It is utterly impossible to maintain that any trace whatever of ignorance—even by reason of a curse from the great Bhṛgu—could attach to Śrī Rāma, the supreme Lord, the superintendent of ignorance (*māyā*), the supreme soul whose corporeality consists of being, consciousness, and bliss, and who incarnated himself in the form of a man in order to bestow release on all people by way of their listening to these stories of his divine play. Therefore, all such things, his banishment and the like, were performed by Śrī Rāma only to instruct people. And these interpretive guidelines are to be applied to other portions of the poem."

13. "Her breasts are as large as your fruits" *bilvopamastanī*: Cg cites the *Ratirahasya* to prove that this description of Sītā classifies her as the *padminī* or "lotus woman," the finest among the various female types mentioned in the erotological textbooks.

15. "for how lush its vines appear, its shoots and blossoms" *latāpallavapuṣpāḍhyaḥ*: None of the commentators really explains why this statement should justify the surmise of knowledge on the part of the *kakubha* tree. It must be either a general conceit—such flowering (which is often likened to horripilation) could only be the result of seeing the beautiful Sītā—or depend on the specific poetic convention that certain trees flower only when hugged or kissed by a beautiful woman (though I know of no example of the convention with regard to this particular tree).

16. The presence of the bees near the *tilaka* perhaps implies that the sweet Sītā must have passed near the tree (the commentators are silent).

17. "*Aśoka*, 'dispeller of grief' " *aśoka śokāpanuda*: The pun as at 54.31.

19. "rosy-golden glow" *jāmbūnadaprabhā*: The reading has only weak support. The NW (1124*) offers *jambūphaloṣṭhī*, "(her) whose lips are like rose-apples"; many S manuscripts, *jambuphalopamām*, "who is like rose-apples" (Cv, "in point of hue"; Cm, Cg, "with respect to her smoothness, not hue," the fruit of this tree being very dark; cf. McCann 1959, pl. 27).

22. Unlike the previous two verses this one posits no characteristic shared by Sītā and the tiger whereby the animal might recognize her; Cm, Cg do suggest that it is the similarity in their gait that is meant, but despite such later terms as *śārdulavikrīḍitā* ("the woman with the playful gait of a tiger," used as the name of a particular lyric meter), I do not think that is meant here.

"you have nothing to fear" *na te bhayam*: Rāma means to say that he is not now out hunting, and so the tiger need not run from him. There is no reason to assume that he believes the tiger to have devoured Sītā and is here reassuring it that he shall not exact vengeance (so Ck, Ct in essence; Cm, Cg more improbably, "Rāma supposes that all the other creatures have refused to speak because they are afraid; but the tiger 'has no fear' ").

23. "hiding" *ācchādya ca*: Although I leave it untranslated, I understand the particle *ca* as functioning concessively (with respect to *pāda* b, "I saw you, though you are hiding").

26. "the only reason" *hi*: Cm, Cg, Ck read *na* instead (unrecorded in the crit. ed.), "(surely she would) not (ignore . . .)."

29. "pale as the *campaka* flower" *campakavarṇābhā*: Literally, "the color of the *campaka* flower." Those that I have seen are pale white (contrast Ingalls 1965, p. 481, "yellow-red"); Ct reads "the color of sandalwood cream."

33. "compulsively" *balāt*: Literally, "by force," that is, under the power of someone or something else (differently Cr, Ct, "that is, as if driven before the wind"; Cg's interpretation of the verse as a whole is considerably different from mine: " 'In one place,' that is, even where there was no similarity between the object and Sītā, 'he was deluded,' by the 'impetus' of grief, into thinking he saw her; 'elsewhere,' in vines and so on, he was similarly deluded 'by the force' of similarity [between the object and Sītā]").

"wandering (like a madman)" (*unmatta iva*) *bhrāntaḥ*: So I read (with the NE, 1131*) for the crit. ed.'s (*unmatta iv)ābhāti* ("he seemed [like a madman]"). The variant construes reasonably with *kvacit* ("another [place]"), unlike the reading of the crit. ed. The triple anaphora of the verbal root *bhram* is not uncharacteristic of the poet (see notes on 2.25.2, 2.50.10).

35. "his hopes . . . remained unfulfilled" *aniṣṭhitāśaḥ*: Ck, Ct, Cr understand, "his hopes . . . not yet abandoned," but see Ck, Ct on 5.5.37 (they gloss the word *nirvṛtam, nivartitam*); see also *MBh* 2.3.34.

Ct again notes, "This behavior is wholly imitative (on Rāma's part) of the usual behavior of human beings; so much 'darkness and passion' [*tamas, rajas*] cannot be imputed to the Blessed One" (see above, note on verse 10).

Sarga 59

1. This *sarga*, according to Cg, illustrates the ninth stage of lovesickness, stupefaction (see 58.1 note). Ck remarks, "According to scripture, 'A wife is half of oneself' [*TaiS* 6.1.8.5], and so to be separated from a wife—especially one rich in treasures of every description—is nearly like losing half of oneself. The 'darkness' [*tamas*] generated because of this obscures the power of Rāma's 'purity' and 'passion' [*sattva, rajas*], and so the search and lamentation naturally result. For no material body can anywhere come into being that consists of pure *sattva* or pure *rajas*" (he adduces *BhagGī* 18.40). See 58.10 note.

14. "enchanted by the forest" *vanonmattā*: Thus in basic agreement with Cm, Ct, Cr; Ck's explanation strikes me as unlikely: "She has become a touch 'mad from' wandering in 'the forest,' and so has entered it without considering that it is a dangerous place."

15. "fish . . . and . . . rushes" *mīnavañjula-*: The NW reads instead *nīla-*, "dark rushes," perhaps with more propriety, as providing a reason why their vision might be obstructed.

20. "the mountain" *śailam*: Mount Prasravaṇa, cf. 29.21, 60.14 (thus too Cm, Cg).

22. "Bali": The *asura* Bali had gained control of the three worlds, and Viṣṇu, after tricking him (by means of his dwarf incarnation) into giving him as much land as he could cover in three strides, traversed the whole universe, then bound the demon and cast him from heaven (contrast the parallel version noted on 2.12.8). The formulaic, ornamental quality of this kind of simile (see Pollock 1986, p. 38) is again revitalized by the narrative homologies, the correspondences (for the poet and audience, not of course for Lakṣmaṇa) in respect of the characters of the

god(like) Rāma, the demonic Rāvaṇa, and the earth-born Sītā, and the very situation in which all three are found.

28. "tried . . . to comfort" *sāntvayām āsa*: Again the perfect has a conative aspect (see 43.36 note).

Sarga 60

1. Before this *sarga* the SR adds two additional *sargas*, devoid of any narrative interest but containing some attractive verses, including:

> There must be no second person on this earth who has done such evil deeds as I [in former births], for grief upon grief, in an endless series, comes upon me and tears my heart and mind to pieces. . . . The loss of kingship, separation from my people, the death of my father, separation from my mother: Each time I think about these things they fill me anew with grief. All these sorrows were assuaged when I came to the lovely forest; but separation from Vaidehī has rekindled them all, as a fire flares up when another log is added." (App. I, No. 13, lines 51–54, 59–66).

The NR inserts within the verse some lines in which Rāma addressed Śakra, complaining that Sītā has left him at the very time a young man should enjoy his wife, that the ashram has the look of a city when a festival has ended, etc. (1153*).

Ct again (see notes on 29.20 and 58.35) remarks that Rāma's show of grief, which Rāvaṇa would hear about from his spies, is meant to confirm to Rāvaṇa that Rāma is a man, and so to bring about the demon's death.

11. "and Vaidehī's mother" *mātaraṃ caiva vaidehyāḥ*: Probably Janaka's "favorite queen" (2.110.32), who nurtured the earth-born Sītā.

13. "the support of all my kinsmen" *jñātipakṣa-*: I agree with Cg in understanding the compound as a *karmadhāraya* ("kinsmen who are my supporters"); Cr takes it as a *dvandva*, "kinsmen and supporters."

14. "the Godāvarī": The SR reads "Mandākinī" (so the NW here and throughout the *sarga*), which is strange, since that is the river flowing along the slope of Mount Citrakūṭa (cf. 2.86.10–11 and note).

Hereafter the NR adds a speech by Lakṣmaṇa, in which he tells Rāma that Sītā is in none of these places, that he must be strong and realize she has disappeared (1160*); the SR inserts a passage in which Rāma, seeing the animals looking as though they wish to tell him something, asks them where Sītā is, whereupon all of them point south. Lakṣmaṇa reads their meaning and urges Rāma to strike out in that direction. Rāma agrees and sets forth, examining the ground along the way (App. I, No. 14).

18. An interpolation after the first line here in the SR (1163*) is in fact a verse from Kālidāsa's *Vikramorvaśīya* (4.51). It runs as follows: "Rāma spoke . . . : 'Leader of all earth-supporters [that is, mountains] [*sarvakṣitibhṛtām, sic leg.*], has the beautiful woman been seen, left by me . . . by you.' " By reason of the pun and the two equally possible syntactic constructions, the same lines can be understood first as a question asked by Rāma ("Have you seen the woman I left . . ."), and then as an echo taken as the answer of the mountain ("Leader of all earth-supporters [that is,

kings], the woman left by you has been seen by me"). But since the mountain refuses to say anything further, Rāma justifiably grows angry in *pādas* cd.

"puny deer" *kṣudramṛgam*: According to Johnston (1928–1932, p. 143) the compound often means "beast of prey" (that is, *kṣudra-* for *krūra-*, "which are used interchangeably in the epics"), though I find little in the *Rām* to corroborate this view. Here such a signification is evidently less appropriate.

22. "impressed upon" *niṣkrāntam*: Literally, "(footprints) stepped out upon" (a *karmaṇi prayoga*); contrast in verse 23, *parikrāntam* (a *bhāve proyoga*; thus, in both cases, Cg).

23. In an NR insertion hereafter Rāma reasons that the *rākṣasa* must have flown through the air, since no tracks of his arrival or departure are to be seen, and in despair he asks in what direction he is now to proceed (App. I, No. 15.24–27).

26. "have wantonly butchered": The line contains one of the epic's great alliterations (technically a *lalitānuprāsa*): *bhittvā bhittvā vibhaktā vā bhakṣitā vā bhaviṣyati*. See the note on 2.20.32 for comments on the poet's propensity for verbal ornamentation at moments of high drama (also 24.25 note above).

"wantonly butchered" *bhittvā bhittvā*: On the *āmreḍita* here as indicating intensity, see *vārt.* 6 (though this is normally restricted to imperatives) or 7 on *Pā* 8.1.12.

32. "battle standard" *samaradhvajaḥ*: The compound (glossed as "a standard indicating the commander in battle," Cg, Ck, Ct, Cr) I construe as *bahuvrīhi* with *rathaḥ* (with Ct, Cr, *contra* Cm, Cg).

33. "shafts" *viśikhāḥ*: Rather than as a noun standing in apposition, as I understand it, this may be adjectival ("blunted," so Cm, Cg).

"long as a chariot axle" *rathākṣamātrā*: According to Cm (who cites the *Śilpapraśna*), four hundred *aṅgulas*, or about twenty-five feet.

"to do their terrible work" *ghorakarmaṇaḥ*: I take this as nominative plural and modifying *śarāḥ* (*metri causa* for *-karmāṇaḥ*, see 37.12 and note, 420*.3, and Michelson 1904, pp. 113–14). Otherwise, "[To what being] of terrible deeds."

Hereafter the SR adds a verse (1176*) in which Rāma sees Rāvaṇa's dead charioteer (see 49.15 note).

35. "her righteousness no defense at all" *na dharmas trāyate*: Lakṣmaṇa will say the same thing to Rāma in 6.70.14ff. Cm remarks, "The proverb, 'In times of trouble *dharma* saves' had no application on this occasion."

After this verse the NR adds, "When a man has always kept to *dharma*, and *dharma*'s bulwark does not protect him [in times of trouble], then the man's spirit is broken, Saumitri, and he [is prone to] become an atheist" (1179*).

36. "who in this mortal world—or which god—has thought it possible to injure me" *ke hi loke 'priyaṃ kartuṃ śaktāḥ . . . mameśvarāḥ*: Rāma is blaming his tragedy on someone's reckless underestimation of his power. We must read *[a]priyam* in *pāda* c (so Crā, Cg, Ck; though there would, presumably, be no perceptible difference during oral delivery). The verse will otherwise make no sense with respect to the argument advanced in verses 37–39. Moreover, I believe this emendation to be substantiated by 61.11 below, *nālaṃ te [devādayaḥ] vipriyaṃ kartum* ("[the gods . . .] would no more do you an injury"; see also 18.4 for a similar sentiment). Cm, reading with the crit. ed., explains, "No god can do him any 'kindness' [*priyam*]; if the gods had been able they would have offered protection before Sītā had been abducted, and therefore, obviously, they are incapable." The gods could not be of help, Ct notes, because they are ineffectual in a matter that cannot be achieved by

dharma (see the previous verse). One other interpretation, suggested by an N version (App. I, No. 15.16–18): if Sītā is dead, nothing any god might do or give could assuage Rāma's grief and anger—any act of kindness, as Venkatanathacharya notes, would be as useless as watering a tree after cutting it off at the roots (1965, p. 444 note).

37. The śāstric principle at issue here is set forth in the *rājadharma* section of the *MBh*: the king must steer a middle course between leniency and cruelty (12.56, especially verses 21, 37–40), and this, it seems, is precisely one of the lessons that Rāma shall have to learn in the remainder of the poem. (See for instance 6.14.11, when Sāgara fails to appear; and cf. Lakṣmaṇa in 2.18.11, with Rāma's response, 2.18.36, etc.).

"the very master of the worlds" *kartāram api lokānām*: Literally, "maker of the worlds." The optative in *pāda* c shows the statement to be a supposition, and not a direct reference to Rāma (one is therefore reluctant to follow Bhatt in believing that "Rāma calls himself the 'creator of the worlds' evidently on account of mental disturbance," 1963, p. 411; similarly improbable Ck, Ct, who understand this to be a reference to Śiva, the " 'maker,' that is, of the destruction, 'of the worlds' "). It may be that we are to understand the phrase in the sense of "(a hero,) the very maker of his people"; cf. *MBh* 12.92.8, "A king is the very maker of beings (*kartā bhūtānām*) as well as their destroyer: a maker if he is righteous, a destroyer if he is not."

38. Ck here reasons as follows: "Objection: How can a *man* feel resentment toward the gods [as Rāma does here] when he ought rather to worship them? Answer: Precisely because Rāma entertains no notion that he is in fact a man. Objection: If then he knows he is a divinity, he must consequently have [and know that he has] omniscience, whereby he should know precisely what is happening with Sītā; all this lamentation then becomes unnecessary. Answer: He knows absolutely that his real self is *brahma*, for three reasons: his knowledge of his own superhuman power was validated by way of his own experience, when he destroyed Khara and the others; second, he has the firm conviction that he himself is a portion of the energy of the glorious, primordial world-cause, *brahma*, by means of inference, through the principle that 'whatever creature is powerful, glorious, or vigorous, you must understand to have arisen from a portion of My energy' [*BhagGī* 10.41]; and finally, by way of the reasoning that if he really were human, he could in no way deviate from the conditions of the human beings he sees about him. Nonetheless, since Rāvaṇa cannot be slain by a god, the reason for Rāma's *avatāra* would be frustrated [if this self-knowledge of Rāma's were generally known] and so, to achieve his purpose, it is the wish of the Blessed One to veil, by the force of 'darkness' [*tamas*], the fact of his being *brahma*, and having all the traits, omniscience and the like, that pertain to *brahma*. On this reasoning, everything that the poet has said so far, and will say, makes perfect sense."

39. "I will efface it" *saṃhṛtyaiva*: The clause is syntactically problematic. A direct object (that is, the virtue, compassion, for which the cool moonlight is the *upamāna* or standard of comparison) must be supplied; at the same time we must understand the gerund either as a main verb (cf. note on 2.18.32), as I have done, or supply another (as the SR attempts to do, in 1181*).

42–43. Something like *trailokyaṃ . . . kariṣyāmi* (cf. 1184*) must be understood with the eight *bahuvrīhis* of which these two verses consist.

"paralyze both fire and wind" *vipranaṣṭānalamarut*: I follow Cr in taking the second element as a *dvandva*. Or perhaps we should simply understand the compound as a variant on *caṇḍavāta*, "raging wind" (cf. *MBh* 6.67.6).

50. In an SR insertion hereafter (1191*) Rāma, compared to Rudra when he destroyed the Triple City, girds up his loins, takes his bow from Lakṣmaṇa, affixes an arrow, and speaks verses 51ff.

52. "Unless" *purā . . . yadi na*: A sort of tautology, literally, "if not before" (see PW, s.v. *purā* 3; somewhat comparable is *MBh* 3.281.98). Alternatively, we may analyze *puras iva* (standing for *eva*, which is actually read in a number of S manuscripts), with double sandhi (though compare Michelson 1904, p. 102, who records only one such instance), "(show . . .) right before my eyes." Quite differently the commentators: " '(show me Sītā bright-smiling) as before,' that is, smiling as she did when she asked Rāma to catch the deer," Cg; "unweeping (*ca arudatīṃ*) as before," Cr; Ct appears to agree with both of them. Cg here cites Hanumān's later words, "If, for the sake of this woman, Rāma were to lay the earth to waste, all the way to the sea, I would think it more than just" (5.14.13).

Ct here comments, "How can Rāma be so angry, what is the purpose [of this passage]? This is an imitation of human behavior insofar as he is at present possessed of a human body. Then too, if at such a time of sorrow he were to show no anger, Rāvaṇa would think him not to be human [read *'manuṣyabuddhim*], and so it would not be possible to destroy him [read *'śakyaḥ*]."

Sarga 61

2. "sought to slay the victim" *hantukāmaṃ paśum*: A kind of synecdoche, perhaps, for "destroy the sacrifice." According to O'Flaherty, "The sacrifice which Rudra pierces or burns with his glance is personified as the sacrificial animal" (1973, p. 128, citing *TāṇMaBr* 7.9.16). (The vulgate reads instead, "burn the whole world.") For the exclusion of Rudra (Śiva) from the primeval sacrifice of Dakṣa, his father-in-law, and his subsequent disruption of it, see note on 23.27 above.

5. "glory" *yaśaḥ*: Rāma's "grandeur, glory" is a function of, and so nearly synonymous with, his righteousness, particularly his always rendering just punishment (cf. below, verse 9 note), and to this the injustice of his present undertaking—to destroy the whole world because of the crime of one creature—stands in sharp contradiction. (To clarify this train of thought is the function of the SR insertion appearing hereafter, "You must not destroy the worlds because of the crime of one," 1196*). Verses 6–8 are interposed to show that only one creature is responsible for Sītā's disappearance, the conclusion being contained in verse 9. (Cm, Cg, Ct, Cr, wrongly I believe, understand here, "—all this is constant (immutable) in you, as well as. . . .")

7. "must . . . have . . . ended" *nivṛtta-*: The reading has the support of Crā, but perhaps more attractive is the widely attested variant *nirvṛtta-*, "must have taken place."

8. "not two" *na dvayoḥ*: See 60.27. Lakṣmaṇa's reasoning is, somewhat illogically, subordinated to the main point he wishes to make in verse 9. He sees only one chariot and set of equipment, and so concludes that only one *rākṣasa* was involved. The fact that no "great army" (this must be the meaning of *balasya mahataḥ*) appears

to have been present does not, however, support his argument, for there is no reason why *rākṣasas* should always duel with vast army contingents in attendance. One must wonder, therefore, whether the oldest manuscript, Ñ1, has not preserved the correct reading, *parasya*: "(. . . not two . . . for I do not find any footprints left by) another great [sc., *rākṣasa*]." (This is not supported, however, elsewhere in the NR; both Gorresio [3.70.12] and Lahore [3.71.12] support the crit. ed.)

9. Ctr here cites *ManuSm* (8.128): "A king who punishes the innocent and fails to punish the guilty incurs great infamy, and goes to hell."

11. The verse refers back to the argument made by Rāma in 60.36.

"would" *alam*: Cm attributes to the word its common signification, "able to," but how this would fit with the simile I cannot see (for what is at issue there is the will to injure, not the ability, though see below).

"the pious" *sādhavaḥ*: That is, according to Cm, Cg, Ck, priests. An injury in the case of a consecrant would be an act of black magic, like a curse ("or, making the rite defective," Ct). Cm quotes scripture to show that they *could* not injure him: "No grief, no bewitching can take hold of him" (untraced).

12. "your majesty" *rājan*: Although removed by the NR, the reference to Rāma's actual kingship (which is likely the reference here) is supported by other allusions in the *Araṇyakāṇḍa* (see for instance above, 28.10 note).

"and the supreme seers to help us" *sahāyaiḥ paramarṣibhiḥ*: "Those in the forest," says Cg, but the reference remains puzzling; the seers will neither help nor even accompany Rāma. This may perhaps simply imply a generalized moral support: The virtuous are on Rāma's side, and so he need not destroy the worlds.

15. "the thirty gods do not restore" *na . . . pradāsyanti . . . tridaśeśvarāḥ*: "Since it is self-evident that, whether dead or alive, Sītā cannot fail to be somewhere in the three worlds, the lords of the three worlds must, self-evidently, be able to 'restore' her," Ck.

16. "by peaceful means" *śivena*: The reading of the crit. ed., *śīlena*, I find to be meaningless here, and accept in its place the variant reported by all but the S commentators (though it is probably no indication they eliminated it for ill-founded sectarian reasons that Cg here remarks, combating some interpretation no longer extant, "Only an idiot would infer, from the description of Lakṣmaṇa's calming Rāma's anger, that it is Śiva's intention—the god having been propitiated by Rāvaṇa and become his partisan—that Rāma's anger be assuaged").

Sarga 62

3. "brought about you(r birth)" *āsīl labdhaḥ*: The third singular verb is appropriate, since *bhavān* would be understood (as in verse 6; thus Cr).

"great mortifications and a great sacrificial rite" *mahatā tapasā . . . mahatā cāpi karmaṇā*: The rite is described in *Bālakāṇḍa* 11–15; the mortifications are not elsewhere explicitly referred to.

"like the immortal gods obtaining the drink of immortality" *amṛtam ivāmaraiḥ*: The gods obtained nectar only after the great effort of churning the Milk Ocean (cf. note on 45.35 above).

4. "became a god" *devatvam āpannaḥ*: That is, he died (for the idiom see note on 2.98.49).

5. On the paradigmatic dimension of kingly behavior see for instance 48.8 and note above and, for the locus classicus, *BhagGī* 3.21. Ct remarks, "The purpose of Rāma's *avatāra* includes instructing people, as the *Bhāgavata* states, 'His *avatāra* as a mortal was intended to instruct mortals' " (5.19.5).

6. Venkatanathacharya offers another explanation of the verse: If Rāma can find respite from grief only in destroying the worlds, how are weaker people, when similarly pained, to find respite (1965, p. 456 note)? This is perhaps more appropriate to Lakṣmaṇa's argument, though somewhat less naturally indicated by the language.

Before or in place of this verse several S manuscripts read, "Take heart, best of men. What mortal never meets with troubles? Like fire they touch one a moment, but then the next are gone" (1200*), an interpolation called forth to elucidate the "way of the world"—that is, the inevitability of suffering—mentioned in verse 7.

7. "Yayāti, son of Nahuṣa": Yayāti's "misfortune" consisted in pride, which caused him to fall back again to earth (cf. notes on 2.11.1 and 5.9). (For Cg the locution "son of Nahuṣa" suggests the story of Nahuṣa himself, whose pridefulness caused him to be cursed to live as a snake [cf. *MBh* 3.177]; for Ct, a further implication here is this: The verb used in the verse, "touched" [*sámaspṛśat*], indicates merely brief contact, and this suggests that Rāma's own sons [like Yayāti's, see note on 2.71.10] will without delay remove his later sorrow [over the second "loss" of Sītā].)

"misfortune" *anayaḥ*: As in verse 12 below (see note on 2.8.14, and contrast 2.20.5 and note).

8. "A hundred sons were born to him in a single day, but all of them were later killed" *ahnā putraśataṃ jajñe tathaivāsya punar hatam*: The sons of Vasiṣṭha were slain by Viśvāmitra (by a curse in the *Rām* version, cf. 1.58, especially verses 18ff.; by means of a *rākṣasa* in the *MBh*, 1.166). The particle *tathaiva* appears to function concessively ("He was given this great blessing and yet . . ."), not that the sons were slain "the very day" they were born, which is nowhere mentioned.

10. "the two eyes of the universe" *jagatāṃ netre*: In the great revelation at the end of Book Six, the sun and moon are said to be Rāma's eyes (6.105.7), as, in his theophany, they are said to be Kṛṣṇa's (*BhagGī* 11.19, and cf. *MBh* 6.61.54).

"upon which everything is founded" *yatra sarvaṃ pratiṣṭhitam*: Insofar as, in the Indian tradition, the sun is the ultimate cause of rain, the moon the progenitor of crops (so Cg, though perhaps overly clever).

11. "destiny" *daivasya*: Literally, "the divine," which makes the paradox of the gods succumbing to destiny even sharper. Note too how contrary these sentiments are to those expressed by Lakṣmaṇa in 2.20.10ff. Consistency in the world view of the individual characters is here, rather untypically, subordinated by the poet to narrative exigency.

"(other beings), men of flesh and blood" (*sarvabhūtāni*) *dehinaḥ*: The latter item is epexegetical, as in *pādas* ab *devāḥ* is to *bhūtāni*. (Those commentators who try to avoid the absurd in the explanation here fall into the solecistic, as Ct, who would take *dehinaḥ* as a neuter plural, a form for which there is no evidence, in the epics at least).

12. "misfortune . . . good fortune" *nayānayau*: See verse 7 note above (accepting the second sense of the word the commentators gloss " 'folly . . . wisdom,' that is, the sorrow and happiness deriving from these").

13. "lost" *naṣṭāyām*: That this is without question the sense of the verb in this

passage is shown by the juxtaposition *vinaṣṭā—bhakṣitā* in 55.17 (an opposition preserved here in Dt[1], D6, and most of the NE version, *naṣṭā—mṛtā*); observe that in 63.21 the word is used even when it is known that Sītā has only been abducted (see also 5.33.53 for a particularly clear example of this sense of the verb).

14. "see things as they truly are" *satyadarśinaḥ*: Compare Bharata's words in 2.98.42–43.

"(their sight remains) unclouded" *anirviṇṇa(darśanāḥ)*: Literally, "undiscouraged" (the concrete sense appears in 37.2).

15. "distinguish right from wrong" *vijānanti śubhāśubhe*: The phrase is ambiguous: do the wise thereby distinguish or understand "their merit and demerit" (Cm), "the good and ill that are to come" (Cg), "what is proper and improper, what they should and should not proceed to do" (Ck, Ct)? I am inclined to accept the last, for the burden of Lakṣmaṇa's discourse is to dissuade Rāma from wholesale destruction and to urge him to find and kill the single perpetrator.

16. "Without doing this, without carefully weighing an action" *adhṛtānāṃ ca karmaṇām nāntareṇa kriyām*: According to the commentators (Cm, Cg, Ck, Ct, Ctr), this verse concerns *karma* in the technical sense (though I do not know that the word occurs in this sense in the poem): Without the previous performance of *karma* its fruit would not come about, and so, because one is ultimately responsible for one's misery, one must put up with it. But this interpretation does not satisfactorily account for the use in *pāda* a of *-guṇadoṣa-* ("the arguments for and against it"), a phrase generally used in the *Rām* with regard to contemplated action (see, for example, 33.2 above, 6.6.10); at the same time it leaves *iṣṭam* ("desired") in *pāda* d unexplained and is contextually meaningless. The true crux here is *pāda* c, which is otiose or whose only function is to overdetermine the message of *pādas* ab. One might perhaps suspect here an old corruption, for (*nāntareṇa*) *dhiyām*, "(The desired result of action is never attained without) forethought (without weighing)" (compare, in a very similar context, *MBh* 3.33.25, *dhiyā dhīro vijāniyāt*).

19. "your powers, which are as much divine as human" *divyaṃ ca mānuṣaṃ caivam ātmanaś ca parākramam*: I agree with Ck, Ct, Cr on this, the most natural construction of the line (the *ca* in *pāda* b is conjunctive between verses 18 and 19, and those in *pāda* a mean "both . . . and"); the bivalence of Rāma's power is elsewhere noticed (see above, 54.14 and the Introduction, Chapter 4d). Cm, Cg explain quite differently, however: " 'Have regard for the celestial and the human, and [be aware of] your own powers,' that is, Rāma should slay only his enemy, not the celestial creatures and men on earth, and he must realize, too, that he has the power to slay them all."

"those who have shown their hatred of you" *dviṣatām*: The NR variously offers the singular.

Sarga 63

4. "(search . . .) through Janasthāna" *janasthānaṃ . . . anveṣitum*: From 58.34, 60.14ff., and similar passages, Rāma would appear to have already searched Janasthāna. Many N manuscripts accordingly offer "(search) again."

5. "gorges" *nirdarāḥ*: For the sense of this uncommon word, see 2.79.19 note.

6. "carefully" *yuktaḥ*: Or, "armed" (so Cm, Cg).

8. "razor-headed" *kṣuram*: See Belvalkar 1947, p. 789 (so basically Cg, Ck; "razor-sharp," according to Cm, Ct, Cr).

After this verse the oldest manuscript, Ñ1, reads 60.28–33; cf. verse 17 and note below.

9. "illustrious" *mahābhāgam*: Literally, "greatly fortunate." Is this epithet vacuously ornamental, or is it supposed to suggest the nobility and grandeur of Jaṭāyus's death ("because he had given up his life in the cause of his master," Cg)? The NR and several S manuscripts eliminate it, substituting "massive" or "with severed wings."

10. As noted on 48.1, the *Mahābhārata* does not introduce Jaṭāyus until the fight with Rāvaṇa. When Rāma comes upon him nearly dead, he must therefore identify himself (3.263.17). In our version, Rāma oddly does not recognize the vulture, something that would make more sense given the *MBh*'s narrative chronology (though we should recall that when Rāma first meets Jaṭāyus in 13.2 he also takes him for a *rākṣasa*, and moreover, he is at present half mad).

13. "in a desolate, most desolate" *dīnadīnayā*: On the semantic function of the repetition, see note on 60.26.

14. "and long may you live" *āyuṣman*: Again Vālmīki breathes narrative life into a dead epithet (compare for example *kāmarūpin* in 60.34 above): Since Rāma is searching for Sītā as if she were a "healing herb," "may you live long" takes on the suggestion "may you find her."

17. "This . . . bow" *etad . . . dhanuḥ*: Unless Rāma has carried all this equipment with him to where Jaṭāyus is lying, the vulture must be near the equipment (he points to it, *etad*). One wonders then why Rāma did not see him when he first saw the bow and the rest in 60.28ff. (see above verse 8 note).

"shield" *śarāvaram*: See De 1958, p. 1145.

20. "(gasping for breath) . . . in that trackless, inaccessible place" *ekāyane durge* (*niḥśvasantam*): Ck, reading *kṛcchre* (for *durge*), explains, " '(his breathing) is difficult, [going] in one direction only,' that is, out." According to 50.1 Jaṭāyus falls to the ground "not far from Rāghava's ashram."

21. "this bird slain" *hato dvijaḥ*: The NR reads instead "my father dead," but clearly this is a revision (perhaps out of a misplaced sense of filial piety), for the loss of a parent lacks the aspect of unforeseeable contingency exhibited by the other calamities.

On the first half of the verse Cg comments as follows: "Even though debarred from the kingship, Rāma might have been allowed to live as a mendicant in the kingdom [cf. 2.38.4], but that was denied him ('living in the forest'); even though living in the forest, to be with loved ones would have brought happiness, but that was denied him ('Sītā lost'); even though separated from loved ones, one might be able to bear the grief in the company of friends, but that too was denied him ('this bird slain')."

22. I believe the verse to be an allusion to a general proverbial sentiment (everything goes wrong for the luckless man; when it rains, it pours; "When sorrows come, they come not as single spies, but in battalions"; Venkatanathacharya cites an Indian one, "The ocean reaches no higher than the knees of an evil man" [1965, p. 464 note], though this seems less applicable). Additionally it plays upon the later problem of Rāma's trying to cross the ocean to get to Laṅkā (6.13–15). (The com-

mentators suggest, unpersuasively, " 'enter,' or, 'swim in' the ocean, in order to soothe the fire of grief," Cm, Cg, Ck.)

Sarga 64

1. "(Saumitri,) his staunchest friend" (*saumitriṃ*) *mitrasampannam*: Literally, "who had become his friend" (so basically Cr; see PW, s.v. *sam* + *pad*); the epithet is employed principally for alliteration. The commentators suggest, "['Endowed with friends,' that is,] a friend to all people" (so Cm, Ck, Ct), or, with *paranipāta*, "wholly friendly to Rāma" (Cg), and I draw on the latter to some extent for the translation.

3. "though . . . his voice has failed" *tathā svaravihīnaḥ*: I am not wholly certain whether *tathā* should, or can, be taken concessively. Perhaps we should read *tathā-svara-*, "likewise his voice had not yet failed (and he is gazing up, [though] vacantly)."

5. Rāma has a short memory, having apparently forgotten his encounter with, and mutilation of, Śūrpaṇakhā, who identified herself as the sister of Rāvaṇa (16.19 above). This point was also made by Goldman and Masson 1969.

7. "(what) feats (has he accomplished)" (*kiṃ*)*karmā*: This corresponds to *prabhāvam* in 67.20 below, "(the full extent of his [Rāvaṇa's] power)"; *contra* Cg, Ck, Ct, who seem to understand, "What did he do" when he took Sītā.

Rāma here speaks very like Rāvaṇa in 32.2. It is clear that neither has ever heard anything of the other.

9. "he worked a prodigious magic of winds and storms" *māyām āsthāya vipulāṃ vātadurdinasaṃkulām*: That is, presumably, Rāvaṇa raised the wind and darkened the sky in order to hide himself (see 6.67.24, where his son Indrajit does something similar).

11. "My breath is coming harder" *uparuddhyanti me prāṇāḥ*: Note the passive stem with active termination.

"the golden trees" *vṛkṣān sauvarṇān*: See above, 45.33 note.

"spikenard" *uśīra-*: The precise signification of the reference is obscure, though it may be observed that spikenard is used in rites for the dead (a paste of it being smeared on the corpse, which is also draped with a garland of the blossoms, cf. Kane 1962–1975, vol. 4, p. 202), and thus carries funereal connotations.

12–13. "the hour called Vinda" *vindo nāma muhūrto 'sau*: Cm, Cg (so too Ct) etymologize the name, "in this hour one finds [*vindate*] lost wealth." According to Cm, it is the eleventh of the fifteen *muhūrtas* (an "hour" of forty-eight minutes) of the day. See note on 2.83.21. Cm remarks that Vinda is another name for Vijaya (the hour of "Victory," though according to 6.4.3 Vijaya is noon), or a *ghaṭikā* (a smaller measure of time) so named. Ctr appears to understand the word generically, as *bindu* ("a moment"?), and like Cm notes that an act done at such a time (he lists the various moments, citing the *Gauli* section of the *Utpalaparimala*) produces for the agent just the opposite of what he intended—in the case of Rāvaṇa, death. According to the *SkandaP* (3.2.30.22), Sītā was abducted at the hour called Vṛnda (*sic*), on the eighth day of the dark fortnight of Māghā.

"he was unaware" *nābudhat*: An a-aorist, as Ct, Cr also take it, rather than irregular imperfect (so Cg, followed by Bhatt 1963, p. 411).

16. "himself" *sākṣāt*: Cg, Cr join the word closely with *putraḥ*, "the lawful son."

The rest of the information about Rāvaṇa, lost in aposiopesis here, will be supplied by Jaṭāyus's brother Sampāti, who completes the line, "and his name is Rāvaṇa, the *rākṣasa* who inhabits the city of Laṅkā" (so noted also by Cg; some eastern manuscripts, seemingly out of unendurable commiseration with Rāma, actually add here, "the overlord of Laṅkā, on an island in the southern sea," 1238*).

18. Cm, asking how Jaṭāyus could have survived so long after Rāvaṇa's fatal blow, replies that it is a result of Sītā's favor, and cites the *SkandaP* [untraced], "The queen told me I would remain alive, lord of kings, until I had the chance to talk with you."

21. "born a long time ago" *cirakālasamutthitaḥ*: Ck, Ct, Cr support the translation; Cg glosses, "had enjoyed prosperity for a long time."

23. This does not mean that Jaṭāyus somehow abdicated his kingship (see 48.19 and note) when he offered protection to Sītā (13.34). The verse simply contains a slight, and characteristic (cf. note on 24.24 above), hysteron proteron: the bird gave up his life and in so doing "relinquished the kingship," the inversion perhaps indicating that, in a sense, kingship would have been the greater loss.

24. "even among the animals" *tiryagyonigateṣv api*: This certainly hints at the events to be narrated in the coming book, Rāma's alliance with the monkeys.

25. Ct tries to soften Rāma's statement here: "In essence he means that [his grief is greater in Jaṭāyus's case] because there is still a chance to recover Sītā, but none to recover Jaṭāyus." Jaṭāyus, moreover, is like a father (cf. 63.25, 64.26 and 33 below, and *RaghuVa* 12.56), and thus irreplaceable (whereas one can always get another wife, and one as good as Sītā, as Rāma himself will say later when Lakṣmaṇa's life is endangered, 6.39.6; see also 6.2029*.5–6).

29–30. "may you go (to the state) . . . may you proceed to the highest of worlds" *gaccha . . . lokān uttamān . . . vraja*: I understand *tāṃ gatim* with *gaccha*, and construe *lokān uttamān* with *vraja*.

"who do not turn their back in battle" *aparāvartinām*: Thus Ck, Ct; the word is quite rare in this sense (the phrase usually runs [*saṃgrāmeṣu*] *anivartin*, as in 2.58.35), but is corroborated by *MBh* 6.102.17. Most unlikely Cm (first explanation), Ctr, " 'who do not return,' that is, the released," and Cg (first explanation), " 'who do not return,' that is, renouncers."

"on taking leave of me" *mayā tvaṃ samanujñātaḥ*: The commentators all interpret the phrase as "with my permission."

For the type of prayer, see 2.58.34ff. The śāstric discussion of these verses is interesting from a theological perspective, if rather involved. Cm, for example, is concerned to show that Rāma here grants the vulture liberation from rebirth (he cites *Nṛsiṃhapurāṇa* [cf. *NaraP* 49.95–96] and *BhāgP* [11.12.6]), and this act proves that during his *avatāra* Rāma had full consciousness that he is God (so in large part Ck). Ctr, by contrast, cites a parallel from the *MBh* (7.55.20ff.), wherein Subhadrā utters a comparable prayer over her dead son Abhimanyu.

32ff. Verse 32 is out of place; in fact, the entire funeral procedure here is confused. The proper sequence of events, after the construction of the pyre, is this: obtaining and dismembering the *anustaraṇī* or "covering animal" (verse 32; cf. 2.70.18 note); praying (verse 34); cremating (verse 31); the water libation (verse 35); the offering of food to the deceased (verse 33). This is essentially the sequence of events in 2.70–71 (the prayers, verse 18; the water libation, verse 23; the *śrāddha*, *sarga* 71), whereas in 2.95.25–30, the offering of food (almond meal) to Daśaratha takes place after the water libation (cf. also Kane 1962–1975, vol. 4, p. 220). Cm,

Cg, Ck, Ct, Cr are aware of the disorder (Cm, Cg list the proper sequence). They cannot explain the difficulty of having the food offering precede the water offering (and that it is a food offering is strongly suggested by the many manuscripts that read *piṇḍīkṛtya* [*-tvā*] for *peśīkṛtvā* [see also 1250*.2], *piṇḍa-* being the word for the balls of food offered the dead). They do, however, attempt to solve the problem of the impossible postponement of the *anustaraṇī* until after the cremation by eliminating it altogether, interpreting *anu tastāra* as " 'made a spread,' that is, of [holy *darbha*] grass, 'around the bird' " (on which the food offering would properly be placed, cf. 2.95.30; or for other purposes, Kane 1962–1975, vol. 4, p. 206). But the language indicates clearly the rite of the *anustaraṇī* (note that *anu* + *stṛ* seems not to be attested in any but this ritualistic sense; why more than one animal is necessary, however, remains obscure; perhaps for the food offering). The NR, too, tries to eliminate the *anustaraṇī*, replacing it with the water libation, which is obviously impossible insofar as it preserves verse 35 as well. Were we to rearrange the verses as follows: 28, 32, 34, 29–31 (see verse 34 note), 35, 34, things would be in good shape. But we have virtually no manuscript authority for this, and so I am compelled to let the confusion stand in the translation.

33. "an offering" *dadau*: The offering of food is to be made only by the son of the dead man (cf. Kane 1962–1975, vol. 4, p. 206); compare note on verse 25 above. Normally it would be a ball of fine rice or barley and sesame. Perhaps meat is more appropriate for a vulture?

34. "the prayer for reaching heaven" *svargagamanam*: The Yāmyasūkta (*ṚV* 10.14.1–5 and 13–16), according to Cm, Cg, the former adding the Nārāyaṇasūkta (*ṚV* 10.90.1–16; Ctr cites, attributing to "Āpastamba," a statement located in *BhāGS* [p. 2 line 16] that supports these identifications). Ck unconvincingly identifies it as the *mantra* "He who knows *brahma* attains the highest" (*TaiUp* 2.1.1). Ñ1, reading verses 29–30 after verse 34, attempts to make those verses the prayer, rather than any vedic hymns.

35. Cg (so Ctś) here considers in detail the propriety of offering the sacrament of cremation to the vulture (note that the ceremony will be performed also for the monkey-king Vālin in the *Kiṣkindhākāṇḍa*, see especially 24.42), claiming that by his devotion to Rāma, the bird succeeded in transcending his "caste" limitations. Ctr offers a veritable treatise on the whole question (pp. 215–26).

36. "according to the custom of the great seers" *maharṣikalpena*: That is, employing vedic *mantras*. *kalpa-* as in 4.36.9; note how this is "glossed," in the *Padmapurāṇa* version (Bengali recension? the lines are cited by Cm on verse 29), by (*saṃskāram akarot* . . .) *brahmavidhānataḥ*. (Unlikely, "by him [Rāma] who was 'like a great seer,' " Cm, Cg; accepted by Bhatt, who curiously concludes, "The comparison of Rāma with a great sage shows that he is not taken to be identical with Viṣṇu," 1963, p. 412.)

The SR adds a final verse, which compares Rāma and Lakṣmaṇa to Viṣṇu and Indra, respectively (1253*).

Sarga 65

1. "westward" *paścimāṃ* . . . *diśam*: In 64.10 Jaṭāyus had told them that Rāvaṇa headed south. Do they proceed to the west, therefore, simply to return to Jana-

sthāna first? (The NR indeed has them return to Janasthāna, where they pass the night in the ashram and leave at dawn, though even then they still go west [1254*].) Cm, Cg, Ck, Ct, Cr artificially construe "west" here with "south" in the next verse, "southwest."

3. "It was nearly impassable" *durgam*: The particle *tu* in verse 4a suggests that we are to construe these qualifications with *panthānam* ("path") in verse 2 (so Ct). Cm, Cg, Cr would have them modify *araṇyam* ("wilderness") in the following verse, which is of course possible.

5. "dense" *gahanam*: I agree with Cm, Ct in interpreting this adjectivally (as in verse 3); optionally we may take it nominally, as in verse 13 below ("the forest [named Krauñca]," so Cm [second interpretation], Cg, Ck, Cr; cf. *AmaK* 2.4.1). Note that later on, the bards of the southern tradition (unfortunately accepted by the crit. ed.) become confused and locate the slaying of Virādha in the Krauñca forest, and that of Kabandha in the Daṇḍaka wilderness (6.96.26, corrected by the NR).

6. "seemed to bristle with life" *prahṛṣṭam iva*: Here in agreement with the commentators (Cm, Cg, Ct), since the negative connotations (see note on 50.11 above) that might be required by the ensuing action (verses 8ff.) are ruled out by the second half of the verse.

7. An SR addition hereafter has the brothers travel east about six miles, leave the Krauñca forest, and come upon a pit "like hell itself," near which they see a female *rākṣasa* (Ayomukhī, by name), who catches hold of Lakṣmaṇa and invites him to live with her. In response Lakṣmaṇa cuts off her ears and nose and breasts, whereupon she runs away (App. I, No. 17; the incident is known to Bhoja, *RāmāCam* p. 202).

11. "*vañculaka*": Glossed *karṇavāla* by Cm, Cg. I am unable to find any information concerning the bird.

"most ominous" *paramadāruṇaḥ*: See 22.4 note on the clear auguristic connotations of the adjective.

"our [defeat]" *āvayor* [*vijayam*]: Literally, "[victory] over us," obviously an objective genitive. Ct, Cr, with stubborn indifference to the context, appear to take it subjectively ("our victory").

13. "enveloped in wind" *saṃveṣṭitam . . . mātariśvanā*: Cg identifies this occurrence as a portent (*utpāta*).

15. "Kabandha": The word itself signifies, among other things, "headless trunk"; cf. 66.12 below (for the semantic development of the word, see the reference in the note on 22.11), though here it is the creature's proper name, for he retains it even when his form has been changed (see 69.36). For a discussion of the monster typology into which Kabandha would fit, see the Introduction, Chapter 6.

21. "wrapped up in his own arms" *bhujasaṃvṛtam*: Recall that Kabandha's arms are a league in length and that he is contorting them to pick out his animals (verse 19). Cv (first interpretation), Cm, Cg, Ct take the latter element of the compound as *kvibanta*, "encircling [animals] with his arms; Cv (second interpretation), Ck, as *bahuvrīhi*, "by whose arms there was an encircling [of animals]."

23. In an SR insertion here Lakṣmaṇa urges Rāma to forget about him and free himself first (1266*).

24. "foremost of *dānavas*" *dānavottamaḥ*: These are usually (though in the *Rām*, except for Dundubhi [*Kiṣkindhākāṇḍa* 11], not necessarily) malevolent beings; but in the epic the term is rarely if ever applied to *rākṣasas* (see verse 14), however blurred

the difference between the two species becomes in the later literature. Cr remarks, "He was born in the lineage of Danu, but through his bad *karma* became a *rākṣasa*. There is therefore no contradiction in his being called a *rākṣasa* elsewhere." See 67.1 note.

27ff. In the *MBh* version it is Lakṣmaṇa rather than Rāma who gives voice to despair (cf. 3.262.27ff.).

27. In a NW interpolation hereafter Rāma identifies himself to Kabandha, and tells him his story. Kabandha flies into a rage, saying that to live in the forest with one's wife is a corruption of *dharma*, and that a forest hermit should not carry weapons (1270*). See above, 2.10–12, where the monster Virādha, who is in most ways homomorphic with Kabandha, makes the same charge (cf. also Pollock 1986, pp. 67ff., on the antinomian character of Rāma).

29. "against all creatures" *sarvabhūteṣu*: The locative is *viṣaya*, not partitive, as Cm would have it ("Among all creatures doom . . .").

The second line of the verse makes sense only as a question (*pace* Cm, Cr).

30. "(collapse) on the field of battle" *raṇājire* (. . . *sīdanti*): The locative should be construed with *pādas* cd, rather than with ab: Rāma is considering how he could be stricken with such terror and paralysis on the field of battle.

Sarga 66

4. "Any minute (. . . will bolt)" *purā* (*tūrṇam ādatte*): *purā* functions adverbially, with the present (see *Pā* 3.3.4).

5. "his horribly bristling (arms)" *susaṃhṛṣṭau* (*bāhū*): The adjective is perhaps to be construed with *rāghavau*, "(the Rāghavas . . . cut off his arms) with a violent shudder" (though it is unlikely, despite a parallel in 52.6 above, that we should follow Cg, Ck, Ct, " 'shuddering,' with joy, because the arms were so easy to cut off").

6. "skillful Rāma . . . his right arm" *dakṣiṇo dakṣiṇaṃ bāhum . . . rāmaḥ*: Instead of "skillful" (so Cv, Cm, Cg, Ct, Cr), Ct, Cr also suggest, "standing at his right." Cg notes, "Lakṣmaṇa always goes to the right side of Rāma, and so faces an opponent's left side, while Rāma faces his right" (see above, 3.15 and note; in the *MBh*, conversely, Rāma cuts off Kabandha's left arm, Lakṣmaṇa his right, 3.263.32).

Sarga 67

1ff. Kabandha's exposition of his history in this *sarga* appears to be a fusion of two separate stories, one contained in verses 1–6, another in verses 7–16, and a reasonable narrative connection between them is hard to establish. The condition created by Indra in verse 13 contradicts the previous version, and the setting of a limit in verse 15 is purely redundant. Thus it becomes difficult to accept the explanation offered by Cm, Cg, Ct that verses 7–16 are meant to clarify how Kabandha acquired his headless form; or that of Ck, Ct that the despicable form acquired by the seer's curse is different from the headless trunk (how *idaṃ rūpam* of verse 2 can be thought to refer to something other than the *idaṃ rūpam* of verse 7 I do not know; see verses 4 and 27). Insofar as Lakṣmaṇa had asked the pertinent question

(66.12), Kabandha's narration would most naturally begin with a nod to the younger prince, as in verse 7. Moreover, the version of verses 1–6 is otherwise inferior, explaining less of the peculiar features of Kabandha's appearance. It has the character of an addition, but one for whose presence no explanation is ready to hand (it is the one version that Bhoja knows, who excludes the Indra story, *RāmāCam* p. 202). All manuscripts offer the two versions, both of which thus *ex hypothesi* revert to the monumental poem of Vālmīki. Still, were we to insist on bracketing verses 1–6 as an "interpolation"—an ancient one piously retained—there is nothing to do about the reference to the seer in verse 16 (though see the note there). The problem is further complicated by the fact that a similar apparent doubling of stories is found in the Virādha episode (see 3.18 note).

5. "insulting" *abhiśāpa-*: For this sense of the word (though the substantival form is not found) cf. *HariVaṃ* 12.28. Not too different the commentators, "assault" (Cm, Cg, Ck, Ct).

7. "radiantly handsome" *śriyā virājitam*: This cannot be interpreted, with Cm, as "son of Śrī (of the lineage of Danu)," in order to accord with 4.4.12, "A son of Śrī [v.l., "of Diti"] named Danu (who had become a *rākṣasa* because of a curse)." (Note, however, that he is called Danu in verses 18 and 24 below, and in 70.15, and "foremost of *dānavas*" in 65.24; in both the *MBh* [3.263.38] and the *HariVaṃ* [31.119], Kabandha, like Virādha [cf. 3.18], is a *gandharva* [named Viśvāvasu].) A number of manuscripts attempt to alter the reading.

10. Because of Kabandha's boon, the thunderbolt only wounds him and fails to kill him.

16. "the great seer" *maharṣiṇā*: Ñ1 reads, "I, my lord (have spoken truly)," eliminating the one problematic vestige of the "interpolated" version (see verses 1ff. note), but unsupported by other manuscripts. The omission of the verse in the NW version appears to result from scribal error, and thus probably has no text-critical significance.

19. "at his leisure" *yathāsukham*: Thus in accordance with Ck, Ct, and as at 38.17; less likely Cg, Cr, "(when I was absent, had left) at my leisure," that is, presumably, off on a leisurely hunt.

20. "we" *vayam*: The plurals here and in verses 21–22, when the dual is expected, are not unparalleled in the poem (compare 6.114.12, where in recounting the incident of Virādha's burial the plural is curiously again employed; see also 2.31.17 and note; 3.10.58, 15.38, 50.5).

22. "broken off over time" *kāle bhagnāni*: As forest hermits Rāma and Lakṣmaṇa may only use branches naturally broken off trees (see note on 2.25.7).

"prepare a . . . pit" *śvabhre . . . kalpite*: Perhaps they are going to cremate him and then bury the remnants (cf. the case of Virādha, 3.24 note).

23. Rāma and Kabandha are cleverly wrangling over who must go first. Rāma insists on Kabandha's telling him before he cremates him, reasonably supposing he will be unable to do so afterward (so Ck on verse 18); whereas Kabandha suspects that once Rāma receives the information, there will be no incentive for the prince to cremate him (so Cg on verse 31). It is to this dispute that the next verse refers.

24. "one clever speaker to another" *kuśalo vaktuṃ vaktāram*: The *tṛ* suffix here denotes "a worthy or fit speaker" (cf. *KāśiVṛ* on *Pā* 3.3.169).

26. "until I am cremated" *adagdhasya*: Yet even then Kabandha will know virtually nothing. We must not, however, pay too close attention to the epistemological prob-

lem posed by his partial knowledge (verse 17, not to speak of his full knowledge of his life prior to the curse, verses 1ff.) when he should know nothing (verse 27), and his total ignorance later when he should know everything. The speech may simply be more of the dispute over who should start and constitute a (false) inducement to get Rāma to be the first. But in any case, the whole episode is in great part a divertissement (as *sarga* 68 demonstrates all the more clearly) after the harrowing madness and grief of *sargas* 55–64, and is not meant to receive too exacting an analysis.

28. "before the sun drives . . . home" *yāvan na yāty astaṃ savitā*: Cremations must take place before sundown (noted also by Bhatt 1963, p. 412).

29. "one who will know" *yaḥ . . . jñāsyati*: The monkey-king Sugrīva is meant. The story of Rāma's alliance with him is narrated in the *Kiṣkindhākāṇḍa*. Perhaps it is because of Danu's still "impaired knowledge" that he claims Sugrīva will know about Rāvaṇa, when in fact he will know nothing.

30. "He adheres to established usage" *nyāyyavṛttena*: Rāma need have no fear in forming an alliance with Sugrīva, for he respects the reciprocal obligations of such a union (as indeed he will, but only after considerable prompting; see Book Four, *sarga* 29).

31. "for some reason or other," *kāraṇāntare*: Despite the fact that the compound clearly implies political conflict in 46.4 above, and that in the case of Sugrīva and Vālin, too, the same sort of conflict is at issue, I translate it here as expressing indefiniteness, since Kabandha's knowledge is still impaired. He will later explain fully what the reason was (68.16).

Sarga 68

1. "went to find," *āsādya*: Cg, Ck, Ct understand the verb causatively, "they moved (Kabandha to a cleft)."

3. "solid fat" *mahat medasā*: Not unobjectionable, though I see no other way to construe the instrumental. Cg takes it closely with *pacyamānasya*, glossing "dense with fat," but I doubt strongly whether the verbal can bear this sense (Cm, Ct, Cr all supply *pūrṇasya*, "full," to govern the instrumental).

4. "spotless garments" *araje vāsasī*: That is, to which dust does not adhere; a sign of divinity (cf. above, 4.5–6).

6. "aerial chariot harnessed with geese" *vimāne . . . haṃsayukte*: To Cm, Cg, Ck this detail suggests that through Rāma's purification of him, Kabandha has reached the world of Brahmā (the goose being Brahmā's mount).

8. "But when the wick runs out on a man (he is hounded by adversity)" *parimṛṣṭo daśāntena (daśābhāgena sevyate)*: Literally, "when one is touched by the end of a wick," or so I suppose, but the verse is obscure. Hesitatingly I suggest this: There are six "measures of royal policy" (war, peace, neutrality, etc.; cf. *MBh* 12.69.65ff., *ArthŚā* 7.1.1ff., *ManuSm* 7.160–61; this is how all commentators understand the phrase; Pārthasārathi in *ŚāstiDī* p. 87 interprets it as referring to the six *pramāṇas*). But Kabandha is not going to give Rāma a long lecture on them, for a man who, like Rāma, is at the end of his rope is going to be harassed by continuing disaster if he persists in acting alone (verse 9ab). Therefore, Kabandha simply advises him to make friends with Sugrīva (verse 10). The commentators do not supply convincing

alternatives; the solution of Cm, Cg, Ct, for example, runs: A man touched by adversity is served by, or naturally allied with, "one who has had a reversal of fortune," taking *daśābhāgena* as *bahuvrīhi*. But why should the same compound be a *bahuvrīhi* in verse 8d and a *tatpuruṣa* in 9a; and *daśānta* in the same line a *tatpuruṣa*? Furthermore, why should a man in trouble seek an alliance with someone else whose principal qualification is that he too is in trouble? (Ctr tries unsuccessfully to answer this question, pp. 243–44.)

12. "Ṛśyamūka": I spell the word thus, with palatal instead of retroflex *s*, here and throughout, in accordance with Bhatt 1963, p. 412.

14. "honors claims of gratitude" *kṛtajñaḥ*: Probably thus, rather than "skilled in practice" (see 2.1.20, 16.31, 23.4; 3.31.19 and notes), that is, an effective ally; for it appears to be this gratitude to which verse 15 is making reference.

16. "the son of Ṛkṣarajas" *ṛkṣarajasaḥ putraḥ*: Cg reports that some commentators hold Ṛkṣarajas to be the mother's name. Like Ck, Ct, Cr, I take it to be that of his putative father.

"ever since he wronged him" *kṛtakilbiṣaḥ*: Ever since, that is, Vālin wronged Sugrīva (cf. 4.8.23, *vālinaṃ kṛtakilbiṣam*, which given the context must mean, "Vālin, who committed this wrong"; see also 4.2.13 and, for a clear statement from the poet on who has wronged whom, 4.4.19). Nonetheless, the compound is inherently ambiguous; Cr in fact glosses, "Sugrīva committed a wrong against Vālin" (Cg neutralizes the question, "being engaged in hostilities with Vālin," cf. 4.4.19). The uncertainty as to who is at fault in the fratricidal struggle between the monkeys is discussed in Masson 1975.

17. Cm, Ck, Ct, Cr suppose the verse to mean that Rāma is to lay down his weapon before the fire when he makes the pact with Sugrīva. This is not, however, what happens (see *Kiṣkindhākāṇḍa* 5). (Venkatanathacharya [1965, pp. 503–4 note] makes the following suggestion: Since Sugrīva is terrified of his brother and suspects warriors to be sent out against him, the advice here is probably simply for Rāma to unstring and deposit his weapons somewhere [he has been advancing in full battle readiness up till now; see 63.8 above], in order to show his peaceful intention, lest Sugrīva flee at once; or, since Rāma does remain armed (4.2.15), the advice here must be for him to proceed with a non-belligerent bearing.)

18. "has discovered" *adhigacchati*: I understand the tense aspect as perfective (cf. 67.31; 4.45.1), though it may as easily be future ("will discover," as the NW version seeks to make clear, reading *vetsyati*; see verses 20ff. below); in 4.7.2 Sugrīva confesses that he has no knowledge whatever of Rāvaṇa.

22. "flawless" *aninditām*: A general commendatory epithet, probably, although according to Cg, Ck, Ct, Rāma is hereby meant to infer that Sītā's chastity has not been violated.

Sarga 69

4. Here and in verses 8ff., in what is surely intended to be a humorous passage, Kabandha—as if he still bore within him the vivid recollection of the gnawing hunger of his previous existence—enticingly describes the gustatory delights awaiting Rāma.

5. "lotus-covered lake known as Pampā" *puṣkariṇīṃ . . . pampāṃ nāma*: Elsewhere it is called a river (see 5.16 and note).

6. "free from . . . pitfalls" *avibhraṃśām*: The substantive is rare; Ck, Ct gloss, " 'anything to trip up one's feet,' that is, there are no entangling weeds" (Cg, "without soft banks").

9–10. "redfish and crooked-snouts and reedfish" *rohitān vakratuṇḍāṃś ca nalamīnāṃś ca*: The translation of fish names are best guesses; the commentators here and elsewhere (*MBh* 12.29.84, *Śāk* 6.14.3, *ManuSm* 5.16) are unhelpful.

"fins" *-pakṣān*: The word appears to be unrecorded in this sense. The line could refer to the birds mentioned in verse 8, though the other qualifications seem less appropriate to them (see also verse 11). Moreover, the image of roasting fish on iron spits is found elsewhere (cf. *MBh* 12.15.30, *ManuSm* 7.20).

14–15. "trees" *viṭapī*: This anomalous form is widely supported by both recensions (for the NR cf. 1304*); the commentators gloss it as irregular accusative plural. Böhtlingk long ago conjectured (the also irregular but at least intelligible) *viṭapīn* (1887, p. 215), and this is found in several S manuscripts.

16. "those are garlands" *tāni . . . mālyāni*: Presumably the ones mentioned in verse 14 above, though Cm, Cr understand thereby merely "flowers" (in order to avoid the problem Cg must solve in verse 18; see note there); the flowers will never be worn, they say, because the forest is so isolated that men never come there (so too Ck, Ct), but undoubtedly Cg is correct in attributing this to their miraculous origin.

"Matañga": Literally, "Elephant," this perhaps having something to do with what we learn in verses 22, 24, 27ff. (in *RaghuVa* 5.53, Matañga curses a *gandharva* to become an elephant). In *Rām* 4.11.41ff. (cf. 4.45.14) the story is told that when Vālin fought the *dānava* Dundubhi, he threw the demon's body so hard and far that drops of blood from its mouth were sprayed over the ashram of Matañga. The sage cursed the monkey-king that he would die should he ever approach the ashram, and Sugrīva consequently, when fleeing from his brother, took up his residence there. In *MBh* 13.29.22ff. Matañga is identified as a low-caste who was turned into a bird by Indra, and similarly in the *Suttanipāta* (1.7.137ff.; cf. Nīlakaṇṭha on *MBh* 14.54.15, and verse 31), Mātañga (*sic*) is a *caṇḍāla* "who gained the highest fame, and embarked on the path to the gods." Both accounts would fit, to some degree, with the fact that a tribal woman (verse 19 and note below) is an acolyte of his.

17–18. As Cg reminds us (see verse 16), the wind must have carried the beads of sweat from the ground to the trees.

19. "Śabarī": Literally, "a female Śabara." The Śabaras are one of the various indigenous tribes of the Deccan.

22. "Elephants" *nāgāḥ*: Or perhaps, "the elephants," those mentioned in verses 24, 27ff. (a number of S manuscripts insert a line to account for them, 1312*).

"because of the provisions of the seer" *ṛṣer . . . vidhānāt*: It is not clear what these provisions are; Ct glosses simply "by the power of the seer." (The divergent explanation of Cm, Cg, Cr results from the interpolated line 1313*.)

24. "fashioned . . . by Brahmā" *brahmaṇā . . . vinirmitaḥ*: Ck notes, "Since everything indeed is 'created by Brahmā,' the purpose of this qualification is to intimate the extraordinary nature of the mountain" (as in verse 25).

28. "in herds or all alone . . . ichor" *rudhira- . . . saṃhatya . . . pṛthakkīrṇāḥ*: I agree in my interpretation with Ck, Ct (for this sense of *saṃhatya* see 10.58 or 25.11),

though *rudhira-* is rare enough in the sense required that Cm, Cg understand, and the NE version reads, "striking (each other and so running with) blood."

30. "blocked by a boulder" *śilāpidhānā*: Cm takes this as the proper name of the cave.

36. "(spoke . . .) word of advice" *nidarśayan* (. . . *uvāca*): Essentially the same sense as in verse 1 above, though here used absolutely (thus also Cr; against Cg, who construes with *rūpam*, "displaying his form," and Cv, Cm, Ct, who supply another object, "[pointing out] the road, etc.").

Sarga 70

1. According to Cg, the episode of the female mendicant recounted in this and the following *sarga* is interpreted in the tradition of Vaiṣṇava allegoresis as exemplifying the state of absolute confidence in (or attachment to) one's spiritual preceptor (*ācāryābhimānaniṣṭhā*), and the rewards it confers (here Śabarī's vision of the Blessed Rāma as a result of her absolute faith in the admonitions of her gurus [verses 11–12]).

3. "the western shore" *paścimaṃ tīram*: It is odd that, proceeding westward, the princes reach the *western* shore of the lake (without being said to have first reached the eastern shore, and crossing the lake). Perhaps because of this the NR in verse 1 has them travel east (despite Kabandha's explicit directions in 69.2).

7. "obstacles" *vighnāḥ*: Such as desire (Cm, Cg, Ck, Ct).

8. "soft-spoken lady" *cārubhāṣini*: "The appropriate form to be used in addressing a holy woman," Cg.

Various N manuscripts add hereafter (or read in place of verse 8) a verse in which Rāma asks where those great seers have gone whom Śabarī had been serving (1328*, 1330*).

9. "won her the esteem of perfected beings" *siddhasaṃmatā*: Or, "estimable as a perfected being" (a similar choice between *tatpuruṣa* and *karmadhāraya* in 2.87.24; see the note there).

An SR insertion hereafter has Śabarī answer Rāma's questions: "It is today that I have achieved perfection in asceticism, by seeing you; today that my birth is rewarded . . . O best of gods" (1332*).

13. According to the "tradition" reported by Cg, Śabarī has been collecting and carefully storing food ever since Rāma reached Mount Citrakūṭa (and thus it is ready on his arrival).

14. "kept in ignorance" *vijñāne . . . abahiṣkṛtām*: I take this to mean (as the NE recension also suggests) that the ascetics had never withheld knowledge from Śabarī about their own activities, and thus Rāma can ask her the question he poses in verse 15 (or, less likely, that she is not ignorant about what was to befall her, pointing back to verses 10–13). Predictably the commentators find theological significance in the phrase, for example, Cg: "This means that she is worthy of the Blessed One's regard because, though she is a low-caste, she 'has gained knowledge' of *brahma* by the grace of her spiritual preceptor"; more elaborately Ck, "She is indisputably 'qualified for knowledge' of *brahma* because, like Vācaknavī [cf. *ŚatBr* 14.6.6.1, 8.1], Maitreyī [cf. *BṛĀraU* 2.4], and other [great female ascetics], she is [must be?] a highborn woman of a family of ascetic brahmans. This has been explained in the intro-

ductory verse to [my?] commentary on the *Bṛhadāraṇyakopaniṣad* and in the *Śrīhaṃsabhāṣya*."

15. "of those great ascetics" (*me*) *mahātmanām*: So I read, for the crit. ed.'s *te mahātmanaḥ* ("of your great [guru]"), adopting a variant that has support in the S and NE recensions, and finds further corroboration in (*prabhāvaṃ taṃ*) *mahātmanām* in 71.2. The feats the female ascetic proceeds to describe in the following verses concern the students, not Matañga himself, and it is moreover unlikely that she should start speaking of Matañga when she has been talking about the "great seers" in verses 10–12. Recall also that Danu-Kabandha spoke of the students (69.17–18) no less than the guru (69.22).

18. "offer it [the shrine] sacrifice" *juhavāñ cakrire tīrtham*: A very peculiar phrase, though the translation offered appears to be supported by Cg. Cm, Cr explain *tīrtha-* as "sacrifice," a meaning unrecorded for the word; Ck, Ct read instead *nīḍam*, "they offered up the cage [of their bodies] in sacrifice," but it is difficult to believe that Śabarī would begin her description of the ascetics' great deeds with the last of them. Perhaps the word has a sense hitherto recorded only in lexica, "fire": "they made offering to the sacrificial fire" (for which Ñ1's *analam* is perhaps a gloss). The causative here seems to be *svārthe* (see note on 26.20 above).

19. "sloping westward" *pratyaksthalī*: So Cg and apparently Cm ("lower at the west, insofar as Viṣṇu's position is in the east, facing west"?); contrast 2.93.23 and note, where Rāma's altar is said to slope toward the northeast.

20. "altars" *vedyaḥ*: Much of the SR reads the singular in place of the plural (see verse 19).

For the second half of the verse the NR offers, "Neither the flowers nor the *kuśa* grass have faded or dried up (even now)" (1341*).

21. The seas would have been brought by the sages in order for them to perform the ritual ablutions (as in the next verse) appropriate at such pilgrimage sites (*tīrtha*).

22. Their clothes have not yet dried because of both the spiritual powers of the sages and the power of the sacred bathing places (the oceans), according to Ct (so Ck).

27. "those" *te*: The pronoun probably refers to the seers Śabarī had previously served (as in verse 24), and not to *maharṣis* in general.

"by virtue of her meditation on the Self" *ātmasamādhinā*: Or, of course, simply, "by virtue of her own meditation."

Sarga 71

1. "by her own act" *svena karmaṇā*: Or, less likely, "by virtue of her merit, her good karma" (see above, note on 62.16).

5. Hereafter NE manuscripts insert seven verses detailing some of the good omens Rāma sees (e.g., animals moving on his right side [that is, left to right], and Lakṣmaṇa's brightening face), 1357*.

11. "peacock" *arjunaka-*: So Cr; the word appears to be unattested in this sense.

"parrot" *kīcaka-*: Thus glossed by Cg.

12–13. These verses are absent in the NR (which in fact has a separate, if not totally divergent, version for most of the *sarga*), and should probably have been omitted from the constituted text. In any case, though this is essentially the version of Ct, the verses appear to me to be out of order (as is the case with other stanzas here, verses 21-22, for example); the sequence of verses is explicitly raised as a matter of dispute in Ck, whereas Cm, Cg show a totally different order from what the crit. ed. has established (Cg remarks, on verse 26, that the codices in his possession displayed a widely discrepant number of lines for the *sarga*). Things seem hopelessly muddled; as they stand, we are required to understand *hradam* ("pool") in verse 12 to mean Lake Pampā itself, part of which is also known as the Pond of Matañga (Cm, Ck, Ct, Cr in fact claim that Matañga's pond is a region of Lake Pampā); the feminines in verse 13 would then refer to Pampā. (The pool has nothing to do with that one mentioned in 69.31, which is on the mountain itself.)

"Rāma felt a pang of desire" *sa rāmo . . . kāmābhisaṃtaptaḥ*: As the poet will explain in the first *sarga* of the following book (which incidentally the NR includes in the *Araṇyakāṇḍa*), it is springtime, "the season that quickens lust and desire" (2.57.10), which Rāma feels to be doubly painful because Sītā is gone from him (4.1.12ff.).

Rāma proceeds to bathe in the pool because it is a holy place (Cg).

20. "he began to lament" *vilalāpa*: Rāma's grief here is alluded to by Bhavabhūti in *UttaRāC* 1.30.15–16.

23. "mentioned before" *pūrvoktaḥ*: An unusually prosaic phrase, not found elsewhere in the *Rām*, I believe, but certainly in keeping with the general negligence of literary art in the *sarga*.

The texts of Cm, Cg, Ck, Cr include verses 23–25 in Rāma's direct discourse (by "adding" the lines marking quotation closure, 1371*).

25. In 4.1.49 we will be told that the brothers proceed together toward Mount Ṛśyamūka (so also according to *MBh* 3.264.8), and later (*sarga* 4) Hanumān comes upon them together. This verse stands in contradiction with the later events; the NR, perhaps justly, omits it (as well as verses 23–24).

26. "the forest" *vanam*: That is, the one between Kabandha's residence and Lake Pampā (so suggested by Cg), not the one by Pampā itself (Ct, Cr).

Glossary of Important Sanskrit Words, Proper Nouns, and Epithets

Agastya: famous sage, son of Mitra-Varuṇa and Urvaśī
Agni: god of fire
Aikṣvāka: "descendant of Ikṣvāku," used mainly of Daśaratha and Rāma
Airāvata: an elephant, Indra's mount
Amarāvatī: the city of the god Indra
apsarases: celestial maidens or nymphs, known for their beauty; frequently seen in the service of superior gods, especially Indra
asuras: a class of demons, the elder brothers of the gods
Ayodhyā: capital city of the Ikṣvākus
Bala (v.l. Vala): demon slain by Indra. "Slayer of Bala" is a common epithet of Indra
Bharata: Daśaratha's second son, by Kaikeyī
Bhogavatī: city of the serpents conquered by Rāvaṇa
Brahmā: creator divinity of the Hindu "trinity," who is regarded as the "Grandfather" of all living creatures
Bṛhaspati: family priest of Indra and the gods
Caitraratha: Kubera's pleasure garden on Mount Meru
cāraṇas: celestial bards
Citrakūṭa: mountain where Rāma, Sītā, and Lakṣmaṇa first live during their exile
daityas: a class of demons descended from Diti
Dakṣa: one of the ten mind-born sons of Brahmā; he is said to have had many daughters
dānavas: a class of demons descended from Danu
Daṇḍaka: the forest where Rāma, Sītā, and Lakṣmaṇa spend part of their exile
Danu: a name of Kabandha
Daśaratha: Rāma's father and king of Ayodhyā
Dāśarathi: "descendant of Daśaratha," used of Daśaratha's four sons, especially Rāma
Dūṣaṇa: a general in Khara's army in Janasthāna, slain by Rāma
gandharvas: a class of semi-divine beings known for their musical abilities. *Gandharva* women are noted for their beauty
Ganges: a famous and important river of ancient and modern India, which is personified as the daughter of Mt. Himalaya. She is the sister of Pārvatī
Garuḍa: the king of the birds; Viṣṇu's mount
Godāvarī: a river in the Deccan
guhyakas: see *yakṣas*
Himalaya: name of a mountain range and king of the mountains
Ikṣvāku: family name of the royal House of Ayodhyā
Ilvala: a *rākṣasa*; brother of Vātāpi
Indra: king of the gods who leads their hosts into battle against the *asuras*

Janaka: lord of Mithilā, father of Sītā
Jānakī: "daughter of Janaka," epithet of Sītā
Janasthāna: part of the Daṇḍaka forest and the residence of Śūrpaṇakhā, sister of Rāvaṇa, and her brother Khara
Jaṭāyus: a vulture, friend of Daśaratha
Jaya: father of Virādha
Kabandha: a *rākṣasa* slain by Rāma
Kaikeyī: junior wife of Daśaratha and the mother of Bharata
Kailāsa: mountain peak in the Himalayas where Śiva and Pārvatī reside
Kākutstha: "descendant of Kakutstha," a common epithet of princes of the Ikṣvāku dynasty, especially Rāma and his brothers
Kāma: god of love
Kandarpa: epithet of Kāma
Kausalyā: senior wife of Daśaratha, mother of Rāma
Khara: brother of Rāvaṇa and Śūrpaṇakhā
kinnaras: mythical creatures with the head of a horse and a human body; *kinnara* women are famed for their beauty
Kosala: kingdom of the Ikṣvākus
Krauñca: a mountain or forest south of Janasthāna
Kubera: god of wealth, son of Viśravas and half-brother of Rāvaṇa. Kubera is the king of the *yakṣas*
Kumbhakarṇa: brother of Rāvaṇa, known for his great size
Lakṣmaṇa: son of Daśaratha by Sumitrā, Rāma's constant companion
Laṅkā: Rāvaṇa's capital city, scene of Sītā's confinement and the epic's culminating battle
Maithilī: "woman of Mithilā," epithet of Sītā
Māṇḍakarṇi: a sage who lived on air for ten thousand years
Mandākinī: tributary of the Ganges; sometimes an epithet of the Ganges
Mandara: a mountain used as the churning rod in the mythical churning of the ocean
Manmatha: epithet of Kāma
Mārīca: a *rākṣasa*, son of Sunda and Tāṭakā
Maruts: storm gods, companions of Indra
Mataṅga: a sage whose ashram is near Ṛśyamūka mountain
Meru: a mythical mountain; thought to be the *axis mundi*
Namuci: an *asura* slain by Indra
Nandana: the pleasure garden of Indra
Nandi: a bull, Śiva's mount
Niṣādas: forest-dwelling hunters and fishermen
Pāka: a demon slain by Indra; the deed gives rise to the common epithet of the great god: Pākaśāsana, "chastiser of Pāka"
Pampā: the lake or river where Rāma and Lakṣmaṇa first encounter Hanumān and Sugrīva
Pañcavaṭī: a forest where Rāma, Sītā, and Lakṣmaṇa live during their exile
piśācas: a class of demons of a particularly low order
Prasravaṇa: mountain where Rāma, Sītā, and Lakṣmaṇa reside for part of their exile
Pulastya: mind-born son of Brahmā, ancestor of the *rākṣasas*

Puṣpaka: the aerial chariot stolen by Rāvaṇa from Kubera
Rāghava: any descendant of Raghu, used especially of Rāma and his brothers
Raghu: son of Kakutstha, ancestor of Rāma
Rāhu: the *asura* who causes eclipses by swallowing the sun and moon
rākṣasa: a class of violent and bloodthirsty demons
Rāma: eldest son of Daśaratha by Kausalyā
Rambhā: an *apsaras* with whom Tumburu is in love
Rāvaṇa: main antagonist of the *Rāmāyaṇa*; the *rākṣasas*' ten-headed overlord who abducts Sītā
Ṛkṣarajas: a monkey, father of Sugrīva
Rohiṇī: daughter of Dakṣa, favorite consort of the moon
Ṛśyamūka: the mountain where Rāma meets the monkey Sugrīva
Rudra: epithet of Śiva
Rudras: sons or companions of the storm god
Śabarī: hermit woman who shows hospitality to Rāma
Śacī's lord: a common epithet of Indra; Śacī is Indra's wife
Śakra: a common epithet of Indra
Śarabhaṅga: an ascetic whom Rāma, Sītā, and Lakṣmaṇa seek out after their encounter with the *rākṣasa* Virādha
Sarayū: a river that flows through the kingdom of Kosala
Śatahradā: mother of Virādha
Saumitri: "son of Sumitrā," matronymic epithet of Lakṣmaṇa
Sītā: daughter of Janaka, wife of Rāma
Śrī: goddess of royalty, consort of Viṣṇu
Sthūlaśiras: sage who curses Kabandha to retain his hideous form
Śukra: preceptor of the *asuras*
Sumitrā: juniormost wife of Daśaratha, mother of Lakṣmaṇa and Śatrughna
Suparṇa: epithet of Garuḍa
Śūrpaṇakhā: a *rākṣasa* woman, sister of Rāvaṇa
Sutīkṣṇa: a sage who shows hospitality to Rāma
Takṣaka: serpent lord defeated by Rāvaṇa
Triśiras: a *rākṣasa* lieutenant of Khara, slain in single combat by Rāma
Tumburu: a *gandharva* cursed to become the *rākṣasa* Virādha
Vaidehī: "woman of Videha," epithet of Sītā
Vaiśravaṇa: "descendant of Viśravas," epithet of Kubera
Vaivasvata: "descendant of Vivasvān," patronymic epithet of Yama
Vālin: king of the monkeys, husband of Tārā, and son of Indra; he is the elder brother of Sugrīva
Varuṇa: god of the ocean
Vāsava: an epithet of Indra
Vāsuki: serpent lord defeated by Rāvaṇa
Vasus: a class of gods
Vātāpi: a *rākṣasa*, brother of Ilvala, slain by the sage Agastya
Vāyu: god of the wind
Vibhīṣaṇa: a *rākṣasa*, brother of Rāvaṇa, ally of Rāma
Vindhya: a mountain range in central India
Virādha: a *rākṣasa*, who, having attempted to abduct Sītā, is slain by Rāma

Viṣṇu: one of the three main gods of the Hindu "trinity," along with Brahmā and Śiva

Viśvakarman: god of craft, architect of the gods

Viśvāmitra: a sage who serves as teacher and friend to Rāma

Vṛtra: a demon slain by Indra

yakṣas: semi-divine beings associated with Kubera; the women are known for their beauty

Yama: god of death

Emendations and Corrections of the Critical Edition

Below are listed the emendations and corrections of the text of the crit. ed. that have been adopted by the translator. For specific discussions the reader may consult the notes to the translation. Question marks identify conjectures.

	READING OF THE CRITICAL EDITION	*TRANSLATOR'S READING*
3.17	kausalyā suprajās	kausalyāsuprajās
4.36	bhuvane	bhavane
5.7	mahārathaḥ	mahāratha
6.3	satatam	saṃtatam
10.10	prabhāvam	prabhavam
10.24	adhikān māsān	adhikaṃ māsam
11.15	-vacanam	-vacanād
13.25	tapasvinaḥ	tarasvinaḥ
13.25	golāṅgulāṃś ca	golāṅgulāś ca
13.35	ātmavāñ	ātmano
17.9	-varṇinī	-varṇini
17.13	karālā nir-	karālānir-
19.10	saṃtuṣṭā	saṃduṣṭā
27.2	dūṣaṇas triśirā	dūṣaṇatriśirā
33.1	buddhvā	buddhyā
34.22	mahāvane	mahāhave
36.6	ūnaṣoḍaśavarṣo	bālo dvādaśavarṣo
40.30	-oṣṭham	-oṣṭhī
41.24	-saṃśraye	-saṃśrave (?)
42 7	muhur dūrāt,	muhūrtān na
42.12	sa bhṛśam	sadṛśam
44.18	sahitau	saṃhatau
44.18	saṃpragalbhitau	saṃpravalgitau
45.4	saṃvatsaraṃ cādhyuṣitā	uṣitvā dvādaśa samā
45.5	saṃvatsarād ūrdhvam	trayodaśe varṣe
45.10		add 874*
47.26	nanu	na tu
48.11	kāma-	kāmaṃ
48.11	ārya mā vasaty	ārya āvasaty
50.33	gatotsāhām	jalocchvāsāḥ
53.32	daiva-	devi

55.5	ālakṣya	ālambya
58.33	ivābhāti	iva bhrāntaḥ
60.36	priyam	'priyam
61.16	śīlena	śivena
70.15	te mahātmanaḥ	me mahātmanām

Bibliography of Works Consulted

TEXTS OF THE *VĀLMĪKI RĀMĀYAṆA*

Ramayana. (1928–1947). 7 vols. Lahore: D.A.V. College. Northwestern recension critically edited for the first time from original manuscripts by Vishva Bandhu. D.A.V. College Sanskrit Series, nos. 7,12,14,17–20.

Ramayana id es carmen epicum de Ramae rebus gestis poetae antiquissimi Valmicis opus. (1829–1838). 3 vols. Bonn: Typis regiis. Edited and translated by August Wilhelm von Schlegel. Volumes numbered 1.1, 1.2 (text); 2.1 (translation).

The Rāmāyaṇa of Vālmīki. (1909). 3rd ed. Bombay: Nirṇayasāgar Press. With the commentary (Tilaka) of Rāma. Edited by Vāsudev Lakshman Shāstrī Paṇśīkar.

Rāmāyan of Vālmīki. (1914–1920). 7 vols. Bombay: Gujarati Printing Press. With three commentaries called Tilaka, Shiromani, and Bhooshana. Edited by Shastri Shrinivasa Katti Mudholkar.

Śrīmadvālmīkirāmāyaṇam. (1911–1913). 7 vols. Bombay: Nirṇayasāgar Press. Also called the Kumbakonam Edition. Edited by T. R. Krishnacharya and T. R. Vyasacharya.

Śrīmadvālmīkirāmāyaṇam. (1935). 3 vols. Bombay: Lakṣmīveṅkateśvara Mudraṇālaya. Edited by Gaṅgāviṣṇu Śrīkṛṣṇadāsa. With the commentaries of Govindarāja, Rāmānuja, and Maheśvaratīrtha and the commentary known as Taṇiślokī.

Śrīmadvālmīkirāmāyaṇam. (1958). Mylapore, Madras: n.p. Second edition revised by K. Chinnaswami Sastrigal and V. H. Subrahmanya Sastri.

Śrīmadvālmīkirāmāyaṇam. (1960–). Mysore: University of Mysore, Oriental Research Institute. With Amṛtakataka of Mādhavayogi. Edited by K. S. Varadacharya et al.

The Vālmīki Rāmāyaṇa: Critical Edition. (1960–1975). 7 vols. Baroda: Oriental Institute. General editors: G. H. Bhatt and U. P. Shah.

SANSKRIT TEXTS

Commentators are specified only when cited in the notes.

The Abhijñāna-Śākuntala of Kālidāsa. (1891). 3rd rev. ed. Bombay: Nirṇayasāgara Press. Edited by Nārāyaṇa Balakṛishṇa Godabole and Kāśīnāth Pāṇḍuraṅg Parab.

Ahirbudhnya-saṃhitā of the Pāñcarātrāgama. (1966). 2 vols. Madras: Adyar Library and Research Centre. Edited by M. D. Ramanujacharya. 2nd ed. rev. by V. Krishnamacharya.

The Amarakośa. (1940). 11th ed. Bombay: Nirṇayasāgar Press. Edited by W. L. Śāstrī Paṇśikar.

The Aṅguttaranikāya. (1885–1910). Edited by the Rev. Richard Morris (vols. 1, 2), Prof. E. Hardy (vols. 3–5), Mabel Hunt (vol. 6, indexes). London: Pali Text Society. Pali Text Society, nos. 10, 20, 35, 44, 46.

Āpastambaśrautasūtram. (1945). 2 vols. Mysore: University of Mysore. Edited by

S. Narasiṃhācār. Mysore University Oriental Library Publications, Sanskrit Series, nos. 87, 93.

Āruṇikopaniṣad in *Upaniṣatsaṃgraha*. (1970). Delhi: Motilal Banarsidass. Edited by J. L. Shastri.

Āśvalāyanagṛhyasūtram. (1938). Poona: Ānandāśrama Press. Ānandāśrama Sanskrit Series, no. 105. Reprint 1978.

Āśvalāyanaśrautasūtra. (1874). Calcutta: Asiatic Society of Bengal. Edited by Rāmanārāyaṇa Vidyāratna. Bibliotheca Indica, no. 49.

Atrismṛti. (1905). Poona: Ānandāśrama Press. Ānandāśrama Sanskrit Series, no. 48.

Atharvaveda (Śaunaka). (1960–1964). 4 vols. Hoshiarpur: Vishveshvaranand Vedic Research Institute. With the Commentary of Sāyaṇācārya. Edited by Vishva Bandhu et al. Vishveshvaranand Indological Series, no. 13.

Bālarāmāyaṇa. (1869). Benares: Medical Hall Press. Edited by Govinda Deva Shastri.

Baudhāyanadharmasūtra. (1983). Varanasi: Chowkhamba Sanskrit Sansthan. Edited by Umeśa Chandra Pāṇḍeya. Kashi Sanskrit Series, no. 104.

The Bhagavad-Gītā. (1935). Bombay: Gujarati Printing Press. With eleven commentaries. Edited by Sastri Gajānaṇa Shambu Sadhale.

Bhāgavatapurāṇam. (saṃvat 1965 [=A.D. 1908]). Bombay: Veṅkateśvara Press.

Bhāradvājagṛhyasūtra. (1913). Leiden: E. J. Brill. Edited by Henriette J. W. Salomons.

Brahmapurāṇam. (1895). Poona: Ānandāśrama Press. Ānandāśrama Sanskrit Series, no. 28.

Bṛhadāraṇyakopaniṣat. (1891). Poona: Ānandāśrama Press. Edited by Kāśīnāth Śāstrī Āgāśe. Ānandāśrama Sanskrit Series, no. 15. Reprint 1939.

Bṛhad-dharma-purāṇam. (1888–1897). Calcutta: Asiatic Society of Bengal. Edited by Haraprasād Śāstrī. Bibliotheca Indica, no. 120. Reprint Varanasi: Chaukhamba Amarabharati Prakashan, 1974.

Bṛhatsaṃhitā. (1865). Calcutta: Asiatic Society of Bengal. Edited by H. Kern. Bibliotheca Indica, no. 48.

The Buddhacarita or Acts of the Buddha. (1936). Lahore: Motilal Banarsidass. Edited by E. H. Johnston. Reprint Delhi, 1972.

The Çatapatha-Brāhmaṇa in the Mādhyandina-Çākhā. (1855). Berlin: Ferd. Dümmler's Verlagsbuchhandlung. Edited by Albrecht Weber. Reprint Varanasi: Chowkhamba Sanskrit Series Office, 1964.

The Champū-Rāmāyaṇa of King Bhoja (1–5 Kāṇḍas) and Lakshmaṇa Sūri (6th Kāṇḍa). (1917). 5th ed. Bombay: Nirṇayasāgar Press. With the commentary of Rāmachandra Budhendra. Edited by Wāsudev Laxmaṇ Śāstrī Paṇśīkar.

Chāndogyopaniṣat. (1934). Poona: Ānandāśrama Press. Edited by Kāśīnāth Śāstrī Āgāśe. Ānandāśrama Sanskrit Series, no. 14.

The Çrautasūtra of Kātyāyana. (1859). Berlin: Ferd. Dümmler's Verlagsbuchhandlung. Edited by Albrecht Weber.

Daśakumāracarita. (1889). Bombay: Nirṇayasāgar Press. Edited by Kāśīnāth Pāṇḍuraṅg Parab.

Devībhāgavatapurāṇa. (1954). Bombay: Veṅkateśvara Press.

Dharmākūtam, vol. III: Araṇyakāṇḍa, by Tryambakarāya Makhi. (1955). Tanjore: S. Gopalan. Tanjore Saraswati Mahal Library Series, no. 70.

Dhātupāṭha. In *Pāṇini's Grammatik, q.v.*

Dhvanyāloka. (1965). Varanasi: Chowkhamba Vidyabhawan. Edited by Jagannath Pathak. Vidyabhawan Sanskrit Granthamala, no. 97.

Dūtavākya. (1962). In *Plays Ascribed to Bhāsa*. Poona: Oriental Book Agency. Edited by C. R. Devadhar. Poona Oriental Series, no. 54.

Gautamapraṇītadharmasūtrāṇi. (1910). Poona: Ānandāśrama Press. Edited by Naraharaśāstrī Talekar. Ānandāśrama Sanskrit Series, no. 61. Reprint 1966.

Harivaṃśa, see *Mahābhārata*.

The Institutes of Nārada. (1885). Calcutta: Asiatic Society of Bengal. Edited by Julius Jolly. Bibliotheca Indica, no. 102.

Kālikāpurāṇa. (1907). Bombay: Veṅkateśvara Press.

Kāmandakīyanītisāra. (1964, 1977). 2 vols. Poona: Ānandāśrama Press. With the Jayamaṅgalā and Upādhyāyanirapekṣā Commentaries. Ānandāśrama Sanskrit Series, no. 136.

Kāśikā of Vāmana and Jayāditya. (1969). 4th. ed. Varanasi: Chowkhamba Sanskrit Series Office. Edited by Nārāyaṇa Miśra. Kashi Sanskrit Series, no. 37.

Kāṭhakopaniṣat. (1914). Poona: Ānandāśrama Press. Edited by Vaijaṇātha Rājavāde. Ānandāśrama Sanskrit Series, no. 7.

The Kauṭilīya Arthaśāstra, Part I. (1969). 2nd ed. Bombay: University of Bombay. Edited by R. P. Kangle. University of Bombay Studies Sanskrit, Prakrit and Pali, no. 1.

Kirātārjunīya. (1917). Bombay: Nirṇayasāgar Press. Edited by T. Śrīnivāsa Veṅkatarāma Śarma.

Kumārasaṃbhava of Kālidāsa. (1886). Bombay: Nirṇayasāgar Press. With the commentary (the Sañjīvanī) of Mallinātha (1–8 sargas) and of Sītārāma (8–17 sargas). Edited by Nārāyaṇa Bhaṭṭa Parvaṇīkara and Kāśīnāth Pāṇḍuraṅg Parab. 9th ed., 1923. Edited by Vāsudeva Laxmaṇ Shāstrī Paṇsīkar.

The Kūrmapurāṇam. (1971). Varanasi: All-India Kashiraj Trust. Edited by Anand Swarup Gupta.

Liṅgapurāṇa. (1885). Calcutta: New Valmiki Press. Edited by Jibananda Vidyasagar.

Mahābhārata: Critical Edition. (1933–1971). 19 vols. Poona: Bhandarkar Oriental Research Institute. With *Harivaṃśa* (1969–1971). Critically edited by V. S. Sukthankar et al.

Mahābhārata. (1929–1933). 6 vols. Poona: Chitrashala Press. With the commentary of Nīlakaṇṭha. Edited by Ramachandrashastri Kinjawadekar.

Mahābhāratam—Part VII, Harivanshaparvan. (1936). Poona: Chitrashala Press. With the Bhārata Bhāwadeepa by Neelakantha. Edited by Ramachandrashastri Kinjawadekar.

Mahābhāṣya: Vyākaraṇamahābhāṣye navāhnikam. (1951). Bombay: Nirṇayasāgar Press. Edited by Bhārgava Śāstrī Joshi.

Mahānāṭaka. (1890). Calcutta: Narayana Press. Edited by Jibananda Vidyasagara.

Maitrāyaṇī Saṃhitā. (1881–1886). 4 vols. Leipzig: F. A. Brockhaus. Edited by Leopold von Schroeder. Reprint in 1 vol. Amsterdam: Philo Press, 1971.

The Maitri or Maitrāyaṇīya Upanishad. (1870). Calcutta: Asiatic Society of Bengal. Edited by E. B. Cowell. Bibliotheca Indica, no. 42.

The Majjhimanikāya. (1888–1925). 4 vols. Edited by V. Trencker (vol. 1), Robert Chalmers (vols. 2, 3), Mrs. Rhys Davids (vol. 4, index of words). London: Pali Text Society. Pali Text Society nos.17, 39, 43, 45, 47, 51, 99.

Mālatīmādhava. (1905). Bombay: Government Central Book Depot. Edited by R. G.

Bhandarkar. Third Edition, revised with additional notes, by V. V. Mirashi. Bombay Sanskrit and Prakrit Series, no. 15.

Mānava-dharma Śāstra. (1886). Bombay: Ganpat Krishnaji's Press. With the Commentaries of Medhātithi [etc.]. Edited by Vishvanāth Nārāyan Mandlik.

Manusmṛti. (1929). Bombay: Nirṇayasāgar Press. With the commentary of Kullūka. Edited by Vāsudevaśarma Paṇaśīkar.

Matsyapurāṇam. (1907). Poona: Ānandāśrama Press. Ānandaśrama Sanskrit Series, no. 54.

Meghadūta. (1957). New Delhi: Sāhitya Akademi. Edited by S. K. De.

Mitākṣarā, see *Yājñavalkyasmṛti*.

Mṛcchakaṭika of Śūdraka. (1896). Bombay: Government Central Book Depot. Edited by Nārāyaṇa Bālakṛṣṇa Goḍabole. Bombay Sanskrit Series, no. 52.

Mudrārākṣasa by Viśākhadatta. (1893). Bombay: Nirṇayasāgar Press. With the commentary of Ḍhuṇḍhirāja. Edited by Kāśīnāth Trimbak Telang. Bombay Sanskrit Series, no. 27.

Mūlamādhyamikakārikā. (1977). Madras: Adyar Library. Edited by J. W. de Jong.

Nala Caritra Nāṭaka of Nīlakaṇṭha Dīkṣita. (1925). Madras: Sri Balamanorama Press. Edited by C. Sankararama Sastri. Sri Balamanorama Series, no. 8.

Nāradasmṛti, see *Institutes of Nārada*.

Narasiṃhapurāṇa. (1911). 2nd ed. Bombay: Gopala Narayana Co. Edited by Uddhavacarya Ainapure.

Nāṭyaśāstra. (1926–1964). Baroda: Oriental Institute. Edited by M. Ramakrishna Kavi and J. S. Pade. Vol. 1, 2nd rev. ed., 1956. Reprint 1980. Gaekwad's Oriental Series, nos. 36, 68, 124, 145.

Nāṭyaśāstra. (1971–1983). 3 vols. Varanasi: Banaras Hindu University. Edited by Madhusudhan Shastri.

Nītisāra, see *Kāmandakīyanītisāra*.

Pāda-Index of Vālmīki-Rāmāyaṇa. (1961–1966). 2 vols. Baroda: Oriental Institute. Edited by G. H. Bhatt. Gaekwad's Oriental Series, nos. 129, 153.

Padmapurāṇam. (1893–1894). 4 vols. Poona: Ānandāśrama Press. Edited by Viśvanātha Nārāyaṇa Maṇḍalik. Ānandāśrama Sanskrit Series, no. 131.

Pañcaviṃśabrāhmaṇa, see *Tāṇḍya Mahābrāhmaṇa*.

Pāṇini's Grammatik. (1887). Leipzig: Haessel. Edited by Otto Böhtlingk. Reprint Hildesheim: Olms, 1964.

Paramāsaṃhitā. (1940). Baroda: Oriental Institute. Edited by S. Krishnaswami Aiyangar. Gaekwad's Oriental Series, no. 86.

Prasannarāghava. (1894). Poona: Shiralkar and Co. Edited by S. M. Paranjpe and N. S. Panse.

Pratīka-Index of the Mahābhārata and Harivaṃśa. (1967–1972). 6 vols. Poona: Bhandarkar Oriental Research Institute. Edited by Parashuram Lakshman Vaidya.

Raghuvaṃśa of Kālidāsa. (śāka 1808 [=A.D. 1886]). 3rd ed. Bombay: Nirṇayasāgar Press. With the commentary of Mallinātha. Edited by Kāśīnāth Pāṇḍuraṅg Parab.

Rahasyatrayasāra of Vedāntadeśika. (1986). Madrapuri: n.p. Edited by Uttamūr Ti. Vīrarāghavācārya. Translated from the Maṇipravāla into Sanskrit by Ku. V. Nīlameghācārya.

Rāmāyaṇacampū, see *The Campū-Rāmāyaṇa*.

Rāmāyaṇasārasaṃgraharaghuvīrastava. (1967). In *Oeuvres poétiques de Nīlakaṇṭha Dī-*

kṣita, vol. 1. Pondicherry: Institut français d'Indologie. Edited and translated by Pierre-Sylvain Filliozat. Institut français d'Indologie Publication Series, no. 36.

Rasagaṅgādhara. (1947). Bombay: Nirṇayasāgar Press. Edited by Bhaṭṭa Mathurānātha Śāstrī. Kāvyamālā, no. 12.

Ratirahasya. (n.d.). Lahore: Punjab Sanskrit Book Depot. Edited by Devidatta Parajuli.

Ṛgveda-Saṃhitā. (1933). 5 vols. Poona: Vaidic Samshodhan Mandal. With the commentary of Sāyaṇāchārya.

Saddharmalaṅkāvatārasūtra. (1963). Darbhanga: The Mithila Institute. Edited by P. L. Vaidya. Buddhist Sanskrit Texts, no. 3.

Ṣaḍviṃśabrāhmaṇa. (1908). Leiden: E. J. Brill. Edited by Frederik Eelsingh.

Sāhityadarpaṇa of Viśvanātha Kavirāja. (1967). Varanasi: Chowkhamba Sanskrit Series Office. Edited by Āchārya Kṛṣṇamohan Śāstrī. Kashi Sanskrit Series, no. 145.

Śāstradīpikā. (1915). Bombay: Nirṇayasāgar Press. Edited by Dharmadatta Sūri.

Śatapathabrāhmaṇa, see *The Çatapatha Brāhmaṇa*.

The Śrauta Sūtra of Āpastamba. (1882–1902). 3 vols. Calcutta: Asiatic Society of Bengal. Edited by R. Garbe. Bibliotheca Indica, no. 92.

The Śrauta Sūtra of Kātyāyana, see *The Çrautasūtra of Kātyāyana*.

Subhāṣitaratnabhāṇḍāgāra. (1952). Bombay: Nirṇayasāgar Press. Edited by Nārāyaṇa Rām Ācārya.

Sūktiratnahāra of Sūrya. (1938). Trivandrum: Government Press. Edited by K. Sāmbaśiva Śāstrī. Trivandrum Sanskrit Series, no. 141.

Suśrutasaṃhitā, see under Bhishagratna, K. K. in Secondary Sources.

Taittirīya-brāhmaṇa. (1898). 3 vols. Poona: Ānandāśrama Press. With the commentary of Sāyaṇācārya. Edited by Nārāyaṇaśāstrī Goḍbole. Ānandāśrama Sanskrit Series, no. 37. Reprint 1979.

Taittirīya Saṃhitā. (1900–1908). 9 vols. Poona: Ānandāśrama Press. Edited by Kāśīnāth Śāstrī Āgāśe. Ānandāśrama Sanskrit Series, no. 42. Reprint 1961.

Taittirīyopaniṣat. (1889). Poona: Ānandāśrama Press. Edited by Vāmana Śāstrī Islāmpurkar. Ānandāśrama Sanskrit Series, no. 12. Reprint 1929.

Tāṇḍya Mahābrāhmaṇa (=Pañcaviṃśabrāhmaṇa). (1870–1874). 2 vols. Calcutta: Asiatic Society of Bengal. Edited by Ānandachandra Vedāntavāgīśa. Bibliotheca Indica, no. 62.

The Thera- and Therī-Gāthā: (stanzas ascribed to elders of the Buddhist order of recluses). (1883). Edited by Hermann Oldenberg and Richard Pischel. London: Pali Text Society. Pali Text Society, no. 5.

Unmattarāghava. (1889). Bombay: Nirṇayasāgar Press. Edited by Durgāprasād and Kāśīnāth Pāṇḍuraṅg Parab. Kāvyamālā, no. 17.

Uttararāmacarita of Bhavabhūti. (1948). Bombay: Nirṇayasāgar Press. Edited by Nārāyaṇa Rām Ācārya.

Vallabhadeva's Kommentar (Śāradā-Version) zum Kumārasambhava des Kālidāsa. (1980). Wiesbaden: Franz Steiner Verlag. Edited by M. S. Narayana Murti in collaboration with Klaus L. Janert. Verzeichnis der orientalischen Handschriften in Deutschland, Supplementband 20, 1.

Vāyupurāṇam. (1905). Poona: Ānandāśrama Press. Ānandāśrama Sanskrit Series, no. 49.

Vikramorvaśīya. (1961). New Delhi: Sāhitya Akademi. Edited by H. D. Velankar.

Viṣṇupurāṇam. (saṃvat 1967 [= A.D. 1910]). Bombay: Veṅkateśvara Press.

Vyākaraṇamahābhāṣya. (1967). 3 vols. Delhi: Motilal Banarsidass. (Reprint [?] of the 6 vol. ed., Bombay: Nirṇayasāgar Press, 1935–).

Yājñavalkyasmṛti of Yogīśvara Yājñavalkya. (1949). 5th ed. Bombay: Nirṇayasāgar Press. With the commentary Mitākṣarā of Vijñāneśvara. Edited by Nārāyaṇa Rām Ācārya.

SECONDARY SOURCES

Auden, W. H. (1967). *Enchafed Flood: or the Romantic Iconography of the Sea*. New York: Vintage Books.

Basham, Arthur Llewellyn. (1954). *The Wonder That Was India: A Survey of the Culture of the Indian Sub-continent before the Coming of the Muslims*. London: Sidgwick and Jackson. 3rd rev. ed. New York: Taplinger, 1968.

Basu, A. (1959). "Hindu Doctrine of Divine Kingship." In *The Sacral Kingship*. Leiden: Brill. Studies in the History of Religions, 4, pp. 167–71.

Belvalkar, Shripad Krishna, ed. (1947). *The Bhīṣmaparvan*. Poona: Bhandarkar Oriental Research Institute. Vol. 7 of the critical edition of the *Mahābhārata*.

Bhatt, G. H. (1963). *Introduction to the Araṇyakāṇḍa: The Third Book of the Vālmīki Rāmāyaṇa: The National Epic of India*. Baroda: Oriental Institute. Critically edited by P. C. Divanji.

Bhishagratna, Kunja K., ed. and trans. (1907–1916). *Sushruta Samhita*. 3 vols. Calcutta: K. K. Bhishagratna. Reprint Varanasi: Chowkhamba Sanskrit Series Office, 1963. Chowkhamba Sanskrit Studies, vol. 39. Vol. 3, *Uttara-Tantra*, 1916.

Biardeau, Madeleine. (1972). *Cléfs pour la pensée hindoue*. Paris: Éditions Seghers.

Bloomfield, M. (1893). "Contributions to the Interpretation of the Veda, I: The Story of Indra and Namuci." *JAOS* 15, pp. 143–63.

———. (1924). "On False Ascetics and Nuns in Hindu Fiction." *JAOS* 44, pp. 202–42.

Bodewitz, H. W. (1976). *The Daily Evening and Morning Offering (Agnihotra) according to the Brāhmaṇas*. Leiden: E. J. Brill.

Böhtlingk, Otto. (1879–1889). *Sanskrit-Wörterbuch im kürzerer Fassung*. 3 vols. St. Petersburg: Kaiserliche Akademie der Wissenschaften. Reprint Graz: Akademische Druck u. Verlagsanstalt, 1959.

———. (1887). "Bemakenswerthes aus Rāmājaṇa, ed. Bombay Adhyj. [*sic*] I–IV." *Berichte über die Verhandlungen der Königlich sächsischen Gesellschaft der Wissenschaften zu Leipzig, philol-hist.* Klasse, vol. 39, pp. 213–27.

Böhtlingk, Otto, and Rudolph Roth. (1855–1875). *Sanskrit-Wörterbuch*. 7 vols. St. Petersburg: Kaiserliche Akademie der Wissenschaften. Reprint Osnabrück-Wiesbaden: Otto Zeller Verlagsbuchhandlung-Antiquariat Otto Harrassowitz, 1966.

Botto, Oscar. (1969). *Storia delle Letterature d'Oriente*. Milan: F. Vallardi. 4 vols. Vol. 3, *Letterature antiche dell' India*.

Brockington, J. L. (1984). *Righteous Rāma: The Evolution of an Epic*. New York: Oxford University Press.

Chaney, Wm. A. (1970). *The Cult of Kingship in Anglo-Saxon England*. Berkeley: University of California Press.

Daṣ Gupta, Tapan Kumar. (1975). *Der Vajra: Eine vedische Waffe*. Wiesbaden: Franz Steiner Verlag.

Dave, K. N. (1985). *Birds in Sanskrit Literature*. Delhi: Motilal Banarsidass.

De, Sushil Kumar, ed. (1958). *The Droṇaparvan*. Vol. 8 of the critical edition of the *Mahābhārata*. Poona: Bhandarkar Oriental Research Institute.

Dean, John. (1979). *Restless Wanderers: Shakespeare and the Pattern of Romance*. Salzburg: Institut für Anglistik und Amerikanistik.

Derrett, J. Duncan M. (1975). "Social and Political Thought and Institutions." In *A Cultural History of India*. Edited by A. L. Basham. Oxford: Clarendon Press, pp. 124–40.

Dubuisson, D. (1979). "Trois thèses sur le Rāmāyaṇa." *Annales* 34, pp. 464–89.

———. (1986). *La Légende Royale dans l'Inde ancienne: Rāma et le Rāmāyaṇa*. Paris: Economica.

Dumézil, Georges. (1948). *L'Héritage Indo-Européen à Rome: Introduction aux séries "Jupiter, Mars, Quirinus" et "Les Mythes Romains."* Paris: Gallimard. La Montagne Sainte-Geneviève, 9.

Edgerton, Franklin. (1953). *Buddhist Hybrid Sanskrit Dictionary*. New Haven: Yale University Press.

Emeneau, M. B. (1962). "Barkcloth in India—Sanskrit *valkala*." *JAOS* 82, pp. 167–70. Reprinted in *Sanskrit Studies of M. B. Emeneau*, edited by B. A. van Nooten. Berkeley: Center for South and Southeast Asian Studies, 1988, pp. 85–88.

Falk, Nancy E. (1973). "Wilderness and Kingship in Ancient South Asia." *HR* 13, pp. 1–15.

Feder, Lillian. (1980). *Madness in Literature*. Princeton: Princeton University Press.

Felman, Shoshana. (1978). *Le folie et la chose littéraire*. Paris: Éditions du Seuil.

Filliozat, Pierre-Sylvain. (1967). *Oeuvres poétiques de Nīlakaṇṭha Dīkṣita*, vol. 1. Pondicherry: Institut français d'Indologie. Institut français d'Indologie Publication series, no. 36.

Friedman, John Block. (1981). *The Monstrous Races in Medieval Art and Thought*. Cambridge: Harvard University Press.

Frye, Northrop. (1976). *The Secular Scripture: A Study of the Structure of Romance*. Cambridge: Harvard University Press.

Geertz, Clifford. (1983). *Local Knowledge: Further Essays in Interpretive Anthropology*. New York: Basic Books.

Gerow, Edwin. (1971). *A Glossary of Indian Figures of Speech*. The Hague: Mouton.

Ghatage, A. M., ed. (1976–). *An Encyclopaedic Dictionary of Sanskrit on Historical Principles*. Vol. 1, parts 1, 2, 3; vol. 2, parts 1, 2 (all published to date). Poona: Deccan College Postgraduate and Research Institute.

Ghoshal, U. N. (1959). *A History of Indian Political Ideas: The Ancient Period and the Period of Transition to the Middle Ages*. New York: Oxford University Press. Reprint, with corrections. London, 1966.

Ghurye, G. S. (1979). *Legacy of the Rāmāyaṇa*. Bombay: Popular Prakashan.

Goldman, Robert P. (1980). "Rāmaḥ Sahalakṣmaṇaḥ: Psychological and Literary Aspects of the Composite Hero of Vālmīki's Rāmāyaṇa." *JIP* 8, pp. 149–89.

——— ed. and trans. (1984). *The Rāmāyaṇa of Vālmīki: An Epic of Ancient India*. Vol. 1, *Bālakāṇḍa*. Introduction by Robert P. Goldman. Annotation by Robert P. Goldman and Sally J. Sutherland. Princeton: Princeton University Press.

Goldman, Robert P., and J. L. Masson. (1969). "Who Knows Rāvaṇa: A Narrative Difficulty in the *Vālmīki Rāmāyaṇa*." *ABORI* 50, pp. 95–100.

Gombrich, Richard. (1985). "The Vessantara Jātaka, the Rāmāyaṇa, and the Dasaratha Jātaka." *JAOS* 105, pp. 427–37.

Gonda, Jan. (1954). *Aspects of Early Viṣṇuism*. Utrecht: A. Oostoek. 2nd ed., Delhi: Motilal Banarsidass, 1969.

———. (1956). "Semantisches zu idg. *reg-* 'König' und zur Wurzel *reg-* (sich aus) strechen." *KZ* 73, pp. 151–67. Reprinted in *Selected Studies*. Vol. 1, *Indo-European Linguistics*. Leiden: E. J. Brill, 1975, pp. 415–31.

———. (1960–1964). *Die Religionen Indiens*. 3 vols. Stuttgart: W. Kohlhammer. *Die Religionen der Menschheit*, vols. 11–13. Vol. 1, *Veda und alterer Hinduismus*, 1960, and 2, *Der jungere Hinduismus*, 1963.

———. (1966). *Ancient Indian Kingship from the Religious Point of View*. Leiden: E. J. Brill. Reprinted from NUMEN III and IV with addenda and index.

———. (1975). *Vedic Literature (Saṃhitās and Brāhmaṇas). A History of Indian Literature*, vol. 1. Wiesbaden: Harrassowitz.

Gorresio, Gaspare. (1843–1848). *Ramayana, Poema indiano di Valmici*. 7 vols. Paris: Dalla Stamperia Reale. Vol. 5, *Sundarakandam: Eastern Rescension*, 1848. Reprint Madras: Indian Heritage Trust, 1980–1982.

Grierson, George. (1912). "Paiśāci, Piśācas, and 'Modern Piśāca'." *ZDMG* 66, pp. 49–86.

Hacker, Paul. (1959). *Prahlāda, Werden und Wandlungen einer Idealgestalt: Beiträge zur Geschichte des Hinduismus*. 2 vols. Mainz: Verlag der Akademie der Wissenschaften und der Literatur in Mainz. Abhandlungen der Geistes- und Sozialwissenschaftlichen Klasses, no. 9, 13.

———. (1960). "Zur Entwicklung der Avatāralehre." *WZKSOA* 4, pp. 47–70.

Heesterman, J. C. (1957). *The Ancient Indian Royal Consecration: The Rājasūya Described According to the Yajus Texts and Annoted* [*sic*]. Disputationes Rheno-Trajectinae, vol. 2. The Hague: Mouton.

———. (1985). *The Inner Conflict of Tradition. Essays in Indian Ritual, Kingship, and Society*. Chicago: University of Chicago Press.

Hillebrandt, Alfred. (1927–1929). *Vedische Mythologie*. 2 vols. Breslau: M. & H. Marcus.

Hopkins, Edward Washburn. (1915). *Epic Mythology*. Grundrisse der Indo-arischen Philologie und Altertumskunde, vol. 3, no. 1B. Strassburg: K. J. Trübner.

———. (1931). "The Divinity of Kings." *JAOS* 51, pp. 309–16.

Ingalls, Daniel H. H. (1965). *An Anthology of Sanskrit Court Poetry: Vidyākara*'s "Subhāṣitaratnakoṣa." Harvard Oriental Series, vol. 44. Cambridge: Harvard University Press.

———. (1968). "The Harivaṃśa as a Mahākāvya." *Mélanges d'Indianisme à la mémoire de Louis Renou*, vol. 28. Paris: L'Institut de Civilisation Indienne.

Jackson, W.T.H. (1974). "The Nature of Romance." *Yale French Studies* 51, pp. 12–25.

Jacobi, Hermann. (1893). *Das Rāmāyaṇa: Geschichte und Inhalt, nebst Concordanz der gedrückten Recension*. Bonn: Friedrich Cohen. Reprint Darmstadt: Wissenschaftliche Buchgesellschaft, 1976.

———. (1897). "Ein Beitrag zum Rāmāyaṇa—Kritik." *ZDMG* 51, pp. 605–22. Reprinted in Jacobi (1970), vol. 1, pp. 307–11.

———. (1970). *Kleine Schriften*. 2 vols. Wiesbaden: Franz Steiner Verlag. Edited by Bernhard Kölver.

Jacob, G. A. (1907). *Laukikanyāyāñjali: A Handful of Popular Maxims*. Vol 1. 2nd ed., rev. Bombay: Nirṇāyasāgar Press.

Jaini, Padmanabh. (1977). "Saṃskāra-Duḥkhata and the Jaina Concept of Suffering." In *Revelation in Indian Thought: A Festschrift in Honor of T.R.V. Murti*. Edited by H. Coward et al. Emeryville, Calif.: Dharma Publishing, pp. 153–57.

———. (1979). *The Jaina Path of Purification*. Berkeley: University of California Press.

Jhala, G. C., ed. (1966). *The Sundarakāṇḍa: The Fifth Book of the Vālmīki Rāmāyaṇa: The National Epic of India*. Baroda: Oriental Institute.

Johnston, E. H., ed. (1928–1932). *The Saundarananda of Aśvaghoṣa*. 2 vols. Lahore: Oxford University Press. Panjab University Oriental Publications, no. 14. Reprint in 1 vol. Delhi: Motilal Banarsidass, 1975.

Jolly, Julius. (1901). *Medicin*. Strassburg: K. J. Trübner. Translation, with notes, by C. G. Kashikar as *Indian Medicine*. Poona: C. G. Kashikar, 1951. 2nd ed., Delhi: Munshiram Manoharlal, 1977.

Jordan, Winthrop D. (1968). *White over Black*. Chapel Hill: The University of North Carolina Press.

Kakar, Sudhir. (1978). *The Inner World: A Psychoanalytic Study of Childhood and Society*. Delhi: Oxford University Press. 2nd ed., revised and enlarged, 1981.

———. (1982). *Shamans, Mystics and Doctors: A Psychological Inquiry into India and Its Healing Traditions*. New York: Knopf.

Kane, Pandurang V. (1962–1975). *History of Dharmaśāstra*. 8 vols. Poona: Bhandarkar Oriental Research Institute. Government Oriental Series, class B, no. 6. Vol. 3, 2nd ed., 1973.

Kantorowicz, Ernst. (1957). *The King's Two Bodies: A Study in Medieval Political Theology*. Princeton: Princeton University Press.

Keith, A. B., trans. (1920). *The Aitareya and Kauṣītaki Brāhmaṇas of the Rigveda*. Cambridge: Harvard University Press. Harvard Oriental Series, vol. 25. Reprint Delhi: Motilal Banarsidass, 1971.

Kinsley, David. (1974). " 'Through the Looking Glass': Divine Madness in the Hindu Religious Tradition." *HR* 13, pp. 270–305.

Kirfel, Willibald. (1920). *Die Kosmographie der Inder nach Quellen dargestellt*. Bonn-Leipzig: K. Schroeder. Reprint Hildesheim: Olms, 1967.

Kosambi, D. D. (1951). "Urvaśī and Purūravas." *JBBRAS* 27.1, pp. 1–30.

Lassen, Christian. (1866). *Indische Alterthumskunde*. 4 vols. 2nd rev. ed. Bonn: H. B. Koenig. 1st rev. ed., 1843.

Lattimore, Richmond, trans. (1967). *The Odyssey of Homer*. Introduction by R. Lattimore. New York: Harper & Row.

Liebich, Bruno. (1936). *Die Vier indischen Āśrama's*. Breslau: Preuss und Junger.

Lingat, Robert. (1967). *Les sources du droit dans le système traditionnel de l'Inde*. Les Systèmes de Droit Contemporain, vol. 20. The Hague: Mouton & Co. Translated by J. Duncan M. Derrett as *The Classical Law of India*. Berkeley: University of California Press, 1973.

McCann, Charles. (1959). *100 Beautiful Trees of India*. Bombay: D. B. Taraporevala Sons and Co.

Macdonell, A. A. (1897). *Vedic Mythology*. Strassburg: K. J. Trübner. Grundrisse der Indo-arischen Philologie und Altertumskunde III, vol. 1, A.

Macdonell, A. A., and A. B. Keith. (1912). *Vedic Index of Names and Subjects*. 2 vols. (Indian Texts Series). London: J. Murray. Reprint Delhi: Motilal Banarsidass, 1967.

Mack, M. (1970). "The Jacobean Shakespeare." In *Essays in Shakespearean Criticism*. Edited by James L. Calderwood and Harold E. Toliver. Englewood Cliffs, N. J.: Prentice-Hall, pp. 40–47.

Masson, J. L. (J. Moussaief Masson). (1975). "Fratricide among the Monkeys: Psychoanalytic Observations on an Episode in the Vālmīkirāmāyaṇa." *JAOS* 95, pp. 672–78.

Mayrhofer, Manfred. (1956–1980). *Kurzgefasstes etymologisches Wörterbuch des Altindischen*. 4 vols. Heidelberg: Carl Winter Universitätsverlag.

Meyer, Johann Jakob. (1930). *Sexual Life in Ancient India: A Study in the Comparative History of Indian Culture*. 2 vols. London: Routledge and Kegan Paul. Reprint in 1 vol., 1952. Translated from the German.

Michelson, Truman. (1904). "Linguistic Archaisms of the Rāmāyaṇa." *JAOS* 25, pp. 89–145.

Miller, B. S. (1974). "The Rāmāyaṇa." In *Dictionary of Oriental Literatures*. Vol. 2, *South and South-east Asia*, pp. 132–33. Edited by Jaroslav Prusek and Dusan Zbavitel. New York: Basic Books.

Muir, John, trans. (1872–1874). *Original Sanskrit Texts on the Origins and History of the People of India, Their Religion and Institutions*. 5 vols. London: Trübner & Co. Reprint Amsterdam: Oriental Press, 1967. Vol. 4, *Comparison of the Vedic with the Later Representations of the Principal Indian Deities*, 2nd rev. ed. 1874.

Nilakantha Diksita. (1967). *Oeuvres poètiques de Nīlakaṇṭha Dīkṣita*, vol. 1. Edited by Pierre-Sylvain Filliozat. Pondicherry: Institut français d'Indologie. Institut français d'Indologie Publication Series, no. 36.

O'Flaherty, Wendy Doniger. (1973). *Asceticism and Eroticism in the Mythology of Śiva*. London: Oxford University Press.

———. (1976). *The Origins of Evil in Hindu Mythology*. Berkeley: University of California Press. Studies in the History of Religions, no. 6.

Oldenberg, Hermann. (1917). *Die Religion des Veda*. Stuttgart: J. G. Cotta.

———. (1923). *Die Lehre der Upanishaden und die Anfänge des Buddhismus*. Göttingen: Vandenhoeck and Ruprecht.

Page, Sir Denys Lionel. (1966). *The Homeric Odyssey*. 2nd ed. Oxford: Clarendon Press. "From corrected sheets" of the 1st ed., 1955.

Pant, G. N. (1978). *Indian Archery*. Delhi: Agam Kala Prakashan.

Parpola, Asko. (1981). "On the Formation of the Mīmāṃsā and the Problems concerning Jaimini." *WZKSA* 25, pp. 145–77.

Pax, Wolfgang. (1936). "Zum Rāmāyaṇa." *ZDMG* 90, pp. 616–25.

Pollock, Sheldon I. (1983). "Some Lexical Problems in Vālmīki Rāmāyaṇa." *Ṛtam, B. R. Saxsena Special Volume*, pp. 275–88.

———. (1984a). "Ātmānaṃ mānuṣaṃ manye: *Dharmākūtam* on the Divinity of Rāma."*JOIB* 33, pp. 505–28.

———. (1984b). "The Rāmāyaṇa Text and the Critical Edition." In *The Rāmāyaṇa of Vālmīki: An Epic of Ancient India*. Vol. 1, *Bālakāṇḍa*. Translated and edited by Robert P. Goldman. Princeton: Princeton University Press, pp. 82–93.

———, trans. (1986). *The Rāmāyaṇa of Vālmīki: An Epic of Ancient India*. Vol. 2, *Ayodhyākāṇḍa*. Edited by Robert P. Goldman. Introduction and annotation by Sheldon Pollock. Princeton: Princeton University Press.

Puhvel, J. (1974). "Transposition of Myth to Saga in Indo-European Epic Narrative." In *Antiquitates Indogermanicae: Gedenkschrift für Hermann Güntert*. Edited by M. Mayrhofer et al. Innsbruck: Institut für Sprachwissenschaft d. Univ. Innsbruck, pp. 175–84.

Rabkin, Eric S., ed. (1979). *Fantastic Worlds*. New York: Oxford University Press.

Rabkin, Norman. (1982). *Shakespeare and the Problem of Meaning*. Chicago: University of Chicago Press.

Raghavan, V. (1973). *The Greater Ramayana*. Varanasi: All-India Kashiraj Trust.

———, ed. (1980). *The Ramayana Tradition in Asia: Papers Presented at the International Seminar on the Ramayana Tradition in Asia*. New Delhi: Sahitya Akademi.

Rapson, E. J., ed. (1922). *The Cambridge History of India*. Vol. I, *Ancient India*. Cambridge, England: Cambridge University Press.

Rau, Wilhelm. (1973). "Metalle und Metallgeräte im vedischen Indien." *Akademie der Wissenschaften und der Literatur*. (Mainz), Abhandlungen der Geistes- und Sozialwissenschaftliche Klasse, no. 8, pp. 37–46.

———. (1980–1981). "A Note on the Donkey and the Mule in Early Vedic Literature." *ALB* 44–45, pp. 179–89.

Renou, Louis. (1939). "Les éléments védiques dans le vocabulaire du Sanskrit classique." *JA* 231, pp. 321–404.

———. (1968). *Grammaire Sanscrite*. Paris: Adrien-Maisonneuve.

Rhys Davids, C.A.F. (1950). *The Book of Kindred Sayings, Part 1*. London: Pali Text Society.

Rhys Davids, T. W., and William Stede. (1921–1925). *The Pali Text Society's Pali-English Dictionary*. London: Pali Text Society. Reprint 1972.

Risley, Sir Herbert Hope. (1891). *The Tribes and Castes of Bengal: Ethnographic Glossary*. 2 vols. Calcutta: The Bengal Secretariat Press. Reprint Calcutta: Firma Mukhopadhyay, 1981.

Roussel, Alfred. (1910). "Les anomalies du Rāmāyaṇa." *JA* 10, no. 15, pp. 5–69.

———. (1910–1912). *Rāmāyaṇa: études philologiques (Extrait du Muséon)*. Louvain: J. -B. Istas.

Ruben, Walter. (1936). *Studien zur Textgeschichte des Rāmāyaṇa*. Stuttgart: W. Kohlhammer. Bonner Orientalistische Studien, vol. 19.

———. (1939). *Eisenschmiede und Dämonen in Indien*. Leiden: E. J. Brill. Internationales Archiv für Ethnographie, vol. 37.

Satya Vrat. (1964). *The Rāmāyaṇa. A Linguistic Study*. Delhi: Munshi Ram Manoharlal.

Scheuer, Jacques. (1982). *Śiva dans le Mahābhārata*. Paris: Presses Universitaires de France. Bibliothèque de l'École des Hautes Études, Section des Sciences Religieuses, vol. 84.

Schlingloff, Dieter. (1969). *Die altindische Stadt, Eine vergleichende Untersuchung*. Mainz: Akademie der Wissenschaften und der Literatur. Abhandlungen der Geistes- und Sozialwissenschaftlichen Klasse, Nr. 5.

Sircar, Dines Chandra. (1965). *Select Inscriptions Bearing on Indian History and Civilization*. Vol. 1. Calcutta: University of Calcutta. 2nd ed. rev. and enlarged.

Smith, J. D. (1980). "Old Indian: The Two Sanskrit Epics." In *Traditions of Heroic and Epic poetry*. Vol. 1, *The Tradition*. Edited by A. T. Hatto. London: Modern Humanities Research Association, pp. 48–78. Publications of the Modern Humanities Research Association, vol. 9.

Sparreboom, M. (1985). *Chariots in the Veda*. Leiden: E. J. Brill.

Speijer, J. S. (1886). *Sanskrit Syntax*. Leiden: E. J. Brill.

Spellman, John W. (1964). *Political Theory of Ancient India: A Study of Kingship from the Earliest Time to Circa A.D.* 300. Oxford: Clarendon Press.

Srinivasachari, P. N. (1970). *The Philosophy of Viśiṣṭādvaita*. 2nd ed. Madras: Adyar Library and Research Centre. Adyar Library Series, vol. 39. 1st ed. 1943.

Stevenson, John Allen. (1988). "A Vampire in the Mirror: The Sexuality of *Dracula*." *PMLA* 103.2, pp. 139–49.

Sukthankar, Visnu S. (1929). "Epic Studies II." *ABORI* 11, pp. 165–91.

———. (1942). *The Āraṇyakaparvan, Part 2*. Poona: Bhandarkar Oriental Research Institute. Vol. 4 of the critical edition of the *Mahābhārata*.

Thapar, R. (1978). *Exile and the Kingdom: Some Thoughts on the Rāmāyaṇa*. Bangalore: Mythic Society.

Todorov, Tzvetan. (1973). *The Fantastic: A Structural Approach to a Literary Genre*. Translation by Richard Howard of *Introduction à la littérature fantastique*. Cleveland: The Press of Case Western Reserve University. CWRU Press Translations.

Tripathi, Gaya Charan. (1968). *Der Ursprung und die Entwicklung der Vāmana-Legende in der indischen Literatur*. Wiesbaden: Otto Harrassowitz.

van Buitenen, J.A.B. (1974). "The Indian Epic." In *Literatures of India*. Edited by Edward Dimock, Jr., et al. Chicago: University of Chicago Press, pp. 47–72.

van Daalen, L. A. (1980). *Vālmīki's Sanskrit*. Leiden: E. J. Brill. Orientalia Rheno-Traiectina, vol. 25.

Venkatanathacharya, N. S., ed. (1965). *Śrīmadvālmīkirāmāyaṇam with Amṛtakataka of Mādhavayogī: Araṇyakāṇḍa*. Mysore: University of Mysore, Oriental Research Institute.

Vinaver, Eugène. (1966). *Form and Meaning in Medieval Romance*. Cambridge, England: Modern Humanities Research Association.

Vrat, Satya. (1964), see Satya Vrat.

Warder, A. K. (1975). "Classical Literature." In *A Cultural History of India*. Edited by A. L. Basham. Oxford: Clarendon Press, pp. 170–96.

Weber, A. (1870). *Ueber das Rāmāyaṇa*. Berlin: F. R. Dümmler. Printed in *Akademie der Wissenschaften* (pp. 1–88). (*Philogische & Historische Abhandlungen)*, vol. 55. Berlin: Abhandlungen Berlin, 1870.

Weimann, Robert. (1978). *Shakespeare and the Popular Tradition in the Theater: Studies in the Social Dimension of Dramatic Form and Function*. Edited by Robert Schwartz. Baltimore: Johns Hopkins.

Whaling, Frank. (1980). *The Rise of the Religious Significance of Rāma*. Foreword by E. G. Parrinder and Preface by D.H.H. Ingalls. Delhi: Motilal Banarsidass.

Wheeler, James Talboys. (1867–1881). *The History of India from the Earliest Ages*. 4 vols. London: Trübner. Vol. 2, *The Rāmāyaṇa and the Brāhmaṇic Period*, 1869.

Whitman, Cedric H. (1958). *Homer and the Heroic Tradition*. Cambridge: Harvard University Press.

———. (1982). *The Heroic Paradox: Essays on Homer, Sophocles, and Aristophanes*. Edited with an introduction by Charles Segal. Ithaca: Cornell University Press.

Wilson, H. H. (1840). *The Vishnu Purana*. London: J. Murray. Reprint Calcutta, 1961.

Winternitz, Moriz. (1904–1920). *Geschichte der Indischen Literatur*. 3 vols. Leipzig: C. F. Amelang. English translation (vols. 1–2): *A History of Indian Literature*, Calcutta: University of Calcutta, 1927–1933. Reprint Delhi, 1972.

Wright, J. C. (1967). "Purūravas and Urvaśī." *BSOAS* 30, pp. 526–47.

Zimmer, Heinrich. (1948). *The King and the Corpse*. Edited by Joseph Campbell. Princeton: Princeton University Press. The Bollingen Series, 11.

Index

abduction of Sītā, 69, 79; attempted by Virādha, 7; chronology of, as controversial, 276, 304; as outrage against heroine, 68; by Rāvaṇa, 8, 56, 81, 188–201; Rāvaṇa tells Mārīca his plan for, 159; time of, 304
aboriginals: identified with *rākṣasas* and *asuras*, 69
adharma: as violence, 57
adulteress: Surpaṇakhā behaves as, 274
adultery: mutilation as punishment for, 79n, 276
aesthetic sentiment. See *rasa*
aesthetic theory of India. See *rasa*
Agastya, 7, 261; directs Rāma to Pañcavaṭī, 114; gives Rāma bow, 113; harassed by Mārīca, 164; kills Vātāpi and Ilvala, 108, 262; kills Vātāpi as demon ram, 108, 174; location of ashram of, 267; practices austerities, 121–22; praises Rāma, 114; praises Sītā, 149; removes *rākṣasas* from South, 109–10; story of, in *Mahābhārata*, 261; tells Rāma of coming to the South, 265; tells Rāma the story of Śveta, 264; visited by Rāma, Lakṣmaṇa, and Sītā, 110–15
Agastya's brother: identified as Idhmavāha, 261; visited by Rāma, 107–9
Ahalyā: and Indra, 51n, 77n
Ahirbudhnyasaṃhitā: on divinity of king, 49–50
Akampana, 291
Araṇyakāṇḍa: articulates duty of king, 57; complementarity of, 13–14; episodic quality of, 10; informed by authority and social function, 13; power of king in, 50; *rākṣasas* first encountered in, 68; *raudra* as *rasa* of, 66; romance genre as thematic feature of, 11; romance in, 12; sexual-political message of, 80; shifts domain of action for king, 55; *tīrthayātra* in, 10; tone of, set by ascetics, 13; transition from *Ayodhyākāṇḍa* to, 3; and unity of *Rāmāyaṇa*, 53
archery: skill of Rāma in, 283
arrow(s): as fiery, 289; for the killing of Khara and Rāvaṇa, 265. See also *gāndharva* arrow
artha: as complement of *dharma*, 53
ascetics: ask Rāma for protection, 96–97; austerities of, obstructed by Indra, 258; bark garments of, 247; curse of, draws force from penance, 260; dwell in Daṇḍaka wilderness, 87; as false, 311; fear *rākṣasas*, 103; Hanumān as, 311; harassed by Mārīca, 164; killed by *rākṣasas*, 96; know divinity of Rāma, 247; liberated by Rāma, 50; power of, 260, 298; practices of, 95; praise Rāma, 149; protection of, 103; Rāvaṇa as false, 179–84, 311; rescued by Garuḍa, 157; set tone of *Araṇyakāṇḍa*, 13; show hospitality to Rāma in Daṇḍaka, 7, 87–88; types of, 253–54; visit Sutīkṣṇa, 97; of Viśvāmitra's ashram attacked by Mārīca, 298
ashram: of Agastya, 7, 110–15, 267; of Agastya's brother, 107–9; of ascetics in Daṇḍaka wilderness, 87; of Gokarṇa as Śaivite pilgrimage site, 292; Mārīca attacks Viśvāmitra's, 163, 298; of Mataṅga, 238–39; Rāma returns to Sutīkṣṇa's, 106; Rāma sets out for Sutīkṣṇa's, 97; of Śabarī, 240–42; of Śarabhaṅga, 93. *See also* motif of sham ascetic
astrology, 311
astronomical similes, 311
asuras, 35; as allusions to real personalities, 69; conditions of boons of, 36. See also *rākṣasas*
austerities: of ascetics, 258, 269; of

austerities (*cont.*)
Bharata, 121–22; compel boons, 35; of Rāvaṇa, 292
authority and social function: inform *Araṇyakāṇḍa*, 13; inform *Rāmāyaṇa*, 12
avatāra, 66, 347; delusiveness of, 77; instructional purpose of, 343; theory of, 52. *See also* Rāma; Viṣṇu
Ayodhyā: similar to Laṅkā, 74
Ayodhyākāṇḍa, 10, 12; central problems of, as antiromantic, 13; concerned with sociopolitical behavior, 3; depicts Rāma as imperturbable, 55; on divinity of kings, 45; as inappropriate arena for revelation of Rāma's divinity, 31; as study of kingship, 53; transition to *Araṇyakāṇḍa* from, 3; violence eschewed in, 55

Bālarāmāyaṇa of Rājaśekhara, 59n
Bali: granted boon by Brahmā, 39; grants boon to Viṣṇu, 40; story of, 39–40; story of, known to Vālmīki, 42n
bark garments, 247
beauty: as sign of virtue, 258
behavior: sociopolitical, 3
Bhāgavatapurāṇa, 59, 335; explanation of Rāma's madness in, 60
Bharata, 258; anger of Lakṣmaṇa toward, 90, 249, 250; attitude of Lakṣmaṇa toward, 272; on divinity of king, 53
Bhāskara Bhaṭṭa, 59n
Bhaṭṭa, Bhāskara. *See* Bhāskara Bhaṭṭa
Bhavabhūti, 59n; inspired by Vālmīki, 335
Bhīma: in *Hiḍimbavadhaparva*, 80; relationship to Hiḍimbā, 80
Blemmyae, 73
boon motif. *See* motif of boon
boon of Rāvaṇa, 20, 21–29; formulation of, 35; grants invulnerability, 34–35
boon(s): of Bali, 39–40; Bali grants to Viṣṇu, 40; Brahmā as granter of, 36; compelled by austerities, 35; conditions of, familiar, 36; of Dhundhu, 42; formulation of, 35; of Hiraṇyakaśipu, 37–38; of Kabandha, 351; of Kaikeyī, 90, 182–83; of Kaikeyī in *Rāmopākhyāna*, 313; of Kumbhakarṇa, 274; of Mataṅga, 238–39; of Namuci, 39n; of Śabarī, 241; in story of Sunda and Upasunda, 35, 36; as structural feature in epic myth-making, 35; of Sunda and Upasunda, 36; of Tāraka, 37; of Virādha, 91, 250. *See also* boon of Rāvaṇa; perfect wish
Botto, Oscar: on divinity of Rāma, 17n
bow: given by Agastya to Rāma, 113; as Vaiṣṇava attribute of Rāma, 278; of Viṣṇu, 264
Brahmā: gives arrow to Indra, 265; grants boon to Bali, 39; grants boon to Dhundhu, 42; grants boon to Hiraṇyakaśipu, 38; grants boon to Kumbhakarṇa, 274; grants boon to Rāvaṇa, 21–22, 34; grants boon to Sunda and Upasunda, 36; grants boon to Tāraka, 37; grants boon to Virādha, 91; Rāvaṇa cuts off heads as offering to, 151; refuses immortality to Sunda and Upasunda, 36; world of, 252, 253; world of, attained by Kabandha, 352; world of, attained by Śarabhaṅga, 95
brahma: identified with Rāma, 253
brahman: Hanumān as, 311; Ilvala as, 108; Rāvaṇa as, 76, 179–84. *See also* ascetic; motif of sham ascetic
brahmans: killed by Vātāpi and Ilvala, 108; know true nature of Rāma, 248; slaughtered by *rākṣasas*, 96; violence of *rākṣasa* toward, 75–76
brahma-rākṣasas, 74
Bṛhadaśva: requested by Uttaṅka to help kill Dhundhu, 42
Brockington, J. L.: on divinity of Rāma, 17n

chastity of Sītā, 331, 353
chronology: of abduction of Sītā, 276, 304; of events in *Rāmāyaṇa*, 273; of

narrative, 303–4, 313, 334; of Rāma's age, 314, 332
churel, 81
Citrakūṭa, 98
city: as opposed to forest, 12
city books: of *Rāmāyaṇa* and *Mahābhārata*, 68
complementarity of *Araṇyakāṇḍa*, 13–14
contradiction: sense of, needs rethinking, 20
contradictory aspects: of Rāma, 20
cosmic background: of *Rāmāyaṇa*, 32
cosmic destruction, 66; threatened by Rāma, 56, 65, 220–21
cosmic evil: Rāvaṇa as incarnate of, 69
cosmic plan: Rāma's tragedy as part of, 31
cremation, 351; of Jaṭāyus, 229, 347–48; of Kabandha, 235, 351–52. *See also* funeral practices
critical edition: of *Rāmāyaṇa*, 17
cruelty: of Rāma and Lakṣmaṇa toward Śūrpaṇakhā, 275
curse: of ascetics draws force from austerities, 260; of Śiva on Khara, 278; of Sthūlaśiras on Kabandha, 233; of Vaiśravaṇa on Tumburu, 92
cyclops: Kabandha resembles, 73. See also *rākṣasas*

Dakṣa: sacrifice of, destroyed by Śiva, 283
dānavas: contrasted with *rākṣasas*, 349–50. See also *rākṣasas*
daṇḍa. See *artha*
Daṇḍaka: etymological pun on, 258; as name of king, 247; wilderness of, 87, 89, 248, 278, 298
Danu: becomes Kabandha, 73n
darśana: of divine king, 51
Daśaratha: aid of, requested by Viśvāmitra, 162; Kaikeyī's rank among the wives of, 249, 273; lust of, compared with Rāvaṇa's, 330; spirit of, seen by Rāma, 19, 33
Dasaratha Jātaka, 4
deer. *See* Mārīca
deification of Rāma. *See* divinity of Rāma
demonic transfiguration; motif of. *See* motif of demonic transfiguration
demons. See *asuras*; cyclops; *dānavas*; monsters; *rākṣasas*
destruction. *See* cosmic destruction
devil: sexuality as trait of, 82
dharma, 3; as complement of *artha*, 53; king as repository of, 47; king as source of, according to *Mahābhārata*, 322; of kings is protection, 47; as part of cosmic destruction, 66
Dharmaśāstras, 45; silent on divinity of kings, 45
Dhundhu: granted boon by Brahmā, 42; killed by Kuvalāśva, 42
Dhundhumāra: absorbs Viṣṇu's power, 48; as new order of being, 43; story of, 41–43. *See also* Kuvalāśva
discontinuity of *Rāmāyaṇa*, 3, 4; *Dasaratha Jātaka* used as evidence of, 4; Jacobi on, 4; Keith on, 5n
disqualified elder: theme of, 322
divine king: activities of, 54; *darśana* of, 54. *See also* divinity of kings
divine plan: narrative of *Rāmāyaṇa* as part of, 34; Rāma's ignorance of, 63; Rāma's tragedy as part of, 31; underlies action of epic, 20, 297, 308, 325
divine power: king a synthesis of, 64; of Rāma, 28
divine status of Rāma. *See* divinity of Rāma
divinity: ethnocentricity of Western interpretations of, 19
divinity of kings, 44, 300; *Ahirbudhnyasaṃhitā* on, 49–50; *Ayodhyākāṇḍa* on, 45; Bharata on, 53, 248; denials of, 45; early *Dharmaśāstras* silent on, 45; found elsewhere, 45; *Kiṣkindhākāṇḍa* on, 46; *Mahābhārata* on, 45; as matter of dispute, 43; politico-theological doctrine of, 300; *Rāmāyaṇa* on, 45; residing in office rather than in king, 46; subject of contradiction, 45;

divinity of kings (*cont.*)
theme of, authentic to Vālmīki's poem, 20
divinity of Rāma, 14–19, 247, 248, 249, 252, 302, 340, 341; authenticity of, questioned by Lassen, 15; Botto on, 17n; brahmans bow before Rāma because of, 248; Brockington on, 17n; as central feature of *Rāmāyaṇa*, 52; commentarial tradition on, 18; compared to Kṛṣṇa's, 20n; as constitutive feature of poem, 53; interpolations rare concerning, 18; known by ascetics, 247; known by Khara, 278; known through his powers, 28; pervades epic, 19; related to nature of king, 14; Ruben on, 18; self-knowledge of, 340, 347; Smith on, 17n; suppressed in Books 2–6, 18; as tempered with mortality, 344; unknown to Rāma, 32; unknown to Virādha, 249; Western scholars question, 15; Winternitz on, 17n
Dracula: shares traits with Rāvaṇa, 83n
Draupadī: outrage against, 68
Dūṣaṇa: addressed by Khara, 132; attacks Rāma, 140; killed by Rāma, 140; Mārīca told of killing of, 159; rallies *rākṣasas*, 139–40; Rāvaṇa told of death of, 152
duty: of king, 57; renounced by Rāma, 56. See also *dharma*
dwarf: granted boon by Bali, 40; as new order of being, 40; Viṣṇu takes form of, 39–40

elements: fear Rāvaṇa, 317; grieve for Sītā, 197–98
epic: contrasted with romance, 11; divine plan underlies action of, 20; hyperbole of, 28
equanimity of Rāma, 55
ethnocentricity: in interpretations of divinity, 19
evil: formulated on cosmic plane, 30

fairy bride: as male fantasy, 81
fantasy. See *churel*; male fantasy
flying chariot: Rāvaṇa's as different than the chariot Puṣpakavimāna, 295. *See also* Puṣpakavimāna
forest: connotations of, 12; as domain of kingly function, 14; as locale of romance, 12; as opposed to city or town, 12
Forest Book. See *Araṇyakāṇḍa*
Frye, Northrop: on distinction between romance and myth, 11–12; on social function of myth, 41
funeral practices, 347; of *rākṣasas*, 251. *See also* cremation
funeral sacraments: propriety of, for animals, 348

gāndharva arrow: Kālidāsa on, 284; released by Rāma, 284
Garuḍa: eats Niṣādas, 296; kills Niṣādas, 296; legend of, in *Mahābhārata*, 296; as mount of Viṣṇu, 295; ravages Niṣādas' kingdom, 158; rescues ascetics, 157; steals nectar, 158
Gāyatrīmantra, 314
genealogy of creatures: as recited by Jaṭāyus, 115–17
genetic history of *Rāmāyaṇa*, 5. *See also* unity
Godāvarī River, 114
god-king, 76–77
god-man, 35, 52; as effective foe of Rāvaṇa, 28; Rāma's status as, 29
gods: kings as, 43; seek aid of Agastya, 108
Gokarṇa: ashram of, 292
golden deer. *See* Mārīca
golden tree. *See* omen(s)
Goldman, Robert P.: on complementarity of Rāma and Lakṣmaṇa, 58n
Grandfather. *See* Brahmā
Grierson, George: on historicization of *rākṣasas*, 69–70

Hanumān: as mendicant, 311
harem: women of, enchanted with Rāvaṇa's charms, 81
heroine: Draupadī as, 68; outrage against, 68

Hiḍimba, 80
Hiḍimbā: compared to Śūrpaṇakhā, 274; as *rākṣasa* woman, 78; relationship of, with Bhīma, 80; story of, 80
Hiḍimbavadhaparva: contrasted with Śūrpaṇakhā episode, 80; sexual-political message of, 80
Hiraṇyakaśipu, 35–36, 37; boon of, 38
historicization of *rākṣasas*, 69–71
holy people. *See* ascetics
Homer, 28
Homeric poems: interpretive history of, contrasted with *Rāmāyaṇa*, 19n
horses of Indra, 93
humanness of Rāma, 289
humor: as cruel, 274, 275
hunting: Rāma's fondness for, 256; as vice, 305

Iliad, 28
Ilvala, 10; as a brahman, 108; and Vātāpi kill brahmans, 108; and Vātāpi killed by Agastya, 108
immortality: never granted by gods, 35; refused to Sunda and Upasunda, 36
imposture, motif of. *See* motif of imposture
Indra: and Ahalyā, 51n, 77n; avoids Rāma, 251–52; deforms Kabandha, 234; fears Rāvaṇa, 252; foretells Rāma's great feat, 94; given arrow by Brahmā, 265; horses of, 93; kills Namuci, 286; king as a fourth part of, 88; as king of Indian pantheon, 47; obstructs austerities, 258; Pākaśāsana as epithet of, 277; reassures Sītā, 332; reveals himself to Rāma, 93; as similar to Rāvaṇa, 77n; story of Namuci and, 39n; takes guise of soldier, 10
Indrajit: Lakṣmaṇa wishes to kill, 58n; sacrifice of, 74n
interpolations: of Akampana as a *rākṣasa* spy, 291; concerning divinity of Rāma, 18; as expansion not innovation, 18; of oral poem of Vālmīki, 17; of Rāma's first encounter with Jaṭāyus, 267; Rāma's interview with Daśaratha's spirit as, 19; in *Rāmāyaṇa* posited by Western scholars, 16; revealed by critical edition, 17; Ruben on, 18; in story of Śabarī, 355
inter-racial conflict, 83n; as metaphor for sexual theft, 83
irony, 334

jackal. *See* omen(s)
Jacobi, Hermann: on discontinuity of *Rāmāyaṇa*, 4; on divinity of Rāma, 16
Jain *Rāmāyaṇas*, 297
Janaka, 89
Janaka's daughter. *See* Sītā
Jānakī. *See* Sītā
Janasthāna: location of, 276, 309; name of, explained, 289
Jaṭāyus: admonishes Rāvaṇa, 190–91; battles Rāvaṇa, 192; challenges Rāvaṇa, 192; chronology of story of, in *Mahābhārata*, 345; cremation of, 229, 348; death of, 228; destroys Rāvaṇa's chariot, 193; evidence of battle between Rāvaṇa and, 56, 219–20; first encounter with, as interpolation, 267; hears Sītā's cries, 190; knows Rāvaṇa, 321; meets Rāma and Lakṣmaṇa, 7, 115; moral of story of, 321; *Rāmopākhyāna* and story of, 345; reassures Rāma, 227–28; recites genealogy of all creatures, 115–17; sees Rāma, 225; tells Rāma of Sītā's abduction, 226–27; wounded by Rāvaṇa, 8, 195
Jayadeva, 59n

Kabandha, 73; arms of, cut off by Rāma and Lakṣmaṇa, 232; boon of, 351; complex story of, 251; cremated by Lakṣmaṇa, 235–36, 351–52; cursed by Sthūlaśiras, 233; deformed by Śakra, 234; described by Lakṣmaṇa, 232; describes Pampā, 238; description of, 230–31; directs Rāma to Śabarī, 238–39; directs Rāma to Sugrīva, 236; encountered by Rāma and Lakṣmaṇa, 9; freed from curse

Kabandha (*cont.*)
by Rāma and Lakṣmaṇa, 234; history of, 350–51; history of, related to Rāma and Lakṣmaṇa, 233–35; impaired knowledge of, 352; name of, explained, 281, 348; obtains world of Brahmā, 352; originally the *dānava* Danu, 73n; as *rākṣasa*, 71–72; Rāma identifies himself to, 350; resembles cyclops, 73; seizes Rāma and Lakṣmaṇa, 231; spiritual salvation of, 50; urges alliance between Rāma and Sugrīva, 236, 240; violence of, 75
Kaikeyī, 72, 259; boon of, 90, 182–83, 313–14; criticized by Lakṣmaṇa, 122; Rāma's true feelings toward, 333; rank of, among Daśaratha's wives, 249, 273
Kailāsa, Mount: lifted by Rāvaṇa, 293, 303, 316; visited by Rāvaṇa, 151
Kakar, Sudhir: on disfigurement of Śūrpaṇakhā, 80n
Kākutstha. *See* Rāma
Kālidāsa, 59; on death of Kumbhakarṇa, 274; episode of fourteen *rākṣasas* unknown to, 278; episode of Śūrpaṇakhā in, 27; on *gāndharva* arrow, 284; inspired by Vālmīki, 335
kāmarūpin, 76; Mārīca as, 76; *rākṣasas* as, 78; Rāvaṇa as, 76; Vātāpi as, 76
karmic retribution: theme of, 287
Kausalyā, 259
Kauṭilya: on political theology, 51n
Keith, A. B.: on discontinuity of *Rāmāyaṇa*, 5n
Khara: admonished by Rāma, 145–46; army of, attacks Rāma, 138–41; army of, destroyed by Rāma, 141; arrow of, used to kill, 265; as Candrakānta, 278; cursed by Śiva, 278; death of, reported to Rāvaṇa, 152; discovers mutilation of Śūrpaṇakhā, 126–27; doom of, presaged by omens, 133–35; episode of, explained theologically, 290; fights with Rāma, 7, 143; invincibility of, to all but Rāma, 290; killed by Rāma, 149; killing of, told to Mārīca, 159; leads *rākṣasa* army against Rāma, 133; mocked by Rāma, 147–48; name of, explained, 276; orders Dūṣaṇa to prepare for battle, 132; orders *rākṣasas* to attack Rāma, 128; relationship of, to Śūrpaṇakhā, 7, 276; shatters Rāma's bow, 144; taunted by Śūrpaṇakhā, 131; taunts Rāma, 146–47; tells of death of the *rākṣasas*, 130–31; understands divinity of Rāma, 278; wounded by Rāma, 145; wounds Rāma, 144
king: *Araṇyakāṇḍa* shifts domain of action of, 55; becomes Viṣṇu, 48; *dharma* of, is protection, 47; divinity of, disputed, 43; duty of, to protect, 96, 260; as fourth part of Indra, 88; function and origin of, 47; gains merit and wealth by protecting subjects, 254; god in form of man, 43; identification with Viṣṇu, 49; identity of spiritual and social functions of, 50; invested with divinity, 44; liberating power of, 50; obligation of, to punish, 79n; power of, in *Araṇyakāṇḍa* to effect spiritual salvation, 40; as source of *dharma*, 47, 322; spies needed by, 293; as synthesis of divine power, 64
kingship: *Ayodhyākāṇḍa* as study of, 53; *Mahābhārata's Rājadharma* section on, 44; in traditional Sanskrit culture, 14; as unifying theme of epic, 53
Kiṣkindhākāṇḍa: on divinity of kings, 46; Rāma's alliance with Sugrīva in, 352
Kṛṣṇa: cycle of legends of, 59; divinity of, compared with Rāma's, 20n
kṣatradharma, 55
Kubera: complex story of, 250; curses Rāvaṇa, 317; defeated by Rāvaṇa, 151, 292; kingdom of, usurped by Rāvaṇa, 298, 317; kinship of, with Rāvaṇa, 317; Puṣpakavimāna of, stolen by Rāvaṇa, 186; Vaiśravaṇa as another name of, 250
Kumbhakarṇa: boon of, 274
Kuntī: in *Hiḍimbavadhaparva*, 80

Kuvalāśva: called Dhundhumāra, 42; helps Uttaṅka kill Dhundhu, 42

Lake Pampā. *See* Pampā
Lakṣmaṇa: accused of treachery by Sītā, 177, 178, 309; anger of, toward Bharata, 90, 249, 250; ascetics show hospitality to Rāma and, 87–88; attitude of, toward Bharata, 272; breaks arm of Virādha, 91; builds hut for Rāma and Sītā, 119; comforts Rāma, 217, 222, 223; cremates Kabandha, 235–36; criticizes Kaikeyī, 122; cuts Kabandha's arm off, 232; described by Śūrpaṇakhā to Rāvaṇa, 154; directed by Rāma to find Sugrīva, 244; directed by Sutīkṣṇa to visit ashrams of Agastya and Agastya's brother, 106–7; enters Daṇḍaka with Rāma, 87; frees Kabandha from curse, 234; goes to aid of Rāma, 56; goes to Pampā with Rāma, 240; marital status of, 275; mutilates Śūrpaṇakhā, 7, 126; ordered by Rāma to guard Sītā, 174–75; propositions Śūrpaṇakhā, 125; and Rāma encounter Virādha, 89–90; and Rāma meet Jaṭayus, 115; and Rāma rescue Sītā, 92; and Rāma seize Kabandha, 231–32; and Rāma welcomed by Śabarī, 240; rebuked by Rāma, 208, 212; rebukes Sītā, 178; rejects Śūrpaṇakhā, 125; resists request of Sītā to follow Rāma, 177; reverses roles with Rāma, 58; sent by Rāma into hiding, 137; sets out to follow Rāma, 179; Sītā sends, to rescue Rāma, 8, 176–77; stands to Rāma's right, 250; tells Kabandha of Rāma, 232; urges search for Sītā, 222; visits Agastya, 110–15; visits Agastya's brother, 107–9; visits Śarabhaṅga, 94; visits Sutīkṣṇa, 97; warns Rāma of golden deer, 171; wishes to release Brahmā's weapon, 58n
lament of Rāma, 213–22
Laṅkā: city of the *rākṣasas*, 74; as maze similar to those found in European romance, 329; Puṣpaka in, 317; Rāvaṇa takes Sītā to, 201; shown to Sītā by Rāvaṇa, 203; similar to Ayodhyā, 74; sovereignty over offered to Sītā, 330; Śūrpaṇakhā sets out for, 150
Lassen, Christian: on divinity of Rāma, 15
love-in-union. See *rasa*

madness: in Shakespeare, 61–62; of Śiva, 65n. *See also* madness of Rāma
madness of Rāma, 8, 55–67, 218–21, 335–37; as an act, 335; descent into, 56; didactic purpose of, 335; explanation of, in *Bhāgavatapurāṇa*, 60; to instruct people, 336; as mimetic quality, 336; Śiva manifested in, 66
magical form of *rākṣasas*. See *kāmarūpin*; motif of demonic transformation; *rākṣasas*
magical form of Sītā. *See* Māyā Sītā; motif of magical form of Sītā; Sītā
magical weapons. *See* weapons
Mahābhārata, 51; chronology of Jaṭāyus in, 345; city books of, 68; on divinity of kings, 45; *Hiḍimbavadhaparva* of, 80; on king as source of *dharma*, 322; Kṛṣṇa's divinity in, compared with Rāma's, 20n; legend of Garuḍa in, 296; on *māyā* as power inherent in *rākṣasas*, 76; outrage against Draupadī in, 68; *Rājadharma* section of, 44, 47, 65; story of Agastya in, 261; story of Sunda and Upasunda in, 35–36; *tīrthayātra* in, 10
Maithilī. *See* Sītā
Mālatimādhava of Bhavabhūti, 59n, 335
male fantasy of fairy bride, 81
Māṇḍakarṇi: fashions Pañcāpsaras Pond, 105; story of, 261
man-lion: as new order of being, 38; story of, 37–38. See also *avatāra*; Viṣṇu
Mantharā, 72
Märchen: genetic similarity of, to *Rāmāyaṇa*, 10
Mārīca: admonishes Rāvaṇa, 166; asked by Rāvaṇa for aid, 158; asks

Mārīca (*cont.*)
Rāvaṇa to consult with Vibhīṣaṇa, 161; attacks Rāma, 165; attacks Viśvāmitra's ashram, 163, 298; as devotee of Rāma, 296; diminishes Rāma's age, 298; escapes from Rāma's arrows, 165; fears Rāma, 165; foretells *rākṣasas'* destruction, 163, 168; foretells Rāvaṇa's death, 168; as golden deer, 56, 303; as golden deer description of, 170; as golden deer, eludes Rāma, 175; as golden deer, entices Sītā, 171; as golden deer, killed by Rāma, 176; harasses ascetics, 164; as *kāmarūpin*, 76; ordered by Rāvaṇa to become a golden deer, 159, 167; praises Rāma, 160–61; prefers to die at hands of Rāma, 302, 303; previous encounters of, with Rāma, 8; pursued by Rāma, 175; and Rāvaṇa proceed to Rāma's ashram, 169; Rāvaṇa rejects counsel of, 166; residence of, in Gokarṇa's ashram, 292; stunned by Rāma's arrow, 163; takes form of golden deer, 8, 170; threatened by Rāvaṇa, 167; told by Rāvaṇa of his plan to abduct Sītā, 159; told by Rāvaṇa of the killing of Khara, Dūṣaṇa, and Triśiras, 159; visited by Rāvaṇa, 158; warns Rāvaṇa, 8, 160, 164
Maruts: as companions of Indra, 251
Mataṅga: ashram of, 238–39; forest of, 10; name of, explained, 354; Vālin cursed by, 354
māyā: as power inherent in *rākṣasas*, 76
Māyā Sītā, 310, 328. *See also* motif of magical form of Sītā
meaning of text, 19
meat: eating of, 262, 308, 314
mendicants. *See* ascetics; motif of sham ascetic
metamorphosis: as theme of *Rāmāyaṇa*, 76
monkeys: live with Sugrīva at Pampā and Mount Ṛśyamūka, 236, 239, 243, 244; witness Sītā's abduction, 200
monogamy: in *Rāmāyaṇa*, 82
monsters: Blemmyae as, 73; Kabandha as, 349; Kabandha and Virādha as, 71; liberated by Rāma, 50. *See also* cyclops; *rākṣasas*
moon: compared to Rāma, 247
moral deformity: physical deformity as index of, 72
mortality of Rāma, 287, 318. *See also* Rāma
mortifications. *See* austerities
motif of boon: explanation of, 24; formulation of, 35; morphology of, 29, 52; as motif of perfect wish, 35; purpose of, 24–25; in story of Sunda and Upasunda, 36; as structural feature in epic myth-making, 22, 35
motif of demonic transfiguration, 77
motif of imposture, 77n
motif of magical form of Sītā, 328
motif of perfect wish, 35
motif of *rākṣasa* women's beautiful form, 78
motif of sham ascetic, 77, 311; Rāvaṇa's character used as, 77, 179–84, 311
Mount Kailāsa. *See* Kailāsa, Mount
Mount Ṛśyamūka. *See* Ṛśyamūka, Mount
Mount Vindhya. *See* Vindhya, Mount
Mudrārākṣasa of Viśākhadatta: on identity of king and Viṣṇu, 49
mutilation: as punishment for adultery, 79n, 276; of Tāṭakā, 276
myth: Northrop Frye on, 11–12, 41; as patterned representation of the world, 41; *Rāmāyaṇa* as, on nature of king, 14; and romance, 11
mythic reading of *Rāmāyaṇa*, 68

nāgas, 292; as distinguished from *pannagas*, 268
Nalakūbara: curses Rāvaṇa, 331
Namuci: attacks Indra, 286; boon of, 39n; story of, known to Vālmīki, 41
narasiṃha. *See* man-lion
narrative: prefiguration of events of,

333–34; of *Rāmāyaṇa* as part of divine plan, 34
narrative coherence, 4
narrative feature: boon as higher order of, 20; meaning of text in various orders of, 19. *See also* chronology of narrative
nature myth: *Rāmāyaṇa* as, 4
nectar: stolen by Garuḍa, 158
Niṣādas: eaten by Garuḍa, 296; killed by Garuḍa, 296; kingdom of, ravaged by Garuḍa, 158; legend of, in *Mahābhārata*, 296

omen(s), 230, 249, 281; in battle, 282; golden trees as, of impending death, 227, 315, 327, 346; good, seen by Rāma, 356; interpreted by Rāma, 136; jackals as, 208; left eye throbbing as, 334; presage Khara's doom, 133–35; presage loss of Sītā, 208–9, 211; tripping at the beginning of a journey as, 335; twitching of left side of body as, 335
otherness of *rākṣasas*, 79
Others: and *rākṣasas*, 68–84
outrage: of Draupadī as, 68; against heroine, 68; of Sītā as, 68

Pākaśāsana: as epithet of Indra, 277
Pampā, 9, 236, 255; described by Kabandha, 238, 243–44; as lake and river, 354; Mount Ṛśyamūka located east of, 239; as residence of Sugrīva and monkeys, 236, 239, 243, 244
Pañcāpsaras Pond, 10; fashioned by Māṇḍakarṇi, 105
Pañcavaṭī: army of *rākṣasas* enters, 135; described by Rāma, 117–19; Rāma directed to, by Agastya, 114; region of, 7
pannagas: as type of snake, differentiated from *nāgas*, 268
Pax, Wolfgang: first to view *Rāmāyaṇa* as romance, 10; views Laṅkā as maze similar to those found in European romance, 329
penances. *See* austerities
perfect wish: as folkloric motif, 35. *See also* boons; motif of perfect wish
physical deformity: as index of moral deformity, 72
Pliny, 73
political theology, 65, 67, 68; according to Kauṭilya, 51n; of divinity of kings, 300; as doctrine, 45, 47, 51; of Vālmīki, 51
Polyphemus: resembles Kabandha, 73
portents. *See* omens
power, of ascetics. *See* ascetics, power of
pralaya, 66. *See also* cosmic destruction
Prasannarāghava of Jayadeva, 59n
prefiguration of narrative events, 333–34
Primal Being. *See* Rāma
protection: of ascetics by force, 103; asked for by ascetics, 96; as *dharma* of kings, 47, 96, 254, 260
Pṛthu: Viṣṇu enters, 48
pūjā: rarely offered in *Rāmāyaṇa*, 261
Pulastya, 293
punishment: divine institution of, 51n; mutilation for adultery as, 79n; as obligation of king, 79n
purāṇas, 49. See also *Bhāgavatapurāṇa; Viṣṇupurāṇa*
Purūravas, 59, 318
Puṣpakavimāna: belongs to Kubera, 186; different than the chariot used in the abduction of Sītā, 295; in Laṅkā, 317; Rāvaṇa offers Sītā use of, 204; Rāvaṇa views earth from, 156–57; stolen by Rāvaṇa, 151

Rāghava. *See* Rāma
rājadharma, 47
Rājadharma section of *Mahābhārata*, 44, 51; as gloss on *Rāmāyaṇa*, 41, 47, 65; on kingship, 44
Rājaśekhara, 59n
rākṣasas, 7, 8, 68–84; aboriginals identified with, 69; army of, enters Pañcavaṭī, 135; army of, led by Khara, 133; army of, rallied by Dūṣaṇa, 139–40; army of, slaughtered by

rākṣasas (*cont.*)
Rāma, 139; army of, wounds Rāma, 138–39; attack Rāma, 129; contrasted with *dānavas*, 349; destruction of, foretold by Mārīca, 163, 168; dispatched by Rāvaṇa, 202; as eaters of human flesh, 317; as embodiments of absolute terror, 78; feared by ascetics, 103; first encountered in *Araṇyakāṇḍa*, 68; fourteen killed by Rāma, 130; fourteen thousand killed by Rāma, 141; funeral practices of, 251; Grierson on historicization of, 69, 71; hostility of, 63; as index of primal terror and desire, 84, 89; as *kāmarūpins*, 76, 78; kill ascetics, 96; Laṅkā capital city of, 74; *māyā* as power inherent in, 76; ordered by Khara to attack Rāma, 128; otherness of, 79; as representatives of desire, 83; sexuality of, 79, 299; similarity of, to European monsters, 74; Sītā born for destruction of, 34; Vibhīṣaṇa and Trijaṭā as good, 75; violence of, toward brahmans, 75, 76
rākṣasa women: assume beautiful forms, 78; censure Śūrpaṇakhā's conduct, 274; guard Sītā, 201; terrorize Sītā, 207. *See also* motif of *rākṣasa* women
ram: Vātāpi as, 108, 262. *See also* Vātāpi
Rāma, 7, 8, 88; admonishes Khara, 145–46; Agastya's story told to, 265; age of, 314; age of, diminished by Mārīca, 298; aided by Lakṣmaṇa, 56; alliance of, with Sugrīva, 352; antinomian character of, 274, 350; ascetics seek protection of, 96–97; attacked by Khara, 141, 143; attacked by Mārīca, 165; attacked by *rākṣasas*, 129; attacked by Triśiras, 142; attacks Khara's army, 138–41; *avatāra* of Viṣṇu, 247, 336, 347; begged by Sītā for golden deer, 8, 172; bow of, 279; breaks Virādha's arm, 91; calmed by Lakṣmaṇa, 217, 222, 223; compared to moon, 247; compared to Rudra, 66; contradictory aspects of, 20; cremates Jaṭāyus, 229; cuts off Kabandha's arm, 232; described by Śūrpaṇakhā, 154; describes Pañcavaṭī, 117–19; describes winter, 120–21; directed by Sutīkṣṇa to visit ashrams of Agastya and Agastya's brother, 106–7; directed to Pañcavaṭī by Agastya, 114; divine powers of, 28; does not know divine plan, 63; does not know own divinity, 32; eluded by Mārīca, 175; encounters Virādha, 89–92; enters Daṇḍaka wilderness, 87; entertained by Sutīkṣṇa, 99; equanimity of, 55; fights Khara, 149; fondness of, for hunting, 256; frees Kabandha from curse, 234; given great bow by Agastya, 113; glorified by Rāvaṇa, 318; goes to Pampā with Lakṣmaṇa, 243; great feat of, foretold by Indra, 94; grief of, 217–18; grieves for Jaṭāyus, 228; helped by Śarabhaṅga, 7, 94; humanness of, 289; identified with *brahma*, 253; identified with Viṣṇu, 52, 278 (see also *avatāra*; Viṣṇu); identifies himself to Kabandha, 350; imperturbable in *Ayodhyākāṇḍa*, 55; Indra avoids meeting, 251; Kabandha directs, to Śabarī, 238–39; Kabandha directs, to Sugrīva, 236; Khara fought by, 144–45; kills Dūṣaṇa, 140; kills fourteen *rākṣasas*, 130, 159; kills fourteen thousand *rākṣasas*, 141; kills Khara's army, 139; kills Mārīca, 176; kills *rākṣasas*, 7; kills Triśiras, 143; kills Virādha, 7, 92; knows Rāvaṇa's boon, 22; Lakṣmaṇa builds hut for, 119; and Lakṣmaṇa seized by Kabandha, 231–32; Lakṣmaṇa sets out to find, 179; Lakṣmaṇa stands to the right of, 250; and Lakṣmaṇa welcomed by Śabarī, 241; laments for Sītā, 213–16; liberates ascetics, 50; liberates *rākṣasas*, 50; limited self-knowledge of, 63; lives in region of Pañcavaṭī, 7; madness of, 8, 55, 218–21; Mārīca as devotee of, 296; Mār-

īca dodges arrows of, 165; Mārīca prefers to die at hands of, 302, 303; Mārīca stunned by arrow of, 163; as meat eater, 308, 314; meets Jaṭāyus, 115; mimetic quality of anger of, 341; mimetic quality of grief of, 338; mimetic quality of madness of, 336; mocks Khara, 146–48; mortality of, 25, 26, 287, 318; as new order of being, 29, 41, 43; offers salvation, 51, 51n; orders Lakṣmaṇa to find Sugrīva, 244; orders Lakṣmaṇa to guard Sītā, 174–75; praised by ascetics, 149; praised by Mārīca, 160–61; as Primal Being, 302; Rāvaṇa hears of the killing of Khara, Dūṣaṇa, and Triśiras by, 159; reassures Jaṭayus, 227–28; rebukes Lakṣmaṇa for leaving Sītā, 208, 212; recovers sense of equanimity, 58n; renounces duty, 56; restrains his anger, 225; reverses roles with Lakṣmaṇa, 58; seduced by Śūrpaṇakhā, 79, 123–26; sees Daśaratha's spirit, 19, 33; sees Jaṭāyus wounded, 225; sees omens, 136, 208–9, 334; sees vision of Indra, 93; sends Lakṣmaṇa and Sītā into hiding, 137; shoots *gāndharva* arrow, 284; Sītā requests Lakṣmaṇa to rescue, 8, 175–76; Śiva manifest in madness of, 66; skill of, in archery, 283; status as god-man, 29; supreme Lord, 323; Śūrpaṇakhā appears to, 78; Śūrpaṇakhā requests death of, 155; Śūrpaṇakhā speaks positively of, 277; teases Śūrpaṇakhā, 125; tells Sītā of need to protect ascetics, 103; threatens cosmic destruction, 56, 65, 220–21; threatens Tāṭakā's mutilation, 276; told of Sītā's abduction, 226–27; told story of Śveta by Agastya, 264; tragedy of, as part of cosmic plan, 31; true feelings of, toward Kaikeyī, 333; true nature of, known by brahmans, 248; urged by Sītā to abjure violence, 102; urged to form alliance with Sugrīva, 236, 240; urged to search for Sītā, 222; views sidestepping of Khara as retreat, 289; visits Agastya, 7, 110–15; visits Agastya's brother, 107–9; visits Sutīkṣṇa, 97; visits Sutīkṣṇa's ashram again, 106; wants to kill Indrajit, 58n; warned by Lakṣmaṇa, 171; warned by Sītā of the perils of violence, 100–101, 257–58; wounded, 286; wounds *rākṣasas*, 138–39. *See also* divinity of Rāma; madness of Rāma

Rāmāyaṇa: chronology of events in, 273; city books of, 68; cosmic background of, 32; discontinuity of, 3; divine king as theme of, 20; divine plan underlies action of, 20; on divinity of kings, 45; divinity of Rāma integral feature of, 15; genetic similarity to Märchen, 10; informed by authority and social function, 12; informed by paradigmatic collective values, 12; insistence of, on monogamy, 82; interpolations in, posited by Western scholars, 16; interpretation of, in global sense, 53; interpretive history of Homeric poems contrasted with, 19n; Jacobi on discontinuity of, 4; Keith on discontinuity of, 5n; *Mahābhārata's Rājadharma* section as gloss on, 44; metamorphosis as theme of, 76; as myth of nature of king, 14; mythic reading of, 68; narrative coherence of, 4; narrative of, as part of divine plan, 34; as nature myth, 4; *pūjā* rare in, 261; receptive history of, 5; romance as a genre of, 10; romantic elements of, 54; sexual-political orientation of, 79; unity of, 5; and unity of *Araṇyakāṇḍa*, 53; unity of, never questioned by tradition, 15; viewed as romance, 10

Rambhā, 92

Rāmopākhyāna: on boon of Kaikeyī, 313–14; describes Mārīca's ashram as pilgrimage site, 292; description of Rāvaṇa in, 311; does not know episode of fourteen *rākṣasas*, 278; Kubera curses Rāvaṇa in, 317; Mārīca prefers to die at the hands of Rāma

Rāmopākhyāna (*cont.*)
in, 303; Rāvaṇa questions Śūrpaṇakhā privately in, 294; story of Jaṭāyus in, 278, 345
rasa, 60, 334; in *Araṇyakāṇḍa*, 66, 224
raudra: as *rasa* of *Araṇyakāṇda*, 66
Rāvaṇa: and the abduction of Sītā, 68, 79, 81, 276; abducts Sītā, 8, 79, 188–201; admonished by Jaṭāyus, 190–91; admonished by Śūrpaṇakhā, 7, 152; admonishes Mārīca, 166; approaches Sītā, 180; arrow used to kill, 265; asked by Śūrpaṇakhā for Rāma's death, 155; asked to consult with Vibhīṣaṇa, 161; asks for Mārīca's aid, 158; assumes guise of ascetic, 179–84, 311; assumes true form, 188; austerities of, 292; beauty of, 82; boasts of his power to Sītā, 186; boon of, 20, 21–29, 291 (*see also* boon of Rāvaṇa); as brahman, 76; chariot of, destroyed by Jaṭāyus, 193; compared to Milton's Satan, 82; converses with Sītā, 77; as cosmic evil incarnate, 69; crimes of, 151; cursed by Kubera, 317; cursed by Nalakūbara, 331; cuts off own heads as self-mortification, 151; death of, foretold by Mārīca, 168; death of Khara and Dūṣana reported to, 152; defeats Kubera, 292; defied by Sītā, 205; as demonic antagonist, 69; description of, 150–51; as devotee of Sītā, 315; dispatches *rākṣasas*, 202; doom of, foretold by Sītā, 206; as false ascetic, 77; as father of Sītā, 297; feared by elements, 317; feared by Indra, 252; fights Jaṭāyus, 8, 56, 192; glorifies Rāma, 318; god-man only effective foe of, 28; goes to Mount Kailāsa, 151; goes to Rāma's ashram with Mārīca, 169; grandson of Pulastya, 293; hears description of Rāma, Lakṣmaṇa, and Sītā, 154–55; hears description of Sītā, 81; invulnerable to superhuman beings, 34–35; and Jaṭāyus in *Rāmopākhyāna*, 345; as *kāmarūpin*, 76, 82; kinship of, with Kubera, 317; known to Jaṭāyus, 321; lifts Mount Kailāsa, 293, 303, 316; as lover, 78; name of, explained, 292; offers Sītā sovereignty over Laṅkā, 330; orders Mārīca to become a golden deer, 159, 167; passion of, for Sīta inflamed by Śūrpaṇakhā, 155; plan of, to abduct Sītā, 159; power of, 29, 30, 151; praises Sītā's beauty, 180–81; proposes marriage to Sītā, 204; questions Śūrpaṇakhā, 154, 294; rebuked by Sītā, 199–200; rejects Mārīca's counsel, 166; reveals identity to Sītā, 184; reviled by Sītā, 184; scorns men, 292; sexuality as dominant trait of, 81, 82; sexuality of, compared to Daśaratha's, 330; shares traits with Dracula, 83n; shows Sītā Laṅkā, 203; similarity to European monsters, 74; son of Viśravas, 293; steals Puṣpakavimāna, 151; takes Sītā to Laṅkā, 201; tells Mārīca of the killing of Khara, Dūṣaṇa, and Triśiras, 159; threatens Mārīca, 167; threatens to devour Sītā, 206–7; usurps Kubera's kingdom, 298, 317; views earth from flying chariot, 156; visits Mārīca, 158; warned by Mārīca, 8, 160, 164; welcomed by Sītā, 181–82; women of, 81; wounds Jaṭāyus, 8, 195
religious mystery: contradictory aspects of Rāma as source of, 20
retribution: as a result of karma, 287; for crimes, 287
righteousness. See *dharma*
Ṛkṣarajas: Sugrīva as son of, 244
romance: in *Araṇyakāṇḍa*, 3, 12; contrasted with epic, 11; elements of, in *Rāmāyaṇa*, 54; forest as locale of, 12; Frye on, 11–12; as genre of *Rāmāyaṇa*, 10; maze of Laṅkā as motif of European, 329; and myth, 11; Pax first to view *Rāmāyaṇa* as, 10; as thematic feature found in *Araṇyakāṇḍa*, 11
Ṛśyamūka, Mount, 9; located to the east of Pampā, 239; and Pampā resi-

dence of Sugrīva and the monkeys, 236, 239, 243, 244
Ruben, Walter: on the divinity of Rāma, 18
Rudra, 66; as compared to Rāma, 66n. *See also* Śiva

Śabarī, 9; ascends to heaven, 242; ashram of, 240–41; Rāma directed to, by Kabandha, 238–39; social class of, 355; spiritual salvation of, 50; story of, seen as interpolation, 355; welcomes Rāma and Lakṣmaṇa, 240
sages. *See* ascetics
Śaivite pilgrimage site: ashram of Gokarṇa as, 292
Śakra. *See* Indra
salvation: offered by Rāma, 51, 51n
Samudragupta: identified with Viṣṇu, 49
Śarabhaṅga: advises Rāma and Lakṣmaṇa on place to live, 94; attains world of Brahmā, 95; explains Indra's visit to Rāma, 94; self-immolation of, 95, 252; spiritual salvation of, 50; visited by Rāma and Lakṣmaṇa, 93–94
Saumitri. *See* Lakṣmaṇa
seers. *See* ascetics
sexuality: as dominant character of *rākṣasas*, 79; as dominant trait of Rāvaṇa, 82; of *rākṣasas*, 299; as trait of devil, 82
sexual-political message of *Araṇyakāṇḍa*, 80; contrasted with *Hiḍimbavadhaparava*, 80
sexual-political orientation of *Rāmāyaṇa*, 79
sexual relations: constraints on, 80–81
sexual theft: as a metaphor for interracial strife, 83. *See also* abduction of Sītā
Shakespeare: use of madness by, 61, 62, 73
sham ascetic, 77. *See also* motif of sham ascetic
similies, astronomical. *See* astronomical similies
Sītā, 7, 8, 9, 72; abducted by Rāvaṇa, 8, 56, 188–201, 276; abducted by Virādha, 7, 89; abduction of, 79, 81; abduction of, as outrage against, 68; accuses Lakṣmaṇa of treachery, 177–78, 309; approached by Rāvaṇa, 180; attacked by Śūrpaṇakhā, 126; beauty of, praised by Rāvaṇa, 181–82; begs Rāma for golden deer, 8, 172; born for destruction of *rākṣasas*, 34; chastity of, 331, 353; converses with Rāvaṇa, 77; cries of, 189–90; cries of, heard by Jaṭāyus, 190; described by Śūrpanakhā, 81, 154–55; directed by Sutīkṣṇa to visit ashrams of Agastya and Agastya's brother, 106–7; enticed by Mārīca, 171; foretells Rāvaṇa's doom, 206; grieved for by elements, 197–98; guarded by Lakṣmaṇa, 174–75; guarded by *rākṣasa* women, 201; history of, told to Rāvaṇa, 182; kindliness of, 258; knows Rāvaṇa's boon, 22; Lakṣmaṇa builds hut for, 119; magical form (*māyā*) of, 309, 310, 320; motif of magical form of, 328; praised by Agastya, 114; proposed to by Rāvaṇa, 204; and Rāma approached by ascetics, 87; Rāma laments for, 213–16; and Rāma return to Sutīkṣṇa's ashram, 106; Rāvaṇa as devotee of, 315; Rāvaṇa offers sovereignty over Laṅkā to, 330; as Rāvaṇa's daughter, 297; Rāvaṇa's plan to abduct, 159; reassured by Indra, 332; rebuked by Rāvaṇa, 199–200; recognized by Rāvaṇa, 184; refers to Rāma's divine powers, 28; remorse of, 332; requests Lakṣmaṇa to rescue Rāma, 8, 176–77; rescued from Virādha, 92; retains courtly garments in exile, 312; reviles Rāvaṇa, 184; sent into hiding by Rāma, 137; shown Laṅkā by Rāvaṇa, 203; taken to Laṅkā by Rāvaṇa, 201; terrorized by *rākṣasa* women, 207; threatened by Rāvaṇa, 206–7; told by Rāma of need to use force, 103; urges Rāma to abjure vio-

Sītā (*cont.*)
lence, 102; visits Agastya, 110–14; visits Agastya's brother, 107–9; visits Śarabhaṅga, 94; visits Sutīkṣṇa, 97; warns Rāma of the perils of violence, 100–101, 257–58; welcomes Rāvaṇa, 181–82. *See also* abduction of Sītā; Māyā Sītā
Śiva: curses Khara, 278; destroys Dakṣa's sacrifice, 283; kills Death, 290; madness of, 65n; as manifest in madness of Rāma, 66; unworthy of worship, 263, 264. *See also* Rudra
Skanda: destroys Tāraka, 37; as new order of being, 37; story of birth of, 37
Smith, J. D.: on divinity of Rāma, 17n
snakes. See *nāgas; pannagas*
social function: and spiritual function of kings, 50. *See also* authority and social function
spies: needed by kings, 293
spirit of Daśaratha. *See* Daśaratha
śrāddha, 262
Sthūlaśiras: curses Kabandha, 233
Sugrīva, 9; alliance of, with Rāma, 352; dwells at Pampā and Mount Ṛśyamūka with monkeys, 236, 239, 243, 244; fears Vālin, 236; Kabandha urges Rāma to form alliance with, 236, 240; Lakṣmaṇa directed by Rāma to find, 244; quarrel of, with Vālin, 353; son of Ṛkṣarajas, 244
suicide: of Śarabhaṅga, 252
Śukra: wealth of, 305–6
Sunda and Upasunda: boon of, 36; boon of, as structural feature of epic myth, 35–36; destroyed by jealousy over a woman, 36; immortality refused to, 36; story of, 35–36; story of, in *Mahābhārata*, 35n
Suparṇa. *See* Garuḍa
Śūrpaṇakhā, 7; admonishes Rāvaṇa, 7, 152; adulterous behavior of, 51n, 274, 275; appeals to Rāvaṇa, 150; asks for death of Rāma, 155; attacks Sītā, 126; attempts to seduce Rāma, 79, 123–26; as *churel*, 81; compared to Hiḍimbā, 274; conduct of, censured by *rākṣasa* women, 274; cruelty of Rāma and Lakṣmaṇa toward, 274, 275; departs for Laṅkā, 150; describes Rāma, Lakṣmaṇa, and Sītā, 154–55; describes Sītā to Rāvaṇa, 81, 154–55; fails to assume beautiful form, 78, 274; inflames Rāvaṇa's passion for Sītā, 155; Kakar on mutilation of, 80n; mutilated by Lakṣmaṇa, 7, 126, 276; name of, explained, 274; propositions Lakṣmaṇa, 125; questioned by Rāvaṇa, 154; questions Rāvaṇa in *Rāmopāhkyāna*, 294; rejected by Lakṣmaṇa, 125; relationship of, to Khara, 7, 276; reports death of Khara and Dūṣaṇa to Rāvaṇa, 152; speaks positively of Rāma after mutilation, 277; story of, as related by Kālidāsa, 276; taunts Khara, 131; teased by Rāma, 125; tells Khara of mutilation, 126–28; tells Khara of Rāma killing *rākṣasas*, 130–31; vengefulness of, 76; visits Khara, 126
Sutīkṣṇa: ashram of, 106; converses with Indra, 98; directs Rāma, Lakṣmaṇa, and Sītā to ashrams of Agastya and Agastya's brother, 106–7; does not destroy himself after Rāma's departure, 256; entertains Rāma, 99; Rāma directed to, 7, 94; visited by ascetics, 97; visited by Rāma Lakṣmaṇa, and Sītā, 97
Śveta: story of, told by Agastya, 264

Taittirīyas: Vālmīki's affinities to, 48
Tāraka: boon of, 37; story of, 37
Tāṭakā: threatened with mutilation by Rāma, 276
text: meaning of, 19
theme: of divine king as authentic to Vālmīki's poem, 20; of disqualified elder, 322; of karmic retribution, 287; metamorphosis as, 76
theology of Govindarāja, 298
theory of Indian aesthetics. See *rasa*
tīrthayātra: in *Araṇyakāṇḍa* and *Mahābhārata*, 10

tragedy of Rāma: as part of cosmic plan, 31
transition: between *Ayodhyākāṇḍa* and *Araṇyakāṇḍa*, 3; as epic convention, 3
trees, golden. *See* omen(s): golden trees as
Trijaṭā: as good *rākṣasa*, 75; as great ascetic and perfected being, 298
Triśiras: attacks Rāma, 142; death of, reported to Mārīca, 159; name of, explained, 285; name of two *rākṣasas*, 274, 285; promises to slay Rāma, 142
Tumburu: becomes Virādha, 73n; cursed by Vaiśravaṇa, 92; passion of, for Rambhā, 92

unity: of *Araṇyakāṇḍa* and *Rāmāyaṇa*, 53; of *Rāmāyaṇa*, 5, 15
universal destruction. *See* cosmic destruction
Unmattarāghava of Bhāskara Bhaṭṭa, 59n
Upasunda. *See* Sunda and Upasunda
Urvaśī, 59, 318
Uśanas: wealth of, 306. *See also* Śukra
Uttaṅka: seeks protection from Dhundhu, 42
Uttarakāṇḍa: austerities of Rāvaṇa described in, 292; Rāvaṇa's name explained in, 292–93; story of Kubera and Rāvaṇa recounted in, 298; story of Rāvaṇa's rape of Rambhā in, 331; story of Vedavatī recounted in, 297

Vaidehī. *See* Sītā
Vaiśravaṇa: as another name of Kubera, 250; curses Tumburu, 92. *See also* Kubera
Vālin: cursed by Mataṅga, 354; feared by Sugrīva, 236; quarrel of, with Sugrīva, 353
Vālmīki: affinity to Taittirīyas, 48; and critical edition, 17; motif of demonic transfiguration in, 77; political theology of, 50; stories of Bali and Namuci known to, 41n; style of, 334, 339, 345
vāstuśānti, 269
Vātāpi, 10; destruction of, narrated by Rāma, 174; and Ilvala killed by Agastya, 108; as *kāmarūpin*, 76; killed by Agastya, 262; kills brahmans, 108
Vedavatī: story of, in *Uttarakāṇḍa*, 297
Vibhīṣaṇa: as good *rākṣasa*, 75; Mārīca asks Rāvaṇa to consult with, 161
Vikramorvaśīya of Kālidāsa, 59, 335
Vindhya, Mount; obeys Agastya, 110; story of, 263
violence, 258; as *adharma*, 57; eschewed in *Ayodhyākāṇḍa*, 55; of *rākṣasas*, 75; Sītā urges Rāma to abjure, 102; Sītā warns Rāma of perils of, 100–101, 257
Virādha: abducts Sītā, 7, 89–90; arms of, broken by Rāma and Lakṣmaṇa, 91; boon of, 91, 250; burial of, 92; death of, 250; killed by Rāma, 7, 92; mistakes Rāma for mortal, 249; name of, explained, 250; originally the *gandharva* Tumburu, 73n, 92; as *rākṣasa*, 71–73; spiritual salvation of, 50; urges Rāma and Lakṣmaṇa to visit Śarabhaṅga, 92; violence of, 75
virtue: beauty as sign of, 258
Viśākhadatta. See *Mudrārākṣasa*
Viṣṇu: aids suffering mankind, 48; bow of, 264; as dwarf, 39–40; as dwarf, given boon by Bali, 40; enters Kuvalāśva, 42; enters Pṛthu, 48; Garuḍa as mount of, 295; identification with king, 49; identified with Rāma, 52, 278; identified with King Samudragupta, 49; king becomes, 48; and kingly function, 47; as man-lion, 37–38; Rāma as *avatāra* of, 247, 335–36, 347
Viṣṇupurāṇa, 59, 335
Viśravas: son of Pulastya and father of Rāvaṇa, 293
Viśvakarman: creates a woman to destroy Sunda and Upasunda, 36
Viśvāmitra: ashram of, attacked by Mārīca, 163, 298; asks Daśaratha for Rāma's aid, 162
vulgate edition of *Rāmāyaṇa*, 17

weapons, 257, 265, 283. *See also* arrow; bow; *gāndharva* arrow
winter: described by Rāma, 120–21
Winternitz, Maurice: on divinity of Rāma, 17n
wish. *See* perfect wish
woman: as new order of being, 36
women of Rāvaṇa's harem, 81

Yama: killed by Śiva, 290; Vātāpi goes to house of, 108
Yudhiṣṭhira, 80